THE BILL OF RIGHTS

Its Origin and Meaning

THE
BILL
OF
RIGHTS

Its Origin and Meaning

IRVING BRANT

The BOBBS-MERRILL Company, Inc.
a subsidiary of Howard W. Sams & Co., Inc., Publishers
INDIANAPOLIS · KANSAS CITY · NEW YORK

First printing, 1965
Copyright © 1965 by Irving Brant
All rights reserved
Library of Congress Catalogue Card Number 65:21401
Designed by Charlotte T. Kloberdanz

Printed in The United States of America

CONTENTS

To My Co-Worker
HAZELDEAN

ACKNOWLEDGMENTS

The author wishes to express his deep gratitude for the co-operation he has received from the librarians and staffs of numerous libraries during the nearly four years of research and writing devoted to this book. This has extended far beyond mere access to collections. It has included the use of study-room facilities for both research and writing, and has been marked by a friendly readiness to seek out materials that might not otherwise have come to his attention. His thanks go in particular to the staffs of the Library of Congress, especially the Law and Manuscripts divisions; the Library of the United States Supreme Court; the Alderman and law libraries of the University of Virginia; the Huntington Library of San Marino, California, which is especially rich in early British materials; the law and general libraries of the University of Oregon; the Provincial Library of British Columbia and the library of the British Columbia Bar Association, both at Victoria, B.C.

The author feels grateful also for the encouragement and helpfulness he has met with from many professors of law and libertarian writers in the United States, and members of the judiciary, who may or may not agree with the conclusions here presented.

PART I
The Bill of Rights and Its Background

CHAPTER 1
Sixty-Three Pledges of Freedom

The American people have been blessed with a Bill of Rights at least since 1791, when the ratification of the first ten amendments to the Constitution was completed. There is reason to say "at least" since then, for when a great outcry went up that the Constitution framed in 1787 contained no Bill of Rights, the reply was made that the entire document was a charter of rights and liberties. Both in the character of the original Constitution and in its specific details, that was true to a much greater extent than alarmed citizens realized. Yet as a charter of freedom it was woefully deficient. By oversight and underestimate, great gaps were left in the protective armor against governmental oppression and the tyranny of popular majorities. Responding to a nationwide demand, the first Congress of the United States undertook to supply what was missing. It seemed to have done so with the submission to the states, in 1789, of twelve amendments, all of which were promptly ratified except two of trivial importance relating to the composition and pay of Congress.

The name "Bill of Rights" was at once applied to these ten amendments, but in a truly national sense it was a misnomer. The restraints contained in them were imposed solely upon the federal government: the states were untouched by these prohibitory mandates. That seemed of little moment at the time, since most of the states had their own bills of rights and citizens of those states had varying degrees of double protection.

Seventy years passed. The Civil War came, dividing the nation by its onset and cementing it by force in its outcome. As one result of the struggle, three million Americans of African descent were propelled from slavery into the ranks of freemen. They became citizens with unestablished rights of citizenship—living and destined to live for generations under the political sway of their former masters. A new national responsibility had to be assumed, and one aspect of it was the expansion of the existing Bill of Rights to make its provisions effective against violation by the states as well as by the national government. The result was the addition, in 1865, 1868 and 1870, of the "Civil War Amendments"—the Thirteenth, Fourteenth and Fifteenth—primarily designed to protect the freedmen and their descendants, but aimed also at a broader guarantee of liberty and equality for all of the people. Half a century later another amendment, the Nineteenth, wiped out a remaining inequality by extending the right of suffrage to women, and in 1964 the Twenty-Fourth Amendment struck down the poll tax as a device to restrict the right to vote.

Thus, by subsequent growth as well as by antecedent beginnings, the identification of the first ten amendments as the American Bill of Rights became grossly inadequate. The American Bill of Rights as it exists today has to be brought together from all its sources—a compendium derived from the original Constitution, the first ten amendments and the subsequent amendments. When this operation is performed, it is like bringing together the scattered works of a great master of painting, sculpture or music. Design and harmony emerge. In all the world's history there is nothing to compare with the pledges of human rights and freedom that have been worked into our charter of government at the great moments of national history.

It is only at great moments that such advances are possible. Between such moments there is most likely to be, first, a contented coasting on a path made smooth by established rights; then forgetfulness of those rights; finally, a challenge of them fired by passions made dangerous by ignorance. That leads either to loss of liberty or to the restoration of freedom through the resurging spirit of the people.

This book is being written at a moment when forgetfulness (outside the seething area of race relations) has made the Bill of Rights the victim of prejudice and passion, among an active minority, abetted by ignorance and passivity among the majority. It is being written at a moment, also, when the most enlightened Supreme Court in American history is moving against the blind forces of prejudice and apathy to restore freedoms lost by all, and to establish rights that the descendants of slaves have owned but never have been able to exercise.

The swift ratification of the anti-poll-tax amendment, and the awakening of Congress revealed by passage of the Civil Rights Act of 1964, provided the first evidence of a relinking of freedom with justice in American public opinion. But the continuing assaults on the Supreme Court, for decisions deserving the highest praise, produced no general uprising in defense of the liberties implanted in the Constitution in the period of its adoption. Apathy due to ignorance, interacting with ignorance due to apathy, continued to be the outstanding feature of the popular reaction.

Again and again, alarmed individuals have taken samplings of popular knowledge and opinion, and the results hardly vary from year to year or place to place. On July 4, 1951, the Madison, Wisconsin, *Capital-Times* sent out two reporters to ask people encountered at random to sign a petition saying that they believed in the Declaration of Independence. Out of 112 persons interviewed, all but one refused to sign. The common ground of refusal was not the obvious fact that such a petition is useless. "They were afraid," the newspaper reported, "that it was some kind of subversive document and that they would lose their jobs or be called Communists." This inspired the New York *Post* to circulate a similar petition and the big city with its foreign-born population did a little better. Nineteen out of 161 were willing to sign, but the prevailing reaction was "suspicion, distrust and hostility."

Fear has to be combined with ignorance to produce such a state of mind, which allows active play to an equal ignorance inflamed by passion. Far fewer than half of the American people have the remotest idea of what their personal and political rights embrace. Still less do they know their neighbors' rights. People will answer Yes, when asked if they believe in a certain form of liberty guaranteed by the Constitution. Then, when a hypothetical case is put before them, involving that right, they are likely to approve the denial of it. Those who respond in this paradoxical fashion are not illiterate ignoramuses. They include, in a generally ascending order of affluence, farmers, street sweepers, gas-tank fillers, clerks, stenographers, merchants, bankers, brokers, corporation executives, head waiters and plumbers. They include in heterogeneous disorder, doctors, preachers, teachers, editors, lawyers, state legislators, congressmen, governors, and entirely too many judges of state and federal courts. Not at all levels, of course, can this be ascribed completely to naïveté.

What, then, is the Bill of Rights? What does it contain? Some years ago, when the editors of a famous encyclopedia invited the author of this book to prepare an article for them on the "Bill of Rights—United States," he looked in the current edition of that work to see what it contained on the subject. There was nothing under that or any other heading. Other reference works, histories and libertarian books consulted by him disclosed no adequate compilation of constitutional rights, liberties, privileges and immunities. Strangely enough, the nearest approach to a full listing of popular rights, as they stood at the moment they were being described, was that of Alexander Hamilton in *The Federalist* No. 84, when he sought to head off the demand of the people for more safeguards by telling them what they would get by ratifying the Constitution as it came from the Convention of 1787.

Hamilton's argument was not wholly flawless, when he disparaged the impotent "should's" and "ought to's" of existing state declarations of rights. But there was a basic rightness in his assertion that such ethical aphorisms did less to secure recognition of popular rights than the Preamble to the Federal Constitution, whose wording he capitalized and italicized:

"WE, THE PEOPLE of the United States, in order to . . . secure the blessings of liberty to ourselves and our posterity, do *ordain* and *establish* this CONSTITUTION for the United States of America."

Ordain and establish! Hamilton was saying that here, in the new Federal Constitution, were not only the popular rights which he had just listed from its pages, but the instrument of government with which to enforce them, and the command of the sovereign—the sovereign people, not a kingly sovereign—that they be enforced.

In the years since the 84th *Federalist* was written (1788), the constitutional guarantees of liberty have been enormously enlarged. But the fundamental protection remains what it was in the beginning—the action of "We the People" in *ordaining* and *establishing* the Constitution. In other words, the first and foremost element in the American Bill of Rights is the fact that we have a *written* Constitution, enforceable as it stands, and unchangeable by ordinary acts of legislation.

For the real significance of that fact, compare the American Bill of Rights with England's great document, Magna Carta, of which its leading analyst, McKechnie, wrote: "The great weakness of the Charter lay in this, that no adequate sanction was attached to it, in order to ensure the enforcement of its provisions." There could be no adequate sanction, because the Charter was not a constitution enforceable against king and parliament. King John did indeed make it law by his acceptance of it in A.D. 1215. Henry the Third, after intervening lapses, did so again in 1217. Edward I repeated the restoring operation in 1297. Edward the Third added his mite, or might, in 1351. Then Parliament took it up. Again and again, as century followed century, the Commons and Lords affirmed and English kings acknowledged that Magna Carta was the law of the land. Thirty-two times, wrote Sir Edward Coke in his *Second Institute*, the Charter had been enacted into law. The necessity to enact it thirty-two times could only mean that thirty-one times it had fallen out of the unwritten British Constitution.

This in-again, out-again, in-again record does not cancel the immense influence Magna Carta has exercised in maintaining both the rights established in it and those to which the same illustrious paternity has been less authentically traced, partly by Lord Coke himself. Also, it is only fair to point out that between 1950 and 1960, certain written guarantees of the American Bill of Rights went in and out of the United States Constitution with an ease and frequency that made some Englishmen and Americans gasp, due chiefly to changes in the personnel of the Supreme Court.

But there is always this great difference. In England, all acts of Parliament are the validly enforceable law of the country, binding on the courts. A British law may play havoc with the British Constitution, and it is still a valid law. If laws of the same sort continue to be passed, they ultimately become part of antiquity, and that makes them part of the Constitution. Legalists may pick flaws in this illustration, as mixing up statutory and unwritten law, but for the layman it is a plain statement of fact.

In the United States, on the other hand, the Constitution is fixed and definite in wording. The meaning of the words is not always plain, but that is not what causes trouble in relation to the Bill of Rights. The question in that respect more often is: shall the clear and ordinary meaning of words be followed or disregarded? The written Constitution stands like a tablet on Mt. Sinai, reading, "This is the law." The problem is to keep the law in the custody of prophets who know how to read the language of liberty.

Seven principles of government, the first of which is the existence of a written Constitution, buttress and form part of the American Bill of Rights. The second is expressed in these words of the Constitution: "The judicial power of the United States shall be vested in one Supreme court, and in such inferior courts as the Congress may, from time to time, ordain and establish. The judges, both of the supreme and inferior courts, shall hold their offices during good behavior . . ."

By these provisions, the United States is given an independent judiciary—totally independent of the President after he nominates the judges; independent of Congress except through the power of removal by impeachment for high crimes or misdemeanors. To realize the importance of judicial independence, the framers of the Constitution had only to look at the progressive degeneration of the English courts during the reigns of the Stuart kings. On account of decisions unfavorable to the crown, or because judges would not agree in advance to decide as the monarch wished, Charles I removed three judges, Charles II removed ten, and James II got rid of thirteen during the three short years before his manifold follies caused the British people to drive him from the throne. If the framers needed anything more than the Stuart record to decide their course, they found it in the notorious subservience of colonial judges to royal governors.

Underpinning the entire structure of American government—essential, indeed, to the very existence of the nation—is a clause so important to ordered liberty that it may fairly be called the third principle of the Bill of Rights. Article VI provides: "This Constitution, and the laws of the United States which shall be made in pursuance thereof; and all treaties made, or which shall be made, under the authority of the United States, shall be the supreme law of the land; and the judges in every State shall be bound thereby, anything in the Constitution or laws of any State to the contrary notwithstanding." Without this grant of supreme power by "We the People" to their national government, the United States would either fly to pieces in a swirling instant, or be reduced to such chaotic disorder and impotence that democratic self-government would give way to a dictatorship.

Taken together, the Judiciary Article and the Supremacy Clause enable the Supreme Court to determine, in cases that come within judicial purview, whether acts of Congress and state legislatures are valid or invalid. The test in either instance is the same: does the state or federal statute conform to the requirements of the Constitution of the United States? Unless a federal question is involved, the state courts have the final decision as to a state law's validity.

It was not until 1803 that the United States Supreme Court held an act of Congress invalid. The litigated matter involved in *Marbury* v. *Madison* was trivial—a mere detail of the duties imposed on the Court by law—but the way the decision was reached was momentous. Chief Justice Marshall's opinion settled for all time that the power of judicial review includes the power to set aside acts of Congress on constitutional grounds. Not until 1857 was this power exerted a second time. Then, in the famous *Dred Scott* case, the Supreme Court held in effect that Negroes were subhuman. That lighted the short-fused time bomb that set off the Civil War. In the century that followed, decisions on constitutionality became a commonplace. Abused as the power has been, in long and recurring periods of judicial darkness, it has been a potent force in holding the nation firm against centrifugal economic and political pressures. And in spite of glaring lapses, too long continued and repeated, it has on the whole given increasing vitality to the guarantees of liberty and equality embodied in the charter of government. In that field, however, potentiality has far exceeded performance, when both are measured by national need and constitutional duty.

A fourth principle in the federal Bill of Rights has to be expressed in words the Constitution does not contain. It is the unstated but omnipresent rule of separation and balance of powers. It is to ensure *separation* of powers that the Constitution says: "All legislative powers herein granted shall be vested in a Congress of the United States. . . . The Executive power shall be vested in a President. . . . The judicial power . . . shall be vested in one Supreme Court. . . ." *Balance* of power is obtained in part by blending power, but not so far as to destroy the separation. As an example, the President and Congress have separate and distinct functions—one executive, the other legislative. If they were left wholly apart, Congress would be sole and absolute in the making of laws, and its control of money would enable it to dominate the Executive. Balance is achieved by giving the President a limited veto power over bills passed by Congress, countered by the power of Congress to override a veto by a two-thirds vote. The result is both separation and balance, each branch of government having power to protect itself against the other, with resultant protection of the people against arbitrary action from either source.

Both separation and balance were achieved by giving the President power to appoint the officers of government, subject to confirmation by the Senate. So it was, also, in placing foreign relations in the hands of the President, subject to senatorial ratification of the treaties he may make. The judiciary, though partially dependent on Congress for its organization and jurisdiction, escaped functional balancing for two reasons. To perform its duties it must have assured tenure and complete discretion.

A fifth protection of liberty is found—or logically should be found—in the delegation to Congress of a limited power to uphold its privileges. The British Parliament is subject to no limitations in this regard except those it created and voluntarily observes in the *Lex et Consuetudo Parliamenti*—the law and custom of Parliament. Any restraints imposed by the British courts—and they do impose some—can be taken away by a simple act or resolution of Parliament itself. In contrast, the privileges of Congress are fixed in the Constitution, with these specifications set forth in Article I:

"Each House shall be the Judge of the Elections, Returns and Qualifications of its own Members . . . and may . . . compel the attendance of absent Members. . . . Each House may determine the

Rules of its Proceedings, punish its Members for disorderly Behavior, and, with the Concurrence of two thirds, expel a Member. . . . The Senators and Representatives . . . shall in all cases, except Treason, Felony and Breach of the Peace, be privileged from Arrest during their attendance at the Session of their respective Houses, and in going to and returning from the same; and for any Speech or Debate in either House, they shall not be questioned in any other Place."

The protections thus given the members of Congress may well be termed a part of the Bill of Rights of the people as a whole, for they are a necessary safeguard of congressional freedom of thought and action. But they confer no power on Congress to take any action against nonmembers, except through the passage of legislation necessary and proper to protect the legislative function. Under the ordinary rules of construction, the enumeration of these privileges excludes all others that are not indispensably necessary to performance of the constitutional duties of Congress. The extent of this restriction raises one of the great questions in American law—how far does the power of congressional committees extend?—a question made critical by two world wars and the tide of political repression that accompanied and followed them.

All of these instruments for the preservation of freedom, worked into the substantive features of the Constitution, would fail were it not for the sixth and highest characteristic of American government—the right of the people to elect their President and Congress, their governors and state legislatures. This is what makes the federal system of states and nation a workable instrument of self-government instead of a collection of warring satrapies or Roman provinces.

Underneath all of this is a seventh principle of American government—the constitutional right of the people to amend, alter or abolish the government they live under. Still more fundamental is the right of revolution, but that is a natural, not a constitutional, right. Its legal status is akin to treason except when successfully employed, as it was in our own national beginnings.

It is on the broad foundation of these seven constitutional principles that we may enumerate the detailed provisions of the Bill of Rights. Here are the specific libertarian articles in the original Constitution: "The privilege of the writ of habeas corpus shall not be suspended, unless when in cases of rebellion or invasion the public safety may require it."

"No bill of attainder or *ex-post-facto* law shall be passed."

"No title of nobility shall be granted by the United States."

"No State shall . . . pass any bill of attainder, *ex-post-facto* law, or law impairing the obligation of contracts; or grant any title of nobility."

"The trial of all crimes, except in cases of impeachment, shall be by jury; and such trial shall be held in the State where the said crimes shall have been committed . . ."

"Treason against the United States shall consist only in levying war against them, or, in adhering to their enemies, giving them aid and comfort. No person shall be convicted of treason unless on the testimony of two witnesses to the same overt act, or on confession in open court."

"The Congress shall have power to declare the punishment of treason, but no attainder of treason shall work corruption of blood, or forfeiture, except during the life of the person attainted."

"Judgment in cases of impeachment shall not extend further than to removal from office, and disqualification to hold and enjoy any office of honor, trust, or profit under the United States . . ."

"Full faith and credit shall be given in each State to the public acts, records, and judicial proceedings of every other State. . . ."

"The citizens of each State shall be entitled to all privileges and immunities of citizens in the several States."

"The United States shall guarantee to every state in this Union a republican form of government, and shall protect each of them against invasion; and on application of the legislature, or of the Executive (when the legislature cannot be convened), against domestic violence."

"No religious test shall ever be required as a qualification to any office or public trust under the United States."

Including the seven basic provisions for free government previously outlined, and taking account of multiple provisions in a single clause, that makes twenty-four elements of a Bill of Rights in a Constitution that is said to contain none. Next come the original Ten Amendments, the first eight of which cover definite rights, liberties, privileges and immunities:

"I. Congress shall make no law respecting an establishment of religion, or prohibiting the free exercise thereof; or abridging the freedom of speech, or of the press; or the right of the people peaceably to assemble and to petition the government for a redress of grievances.

"II. A well regulated militia, being necessary to the security of a free State, the right of the people to keep and bear arms, shall not be infringed.

"III. No soldier shall, in time of peace be quartered in any house, without the consent of the owner, nor in time of war, but in a manner to be prescribed by law.

"IV. The right of the people to be secure in their persons, houses, papers, and effects, against unreasonable searches and seizures, shall not be violated, and no warrants shall issue, but upon probable cause, supported by oath or affirmation, and particularly describing the place to be searched, and the persons or things to be seized.

"V. No person shall be held to answer for a capital, or otherwise infamous crime, unless on a presentment or indictment of a grand jury, except in cases arising in the land or naval forces, or in the militia, when in actual service in time of war or public danger; nor shall any person be subject for the same offence to be twice put in jeopardy of life or limb; nor shall be compelled in any criminal case to be a witness against himself; nor be deprived of life, liberty, or property, without due process of law; nor shall private property be taken for public use, without just compensation.

"VI. In all criminal prosecutions, the accused shall enjoy the right to a speedy and public trial, by an impartial jury of the State and district wherein the crime shall have been committed, which district shall have been previously ascertained by law, and to be informed of the nature and cause of the accusation; to be confronted with the witnesses against him; to have compulsory process for obtaining witnesses in his favor, and to have the assistance of counsel for his defence.

"VII. In suits at common law, where the value in controversy shall exceed twenty dollars, the right of trial by jury shall be preserved; and no fact tried by jury, shall be otherwise re-examined in any court of the United States, than according to the rules of the common law.

"VIII. Excessive bail shall not be required, nor excessive fines imposed, nor cruel and unusual punishments inflicted.

"IX. The enumeration in this Constitution, of certain rights, shall not be construed to deny or disparage others retained by the people.

"X. The powers not delegated to the United States by the Constitution, nor prohibited by it to the States, are reserved to the States respectively, or to the people."

Again taking account of multiple protections in a single article, that adds thirty to the list, making fifty-four guarantees of freedom that date back to the beginning of our present form of government. Then, as a further portion of the American Bill of Rights, come the three Civil War amendments:

"XIII. Neither slavery nor involuntary servitude, except as a punishment for crime whereof the party shall have been duly convicted, shall exist within the United States, or any place subject to their jurisdiction.

"XIV. Section I. All persons born or naturalized in the United States, and subject to the jurisdiction thereof, are citizens of the United States and of the State wherein they reside. No State shall make or enforce any law which shall abridge the privileges or immunities of citizens of the United States; nor shall any State deprive any person of life, liberty, or property, without due process of law; nor deny to any person within its jurisdiction the equal protection of the laws.

"Section 2. Representatives shall be apportioned among the several States according to their respective numbers, counting the whole number of persons in each State, excluding Indians not taxed. . . .[1]

"XV. The right of citizens of the United States to vote shall not be denied or abridged by the United States, or by any State on account of race, color, or previous condition of servitude."

To leave no opening for doubt, each of these three amendments was given a section providing that Congress should have power to enforce it "by appropriate legislation." These Civil War amendments were ratified in 1865, 1868, and 1870. In 1919 came the Nineteenth Amendment, extending the right of suffrage to women. The year 1964 witnessed the quick ratification of the unneeded

Twenty-Fourth Amendment, forbidding the restriction of suffrage by means of a poll tax or any other tax.[2]

These five post-Civil War amendments contain nine libertarian provisions, asserted either as positive rights or as restraints upon state action. The grand total reveals an American Bill of Rights containing sixty-three specific guarantees. Seen as a connected whole, the spirit is the same throughout. It is a spirit of unqualified devotion to human rights, human dignity, the liberty and equality of free men. The mere listing of them, in their full proportions, is enough to blow into cosmic dust two ancient misconceptions concerning the founders of the American Republic. It is utter fallacy that the spirit of the Constitution is opposed to the spirit of the Declaration of Independence. Equally fallacious is the notion that the framers of the Constitution did not share the devotion to freedom of the congressmen who framed and submitted the 1789 amendments.

With that superficial judgment overthrown by the unified record of what both groups did, the study of the Bill of Rights must have a new beginning. The first necessity is to re-examine that subject in the Constitutional Convention of 1787.

CHAPTER 2
Thinking Back to Edward III

Convening in Philadelphia on May 28, 1787, the Federal Convention spent the next two months debating and revising, but generally adopting, fifteen resolutions written by James Madison and offered by Governor Edmund Randolph as titular head of Virginia's seven-man delegation. Known as the Virginia Plan, it furnished the groundwork of the new Constitution of the United States. During a ten-day recess ending on August 6, these resolutions were converted and expanded by a Committee of Detail into a full charter of government which was then taken up item by item for final consideration. On August 20, the Convention dealt with the treason clause, worded as follows in the tentative draft:

"Treason against the United States shall consist only in levying war against the United States, or any of them; and in adhering to the enemies of the United States, or any of them. The Legislature of the United States shall have power to declare the punishment of treason. No person shall be convicted of treason, unless on the testimony of two witnesses. No attainder of treason shall work corruption of blood, nor forfeiture, except during the life of the person attainted."

The debate that followed, like everything else that was said during the convention, is known almost entirely from the voluminous notes kept by Madison and first published in 1840. Here are excerpts from them, all bearing on one point in the discussion of treason.

"Mr. Madison thought the definition too narrow. It did not appear to go as far as the Stat. of Edward III."

"Mr. Mason was for pursuing the Stat. of Edward III."

"Mr. Randolph thought the clause defective in adopting the words 'in adhering' only. The British Stat. adds, 'giving them aid and comfort' which had a more extensive meaning."

"Mr. Ellsworth considered the definition as the same in fact with that of the Statute."

"Mr. Gouverneur[1] Morris 'adhering' does not go as far as 'giving aid and comfort' or the latter words may be restrictive of 'adhering,' in either case the Statute is not pursued."

"Mr. Gouverneur Morris and Mr. Randolph wished to substitute the words of the British Statute and moved . . . the following . . . 'that if a man do levy war against the U.S. within their territories,[2] or be adherent to the enemies of the U.S. within the said territories, giving them aid and comfort within their territories or elsewhere, and thereof be provably attainted of open deed by the people of his condition, he shall be adjudged guilty of Treason.' "

Twelve delegates took part in that 1787 debate. Every one of them showed complete familiarity with an English treason statute written in 1351. Their manner of discussing it presupposed equal familiarity by the other delegates. How many Americans today know that the treason clause in our Constitution was lifted almost verbatim out of a fourteenth-century English statute? How many could even remotely guess the reason why this was done?

The lapse of knowledge is accounted for by more than differences in education. Treason was a vital topic among the members of the Constitutional Convention, for virtually every member had been guilty of it less than ten years earlier. But that was incidental. To Americans of the eighteenth century, English history was part of American history. Madison, Mason, Randolph, Ellsworth and Morris were talking about one of their own kings when they spoke of Edward the Third. If we disregard the national origins of individuals, Edward III and his treason statute are directly in the line of the universal American inheritance. The bearing of this common lineage extends far beyond the treason clause. Every item in the English heritage of freedom was a natural part of the American heritage. Before 1776 every loss of freedom in England, every perversion of justice there, was a blow to liberty and justice in the American colonies. The Stuarts were American as well as English kings. They were oppressors on the American side of the Atlantic even when their acts of oppression did not extend across the sea. For the potential of injury was there; the loss of rights was co-extensive with British sovereignty.

Reading American court reports recorded during the first half century of national independence, one is struck by the fact that nearly all the cases cited to support decisions are English cases. The line runs backward, not across state lines. If this marks a continuity in English and American legal thinking, as it undeniably does, it is accompanied by a parallel phenomenon in the struggle of the people for the retention, the restoration and the development of their own rights as human beings. The line of struggle in the United States to gain and preserve rights and liberties, privileges and immunities, is to be traced not from the colonies to the states, except as the colonists were the victims of maladministration imposed from overseas or as they imitated bad examples. The American struggle was bound up with the struggle in England, and that was in great part a contest between the people and the courts and cabinets. When English judges are cited as authorities, *for the purpose of narrowing the legal scope of American rights and liberties,* it is a citation of those against whom English minorities had been struggling for centuries. They fought with an ardor no less intense and infinitely riskier than that which put the guarantees of freedom into the American Constitution, but the efforts in England were attended with far less possibility of success.

It was in that affirmative spirit that the framers took up the proposed treason clause. Madison, after his initial comment about the Statute of Edward III, broadened the definition by changing "and" to "or" in the opening sentence. Otherwise it might be thought necessary to prove both levying of war and adhering to the enemy in order to obtain a conviction. At his instigation the words "or any of them" (the states) were struck out to remove the opening for double jeopardy.

John Dickinson thought "that proof of an overt-act ought to be expressed as essential in the case." The motion that passed went further: there must be "two witnesses to the same overt act." Benjamin Franklin, long a resident of England as colonial agent, gave the motion strong support: "Prosecutions for treason were generally virulent; and perjury too easily made use of against innocence." That was in fact the precise reason for adoption of the two-witness rule (not to the same act) in England. There had been such a requirement in ecclesiastical law for centuries, made statutory in 1547, but Queen Mary's judges nullified it by dubious decisions that held throughout a passion-torn century. Then contrary decisions restored the law and it was stiffened by statute after the revolution of 1688. Unless upon willing confession in open court, no person was to be tried for high treason "but by and upon the oaths and testimony of two lawful witnesses, either both of them to the *same overt act,* or one of them to the one and the other of them to another overt act of *the same treason."*

Minus the weakening alternative, that was the restrictive pattern followed at Philadelphia. The same motive governed George Mason when he moved the inclusion of the words "giving them aid and comfort." He offered them "as restrictive of 'adhering to their enemies, etc.,' " which otherwise would be too indefinite.

All through the debate it was evident that the delegates wanted a rigorously limited definition of treason. The clause on corruption of blood and forfeitures revealed a knowledge of what modern scholarship has concluded—that the struggle over treason in the Middle Ages was not primarily concerned with liberty but with property. Kings expanded the punishable acts in order to confiscate the lands and movables of the barons, who on their part robbed the people. The barons, when they had strength enough, forced the kings to restore their inheritances and safeguarded them by narrowing the crime of treason. In the resistance to it, life, liberty and property were all wrapped up in the same package, and the American framers were primarily thinking of life and liberty, including their own.

The idea of ancient English rights stamped out by royal tyranny or baronial oppression is to some extent a demonstrable truth, related to Norman recognition and violation of Saxon law. In part it is a fiction grounded in human nature. In relation to treason, this idea goes back to the earliest case that has impressed itself in English history. That was the trial and conviction of Thomas Becket, Archbishop of Canterbury, for failing to appear before Henry II (one of the better kings) on the day set for deciding a quarrel between Thomas and John the Marshal. On the second day, before the bishops, earls and barons of England (so relates the ancient narrative), "the Archbishop was accused of treason, because as is said before, he was cited . . . and neither came, nor made a sufficient excuse . . . and they condemned him to be in the king's mercy for all his movable goods." Trying to save his goods from this decree of confiscation, the archbishop appealed to the Pope, saying that "they had unjustly condemned him, contrary to the custom and example of antiquity." Ancient custom was still more rudely violated when four of the king's followers murdered the archbishop in his own cathedral.

Thomas's crime was "accroaching the royal power." The king had fixed the day for the litigant to appear, and in altering the day Becket had usurped the power of the king. That was almost two hundred years before the barons who made up Parliament induced Edward III to wipe out the excrescences of treason by converting it from a common-law to a statutory crime.

The framers of the United States Constitution knew the history of those two centuries. Compulsory reading for every lawyer was Sir Matthew Hale's *Pleas of the Crown,* in which the great Chief Justice wrote that "accroaching of royal power was a usual charge of high treason anciently," though so uncertain and arbitrary it was, prior to the statute of Edward III, "that almost every offense, that was, or seemed to be a breach of the faith and allegiance due to the king, was by construction, and consequence and interpretation raised into the offense of high treason."

Lord Hale told how, in subsequent reigns, the admirable statute of Edward III was broken down by judicial construction and expanded by new acts of Parliament. Political factionists used the charge of treason to send their adversaries to the scaffold, then lost their own heads when royal favor shifted. "These were the unhappy effects," wrote Hale, "of the breaking of this great boundary of treason, and letting in of constructive treasons, which . . . mischieved all parties first or last, and left a great unquietness and unsettledness in the minds of the people."

Parliaments did their full part in breaking that boundary between real treason and the constructive variety, in which the presumed intent of nontreasonable words or actions was sufficient for a death sentence. New treasons were added to the statutory list with no requirement that an overt act be proved. This omission, said Lord Hale, "subjected men to the great punishment of treason for their very thoughts." In the reign of Richard II, to support a vast structure of new treasons, it was enacted that any member of Parliament making a motion to repeal these laws should be executed as a traitor. That monstrous act was itself repealed, and all the treason statutes of Richard II along with it, in the first Parliament after that hated monarch was deposed. The act of repeal, in 1399, anticipated by four hundred years the debate over the American treason clause:

"Whereas, in the said Parliament [of Richard II] . . . divers pains of treason were ordained by statute, inasmuch that there was no man that did know how he ought to behave himself, to do, speak, or say, for doubt of such pains. It is accorded and assented, by the King, the Lords and Commons aforesaid, that in no time to come any treason be judged otherwise than it was ordained by the statute in the time of his noble grandfather King Edward III, whom God assoil."

"IN NO TIME TO COME!" The thought was common to Englishmen and Americans, but the former possessed no legal sanction to support the thought. The act of 1399 recorded the wish of Englishmen to protect themselves and posterity from treason laws so broad and lax that they assailed the most elemental rights of speech and action. But there it ended. They possessed no written Constitution, based on the sovereignty of the people, that would reach into all "time to come" and say to King and Parliament with enforceable authority: "Thou shalt not."

That English law designed for all future time had a working life of twenty-three years. It remained on the statute books, majestically untouched, still validating the statute that caused Edward the Third (so said Lord Coke) to be called *Benedictum*—the Blessed. But as a limitation of the crime of treason it was as dead as King Edward himself.

For when an outlawed felon broke jail in 1422 and assisted two known traitors to escape, there was no ground for charging him with treason. The judges then made a great discovery. They found that the Statute of Edward III was not an all-embracing limitation, but merely a declaratory act, telling what the law was that was included in it. There were other treasons at common law, and they were not repealed by the statute of 1351, so the jailbreaker was hanged, drawn and quartered. That interpretation stuck. When Sir Nicholas Throckmorton was tried 132 years later, and contended that the Statute of Edward III did not make it treason for him to say that he disliked Queen Mary's Spanish marriage, Serjeant Stanford of the Queen's counsel replied to him:

"You are deceived . . . there doth remain divers other treasons at this day at the common law, which be not expressed by that statute, as the Judges can declare."

And the judges had been so declaring during all those 132 years. Men were disemboweled and beheaded under Edward's statute when they could be pulled within its compass. Otherwise they were disemboweled and beheaded under the common law which the statute was designed to annul. This, however, was not enough for Mary's father, Henry the Eighth. The treasons he created were more numerous than his wives and some concerned them. It was treason one year to call one of his marriages invalid; treason the next year to say the opposite. By one law his daughter Elizabeth was declared legitimate, by a later one illegitimate, and woe to the unlucky subject who called her a bastard in the wrong year.

Almost as an incident of Henry's marital tangles, but with a rising public sentiment to support him, the king detached England from the Church of Rome and became an exceedingly noncelibate Pope in his own right. Heresy was now a magnified terror for Catholics and a rising menace to Protestant Dissenters. All of this came within the compass of treason laws expanded to fit the girth of a monarch against whom *lèse majesté* could be committed as head of either Church or State. It was unwise to take chances with Henry the Eighth even when he lay dying, as his physicians decided when they refused to reveal his condition lest they be found to violate the law that made it treason to predict his death.

Such conduct surpassed the aberrations of the late Plantagenets, in whose reigns, it must be said, some of the executions for treason were more than normally necessary and proper. Who could decry the fate of Jack Cade, put to death for rearing up the devil "in the semblance of a blak dogge in his chambre"? There was no hesitation in cutting off the head of Thomas Burdett, who, on hearing that Edward IV had put an arrow through an admired white buck, said he wished that the animal, horns and all, were in the king's belly. That was held to be "compassing or imagining the death of the king." The degree of guilt was debatable, considering what a fifteenth-century king's belly could hold, but no such doubt attended another charge against Burdett. By "art, magic, necromancy and astronomy," he had fixed a day on which Edward Prince of Wales was to die. Sharing both his guilt and his fate was the king's brother, the Duke of Clarence, who, seeking to gain the throne for himself (so testified the king) had by magic caused the Prince of Wales "to waste away as a candle is consumed by burning."

In the higher moments of English justice, "compassing or imagining the king's death" was construed to mean "attempt" or "contrive." "Treason, gentlemen," said Solicitor General Sir John Somers to a jury in 1691, "consists in the imagination of the heart; but because that imagination of the heart can be discovered in no other way but by some open act, therefore the law doth require, that some overt act, manifesting that intention and imagination, be assigned and proved." That was said in the ignominious days of Charles the Second, and even in that period the "two-witness rule" was adhered to.

Cited again and again in English law reports, during the century that preceded American independence, was the trial in 1668 of Peter Messenger and fourteen others, eight of whom were found guilty and four were put to death for high treason. The brand of treason was waging war on the king and accroaching the royal power "under colour of pulling down bawdy houses"—a power that belonged to the king alone, though it is doubtful if anybody expected Charles II to do much in that sort of moral crusade. "Down with the Bawdy Houses, Down with the Red-Coats," shouted "this rabble" of 400 men and boys on Easter Monday holiday. And some of them signed the death warrant of their leaders by calling out to the commander of royal troops, "If the king will not give us liberty of conscience, May-day shall be a bloody day." In other words, the tumultuous assembly in Moor-fields was a protest by Protestant Dissenters against the immorality of King Charles's court, and a symbolic uprising against the royal proclamation forbidding "conventicles"—private and secret religious meetings.

The conclusion that this was treason was reached by ten of the highest judges of England (over the dissent of Sir Matthew Hale) after a jury of "knights, esquires and gentlemen" had determined whether there were two good witnesses against each defendant to the overt acts charged in the indictments. The inquiry reached its peak, legally and otherwise, when Lord Chief Justice Kelyng called Richard Woodward up for examination. One witness had sworn to seeing him, carrying a stick, in the crowd that pulled down "Madam" Burlingham's house after "the redheaded man," Limerick, dragged her out of it.

"Lord Chief Justice: . . . Woodward, what say you?

"Woodward: My Lord, there was a whore clapped hands on me, and I wrung myself from her, and told her that her house should [i.e. would] be pulled down.

"Lord Chief Justice: You gentlemen of the jury, in this case take notice: as for Woodward, they say he was there with a stick in his hand. I would have you take notice that there is but one witness: for the other [witness] you have his own brags, if you will believe him, that he pulled down a house, you have no other; if you will take him to be a bragging fool you may."

The jury did take him to be one. Limerick went to the gallows; Woodward was acquitted because a Stuart judge was intrigued by his folly. This case, so revealing in its nuances, fortified the requirement of two witnesses to overt acts of treason. To offset that, it set up the principle that voluntary confession, not to treason but to an overt act held to be treasonable, could convert a defendant into one of the two witnesses required to convict him. To Americans in particular, it brought home the deadly connection between treason and heresy, wherever the government assumed the right to control the religious thinking of the people.

It may be said that these particular forms of treason became foreign to American affairs the moment national ties with England were cut. How could people living under a republican form of government be charged with "accroaching the royal power" or "compassing or imagining the death of the king"? They could not. But if the framers had approached this subject in the spirit that ruled England they would have made it treason "to compass or imagine the death of the Republic."

Those words stayed out; so that is that. Or is it? What was it that really happened at one minute past midnight on January 2, 1920, when, at the clang of a bell in the mind of Attorney General A. Mitchell Palmer, several hundred agents of the federal Bureau of Investigation swept out and filled the jails with 3,000 bewildered Russian, Finnish, Polish, German, Italian and other alien workmen? They being aliens, there could be no technical charge of treason against these hapless victims of the "Red Raids" of 1920. But the actual substance of their supposed crime was nothing more nor less than "compassing or imagining the death of the Republic." What was "McCarthyism" but a longer-lasting and equally virulent epidemic of the same disorder? Do not the same words apply, with complete logic, to the punitive actions of House and Senate committees that probe into people's thoughts and feelings, and to state investigators whose imputations of criminality drive socialistic college students into brooding cynicism?

The resemblance is so close to the ancient English form of treason, rejected by our constitution makers (and now obsolete in England), that it amounts to coidentity in everything but the severity of the punishment. There is no death sentence for "compassing or imagining the death of the Republic," though sometimes the pains and penalties do not run far short of that. The similarity extends to the location of the imagination. In a great proportion of the recorded English treason trials based on this feature of the law, the imagining was in the minds of kings, cabinet ministers and prosecutors. So it was here in the Palmer Raids, and so it has been in the later American manifestations. In many instances, no doubt, the hostile imagination is a reality. What is lacking is the action that transforms imagination into a crime, although nothing is easier for a prosecutor than to conjure an action out of the oral or written expression of a state of mind.

If anyone doubts that we have today an unenacted but enforceable law to punish people for "compassing or imagining the death of the Republic," let him ask himself this question: would all Americans recoil from the thought of having such a *written law?*

There are probably several millions who would defend that law with fanatic zeal if it were in the statute books, and a good part of them would like nothing better than to put it there.

But what has this to do with the framing of the treason clause of the Constitution and the attitude of the framers toward the Bill of Rights? It has everything to do with it if their thoughts spilled over into the areas they excluded from the definition of treason. The very fact of the limitation proves that they did spill over, and the history of England determines the nature of the spilling.

Henry VIII died in 1547. Upon the accession of Edward VI, an act was passed that wiped out all forms of treason except those contained in the statute of Edward III. The act then made it treason for any person to affirm "by open preaching, express words or saying" that the new king "is not or ought not to be supream head in earth of the Church of England"; treason also to say that Edward VI was not or ought not to be king. The punishment was graded— jail and confiscation for the first such remark, life imprisonment for the second and death for the third time it was said. If similar opinions were expressed by writing, printing or overt deed, the action was high treason from the start.

In the vibrations of power that followed, Catholic Queen Mary obtained the throne, and began to kill off the Protestants. Protestant Elizabeth succeeded her and slaughtered the Catholics (getting rid also of her rivals and some of her lovers). The queen's viceroy to Ireland was convicted of high treason for failing to prevent the escape of the traitor O'Rourke, who compassed and imagined the queen's death by writing her name on a picture, dragging the paper tied to a horse's tail and cutting it to pieces with a head-chopper's ax.

After Elizabeth came the eighty-five-year epoch of the Stuarts, with Cromwell's Puritan Revolution sandwiched in. It was a period in which the orgy of persecution continued, with Catholics and Protestant Dissenters as victims of the Anglicans except when Cromwell's Puritans had their go at everybody else. Gallows, pillory, knotted whip and prison were used, by every faction that gained power, in an effort to determine which Christian denomination best represented the loving spirit of the Nazarene and the merciful benignity of God.

Elizabeth, Cromwell and the Stuarts all put heavy emphasis

on the criminality of the *written* word. This marked the impress of a new force in the world. From the time William Caxton set up the first printing press in England, in 1477, until Henry VIII broke with the Roman church, printed books were almost entirely religious in subject and orthodox in tone. But the rupture among English Catholics coincided with a broad spreading of Wycliffite dissent. By the time Elizabeth picked up Mary's bloody sword, the Church of England was beset on both sides and printing had become a tuppenny trade. With concealed backing from Sir Charles This or Squire Humphrey That, anybody with nimble fingers and a knowledge of the alphabet could set up a basement publishing house and convert the manual scrawl of his patron or his patron's parson into a readily distributed pamphlet, discreetly anonymous. The way to heaven being the principal thing in people's minds, except how to postpone going there, the country was soon flooded with Anabaptist, Presbyterian, Quaker and Papist tracts that singed the hides and seared the souls of Anglican bishops and archbishops.

To deal with the Catholics, Elizabeth and her Parliament created numerous new treasons. The death penalty was imposed upon "Romish priests," upon anybody who sheltered a Jesuit, upon anybody who should defect from the Anglican to the Roman church. It was made high treason to imagine bodily harm to the queen, or to call her a tyrant, usurper or heretic, and under these laws it was no longer necessary to prove an overt act. Mere expression of an opinion was enough for conviction and death. Here was, in fact, a total reversal of a later axiom of Sir Edward Coke, which became true in time partially because he said it when it was not true, that "Bare words may make an heretick but not a traytor without an overt act."

Protestant Dissenters furnished Elizabeth with no Mary Queen of Scots to torment her with dreams of deposition and death. Anabaptists and Calvinists thrust their thorns into the flesh of the clergy rather than of the queen, who responded willingly but futilely when asked to pull them out. Here, much more than in the contention with the Catholics, repression took the form of supression of freedom of speech and of the press.

Restriction of the press was a relatively late development. Printing had to be invented before it could be restrained, and it had to become a mass product before the need of restraint was felt. Queen Elizabeth and her churchly advisers recognized this need, and treason, felony and heresy statutes directed against authors and publishers became a new underpinning of monarchy in a country where Church and State were one. When these proved unavailing, they were supplemented by a licensing system to control the actual printers and their presses. The government and its minions alone were free to express opinion through the spoken or written word.

This blow to human liberty was struck first by the Tudors a few years before the earliest settlers sailed for the New World. During the next two centuries the savagery of the laws abated, but the repression of freedom became more general as it was systematized in the courts. The whole record was known to the men who built the government of the United States on the sovereignty of the people and their rights as citizens of a republic. Most of it they knew by their reading of history, part of it by observation, and some by going through a revolutionary struggle in which the possible alternatives were the laurel wreath of victory and the hangman's noose.

The united influence of history, observation and experience explains the determination of the framers to restrict the definition of treason to the part of the Statute of Edward III that was applicable to a republic. It explains the exclusion of constructive treason by making an overt act of war, or active adherence to an enemy, the essential elements of that restricted crime. It explains the added requirement, going beyond the ancient English statute, of proof by two witnesses to the same overt act. It makes natural, even inevitable, the most important word in the article: treason was to consist ONLY in what was there defined. In a closely related field, it explains the prohibition of religious tests for office.

But the very nature and scope of this prevailing knowledge gives rise to other questions. What did the framers expect to accomplish by other restraining clauses of the Constitution they drafted in 1787? And why did they not give specific protection to the great rights that were declared untouchable in later amendments? That calls for further inquiry into the work of the Philadelphia convention.

CHAPTER 3
Textbooks on Tyranny

It is not enough merely to assert, without supporting evidence, that the framers of the Constitution of 1787 had intimate knowledge of the 500-year struggle between tyranny and freedom that had been going on in England. Still less may one guess at their reaction to that knowledge, except where it involved the causes of the American Revolution. They were educated men and college degrees denoted more then than they do now, even apart from the major shift from theology to football scholarships. Consider the correspondence between young William Bradford of Philadelphia (later President Washington's Attorney General) and James Madison, when Bradford consulted his elderly friend (Madison was nearly twenty-three) about the formation of "a library of books which I intend shall be my companions thro' life." Bradford was already intent on "history and morality," but had made the mistake after leaving college of mastering the subjects in chronological stages and was just emerging from ancient Rome. He asked his mentor to draw up a list of books suitable for a "gentleman's library," with emphasis on the British constitution. Madison furnished the list (now lost) and followed it with the comment:

"I am pleased that you are going to converse with the Edwards and Henrys and Charles etc. etc. who have swayed the British Sceptre though I believe you will find some of them dirty and unprofitable companions unless you will glean instruction from their follies and fall more in love with liberty by beholding such detestable pictures of tyranny and cruelty."

That observation came from a young man who was to be the

29

principal working architect of our constitutional guarantees of liberty. It furnishes clear evidence that Madison thought of English history primarily as a contest between liberty and tyranny, and his thoughts were focused on the periods when tyranny ruled. As the scroll of the centuries unrolled, he beheld a warning against dire examples rather than a model to be followed. It was a one-sided appraisal, but his was a one-sided approach—the side of liberty.

For that fact the reading of history was only in part responsible. On a smaller scale, the Old World story of tyranny and cruelty was being acted out, almost in Madison's front yard, by the established Anglican Church in its prosecution of Dissenters. "Slavery and subjection," he wrote to Bradford in 1774, would he believe be the fate of all the colonies if the Church of England held sway throughout the continent as it did in Virginia. Of conditions in that commonwealth he wrote:

"Poverty and luxury prevail among all sorts; pride, ignorance, and knavery among the priesthood, and vice and wickedness among the laity. This is bad enough, but it is not the worst I have to tell you. That diabolical, Hell conceived principle of persecution rages among some and to their eternal infamy, the clergy can furnish their quota of imps for such business."

Two years later, as a delegate to Virginia's revolutionary convention, Madison planted in the new state's Declaration of Rights the first constitutional guarantee ever written of complete freedom of conscience. By discarding the half-servile doctrine of religious toleration by grace of those in power, he set the pattern not only for genuine freedom of religion as a natural human right, untouchable by government, but for the extension of that same principle to all the other rights and liberties that give dignity to human life. In 1784-85, after the Anglican Church was disestablished, Madison led and won the fight against re-establishment through tax support of all religious teachers.

Edmund Randolph, another participant in the 1787 treason debate, had shown himself in advance of his times during the Revolution. As Virginia's Attorney General, having the easy opportunity of disposing of a captured outlaw by enforcing a bill of attainder passed by the legislature, he gave Josiah Phillips a chance for his life by putting him on trial for robbery before a jury. The result was the same—a death sentence. But the course he followed gave him the opportunity to ask, when the Phillips attainder became a factor in Virginia's ratification of the Constitution: "Was this arbitrary deprivation of life, the dearest gift of God to man, consistent with the genius of a republican government?"

Benjamin Franklin, at the age of sixteen, had seen and felt transplanted tyranny in another field of human liberty. His brother James, founder in Boston of the second newspaper on the continent, published an anonymous article hinting that the Massachusetts Assembly was soft on piracy. James was imprisoned for a month by the arbitrary order of the colonial lawmakers. Benjamin, his apprentice, received a reprimand from the colony council, either for not knowing who wrote the article or for having such a brother. On the latter point Benjamin did some wondering himself. James had treated him with persistent cruelty, but Benjamin stood by him in this crisis and put out the *New England Courant* by himself, inserting in it covert criticism of the colonial government's assault on freedom of the press. Sixty years later, describing the misconduct of the Assembly but referring particularly to the cruelty of his brother, he wrote in his *Autobiography*: "This severe and tyrannical treatment contributed, I believe, to imprint on my mind that aversion to arbitrary power, which, during my whole life, I have ever preserved."

Educated Americans of the eighteenth century were as well versed in history and political theory as in the classics. In 1783, when Madison was a leading member of the Continental Congress, he obtained authority to "report a list of books proper for the use of Congress." Among the hundreds he recommended were works on politics and religion which, if converted into corresponding modern issues and listed for student reading by a university professor, would provide a year's sensation for congressional investigators of un-American activities. In the more orthodox field of British history, the suggestions included Hume, who exposed the misdeeds of conservatives in apologizing for them; Clarendon, a Stuart royalist who damned the Commonwealth and was not easy on his friends; and the two iconoclasts, Rapin-Thoyras and Kennett, who cracked the heads of kings. One paragraph from Rapin, descriptive of the reign of Richard II, was enough to set off a shower of sparks in the mind of almost any American Revolutionist:

"The Parliament strove to carry the Prerogative Royal to a greater height than any King of England had ever pretended to stretch it, and established such maxims as were destructive of the constitution and liberties of the people. . . . Pursuant to this principle, the judges who attended during the sitting of the Parliament, decided, that *When the King proposed any Articles to be debated in Parliament, it was High-Treason to bring in others before the King's were first dispatched.* By this and the like decisions, the cases of High-Treason were so multiplied, that hardly was it possible to prevent falling into that crime, unless by making the King's will and pleasure the sole rule of action."

Madison's book list for Congress provided the usual sets of parliamentary histories and debates, and two great stores of ammunition against royal, ministerial and judicial oppressions: *Cabala: Mysteries of State, in letters of the great ministers of King James and King Charles*; and Rushworth's *Historical Collections.* Familiarity with Rushworth's eight folio volumes was taken for granted among educated Americans. Jefferson wrote as casually about "looking into Rushworth" as one would today about the *Federalist.* The crown-piece of the *Collections* was its final volume, whose entire 786 pages were devoted to the bill of attainder—that is, condemnation of a man to death by direct vote of a legislature— against the Earl of Strafford. Evil though Strafford's influence had been, the circumstances under which Parliament sentenced him to death without a judicial trial went far toward fixing American sentiment against that iniquitous instrument of tyranny and against constructive treason. In Rushworth, too, one found the detailed record of John Lilburne's epochal fight for freedom of speech and press, freedom of religion, and the guarantees of fair trial that were being violated by Stuart judges.

Madison's section on politics included the works of Sidney, Locke, Harrington and Priestley, apostles of liberty; also the ultra-monarchic Hobbes and Selden. In the list was the Italian Beccaria, who did more than any other man to arouse Europe to the monstrous nature of torture and other forms of compulsory self-incrimination. Burnet's *History of His Own Time*—a familiar reference work in America—revealed the reaction of a fair-minded Anglican bishop against the excesses produced by the anti-Catholic feeling that he shared. Burnet helped to tell the story of death and terror that resulted from the fictitious "Popish Plot" invented by Titus Oates and his crew of perjured informers—a story swallowed whole by Parliament and the public and utilized by an Administration that knew it to be false.

The books recommended to Congress covered the whole field of international law. Though including Justinian, Coke and the newcomer Blackstone, Madison's report made no attempt to duplicate the library of a practicing lawyer, which commonly ran into hundreds of volumes[1] that were of necessity owned by a large percentage of the members of Congress.

As the Treasury contained many million dollars less than nothing, Madison could not get a clipped shilling for his project even though the objective won sympathy. There was in fact no need of buying these books except for the future. The greatest American library of the eighteenth century—that of the Library Company of Philadelphia—had been in use since 1774 as an unofficial Library of Congress. Housed but a few yards away in Carpenters' Hall, it was constantly resorted to for governmental, legal and historical material. On its shelves was the whole story of English kings and parliaments and courts, of guilt and innocence alike condemned, of immemorial rights and memorials of wrong.

Under a charter granted in 1742 by the Pennsylvania proprietaries, Benjamin Franklin and seventy-four others were authorized to establish this library especially intended for mechanics and others who could not afford a college education. The noted lawyer Andrew Hamilton was one of the founders. Under Franklin's guidance it went far beyond its original purpose. Other Philadelphia libraries merged with it. Peter Collinson of London, a friend of Franklin, acted for thirty years as its London purchaser, as Franklin himself did during his years as colonial agent in England. The idea spread and similar smaller libraries were established in other cities. That process was still going on when Dr. George Stueber wrote about it in his continuation of Franklin's *Autobiography:*

"This will be the best security for maintaining our liberties. A nation of well-informed men, who have been taught to know and prize the rights which God has given them, cannot be enslaved. It is in the regions of ignorance that tyranny begins."

From the beginning the Library Company of Philadelphia put dual emphasis on science and on the great political clash of the eighteenth century—the contest between governments striving for power and men struggling for liberty. As a matter of course, the library contained Emlyn's 1730 enlargement of Salmon's *State Trials*, and supplemental volumes up to 1765. Here, in ten great folios, was the chronicle of tyranny and cruelty that darkened the courts through the centuries—yet centuries that marked the slow and painful advance in England toward justice and freedom.

The *State Trials* are not official lawbooks. Yet they are still cited today, and rightly so, by English and American judges. The heaviest damage they inflict on the reputations of jurists and prosecutors is by allowing them the privilege of voluntary self-incrimination. High praise was bestowed on these books in 1770, for factual accuracy, *by a defender of crown judges,* when a parliamentary critic of the courts asserted that they made the record of some judicial rulings better than they were. Said Alexander Wedderburn (afterward Lord Chancellor) in rebuttal:

"I take the *State Trials* to be books of good credit. At least men of as great penetration and judgment as any person in this House have viewed them in that light. . . . For the *State Trials* do not relate to things done in a corner. They record transactions that passed on a public theatre, before the nation at large. Falsehood, therefore, in such great and essential points could not creep into them without detection. . . ."

By 1787, many American libraries and individuals possessed this work. Eight Americans were among the prepublication subscribers whose advance support made possible the issuance of the 1730 edition, and some of the names have lasting significance. One subscriber was Chief Justice Lewis Morris of New York, who was removed from office three years later for refusing to make decisions demanded of him by royal Governor Cosby. Another was William Smith, one of the counsel for Peter Zenger in the most famous "freedom of the press" case in American history. Still another subscriber was Chief Justice Nicholas Trott of South Carolina, who, when Speaker of the House of Representatives, had been arrested for seditious libel by the royal governor. Also among the American subscribers was Mann Page of Virginia, father of Congressman John Page, Madison's most helpful associate in stirring the House of Representatives to take up the subject of amending the Constitution.

But this great collection of treason, heresy and sedition trials was not the major source of American information on the subject. Almost every notable political or religious trial in those two hundred years was put before the English and American public in pamphlets that sold in thousands. At the time of the Constitutional Convention, the Philadelphia library used by the delegates contained sixty-three pamphlets on criminal trials published before 1780, nearly all of them political prosecutions. All but two—those dealing with the Zenger case and the "Boston Massacre" murder trials—were imported from England, where, also, the Zenger pamphlets were reprinted and sold in countless numbers. It was more from the pamphletized record than from formal law reports that the great collection of *State Trials* was compiled by its successive editors.

From this broad background of historical knowledge, the framers of the Constitution considered the various dangers to liberty. The effect is visibly evident in the debate on treason. It is invisibly evident in the fact that the clause forbidding Congress to pass bills of attainder went into the Constitution without a word of debate or a single adverse vote, and that the prohibition was extended to the states. During the Revolution, a number of state legislatures had resorted to bills of attainder, mixing patriotic motives with the covetous purpose of confiscating the property of British Loyalists. They were recognized in retrospect as one of the vicious accompaniments of civil strife, putting accusation, judgment and punishment into the hands of impassioned legislators. With similar unanimity of purpose, the framers approved a clause forbidding the states to pass *ex post facto* laws. All agreed that it was unjust to punish a person for an action that was not a crime when it was committed, but was made so by a later law.

There was unanimous action and no debate in requiring that the trial of all crimes (except in impeachment) be by jury. Dividing a motion into two parts, the delegates voted unanimously that "The privilege of the writ of Habeas Corpus shall not be suspended." Seven states to three, they added the proviso, "unless in cases of rebellion or invasion the public safety may require it." North and South Carolina and Georgia wanted the guarantee to be absolute, as did Wilson of Pennsylvania. Invisibly, England's anti-Stuart Habeas Corpus Act of 1679 fortified the general distrust of power, passion and judicial subservience.

Religious tests for public office were forbidden without an opposing vote, and with the sole dissenting remark that Congress could be trusted not to impose them. Titles of nobility were prohibited with no comment and no contradiction. With similar unanimity, citizens were assured of equal privileges and immunities in all the states, and all states were guaranteed a republican form of government and federal protection against rebellion.

That is the record of what the framers of the Constitution did to safeguard the rights and liberties of citizens. Now for what they did not do. On September 12 the Committee on Style and Arrangement reported the final draft of the Constitution. A motion to provide for jury trial in civil cases brought the objection from Nathaniel Gorham of Massachusetts that this would include equity cases, to which the jury system did not properly apply. Madison's notes then record:

"Col. Mason perceived the difficulty mentioned by Mr. Gorham. The jury cases cannot be specified. A general principle laid down on this and some other points would be sufficient. He wished the plan had been prefaced with a Bill of Rights, and would second a motion if made for the purpose. It would give great quiet to the people; and with the aid of the State declarations, a bill might be prepared in a few hours.

"Mr. Gerry concurred in the idea and moved for a Committee to prepare a Bill of Rights. Col. Mason seconded the motion.

"Mr. Sherman was for securing the rights of the people where requisite. The State Declarations of Rights are not repealed by this Constitution; and being in force are sufficient. There are many cases where juries are proper which cannot be discriminated. The Legislature [Congress] may be safely trusted.

"Col. Mason. The laws of the U.S. are to be paramount to State Bills of Rights."

The Journal recorded the vote: "unanimously in the negative."

Two days later, on the next to the last working day of the convention, Charles Pinckney and Gerry moved to insert a declaration "that the liberty of the press should be inviolably observed." This was the reception:

"Mr. Sherman. It is unnecessary. The power of Congress does not extend to the press. On the question, it passed in the negative." Massachusetts, Maryland, Virginia and South Carolina voted Aye.

Haste and fatigue, Madison wrote at a later time, caused the convention to pay less attention to Mason's proposal than if he had made it earlier in the convention. That was true, no doubt, but hardly basic. The evident fact was that the delegates did not regard a Bill of Rights as essential. Sherman offered three reasons for this. (1) The State Declarations were in effect and adequate. (2) The power of Congress did not extend to the press. (3) Congress could be trusted.

But Congress was not trusted when it came to treason, bills of attainder, *ex post facto* laws, trial by jury for crime, religious tests for federal office, titles of nobility, and only in part on habeas corpus. Those were subjects *to which the power of Congress unquestionably did extend*, and that may fairly be taken as the crucial factor. Had there been any similar belief that congressional power extended to religion, the demand to eliminate it would have been quick and decisive. The framers created a partial Bill of Rights by limiting or prohibiting certain legislation which otherwise would clearly lie within the federal power. But they did not extend these prohibitions to areas in which they believed federal power to be nonexistent.

Another fact needs to be pointed out. Every restriction put in the body of the Constitution was worded as an unqualified command. Treason as defined was to be the ONLY treason. There were to be NO bills of attainder, NO test oaths, NO titles of nobility. The trial of ALL crimes was to be by jury. ALL governments were to be republican in form, kept so by forcible intervention.

The Bill of Rights asked for by Mason was to be quite different: "A general principle laid down . . . would be sufficient." The article proposed by Pinckney was of the same sort. Liberty of the press SHOULD BE inviolably preserved. That would not be a mandate. It would be a maxim of good government, which Congress could heed if it felt like doing so, or trample underfoot without the least probability of being restrained by the judges.

The delegates at Philadelphia could indeed have prepared a nonmandatory Bill of Rights within a few hours. They could have adopted Mason's own Virginia Declaration of Rights, and it would have been a noble expression of the principles of free government. But they could not in a few hours convert those principles into binding commands enforceable in the courts. That would be a work of days or even weeks, if the commands were to be both safe and comprehensive.

When this is realized, it becomes evident that the defeat of the Mason-Gerry motion for a Bill of Rights opened the surest road to an adequate one. At every point where the framers of the Constitution saw a menace to life and liberty, lying within the *admitted range* of the powers delegated to Congress, they said to that body: "Thou shalt not." But the task was not complete.

The restrictions and prohibitions of the Constitution covered the instrumentalities and practices by which the Edwards and the Henrys and the Charleses had kept themselves in power and ringed the city of London with quartered bodies fixed on poles. The affirmative mandates guaranteed the safeguards, trial by jury and habeas corpus, which had proved the bulwark of English freedom when the odds were not too great. This much was accomplished in the Philadelphia Convention. It remained for the American people and for Congress itself, including many of the framers, to broaden the commands. They had yet to deal with the *unadmitted* but *possible* powers of the national government in the area of civil rights and liberties.

CHAPTER 4
Ten Pillars of Freedom

No sooner had the Continental Congress laid the proposed Constitution before the people for ratification than a great cry went up: it contained no Bill of Rights. Two of the framers, George Mason and Elbridge Gerry, opposed adoption partially on that ground. The cry for a Bill of Rights came loudest from state-minded politicians who hoped to defeat the Constitution altogether, or had dreams of a second convention in which Congress would be denied the power to lay taxes or to regulate commerce. However, their expressions of alarm would have had no force if they had not touched a sensitive nerve among the masses of the people throughout the thirteen states.

In five states—Delaware, Pennsylvania, New Jersey, Georgia and Connecticut—the Constitution was ratified too speedily for organized protest to muster strength. But when the Massachusetts convention acted in February 1788, it enjoined upon its future representatives in Congress that they work for certain amendments and alterations that "would remove the fears and quiet the apprehensions of many of the good people of this Commonwealth and more effectually guard against an undue administration of the Federal Government." What they feared most, apparently, was the power of Congress to levy direct taxes, but three amendments they wanted were germane to civil rights—a requirement of indictment by a grand jury for any crime involving infamous punishment or loss of life; jury trial in civil cases if asked for by either party; and a declaration reserving to the states all powers not expressly delegated to Congress.

Maryland ratified without reservations, after a hard fight produced by the clause forbidding the states to emit paper money. No action was taken on a committee report calling for libertarian amendments. South Carolina sought to retain state control of federal elections and to weaken the taxing power of Congress. New Hampshire took over the entire body of Massachusetts proposals, and on June 21, 1788, became the ninth state to ratify. The Constitution, by its own terms, had been adopted by enough states to be effective as to them.

But the great fight was not ended, for it was inconceivable that the new government could function or the nation exist without Virginia and New York. With the New Hampshire result unknown, the June conventions of those two states were rocked by struggles in which civil liberty was on the lips of orators and the location of power was uppermost in their thoughts. Personally, it became in New York a battle between Governor George Clinton and Alexander Hamilton, and in Virginia between Patrick Henry and James Madison. Clinton, head of a powerful political machine, was trying to preserve New York's tremendous economic asset—its semimonopolistic power to levy duties on all goods brought in through America's greatest seaport, regardless of their ultimate destination. Patrick Henry was fighting against abolition of the state powers that had been the basis of his political supremacy— the power to issue paper money whose depreciation would ease the payment of debt, and the power to impair the value of contracts by laws postponing payments under them. Hamilton and Madison had nothing to gain or lose in state politics. They were working to save the nation from chaos and collapse.

For more than five months, until March 4, 1788, Madison had remained in New York City to collaborate with Hamilton in the writing of the *Federalist Papers,* published in New York newspapers and republished throughout the country as an aid to ratification. In June each man took the leadership in his own state convention, and with able colleagues sustained the necessity of a new government with ample powers. Virginia's action, Hamilton wrote to Madison, would determine the outcome in New York.

In Virginia, opponents of the Constitution hammered upon the theme of a Bill of Rights. Its supporters replied that such a declaration was not needed and might be dangerous, jeopardizing the rights not specified in it. A year later, referring to the ratification debates when speaking in Congress, Madison said: "Some policy has been made use of, perhaps, by gentlemen on both sides of the question." His evident meaning was that those who demanded prior amendments were using the apprehensions of the people to defeat the Constitution, and those who replied that a Bill of Rights was dangerous had no belief that it need be so.

The odds changed in Virginia when the advocates of ratification adopted the strategy worked out by Madison and George Nicholas. The convention should ratify the Constitution without reservation, and ask for subsequent amendments. Madison pledged himself to help secure any amendments that would give satisfaction and were not harmful. These assurances did not win the antis, but swung the doubtful and brought victory.

George Mason itemized the guarantees to be asked for by Virginia. Fourteen of Mason's twenty articles were taken from the Virginia Declaration of Rights, and the language of Magna Carta was drawn upon to protect life, liberty and property and assure fair trials in accord with the law of the land. But the entire document had the defect of being admonition, not command. In thirty-three places it said that something "ought" or "ought not" to be done, or used some similar adjuration. Not once was there a "shall not," such as the Constitution itself contained where it touched on rights and liberties.

Most significant in the Virginia convention's action was the double emphasis placed on rights vital to self-government and personal dignity: freedom of speech, of the press, and of religion. Mason's amendments called them bulwarks of liberty: they *ought not* to be violated. The actual resolution of ratification, drafted by the supporters of the Constitution, used far stronger language. It asserted "in the name and in behalf of the people of Virginia . . . that no right of any denomination can be cancelled, abridged, restrained, or modified, by the Congress . . . by the President, or any department or officer of the United States, except in those instances in which power is given by the Constitution for those purposes; and that among other essential rights, the liberty of conscience and of the Press cannot be cancelled, abridged, restrained, or modified, by any authority of the United States."

Had that stood by itself, separate from the resolution of ratification, it would have received unanimous approval. It declared the meaning of the Constitution as it stood then, without amendment. But far more than that, it revealed the intensity of the desire for amendments specifically protecting these three primary freedoms, and the absolute sweep of the protection demanded. It was the mandate under which Representative James Madison of Virginia acted when he moved on June 8, 1789, in the first Congress of the United States, that the House take up the subject of constitutional amendments. As described in the *Annals of Congress*, Mr. Madison rose and reminded the House that this was the day that he had heretofore named for this action:

"As I considered myself bound in honor and in duty to do what I have done on this subject, I shall proceed to bring the amendments before you as soon as possible, and advocate them until they shall be finally adopted or rejected by a constitutional [two-thirds] majority of this House."

He then moved that the House resolve itself into a Committee of the Whole on the state of the Union, that he might "bring forward some propositions, which I have strong hopes will meet with the unanimous approbation of this House, after the fullest discussion and most serious regard." The insistent manner in which he spoke, quite different from his usual tactics, reflected the renewed agitation in Virginia for a second constitutional convention.

The motion met instant opposition as an interruption of the work of organizing the new government. Either appoint a select committee on amendments, advised William Smith of South Carolina, or let the Madison amendments be printed for study and later consideration. James Jackson of Georgia wanted a year's postponement. Examine the Constitution by experience, "discover by that test what its errors are, and then talk of amending." This "go-slow" position was taken by two men whose later records put them poles apart—Smith a notorious speculator in public securities, Jackson the indignant foe of the Yazoo land frauds.

Madison reminded the House that he had consented to one postponement for the dispatch of business, but the business was not dispatched. He wished now merely to bring the amendments before the House, "that our constituents may see we pay a proper attention to a subject they have much at heart." Continual postponements might inflame or prejudice the public mind against the work of Congress.

White of Virginia urged speedy action "to tranquillize the public mind," but the debate dragged on until John Page of Virginia remarked in a tone of disgust that rose to vehemence:

"If no objection had been made to his [Madison's] motion, the whole business might have been finished before this. . . . I venture to affirm, that unless you take early notice of this subject, you will not have power to deliberate. The people will clamor for a new convention; they will not trust the House any longer."

Madison then shifted tactics, withdrew his motion to go into Committee of the Whole, and moved the appointment of a select committee to consider and report amendments. This gave him the opportunity, as an argument for adoption of his motion, to submit and support his sheaf of proposals.

The House was bound by every motive of prudence, Madison said, not to let the first session pass without submitting amendments acceptable to the people. Among other reasons, he wished the friends of the Constitution to prove to those who opposed it, that its supporters were just as devoted to liberty and republican government as those who accused them of trying to lay the foundation of an aristocracy or despotism:

"It will be a desirable thing to extinguish from the bosom of every member of the community, any apprehensions that there are those among his countrymen who wish to deprive them of the liberty for which they valiantly fought and honorably bled."

That statement had more in it than patriotic oratory. It stands as a challenge, today, to those who contend that the Declaration of Independence did nothing but sever the political ties binding the American colonies to England, and that the people of the new nation automatically adhered to the folkways of the mother country, including the iniquities and shortcomings that had been perpetuated in the English common law. If the revolting colonists fought and bled for the rights and liberties they now thought to be still in jeopardy, they fought and bled for freedom of speech, press and religion, for protection of life, liberty and property against all arbitrary acts of government. Couple that with the declaration in the Virginia Act of Ratification that "the liberty of Conscience and of the Press cannot be cancelled, abridged, restrained, or modified, by any authority of the United States," and it carries those freedoms infinitely beyond the English common law, which offered no freedom whatever to religion, speech or press.

Although emphasizing the need to conciliate public opinion, Madison expressed his own belief that, all power being subject to abuse, amendments were desirable to strengthen the defenses against abuse of power. "I will not propose a single alteration," he promised, "which I do not wish to see take place, as intrinsically proper in itself, or proper because it is wished for by a respectable number of my fellow-citizens." Some objections had been leveled against the structure or powers of government, but he believed the great part of the people who opposed the Constitution disliked it because it did not contain effectual provisions against the encroachments on particular rights. By proper amendments they could "satisfy the public mind that their liberties will be perpetual," without endangering any essential part of the Constitution.

Madison then proposed eight amendments, one of them containing nine guarantees, and explained each amendment as he presented it. The first of them consisted of three general articles on the principles of government taken from the Virginia Declaration of Rights: that all power is vested in and derived from the people; that government ought to be exercised for their benefit; and that the people have a right to reform or change their government. This he presented with the comment:

"The first of these amendments relates to what may be called a bill of rights. I will own that I never considered this provision so essential to the Federal Constitution as to make it improper to ratify it, until such an amendment was added; at the same time I always conceived, that in a certain form, and to a certain extent, such a provision was neither improper nor altogether useless."

These three aphorisms, offered to satisfy George Mason, were dropped in committee. Although Madison's comment appeared to be directed only against them, he probably was thinking of the proposals in general. In October 1788 he had written to Jefferson that his opinion "had always been in favor of a bill of rights," but there was "great reason to fear that a positive declaration of some of the most essential rights could not be obtained in the requisite latitude." At that time he was not anxious to supply the omission "for any other reason than that it is anxiously desired by others." Now he was striving to satisfy both the anxiety of others and his own desire to give adequate protection to the most essential rights.

Madison's second and third amendments fixed the size of the House of Representatives and provided that no law varying the compensation of Congress should take effect until after the next election. Both were submitted to the states and neither one was ratified.

The remaining five proposals contained the complete substance of what became the first ten amendments of the Constitution. As proposed by Madison, these were to be scattered through the body of the instrument, wherever they fitted the original articles. This plan was altered, on motion of Roger Sherman of Connecticut, in favor of numbered articles of amendment to be appended to the original document. Thus the ten amendments took on the appearance of a formal Bill of Rights—a fact which gave these articles deserved prestige, but tended to obscure the guarantees of liberty already in the Constitution.

Madison then discussed the amendments that laid enforceable injunctions on the government. He was aware that a great many "champions for republican liberty" had held such a provision not only unnecessary but even improper. "I believe some have gone so far as to think it even dangerous." But these he suggested were policy statements, employed to promote ratification without prior amendments. There had been ingenuity, he conceded, in the arguments against the Constitution, drawn from the absence of something corresponding to the British Declaration of Rights of 1688. But that document merely raised a barrier against the power of the Crown. The power of Parliament remained indefinite in extent and the most valuable rights received no protection whatever:

"Although I know whenever the great rights, the trial by jury, freedom of the press, or liberty of conscience, come in question in that body, the invasion of them is resisted by able advocates, yet their Magna Charta does not contain any one provision for the security of those rights, respecting which the people of America are most alarmed. The freedom of the press and rights of conscience, those choicest privileges of the people, are unguarded in the British Constitution."

It might not be thought necessary to restrain the legislative power in England, Madison went on, but "a different opinion prevails in the United States." The people of many states had thought it essential to raise barriers against power in all forms and departments of government. If bills of rights were once established in all the states, as well as in the Federal Constitution, he was inclined to believe that even though some of the provisions were "rather unimportant, yet, upon the whole, they will have a salutary tendency." (That is, the general effect would be good even if "the great rights" were mixed with "rather unimportant" ones.) The contents of bills of rights he divided into five categories:

1. Those that "do no more than state the perfect equality of mankind . . . an absolute truth, yet . . . not absolutely necessary to be inserted at the head of a Constitution."

2. Those asserting the rights exercised by the people in establishing a plan of Government.

3. Those specifying the rights retained by the people when particular powers are given up to be exercised by the Legislature.

4. Those that seem to result from the nature of the social compact, such as trial by jury, which cannot be considered as a natural right yet is no less essential to securing the liberty of the people.

5. Those that lay down dogmatic maxims respecting the construction of the government, as that the legislative, executive and judicial branches shall be kept distinct and separate.

When these are regrouped according to Madison's estimate of their importance, the third and fourth categories stand out.

The first, asserting the equality of mankind, may have seemed self-evident under that day's assumptions, but the need to state it became imperative when slavery was abolished. The second group included the general propositions taken over from the Virginia Declaration of Rights, which Madison already had labeled unimportant. The same was true of the "dogmatic maxims" of the fifth category. The principle of separation of government into distinct departments was sound, he said, but he thought it more effective to plant actual safeguards in the Constitution, against the encroach-ment of one department upon another. As that already had been done, he was in effect saying that he was proposing an unnecessary amendment in order to satisfy the public. It was dropped.

Very different was Madison's appraisal of the guarantees in his third and fourth categories. The great object in view was "to limit and qualify the powers of government by excepting out of the grant of power those cases in which the government ought not to act, or to act only in a particular mode." He had already identified certain untouchable rights—freedom of religion, freedom of the press, trial of crimes by jury. To these could logically be added protection against general warrants, unreasonable search and seizure, denial of the right to counsel, assurance of habeas corpus and various other guarantees in the body of the Constitution.

The position Madison took might be called "the doctrine of the pre-eminence of the great rights." It furnishes a complete refuta-tion, dated 1789, of the contention sometimes made that all guaran-tees of the Bill of Rights are on an exact parity with each other in constitutional importance and enforceability. This tends to the conclusion that there is no more forcefulness to the words, "Congress shall make no law abridging the freedom of the press," than to the clause preserving jury trial in civil suits involving more than $20.00. This makes it easier to strip away the mandatory quality of the First Amendment and to leave the great freedoms subject to any abridgment that does not shock five members of the Supreme Court.

Quite different ideas were laid before Congress in 1789, when Madison asked that "the great rights" be placed beyond the reach of any branch of government. Sometimes, he said, the guarantees had to be directed against abuse of executive power, sometimes of legislative power. And in some cases, the prohibitions must be directed "against the community itself; or, in other words, against the majority in favor of the minority."

In the United States, Madison thought, it was perhaps less necessary to guard against abuse in the Executive Department, because it was the weakest branch of the system. "It must therefore be leveled against the Legislative, for it is the most powerful, and most likely to be abused, because it is under the least control." Yet he would confess that in a government modified like that of the United States, he saw the greatest danger of all in the abuse of power by the community itself.

"The prescriptions in favor of liberty ought to be leveled against that quarter where the greatest danger lies, namely, that which possesses the highest prerogative of power. But this is not found in either the Executive or Legislative departments of government, but in the body of the people, operating by the majority against the minority."

It might be thought "that all paper barriers against the power of the community are too weak to be worthy of attention." But at least the declaration of rights would have a tendency to impress respect for them, to establish public opinion in their favor, and rouse the attention of the whole community. It might therefore "be one means to control the majority from those acts to which they might be otherwise inclined." In other words, he was saying that the Bill of Rights by moral force might restrain part of the people from doing what all of the people have forbidden their government to do.

Some people, Madison remarked, believed that because the powers of the Federal Government were limited and enumerated, there was no need of a Bill of Rights, "the great residuum being the rights of the people." These arguments were not without foundation, said Madison, but they took no account of the fact that Congress had power to pass all laws "necessary and proper" to carry the enumerated powers into effect. That included the *means* of doing so. Might not, for example, general warrants be considered necessary for the enforcement of revenue laws? For analogous reasons general warrants were prohibited in state constitutions and there was like reason for restraining the Federal Government.

That argument by Madison is in total conflict with the contention of some judges that the grant of power to Congress to legislate in a particular field carries with it, by implication, the power to use a means that Congress is generally forbidden to use. Such decisions say in effect that Congress *may do lawfully, in spite of the prohibition,* what the framers feared Congress would do *unlawfully, without the prohibition.* There could hardly be a more glaring perversion either of the words or purpose of the Bill of Rights.

The next contention Madison took up was that a federal Bill of Rights was not needed because state declarations of rights were still in force. The solemn acts of the people in putting such declarations in their state constitutions, it had been said, could not be annihilated by their later establishment of a general government whose express purpose was "securing to themselves and posterity the liberties they had gained by an arduous conflict." (Here again the objectives of the American Revolution were defined in terms of the guarantees contained in bills of rights.)

Madison found this objection inconclusive. In the first place it was too uncertain ground on which to leave a matter considered so important by the people. "Besides, some States have no bills of rights, there are others provided with very defective ones, and there are others whose bills of rights are not only defective, but absolutely improper; instead of securing some in the full extent which republican principles would require, they limit them too much to agree with the common ideas of liberty."

Here Madison refuted in advance an argument later utilized to undermine the basic freedoms—the contention that the defects in state bills of rights should be used to measure the purpose, force and extent of the federal guarantees. In reality, those defects were used as an argument for adoption of a strong federal bill of rights, instead of being evidence of weakness in the one adopted.

This brought Madison to the question of enforcement. It had been said that a federal provision would be useless "because it was not found effectual in the constitution of the particular States." True it was that there were few states in which the most valuable rights had not been violated. But it did not follow that they had no salutary effect against the abuse of power. He saw two great protective agencies that would support the federal guarantees of liberty:

"If they are incorporated into the Constitution, independent tribunals of justice will consider themselves in a peculiar manner the guardians of those rights; they [the courts] will be an impen-

etrable bulwark against every assumption of power in the Legislative or Executive; they will be naturally led to resist every
encroachment upon rights expressly stipulated for in the Constitution by the declaration of rights."

The other protection was to come from the states:

"Besides this security, there is a great probability that such a
declaration in the federal system would be enforced; because the
State Legislatures will jealously and closely watch the operations of
this Government, and be able to resist with more effect every
assumption of power, than any other power on earth can do; and
the greatest opponents to a federal government admit the State
Legislatures to be sure guardians of the people's liberties."

Madison's word "admit" appeared to make him a sharer of the
opinion that the state legislatures were sure defenders of civil rights
and liberties. His next proposal made it evident that this was not
the case. The Constitution, he told the House, already contained
wise and proper restrictions on the states in the words "No State
shall pass any bill of attainder, *ex post facto* law, etc." There was
more danger, he thought, of those powers being abused by state
governments than by that of the United States. The same could
be said of other powers of equal or greater importance which the
states possessed, unless they were brought under control by the
general principle that laws are unconstitutional which infringe
the rights of the community. Then came his proposal:

"I should, therefore, wish to extend this interdiction, and add,
as I have stated in the fifth resolution, that no State shall violate the
equal rights of conscience, freedom of the press, or trial by jury in
criminal cases; because it is proper that every Government should
be disarmed of powers which trench upon those particular rights.
I know, in some of the State constitutions, the power of the Government is controlled by such a declaration; but others are not. I
cannot see any reason against obtaining even a double security
on those points . . . it must be admitted on all hands that the State
Governments are as liable to attack these invaluable privileges as
the General Government is, and therefore ought to be as cautiously
guarded against."

Broadened in committee to include freedom of speech, the
amendment was approved by the House but failed to receive a two-

thirds vote in the more state-minded Senate. Madison's apprehension of state violations of these freedoms was more than fulfilled, but in regard to Congress his look into the future did not extend to the twentieth century nor even to the end of the eighteenth. He did not foresee that nine years after he spoke, he would be calling upon his own state to resist an unconstitutional assumption of power against which the federal tribunals of justice made not the slightest attempt to be a bulwark. Still less did he look ahead to the more distant day when Supreme Court justices, equally sincere, would engage in forensic battles over the meaning of words which in themselves are clear and unequivocal: "Congress shall make no law abridging the freedom of speech or of the press."

What does that prohibition mean? Some judges say: The words "Congress shall make no law" mean that Congress shall make no law.

Another group says: The words "Congress shall make no law" mean that Congress shall make no law unless, balancing the needs of the country against the command of the Constitution that such a law shall not be made, the legislators conclude that the reasons for making the law outweigh the reasons for not making it.

That is known as the "balancing test." Under it, a law abridging freedom of the press is a valid law unless the Supreme Court finds some compelling reason for concluding that the judgment of Congress is incorrect. That, in one small and one large nutshell, is a condensation of tens of thousands of words embodied in Supreme Court opinions written since the First World War and the Russian Revolution duplicated the effect of the French Revolution and knocked Congress and the courts and the people off their feet. Between these extreme positions there is a middle ground which many jurists and commentators have sought to occupy. But every decision not based on the words of the Constitution is forced to a rejection of them, which opens the way to annihilation both of the declaration of rights and of the rights themselves. Let us test the reasoning by the actual words of those who put these guarantees into the Constitution.

Would the Revolutionary generation have recognized the "balancing test" as "the liberty for which they valiantly fought and honorably bled"?

What room is there for the "balancing test" in the declaration of the Virginia ratifying convention "that among other essential rights the liberty of Conscience and of the Press cannot be cancelled, abridged, restrained, or modified, by any authority of the United States"?

Did Representative Page think that congressional power to "balance freedom against other interests" was in the thoughts of the American people when he told his colleagues that unless there was speedy action "you will not have power to deliberate"?

Is it through such a concept that the government is *"disarmed* of powers which *trench upon* those particular rights"?

Was the "balancing test" what Madison had in mind when he said that an independent judiciary would be an "impenetrable bulwark" against every assumption of power, resisting "every encroachment" upon rights expressly set forth in the declaration of rights?

The American people are caught up today, like the rest of humanity, in the world-wide confrontation of democratic self-government and Communist or Fascist totalitarianism. Democratic self-government cannot endure *without* freedom; totalitarian government cannot endure *with* it. To destroy freedom for the purpose of preserving democracy is like cutting out a man's heart to reduce his blood pressure.

The commands to Congress are in the Constitution, mandates of liberty put there by the American people at a time when the dangers inherent in unchecked power were made acute in their minds by the memories of tyranny. And the words addressed to the judges are in the record, pointing the way of moral obligation and judicial duty to those who make up the independent tribunals of justice.

CHAPTER 5
Hats On and Hats Off

Watching for an opportunity to bring up his amendments, Madison found a lull in business on July 21 and moved to go into Committee of the Whole to consider them. The motion produced the same opposition as before and some new support that was disturbing. Gerry of Massachusetts and Thomas Tudor Tucker of South Carolina wanted action in that manner so that they could bring up amendments that might not (and certainly would not) be reported by a select committee. Fisher Ames of Massachusetts sensed their purpose. He was sorry to hear an intention avowed of "considering every part of the frame of this Constitution. It was the same as forming themselves into a convention of the United States." Madison's motion was defeated 34 to 15 (possibly to his unspoken satisfaction) and his amendments were referred to a committee of one from each of the eleven states that were represented in Congress.

It was a friendly committee with Madison representing Virginia. Several members, like Chairman Vining of Delaware, thought no amendments were necessary, but agreed that if any were to be submitted they should be of a kind that would satisfy the people. Thus the friendly disbelievers were ready to go as far as Madison, Egbert Benson of New York, Thomas Burke of North Carolina, Gerry and other active advocates of strong safeguards against federal infringements of liberty. The committee made its report in a week, and August 13 was set for its consideration.

On that day, when Richard Bland Lee of Virginia moved to go into Committee of the Whole to consider the report, Sedgwick of Massachusetts opposed the motion with evident dislike of the entire proposition. "Is it desirable," Madison said in reply, "to keep up a division among the people of the United States on a point in which they consider their most essential rights are concerned?" He put it up to the House, "in point of candor and good faith, as well as policy, to be incumbent on the first Legislature of the United States, at their first session, to make such alterations in the Constitution as will give satisfaction, without injuring or destroying any of its vital principles." If action was delayed until other business was out of the way, he feared that "gentlemen's patience and application will be so harassed and fatigued" as to cause a postponement to the next session.

Chairman Vining urged immediate action on the report, saying he was so impressed by Madison's anxiety that he would consent to postpone a bill of great interest to him, which had priority. The motion carried, and a fight started as soon as the House took up the shortened and sharpened committee revision of Madison's article on freedom of opinion:

"The freedom of speech and of the press, and the right of the people peaceably to assemble and consult for the common good, and to apply to the Government for redress of grievances, shall not be infringed."

Sedgwick scoffed at the amendment. It would make them appear trifling in the eyes of their constituents.

"What, said he, shall we secure the freedom of speech, and think it necessary, at the same time, to allow the right of assembly? If people converse freely, they must assemble for that purpose; it is a self-evident, unalienable right which the people possess; . . . it is derogatory to the dignity of the House to descend to such minutiae; he therefore moved to strike out 'assemble and.' "

Benson replied. The committee, he said, "proceeded on the principle that these rights belonged to the people; they conceived them to be inherent and all that they meant to provide against was their being infringed by the Government." Sedgwick came back with sarcastic ridicule:

"If the committee were governed by that general principle, . . . they might have declared that a man should have a right to wear his hat if he pleased; that he might get up when he pleased, and go to bed when he thought proper; but he would ask the gentleman whether he thought it necessary to enter these trifles in a declaration of rights, in a Government where none of them were intended to be infringed."

Tucker, Gerry and Page challenged Sedgwick's argument, and the two latter congressmen got down to cases. The right of assembly, said Gerry, was an essential right, "and though it had been abused in the year 1786 in Massachusetts, yet that abuse ought not to operate as an argument against the use of it. The people ought to be secure in the peaceable enjoyment of this privilege, and that can only be done by making a declaration to that effect in the Constitution."

Gerry's remarks sound today like vigorous generalities, but everybody in the House knew what he was talking about. Had Gerry uttered his actual thoughts they would have run about like this: We know very well, Mr. Sedgwick, why you don't want the right of assembly to be given protection in the Constitution. We are well aware that in 1786, your excessive zeal against the Shaysites caused the farmers of your county to assemble with the intention of destroying your house.

Page of Virginia took up Sedgwick's scoffing illustration of superfluous guarantees:

"The gentleman from Massachusetts . . . objects to the clause, because the right is of so trivial a nature. He supposes it no more essential than whether a man has a right to wear his hat or not; but let me observe to him that such rights have been opposed, and a man has been obliged to pull off his hat when he appeared before the face of authority; people have also been prevented from assembling together on their lawful occasions. . . . If the people could be deprived of the power of assembling under any pretext whatsoever, they might be deprived of every other privilege contained in the clause."

That statement means nothing to twentieth-century America in the way of historical allusion. Was it equally meaningless to the men who listened to the spirited exchange between Page and Sedgwick? Why did Page say no more and why did no member of Congress ask what he was talking about? There was no need to do so. The mere reference to it was equivalent to half an hour of oratory.

William Penn loomed large in American history, but even if he had never crossed the Atlantic, bringing the Quaker religion with him, Americans would have known about his "tumultuous assembly" *and his hat.* Few pamphlets of the seventeenth century had more avid readers than the one entitled "The People's Ancient and Just Liberties, asserted, in the Trial of William Penn and William Mead at the Old Bailey, 22 Charles II 1670, written by themselves." Congressman Page had known the story from boyhood, reproduced in Emlyn's *State Trials* to which his father subscribed in 1730. It was available, both in the *State Trials* and as a pamphlet, to the numerous congressmen who had used the facilities of the City Library of Philadelphia. Madison had an account of it written by Sir John Hawles, a libertarian lawyer who became Solicitor General after the overthrow of the Stuarts in 1688. Connected with the Penn-Mead case and no less familiar was the momentous one that resulted from it, the "Case of Edward Bushell for alleged misconduct as juryman." These two cases, taken together, involved a major portion of the basic freedoms guaranteed in the American Bill of Rights. The Penn-Mead preface addressed to "The English Reader" castigated the system of injustice under which they were prosecuted:

"Liberty of Conscience is counted a pretence for Rebellion, and religious assemblies [are called] routs and riots. . . . Oh, what monstrous, and illegal proceedings are these? . . . When all pleas for liberty are esteemed sedition, and the laws, that give, and maintain them, so many insignificant pieces of formality.

"And what do they less than plainly tell us so, who at will and pleasure break open our locks, rob our houses, raze their foundations, imprison our persons, and finally deny us justice to our relief; as if they then acted most like christian men, when they were most barbarous, in ruining such, as really are so."

Forbidden to preach inside any building, William Penn delivered a sermon to a quiet, orderly assembly of Quakers in Gracechurch Street, London. He was at once committed to jail, along with William Mead (a listener unknown to him before the meeting), who was included in order to obtain an easier conviction by charging conspiracy. The indictment averred that Penn and Mead and three hundred unknown did unlawfully and tumultuously assemble and Penn "did take upon himself to preach and speak . . . to the great disturbance of [the king's] peace; to the great terror and disturbance of many of his liege people and subjects." Both pleaded not guilty.

The magistrates in the London Court of Sessions were Lord Mayor Samuel Starling, the Recorder and five aldermen. Although the narrative was Penn's, there was no challenge of his account of what followed the entry of the two men, bareheaded, for their trial.

"Mayor. Sirrah, who bid you put off their hats? put on their hats again."

An officer of the court enforced this order and the men were brought to the bar, hatted.

"Recorder. Do you not know there is respect due to the court?
"Penn. Yes.
"Recorder. Why do you not pay it then?
"Penn. I do so.
"Recorder. Why do you not pull off your hat then?
"Penn. Because I do not believe that to be any respect.
"Recorder. Well, the court sets forty marks apiece upon your heads, as a fine for your contempt of the court.
"Penn. I desire it might be observed, that we came into the court with our hats off (that is, taken off), and if they have been put on since, it was by order from the bench; and therefore not we, but the bench should be fined."

Three or four Crown witnesses testified to Penn's speaking and Mead's presence at the religious assembly, but when one of them said he did not see Mead, the Recorder asked the defendant a question (unrecorded) that brought this reply:

"Mead. It is a maxim of your own law, *'Nemo tenetur accusare seipsum,'* which if it be not true Latin, I am sure it is true English, 'That no man is bound to accuse himself.' And why dost thou offer to insnare me with such a question? Doth not this show thy malice? . . .

"Recorder. Sir, hold your tongue. I did not go about to insnare thee."

Penn now broke in to say that he would never recant "nor shall all the powers upon earth be able to divert us from reverencing and adoring our God who made us." He asked to know "upon what law you ground my indictment."

"Recorder. Upon the common-law.
"Penn. Where is that common-law?"

Repeating the question and getting only abusive answers he

quoted from Coke's *Third Institute* that "Common-Law is common right," and complained that "You have not answered me; though the rights and privileges of every Englishman be concerned in it."

"Recorder. Take him away. My Lord, if you take not some course with this pestilent fellow, to stop his mouth, we shall not be able to do anything tonight.

"Mayor. Take him away, take him away, turn him into the bale-dock."

Denied the right to defend himself or to face his accusers, Penn was taken to the bale-dock, a walled-off corner of the courtroom with partitions that did not reach the ceiling. As he was led away he called out to the jury:

"Must I therefore be taken away because I plead for the fundamental laws of England? However, this I leave upon your consciences, who are of the jury (and my sole judges) that if these ancient fundamental laws, which relate to liberty and property . . . must not be indispensably maintained and observed, who can say he hath right to the coat upon his back?"

William Mead was then examined, and told the jury that he stood there to answer to an indictment full of lies and falsehoods. He was a peaceable man, but was accused of meeting with force and arms in an unlawful rout. "The lord Coke tells us what makes a riot, a rout and an unlawful assembly. A riot is when three or more, are met together to beat a man," or to enter his land by force to cut his wood or break down his pales.

The recorder thanked Mead with mock deference for telling "what the law is." The mayor added, "You deserve to have your tongue cut out," and the prisoner was sent to join Penn in the bale-dock. The mayor and recorder then charged the jury in the absence of the defendants—a clear violation of the common law. It was proved, the recorder said, that Penn preached, Mead had "allowed of it," and the jury was to keep to and observe "what hath been fully sworn, at your peril." The court was telling the jurors that their sole duty was to return a verdict of "guilty as charged" if they found that Penn did preach in the street. If they went farther and decided that his preaching did not violate the law against rioting and tumultuous assembly, they would be subject to summary punishment. At this point, William Penn climbed above the wall of the bale-dock and cried out:

"I appeal to the jurors who are my judges, and this great assembly, whether the proceedings of the court are not most arbitrary, and void of all law, in offering to give the jury their charge in the absence of the prisoners . . . as Coke in the *Second Institute* . . .

"Recorder. Pull that fellow down, pull him down.

"Mead [also appearing above the wall]. Are these according to the rights and privileges of Englishmen, that we should not be heard, but turned into the bale-dock, for making our defence . . .

"Recorder. Take them away into the Hole."

The prisoners were pushed into the Black Hole and the jury went out. Learning after an hour and a half that they were divided the judges sent for them. "Mr. Bushell," said Alderman Robinson, "you have thrust yourself upon this jury . . . You deserve to be indicted more than any man that hath been brought to the bar this day."

"Bushell. No, Sir John, there were three-score before me, and I would willingly have got off, but could not.

"Mayor. Sirrah, you are an impudent fellow. I will put a mark upon you."

The jury was sent off again and soon returned. The prisoners were brought in. The clerk asked the required question: was William Penn guilty *in the manner and form* of the indictment, or not guilty?

"Foreman. Guilty of speaking in Gracechurch street.

"Recorder. You had as good say nothing.

"Mayor. Was it not an unlawful assembly? You mean he was speaking to a tumult of people there?"

Some of the jurors "seemed to buckle," the report of the trial records, but Bushell and others "allowed of no such word as an unlawful assembly in their verdict." Sent out again, they came back with the same verdict about Penn and a complete acquittal of Mead. The mayor scored them for being led by such a silly, impudent, canting fellow as Bushell. The recorder demanded "a verdict that the court will accept; and you shall be locked up, without meat, drink, fire, and tobacco; . . . we will have a verdict, by the help of God, or you shall starve for it."

"Penn. My jury, who are my judges, ought not to be thus men-aced; their verdict should be free, and not compelled . . .

"Recorder. Stop that prating fellow's mouth, or put him out of the court.

"Penn. . . . (Looking at jury) You are Englishmen, mind your privilege, give not away your right.

"Bushell and others. Nor will we ever do it."

The jury was kept "all night without meat, drink, fire, or . . . so much as a chamber-pot though desired." At seven o'clock Sunday morning they repeated the verdict, Penn was "guilty of speaking in Gracechurch Street."

"Mayor. To an unlawful assembly?

"Bushell. No, my Lord . . .

"Mayor. You are a factious fellow. I'll take a course with you. . . .

"Bushell. Sir Thomas, I have done according to my conscience.

"Mayor. That conscience of yours would cut my throat. . . . I will cut yours so soon as I can."

Twice more the jury went out and twice it came back, its verdict stubbornly unchanged. Said the mayor, referring to Bushell: "Have you no more wit than to be led by such a pitiful fellow? I will cut his nose."

"Penn. It is intolerable that my jury should be thus menaced. Is this according to the fundamental laws? Are not they my proper judges by the Great Charter of England?

"Mayor. Stop his mouth, gaoler, bring fetters, and stake him to the ground."

Ordered to go out again the jurors refused, the foreman saying: "We have given our verdict, and all agreed to it; and if we give in another, it will be a force upon us to save our lives." However, yield-ing to a sheriff's friendly plea, they deliberated through a fireless night in Newgate Prison and came back next day with a shorter ver-dict: William Penn, "Not Guilty." William Mead, "Not Guilty." The jury was polled: every man repeated the verdict as his own. Said the recorder:

"God keep my life out of your hands, but for this the Court fines you forty marks a man; and imprisonment till paid."

As this was an acceptance of the verdict, William Penn de-manded his release. "No," replied the mayor, "you are in for your fines."

"Penn. Fines, for what?

"Mayor. For contempt of the Court.

"Recorder. Take him away, take him away, take him out of the Court."

So, acquitted by a jury that refused to look upon public worship as riot or tumultuous assembly, Penn and Mead went to Newgate Prison *for having obeyed the court's order to put on their hats.* The twelve jurors went to prison for disobeying the court's order that the two Quakers be convicted.

This was the story that lay behind the verbal exchange between Congressmen Page and Sedgwick in the framing of the First Amendment. Every Quaker in America knew of the ordeal suffered by the founder of Pennsylvania and its bearing on freedom of religion, of speech, and the right of assembly. Every American lawyer with a practice in the appellate courts was familiar with it, either directly or through its connection with its still more famous aftermath, the habeas corpus proceedings in behalf of Edward Bushell and the eleven other jurors. Their imprisonment was fully in line with Tudor and Stuart practices, but came at a time when many Englishmen of all sects were getting sick of this perversion of the ancient jury system. It came at a rare moment also when high judges shared that feeling, and dared to express it.

Ten judges, headed by Chief Justice Vaughan of the Court of Common Pleas, were called together to pass on Bushell's writ. The "return" against it accused the jury of acquitting Penn and Mead "against full and manifest evidence and against the direction of the court in matter of law." Such a return, said Vaughan, did not inform the court whether the evidence was full and manifest "or doubtful, lame and dark." Furthermore, it was no crime to free the men against "full and manifest" evidence unless the jury did so knowing the evidence to be full and manifest. What was more common than for two judges to reach opposite conclusions on the same set of facts?

With equally scathing logic, the ten high judges dismissed the charge—factually correct—that the jury acquitted Penn and Mead against the direction of the court in the matter of law. If the meaning was, that the judge having heard the evidence should say that it placed the law on the side of the plaintiff, or of the defendant, and the jurors were to find accordingly, then—said Vaughan—"the jury is but a troublesome delay, great charge, and of no use in determining right and wrong." The proper course was for the jury to find out what the fact was, and for the judge to give discreet hypothetical suggestions of what the verdict should be if they find the fact to be thus or so.

In other words, Vaughan was *applying to freedom of speech and religion* the common-law principle in felony trials, that the judge *advises* the jury as to the law, but the jury *decides* both fact and law —whether, for example, a defendant charged with murder did the killing, and if so, whether it was murder, manslaughter or justifiable homicide. Chief Justice Vaughan and his fellow judges set a standard that emancipated jurors from the coercive pressure of the Crown. But Americans devoted to human liberties were well aware, in 1789, that the power of English juries to determine both law and fact in cases of the Penn-Mead variety was soon swept away in a heightened torrent of religious and political repression. Eighteenth-century England barely rose above the mockeries of freedom that caused Madison to decry the "detestable pictures of tyranny and cruelty" presented by Stuart and Tudor kings.

Congressman John Page spoke for an alarmed people and an informed people, and he spoke to an informed Congress, when he reached back into English history and brought forward, without needing to name it, one of the great examples of judicial tyranny founded on pretended law. Following the exchange between Page and Sedgwick, Representative Hartley turned to Sedgwick's motion to strike out "and assemble" from the guarantee of the right to consult and petition for redress of grievances. It was his personal belief that the words were not essential, but as four or five states had called for an express declaration in the Constitution, he was disposed to gratify them:

"He thought[1] every thing that was not incompatible with the general good, ought to be granted, if it would tend to obtain the confidence of the people in the Government; and, upon the whole, he thought these words ["and assemble"] were as necessary to be inserted in the declaration of rights as most in the clause."

This debate makes it clear that in framing the amendments, some members of Congress were going beyond their own ideas of necessity and accepting the more extreme views of the people at large. Sedgwick's motion to strike out "and assemble" as unnecessary "lost by a considerable majority."

A similar argument of "no necessity" came from Roger Sherman when the committee reported the reworded clause: "No religion shall be established by law, nor shall the equal rights of conscience be infringed." Congress, Sherman declared, "had no authority whatever delegated to them by the Constitution to make religious establishments." His motion to strike out the article was opposed by Daniel Carroll, a leading Catholic layman of Maryland:

"As the rights of conscience are, in their nature, of peculiar delicacy, and will little bear the gentlest touch of governmental hand; and as many sects have concurred in opinion that they are not well secured under the present Constitution, he said he was much in favor of adopting the words. He thought it would tend more towards conciliating the minds of the people to the Government than almost any other amendment he had heard proposed."

Madison undertook to calm New England fears that this would give Congress an opening to interfere with the state church (Congregational) established there. The meaning he apprehended "to be, that Congress should not establish a religion, and enforce the legal observation of it by law nor compel men to worship God in any manner contrary to their consciences." He thought if the word "national" were inserted, it would eliminate the widespread fear that "one sect might obtain a pre-eminence, or two combine together, and establish a religion to which they would compel others to conform."

A protest by Gerry, that the word "national" savored of consolidation of the states, caused Madison to withdraw his motion. The House then approved, 31 to 20, a more drastic substitute (later abandoned) offered by Livermore of New Hampshire: "Congress shall make no law touching religion, or infringing the rights of conscience."

Coming to what is now the Fifth Amendment, House members spoke not a word against the well-established principle of English law that no person shall be compelled to be a witness against himself. The prohibition of double jeopardy for the same offense was so worded as to prevent a second trial of a person, who, though guilty, had been improperly convicted. A motion to revise the wording failed, but Congress switched later to the simple and more elastic guarantee of the Articles of Confederation: "nor shall any person for the same offense be twice put in jeopardy of life or limb."

More significant was the defeat of a motion by George Partridge of Massachusetts to add the words, "by any law of the United States." Had that addition been made, it would have implied that a person tried and acquitted under federal law could later be tried and convicted of the same offense in a state court. The Supreme Court in a number of instances has upheld the power of a state to try and to convict a person after a federal acquittal of the same offense. The defeat of the Partridge amendment stamps every such double jeopardy as a perversion of the Constitution. The first eight amendments, in general, were meant to be binding only on the federal government. But the one forbidding double jeopardy has to cover both federal and state courts in order to fulfill its declared purpose. Partridge's motion certainly would have been adopted if Congress had shared his desire to open this loophole.

"Due process of law" was guaranteed without debate or an opposing vote. One voice, that of Livermore, was raised against the article forbidding cruel and unusual punishments. "It is sometimes necessary," said he, "to hang a man, villains often deserve whipping, and perhaps having their ears cut off, but are we in future to be prevented from inflicting these punishments because they are cruel?" The significant fact about Livermore's comment is that he believed these punishments would be abolished by the amendment, although he wished them to be continued.

When the clauses were taken up forbidding general warrants and unreasonable searches and seizures, the criticism was made that their wording did not achieve their full purposes. That was corrected, partly at this time, partly on a later day, with every evidence of repugnance to these pre-Revolutionary malpractices. There was no opposition to the clause requiring indictment or presentment by a grand jury, as a prelude to any trial "for a capital, or otherwise infamous crime." But Thomas Burke of North Carolina was beaten in an effort to forbid trials "by information"—that is, on simple accusation by a prosecutor—in any criminal case whatsoever. Thus Congress sensibly excluded minor misdemeanors.

The House came at length to Madison's proposed article: "No State shall infringe the equal rights of conscience, nor the freedom of speech, nor the right of trial by jury in criminal cases." Opposition came from South Carolina. This, said Tucker, "goes only to the alteration of the constitutions of particular States." These were already too much interfered with. His motion to strike out the words brought the author of them to his feet:

"Mr. Madison conceived this to be the most valuable amendment in the whole list. If there were any reason to restrain the Government of the United States from infringing upon these essential rights, it was equally necessary that they should be secured against the State Governments. He thought that if they provided against the one, it was as necessary to provide against the other, and was satisfied that it would be equally grateful to the people."

Livermore had "no great objection to the amendment," but wished to give it an affirmative cast: "The equal rights . . . shall not be infringed by any State." That was accepted. So ended the recorded debate on one of the most significant libertarian proposals in American history, made in a Congress elected—according to State Rights mythology—at a period of the highest devotion to state sovereignty. The clause was adopted, but failed to receive a two-thirds vote in the Senate. Ultimately it was in effect embodied in the Fourteenth Amendment and put in force by Supreme Court decisions holding that the Fourteenth made the guarantees of the First Amendment binding on the individual states.

South Carolina made one more effort to enlarge state powers when Madison's final amendment came up: "The powers not delegated by the Constitution, nor prohibited by it to the States, are reserved to the States respectively." That changed nothing, but was a declaration of existing fact. Tucker moved to make it read, "The powers not *expressly* delegated," which would have altered the Constitution profoundly. Madison protested:

"It was impossible to confine a Government to the exercise of express powers; there must necessarily be admitted powers by implication, unless the Constitution descended to recount every minutiae. He remembered the word 'expressly' had been moved in the convention of Virginia, by the opponents to the ratification, and, after a full and fair discussion, was given up by them, and the system allowed to retain its present form."

Sherman supported Madison and Tucker's motion was defeated. The Committee of the Whole, on Carroll's motion, added "or to the people," and Sherman sponsored the same change in later proceedings. This addition to the Tenth Amendment strengthened the implication that gives value to the Ninth—that there are rights and powers belonging to the people, beyond those embraced in state or federal constitutions. These, whenever they can be defined, are not to be infringed by any government.

All of the amendments approved in Committee of the Whole had to be acted on again in formal session of the House. Here the only significant change was a revision of the clause on religion. Offered by Ames but probably (from its wording and Ames's previous lack of interest) emanating from Madison, it read: "Congress shall make no law establishing religion, or to prevent the free exercise thereof, or to infringe the rights of conscience." This achieved the purpose of Madison's original clause and avoided the far-reaching ambiguity of Livermore's ban on any law "touching religion."

Before final adoption by the House, the amendments were slightly recast to fit the decision that they be added to the Constitution instead of being placed in the various articles of government to which they related. In select committee and on the floor, Madison's original wording had been improved and the meaning retained. Not one guarantee was weakened, except by dropping the exclusion of conscientious objectors from military service.

Changes made by the Senate were mostly minor and acceptable to the House, but the article forbidding an establishment of religion was thoroughly emasculated. It was cut down to read that Congress should "make no law establishing articles of faith or a mode of worship or prohibiting the free exercise of religion." The purpose was obvious: to open the way to financial support of religious institutions by the federal government. Madison could not fail to recognize the hand behind this. Senator Richard Henry Lee, a zealot of Anglican church establishment, had teamed up with New England Congregationalists to prohibit a national church yet open the way to duplication, on a national scale, of Patrick Henry's 1784 "Bill establishing a provision for teachers of the Christian religion." Madison had defeated Henry and Lee on that issue in the Virginia legislature, largely through the effect of his famous "Memorial and Remonstrance against Religious Assessments." He was named now as one of three House members appointed to settle the difference with the Senate. The result was a complete victory for the House.

The conference report produced a stronger and clearer command for separation of state and church than was to be found in any previous draft: "Congress shall make no law respecting an establishment of religion or prohibiting the free exercise thereof." The wording, completely in line with Madison's ideas, undoubtedly came from him, since his House associates (Vining and Sherman) had taken no part in shaping or discussing previous drafts of the article, and it was repugnant to the views which the Senate members were appointed to defend.

The clear and mandatory wording, "Congress shall make no law," was applied to all the guarantees of the First Amendment—on religion, speech, press, assembly and petition—when these were revised to fit the decision that all amendments be appended to the Constitution. Madison and his colleagues knew what they were doing. English history had demonstrated to them that without complete religious liberty, without freedom of conscience and separation of church and state, there could be no freedom of speech, or of the press, or the right of assembly. Both English and American experience had taught them that without all these freedoms there could be no free government. And they had learned that even in a country where the people are sovereign, no words of lesser force than "shall not"—enforceable in independent courts of law—could restrain the servants of the people from acting as if they were the masters.

CHAPTER 6
Mandates or Admonitions

Submitted to the thirteen states for ratification on September 25, 1789, the first ten amendments sailed through nine legislatures at their next sessions. On June 2, 1790, after Rhode Island made No. 9, action by one more state was needed to produce the required three fourths. The Virginia House of Delegates had given almost unanimous approval in the previous December and sent the ratification resolution to the antifederal little Senate. Eight of the fifteen senators in attendance were hard-core opponents of a strong federal government. They were fortified by a vitriolic letter from United States Senators Richard Henry Lee and William Grayson denouncing Congress and especially Madison for paying no heed to Virginia's call for restriction of the power of Congress to levy direct taxes. Eight to seven, the Senate voted to amend the House Resolution by striking out the most popular amendments. That threw all of them over to the next session.

The eight then placed a declaration in the Senate Journal that they killed the resolution because the guarantees of liberty were too weak. The one forbidding an establishment of religion, they said, did not prohibit financial aid to churches. This was a fictional alarm. Three of the eight protesting senators were conspicuous advocates of a union of church and state. Every senator who had made a record as a champion of religious liberty voted for immediate ratification. The purpose of the obstructing majority was recognized instantly: to frighten Virginia Baptists into opposition and send all the amendments back to Congress in order to open the way to destruction of the taxing power. Baptist leaders who had helped kill the tax support of teachers of religion in 1785 sent word to Madison that they were completely satisfied with the amendment. Two years elapsed, however, before a Senate chastened by public opinion and election results completed the ratification. That brought the ten amendments into force on December 15, 1791. A shift of one vote in the original action of the Virginia Senate would have put the effective date a year and a half earlier, when Rhode Island ratified.[1]

Massachusetts, Connecticut and Georgia took no action on the amendments. The Massachusetts legislature became deadlocked in a struggle over the taxing power, similar to that in the Virginia Senate, and the two other states adhered to their belief that amendments were unnecessary or premature. The affirmative speed of the great majority of states, reinforced by the popular reaction against senatorial obstruction in Virginia, testified both to the general anxiety of the American people for strong safeguards and to their satisfaction with those they obtained. But how strong and enduring were the guarantees of freedom? What did they mean at that time and what would they come to mean? Only time could answer, and some of the answers were still uncertain in the second half of the second century of trial and discussion.

It is easy enough to dispose of the conflict between those who consistently support the free expression of thought and those who consciously desire to restrain it. Judgment is equally easy upon the disagreement between those who believe in fair treatment of all men accused of crime and those who regard such sentiment as the coddling of malefactors. Difficulties become acute when persons who have or think they have an equal regard for human rights disagree radically on the meaning and force of the guarantees for their protection.

It would be hard to find two men who were more sincerely devoted to the objectives sought in the American Bill of Rights than the late Judge Learned Hand, of the United States Circuit Court of Appeals in New York, and the late Dean Roscoe Pound of the Harvard Law School. Yet the basic conflict over the legal force of these constitutional guarantees can be set forth with the sharpest clarity in their opposing utterances. Said Judge Hand in an address before the New York State Board of Regents in October 1952:

"What is 'freedom of speech and of the press'; what is the 'establishment of religion and the free exercise thereof'; what are 'unreasonable searches,' 'due process of law,' and 'equal protection of the law'? . . . Indeed, these fundamental canons are not jural concepts at all, in the ordinary sense; and in application they turn out to be no more than admonitions of moderation, as appears from the varying and contradictory interpretations that the judges themselves find it necessary to put upon them."

Continuing, Judge Hand said that as long as there are "any plausible arguments in support of a measure," the courts must abstain from intervening. It is the voters, speaking through their delegates, who have the final word: they alone "can and will preserve our liberties, if preserved they are to be." Since plausible arguments can be found in support of almost any law, Judge Hand reduced the constitutional command to a virtual nullity. Dean Pound may well have had this speech in mind when he set forth a sweeping rebuttal of the "admonition" doctrine five years later, in the preface to his book, *The Development of Constitutional Guarantees of Liberty:*

"The guarantees of liberty in American constitutions are not and are not thought of as exhortations as to how government should be carried on or its agencies will operate. They are precepts of the law of the land backed by the power of the courts of law to refuse to give effect to legislative or executive acts in derogation thereof. Thus violation of these secured liberties must amount in effect to a revolution in order to overthrow them. Any considerable infringement of guaranteed individual or minority rights appears to involve much more than overriding a pronouncement of political ethics in a political instrument. It involves defiance of fundamental law; overthrow of established law upon which the maintenance of the general security rests."

Which of these conflicting concepts comes closer to fulfilling the assurance given by Madison to Congress in 1789? Incorporate these guarantees of liberty in the Constitution, said he, and through their enforcement of them, independent tribunals of justice will "be an impenetrable bulwark against every assumption of power" by Congress or the Executive. So the mandates were placed in the Constitution, and what followed? "The varying and contradictory interpretations" of the judges made them "no more than admonitions of moderation."

The guarantees are not worded as admonitions. They are un- qualified commands. They sank to the level of admonitions because that was the way Congress and the judges treated them. It is the rejection of the mandate that has created the problem and made it look insoluble. When "no abridgment" becomes abridgment at the discretion of Congress and the courts, *freedom* becomes a *degree of freedom*, and the degree varies with the temper of the times and the varying insight and stamina of the judges. In effect, the Bill of Rights is amended in one direction when strong judges, devoted to liberty, become a majority on the Supreme Court; amended in the other direction when the majority is weak, hesitant, or unaware of the essentials of freedom; and open to annihilation should a strong antilibertarian Supreme Court ever unite with a like-minded Congress (as all the individual justices did in 1798-1800) in follow- ing the road of tyranny.

Let the *wording* of the Bill of Rights be accepted as its true *meaning* and every deviation from it will be recognized for what it is. There will be no need to ask, after each new appointment to the Supreme Court: what additional degree of freedom will this give to the American people or take away from them? Against a tyrannical union of courts and Congress there is indeed no resort except to the electorate, who ended such a tyranny in 1800. But when Judge Hand turned to the people as the sole protectors of liberty against "the varying and contradictory interpretations" of the judges, he took no heed of what the author of the ten amend- ments said in presenting them to Congress. "The prescriptions in favor of liberty," said Madison, "ought to be leveled against the quarter where the greatest danger lies, namely . . . in the body of the people, operating by the majority against the minority." Yet in effect, Judge Hand recognized the truth of that statement, and destroyed his own contrary position, when he said to the Board of Regents with obvious reference to McCarthyism:

"I believe that that community is already in process of dissolution where each man begins to eye his neighbor as a possible enemy, where nonconformity with the accepted creed, political as well as religious, is a mark of disaffection; where denunciation, without specification or backing, takes the place of evidence; where orthodoxy chokes freedom of dissent; where faith in the eventual supremacy of reason has become so timid that we dare not enter our convictions in the open lists, to win or lose."

That is a description of the distemper of our own times in our own country—a description of majority rule unchecked by effective constitutional curbs on passion. It can be expected to pass away in time as did the distempers of earlier centuries. But what of its victims? It was for their protection that the mandates were placed in the Constitution. Are the victims of unconstitutional laws saved from the ruinous effect of them by mere admonitions that such laws ought not to be enacted? Does ultimate repeal of them wipe out the prison terms unjustly served, the fines unlawfully exacted, the financial losses and social infamy cruelly inflicted on whole families? Because Judge Hand was so clearly a believer in the just rights of all men, the inadequacy of his view of the Bill of Rights has been more damaging than the similar contentions of higher judges whose devotion to liberty is less manifest. His own recital of the evils visible to him is enough to condemn the wrist-tapping remedy he looked to, unless one believes that constitutional guarantees of liberty are to be construed primarily for the convenience and comfort of those whose rights have not been assailed.

Following the resounding presentation of Dean Pound's contrary doctrine, and after U.S. Circuit Judge Jerome Frank (Hand's immediate colleague and admirer) took issue with him in lectures at the Yale Law School, Judge Hand restated and modified his position in lectures at Harvard on the Bill of Rights. Not a word more was said about those mandates being mere admonitions. To settle disputes between the departments of government, he said, the "authority of courts to annul statutes (and *a fortiori*, acts of the Executive) may, and indeed must, be inferred, although it is nowhere expressed. . . . However, this power should be confined to occasions when the statute or order was outside the grant of power to the grantee, and should not include a review of how the power has been exercised." If the statute "is the result of an honest effort to embody that compromise or adjustment that will secure the widest acceptance and most avoid resentment, it is 'Due Process of Law' and conforms to the First Amendment."

Let us reword the First Amendment in strict harmony with the meaning thus given to it: "Congress shall make no law . . . abridging the freedom of speech, or of the press, but this shall not debar the making of a law that is the result of an honest effort to embody a compromise or adjustment that will secure the widest acceptance and most avoid resentment." Suppose that James Madison had offered such an amendment in 1789. His political career in Virginia, and therefore nationally, would have ended at that moment. Suppose it had been submitted to the states by Congress. Can anybody believe it would have been ratified? Suppose that in some later period of internal fear and strife those qualifying words were put into the First Amendment. They would be considered, on the recovery of reason, either to vitiate entirely the freedom of speech and press or to impose an impossible burden upon the courts. Yet those words are in effect implanted in the Constitution, by judicial construction, whenever the courts use such a criterion to determine whether Congress *may do* what the Constitution says Congress *shall not do.*

Judge Hand recognized that the Supreme Court had taken a broader view of the Bill of Rights than he did: "I am well aware that the decisions do not so narrowly circumscribe the power of courts to intervene under the authority of the First Amendment and the 'Due Process Clause.' " But he would not undertake to say how far the judges had extended the scope of those clauses. "Frankly, I should despair of succeeding." It seemed to him that the Supreme Court was merely reviewing the merits of legislation and approving or annulling it on that basis. This was inexpedient because it was bound to project the judges into political questions and into decisions based on their personal convictions and predilections. Nevertheless (and here he abandoned a considerable part of his "admonition" theory) he would concede one field to those who wished constitutional decisions to be based on the merits of legislation:

"I agree that they have the better argument so far as concerns Free Speech. The most important issues here arise when a majority of the voters are hostile, often bitterly hostile, to the dissidents against whom the statute is directed; and legislatures are more likely than courts to repress what ought to be free. It is true that the periods of passion or panic are ordinarily not very long, and that they are usually succeeded by a serener and more tolerant temper; but, as I have just said, serious damage may have been done that cannot be undone, and no restitution is ordinarily possible for the individuals who have suffered."

It seems obvious that Judge Hand referred to "Free Speech" in its broad sense, to include freedom of press, assembly and association, because he was speaking in general terms of the majority attitude toward dissidents. When he came "to the other interests covered by the 'Bill of Rights,' " he was unable to say whether the advantage lay with or against the power of the courts to annul a statute. He was certain, though, that if such a power was desirable, it should be exerted openly by the courts as a third chamber of the legislature. At present, he said, they do not and cannot speak right out and say that the solution offered by Congress is too strong for the judicial stomach:

"On the contrary they wrap up their veto in a protective veil of adjectives such as 'arbitrary,' 'artificial,' 'normal,' 'reasonable,' 'inherent,' 'fundamental,' or 'essential,' whose office usually, though quite innocently, is to disguise what they are doing and impute to it a derivation far more impressive than their personal preferences, which are all that in fact lie behind the decision."

These words, spoken with the freedom that came with retirement from the bench, voiced the reaction of an appellate judge, below the highest level of authority, to the conflicting and confusing Supreme Court decisions he had been trying to follow. But the striking fact is that he was not debating with those who believe that the Bill of Rights means what it says. His argument was with those who use the adjectives "reasonable," "arbitrary," etc., to convert the mandate, "Congress shall make *no law* abridging" the freedoms, into "Congress shall make no law *unreasonably* abridging" them. Under this judicial concept, powers unqualifiedly forbidden to Congress by the Constitution become powers selectively permitted to Congress by the Supreme Court. By their own invention of the "balancing test," which makes *forbidden laws* permissible or invalid according to the location of the greater good to society, the judges forced themselves to base decisions on the merits of legislation. In doing so they had either to rely on their own ideas of merit, or accept the ideas of Congress. Laws were valid if the two bodies agreed on merits or disagreed but slightly; invalid if the disagreement was large and sharp. No wonder the Court gets into all sorts of anomalies and contradictions, and that the meaning of the Constitution changes almost as often as there is a change in the personnel of the high tribunal.

There are areas where the Supreme Court is compelled to decide the constitutionality of a law, or of an executive action, on the basis of its reasonableness. How otherwise could it enforce the clause of the Fourth Amendment protecting the people "against *unreasonable* searches and seizures"? There is judicial latitude, likewise, in the associated requirement that "no warrants shall issue but upon probable cause." In case of challenge, that which is "probable" has to be determined judicially. The courts have wielded discretionary power, and rightly, in holding that the strict and detailed limitations placed upon warrants of arrest are an implied prohibition of arrest without a warrant, except of persons caught in acts of crime or in flight from justice. But try to collect damages for such illegal arrests!

The constitutional requirement that "No person shall . . . be deprived of life, liberty, or property, without due process of law," also is something whose scope has to be determined by the courts. This clause is found both in the Fifth Amendment, where it binds the federal government, and in the Fourteenth, where it applies to the states. In the Fifth, it is accompanied by many specific protections of the rights of persons accused of crime. In the Fourteenth it has no such accompaniments. This has produced a sharp division in the Supreme Court, beginning in 1884. The Court held at that time, in *Hurtado* v. *California,* that the Due Process Clause of the Fifth Amendment does not include the specific safeguards of fair trial accompanying it, because if it did include them, there would have been no need to specify them. "Due process" in the Fourteenth Amendment must have the same meaning as in the Fifth, so, the Court reasoned, it does not include the specific safeguards of fair trial contained in the earlier amendments. The two clauses, therefore, cover whatever the judges conclude to be "due process," and if the same things are required by other clauses of the Constitution, that is merely a coincidence.

With increasing emphasis and in growing numbers minority judges have dissented from this construction, contending that whatever else may be included in "due process," it contains as a minimum the specific requirements of a fair trial that are set forth in the Bill of Rights. The effect of the majority position proved anomalous. It led, on the one hand, to deprivation in state courts of protections that are mandatory in federal tribunals. But it left the way open, in the Fourteenth Amendment, to certain expansions of "due process" that would have been equally logical and might have come earlier under the minority interpretation. Beginning in the 1920s, successive court decisions placed freedom of speech, press, assembly and religion within the compass of "due process of law." In substance, this incorporated the First Amendment liberties in the Fourteenth, protecting them against violation by the states. In immediate effect and in its potential, this was one of the greatest gains for freedom in American history. It achieved what Madison asked for, and the House of Representatives voted for, in 1789, in a proposed amendment that failed to win a two-thirds vote in the Senate.

With such a recognition of the primacy of the First Amendment rights, one might expect corresponding judicial vigor in the definition of them. But that did not prove true of the freedoms of speech and press, in relation to either states or nation. The "balancing test" put them on a teeter-totter—one end weighted with the constitutional command, "Congress shall make no law," the other with the judicial amendment of it, "except when there is sufficient reason for doing so." When such a balance is perfect, the mandate is half enforced, but in the actual distribution of weight, the guarantees of freedom have oftener been up in the air than solidly on the ground.

In varying degrees, this weakening tendency has reached at times nearly every phase of judicial review that touches political and civil rights—but with a momentous and fortunate upturn, in the mid-twentieth century, in cases involving the equal protection of the laws. In relation to the lives of individuals, the guarantees of the Bill of Rights may be said to fall into two general categories. There are those that directly concern a person's contact with the government as an adversary. These furnish the protections thrown around persons accused or suspected of crime, or whose homes might be invaded for political or personal reasons unconnected with crime. It is to guard the privacy and other social rights of every individual, as much as to prevent compulsory self-incrimination, that search warrants are required and the indiscriminate seizure of private papers is forbidden. Such rights and immunities are expressed in the maxim that "Every man is considered innocent until proven guilty," and in the aphorism, "An Englishman's home is his castle." Procedural due process covers these rights.

Other rights—substantive—are protected by the guarantees of the First Amendment—freedom of religion, speech, press, assembly, petition, association. Closely related are voting rights. To the list should be added, either as elements of these privileges and immunities or under the Ninth Amendment, the right of silence and the right of travel. Collectively, all these rights and privileges not only govern a man's normal, day-to-day relations with his fellowmen: they also determine his place in the community and his participation in what we know in America as government of and by the people. Through the maintenance of these rights, or by the loss of them, a man is either a self-respecting human being or a serf.

Having separated these rights into two categories, what then? Invasion of the first group does not necessarily jeopardize the second. Indeed, mistreatment of persons accused of crime commonly stimulates a stronger expression of public opinion against such evils. But whenever freedom of opinion is invaded, so too are the guarantees of fair procedures, and the two categories coalesce. Suppression of religious freedom in past ages, suppression of free speech and freedom of the press in past and present, has led and invariably leads to unlawful searches and seizures, to arbitrary arrest without probable cause, to tragi-farcical trials before prejudiced judges and juries, and to vindictive punishments. Such periods are usually marked by appellate decisions in which some judges either share or bow to the prevalent passions, while others win the execration of the many and the praise of a few by endeavoring to maintain the shattered constitutional rights of the victims.

In England, the protection of procedural rights developed hundreds of years in advance of freedom of the mind. That was due to the centuries-long conflict between a monarchical government and the people. This conflict took different shapes at different times: king against people, nobles against people, king against nobles, church against part of the people. Always, however, in the long period before the sovereignty of the people was recognized, The Establishment felt the need to protect itself. It did so, in basic policy, by denying the right of the people to express their thoughts, by treating accusatory political discussion first as treason and then as seditious libel.

Harsh methods were needed to carry out harsh policies, so in English trials of this sort there were many violations of the procedural processes that had grown up in the common law. Consequently, the defense in cases involving political or religious freedom was likely to center on procedural "due process." Indeed, trials were forced into this pattern. The minuscule extent to which speech, press and religion were protected in English law made it utterly futile to contend in court for total freedom. In many cases the defendant and his lawyers were compelled for strategic reasons to accept or even to approve a hated limitation in order to secure acquittal under it.

It is often said that the case of John Wilkes, whose prosecution and triumph in England made such a tremendous impression in the American colonies and infant nation, did not involve freedom of the press at all, because he did not make it the basis of his defense. He would have been a fool to do so, in the face of judges who were consistently crushing that freedom, when he had a valid defense in the violation of his privileges as a member of Parliament and an effective counterweapon in the lawless invasion of his home. Yet freedom of the press was at the very heart of the conflict, and what he did in support of it went into the blood, bone and sinew of our constitutional protections.

In considering the meaning of the Bill of Rights, we must look at all of it at once. Treason, constructive treason, heresy, bills of attainder, test oaths, seditious libel, trial by jury, self-incrimination, double jeopardy, confrontation of one's accusers, habeas corpus, general warrants, search and seizure—these and the great freedoms of the First Amendment are all bound up together. They are bound together both in the violations of liberty and in the development of it through the ages.

This brings up the question: is the force of the Bill of Rights to be limited, in the twentieth century, to the meaning it may have had in the minds of the men who framed and submitted the guarantees; of the greater number who ratified them, and the judges— English, colonial, state and federal—who made early decisions bearing on these rights and immunities? *Stare decisis*, says one group: that which has been decided, shall stand. But the true answer, most assuredly, must be No. Freedom either is a growing thing or it is not freedom. The world did not come to a standstill in 1787, or 1789, or 1791, or 1868. Principles remain unchanged while the understanding of them grows and their application enlarges.

But if it is true that freedom is a growing thing, it cannot have a lesser meaning today or tomorrow than it had at the birth of our nation. For more reasons than one, it is vitally important to know what the framers of the Bill of Rights thought they were doing. First, such facts firmly established will form a barricade against retreat. In any human society, progress is made by an excess of forward over backward steps, but progress is not automatically achieved. In the second place, we need to discover how great a growth of freedom there was in the work of the framers themselves —how far they went beyond the limited concepts that preceded the American Revolution or even survived it in a considerable part of the population. If that is demonstrated, the views of the framers, and of the great mass of the people who inspired them, will furnish a powerful leverage toward a fuller realization of the rights and privileges that belong to human beings either by natural law or by man's conquest of his social and physical environment.

CHAPTER 7
Old Rights and Later Wrongs

Fisher Ames of Massachusetts believed throughout his life that true liberty was maintained by orderly acceptance of an elected aristocratic government. In helping to perfect and submit the first ten amendments he acted in the belief that they might do "some good towards quieting men who attend to sounds only." With much labor and research, wrote Ames, Mr. Madison had "hunted up all the grievances and complaints of newspapers, all the articles of conventions, and the small talk of their debates." This "may get the mover some popularity, which he wishes."

This disparaging account of the origin of the amendments tells far more than it seems to. More eloquently than any assertion by a zealot of liberty, it reveals the force of public opinion in persuading lawmakers to do what many of them had no wish to do. It points, accurately, to the tie between federal guarantees of freedom and those pronounced earlier in the states, either in their own constitutions or in the conventions that ratified the new federal charter. Eight states then had bills of rights, and exactly half of Madison's twenty-eight specific proposals (twenty-two of which went into the adopted amendments) had their counterparts in state constitutions. But since the states themselves had been in existence for only thirteen years, the real link is with the American revolutionary movement in general: that is, with the grievances engendered by colonial vassalage and the spectacle of monarchic misrule in England; also with the cherished but abused heritage that had become the property of Americans as subjects of the British crown.

The argument has been advanced from time to time that the

American Revolution was merely a territorial secession from the English Motherland; that the Constitution of the United States did little more, apart from eliminating a king, than write into basic law the fundamentals of the British constitution.[1] Such a theory permits the conclusion that the American Revolution was fought to preserve an established church, a hereditary peerage and the House of Lords; to restore Parliament to the supremacy it misused before George III made matters worse, and to suppress the freedoms of religion, speech and press. A revolution very different from mere territorial secession was in Madison's mind when he said to Congress: "The freedom of the press and rights of conscience, those choicest privileges of the people, are unguarded in the British Constitution."

Numerous important safeguards, such as trial by jury, habeas corpus, protection against self-incrimination, due process of law, are a portion of our English heritage. But the constitutional protection given in the United States to freedom of religion, speech and press presents a wide deviation from the law and custom that make up the British Constitution. The same is true of our banning of bills of attainder, test oaths and titles of nobility.

In searching for American attitudes that help to define the original meaning of the Bill of Rights, one must start by throwing out the opinions of those who were consciously opposed to the maintenance of civil rights and liberties. No apologist for tyranny or slavery ever gave a true definition of freedom. For the rest, there were varying degrees of advocacy among laymen and lawyers. As far as laymen are concerned, it is fair to infer that the intensity of their demand for guarantees was matched by their desire for strength in those demanded. Among lawyers and judges who favored the guarantees, many had actively combatted the outstanding restrictions on liberty entrenched in judicial decrees. Others accepted the restrictions and gave the name of freedom to mere palliatives of greater evils. It was not from this last group, nor from their English counterparts, that we obtained the constitutional guarantees, nor is it through their restricted vision that they are to be defined. To get their true meaning, it is necessary to pursue the struggle to free men's minds, particularly as it came down in English history, with minor repetition in American colonial experience. On both sides of the Atlantic it is far more a story of cruelty and oppression—of denials of liberty and perversions of the institutions of justice—than it is of willing recognition of the rights of man.

Magna Carta played as great a role in American as in English thought, and in the eighteenth century it was known almost entirely through the interpretations of Sir Edward Coke. His influence reached far beyond the legal profession. Few except hapless students of law read *Coke on Littleton*, but his *Second Institute* on Magna Carta was required material for any man who wanted to know the origins of his own institutions. Secondary knowledge could be drawn from a myriad of sources in newspapers, magazines, books and pamphlets.

Coke was three men in one. He was the ruthless Attorney General who, accepting the standards of the Elizabethan age, sent Sir Walter Raleigh to the gallows by methods that reduced the trial to a mockery of justice. He was the fair-minded, incorruptible Chief Justice who stood up to King James the First and was thrown out of office for refusing to become a stooge of the Crown. Finally, he was the political rebel in Parliament who risked his life (and maybe saved it and the lives of others) by heading the courageous band that imposed the Petition of Right on Charles the First in 1628.

The *Second Institute* (published that same year) was a late product of this transition. Modern scholarship has convicted Coke of finding popular rights in Magna Carta that are not there, and of enlarging others that are there in embryo. Some suspect that he deliberately used his unrivaled prestige to dignify those rights by carrying them back (as people do their family trees) some centuries closer to William the Conqueror than legitimacy warranted. If that was the purpose, the crime hardly amounted to a felony. Is the command of the writ of habeas corpus any less compelling because Coke confounded it with the older writ *de odio et atia*, used likewise to release a person wrongfully held in prison? Is it material that Coke made "due process of law" identical with Magna Carta's "law of the land," when in fact "due process" supplanted the earlier phrase in the reign of Edward III, something over a century later? Who can read the most vital chapter of Magna Carta today without sensing the powerful thrust toward justice and equality in King John's reluctant pledge, as re-affirmed by Edward the First:

"No freeman shall be taken, or imprisoned, or be disseized of his freehold, or liberties, or free customs, or be outlawed, or exiled, or any other wise destroyed, nor will we not pass upon him, nor condemn him, but by lawful judgment of his peers, or by the law of the land."

Modern scholarship can tear parts of this into irrelevant shreds, as applied to society today. Coke himself correctly identified "liberties" with gifts of property rights by the king. Dr. McKechnie (with some aid from Henry III) concluded that "free customs" meant principally the right to levy tolls. The "law of the land" in King John's day commonly signified trial by battle or by ordeal. A man's "peers" (above the peasant level) were his social equals, whose function in law was to referee the battle or decide whether the defendant's reaction to a red-hot iron denoted guilt or innocence.

Antiquarians may rightly gloat over such discoveries, but they mean nothing in measuring the accrued force of ancient law. *Magna Carta became more sacred as its contents broadened in the people's minds.* There was in actuality a mighty advance when "the law of the land" in 1215 became the "due process of law" of 1344. But to Americans of 1776 they were synonymous terms and the earlier one had the more impressive wording. Of the eight states that adopted bills of rights in the ensuing decade, seven required procedures in accordance with "the law of the land." No matter what these terms meant to the barons at Runnymede, to generations of Englishmen and to Americans setting forth their inalienable rights, they included a fair trial by an impartial jury.

That was a historical error, to be sure, and legal scholars have had great fun tracing it back to its origin. The mistake was first made (Pollock and Maitland discovered) in 1302, only eighty-seven years after the signing of Magna Carta. Nearly six hundred years elapsed before the error was detected by jubilant legal sleuths. What this really testifies to is the antiquity of the jury system, the rapidity with which it developed after trial by combat began to fade, and the depth to which it is implanted in English and American constitutional law.

This development began before Magna Carta and coincided

with the organization and growth of the English courts. Although the barons wrung the Great Charter from King John primarily for their own protection, the words "no freeman" in it had broad application and an honorable heredity. A hundred years earlier, Henry I, bidding for popular support against feudal barons, proclaimed a Charter of Liberties that pledged protection to tenants of the barons and required the barons to "hold themselves in check towards their tenants." Henry the Second's Assize of Clarendon (1166) put trial by jury on the road of development as a substitute for the official duel. It acquired even greater antiquity in the minds of the English and the American people. Few would have disputed the assertion of Sir John Hawles, William the Third's solicitor general, that the system much as known in his day was brought to England by Saxon invaders.

Henry the Second's extension of the judicial functions of the king's council (*Curia Regis*) gave the machinery of the law a more tangible start toward its modern structure. The Court of Exchequer, the Court of King's Bench and the Court of Common Pleas all were split off from the council before the end of the thirteenth century. Organization of the British judiciary gave substance, form and force to the common law. It was lifted from a vague memory of Saxon and Norman rights, expressed in nostalgic protests against their violation, to a body of law from whose limitations the king himself was not wholly exempt. Above all, it promoted a belief in the supremacy of law which has proved the most stabilizing factor in Anglo-American society. In England it has survived impairment by many kings. In the United States today it is under double strain: from King Coin, his courtiers and satellites, and collectively and individually from the followers of King Mob.

By the end of the thirteenth century, the English Parliament had popped into being from who knows where. There are indications that it grew from acorns of the *Quercus Witanagemotii*, brought from the forests of Germany before the 1066 Conquest. Some find Norman roots in the *Curia Regis*, or in the great assemblies called from time to time to find money for the kings to squander in foreign wars. But in 1275 and afterward, there it was, the High Court of Parliament—nobles, clergymen and commoners forming three estates in a single chamber—doing what strong kings ordered it to do and telling weak kings what they must or must not do. The making of laws—*by the king* with the assent of Parliament—was a game of pressure and counterpressure.

During this evolutionary process, Magna Carta did not stand forth either as an English Constitution or as a king's action automatically binding his successors. Originally a contract between John and the barons, it was becoming a statutory charter of liberties which later kings were induced or compelled to reaffirm. Edward I, in his unwilling confirmation of it in 1297, referred to it and King John's Charter of the Forest as "made by common assent of all our realm." He pledged himself to send these charters to all his justices and other officers throughout the kingdom. And those who "have to administer the laws of our land, shall allow the said charters . . . in all their points . . . for the relief of our people." His final order was "that archbishops and bishops shall pronounce sentence of greater excommunication against all those that by word, deed, or counsel, shall go against the said charters, or that in any point break or go against them."

There was no "balancing test" in this command for the enforcement of Magna Carta. It was the most absolute sort of an absolute decree, actually directed against the law-breaking monarch who put it forth. The sanction—excommunication—was one that would have struck terror into all officialdom if the king had felt any real desire to enforce the curtailment, through Magna Carta, of his own prerogatives. The action forced on him revealed both the contemporary strength of the parliamentary estates and the weakness of the British Constitution. It found place among many warnings to the American people to put stronger sanctions in their own Great Charter—the Constitution of the United States—by permanent and enforceable commands.

The rule of law weakened still more under Edward II, yet a broadening concept of justice can be seen in what followed the attainder and execution of Thomas, Earl of Lancaster, in 1322. A perennial rebel, he was taken in arms, tried before Edward II in person and condemned to death by the king himself. On the accession of Edward III, Thomas's brother Henry became guardian of the under-age monarch and petitioned Parliament in 1327 for a reversal of his brother's attainder and restoration of his estates.

Parliament did what was asked. The significant feature was the ground of reversal—three violations by the monarch of English law. The king himself had decreed Thomas's death *although the courts were open.* (A principle and precedent cited to restrict martial law in the American Civil War.) The law of the land was disregarded in the omission to arraign the earl and put him to question. Magna Carta was violated again through failure to let him be tried by his peers. That meant trial by the High Court of Parliament, but all free subjects had their peers. The Great Charter's mandate said that "no freeman," not that "no member of the peerage," was to be denied such a trial. That was made clear in 1344, when Edward III bowed to the demand of Parliament that he accept a law aimed against his own excesses:

"No man of what estate or condition that he be, shall be put out of land or tenement, nor taken nor imprisoned, nor disinherited nor put to death without being brought in answer by due process of law."

The "law of the land" was shaping into "due process." The grand jury too was taking form as a protective agency of due process. In 1331 the sheriff of London found three goldsmiths "at work in a round ring upon invocations of evil spirits." In front of them they had placed human figures molded of virgin wax, under which were written the names of Robert of Ely (the king's minister) and Marjery. They had formulas "for killing whom they would and making better whom they would," by sticking wooden nails into the wax figures, or pulling them out. Taken before nineteen-year-old Edward III, the goldsmiths offered a logical if not convincing defense. Their object was not to kill Robert of Ely, but to win his friendship for the benefit of John of Gloucester, who was being oppressed by a protégé of the minister. John had paid a magician twenty shillings to furnish the charms.

The king ordered the sheriff of Surrey to bring "twenty-four upright and law-abiding men" to inquire into the affair for the Court of King's Bench. This grand jury credited the charge of intended killing, and put the finger on John, but since nobody was killed, all they did was indict the magician for plying his damnable art. Something might be said, perhaps, against the science of 1331, but the grand jury lacked hardly anything of its modern form and function.

The next two hundred years witnessed the almost complete destruction of the feudal nobility, through family and factional struggles for possession of the crown. The War of the Roses removed the most effective check on the powers of whoever secured the throne. It weakened the position of Parliament, depressed the common-law courts, re-exalted the king's council, and gave Tudor monarchs an ascendancy higher than that of the early Edwards. It was a throwback toward the personal rule of the Normans, but without royal armies to put the nation in subjection to the king, and without feudal armies to hold the king himself in check.

After the King's Bench and other courts were split off from the *Curia Regis*, the king's council became primarily an executive and advisory body. It retained judicial powers, however, and with the Tudor uplift of royal prerogative, this feature of conciliar power was expanded to offset the growing independence of the common-law courts. The ultimate effect was devastating. The main crimes against liberty were the development, first of the Court of Star Chamber, then of the Court of High Commission, another branch of the Privy Council. The avowed purpose of the Star Chamber was to make justice swift and sure in secular trials, that of the High Commission to do the same in offenses against the Church. Justice was being arrayed in new unspotted robes.

The Court of the Star Chamber was made up of the Lord Chancellor, two common-law judges, a high prelate and an indefinite number of the king's councillors. Formalized by act of Parliament in the third year of Henry VII (1487), it enabled king and council to bypass nearly all the processes and safeguards of the common law. Grand-jury indictments were dispensed with. For speed and certainty the Star Chamber resorted to the "information *ex officio,*" holding people to trial "by virtue of its office." Coupled with this was the "oath *ex officio*" which men suspected of crime were compelled to take. It bound them to answer all questions that might be asked, thus taking away the common-law privilege against compulsory self-incrimination. The judges did the trying, determined the guilt and imposed the sentence. There was no such nonsense as a jury of twelve good men of the vicinage, though in a partial return to constitutional principles this arbitrary tribunal was not allowed to impose the death penalty. Life imprisonment (which meant a slow and cruel death), fines, pillory, whipping, branding and mutilation were its modest prerogatives.

The Star Chamber did indeed prove efficient, and for many years its popularity was high. It won applause by striking down the castle-owning "maintainers" of robber bands that infested the country and terrorized rural courts. But like all possessors of arbitrary power, it was corrupted by its own authority and its methods. Turning from the chastisement of robbers to the suppression of political and religious freedom, it made *injustice* swift, sure and terrible. Men who made the slightest deviation from orthodoxy as to king or church were liable to be dragged off to London, and put on trial by the fiat of a prosecutor. Defendants were forced to answer incriminating questions. Confessions were obtained by torture. Punishment was as certain as death and lacked little of its terrors. The preliminary procedures—torture, etc.—spread to the common-law courts. King's Bench jurors who found political defendants not guilty were dragged to the Star Chamber for punishment.

The arbitrary processes of the tribunal had tainted the whole judicial system when Edward Peacham, accused of treason, was interrogated in 1615, preliminary to trial in the Court of King's Bench. Eight Crown officials headed by Attorney General Sir Francis Bacon made this report to King James:

"Upon these interrogatories, Peacham this day was examined before torture, in torture, between torture, and after torture; notwithstanding, nothing could be drawn from him, he still persisting in his obstinate and insensible denials, and former answers."

The excuse for compulsory self-incrimination by torture in a King's Bench case (no excuse was needed in Star Chamber) was that it was permissible to discover whether he had any accomplices in his treason. Just how Peacham could have had accomplices—though he obviously needed informants—is a bit perplexing. Officers rummaging his room on another matter found a sermon in his handwriting saying that James the First "is the greatest whoremonger in the kingdom." Also the greatest drunkard. Peacham's hypothetical defense in the trial, generally regarded as the truth, was that this was written in a sermon not delivered and not intended for delivery. A partial confession of his handwriting was repudiated as made—if made at all—"wholly out of fear, and to avoid torture." Sir George Croke, later a noted judge, wrote that Peacham was found guilty but not executed, "that many of the judges were of opinion, that it was not treason."

Peacham's case acquired notoriety because of Bacon's casual avowal of torture, the picaresque tribute to the king's sexual morality, and the apparent conclusion of the judges that such defamation of the king was not treason. Finally, it was made memorable by Bacon's use of it in his efforts to throw his hated rival Coke out of his position as Lord Chief Justice of the King's Bench. King James directed Sir Francis to poll the twelve high judges of England secretly and separately, on the treasonableness of Peacham's sermon. Bacon advised the king that he would leave Coke to the last, to prevent him from calling a judicial conference. By this strategy he would make sure of the others and might finally win "my lord Coke himself, when I have in some dark manner put him in doubt that he shall be left alone." Eleven judges capitulated. Coke vehemently protested "this auricular taking of opinions, single and apart" as new and dangerous, and finally gave an opinion that meant nothing.

The impact of the failure to behead Peacham after his conviction was felt thirteen years later, when all the judges of England were called together to give an opinion upon the treason charge against Hugh Pine. This farmer had been heard to say that Charles the First was carried from place to place by those around him, "as one would carry an apple," and "Before God, he is no more fit to be king than Hickwright"—the farmer's simple shepherd. At the trial, the Solicitor General put twenty-two precedents before the judges, including four instances in which men were hanged, drawn and quartered for speaking ill of a king. The judges held together and stood their ground. This was their recorded answer:

"Upon consideration of all which precedents, and of the statutes of treason, it was resolved by all the judges before-named, and so certified to his majesty, that the speaking of the words before-mentioned, though they were as wicked as might be, were not treason. For . . . there is no treason at this day but by the statute of 25 Edw. 3, c. 2, for imagining the death of the king, etc. . . . To charge the king with a personal vice, as to say of him, 'That he is the greatest whore-monger or drunkard in the kingdom,' is no treason; as Yelverton said it was held by the judges, upon debate of Peacham's case." (Yelverton, now a judge, prosecuted Peacham.)

The transgressions of the Crown in Peacham's prosecution involved more than a dozen violations of principles at stake in the long struggle for justice and liberty both in America and England:

Independence of the Judiciary; advance opinions of judges on pending case;

Secret pressure of the Crown on judges;

Distortion of the treason statute of Edward III; resort to constructive treason;

Seditious libel; publication as proof of guilt; private possession of manuscript as proof of publication;

Unreasonable search and seizure; wrongful use of evidence illicitly obtained;

Compulsory self-incrimination; torture;

Denial of defendant's right to counsel or to present *sworn* testimony of himself or witnesses.

Putting the Peacham and Pine cases together, it is seen that the judges (not all the same ones) first yielded to royal pressure, individually applied; then collectively redeemed themselves in the same trial; and later stood courageously together against similar pressure from another king. Before the Stuarts were driven from the throne, judicial independence and integrity dropped to their lowest level in English history. But as these cases show, the record would have been infinitely better if the British Constitution had been such as to give judges effective protection against pressures from the Crown and Parliament. It was an example that did not go unheeded in the United States.

In relation to the American Bill of Rights, these two cases have a significance not limited to executive abuse of the courts or to the monstrosity of constructive treason and the manifold violations of due process. The accusation was treason, but the underlying issue in Peacham's case was freedom of writing and in Pine's case freedom of speech. In substance though not in law, these were cases of seditious libel, of the sort that were common and notorious a century later. Classing them as treason made the link with libel all the more ominous.

But in 1615, "seditious libel" was a term just creeping into English law. Slander, by its own name, had been known to English law from the earliest days. It was almost entirely an offense of person against person, to be remedied by civil damage suits at common law or punished by criminal action in the ecclesiastical courts. From the Norman period downward, slander of the king, the government, or high officials was punishable as treason, felony, misprision of treason, or contempt, depending on the rank and office of the person slandered and the degree of guilt. In 1275 this system of royal justice produced the statute later called *De Scandalis Magnatum,* an edict by which Edward I, to reduce strife, commanded "that from henceforth none be so hardy to cite or publish any false news or tales whereby discord or occasion of discord or slander may grow between the king and his people or the great men of the realm; and he that doth so shall be taken and kept in prison until he hath brought him into the court which was the first author of the tale."[2]

This royal edict has sometimes been put forward as the earliest record of the common law of libel. It was nothing of the sort. The king's palace would be a strange birthplace for a common law synonymous with immemorial custom, and doubly so for a law specifically directed against the printed word two hundred years before the invention of printing.

Sir James Fitzjames Stephen wrote in his *History of the Criminal Law* that he could "say nothing as to the way in which this enactment [of Edward I] may have been used." It was natural that he could find no record of its use, for it was not primarily a slander statute but an instrument of compulsory discovery. The penalty, potential life imprisonment, could be totally escaped by the "publisher" (i. e. the spreader) of the "false news or tale" by bringing into court "the first author of the tale." The author's crime would not be slander or libel, but high treason, and any "publisher" who failed to bring in the author could as readily be hanged for presumed authorship of the falsehood as imprisoned for repeating it.

No legal distinction was made between spoken and printed

slander until a hundred years after the invention of printing. Then, based on the wider circulation of the printed word and the greater presumption of malice in it, written slander became "libel," or "seditious libel" if the words concerned the government or public men. To criticize them was seditious.

Theoretically, this new crime was in the line of ecclesiastical jurisdiction, which was based on civil (Roman) law instead of the common law. But the temper of the times called for speed as well as severity. So personal damage suits were left to the common law, while seditious libel had its birth in the Court of the Star Chamber, which built its rigorous procedures on Roman practice.

Referring to libels between private persons, W. Hudson wrote in his *Treatise of the Star Chamber* that "in all ages libels have been severely punished in this court; but most especially they began to be frequent about 42 and 43 Elizabeth when Sir Edward Coke was her Attorney General." I. S. Leadam, editing his *Select Cases before the Court of the Star Chamber, 1477-1509*, quoted this statement and remarked that jurisdiction was probably based on the theory that the Star Chamber supplemented the defects of common and statutory law. As evidence, he cited the earliest such case in the Star Chamber records. That was *Vale* v. *Broke,* in which Simon Vale complained that he could get no relief at common law against John Broke, a bailiff, who maintained thieves, vagabonds and "common quenes pristes lemans," and openly slandered Vale and his kin by calling them strong thieves and common robbers.

Spoken slander had been triable at common law, between person and person, from before the Norman Conquest. If, in the fifteenth century, common-law relief was ineffective in that field, it is hardly surprising that after the development of printing the Star Chamber should have created the crime of seditious libel, and monopolized the trials. How then, in a later century, did lawyers and judges come to talk about a "common law of criminal libel"? Thomas Starkie described the development in his 1812 *Treatise on the Law of Slander and Libel:*

"The offense of libel fell principally under the jurisdiction of the Star Chamber, which, in part at least, adopted the rules of the civil law, and which, *when that jurisdiction was abolished, were incorporated into the common law practice."* (Italics added.)

Starkie did not explain what he meant by "fell *principally*" to the Star Chamber. Beyond a doubt, however, he was referring to a statement by Sir Edward Coke in his 1606 *Reports* of English trials. Describing a Star Chamber case, Coke gave the earliest known description of seditious libel, and said it could be prosecuted either by indictment in the Court of King's Bench (that is, prosecuted at common law), or by bill in the Star Chamber. Coke did not say it ever had been prosecuted at common law, and he evidently knew of no such trial. For twenty-two years later, in his *Third Institute*, he said he had discovered two libel prosecutions in the king's court in 1336 and 1344. As will be shown in a later chapter, these were not libel or slander trials at all. Even if they had been, the ensuing hiatus of 284 years, with these cases unknown and no others recorded, would have stripped them of value as an indication of legal custom, which is the basic characteristic of the common law.

If seditious libel has any genuine common-law affiliation, it is by descent from constructive treason and heresy, both of which are totally repugnant to the Constitution of the United States. What is called today the common law of seditious libel is in fact the creation of the Court of Star Chamber, the most iniquitous tribunal in English history. It has been injected into the common law solely by the fiat of Coke, and subsequent decisions and opinions of English judges, who chose this method of perpetuating the vicious procedures by which the Star Chamber stifled criticism of the government and freedom of political opinion.

The transfer of the spurious doctrine to America, however, came about chiefly through the medium of Sir William Blackstone, whose *Commentaries on the Laws of England*, published 1765-1769, became an important part of American legal equipment after an American edition was put out in 1771. Blackstone, a clear expositor rather than a philosopher of the law, has fallen into deep discredit in the twentieth century. It is recognized that his unthinking devotion to the governing forces in England caused him to present contemporary practices as if they represented the enduring realities of English law and justice. But his *Commentaries* had a tremendous vogue in the United States from late in the eighteenth century until late in the nineteenth. From this the argument arose, and is still heard today, that even though he was a false guide, he was a recognized guide: therefore his definition of freedom of the press must be what the framers of the First Amendment had in mind when they drafted the mandate that "Congress shall make no law" abridging that freedom. Here is Blackstone's definition:

"The liberty of the press is indeed essential to the nature of a free state; but this consists in laying no *previous* restraints upon publications, and not in freedom from censure for criminal matter when published. Every freeman has an undoubted right to lay what sentiments he pleases before the public: to forbid this is to destroy the freedom of the press; but if he publishes what is improper, mischievous, or illegal, he must take the consequences of his own temerity."

Blackstone gave an account, technically correct yet so far from the facts of life as to be utterly misleading, of how this brand of freedom came into being. The art of printing, he said, was looked upon from early days as subject to the coercion of the crown, and was regulated by royal proclamations and prohibitions "and finally by the decrees of the court of star-chamber, which limited the number of printers and of presses which each should employ, and prohibited new publications, unless previously approved by proper licensers." On the demolition of this "obnoxious jurisdiction," in 1641, Parliament "assumed the same powers as the star chamber exercised with respect to the licensing of books." By successive ordinances and statutes, the system was continued for half a century, until Parliament refused a renewal. So "the press became properly free in 1694, and has ever since so continued."

That is surely a strange ancestry for the *common law* of freedom of the press. First there is restraint by the king, then restraint by the Star Chamber, finally restraint by Parliament. The lifting of these executive, judicial and statutory restraints constitutes freedom of the press by virtue of the immemorial usages that make up the common law of England. What a mass of incongruities! And what was the situation of the British press after it achieved this blessed state of common-law freedom? Thomas Erskine May has told the story in his *Constitutional History of England*. After 1694, he wrote, every writing could be freely published, but at the peril of a rigorous execution of the libel laws:

"To speak ill of the government was a crime. Censure of ministers was a reflection upon the king himself. Hence the first aim and use of free discussion was prohibited by law. . . . And the war which rulers had hitherto waged against the press, was now taken up by parties. Writers in the service of rival factions had to brave the vengeance of their political foes, whom they stung with sarcasm and lampoon. They could expect no mercy from the courts, or from Parliament. Every one was a libeler who outraged the sentiments of the dominant party. The Commons, far from vindicating public liberty, rivalled the Star Chamber in their zeal against libels."

That was England, operating under Blackstone's definition of a *"properly* free" press. Educated Americans of the eighteenth century did not need Mr. May to tell them what had been happening to the British press. The story had been streaming across the Atlantic year after year, in books, pamphlets, magazines, newspapers and parliamentary proceedings. Was it on such a model that James Madison and his associates built the American concept of freedom of the press? That they would have done so transcends belief.

It need occasion no surprise that the Blackstone definition was seized on with alacrity by the Federalist judges who enforced the Sedition act of 1798 with fanatic zeal. The almost incredible fact is that the "previous restraint" definition was cited with approval by the United States Supreme Court (over Justice John Marshall Harlan's dissent) as late as 1907. And the opinion was written by none other than Justice Oliver Wendell Holmes, who rather reluctantly confessed his error a dozen years later and ultimately rejected the whole idea that the First Amendment was built on the common law of England.

The past damage and future danger lie not in the absurd contention that an unlicensed press is *ipso facto* a free press, but in acceptance of the theory that *any* abridgment of freedom is permitted by an article of the Constitution that says there shall be *no* abridgment. American experience in 1798-1800 and in the twentieth century has revealed the fatal weakness of such an interpretation, which in effect has meant abridgment at the discretion of Congress, with the courts inadequately checking or even furthering the abridgments. In relation to our constitutional system, it amounts to a rejection of the plain meaning of mandatory words—a rejection due either to fear of freedom or hostility to it. But the origins of the matter go far back in English history. It is there, in the history of seditious libel and the *unsuccessful* British struggle for legally established freedom of speech and press, that we must go to discover what lies behind the guarantees of freedom in the American Bill of Rights. For its bearing on national intentions, it is necessary to view the scene as it was known to Americans in the last quarter of the eighteenth century.

CHAPTER 8
The Diabolical Art of Printing

Repression of opinion in England had a long history before it took the form of statutory restrictions on the press. Familiar to all educated Americans was the prosecution of John Wycliffe in the fourteenth century for "writings and preachings" that produced a bull against him from Pope Gregory XI. The Pope commanded the University of Oxford to take this parson of Lutterworth into custody and deliver him to the Archbishop of Canterbury for punishment. King Richard II disliked papal infringement of his sovereignty, and Wycliffe's supporters gave him effectual asylum. Nobody, however, questioned the power of State and Church to punish either spoken or written heresy under ecclesiastical law.

"In the sixteenth century," wrote T. E. May, "the history of the church is the history of England." Catholics and Protestants alike "recognized the duty of the state to uphold truth and repress error . . . conformity with the new faith as with the old, was enforced by the dungeon, the scaffold, the gibbet, and the torch." Bishop-Historian Burnet recorded the rule of law, as stated with convincing clarity by Archbishop Cranmer to Edward VI: "A prince being God's deputy, ought to punish impieties against God."

Sixteenth-century history was lighted with flaming human faggots, the brightest of which was Sir Thomas More. He could have saved his life in 1535 by approving the Statute of Succession (which legalized the second marriage of Henry VIII) and the Statute of Supremacy, which made Henry supreme head of the Catholic Church in England. More's story was known in the American colonies through every English history and the *State Trials*. The

97

Statute of Succession, he told the Lord Chancellor and other examiners, "was like a two-edged sword," for if he spoke against it, he should be the cause of the death of his body; and if he assented to it, he should purchase the death of his soul. This he believed, he told the king himself, "according to the dictates of my conscience," which it was no treason to the king to reveal but would be perfidious treason to God to conceal.

As to the Statute of Supremacy, Sir Thomas chose silence, for neither this statute "nor no other law in the world can punish a man for his silence, seeing they can do no more than punish words or deeds; 'tis God only that is the judge of the secrets of our hearts." The Attorney General replied that More's silence was "an evident sign of the malice of your heart." But he tacitly acknowledged the contrary by taking the testimony of Solicitor General Richard Rich (known from youth as a notorious liar and reckless gambler) that More made treasonable remarks when his library was seized by the Crown. To which More replied: "In good faith, Mr. Rich, I am more concerned for your perjury, than for my own danger."

Who, on reading this account, can doubt where the words came from in the Virginia Declaration of Rights, "according to the dictates of conscience"? Who can fail to observe the antiquity of the "right of silence," which some people in the United States have called a new discovery by radical libertarians of the mid-twentieth century? It was largely by way of heresy trials, with their unspeakable cruelty and injustice, that England moved into the repression of religion, speech and press, and the American people—in contrast —found overwhelming need to fashion guarantees of freedom.

If, as Blackstone contended, the British press became free when licensing was abolished, it must have been free before licensing was established. Was that the case? That it was not is evident from the preamble to the Star Chamber decree of June 23, 1585, setting up the licensing system:

"Whereas sundry decrees and ordinances have upon grave advice and deliberation been heretofore made and practiced, for the repressing of such great enormities and abuses as of late (more than in times past) have been commonly used and practiced by divers contemptuous and disorderly persons, possessing the Art or Mystery of printing and selling of books: And yet notwithstanding, the said abuses and enormities are nothing abated; but (as is found by experience) do rather more and more encrease, by the willful and manifest breach and contempt of the said ordinances to the great displeasure and offence of the Queen's most Excellent Majesty . . ."

To state the case succinctly: the earlier laws were abridgments of freedom of the press: the licensing system its intended executioner. The framers of the American Bill of Rights had the English story as told in or retold from John Strype's well-known biography, *The Life and Acts of the Most Reverend Father in God, John Whitgift, D.C., the Third and Last Lord Archbishop of Canterbury, in the Reign of Queen Elizabeth.* As might be expected, press censorship by licensing originated in the zeal of the Anglican Church to suppress heresy, and this Most Reverend Father in God was the man who brought it about. Strype tells with sympathetic accuracy of the impetus Whitgift gave to it:

"The liberty of the press now [1585] gave great occasion to the spreading of sects and schisms: So that many disaffected books and scurrilous libels [little books] were daily published and dispersed, against the government, especially against that of the church, in respect of its religious worship, and episcopal jurisdiction; whereby many men became prejudiced against conformity, and a peaceable compliance with the churches orders; and their minds blown up with discontents, and doubts, about the usages and present practices of the church. The Archbishop therefore thought it highly necessary to have a strict watch there, and to stop any copies going to the press, before they had been by the Bishop of the Diocese, or some reverend and able persons, diligently read over, and allowed. And not to permit any to be printed or published, that impugned the doctrine or discipline; or that made any unworthy reflections upon the Queen or the State."

The Archbishop laid the matter before Queen Elizabeth "and she thereupon charged him, and the Lords of her Privy Council, to see her intentions in this point duly performed: And so the Archbishop got a decree in the Star Chamber for restraining such books." Whitgift himself drew up the decree put out by the Star Chamber on June 23, 1585, to restrain the abuses and enormities described by him. The decree confined the printing trade to

London, except for one press in Oxford and one in Cambridge. No book or shorter work could be printed unless the text was first seen, perused and allowed by the Archbishop of Canterbury or the Bishop of London. Book publishers violating the decree were to be punished by six months' imprisonment and banned from printing; their equipment to be destroyed. Wardens were authorized to search wherever "they shall have reasonable cause of suspicion," and to seize all books, etc., printed contrary to the ordinances. All printing equipment so taken was to be destroyed and the printing presses "melted, sawed in pieces, broken or battered at the smith's forge," and returned in that shape to their owners.

These relatively mild penalties were directed at the mechanical side of the trade. Authors of banned books, if discovered, were subject to the greater rigors of trial in the Star Chamber or High Commission for seditious libel or heresy, or at the King's Bench for felony or treason. If more convenient, they could be done to death by Parliament through bills of attainder. Thus punishment for violation of the licensing law was the least of the burdens laid upon the press. The effectiveness of licensing was in controlling the machinery of publication, and the first reaction of the printers of heretical religious tracts was to hide their types and presses.

Whitgift's immediate objective, as reported by Strype, was to identify and punish the authors and printers of the "Martin Marprelate" books, which emanated from an Anglican sect of "Disciplinarians." Their aim was to reform the articles of worship, which they regarded as idolatrous and tyrannous. Their tracts, said Strype, used "very rude and unbecoming expressions" toward the bishops and the archbishop. These godly churchmen were called "a swinish rabble [of] petty Antichrists, petty Popes, proud Prelates, enemies to the Gospel and most covetous wretched Priests."

Notwithstanding all the efforts of Archbishop John to crush this rebellious sect, "they came to that growth [wrote his biographer] that they set up their discipline . . . in Warwick, Northampton, Cambridge, etc. . . . and made orders and decrees for the government of their churches." They had the temerity to petition the Queen to reform the Church of England. "At length, by the industry of the Archbishop and his spies, many of their papers and letters were seized."

This discovery, wrote Strype, "brought the writers of them into the *Star Chamber* in the year 1589 or 1590, when many of them were taken up, and put into prison, and censured." Nevertheless, antiepiscopal books continued to be printed, and these deviations from orthodoxy caused the Queen to issue an additional proclamation, written in Whitgift's best style, "against Seditious and Schismatical Books and Libells." These works tended to "bring in a monstrous and apparent dangerous innovation" of ecclesiastical government, and to the overthrow of Her Majesty's divinely ordained prerogatives.

All persons possessing such books were commanded to deliver them to the "Ordinary" of his diocese (bishop of the ecclesiastical court). Persons knowing of such books possessed by others would escape punishment for that guilty knowledge if they informed on the miscreant within a month. In the enforcement of this system of repression and compulsory espionage, the trials that lived in history were not of printers who violated the licensing act, but of preachers and laymen who exercised the right of conscience and put their unorthodox beliefs on paper. Discovery of hidden presses and prosecution of printers opened the way to identification and arrest of the heretics.

The decrees that gave force to these Elizabethan statutes, and the state trials that resulted, antedated the Constitution of the United States by two hundred years. Does it follow that the trials were unknown to the framers, or that time had dulled their impact? The answer to that lies partly in the published record—the spread in England and America of pamphlets describing individual cases, and the collected *State Trials*—but even more in the universal reach and emotional impact of the religious controversies.

Publication of the Marprelate books and other works of the Anglican Disciplinarians marked an acute flare-up of the revolt against the Episcopacy. It not only contributed to the breakaway of the Presbyterians from the Church of England, but produced a schism among Anglicans in the North American colonies that reached its climax in the quarter century before the American Revolution. The high place held among Virginians by Dr. John Witherspoon, New Light Presbyterian president of Princeton, was due in part to the intense repugnance of Virginia Anglicans to the reputed ambition of President Horrocks of William and Mary College to have the Archbishop of Canterbury make him Bishop of America. Thus, in a far milder way, American Anglicans and Dissenters were making the same fight against centralized church authority that had been a life-and-death matter when waged through the heretical books of "Martin" and other Disciplinarians.

The most famous English trial was that of John Udall, a Puritan minister who remained an Anglican but was forbidden to preach because of his denial of the hierarchy's authority. Suspected of being "Martin Marprelate," he was examined by the Privy Council in 1588. The sole testimony against him came from the archbishop's spy and *agent provocateur* Chatfield, a parish priest, who quoted Udall as saying that if he were stopped from preaching "he would give the Bishops such a blow, as they never had." Udall denied that he was Martin, or that he knew who Martin was, and no charge was made against him. A year and a half later, after more books by Martin and others came from the secret presses, Udall was brought once more before the Council, actively headed by Lord Chief Justice Anderson of the Court of Common Pleas. His defense involved not only freedom of the press but the privilege against self-incrimination.

"You are called hither," said Anderson, "to answer concerning certain books, which are thought to be of your making."

"If it be for any of Martin's books," Udall replied, "I have already . . . cleared myself not to be the author, nor to know who he was."

Anderson asked him if he was not the author of *A Demonstration of Discipline.*

Udall. "I cannot answer thereunto."

Anderson. ". . . You had as good say you were the author."

Udall. "That will not follow . . . I think the author . . . did well . . . and therefore I think it my duty to hinder the finding of him out, which I cannot do better than thus."

Anderson. "And why so, I pray you?"

Udall. "Because if every one that is suspected do deny it, the author at the length must needs be found out . . . besides that if I were the author, I think that by law I need not answer."

Anderson. "That is true, if it concerned the loss of your life."

This was no sign of leniency, for the Chief Justice turned to the Bishop of Rochester and said: "I pray you let us make short work with him, offer him a book." Then to Udall: "Will you swear to answer to such things as shall be demanded of you in behalf of our sovereign lady the queen?"

Here was the dreaded "oath *ex officio*," brought in from ecclesiastical law to evade the privilege against self-incrimination. Udall threw it back at them:

"I will swear an oath of allegiance to her majesty . . . but to swear to accuse myself or others, I think you have no law for that."

Udall was remanded to jail, and denied counsel, yet he had one consolation: Chief Justice Anderson had remarked that the case did not involve loss of life. Unless that was a trick to loosen his tongue, the charge would be no greater than misdemeanor. Six months later the indictment was read to him at the Croyden Assize, where the presence of six judges testified to the importance of the case. The accusation was that he "did maliciously publish a slanderous and infamous libel against the queen's majesty, her crown and dignity." But the crime specified was not libel. It was felony, and carried the penalty of death.

The Crown presented no witnesses against Udall. The informer Chatfield's statement was introduced, about Udall's declared intention to "give the Bishops . . . a blow." The defendant replied that the same words had been used two years before to prove him the author of another book. The Crown next offered the statement of Nicholas Thompkins, a manservant, made before the High Commission, that Udall had told him he was the author of the *Demonstration*. How would he reply to that?

Udall. "My lords, I answer it thus, denying it to be his testimony, for if it be, why is he not present to verify it face to face, according to the law? . . . I am persuaded he was amazed, and answered he knew not what."

The prosecutor lamely explained that Thompkins was "beyond the seas about merchandizes." (A manservant traveling as a continental merchant!) Udall asked leave to present several witnesses who would testify to the diverse accounts Thompkins had given about the things he said to the High Commission. The witnesses pressed forward, repeating the request, but were told that because their testimony "was against the queen's majesty, they could not be heard." Udall's protest availed him not. Thompkins' statement to the High Commission being made under oath, said Judge Clarke, "is to be preferred before his bare report" to others. Thus perished the established right to be confronted with one's accusers, and the prosecution's next move combined absenteeism and hearsay:

"Then was read the confession of Henry Sharpe of Northampton, who . . . had said 'that he heard Mr. Penry[1] say, that Mr. Udall was the author of *The Demonstration.*'"

Udall replied that the Archbishop himself had told him that Mr. Penry wrote the *Demonstration,* which ought to outweigh Sharpe's report. This colloquy followed, vital to the whole subsequent history of freedom of the press:

Daulton (a prosecutor). "You mistake the matter; the force of the matter resteth in Mr. Penry's report, who was one of your great acquaintance and familiars." . . .

Udall. "Here is one man's saying that another said so; let the jury consider of what force this proof is; if you have more, let it appear."

Judge Clarke. "You of the Jury have not to enquire whether he be guilty of the felony, but whether he be the author of the book; for it is already set down by the judgment of all the judges in the land,[2] that whosoever was author of that book, was guilty by the statute of felony, and this is declared above half a year agone."

Here, *in a felony trial based on Elizabeth's statute,* the judges laid down a rule that took away the jury's common-law right to decide whether an action was or was not felony. Years later, after the abolition of the Star Chamber shifted seditious libel cases to the King's Bench, this violation of due process *in felony* was picked up and presented as a part of the common law *in seditious libel,* although seditious libel itself was unknown to the common law at that time.

There was no actual doubt that Udall wrote the heretical *Demonstration of Discipline,* which any man might have written freely in a country possessing religious liberty or freedom of the press. But that was all that the jurors were to decide. At one point, when Judge Clarke said they were to find only whether the defendant was guilty of writing the book, a Udall supporter ventured to add, "and also guilty of a malicious intent in making it." Criminal intent, as every lawyer knew, was a fundamental element in felony. But Prosecutor Daulton interjected: "What have you to do with the matter, Mr. Fulton, to speak to the jury?" That was the nearest approach to representation by counsel.

Udall was found guilty, and the judges sentenced him to death. During the discussion of the sentence an astonishing admission was made. To Udall's assertion that the offense was not considered a felony by the Privy Council, Judge Puckering replied that he had slandered the queen (by slandering her bishops), "and yet I assure you, that your book had been passed over, if there had not come forth presently after it such a number of slanderous libels, as 'Martin Mar-Prelate,' . . . and other such-like; of which your book was judged to be the ring-leader." The Martin books, Udall rejoined, "were never approved by the Godly learned," and he never could learn who Martin was.

So Udall was condemned to death because somebody else used violent invective in advocating the same cause to which he brought analytical reasoning sprinkled with pepper. Yet there was logic in their course, for the real issue then, as always, was liberty of opinion—not the unreal distinction between liberty and license in its expression.

Udall was given a seven months' reprieve to enable him to petition the queen for mercy. Sir Walter Raleigh supported him and his own judges urged him to condemn his book and approve the hierarchy. On his refusal to recant the judges reaffirmed the death sentence. The queen, however, granted another reprieve, and after a time the archbishop began to soften: he would agree to a pardon if Udall would spend the rest of his life in Turkey. Accounts leave it uncertain whether Elizabeth granted a pardon, but they agree that Udall died of prison hardships before a pardon arrived.

In this case, known in eighteenth-century America through the *State Trials* and Udall's pamphletized narrative of his trial, the list of judicial transgressions reads like a Bill of Rights in reverse. The Privy Council led off with an attempt at compulsory self-incrimination. Prosecutors and judges violated freedom of religion, freedom of the press, the right to counsel, the right to face one's accusers, the right to present witnesses for the defense, the right to bail, the right to fair instructions to a jury. Not a solitary witness took the stand for the Crown, or was allowed to take the stand for the defense. The judges invented a crime of "constructive felony," basing a presumption of guilt on an inference drawn from an unproved remark about giving the bishops a blow. The highest judges in the land reached a verdict of guilty six months before the trial, and perverted the jury system by denying the right of the jury to do anything more than decide whether the defendant wrote the book.

Taken by itself, the Udall case would stand as an individual miscarriage of justice, monstrous in nature, but vital only to the victim of it. But it cannot be taken by itself. Later judges transmuted it into the common law of England. Blackstone gave authority to its false doctrines. Two hundred years after Udall died, libertarians in Parliament were still denouncing his judges. Yet some of these perversions came across the Atlantic to be accepted by American courts and undermine constitutional barriers against these very evils.

It was a few years after the felony trial of Udall in the King's Bench that Sir Edward Coke began his series of Star Chamber prosecutions for seditious libel. Here the same men were judges and jury, so they naturally decided both law and fact—against the defendants. In 1634 came the trial in Star Chamber of William Prynne, a lawyer, for publishing "a libelous volume" against plays, masques, dancing, etc. His offense could have been described as "guilt by coincidence." He had the misfortune to place in the book's table of contents the heading, not wholly inapt in the reign of Charles I, "Women Actors notorious whores." His misfortune lay in the fact that the book (though written four years earlier and approved by the licenser) came off the press only six weeks before the Queen of England displayed her dramatic talents on the amateur stage.

Archbishop Laud carried the book to the equally shocked king, and pointed to passages that would make it a libel of the queen even though the author was unaware of her intended performance on the stage. For Prynne wrote that stage plays ordinarily if not always defiled both actors and spectators "by exciting meretricious, lustful, lewd, adulterous desires and affections." All who did not concur with him were damned, and nobody would deny what he said "but whores, panders, or foul incarnate devils." Lord Cottington, Chancellor of the Exchequer, regarded this last statement as an attack not only on the queen but on the Church, since many clergy-men thought well of stage plays and this would consign them to damnation. The Star Chamber judges sentenced Prynne to stand successively in two pillories, having an ear cut off in each, to pay a fine of £5,000, and to suffer life imprisonment. Being tender-hearted men, they rejected the recommendation of the Earl of Dorset that he also be branded in the forehead and have his nose slit.

Besides its inclusion in Emlyn's *State Trials,* Prynne's case was familiar to Americans through three works which Madison recom-mended for purchase by the Continental Congress: Rushworth's *Collections* and the histories of Kennett and Clarendon. To the framers of the American Bill of Rights it was an eloquent argument also for prohibition of *ex post facto* laws, for the requirement of grand-jury action, the guarantee of trial by jury, the ban on com-pulsory self-incrimination, and the forbidding of cruel and unusual punishments.

Three years later, in December 1637, began the seventeen-year ordeal of John Lilburne, which illumined his name to a dozen later generations of Englishmen and Americans who cherished the liberties for which he fought. In January 1638 he was brought before the Archbishop of Canterbury and other dreaded judges of the Star Chamber, charged with violating the Licensing Act by shipping "factious and scandalous books out of Holland into England." In other words, books that promoted Puritan dissent. There was no proof of transportation by him, and Lilburne denied that he printed the books in question, saying that they were openly on sale in Dutch cities when he went to Holland. The judges never passed on that charge. To avoid incriminating others, Lilburne refused to take the "oath *ex officio*," binding him to answer all questions. For that refusal, which if allowed would topple the whole edifice of Star Chamber power, built on self-incrimination, the judges fined him £500 and ordered him whipped, pilloried, and imprisoned until he should take the oath. Potentially that was life imprisonment.

The underlying issues in this case—deeper than compulsory self-incrimination—were freedom of religion, freedom of speech (he was gagged to silence him at the pillory), and freedom of the press. These were untouched at the trial. It would have been fruitless to base a defense on rights that never had existed—that could not exist in a period of ferocious religious persecution. It was even more hopeless to do so in a court from which there was no effective appeal, and whose principal reason for being was to destroy the freedoms that did exist.

The two hundred bloody welts raised on Lilburne's back, as he was whipped from the Fleet to Westminster, helped to bring about the abolition of the Star Chamber in the first year of the Long Parliament in 1641. In the same year, on Lilburne's petition presented by Oliver Cromwell, Parliament reversed his sentence as "illegal and against the liberties of the subject." The resolution voiced a nationwide sentiment, not limited to Puritans, in declaring the Star Chamber proceedings to be "bloody, wicked, cruel, barbarous and tyrannous."

Lilburne's next dozen years produced enough hazards and excitements to overcrowd a dozen lives. Taking a captain's commission from Parliament at the outbreak of civil war, he was captured by the king's forces and put on trial for high treason. Parliament's threat of instant reprisals saved him from a death sentence, and he re-entered Cromwell's army when exchanged. A strange phenomenon then developed. While reparation bills were being pushed and blocked in Parliament, to cover his Star Chamber losses and suffering, he became embroiled with both houses because of caustic speech and writings. The House of Lords voted him £2,000 reparation, and almost on the heels of that action cited him for slanderous words about the Speaker, fined him £4,000 and sentenced him to seven years in prison. Lilburne appealed to the House of Commons as the only lawful judge of a freeborn English commoner. The Commons gave him a bewildered sort of support, then cited him for contempt when he appealed to the British people to help him "maintain with the last drop of his heart's blood his civil liberties and freedom." His 1648 pamphlet calling for abolition of the House of Lords sent him once more to the Tower, by order of the Commons at the request of the Lords, but both houses freed him to secure his support against usurpations by Cromwell.

A year later Lilburne published *An Agreement of the Free People of England,* the first proposal ever made for a written constitution binding on parliaments and kings. After "cruel, home-bred war" and intolerable oppressions the free people "Agree to ascertain our government, to abolish all arbitrary power, and set bounds and limits to our supreme and all subordinate authority, and remove all known grievances, and accordingly do declare and publish to the world, that we are agreed as followeth." The supreme authority was to reside "in a representative of the people, consisting of 400 persons," to hold office for a year, "and all laws made, or that shall be made, contrary to any part of this Agreement, are hereby made null and void."

It was an unworkable constitution, with no means of enforcement except that in case a parliament should fail to order a new annual election, the parties to the Agreement should choose a new 400 from which all the old members would be excluded. Yet it was a mighty thought, and in its wording there is part of the Supremacy Clause of the United States Constitution and the germ of judicial review.[3]

Cromwell's government took the Agreement seriously enough to send Lilburne back to the Tower on a new charge of high treason, with these passages cited. Released to avert a popular uprising, he immediately called for the impeachment of Cromwell for treason in his recent punishment of mutineers. Parliament replied by ordering Lilburne's delayed treason trial to proceed before a special court set up for that purpose. The trial took place, with Lilburne denouncing the special court as contrary to Magna Carta, and telling the jurors, in repeated defiance of the judges, that they were to decide both law and fact. They did so and acquitted him, amid such popular rejoicings that the judges dared not reject the verdict. Parliament, however, found a trivial excuse, fined him £3,000 and exiled him for life. He returned from the Netherlands within a year, was committed to Newgate prison and appealed to Cromwell for protection. The answer was a treason trial that began at Old Bailey on July 13, 1653.

By this time Lilburne was known throughout England as "Freeborn John." In Rushworth's *Collections,* a 1647 account of one of his controversies has the marginal heading, "Freeborn John Lilburne complains of the House of Peers as his Accusers and Judge." In the upper classes, this nickname was a term of disparagement. Among the masses of the people it came closer to idolatry. Thurloe's *State Papers* contain this passage in a letter dated June 27, 1653, concerning his pending treason trial: "Free born John is turned over to the sessions in the Old Baily, and, I believe, will speedily be hanged." Over the country, Thurloe recorded, houses and taverns rang with a newly written song:

> And what, shall then honest John Lilbourn die?
> Three score thousand will know the reason why.

Cromwell filled London with Roundhead troops as a precaution against mob action to rescue Lilburne from the expected sentence of death. The trial was held, the jury voted, and, it is recorded, "in spite of their officers, the soldiers shouted and sounded their trumpets when they heard that Lilburne was acquitted." That was the end of his troubles. He turned Quaker, abjuring violence, and Cromwell continued the pension that had been allotted for his support in prison.

Although Lilburne was an ardent Puritan Revolutionist and republican, he disapproved the execution of Charles I. And well he might, for the manner in which Charles was prosecuted, by order of Parliament, before a special trial commission, was a fantastic replica of the proceedings against Lilburne himself. The speeches of Charles in his own defense, denying the jurisdiction of that court, were virtual paraphrases of Lilburne. The king's written statement to his judges, which he was not allowed to read, would have richly earned him the title of "Freeborn Charles" if his career had not belied his words. King Charles would say no more, he wrote, if he alone were concerned:

"But the duty I owe to God in the preservation of the true liberty of my people will not suffer me at this time to be silent. For, how can any free-born subject of England call life or any thing he possesseth his own, if Power without Right daily make new, and abrogate the old fundamental ways of the Land?"

It was not the divine right of kings that Charles Stuart invoked, but, like Lilburne, the inborn rights of the British people. Not one tenth of them, Charles declared, had cast their votes for the Parliament that condemned him, "and in this way you wrong even the poorest ploughman, if you demand not his free consent." Except for the royal touch, his ensuing words seemed to be, and probably were, a conscious paraphrase of what Lilburne had been telling the people about their natural rights:

"Thus you see that I speak not for my own right alone, as I am your king, but also for the true liberty of all my subjects, which consists not in the power of government, but in living under such laws, such a government, as may give themselves the best assurance of their lives, and property of their goods. . . . I am against my will brought hither, where since I am come, I cannot but, to my power, defend the ancient laws and liberties of this kingdom, together with my own just right."

This parallel began where a great divergence ended. For Lilburne had been a *victim* of the Star Chamber, King Charles the *employer* of its cruel and arbitrary malpractices. Both of them learned that, even with that nefarious institution abolished, freedom could not flourish in a society inherently intolerant.

Albert Venn Dicey, in his *Law of the Constitution,* put the case well when he said the abolition of the Star Chamber was a stroke for legality, not for liberty:

"Hundreds of Englishmen who hated toleration and cared little for freedom of speech, entertained a keen jealousy of arbitrary power, and a fixed determination to be ruled in accordance with the law of the land. These sentiments abolished the Star Chamber in 1641, and made the re-establishment of the hated Court impossible, even for the frantic loyalty of 1660 [the year of the Stuart Restoration]. But the destruction of the Star Chamber meant much more than the abolition of an unpopular tribunal; it meant the rooting up from its foundations of the whole of the administrative system which had been erected by the Tudors and extended by the Stuarts."

Lilburne's great gift to posterity was the exalting of the thought of liberty as a natural right, but the time was far in the future when men would be free to speak or print their religious or political opinions if they conflicted with those held by Church or State. Licensing of the press outlasted by fifty-three years the court whose decree produced it, and freedom of the British press remained an empty pretense for more than a century beyond that.

In the hundred years from the execution of Sir Thomas More down to the trials of John Lilburne, the freedoms of religion, speech and press were suppressed by the High Commission and the Court of Star Chamber—both of them arbitrary agencies of the king—and by felony and treason trials in the common-law Court of King's Bench. But all charges of seditious libel were tried in the Star Chamber without a jury. Of the four notables tried before juries on account of their writings, Udall was indicted for felony, Peacham, Pine and Lilburne for treason. There was not a single trial of seditious libel at common law. The reason for that becomes manifest when one considers the relationship of Sir Edward Coke to what came to be fallaciously known, owing to him and after his time, as the common law of libel.

CHAPTER 9
Coke's Myth of Seditious Libel

Seditious libel became known to English law through Coke's extended comment in reporting "The Case *de Libellis Famosis, or of Scandalous Libels,*" which was tried in the Court of the Star Chamber in the spring of 1606.[1] Factually, the case was insignificant. Coke as Attorney General (a few months before his elevation to the bench) had obtained the defendant's confession to composing and publishing a scandalous set of verses on two of England's highest clergymen. The case furnished an opportunity to set forth, for the first time, the rules of law concerning libel that were formulated in Star Chamber late in the reign of Queen Elizabeth. Nearly all of these cases involved libel of private persons and were prosecuted by Coke himself, which may account for his desire to furnish the law of libel with an ancient and honorable ancestry. At any rate, he threw it back to the Old Testament. Job, he wrote, "became *quodammodo* impatient when libels were made of him; and therefore it appears of what force they are to provoke impatience and contention."

Those were studied words. The term "libel" itself, thus given antiquity, did not have the meaning Coke gave it until his own day. When books were handwritten scrolls, a short scroll was a "libel," and after the printing press came in, that term was transferred to pamphlets. Its earlier meaning is pointedly revealed in successive renderings of a verse from Numbers 23 in two editions of Wycliffe's Bible: Edition of 1382: "And the preest shall write in a libel . . ." Edition of 1388: "And the preest shall write in a litil book . . . "[2] In saying that the libels (slanders) of Job provoked "impatience and contention," Coke was giving antiquity to the technical device by which the Star Chamber, whose jurisdiction was limited to misdemeanors, created its own power to try libels. They were said to be incitements to disorder and private vengeance. By the same stroke of perverted genius the Star Chamber set up the rule (afterwards solemnly declared to be part of the common law) that because the tendency to cause quarrels was the essence of the crime, the truth of a libel was no defense and might even be an aggravation of criminality.

But accepting Job as complaining witness in the world's first case of criminal libel, the gap thereafter is a clean jump to Coke himself and his description of Star Chamber practices. A libel against a private person, it was resolved in that court, deserved severe punishment because it tended to stir those of the same family or society to revenge and breach of the peace. If made "against a magistrate or other public person, it is a greater offense; for it concerns . . . also the scandal of government," and what greater scandal could there be than to have corrupt or wicked magistrates appointed by the king?

"It is not material," Coke's descriptive account went on, "whether the libel be true, or whether the party against whom it is made, be of good or ill fame; for in a settled state of government the party aggrieved ought to complain for every injury done him in an ordinary course of law, and not by any means to revenge himself" by libeling or assaulting his adversary.

This was a perfect Star Chamber recipe for protecting corrupt or wicked appointees of the king. A private person injured by another private person could indeed seek, and might find, a remedy in the "ordinary course of law." But could a private person sue a king's minister for corruption or wickedness? Against corruption in a monarchy the people could have no possible remedy except exposure of the corruption and the resulting pressure or menace of public opinion. If it was seditious libel to tell the truth about unfaithful public servants, the law that made it so was as much the fortress of wickedness as the castles of the robber barons had been in the days of the Plantagenets.

Continuing his narration, Coke listed the various forms of writing and publishing held criminal by the Court of Star Chamber.

He then widened the jurisdiction over the crime but gave no citation of cases to support its theoretical breadth:

"A libeller (who is called *famosis defamator*) shall be punished either by indictment at the common law, or by bill [i.e. by complaint against him in the Star Chamber], if he deny it, or *ore tenus* [by word of mouth] on his confession in Star-Chamber, and according to the quality of the offence he may be punished by fine or imprisonment; and if the case be extraordinary, by pillory and loss of his ears."

Had Coke known of any libel cases in the common-law courts, he undoubtedly would have cited one to support his statement about an indictment at the common law. In June 1606 he was appointed Chief Justice of the Court of Common Pleas. As a side line, that made him one of the Star Chamber judges. Five years later he elaborated his description of seditious libel in a report of *John Lamb's Case,* brought in the Star Chamber against numerous citizens of the town of Northampton. "It was resolved," wrote Coke, "that every one who shall be convicted in the said case, either ought to be a contriver of the libel, or a procurer of the contriving of it, or a malicious publisher of it, knowing it to be a libel." As an illustration, Coke said that if a man read a libel, or heard it read, and laughed at it, that was no publication; but if he repeated it to another, knowing it to be a libel, he was guilty of publishing it.

These Star Chamber definitions became standard in English courts during the ensuing century, but for a time there was nothing to support Coke's assertion that seditious libel had a common-law background. Then he himself searched and reported in 1628 that he had found it. In words that actually testified to the newness of the subject, he wrote in his *Third Institute*:

"What a libel is, how many kinds of libels there be, who are to be punished for the same, you may find in my reports [Citations of the Star Chamber cases described above]. . . . To these you may add two notable records. By the one, it appeareth that Adam de Ravensworth was indicted in the king's bench for the making of a libel in writing, in the French tongue, against Richard of Snowshill, calling him thereon, *Roy de Raveners, etc.* Whereupon he being arraigned, pleaded thereunto not guilty, and was found guilty, as by the record appeareth. So as a libeller, or as a publisher of a libell committeth a public offence, and may be indicted therefore at the common law."

Coke's citation was to the rolls of the King's Bench in the tenth year of Edward III, which was 1336. His second case of alleged libel was in the same court eight years later. John de Northampton, an attorney of the King's Bench, wrote a letter to John Ferrers, a member of the king's council, saying "that neither Sir William Scot, chiefe justice [of Common Pleas] nor his fellowes the king's justices, any great thing would do by the commandment of our lord the king, nor of queen Philip[pa], in that place, more than of any other of the realme." John confessed the writing of the letter, which, said the king's court in passing judgment, "contains no truth, on which account our lord the king has reason to be indignant, which is in scandal of justice and the courts." So John was committed to the marshal and was required to produce six sureties for his good conduct.

If John of Northampton's letter did in fact subject him to a trial for seditious libel, it would strike down one of the favorite tenets of the Star Chamber, for John's case turned on the truth or falsity of the allegations. But it clearly appears from the words of the judgment, *"quod esset in scandalum justic' et curiae,"* that this was a plain case of contempt of court. It was committed by an attorney (an officer of the court) in derogation of the judges and was punished as contempt. That eliminates one half, but much the weaker half, of the alleged common-law ancestry of seditious libel.

The Ravensworth case, *if stated correctly by Coke,* would indeed constitute seditious libel, and would fully justify Coke's conclusion from it that a libeler "may be indicted therefore at the common law." *But Lord Coke did not state the case correctly.* Adam of Ravensworth did not call Richard of Snowshill "king of raveners" (robbers). *Adam applied the obnoxious words to himself.* His crime was not seditious libel. According to the importance attached to it, it could have been regarded as treason by "accroaching the royal power," or as a high contempt of the king by subjecting him to personal indignity.

Richard of Snowshill, who was pastor of the church of Huntington, Yorkshire, presented Adam's letter to the king and his council when Edward visited York on November 6, 1336. Here is the opening sentence of the French original, as it appears in Sayles' *Select Cases in the Court of King's Bench, Edward III:*

"*Lyonel, roi de la Route de Raueners, a nostre faux et desloiaux Richard de Snaweshill', salutz saunz amours.*"

And here is the translation that accompanies it:

"Lionel, King of the rout of Raveners, to our false and disloyal Richard of Snowshill, greeting without love."

Lionel, king of the band of robbers, then issues orders to his disloyal subject. The parson must allow the abbot of our Lady of Bootham to have his liberty. Richard must confirm the abbot's choice of a vicar for Burton Agnes in place of "him whom you are maintaining" there. "And, if you do not do it, we make our vow, first to the King of Heaven and then to the King of England and to our crown, that you will have and receive from us such orders as the bishop of Exeter had in Cheapside, wherever you may be found." A threat followed to inflict a thousand pounds damages "from us and ours" on the parson's lordly protector (unnamed) if the latter did not "abandon false plottings and confederacies" in relation to the vicarage. In the concluding sentences, Lionel extended the threat of damages to the parson and reasserted his own status as king of the "rout of raveners":

"And if you do not intend to pay attention to our orders, we shall instruct our sheriff of the North to make great distress against you, as is said before. Given at our castle of the Wind in the Greenwood Tower in the first year of our reign."

The parson of Huntington did not need to be told who sent this letter to him. A double pun in the salutation identified the author and the concluding words confirmed the identification. To the parson, Lionel, king of raveners, was *Ravens*worth, king of *Ravens,* writing from his "castle of the Wind in the Greenwood Tower."

This letter was written fifteen years before Parliament persuaded or compelled Edward III to narrow the crime of treason by limiting it to making war on the king or compassing or imagining his death. By the standards of 1336 Adam's aping of royalty smacked of treason and reeked of contempt. His choice of "Lionel" as a name for himself was an assumption of the highest royal status. The reference to "our sheriff of the North" gave a territorial spread to the mock sovereignty and prerogative. Adam knew his risk, and took out insurance against extremities by putting in "our vow . . . to the King of England and to our crown." He was a king below a king, but his act was still a burlesque of the reigning sovereign. The nature of it as an offense against the person of the king, rather than against the parson, was further indicated in the judgment.

Two countrymen who carried the letter (for which one of them was paid a penny) were tried along with Adam. This was the verdict of the twelve jurors: "They say on their oath that Adam of Ravensworth is guilty of making the aforesaid letter and that Geoffrey and Robert of Latham knew nothing about the things contained in the letter nor are they in any way guilty thereof." The judges committed Adam to prison but added: "And because the court here is not yet advised to give full release to Geoffrey and Robert of Latham because this business concerns the royal dignity and is in prejudice of the king," they were released on mainprise. Six Yorkshire men undertook to have the pair "before the king . . . whenever they shall be notified."

All crimes conventionally concerned the royal dignity, but to give the full sentence that limited significance here would be to say that the judges could not accept a jury's verdict of "not guilty" because the defendants were accused of something criminal. The Court of King's Bench had to refer the verdict of acquittal to a still higher authority because, as the judges said in coupled phrases, the business "concerns the royal dignity and *is in prejudice of the king.*" There was no higher authority except the king and his council, before whom personally the case originated.

The closest approach to a similar situation and similar language is found in the case of the Archdeacon of Norfolk and his ecclesiastical subordinate, who were brought before Edward the Second and his council in 1315. They were accused of violating the rule that no summonses should be served within the king's palace of Westminster, and with aggravating the offense by serving one on the king's niece, Joan de Bar, Countess of Warenne. She was to answer the charge (whose nature may easily be guessed) of Matilda of Warford in Matilda's suit for divorce. The citation was made, the king's council declared, "in manifest shame of the king and in contempt of him to the extent of twenty thousand pounds and in derogation of his crown and dignity etc."

Here, as in Adam's case, the conventional derogation of royal dignity was joined with a specific accusation of personal insult to the king, made even more definite by the fixing of monetary damages. So too in the judgment. The subordinate confessed that he issued the summons and was committed to the Tower of London for an action that "redound[ed] to the shame and contempt of the king and [was] in derogation of his crown and dignity etc." Because the archdeacon denied ordering the citation, he was allowed "by special grace of the king" to have a day when he would "hear the king's pleasure" concerning him.

Here is a virtual duplication of the Ravensworth trial, even to the postponement of final action to learn the king's pleasure. The proceedings are similar, the denunciations are both personal and conventional, the offenses are identical in nature—both of them involving personal insult to the king. Coke's error in calling Adam's trial one of seditious libel is made trebly evident by his application of the term *"Roy de Raveners"* to the wrong person, by the words and actions of the judges, and by the fact that in the entire record not a word is said about any offense given to the humble parson of Huntington Church.

So that is the end of Adam of Ravensworth, king of the flock of ravens in the Castle of the Wind, as the supposed libeler of Richard of Snowshill. With his disappearance the crime of seditious libel vanishes completely, as an offense known to the common law of England through any recorded trial of earlier date than the abolition of the Star Chamber in 1641. Its existence depends entirely on the fiat of Lord Coke, totally unsupported by evidence when made, and buttressed later by two cases of alleged libel that vanish on examination.

The straightening out of the record leaves civil damage suits for libel within the scope of the common law. It makes criminal libel entirely the creation of the Star Chamber. And as Starkie says, criminal libel was taken over by the common-law courts after Parliament put the Star Chamber out of existence. But common-law judges, hostile to religious and political freedom in an era of universal and savage intolerance, could not acknowledge that so valuable an instrument of repression was cut from such poisonous wood. Nor would they or the Crown allow it to be given up. The result was a continuation of Star Chamber procedures under the pretense of sanction at the common law.

CHAPTER 10
Judicial Midwives of the Law of Libel

Apparently the rulers of Great Britain hated and feared the press as much as the people hated and feared the Court of the Star Chamber. At any rate, the licensing system lasted for fifty-three years after the abolition in 1641 of that unloved tribunal. Its oppressive decrees perished with its death, but licensing gained a statutory base. At first the control had a temporary look, established by a short-term ordinance of the Long Parliament. Another ordinance followed, and Cromwell renewed the pattern during the Puritan interlude. In 1662, following the restoration of Charles II to the throne, a fifteen-year licensing act was passed. It was renewed on expiration and the system did not come to an end until 1694, six years after the "Glorious Revolution" overthrew the Stuart dynasty. Parliament stubbornly repelled the efforts of William III and his ministers to continue the censorship.

During that half century, Stuart kings, Puritan Protector and Orange Liberator held alike to the central purpose of the licensing system to limit and control the output of books, and to compel the printers of seditious works—usually heretical—to identify their authors. The continuation of the Tudor-Stuart restrictions by Cromwell produced one unforgettable protest—the *Areopagitica* of the poet John Milton—appealing for an unlicensed press and blasting restraint on human thought in terms that resound today more loudly than they did for a hundred years after they were uttered. Indeed, Milton's words broke at last through limitations that he himself placed upon their application, for in that period of universal religious strife no Protestant exhorter on liberty would or safely could attempt to bring Catholics within the range of tolerance that was classed as freedom.

There was no wisdom, wrote Milton, in trying to restrain the press by licensing, "whenas those corruptions which it seeks to prevent, break in faster at other doors which cannot be shut." A forbidden writing was "thought to be a certain spark of truth that flies up in the faces of them who seek to tread it out." For the origin of such restrictions, in the world at large, Milton looked toward Rome and blamed "the most Antichristian Councel,[1] and the most tyrannous Inquisition that ever inquir'd." Free writing and free speaking had been the result of mild, free and humane government in England, a country where liberty had been the nurse of all great wits. The people could grow ignorant, brutish and slavish again, but Parliament must first become as oppressive, arbitrary and tyrannous as the government (of Charles I) from which the House of Commons set the country free. And Milton exclaimed in climax:

"Give me the liberty to know, to utter, and to argue freely, according to conscience, above all liberties."

It is mere carping to decry Milton because his *ideas* of freedom did not match his *ideals*. He was chained to his time, even though his spirit soared, and his time, in terms of Christian brotherhood, was one of saint-eat-sinner, with rapidly alternating labels on devourer and devoured. But his spirit never sank to earth, and when men became worthy of his words, by casting off their own debasing prejudices, Milton became to them the prophet of a greater freedom than any he had visioned.

In his own day, the declared principles of the libertarian poet were cruelly betrayed by the lawmakers in whom he expressed such confidence. In addition to continuing the licensing system, Cromwell's Parliament did its own punishing of major religious offenders. Its most famous victim was James Nayler, an "extravagant Quaker" whose followers regarded him (with considerable help from himself) as a reincarnation of Jesus Christ. On December 5, 1656, after junketing around the country for evidence, a committee of the House of Commons reported that Nayler "did assume the gesture, words, honour, worship and miracles of our blessed Savior."

The most convincing evidence against him was that disciples had kissed his feet, and "As for his doing of miracles particularly,

Dorcas Erbury saith, That she was dead in Exeter gaol two days, and that Nayler laid his hands upon her, and raised her." Asked by the Commons committee if he had indeed raised this woman from the dead, the blaspheming wretch replied: "I can do nothing of myself. . . . There is a power in me from above." No less damnably, he allowed his followers to call him "The Fairest of Ten Thousand," and said to the committee when called on to explain: "if they speak it to that which the Father hath begotten in me, then I dare not deny it; because that, as he said, is beautiful, where-ever it is begotten." The Commons, after hearing Nayler admit that his answers were correctly recorded, voted him guilty of blasphemy. A motion to inflict the death penalty was postponed, 96 to 82, following a powerful argument against it by Lord Commissioner Whitelocke.

The death penalty for heresy, Whitelocke contended, was not a genuine part of the common law, but was brought into existence by Arundel, Archbishop of Canterbury, during the reign of Henry IV (1399-1413). This high churchman invented the writ *De Haere-tico comburendo* in order to execute the Lollards, "who were good Christians, and of the same profession that we are." But even if *heresy* were punishable with death, that would not make *blasphemy* a capital offense. In order to condemn Nayler to death, Whitelocke told the Puritan lawmakers, Parliament would have to choose between two evil courses. It must either act as a court, in which case it must create the law on which it acted; or it must act by bill of attainder, without a law to sanction it. Either way would create a precedent for England "wherein no man can be safe." Impressed by this plea for justice and mercy, the tenderhearted Puritan Parliament merely ordered that the Quaker be exposed in the pillory for two hours at Westminster, be whipped by the hangman from there to Cheapside, be pilloried (for the sport of another mob) at Cheapside for two hours, then have his tongue burned through with a hot iron and the letter B (for Blasphemy) burned into his forehead. Thus did Cromwell's Christians offer the Quakers an example of brotherly love and furnish an illustration (in the view of some twentieth-century Americans) of action that does not conflict with eighteenth-century American ideas of freedom of speech.

In spite of its vicious cruelty the Nayler case actually helps to strike down seditious libel as a common-law offense. For Whitelocke argued—and gained his objective—that a heresy writ which had been in use for more than 250 years was not a part of the common law, even though currently registered as such, because "it is not in the ancient manuscript registers, which indeed is a true part and demonstration of the Common Law."

Nor had seditious libel yet come into the common law in 1663, when John Twyn, a printer, was brought before Chief Justice Sir Robert Hyde, one of the many unadmired appointees of Charles II to the Court of King's Bench. The charge against Twyn was high treason, for printing (not for writing) "a seditious, poisonous and scandalous" book, which proclaimed, as its most treasonable feature, that *a king was accountable to the people*. The three judges, Hyde, Kelyng and Recorder Wilde, agreed "that printing and publishing such wicked positions, was an overt act declaring the treason of compassing and imagining the King's death." Kelyng himself reported the case in sufficient detail to support the more dramatic account in the *State Trials*.

Opening the trial, Lord Hyde directed Prosecutor Lee to read thirteen passages from Twyn's book. Lee read its title and began on the text: "It is one of the scarlet sins of this nation, that the people suffered their rulers—" Choked with emotion, the king's counsel could go no farther. The passages called for, he told the court, "are too impious to be published, and indeed too foul to be repeated, but in substance." So he toned them down to their still-horrifying substance, which was:

"The Supreme Magistrate is made accountable to the people."

Lee managed to get through four other paraphrases of nearly equal horror before the judges stopped him by saying they had heard enough. The Lord Chief Justice then addressed Twyn:

"Now say what you will. But I must tell you, in those particulars that have been compared, there is as much villainy and slander, as it is possible for the devil or man to invent. It is to destroy the king in his person, to rob him of the love and affections of his people; to destroy the whole family, and all government, ecclesiastical and civil."

Twyn was convicted and sentenced to die, but was given hope

of life by the prison chaplain if he would name the author of the book he printed. He refused. The contents of the book had been unknown to him, for the manuscript was brought, put in type and printed when he was sick in bed. But he had promised the author not to reveal his name and it was against his principles to do so. "Better (says he) one suffer, than many."[2]

Twyn's real crime was his refusal to betray the writer of the book. Had he co-operated with the Crown, he might perhaps have escaped trial or been subjected to moderate punishment under the Licensing Act of 1662. But the Crown bypassed the statute and used the device of constructive treason to inflict a death sentence on the only culprit within reach. In every basic element, the prosecution was a violation of freedom of the press and of religion, but in law it was a treason trial, under a perverted application of the benign treason statute of Edward III.

Chief Justice Hyde, however, was the man who opened the door through which seditious libel was brought into the common law of England. He did it in October 1664, two years after the Twyn case, when Benjamin Keach was brought before him at the Aylsbury Assizes. Keach was charged with (and admitted) writing a book entitled *The Child's Instructor; or, a New and Easy Primmer*, containing a number of contradictions of Anglican doctrine. He wrote against infant baptism, asserted that laymen might preach the Gospel, and affirmed that Christ would someday rule personally upon earth. At the preliminary hearing he attempted to explain his teachings to Chief Justice Hyde:

"Keach. My lord, as to those things—

"Judge. You shall not preach here, nor give the reasons of your damnable doctrine, to seduce and infect his majesty's subjects. These are not things for such as you are to meddle with, and to pretend to write books of divinity; but I will try you for it before I sleep."

Hyde admonished the grand jurors that Keach was "a base and dangerous fellow" and called on them to do their duty, which they did. At the trial, the Chief Justice read passages from the book and made this comment: "Because Christ, when he was upon the earth, made choice of tradesmen to be his disciples; therefore this fellow would have ministers to be such now; taylors, and pedlars, and tinkers, and such fellows as he is: But it is otherwise now . . ." Keach attempted to speak, but got no farther than "As to the doctrines—"

"Judge. You shall not speak here, except as to the matter of fact: that is to say, whether you writ this book or not.

"Keach. I desire liberty to speak to the particulars in my indictment, and those things that have—

"Judge. You shall not be suffered to give the reasons for your damnable doctrine here, to seduce the king's subjects."

Hyde's instructions to the jury were not taken down by the reporter, but the nature of them was evident in his passing remarks: the jury was not to decide whether the book was libelous, nor whether the writing and publication of it violated any law, but only whether Keach wrote it—a matter not in dispute. Receiving word that the jurors could not agree, the Chief Justice conferred with one of them and "would frequently shake him as he spoke to him." The jury reported, "Guilty in part," and after a brief exchange Hyde said:

"You must go out again, and agree; and as for you, that say you cannot in conscience find him guilty, if you say so again, without giving reasons for it, I shall take an order with you."

That quelled the revolt. Keach was sentenced to be jailed and fined and to spend two hours in the pillory in two successive weeks, his book to be burned before his face by the common hangman. He would remain in jail until sureties were found for his good behavior and for his future appearance in court "there to renounce your doctrine, and make such public submission as shall be injoined you." Keach replied, "I hope I shall never renounce those truths which I have written in that book." He furnished the sureties, but the Chief Justice dropped dead in court during the next term and he never was called on to recant.

In Keach's case the court adjusted the old Star Chamber rules to fit a jury trial for seditious libel and then coerced the jury after taking away all of its powers that had any meaning. The Lord Chief Justice, without specifically mentioning the common law, was expanding it to bring seditious libel within its scope for the easier punishment of heresy. He condemned Keach's book as false, and denied the right of the jury to pass either on that question or on the innocence or criminality of publishing erroneous doctrine. In a case where the law and the fact were inseparable, they were ordered to reach a verdict of Guilty or Not Guilty on the fact of publication alone. It was exactly as if, in trying an indictment for murder by gunshot, the jurors were forbidden to decide whether the defendant acted in self-defense, or even discharged the gun by accident, but must bring in a verdict of *guilty as charged* if they found that he fired the fatal shot. If homicide cases were tried that way, a claim of self-defense would amount to a confession of murder. Just so, in this libel case, the defendant's attempt to prove the innocence of the publication made his conviction inescapable unless the jurors defied the judge.

In the next great case the jurors did just that and went to prison. It was the famous trial in 1670 of William Penn and William Mead for "tumultuous assembly" (described in Chapter 5), actually a trial for preaching in the street after being forbidden to preach under a roof. Though not in form a trial for seditious libel, it was so closely related that the judges brought in all the violations of fair procedure that were being devised to abridge the freedoms of religion, speech and press. It is worth while to repeat, at this point, the opening words of Penn's account of this ordeal:

"Oh, what monstrous, and illegal proceedings are these? . . . When all pleas for liberty are esteemed sedition, and the laws, that give, and maintain them, so many insignificant pieces of formality."

That was not a characterization of this trial alone. It was directed against all that had been happening in England since the persecution of Protestant Dissenters made religious intolerance universal. It was a protest against the arbitrary actions and distortions of law employed to punish Udall, Peacham, Prynne, Lilburne, Nayler, Twyn, Keach and less conspicuous victims. It was this record of *innovations and inventions* presented as *immemorial customs* that caused Penn to call out so insistently during his trial:

"Where is that common-law? . . . if it be common, it should not be so hard to produce. . . . It is too general and imperfect an answer, to say it is the common-law, unless we know both where and what it is. . . . I have asked but one question, and you have not answered me . . ."

The judges and prosecutors could not answer him, for the

common law they were talking about had no existence. A courageous jury saved Penn and Mead from the fate intended for them, and ten courageous judges braved the wrath of the Crown and released the jurors from prison. But within a few years the British judiciary became once more the abject tool of the Stuart king, as courts and Crown began their catastrophic slump to the lowest level in the nation's history. All this time the Penn-Mead pamphlets were spreading over the country, winning little sympathy for Quakers, but revealing the hollow farce of a common law of libel that could not be located in the common law. The government had to do something about it, and it did.

In 1678, Sir William Scroggs became Chief Justice of the Court of King's Bench. The worst Chief Justice in British history (or call him a close second to the later Jeffreys) was ordered by Charles the Second to call together the twelve high judges of England. By their unanimous voice, they declared seditious libel to be punishable at common law. Had it been truly so, there would have been no need for such a declaration. The evidence of it would have been in lawbooks running back hundreds of years.

Scroggs made the announcement, in threatening terms, to a jury impaneled in 1680 to try Benjamin Harris, a Guildhall bookseller, and the manner of the trial left no doubt of the true ancestry of this alleged common law. The rules it embodied were those of the Star Chamber, modified to give the judges an authority over juries analogous to that possessed by Star Chamber judges without a jury.

Harris was indicted for printing and selling a pamphlet appealing to the country against the repeated proroguing of Parliament by Charles II at a time of crisis. The crisis was imaginary—that of the fictitious "Popish Plot" against the life of the king invented by Titus Oates. But both Chief Justice Scroggs and Recorder George Jeffreys (not yet at the apex of his perverted career) construed its contents as a concerted preparatory plan to put the bastard Duke of Monmouth, King Charles' son, on the throne if the Jesuits should succeed in their nonexistent murder plot.

If such a scheme "be not downright treason," Scroggs told the jury, "I am sure it is just upon the heels of it." As for this publication in particular, "you can hardly read a more base, and pernicious book." He rejected with vehemence the defense offered by Harris's counsel, that book sales without malice violated no law. Said the Chief Justice:

"They would insinuate, as if the mere selling of such a book was no offence: it is not long since, that all the judges met; by the king's command; as they did some time before too: and they both times declared unanimously, that all persons that do write, or print, or sell any pamphlet, that is either scandalous to public, or private persons; such books may be seized, and the person punished by law."

Scroggs instructed the jury that they had nothing to do but decide whether Harris sold the book, returning a general verdict of "Guilty" or "Not Guilty." Since the fact of sale was admitted, this was in effect an order to convict the bookseller of malicious publication, even though the jurors might not regard the publication as malicious. The judges, if they saw fit, could then offset the verdict by granting a stay of judgment. Since they had already pronounced the book to be close to treason, the instructions made an utter farce of the trial, unless the jury ventured to defy the judges. This they could do by returning a special verdict, or a general verdict of "not guilty" in direct disregard of instructions. In everything but name, this was a perpetuation of Star Chamber procedures under the fictitious denomination of a common law of seditious libel.

The Harris jury disregarded the instructions, and brought back the special verdict: "Guilty of selling the book." At this refusal to find Harris guilty *as charged in the indictment*, "there was a very great and clamorous shout." The Lord Chief Justice instantly addressed the jurors: "That was not their business. They were only to determine whether barely Guilty, or not Guilty."

If Scroggs had any uncertainty about how to act, Recorder Jeffreys had none. The future hatchet man of "The Bloody Assizes" asked that the jury be polled. At this foretaste of attaint and imprisonment, "they all unanimously cried out, they were all agreed, and then the foreman gave the verdict again, 'Guilty.'" Harris was led away to prison and Chief Justice Scroggs gave the jury a lecture:

"I am sorry you gave countenance to this cause so much, as to stir from the bar, when the evidence was so full, and when I told you plainly, not only my opinion, but likewise that of all the judges of England, that selling this book was an offence at the common law, for which they ought to be punished; and yet you with your scruples, you give the party (with their halloos and shoutings) to take advantage . . . Would I knew some of those shouters, I would make them know, I would punish them."

That was the way the Star Chamber law of seditious libel was brought into the common law of England, by Stuart judges who endorsed and adopted every detail of Star Chamber injustice and added some of their own for the purpose of coercing freedom-minded juries.

CHAPTER 11
The Popish Plot

Of all the infamies that have darkened Anglo-Saxon justice, first place can hardly be denied to "The Popish Plot" that kept England in a state of panic and vindictive rage from 1678 until its principal inventor was convicted of perjury in 1685. Yet except for the unspeakable barbarities of the punishments inflicted (and those were typical of the times), the history of the plot bears a disquieting resemblance to the excesses of the McCarthy Era in American politics, with its hideous repercussions in all branches of government and on the minds and conduct of the people of the United States. In one prime feature the Popish Plot could have no American counterpart. It was supposed to be a plot to kill the king, but Charles the Second knew better than any other man in the kingdom that the charge was false. He kept still and let his friends and supporters die on the gallows because to speak the truth as he knew it might have put his crown in jeopardy.

In its sectarian aspect the Stuart Restoration gave a new face to an old anomaly. The Puritan Commonwealth was overthrown by an Anglican Church party, strongly anti-Catholic, which nevertheless brought back a ruling family with papal ties and inclinations. Charles the Second, whose mother (Queen Henrietta Maria) was a Catholic, took a Portuguese Catholic wife, Catherine of Braganza, soon after his restoration in 1660. It was a useful marriage for trade and politics which the country reluctantly accepted on that account, but the belief was widely held that Charles himself was an Anglican only because his position required him to be head of the established church. His brother James, Duke of York (later James II), had closer Catholic ties, both of his own and through his Italian wife, Mary of Modena. Laws carrying the death penalty, enacted in Elizabethan days, forbade Catholic priests to say mass in England and barred Jesuits from the country. But these laws were laxly enforced, with no rigid restrictions except against open worship and the wearing of priestly garb. Somerset House, where Queen Catherine held her court, contained a Catholic chapel and she was allowed a private chaplain. Thus Somerset House became a Catholic enclave in a hostile country, and many of the queen's visitors were supposed to be—and were—unrobed priests.

In 1676 an adventurer named Titus Oates, at the mature age of twenty-seven, was finding it hard to make an honest living at that trade. He had recently escaped conviction on a perjury indictment resulting from slanderous charges, with overtones of blackmail, made by him against the morals of a schoolmaster. Concluding that there was big money in bigotry, Oates made a pretended conversion to the Catholic Church in order to gather material for betrayal purposes. To make a thorough job of it he lurked around Somerset House to see who came and went in the queen's circle, and to observe religious procedures. Gaining admission to a Jesuit college in Spain and being expelled for scandalous actions, he was next admitted to and ultimately expelled from the Jesuit school at St. Omer, in France. In this manner he became passably familiar with the affairs of that order. To strengthen his educational standing he called himself "Doctor" Oates, falsely claiming that the University of Salamanca, which he never attended, had given him a degree. His principal working asset was a partial list of Jesuits illegally in England.

Thus equipped, "Doctor" Oates sought out Israel Tonge, a fanatically anti-Catholic doctor of divinity who had hallucinations about religious plots. Oates proposed that they work up the story of a Jesuit conspiracy to assassinate the king. They could publish a sensational book about it and divide the profits. Tonge agreed. In a preliminary move apparently designed to obtain publicity, Tonge carried the tale to the Earl of Danby, Lord High Treasurer and the king's favorite, as a plot whose details could be learned from Oates. Danby, a Protestant who disbelieved the story, sent Oates to Justice of the Peace Sir Edmundbury Godfrey[1] for a preliminary statement, and took him before the king and Privy Council. The results were so sensational that Oates abandoned the book-writing plan and opened a new career for himself as a professional accuser, supported by public funds. Almost instantly he gained power over men's lives and for some years over the government itself.

Before the Privy Council on September 6 and September 31 (Old Style), Oates laid bare the nonexistent plot of the Jesuits to assassinate the king, subject England to the rule of France, overthrow the Protestant religion and restore the dominion of the Pope. He testified that in the previous September, while he was still a student at St. Omer, a letter came from the general order of Jesuits directing nine men including himself to go to London for a Jesuit consult. They were to meet on April 24, 1678, at the White Horse Tavern in the Strand, where they would arrange to carry out the detailed orders, given in the letter, for the killing of the king. His own assignment was to murder "Dr. Tongue" on account of a book he had translated from the French called "The Jesuits Morals." Thus Oates established his position as an informer and yet avoided the regicide role.

King Charles personally conveyed the news of the plot to Parliament, when it reassembled on October 21, in a brief and strangely worded message: "I have been informed of a design against my person by the Jesuits; of which I shall forbear any opinion, lest I may seem to say too much, or too little; but I will leave the matter to the law."

He did indeed say too little, but anything more than he said would have been too much. Seven years later, long after the quartered bodies of the innocent Jesuits pointed to by Titus Oates had rotted away on poles, King Charles heaved a great sigh of relief. A secret that he had kept to himself and his family during all that time could now be cautiously told, and tell it he did, to his close friend and confidant Sir John Reresby, who recorded the revelation in his *Memoirs:*

"[1685] May 8. Waiting on the King in his barge from Whitehall to Somerset House to see the Queen Dowager the day that Doctor Oates, the great evidence in the Popish Plot, was convicted of perjury (it being proved that he was at St. Omers the 24th of April, 1678, when he swore he was at the White Horse Tavern in the

Strand, when Pickering, Groves, Ireland, etc., Jesuits signed the death of Charles the Second), the King said indeed there was a meeting of the Jesuits on that day, which all the scholars of St. Omers knew was to be, but it was well Doctor Oates knew no better where it was, for it was then held in St. James's, where the King then dwelt; for, said the King, if that had been understood by Oates, he would have made ill work for me."

So there was the basic fact, recorded by a man respected in England for his probity. The alleged meeting of Jesuit conspirators, at which the work of assassinating the King was parceled out, was held in St. James's Palace, under the protective supervision of Charles the Second and the Duke of York. It was in reality the periodic triennial conclave of English Jesuits, held to organize the leadership and plan the activities of the order for the next three years. Since British law made it high treason for any Jesuit to enter the country, the meeting place had to be both secret and safe, and where could it be more so than in the palace of the king?

To the Protestant public at large, the Popish Plot was the overwhelming reality of the seventeenth century. It proved, beyond the limit of their imaginings, all that they were ready to believe about the fiendish malignity of Roman Catholic priests. To high ministers of state and parliamentary leaders it was at first a stroke of good fortune by which they could undermine hated rivals. Skeptical of the plot, they used the story with such effect that they dared not stop it: a whisper of disbelief would put them in the jaws of the juggernaut they had helped to create.

In his statement of September 31 to the Privy Council, framed by himself and Tonge, Oates made forty-three charges against groups and individuals. He named three Jesuit priests—Fathers Ireland, Pickering and Grove—whose assignment was to assassinate the king. On the chance that their attempt would fail, £10,000 was to be offered to the queen's physician, Sir George Wakeman, to poison the monarch. Later the offer was raised to £15,000, and Oates had seen Wakeman's receipt for a third of it. The Council called in Dr. Wakeman, who "utterly denied all," whereupon Oates was asked whether he knew anything personally against Sir George. He replied that he did not.

Oates's story was so dubious that the whole thing might have collapsed at this point except for a collateral happening. On Saturday, October 12, Sir Edmundbury Godfrey disappeared. Five days later his body was found in a roadside ditch, transfixed with his own sword. His gold and silver were still in his pocket. The body lay within plain sight of passersby. Physicians found no signs of bleeding at the wounds. Unquestionably it was murder, committed elsewhere, probably by strangulation, and the sword was thrust through to make it look like suicide. As the story of the plot and murder spread far and wide, two thoughts flashed into people's minds: "The priests have done it. Titus Oates is telling the truth." Nobody carried the analysis to its revealing conclusion: that the murderers did not want the death to look enough like suicide to make people think that such it was.

Oates now fed like a gourmet on his own cooking. Four days after Godfrey's body was discovered, Parliament convened in a state of frenzy. Oates, called to tell his story at the bar, enlarged his treason accusations from forty-three to eighty-one. (Senator McCarthy was not the first to prove the truth of a lie by telling a bigger one.) Lords and Commoners listened in horrified fascination as he testified that "five Popish lords" were at the head of the plot. He had seen the commissions issued to them by the Pope, under which they were to head the government that would be set up after the king was murdered. The five—Lords Arundell, Stafford, Powis, Petre and Belasyse—were clapped into the Tower of London, impeached and indicted. Lord Stafford, after long staving off a trial, was hanged as paymaster of a nonexistent army of massacre. Lord Petre died in the Tower, where the three others were held until Oates was convicted of perjury in 1685.

No more immune was Lord High Treasurer Danby, who through the king's favor had been ruling ministers higher than himself. In the articles of impeachment it was charged that he had "traitorously encroached to himself Regal Power. . . . That he is Popishly affected, and hath traitorously concealed (after he had notice) the late horrid and bloody Plot and conspiracy." King Charles halted the impeachment by giving Danby a general pardon and saying he would repeat it ten times over to make it good. Sir Harbottle Grimston suggested that Danby "be hanged, with the pardon about his neck," and the Commons moved in that direction by shifting to a bill of attainder. The king blocked that by proroguing Parliament and refusing to call it back. For almost five years the once mighty Danby languished in the Tower, putting out pamphlets in which he assailed the rivals who kept him there, and piteously appealing to the public to believe that Titus Oates had never said a word against him. Again and again habeas corpus was refused, but at last the twelve judges of England gathered enough united courage, with the king's backing, to release him on bail.

In such an atmosphere, and fortified by the sensational murder of Godfrey, Oates had no difficulty in getting a death sentence for his first chosen victim, Edward Coleman, secretary to the Catholic Duchess of York. In his initial appearance before the Privy Council, Oates made only a casual, nonincriminating reference to Coleman. He had once seen a newsletter that he believed to be in his hand. This remark led to Coleman's arrest, but Oates testified at Coleman's examination that he had never seen the man before. Then a search of Coleman's papers turned up some letters of 1674 and earlier, showing that Coleman had once sought money from France with which to induce King Charles to dissolve the strongly anti-Catholic Parliament. The discovery of these papers brought Titus Oates to life. He swore to the Privy Council, to Parliament, and at Coleman's trial, that he himself had carried letters from Coleman to St. Omer and Paris and brought back an answer directing that £10,000 be paid to "cut off" the king of England. Oates swore that Coleman was present at the White Horse Tavern and took part in planning the king's death. He heard Coleman say that £10,000 would not be enough to induce Dr. Wakeman to poison the king: they should add another £5,000 "that they might be sure to have it done."

In reply to all this Coleman could only say that his abortive intrigues ended in 1674 (the year in which he became secretary to the duchess), and that "I never saw Mr. Oates since I was born," except at the examination after his arrest. Oates "there told the king, he never saw me before."

"Mr. Oates," said Chief Justice Scroggs, "answer to what Mr. Coleman saith."

"Oates. My lord . . . I then said I would not swear that I had seen him before in my life, because my sight was bad by candle-light, and candle-light alters the sight much, but when I heard him speak I was sure it was he, but it was not then my business."

To appreciate that, one needs to read the unforgettable description of Coleman in the *Dictionary of National Biography:* "His sad sunken eyes, his lean, withered countenance, showing more ghastly pale while surrounded by his black peruke, gave him at least the appearance of one zealously affected towards ecclesiastic discipline." What would candle-light do but intensify every identifying feature?

The Lord Chief Justice then asked why Oates did not make heavier charges at that time. Because, replied Oates, "then I was so weak, being up two nights, and having taken prisoners, upon my salvation, I could scarce stand upon my legs." But Coleman being so dangerous, said Scroggs, endeavoring to kill the king, how came Oates to omit this information in two appearances before the king and council?

"Oates. I spoke little of the persons till the persons came face to face."

He was reminded that he accused Wakeman by name without facing him. Why did he not name Coleman? "For want of memory; being disturbed and wearied in sitting up two nights, I could not give that good account of Mr. Coleman, which I did afterwards, when I consulted my papers." What that meant was that he made up his story after consulting Coleman's papers, not his own.

At this point in the trial, Coleman spied Sir Thomas Dolman, clerk of the Privy Council, who had been present at Coleman's examination. He begged Dolman to take the stand and Sir Thomas did so. He testified that Oates had said he "did not well know" Coleman—that is, did not know him at all. Scroggs turned to Oates and asked why he did not come forward, when he recognized Coleman's voice, and say that he *did well know him.*

"Oates. Because I was not asked."

That brought the Chief Justice to a crucial question: "But, Sir Thomas, did he [Oates] say he did not well know him *after Mr. Coleman spake?"*

"Sir T. Dolman. YES."

That question and answer ought to have ended the trial with a directed verdict of acquittal for Coleman and a committal of Oates for perjury. The Crown saved the day by putting on the stand Sir Robert Southwell, who swore that Oates *at that examination* accused Coleman of paying Dr. Wakeman to poison the king. Oates had made no such claim in his present testimony and the statement, as Coleman quickly showed, was preposterous anyway. Southwell himself at the end of that hearing had induced the Privy Council to cancel a commitment of Coleman to Newgate Prison and merely put him in custody of a messenger. Southwell lamely explained that he told the messenger to be very civil to Coleman "but you must keep him safely."

To Chief Justice Scroggs, however, Southwell's testimony reestablished the veracity of Oates. "This," he said, "answers much of the objection upon him." The perjured Bedloe then took the stand. A half-starved adventurer, he had lately been imprisoned and pilloried for a confessed attempt to burn down Westminster. A pardon removed his infamy and qualified him as a witness. Bedloe swore that in 1675 he carried letters from Coleman to the father confessor of the King of France, and listened to conversations between French and English churchmen about "the Plot to subvert the government of England, to destroy the king and the lords of the council." Money, he said, was sent to Coleman for that purpose.

The date of this pretended occurrence—1675—cleverly hooked up Oates's plot with Coleman's actual 1674 intrigue for the dissolution of Parliament. Thus his genuine letters, which had nothing to do with the case, sealed his doom. "Your own papers are enough to condemn you," said Scroggs, after Coleman protested that he was being sent to his death by perjurors.

In measuring the cumulative effect of false testimony, it is a fair estimate that two perjurors have four times the power of one, but there is a concentration point beyond which added numbers strain credulity and Oates kept below it. Now the vultures flew in from every side as they smelled the corpse. With a frankness that has no American counterpart, the *Dictionary of National Biography* lists the notables of the Popish Plot by name and title to remembrance:

Oates, Titus, perjuror;

Bedloe, William, dishonest adventurer and "evidence in the Popish Plot";

Dangerfield, Thomas, false witness;

Dugdale, Stephen, informer;

Turberville, Edward, informer . . . remarked to lawyer that "no trade was good but that of a 'discoverer' ";

Prance, Miles, perjuror. (Usually spelled Praunce.)

These six men worked in pairs, trios and quartets under the skilled direction of Titus Oates. Clever as Oates was in weaving the pattern of evidence, his cloak-and-dagger yarns needed the brutal support of Lord Chief Justice Scroggs and Recorder George Jeffreys to prevent their breakdown. With judges and prosecutors reviling the defendants and castigating and browbeating their witnesses, the tragic farce went on. Group after group of Jesuits were tried, convicted and put to death for complicity in a plot that had not even the shadow of reality.

The great event of the winter of 1678-79, however, was Bedloe's "solution" of the Godfrey murder. The setup for it came when the goldsmith Miles Prance was arrested as a suspect, on a mere report that he was away from home on the Saturday night of Godfrey's disappearance. Bedloe went before the Council with a story that two Jesuit priests offered him £4,000 to kill "a very material man" whom they refused to name. The money, they said, was to come from Lord Belasyse (in the Tower) through Coleman, to get rid of the magistrate who had taken the testimonies of Oates and Tonge. Bedloe told them that he would not kill a man without knowing his name. They asked him to meet them that night at Somerset House, the queen's Catholic resort. There they told him that the deed already was done, by strangulation, and the body was in the house. They would give him half the reward if he would help them carry it off. They showed him the body on the floor, and he recognized it—that of Sir Edmundbury Godfrey. He did not know any of the numerous men who were in the room, but would recognize them on sight.

That was Bedloe's story, as wild and unbelievable as any that ever came out of an opium dream. But this was just a preliminary. Bedloe obtained a copy of his examination and had it placed by stealth on the bed of Miles Prance in Newgate Prison, during Prance's absence. Some time later, Bedloe contrived to pass Prance in a corridor of the prison and cried out to a constable to arrest him —this was a man he had seen in the room with Godfrey's body.

Miles Prance fathomed the significance of the manuscript found on his bed. His choice was to deny participation in the murder, and go to certain death on the perjuries of Bedloe and Oates, or join them and fasten the crime on three male servants of Somerset House whom Bedloe had named as the stranglers of Godfrey. He asked to be taken to a magistrate. Before that astonished official, Prance duplicated almost every detail of Bedloe's account of the murder, and told how he himself acted as a guard at a gate while Godfrey was being choked to death with a silken kerchief. Later he recanted, saying his story was all a lie; then he recanted the recantation and swore it was the truth.

The original pattern was followed in the trial of Robert Green, Henry Berry and Lawrence Hill, three innocent servitors who heard the fantastic and fatal tale unfold before judges and jury. The judges ran true to form. Mrs. Broadstreet, a defense witness, testified that her work took her constantly in and out of the room where Godfrey's body was supposed to have lain in the middle of the floor. "It is well you are not indicted," remarked Justice Dolben. Mary Tilden, housekeeper, testified that the defendant Hill waited on table (Queen Catherine being there at supper) on the evening of the alleged removal of the body and never went out of the house after the queen left. Commented Recorder George Jeffreys:

"I hope you did not keep him company, after supper, all night."

Chief Justice Scroggs brushed aside the defense witnesses with the remark that they would "say anything to a heretic for a papist." It was "no hard thing," he said to the jury, "for the priests to contrive such an action; but for two witnesses to agree on so many material circumstances with one another, that had never conversed together, is impossible." Green, Berry and Hill were hanged, drawn and quartered. Seven years passed before Miles Prance, on trial for perjury, confessed that his whole story was concocted from the Bedloe statement that he found on his bed in Newgate Prison.

The conviction of Godfrey's "murderers" in February 1679 established the credit of Titus Oates and lifted his whole crew of perjurors above the level of successful attack. On June 13 five more Jesuits were tried at Old Bailey—Fathers Fenwick, Harcourt, Whitebread, Gavan and Turner. These five were considered so high in the Jesuit order that "all the judges of England" were

brought together to try them. By this time there were four informers, Prance and Dugdale having joined the stable. The testimony
of this quartet was a mass of inconsistencies, contradicted by defense witnesses whose credibility was destroyed by one brief elicited
answer: "I am a Roman Catholic."

Imposition of sentence on the priests was postponed until after
the trial next day, before the same judges, of Richard Langhorn, a
lawyer and one of the leading Catholic laymen of England. The
same informers appeared against him too, and the pattern of prosecution was much clearer against this solitary defendant. Dugdale
and Prance, who knew nothing about Langhorn, were used to put
the jurors in a proper frame of mind by giving the general design
of the Popish Plot. Dugdale did not hesitate to shock them with
his own villainy.

"Justice Atkins. What were you hired to do?
"Dugdale. I was to kill the king."

After that, said Dugdale, there was to be a massacre. Then an
army would be raised, and "those that did escape the massacre
should [i.e. would] be cut off by the army." And who, asked Atkins,
were to be murdered in the first place?

"All Protestants, and those we could not be sure to be Papists."

If this chilled the blood of the jurors, they could well change to
frozen fury as they listened to Dugdale's answer to another well-
planted question: Had he seen any Jesuit letters concerning Godfrey?

"I do remember a letter that came to Mr. Ewers, from Mr. Harcourt, which did express and begin thus, 'This very night Sir Edmundbury Godfrey is dispatched.' "

And when was this damning letter from Father Harcourt delivered? Three days before Godfrey's dead body was discovered.
With the stamp of guilt placed on a whole church order, it was
hardly necessary for Oates and Bedloe to draw Langhorn into the
picture. Oates presented a crescendo account of pleasant relations
with Langhorn and his family, gradually reaching the climax of
treason and intended regicide. Langhorn was described, not as a
participant in the Jesuit consult at White Horse Tavern, but as
the medium through which the traitorous correspondence passed
and as custodian of the papal commissions that were to put the

"Five Popish lords" in command of the country. When Oates gave him the minutes of the White Horse consult, Langhorn was "very much disgusted that Sir George Wakeman was not contented with the 10,000 pounds . . . to poison the king." Bedloe, following Oates to the stand, took a lesser role in the melodrama. He was the courier who carried the treasonable letters described by Oates, and Langhorn was the man who gave them to him.

Against this fabric of total invention, the lawyer Langhorn was invited to make his defense. Having been eight months in prison without seeing a single friend or knowing the charge against him, he told the Court, all he could do was try to disable the crown witnesses. A fellow prisoner, Reading, had told him Bedloe received £500 from the crown. Was that true? The answer came from Chief Justice North of the Court of Common Pleas. Reading was "an infamous person" who had stood in the pillory, and could not be a witness. But the £500 "was for the discovery of the murderers of Sir Edmundbury Godfrey."[2]

Now into the courtroom trooped sixteen young men, at sight of whom Titus Oates exclaimed in apparent terror: "My lord, here are papists come into the Court with their swords on." The judges soothed his fears. "Dr. Oates, you are safe enough here," said the Lord Mayor of London. All this was a show to impress the jury. The sixteen were students from St. Omer who had appeared as witnesses the day before in the trial of the five priests. Swords, commonly worn, were not illogical, in view of Lord Castlemaine's report to the Court within the next hour that some of the witnesses summoned for the prisoners were being "so beaten and abused without, that they dare not come to give their evidence, for fear of being killed." Oates put Castlemaine on his list for future attention.

From the students came unanimous testimony that Oates was with them at St. Omer on April 24, 1678, the day of the alleged White Horse Tavern gathering, and all the time before and after from December to June. He was conspicuous as an older man who ate at a table by himself. The most important witness, Martin Hilsley, denied the story told by Oates, that the two of them traveled together in the party of Jesuits that came from St. Omer to London. Oates, interrupting the testimony, carried out his perfectly planned finesse, telling how, on their April 24 trip together,

Hilsley was swindled by a stranger at Calais. The truth was that Hilsley told this story in London, on April 29, to a student, Burnaby, who was on his way to St. Omer. Burnaby repeated it there in the presence of Oates and a student now in the courtroom. This youth came forward and told the story, but Scroggs disposed of all sixteen by telling the jury that they were brought up in a religion that teaches "that a lye does God good service, if it be for the propagation of the faith."

The jury found Langhorn guilty, whereupon the five prisoners convicted the day before were brought into the court and Recorder Jeffreys delivered the sentence of the twelve highest judges of England upon all six:

"That you be conveyed from hence to the place from which you came, and from thence you be drawn to the place of execution, upon hurdles; That you be there severally hanged by the neck; That you be cut down alive; That your privy members be cut off; That your bowels be taken out, and burned in your view; That your heads be severed from your bodies; That your bodies be divided into four quarters, and your quarters to be at the king's dispose. And the God of infinite mercy be merciful to your souls."

Richard Langhorn found time, before his execution, to write a poem in twelve parts, entitled "The Affections of my Soul, after Judgment given against me in a Court of Justice, upon the Evidence of False Witnesses." Here are some of its lines:

> O my Father,
> Come now in mercy and receive thy child;
> Give him the kiss of peace;
> Remit unto him all his sins;
> Cloath him with thy nuptial robe;
> Receive him into thy house;
> Permit him to have a place at thy feast;
> And forgive all those who are guilty of his death.

CHAPTER 12
The Fall of the Perjured Informers

Titus Oates was riding high in the summer of 1679. On the very day Richard Langhorn's execution notched No. 14 on his bow, he brought the queen's physician to trial on the charge of accepting £15,000 to murder the king. Inflated with arrogance, and, perhaps, swayed by the feeling that his most dangerous enemy was Queen Catherine, he shaped his testimony to warrant the comment made by Bishop Burnet: "The truth is, that this was looked on as the queen's trial, as well as Wakeman's." To give breadth to the conspiracy, two Benedictine monks and a Jesuit were brought into it and tried along with Sir George.

The trial followed the proven pattern. To inflame the jury, Dugdale and Prance described the general design to kill the king, seize power and "cut off" all Protestants. The shudder-producing line, "This very night Sir Edmundbury Godfrey is dispatched," was repeated with new elaborations. Then Oates took the stand, and swore that he watched Dr. Wakeman write a prescription for the king's poison potion, to be obtained at a pharmacy by Jesuit Father Ashby. He read Wakeman's accompanying letter to Ashby saying "that the queen would assist him to poison the king."[1]

Five days later, said Oates, he went to Somerset House with five Jesuits who had been summoned by the queen. One was Father Harcourt, who was to pay Wakeman for the poisoning job. Oates waited in the queen's anteroom while the others went into the inner chamber. "And I did hear a woman's voice which did say . . . that she would not endure these violations of her bed any longer [the king's adulteries with Lady Castlemaine and others] and that

144

she would assist Sir George Wakeman in the poisoning of the king."
Then, Oates testified, he walked into the queen's chamber and had
"from her a gracious smile." And in the same voice that he had
heard before, the queen (the only woman in the room) asked Father
Harcourt whether he had received the last one thousand pounds.

If this was lunacy, it was no more so than the stories that already
had cost fourteen innocent men their lives. But with the queen involved, Lord Chief Justice Scroggs suffered a sudden stroke of
sanity. Sir Philip Lloyd of the king's Privy Council was put on the
stand to tell what happened after Oates swore to the council that he
had seen a letter from Father Whitebread saying that Wakeman
had agreed to poison the king. The Lord Chancellor, as Lloyd described the scene, "desired Mr. Oates to tell him, if he knew nothing personally of Sir G. Wakeman." To which Oates answered, with
a lifting of his hands:

"No, God forbid that I should say any thing against Sir G.
Wakeman, for I know nothing more against him."

At this testimony by Lloyd, Oates did not wait to be questioned:

"My lord, I believe Sir Philip Lloyd is mistaken; but however
I was so weak, and the king and council were so sensible of it, that
the king himself had like to have sent me away once or twice before, because he found I was so weak."

Here was an almost exact duplication of the scene in which
Oates pleaded physical weakness as a reason for not accusing Edward Coleman of the charges he brought against him later. But in
the Coleman trial Scroggs did not even mention this vital matter to
the jurors. Now the Lord Chief Justice was in another frame of
mind as he addressed the jury. Why, he repeated, did not Oates
accuse Wakeman of writing a letter about the poisoning, when he
was before the king and council?

"He makes an answer (which to me indeed is a very faint one)
as if he were so weak and tired, that he could not speak any word
further. . . . I do not know, if a man be never so faint, could not he
say, I saw a letter under his hand, as well as, I knew nothing more
of him? There are as few words in one, as in the other."

Dr. Wakeman was acquitted, and for good measure, so were
the monks and priest who were tried with him (although two of
them were tried again and hanged after the judges recovered their

insanity). But Fate played a trick on Sir William Scroggs, who for the first time in his life—probably by royal direction—had performed a virtuous act. As Bishop Burnet described the aftermath, "the witnesses saw they were blasted," and turned in fury upon the Lord Chief Justice, aided by all the anonymous pens they could muster on their side of the religious controversy. Scroggs from the bench defended that trial from "those hireling scribblers that traduce it, who write to eat, and lie for bread," but was careful to say nothing against the perjurors themselves, and he willingly assisted in the libel conviction of a servant of Oates who charged that Oates had made homosexual advances to him. This protective service did not mollify Oates and Bedloe, who went before the Privy Council with thirteen treason charges against Scroggs of being soft on popery and hard on witnesses against it. The Wakeman acquittal formed the principal item. Scroggs won a vote of confidence after sending Lionel Anderson and five other Catholics to the gallows on the mere charge of being priests in England. Conviction was easy, since Oates, Bedloe and a new perjuror merely swore that they went to confession before the priests or heard them say mass.

These cases of libel and treason marked the advent as a witness of Thomas Dangerfield, described by Burnet as "a subtle and dexterous man, who had gone through all the shapes and practices of roguery." Far inferior to Oates in cleverness, he excelled in exhibitionism. Although Dangerfield acted in full concert with Oates and Bedloe in dooming these unoffending priests, he was living at the expense of Mrs. Elizabeth Cellier, a retainer of Lady Powis, wife of one of the Popish Lords in the Tower. Burnet called her "a popish midwife, who had a great deal of wit, and was abandoned to lewdness."

No pole long enough to fathom Dangerfield's false tales, perjuries and duplicities has ever been found. With help from Lady Powis, he carried to the king a concocted story of a Presbyterian plot to murder him. If believed, it would discredit Oates and Bedloe. The king sent him to Secretary Coventry, who soon complained that the money paid to the informer was producing nothing but "his own talk" and no papers. Dangerfield then obtained a warrant to search for smuggled goods in the rooms of Colonel Roderick Mansell, in whose house he rented quarters. Accompanying the officers, he had the good fortune to discover a packet of treasonable letters pinned back of the head of Mansell's bed. Some time elapsed before a constable recalled that Dangerfield had not yet opened the packet when he shouted, "Here is treason against his majesty." Mansell proved the papers to be forgeries.

About to be pilloried for the deception, Dangerfield induced Mrs. Cellier to take some dangerous papers from him and hide them in the bottom of her meal-tub. He then denounced her as a traitor and betrayed the hiding place of the evidence. The bizarre location of the "Meal-tub Papers" made them the sensation of the day, but a skeptical public refused to credit a plot of Protestant Dissenters, not to murder the king, but upon his death to establish a commonwealth headed by his illegitimate son, the Duke of Monmouth. Lord Essex, named as one of the plotters, resigned in vexation at the momentary credence given the story, but the absurdity of it soon made the "Meal-tub Plot" a coffeehouse jest.

Disillusioned by the reaction to a Presbyterian insurrection, Dangerfield returned to the reliable field of antipapal discoveries and almost overnight achieved a temporary parity with Titus Oates. His chief targets were the two women who had been supporting him, Lady Powis and Mrs. Cellier, but he also helped Oates fasten a treason trial on the Earl of Castlemaine, who had tried to protect Langhorn's witnesses from beatings by a mob.

Mrs. Cellier was tried for treason in June 1680. In that confrontation of perjuror and midwife, the planter of the "Meal-tub Papers" more than met his match. When Dangerfield displayed the royal pardon that qualified him as a witness, the lady came back at him with evidence of felony and outlawry not covered by the pardon. Lord Chief Justice Scroggs, aware by this time that King Charles was heartily sick of the "Popish Plot," drove the would-be witness from the court with such scathing denunciation that Dangerfield was moved to say: "My lord, this is enough to discourage a man from entering into an honest principle."

Dangerfield's departure deprived the Crown of a second witness to the overt act of treason, which consisted of asking an astrologer when the king would die. Mrs. Cellier was acquitted of "imagining and compassing the death of the king." Next came the treason trial of Roger Palmer, Earl of Castlemaine, husband of the king's favorite mistress. King Charles had forced an Irish earldom on Palmer in payment for his wife, and had no wish to disturb the existing system of peaceful coexistence. But he could not well refuse the broader pardon that now qualified Dangerfield as a witness. Conviction depended on him and Oates, because Bedloe had become so thoroughly discredited that Recorder Jeffreys gave him a permanent dismissal. Scroggs allowed Dangerfield to testify but advised the jury to consider well whether a man guilty of "six great enormous crimes" could suddenly be made a saint by being made a witness. Castlemaine was acquitted.

Unfortunately for himself, Lord Chief Justice Scroggs underestimated the extent to which the "Popish Plot" still dominated the thoughts and feelings of Protestants. He also underrated the power of Lord Shaftesbury. Three days after the Castlemaine acquittal, Scroggs dismissed a grand jury in order to block Shaftesbury's effort to exclude the Duke of York from succession to the throne by indicting him as a "popish recusant"—an Anglican turned Catholic. Upon the reassembly of Parliament, the House of Commons, dominated by the Shaftesbury party, unanimously voted to impeach the Chief Justice for unlawfully discharging the grand jury, and defaming Oates, Bedloe and other witnesses. The king blocked action in the House of Lords by dissolving Parliament. This only heightened the nationwide clamor. To save his faithful satellite from possible execution the king removed Scroggs from office.

Oates was now on top of the world. His showy coach was seen on all the fashionable streets of London. The doors of all great houses were open to him—or else. On the day after Christmas 1680, Sir John Reresby attended chapel with a party to which Oates attached himself and they all dined at the table of the Bishop of Ely. Reresby described what ensued in milder terms than it deserved:

"Doctor Oates . . . blown up with the hopes of running down the Duke [of York], spoke of him and his family after a manner which showed himself both a fool and a knave. He reflected not only on him personally, but upon the Queen his mother, and her present Majesty, till, nobody daring to contradict him for fear of being made a party to the Plot, I at last did undertake to do it, and in such a manner that he left the room in some heat."

In another account of the incident, Reresby refers to Oates "speaking reflectingly on the chastity of the late Queen Mother." What he said at table was that the Duke of York (and he could as well have said the king) was "the son of a whore." On hearing those words a bishop of the Church of England and his Protestant guests (with one exception) dared not utter a word of reproach lest they be accused, tried and put to death as murder agents of the Pope. By their attitude they revealed their belief that Oates was a perjuror and the plot a heinous hoax, but there was a legitimate reason for their apprehension. Three weeks before, Titus Oates had achieved the greatest triumph of his career. The long-staved-off impeachment of Viscount Stafford was brought to trial before the House of Lords. For seven days the peers of England listened to the perjuries of Oates, Dugdale and a fresh accomplice, Turberville, then voted 55 to 31 to send this "Popish Lord" to his death. It strains credulity to believe that a third of them thought him guilty.

The mixture of cynicism and cowardice with which the lords treated the plot at large was revealed a few weeks later when Sir William Temple protested in the Privy Council against the impending trial of the six priests for the treason of being in England. A dormant Elizabethan law, he said, should not be enforced without a previous public warning to priests to leave the country. Lord Halifax (Temple wrote in his *Memoirs)* heatedly replied in private that if Temple "would not concur in points which were so necessary for the people's satisfaction, he would tell everybody I [Temple] was a Papist." The plot, Halifax declared, *"must be handled, as if it were true, whether it were so or not."* Yet Halifax had just shown his own disbelief in the plot by voting to acquit Lord Stafford. He would save an innocent peer, but let lesser victims die to appease a mob.

The plot hung on for five more years, but by 1684 Oates's prestige had diminished so much that it became feasible for the Duke of York to sue him for slander. Witness after witness testified to hearing Oates call the duke a traitor and participant in the plot. Oates defaulted, making no appearance in court, but boasted that England would soon get a Parliament that would reverse any judgment against him. The jury awarded the full amount of damages claimed, £100,000. Oates was sentenced to prison until it should be paid—a potential life term. A year later King Charles died and the Duke of York ascended the throne. By this time Sir George Jeffreys had become Lord Chief Justice of the King's Bench, and he knew which side of his bread carried the jam. Titus Oates was brought to trial on two separate charges of perjury, and Jeffreys managed the trials with as much malignant efficiency in support of truth as he had formerly exerted for the triumph of falsehood. Both trials brought convictions.

The principal charge was that Oates perjured himself in swearing that he was in London on April 24, 1678, and attended a Jesuit consult that day at the White Horse Tavern. Sixteen witnesses swore, as many of them and others had done before, that Oates was with them at that time in St. Omer, France. In the earlier trials this same testimony, supported by infinite detail, had been disparaged by the judges, who insinuated that the Pope gave Catholics dispensation to perjure themselves. Now Jeffreys allowed Oates to ask a simple question about their religion, but rigorously defended them from his attempt to push them into self-incrimination by making them say that they attended a Jesuit school. The key witness, as before, was Martin Hilsley, who repeated his denial that Oates traveled with him from Calais to Dover. Here is the exchange (condensed) that followed between Oates and the Lord Chief Justice:

"Oates. My lord, I would know what was his employment there at St. Omer?

"L.C.J. But, Mr. Oates, you must not ask any such questions: what know I, but by asking him the question, you may make him obnoxious to some penalty, but you must not ask him any questions to ensnare him.

"Oates. I desire you would ask him, Whether there were not priests and Jesuits that governed that house?

"L.C.J. What a question is that! I tell you it is not fit to be asked."

The Chief Justice knew the law, and set it forth truly, but in the different political climate of 1678, no legal scruples had deterred the judges themselves from using the tactics they now decried in Oates. Nor did Jeffreys act as an impartial judge in telling the jury now that "If you think these witnesses swear true, as I cannot see any colour of objection, there does not remain the least doubt, but that Oates is the blackest and most perjured villain that ever appeared upon the face of the earth."

History still gives Titus Oates that accolade. Uncontroverted evidence in the perjury trials heightened his guilt as a condemner of innocent men. Crown witnesses from other trials came forward to tell how he had terrorized them into supporting his perjuries with false testimony of their own. Nevertheless, the needless bias of the judges deprived him of a fair trial. This was compounded by the bizarre savagery of the punishment imposed on him for libel and perjury. In effect he was given two sentences of life imprisonment; the first for inability to pay the judgment of £100,000 for slandering the Duke of York, now king; the second imposed directly for the perjuries. In addition he was fined 2,000 marks, ordered to be pilloried twice and to be whipped from Aldgate to Newgate and later from Newgate to Tyburn. (The hangman almost whipped him to death.) After that, on five specified days each year for the rest of his life, he was to stand an hour in the pillory as "annual commemorations" of his five worst offenses.

The sentences were enforced for fourteen years. After King James was unseated by the Revolution of 1688, nine judges in the House of Lords protested with truth that the Oates convictions were "contrary to law and ancient practice." They violated the declaration in the newly adopted Bill of Rights "that excessive bail ought not to be required, nor excessive fines imposed, nor cruel nor unusual punishments inflicted." The lords reversed the libel judgment, freeing Oates from one threat of life imprisonment. A pardon by the new king, asked for by Parliament, ended both his prison sentence and the annual appearance in the pillory. The lawmakers then restored one third of his former pension of fifteen pounds a week. He married a rich woman, lived on a grand scale, became a Baptist preacher and was expelled by the church for misconduct.

A large part of the populace continued to believe in Oates, although he and his whole stable of informers had been shown up as 100 per cent liars.[2] All was known, indeed, except the deeply buried incident on which the deadly hallucination was built—the secret holding, in St. James's Palace, of a triennial Jesuit Congregation whose date was all that Titus Oates knew about it.

But the state of the public mind banned recognition of reality in that era of religious intolerance, hatred and obsessive fears. This feeling headed up in Parliament, where the House of Commons had been the driving force behind the prosecutions from the very start. In effect though not in form, the pressure of a panicked people on Parliament, and the pressure of a violent Parliament on subservient courts, converted judicial trials into virtual bills of attainder. Neither the people nor the lawmakers could face the fact that they had helped to perpetrate the most diabolical hoax in the country's history. Years passed before those who did realize the truth had the courage to utter it.

What was the impress of all this on the people of America? The colonists knew every detail of the story, believing it at first, and imagining similar Jesuit plots against colonial governments. Fifteen contemporary pamphlets on the "Popish Plot" were in the Philadelphia library used by the Continental Congress and the delegates to the Constitutional Convention. Included among them were stenographic accounts of the great trials, published by authorization of Chief Justice Scroggs, who did not know that he was damning himself. The same narratives were gathered up in Emlyn's *State Trials*, familiar to American lawyers and statesmen. Graphic accounts of the plot, exposing the perjurors, came to America in the historical works of Burnet, Ralph, Rapin, Hume, Clarendon and others.

Yet, paradoxically, scant mention of these trials can be found in American publications of the eighteenth century. Probably the subject was too painful. Colonial America was anti-Catholic and shared the British fear of papacy. The denial of religious freedom never reached the stage of a blood bath, but Catholics nearly everywhere were excluded from office and the right to vote. In Virginia, in 1784, Madison protested that the wording of the 1776 state constitution, continuing the right of suffrage *as it had been in the colony*, might revive the ancient exclusion of "Popish Recusants." Far more vividly, to reinforce his position, he could have harked back to the crimes committed against humanity and the law through fear of the nonexistent Popish Plot.

Historical knowledge worked silently, nevertheless, to strengthen the call for constitutional guarantees—for freedom of religion, speech and press; for protection against self-incrimination and double jeopardy, against excessive fines and cruel punishments; for grand juries and fair trials; for strict limitation of the crime of treason. All these were brought sharply to view in the trials.

The lessons of the Popish Plot come down still more forcefully (if Americans are willing to acknowledge them) in its likeness to the excesses that began but did not end with the career of Senator Joseph McCarthy. In both instances there was a genuine and similar causal element. In England, Catholics and Protestants had been feuding for centuries, with alternate seizures of power and an ever-present desire in each to dispossess the other. In the United States, fears engendered by the dangerous rise of international communism made the domestic Communist mouse look as big as an elephant.

In England, in 1678, there was a thousandfold greater reason to fear a Catholic plot to subvert the government, when no such plot existed, than there was in the United States in 1948 to fear an attempt at Communist subversion, whether it existed or not. It was the absolute fiction of the Popish Plot, the cruel greed of the perjurors, the barbarity of the punishments, the violent bias of the courts, the fantastic planting of evidence (from the body of the murdered Godfrey to the "Meal-tub Papers"), the cynicism and credulity in Parliament, the passions of the populace—it was these that turned innocent Catholic victims into unforgettable martyrs in anybody's religion.

The American counterpart has been much less starkly black and white. Yet take away Jack Ketch's bloody ax, take away the foul invectives of Scroggs and Jeffreys, add three civilizing centuries of education, culture and human brotherhood, and wherein does the twentieth century show itself better than the seventeenth? Above all else, history repeats and worsens itself in the continuation of congressional instruments of persecution after the fictional crisis disappears. It repeats itself even more ominously in the stubborn refusal of the American people to ask themselves, and find out for themselves, what errors they made and what injustices they inflicted during the long night of blacked-out reason.

CHAPTER 13
Eight Saints and a Sinner

Momentous events affecting human freedom were crowded into the terminal period of Charles II and the three short years in which his brother James held the throne. The totally fictitious Popish Plot against Charles was overlapped by the nearly imaginary "Rye-House Plot" against him. After this came a genuine plot—the attempt of the bastard Duke of Monmouth to take the throne from his Uncle James—a plot so fatuous in conception and so frightful in reprisals that it first beggars and then staggers the imagination.

The Monmouth Rebellion gave Lord Chief Justice Jeffreys his unenvied place and name in English history—Jeffreys of the "Bloody Assizes." But to Americans of the eighteenth century, he was Jeffreys the executioner of Algernon Sidney, the most heroic figure in democratic ideology and idealism. Outside the scenes of bloodshed but within the realm of danger stood lesser symbols of resistance to royal tyranny, the Seven Bishops who courageously defied both James the Second and the courts.

Jeffreys was not the immediate successor of Scroggs as Lord Chief Justice of the Court of King's Bench. Sir Francis Pemberton rose to that office and was speedily removed for lack of zeal in the trial of Lord Russell, who was nevertheless done to death (Parliament ultimately called it murder) by a wholly new set of perjurors in the Rye-House affair. The next Chief Justice died five months after taking office. Then came Jeffreys, appointed by Charles in 1682 but a man after James's own lack of heart.

Nobody knows how many hundreds of men, innocent or of unproved guilt, Jeffreys sent to their deaths in the pseudo trials that followed Monmouth's feeble and stupid attempt to seize the throne. When the ordeal ended, scores had been executed and 1,260 were awaiting the hangman in three counties. To be absent from home during the uprising was evidence of guilt. Mere death was considered much too mild for the villagers and farmers rounded up in these raids. The directions to a high sheriff were to provide an ax, a cleaver, "a furnace or cauldron to boil their heads and quarters, and soil to boil therewith, half a bushel to each traitor, and tar to tar them with, and a sufficient number of spears and poles to fix their heads and quarters" along the highways. One could have crossed a good part of northern England by their guidance.

The story of The Bloody Assizes, widely known to Americans, helped to place constitutional limitations on the crime of treason and to produce a bar against cruel and unusual punishments. But in the polemics that led to the various guarantees of freedom, it had no place compared with the tremendous thrust of the trial and execution of Sidney. The hundreds of judicial murders committed by Jeffreys and his fellow judges were totally inconceivable in a free American republic, but any American could imagine himself in Sidney's place—executed for putting on paper, in his closet, words that later on came to express the basic principles of republican government. Unless barred by fundamental law, the legal rulings that permitted this result could easily be employed against any person whose political opinions challenged the party in power.

The story of Algernon Sidney reached eighteenth-century Americans from many sources besides formal histories. It came in Bishop Burnet's *History of His Own Time*, and in the denunciatory words of Charles James Fox, the liberal statesman who wrote a *History of the Early Part of the Reign of James II*. It came in the penetrating legal analysis of Sir John Hawles, King William's solicitor general, whose description of the errors in this and other notable perversions of justice found a place in Emlyn's *State Trials*. "Algernon Sidney" became a pen name to conjure with, used for half a century after the American Revolution as a pseudonym of libertarian writers.

Sidney was dragged by hearsay into the fantastic "Rye-House" treason trials brought about by two frightened crackpots, West and Rumsey. These men, having taken part in drawing up a harebrained plot to kidnap King Charles, undertook to save themselves by agreeing upon a perjured tale based on a germ of truth about the meeting of six peers at the Rye House Tavern. Each named Sidney as among those present. "Yet even here," wrote Bishop Burnet, "they contradicted each other; Rumsey swearing that he had it from West, and West swearing that he had it from him; which was not observed until the trial came out [in print]" and Sidney was dead.

The Rye-House meetings apparently were coffeehouse palavers on England's woes and possible ways of ending them, treasonable in spirit (if the later "Glorious Revolution" was treasonable), but without any plan of action. The Crown, however, broke down one of the sextet, Lord Howard, who became a pliant perjuror in the ensuing trials and went around moaning to his friends (said Sir John Hawles) "that he could not have his pardon, till he swore others out of their lives."[1]

There was no evidence against Sidney in the Rye-House affair except the unsupported oath of Howard. Ten witnesses of high standing refuted Howard by his own words to them. But it was Sidney's death that the Crown desired above all else. His jury, Burnet learned in the household of the Duke of York, was picked largely by a murderer named Parry, who was pardoned for the purpose of rounding up tractable riffraff for the panel. Sidney's real offense was using a pen in behalf of free government.

Agents of the Crown, ransacking Sidney's house, came upon a manuscript he had written many years earlier—an unpublished rebuttal of the well-known book *Patriarcha,* in which Sir Robert Filmer slavishly upheld the divine right of kings. The most damning item in Sidney's indictment for treason was the following appraisal of Filmer:

"He cannot comprehend that magistrates are for or by the people, but makes this conclusion, as if nations were created by or for the glory or pleasure of magistrates, and affects such a piece of nonsense; it ought not to be thought strange, if he represents as an absurd thing, that the heedless multitude may shake off the yoke when they please. But I would know how the multitude comes under the yoke, it is a badge of slavery."

Again Sidney wrote:

"The general revolt of a nation from its own magistrates, can never be called rebellion."

Sidney's manuscript, published after his death under the title *Thoughts on Government,* has become one of the classics of the literature of freedom. Lord Chief Justice Jeffreys, in his perverse way, testified to that merit when he told the jury that "this book contains all the malice, and revenge, and treason, that mankind can be guilty of: It fixes the sole power in the parliament and the people." Having only one witness against Sidney where two were required, the government decided to use this ancient writing as *a second overt act* of the treason charged in the indictment. To achieve this, every abstract reference to a magistrate was declared to mean "the most serene lord, Charles 2, now king of England," and to be written to promote the Rye-House conspiracy. Charles James Fox made no overstatement when he called this "such a compound of wickedness and nonsense as is hardly to be paralleled in the history of juridical tyranny."

In America, attention focused more on the words that sent Sidney to his death than on the techniques of injustice by which this was accomplished. The principles he set forth combined the natural rights on which American independence came to be based and those on which the government of the United States was established. Words and sentiments for which he was beheaded found their way into Virginia's 1776 Declaration of Rights and into Lincoln's Gettysburg Address. In 1804 Washington's early biographer, the Reverend Mason Locke Weems, asked Jefferson's advice about publishing the works of Sidney, "much extolled" by John Taylor, Benjamin Rush and John Dickinson. Jefferson replied that the *Discourses on Government* was "probably the best elementary book on the principles of government, as founded in natural right which has ever been published in any language . . . in such a government as ours . . . it should be put into the hands of our youth as soon as their minds are sufficiently matured for that branch of study."

The crime charged against Algernon Sidney was treason; and the perversion of the treason laws was one of many features that made a shambles of the house of justice. But this aspect of the case (which impressed Fox most deeply) was not what gave Sidney's name a talismanic quality on the western side of the Atlantic. Here was seen the punishing of a man, shockingly compounded by putting him to death, for expressing sentiments close to the heart of every patriotic American. His words made him a symbol of American ideas of liberty; his death made him a martyr to them. Not every man would concede total freedom to those whose opinions were anathema to him. But here was enough to give a firmer fixation to the concept of freedom of thought and expression, a heightened intensity to the emotional support of that concept; and to arouse a corresponding detestation of the laws and legal practices that made Sidney's martyrdom possible. Here, to the extent that it could be brought to one point, was the fertilizing force that produced the First Amendment.

Charles the Second survived Algernon Sidney by only two years. His successor James the Second lasted but three years on the throne. In those three years, James carried Stuart autocracy higher and free government lower than his brother, his father or his grandfather had done. In addition to this, by a remarkable paradox, his downfall was assured by a combination of attempts to *tighten* the restraints on speech, press and petition, and to *loosen* the restraints on religion. But in this last there was no ideological support of freedom of conscience.

King James II, a Catholic reigning over an intensely anti-Catholic national majority, put pressure on his compliant judges (after noncompliant ones were ousted) to decide that he had power to exempt his coreligionists from taking the abhorrent test oath. The 1687 King's Bench decision in *Godden* v. *Hale* put a false label of legality on this power to dispense with the laws. James promptly published a Declaration of Indulgence exempting both Catholics and Protestant Dissenters from *all penal statutes* based on religion. Supported by these two large minorities, his action had more than a forlorn chance to withstand the storm of Anglican protest and become a lasting boon to religious liberty. But he capped it in the spring of 1688 with an act of folly that drove the Anglican clergy into emotional revolt, and followed this with a court action that had an explosive effect in England and a profound and lasting influence on American thought.

The king issued a proclamation commanding bishops and

pastors to read the Declaration of Indulgence in cathedrals and churches throughout the land. To Anglicans of that period, this was hardly short of ordering them to help re-establish papal supremacy. Seven bishops, headed by Dr. William Sancroft, Archbishop of Canterbury, refused to obey and sent a joint petition to the king, thereby bringing on the most famous trial for seditious libel in British history. Their unwillingness to read the declaration in church, the bishops said in humble tones, proceeded not from want of duty and obedience. They were unwilling "because that declaration is founded upon such a dispensing power, as hath been often declared illegal in Parliament," the last time being in James's own reign. It was a matter so momentous "to the whole nation, both in church and state, that your petitioners cannot in prudence, honour or conscience," make themselves parties to it by solemn publication all over the nation, "even in God's house."

The king's answer was to order the seven bishops brought to trial. The information charged that they conspired to diminish the regal authority and for that purpose wrote and published a "false, feigned, malicious, pernicious and seditious libel" under the pretense of a humble petition. They were being prosecuted, Attorney General Thomas Powys told the jury, not as bishops, but as subjects of the kingdom, "for censuring of his Majesty and his government, and for giving their opinion in matters wholly relating to law and government." There was nothing more to be prevented and punished, than such accusations:

"No man can say of the great men of the nation, much less of the great officers of the kingdom, that they do act unreasonably, or unjustly, or the like; least of all may any man say any such thing of the king; for these matters tend to possess the people, that the government is ill administered; and the consequence of that is, to set them upon desiring a reformation; and what that tends to, and will end in, we have all had [in the execution of Charles I] a sad and too dear bought experience."

Powys was a man of strong and independent mind. Otherwise out of place in such a reign, he owed his position to the fact that he had defended the king's dispensing power. His way of presenting the case made no separation of the law from the facts. Instead of telling the jurors that they had nothing to do except decide whether or not the bishops wrote and presented the petition, Powys put the question of "libel or no libel" squarely before them. Earlier in the trial he had shown that he had little stomach for the prosecution and no sympathy with unfair procedures that precedents compelled him to use. In resisting a motion for continuance because of the suddenness of the accusation he gave a partial preview of the American Bill of Rights.

"Sir, there are many things that seem hard in law, but yet when all is done, the judges cannot alter the law. 'Tis a hard case that a man that is tried for his life for treason or felony, cannot have a copy of his indictment, cannot have council, cannot have his witnesses sworn; but this has been long practiced, and the usage is grown to a law, and from time to time it hath been so taken for law; it cannot be altered without a new law made; as it hath been heretofore, so it must be now, till a greater authority alter it."

The bishops' powerful battery of defense lawyers (including ousted Chief Justice Pemberton) attacked the validity of the information, but their main contention was that the king had no power to dispense with the laws on religion. Consequently a petition to be excused from helping him to do so could not be libelous. This attack on the dispensing power—making truth of the alleged libel a defense—struck at the one real tie between Powys and the king. The Attorney General proceeded to close that avenue of defense, but opened a wider one in doing so. Said he:

"Whether the libel be true or not, as to the matter of fact, was it ever yet in any court of justice permitted to be made a question whether it be a libel or not? or whether a party be punishable for it? And therefore I wonder to hear these gentlemen to say, that because it is not a false one, therefore it is not a libel. . . . The only thing that is to be looked into, is, whether there be any thing in this paper that is reflecting and scandalous, and not whether it be true or no."

Though rejecting truth as a defense, the Attorney General clearly indicated his belief that the question of "libel or no libel" was one for the jury. That is where the four judges proceeded to place it, as each of them charged the jury. Two of them called the petition libelous. Two said it was innocent. But only one judge denied the right of the jury to make the decision.

Of the three others, Justices Powell and Holloway acted from principle in affirming the jury's right to decide both law and fact. Lord Chief Justice Wright, a henchman of the crown, was reported by Lord Macaulay to be terrified into silence by the presence of so many hostile earls and barons. He looked, said a spectator, as if he thought they had halters in their pockets. Sole denial of the jury's power came from Justice Allibone, lately hoisted from obscurity to the bench, and generally considered to be without an inferior in British judicial history. Besides taking this narrow stand on jury power, Allibone laid down three general "positions" that accurately represented the extreme Stuart-Tory thinking:

1. Unless a man has leave from the government to write against its actions, any criticism of them is a libel, "be what he writes true or false."
2. "No private man can take upon him to write concerning the government at all; for what has any private man to do with the government, if his interest be not stirred or shaken? It is the business of the government to manage affairs relating to the government; it is the business of subjects to mind only their own properties and interests."
3. "I do agree, that every man may petition the government, or the king, in a matter that relates to his own private interest; but to meddle with a matter that relates to the government, I do not think my lords the bishops had any power to do [that,] more than any others."

For very different reasons, the words of Justice Powell to the jury have also lived in history, standing like an unyielding rock against the submerging torrent of the so-called common law of libel:

"Truly I cannot see, for my part, any thing of sedition, or any other crime, fixed upon these reverend fathers, my lords the bishops. For, gentlemen, to make it a libel, it must be false; it must be malicious, and it must tend to sedition."

The case, said Powell, turned on the question whether the king had power to dispense with the laws concerning ecclesiastical affairs. If that authority did not exist, there could be no libel in saying that the exercise of it was illegal. He knew of no such authority, but if it did exist, there must be equal power to dispense with other laws. "If this be once allowed of, there will need no parliament; all the legislature will be in the king, which is a thing worth considering, and I leave the issue to God and your consciences."

The jurors' consciences may have sufficed to produce the verdict Not Guilty, at which, the chronicle of the trial concludes, "there were several great shouts in Court, and throughout the hall." King James replied by ousting Justices Powell and Holloway from the bench. The dissident peers and the British people, already poised for revolution, replied by ousting King James from the throne. Lord Chief Justice Wright fled, was caught, jailed, and died in Newgate Prison before he could be tried for unlawfully upholding the dispensing power. Justice Allibone died with equal promptness, and thereby, wrote Edward Foss in his *Judges of England,* probably saved himself from inevitable attainder.

The trial and acquittal of the Seven Bishops furnished English liberals with a freedom banner which they never ceased to wave during the long dark years that still lay ahead. Two brave judges and a scared one rejected rules concerning seditious libel that had been injected into British law by the Court of the Star Chamber and carried into common-law proceedings by Chief Justices Hyde, Scroggs and Jeffreys. Truth and nonmalicious intentions were admitted as defenses, and the jury was authorized to decide both law and fact. But this was done *at a moment when power was in the people,* when a vast majority of them were near revolt against their hated government, and when government was using the instrument of seditious libel to paralyze criticism and opposition from top to bottom of the social structure.

The moment of popular revolt against a dying dynasty was no time to test the permanence of a gain of liberty. Nor did the acquittal of the Seven Bishops touch the core of the question—the right of the people *to say what they pleased* about their government, regardless of what the government might think about it. Until that right was established *by the people,* beyond the power of kings and parliaments and judges to change it, the liberty-destroying "positions" of Justice Allibone could at any time become the judicially enforceable law of the land.

After a fair start toward liberty, that is very close to what happened in eighteenth-century England, but not through the machinations of evil men or the dull mentality of better ones. There were dynastic plots aplenty to start the reversal of the libertarian trend, but it gathered momentum from a clash as old as history—that between a changing world and those in command of society who want no change. For Americans, this political conflict culminated in the Revolutionary War and the independence of the United States. In all that bore on civil rights and liberties, the American colonists were major observers and only minor victims. But every denial of liberty in England had its repercussions in America, leading crown judges, bureaucrats and other royalist adherents in one direction and driving the mass of the people in the other. The effect in America of injustice in England was to build up a cumulative zeal for personal freedom, and the feeling was made more intense by colonial imitations of British malpractices.

CHAPTER 14
Such Freedom as the Law Allows

The Revolution of 1688 brought England that year's parliamentary Declaration of Rights, followed in 1689 by the Bill of Rights and its included act of Succession to the Crown. These statutes were designed to assure ancient rights, clear away Stuart usurpations of power and perversions of justice, block a restoration of that hated family, and ensure Protestant succession to the throne. They also gave fair notice to the imported cosovereigns from the House of Orange that King William III and Queen Mary were to rule under Parliament as well as under God.

These acts achieved their limited purposes, but as declarations of principles they fell far short of covering the rights, privileges and immunities of the people. Like Magna Carta, the Bill of Rights was devoted to an immediate protective purpose, but unlike the Great Charter and its later glosses, it had not the breadth of coverage required to chart the course of a national society. It protected several recently violated elements of due process—prohibiting excessive bail, excessive fines or cruel and unusual punishments—but said not a word about freedom of speech except to assure it in the proceedings of Parliament. As an echo from the trial of the Seven Bishops, Englishmen were guaranteed the right of petitioning the government.

Narrow in scope and repealable by law, the Bill of Rights was no guide for Americans except in pointing the direction and furnishing the format for self-protective action. Thomas Paine ignored certain minor values to the people yet held close to political

reality when he admonished the British people in his controversial
Rights of Man:

"The act, called the Bill of Rights . . . what is it but a bargain,
which the parts of the government made with each other to divide
powers, profits, and privileges? . . . and with respect to the nation,
it said, for your share *you* shall have the right of petitioning. . . .
Where is there the constitution either that gives or that restrains
power?"

As if to prove the worst that here was charged, these words were
given a major position in the information *ex officio* on which Paine
was tried and convicted in 1792 of seditious libel against the
Glorious Revolution, the Bill of Rights, the Parliament and King.
There was no foretaste of this, however, when William III appointed Sir John Holt Lord Chief Justice of England in place of
the absconded Wright. For a dozen years the spirit of the Revolution kept England tranquil. After the deaths of Mary and William,
the accession of Queen Anne in 1701 opened the way to plottings
in behalf of the Stuart Pretender and led to a general outburst
of violent writings on both sides.

In 1702 the House of Lords ordered that William Fuller, a
once-pilloried cheat and impostor, be tried at Queen's Bench for
publishing "a false scandalous and defamatory libel." In his
pamphlet Fuller charged that £180,000 of French money had been
distributed among unnamed persons employed by the British government. When examined by the Lords and Commons, he said he
had been told this by somebody named Thomas Jones. Ordered to
produce Jones, he failed even to identify him, whereupon his
prosecution was ordered. In court, Attorney General Sir Edward
Northey told Fuller he could escape serious censure by bringing
in this mysterious Mr. Jones. Lord Holt took over, again and again
inviting Fuller to justify his accusations:

"But can you make it appear that they are true? . . . If you take
on you to write such things as you are charged with, it lies upon
you to prove it at your peril. . . . If you can offer any matter to prove
what you have writ, let us hear it."

The best Fuller could offer was the nonsensical assertion that
Jones could not come without a warrant because, in some court of

unknown location, he had confessed himself guilty of high treason. Government witnesses testified that Fuller published the pamphlet and Lord Holt instructed the jury that "if you believe he did so, you are to find him guilty." This they did.

Holt's reputation as a trial lawyer had been built on his devotion to fair procedures in court and decency in government. Anti-Catholic himself, he had defended two of the "Popish lords" against their unjust impeachment for treason. He had defended Londoners who rioted against dishonest elections. He resigned his first judgeship rather than sentence an army deserter to death. But he shared the prevalent view that unwarranted criticism of the government was punishable as seditious libel. What he insisted on was a fair trial, and he offered Fuller every opportunity to hinge the case on truth or falsity. In doing so, the Chief Justice abandoned some of the outstanding features of Star Chamber practices as described by Coke, and the evil adaptations of them to jury trials by Hyde, Scroggs and Jeffreys. 1. Truth was recognized as a defense, not as a possible aggravation of the alleged libel. 2. As a corollary, both law and fact would have been before the jury if Fuller had offered truth as a defense.

This was a restoration of ancient rights, lifting libel to a parity with felony in allowable defenses. But it went beyond governmental thinking. In the magazine *Rehearsal* (March 15, 1707), Editor Charles Leslie said it was "a wise and good law" that protected high public officials and gentlemen of quality even from truthful accusations of misconduct. "For private men," said he, "are not judges of their superiors. This would confound all government." This apparently private utterance was virtually a declaration by the government itself, since Leslie's paper had been set up to rebut the charges, especially of naval corruption, made in John Tutchin's *Observator*. Leslie's tone of fawning sycophancy is hardly an aid to the argument that the American guarantee of freedom of the press embraces this early British concept of seditious libel. Yet American as well as English judges and lawyers have worked hard to push Lord Holt into that muddy stream.

The principal significance of Holt's attitude in *Fuller's Case* is in the light it throws on a far more noted one that came before him in 1704—the seditious libel trial of Tutchin for a series of articles published in his *Observator*.[1] Running through two years, they reached a climax in the following words:

"At the same time we consider the French king's success in his bribery and corruption, we ought to lament the sad state of our own country, which affords so many instances of treachery. If we may judge by our national miscarriages, perhaps no nation in Europe has felt the influences of French gold more than England."

The question of the jury's power arose at the outset, when a prospective juror asked to be excused because he disliked the *Observator* and did not think he could be impartial. Attorney General Northey said this was immaterial: the jury had nothing to do but decide whether Tutchin wrote and published the articles. That was a point, remarked Chief Justice Holt, that he would rule on if the juror was formally challenged. Both sides agreed, however, to let him go.

Associated with the Attorney General was a predecessor in that office, Sir Thomas Powys, whose fair conduct in the trial of the Seven Bishops caused him to be made a King's Serjeant of Law after the Revolution. Opening for the prosecution, Powys once more, as in the bishops' case, virtually put the question of libel before the jury. What the Crown was to prove was that Tutchin composed and published the article, but, he also said, "I presume there ought to be made a difference between a just liberty and licentiousness."

Attorney General Northey opened with a denunciation of the libel. It would appear in the trial that Tutchin had "taken the greatest liberty, I believe, that ever man took. . . . He censures all mankind; writes magisterially, and defies all authority, and casts the vilest reflections on the government . . . if such mercenary writers may have liberty to reflect on whom they please, no man's reputation can be safe." The Attorney General told the jury that the question of authorship and publication was "the matter you are to inquire into," but his heavy emphasis on the wickedness of the libel implied a feeling that they might do more.

Lord Chief Justice Holt's charge to the Tutchin jury was cited for the next eighty-eight years—until Parliament passed the Libel

Act of 1792—to support both views of the jury power. Two conflicting passages, italicized below, led to the divergence. He began in this fashion:

"So that now you have heard this evidence, you are to consider whether you are satisfied that Mr. Tutchin is guilty of writing, composing and publishing these libels. They say they are innocent papers, and no libels. . . . But this is a very strange doctrine, to say, it is not a libel reflecting on the government, endeavoring to possess the people that the government is mal-administered by corrupt persons. . . . *Now you are to consider, whether these words I have read to you, do not tend to beget an ill opinion of the administration of the government.*"

After inviting the jury to consider the tendency of the publication, Holt turned to the question whether the offense, if committed by Tutchin, was laid in London, or in Middlesex County and thus outside the jurisdiction of this court:

"Now they on his behalf . . . say you do not prove any crime against him in London. Indeed it is not proved that he writ them in London; but the question is, whether there is not proof of the composing and publication in London. . . . *Gentlemen, I must leave it to you; if you are satisfied that he is guilty of composing and publishing these papers at London, you are to find him guilty.*"

Taking the last sentence by itself, it was a clear direction to return a verdict of Guilty if the jury found that Tutchin wrote or published the article in a place where the court had jurisdiction. But this followed an instruction to the jurors to consider whether the writings, called "innocent papers and no libel" by the defense, "do not tend to beget an ill opinion of the government." For what purpose were the jurors to consider whether the words had such a tendency, if it was none of their business whether they did or did not have it? Unless the direction was utterly without significance, it meant that the decision on libel was to come first, and if the jury agreed with the judge that the words were libelous, they were to decide whether Tutchin committed the offense and whether he did so within the jurisdiction of the court.

This view is supported by what followed. The jury found Tutchin "guilty of composing and publishing, but not of writing." Questioning brought out that they meant "in London." On its face this was a special verdict, falling short of conviction. ("They appeal from my opinion," remarked Holt.) But the Solicitor General asked: "Do you find him guilty of the whole charge, except the writing?" The foreman answered "Yes." The defense lawyers then brought forward a procedural blunder by the Crown that vitiated the entire proceeding and Tutchin never was tried again.

Thus it appears that Lord Holt submitted the entire question of libel to the jury and they decided the entire question, with that fact emphasized by the installments in which the verdict was disclosed. He had shown his readiness to do the same in *Fuller's Case,* and he followed a similar course in the 1706 trial of Dr. Brown, described by Holt in his *Reports.* The jury found Brown guilty, and his lawyers moved for a stay of judgment on the ground that the pamphlet charged as libelous praised the persons referred to. Holt answered "that this was laid to be ironical, and whether 'twas so or not, the jury were judges, and they found it so." To decide the question of irony was to decide whether the writing was malicious, and that was a question of law.

So in all of Holt's recorded libel cases he submitted both law and fact to the jury. His death in 1710 prevented the lengthening of the record and made it easier for later judges to ignore or misinterpret his position. The next blow to liberty had damaging effects that rolled down the centuries on both sides of the Atlantic. In 1731 Richard Francklin, publisher of *The Craftsman,* was put on trial before Lord Chief Justice Raymond for publishing "a false, scandalous and malicious libel" in the form of a "letter from Ghent." This supposed dispatch commented on rumors of injurious changes in the relations of the allied nations, England, France and Spain, as a result of ministerial disagreements. The "letter from Ghent," the government alleged, was written in England to sow dissension by creating an impression that King George II intended to violate his treaty.

Any American law student at the Inner or Middle Temple, after visiting a London coffeehouse, could have written home that this "letter from Ghent" came from the pen of Viscount Bolingbroke, who along with the satirist William Pulteney sponsored *The Craftsman* and made it their political outlet. The letter was written not to jeopardize treaty relations, but to bring about the retirement of Prime Minister Robert Walpole. It was a normal part of the intense political partisanship of the period, and the reaction of the ministry was equally typical. Here was a sample of what Thomas Erskine May had in mind when he wrote that after the abolition of licensing, the war against the press continued and "Every one was a libeler who outraged the sentiments of the dominant party." But Bolingbroke ranked too high to be attacked without proof of authorship, so Francklin became the target *in terrorem* and in anger.

At the trial, the influence of Lord Holt's libertarian rulings was evident in the early tactics of the Attorney General and Solicitor General (Sir Philip Yorke and Charles Talbot). They set out to demonstrate that the "letter from Ghent" actually was libelous. "Gentlemen," said Yorke to the jury, "you may plainly observe here, that this is a positive charge of perfidy and breach of faith on these ministers." And Talbot: "Gentlemen, I hope it now plainly appears to you, that this pretended Hague letter is a libel, and I may say, a very malicious and seditious one too." A lengthy discussion followed between Crown and defense counsel, on the controversies among the allies, the defense seeking to eliminate those that were not pertinent to the issue of libel. Lord Raymond, who must have known that the crown lawyers were following Holt, realized at last that they were being pushed out of a case.

"Is this essential or not?" asked the Lord Chief Justice.

The record does not disclose his tone of voice, but Sir Philip Yorke got the message. He answered in one word, "No."

"Lord Chief Justice. Why hath there been then almost two hours spent about it?"

From that moment the prosecution dropped the issue of libel and concentrated on proof of publication and identification of the word "ministers" as meaning the ministers of King George. The defense lawyers gave combat on both points and swung onto the dangerous bearing of the prosecution's tactics on affairs of a public nature. "I mean," said Lawyer Bootle, "the suppression of the liberty of the press, which liberty hath been always esteemed as a great privilege," and was now being jeopardized. "And I submit it to you," he said to the jury after analyzing the articles, "with all deference to my lord's judgment and directions, whether it is not incumbent on them to prove, that this piece of foreign news is false, scandalous and seditious, before you can find it, by your verdict, to be so?"

Lord Raymond's answer came from the Star Chamber out of Coke: "It is not material whether the facts charged in a libel be true or false." He went on, further paraphrasing Coke's narration of rules of the Star Chamber but not saying where they came from, and concluded:

"Therefore I shall not here allow of any evidence to prove that the matters charged in the libel are true; for I am only abiding by what have been formerly done, in other cases of the like nature."

Bootle responded: "My lord, then I must submit it to your lordship, whether this will not tend to the utter suppression of the liberty of the press, which hath been so beneficial to the nation in general." The truth, he pointed out, could be pleaded in libel suits relating to private affairs:

"And why should not the same be allowed with respect to public affairs? As the Star Chamber is now abolished, I don't know how far that doctrine may be adhered to. I should be glad to have one instance or authority of this, and of there being no need to prove news to be true: . . . it will be of dangerous and fatal consequence indeed, if matters of state, or public affairs, are not to be meddled with, or inserted in the news-papers, notwithstanding they are true, but at the peril of him that does it. They may as well, at once, take away the liberty of the press; and then we shall all live in darkness and ignorance, which may occasion disorders enough in the nation."

This challenge had to be met, and Attorney General Yorke defined freedom of the press in terms that anticipated Blackstone by nearly four decades. Liberty of the press, he said, did not "mean a licentious and an unbounded liberty, to libel and scandalize his majesty, or his principal officers and ministers of state, or his magistrates" or even the meanest of his subjects:

"The liberty meant is to be understood of a legal one: he may lawfully print and publish what belongs to his own trade; but he is not to publish any thing reflecting on the character, and reputation, and administration of his majesty, or his ministers; nor yet to stain the character or reputation of any of his subjects; for, as I said before, that to scandalize and libel people is no part of his trade, so I say, that it is only that liberty of the press, which he is to use, that is regulated by law and subjected to it; and if he breaks that law, or exceeds that liberty of the press, he is to be punished for it, as well as for breaking other laws or liberties."

The Attorney General also took up the challenge to cite any precedent outside of the Star Chamber for the Court's ruling that the defendant in a libel action could not base his defense on the truth of all or a part of what he had written. To show the existence of such a law "long before the Star-Chamber," he would quote the statute *"De Scandalis Magnatum,"* made in 1275, in the reign of Edward the First, that "none be so hardy to tell or publish any false news or tales, whereby discord, or occasion of discord, or slander, may grow between the king and his people, or the great men of the realm; and he that do so, shall be taken and kept in prison, etc."[2] "So, gentlemen," he continued, "you see that this of libels is not a new law, or one that came from the Star Chamber; . . . but one that has been almost of 500 years standing."

Just how a penalty for spreading *"false* news or tales" justified the Star Chamber rule that *"truth* is no defense," Sir Philip did not explain. But Francklin's lawyers had no opportunity to point out the absurdity before Lord Raymond charged the jury. On the points of law that had been so vigorously debated, his address made a vice of the virtue of brevity. It was not an opinion, backed by judicial records, but an unsupported fiat. Two questions, he said, were for the jury to decide—whether Francklin published the offending article and whether it referred to the British ministry:

"But then there is a third thing, to wit, Whether these defamatory expressions amount to a libel or not? This does not belong to the office of the jury, but to the office of the Court; because it is a matter of law, and not of fact; and of which the Court are the only proper judges . . . for matters of law and matters of fact are never to be confounded."

The Chief Justice defined the rights of a publisher as the Attorney General had done:

"There is no knowing or proving particular malice, otherwise than from the act itself; and therefore if the act imports as much, it is sufficient; nor is he to take the liberty to print what he pleases;

for the liberty of the press is only a legal liberty, such as the law allows; and not a licentious liberty."

The moderate punishment imposed on Francklin[3] bore no relationship to the lasting impact of this case in British and American courts. The weakness of Lord Raymond's position became in time its strength. Since he cited no common-law authorities whatever to support his assertions, he could not be attacked for presenting faulty precedents. As he did not sustain his stand by arguments, there was no vulnerable reasoning to refute. A brief definition of libel early in the trial emanating from the Star Chamber but unidentified as to origin, and two final dogmatic sentences addressed to the jury, became after a few years the authentic voice of the English judiciary, supposedly summarizing five hundred years of the common law.

CHAPTER 15
The Case of John Peter Zenger

To measure its influence in the United States, the position taken by Lord Raymond in the Francklin case needs to be split into two categories. One relates to the rights of defendants and the powers of juries in trials for criminal libel. The other concerns the question whether libel prosecutions conflict with the guarantees of the First Amendment.

In spite of Lord Raymond's brevity of speech and paucity of argument, the Francklin case throws a brilliant light on this constitutional controversy. For this we may thank Attorney General Yorke, a blunt and honest man, whose more extended remarks the Lord Chief Justice was condensing when he defined the freedom of the press. Read again the salient words of the Attorney General, in reply to Mr. Bootle's charge that the Court was suppressing the right of the press to comment freely on affairs of state. The capitalization below will show its bearing on our constitutional command that Congress shall *make no law* abridging the freedom of the press:

"The liberty meant, is to be understood of [as] a legal one: . . . it is only that liberty of the press which he is to use, THAT IS REGULATED BY LAW AND SUBJECTED TO IT: and if he breaks that law, or EXCEEDS THAT LIBERTY OF THE PRESS, he is to be punished for it. . . . So I hope it appears to you to be very plain that THE LIBERTY OF THE PRESS IS LIMITED AND GOVERNED BY LAW."

Lord Raymond took the same position in similar words:

"Nor is he to take the liberty to print what he pleases; for the liberty of the press is only a legal liberty, SUCH AS THE LAW ALLOWS; and not a licentious liberty."

Against these declarations place the mandate of the First Amendment: "Congress shall MAKE NO LAW . . . abridging the freedom of speech, or of the press." What room is there, in those words, for a freedom of speech that is "regulated by law AND SUBJECTED TO IT"? What room is there for a freedom of the press that is "LIMITED AND GOVERNED BY LAW"? Can liberty be "limited" without being "abridged"? Do the words "NO LAW" mean the same as "ONLY . . . SUCH AS THE LAW ALLOWS"? Under such standards as these, the American people would be better off with a guarantee reading, "Congress shall make no law *protecting* the freedom of the press." That would leave the way open for defense of political freedom as one of the natural and unalienable rights of citizens of a free republic.

The Court's position in *Francklin's Case* gradually became known throughout the English-speaking world. Bolingbroke's invisible connection put it in the storm center of British politics. It was published by pamphlet and in the *State Trials,* approved and condemned in Parliament, endorsed by judges, opposed by defense lawyers, condemned by libertarian writers. One could almost think that the framers of the First Amendment had the words of Sir Philip Yorke in mind, when they drafted so clear a rejection of the doctrine they embodied. But for the next half century colonial America was bound to the basic British rule. In the sedition cases that followed *Francklin,* the outstanding feature was the resistance of juries to the Raymond rule separating law and fact and rejecting truth as a defense. They were not all British juries.

The next great trial after Francklin's came too soon and at too great a distance for the words of Raymond and Yorke to gather authority. The scene was New York, but the case created as great a stir in England as in America. This was the trial of John Peter Zenger, publisher of the New York *Weekly Journal,* whose protest against Royal Governor Cosby's arbitrary removal of Chief Justice Lewis Morris from office led to his prosecution in 1735 for seditious libel. Morris's hand-picked successor, Chief Justice De Lancey, charged the grand jury that it was "high time to put a stop to" such criticisms. He quoted from Hawkins' *Pleas of the Crown* that it was "a very high aggravation of a libel, that it tends to scandalize the government, by reflecting on those who are entrusted with the administration of public affairs." Besides endangering the public peace, this "also has a direct tendency to breed in the people a dislike of their governors and incline them to faction and sedition." For a commentary on these very words, and on this very case, we may bring together some passages in a 1784 booklet of Dr. Joseph Towers, English libertarian writer and compiler of national biography:

"The doctrines concerning libels, which are to be found in some of our lawbooks, are so destitute of any legitimate origin, so evidently sprung from the court of Star-Chamber, and so inconsistent with every principle of a free constitution, that they deserve . . . to be scouted."

Juries, said Dr. Towers, ought to have enough spirit and acuteness to decide for common sense and common justice, "even against Hawkins, or any other solemn reporter or compiler of Star-Chamber law." Farther along, he wrote, in taking up the Zenger case:

"It appears, that attempts have been made to establish the Star-Chamber doctrines concerning libels even in America, and to deprive jurymen there, as well as in England, of the right of determining the law, as well as the fact, in trials for libels."

Even in America! where, Towers evidently believed, such a prosecution represented a stifling of the air of freedom that people breathed. The grand jury would not indict Zenger, so Governor Cosby ordered the Attorney General to bring him to trial by information *ex officio*. As the trial opened, Zenger's lawyers, James Alexander and William Smith, filed an exception to the Chief Justice's power to hear the case because he had been commissioned by the governor without the advice and consent of the British colonial council. Chief Justice De Lancey replied by disbarring both lawyers from the case.

This action brought Andrew Hamilton from Philadelphia to act as unpaid counsel for Zenger. Hamilton invited the prosecution to dismiss the witnesses who were to prove that Zenger published the articles: it would violate his own principles "to deny the publication of a complaint, which, I think, is the right of every free-born subject to make, when the matters so published can be supported with truth." Why, then, replied the Attorney General, "I think the jury must find a verdict for the king; for supposing [these libels] were true, the law says that they are not the less libellous for that; nay indeed the law says, their being true is an aggravation of the crime." Hamilton's response was an echo from the trial of the Seven Bishops:

"Not so neither, Mr. Attorney . . . the words themselves must be libellous, that is, false, scandalous, and seditious, or else they are not guilty."

This was the beginning of a lawyers' battle of authorities and arguments, the Attorney General relying on Coke, Hawkins and lesser commentators. Hamilton took note that his adversary went for his proofs of law to the Court of the Star Chamber. He had hoped that "as that terrible court where those dreadful judgments were given . . . was long ago laid aside . . . that Mr. Attorney knowing this, would not have attempted to set up a Star-Chamber here, nor to make their judgments a precedent to us." Hamilton laid out his defense: he would "prove those very papers that were called libels to be true." At which the Chief Justice interjected:

"You cannot be admitted, Mr. Hamilton, to give the truth of a libel in evidence. A libel is not to be justified, for it is nevertheless a libel that it is true. . . . I pray show that you can give the truth of a libel in evidence."

Hamilton cited, from Coke, the 1344 case of John de Northampton, where the judgment (though it was a case of contempt of court) turned on the falsity of the words; also the *Case of the Seven Bishops* and the words of Lord Holt in *Fuller's Case*. Chief Justice De Lancey gave contrary citations from Coke and Hawkins to prove that the appearance of truth in malicious invective made it more libelous than falsehood. This produced the following exchange:

"Mr. Hamilton. These are Star-Chamber cases; and I was in hopes that practice had been dead with the [abolition of that] court.

"Mr. Chief Justice. Mr. Hamilton, the Court have delivered their opinion . . . you are not to be permitted to argue against the opinion of the Court."

Hamilton hoped he would be permitted to tell the jury that

the Court was against him on that point. "Use the Court with good manners," replied the Chief Justice, "and you shall be allowed all the liberty you can reasonably desire."

"Then, gentlemen of the jury," said Zenger's counsel, "it is to you we must now appeal, for witnesses to the truth of the facts we have offered and are denied the liberty to prove. . . . You are citizens of New York [and the facts] are notoriously known to be true; and therefore in your justice lies our safety."

To this the Chief Justice replied:

"No, Mr. Hamilton; the jury may find that Mr. Zenger printed and published those papers, and leave it to the Court to judge whether they are libellous."

Rejoined Hamilton: "I know, may it please your honour, the jury MAY do so; but I do likewise know they may do otherwise. I know they have the right, beyond all dispute, to determine both the law and the fact; and where they do not doubt of the law, they ought to do so."

Zenger's lawyer granted that it was unmanly and unmannerly to expose personal faults or even vices that did not affect the public peace. But when a ruler brought his faults and vices into his administration, that altered the case mightily. All the things said in favor of rulers and upon the side of power "will not be able to stop people's mouths when they feel themselves oppressed, I mean in a free government." He went back to early cases of revolt by juries, describing the trial of William Penn and Willam Mead for tumultuous assembly, the imprisonment of the Penn-Mead jury for its acquittal of them and the release of Bushell and the others by habeas corpus. Hamilton assailed the Crown's portraiture of libel:

"If a libel is understood in the large and unlimited sense urged by Mr. Attorney, there is scarce a writing I know that may not be called a libel, or scarce any person safe from being called to account as a libeller; for Moses, meek as he was, libelled Cain; and who is it that has not libelled the Devil? For, according to Mr. Attorney, it is no justification to say one has a bad name. Echard has libelled our good king William, Burnet has libelled, among many others, king Charles and king James; and Rapin has libelled them all."

Chief Justice De Lancey saw that he was hopelessly beaten on the issue of the jury's power, but he tried to salvage the case on the scope of libel. Mr. Hamilton's design, he said to the jury, was to cause them to pay little attention to what he had been saying:

"I shall therefore only observe to you, that, as the facts or words in the information are confessed, the only part that can come in question before you is, whether the words, as set forth in the information, make a libel; and that is a matter of law, no doubt, and which you may leave to the Court. But I shall trouble you no more with any thing more of my own; but read to you the words of a learned and upright judge, in a case of the like nature."

He then read, from the charge to the Tutchin jury, Lord Holt's summary of libelous passages and his opinion that no government was safe if people could not be punished for endeavors "to procure animosities as to the management of it." What De Lancey read included Holt's instruction that "you are to consider, whether these words I have read to you do not tend to beget an ill opinion of the administration of the government." Thus, in the Zenger case, De Lancey opened the trial with a flat denial of the jury's right to pass on the question of libel. He then half surrendered by saying they *may* leave that question to the Court, and wound up with the quotation in which Holt left it to the jury.

The jury acquitted Zenger. "Upon which there were three huzzas in the Hall, which was crowded with people." At its next meeting the New York Common Council ordered that Andrew Hamilton be presented with the Freedom of the Corporation. It was formally presented as a testimonial to the remarkable service done by him to the inhabitants of New York "by his learned and generous defense of the rights of mankind, and the liberty of the press, in the case of John Peter Zenger."

The Zenger case firmly established in the American colonies, in 1735, the rights of juries that were not gained in England until 1792. It established, at least in the minds of the people, that truth was a defense in libel. There was no assertion, by Hamilton, of immunity from criminal prosecution for charges alleged to be false. Indeed, he expressly disclaimed that. But it was a tremendous forward step to overset the doctrine that public officers were immune from criticism, true or false, if the criticisms tended to bring the government into disrepute. The influence of this case stretching through almost two centuries was revealed in these words by Justice Steele of the Colorado Supreme Court, dissenting in 1906 from a seditious libel conviction disguised as contempt of court:

"Gouverneur Morris is said to have stated that instead of dating American liberty from the Stamp Act, he traced it to the persecution of Zenger; because that event revealed the philosophy of freedom, both of thought and speech, as an inborn human right, so nobly set forth in Milton's speech for the 'Liberty of Unlicensed Printing.' "

As in the instance of Milton, Andrew Hamilton's spirit transcended the actual stand he took for freedom and helped to enlarge the vision of others. Pamphlets describing the Zenger trial were published and republished in the American colonies and in London. Zenger's own account of it, based on the stenographic record, was reproduced in the continuation of Emlyn's 1730 *State Trials* immediately following *Francklin's Case*. This American trial, said Editor Emlyn, "having made a great noise in the world, is here inserted; though the doctrines advanced by Mr. Hamilton in his speeches are not allowed in the courts here to be law.—See Lord Raymond's opinion in the foregoing trial."

The "great noise in the world" was not due to the New York jury's revolt against British juridical rulings, for British juries had revolted similarly with less dramatic effect. It was due to the advancing concept, among a vocal portion of the people, of the natural right of free men to express their thoughts, no matter what they might be, without either prior restraint or the risk of subsequent punishment. In practical application the defenders of freedom asserted in every instance the right to publish what the judges called seditious.

The Zenger case has often and fallaciously been portrayed as an American break with *long-established* British rulings on the common law of seditious libel. That is on the supposition that Lord Raymond had numerous common-law decisions behind him when he made his undocumented rulings in the Francklin case. In reality he had nothing to bulwark his position except the Star Chamber rulings stated by Coke and the worse-than-nothing decisions of Hyde, Scroggs and Jeffreys, which he did not cite. Neither, for an opposite reason, did Raymond dare to challenge Lord Holt, but overruled him *sub silentio*. De Lancey, moreover, did not refer to Raymond. At the time of the Zenger trial, in 1735, Raymond's undocumented opinion of 1731 was apparently unknown to American lawyers.

It appears, then, that Raymond in England and De Lancey in New York independently resurrected the Star-Chamber rulings on seditious libel and treated them as common law. De Lancey's rendering of the law, torn to shreds by Andrew Hamilton and rejected by the New York jury, has survived in American history only in anathema. Raymond's identical doctrines were ratified by England's Georgian judges—especially Lord Mansfield—through whose freedom-destroying respectability the doctrines came back to the United States a century later. Here, employed to restrict the meaning of the First Amendment, they have been cited with approval by American judges who would have shrunk in horror from presenting the same arguments in the words of De Lancey or of Scroggs.

In the Zenger case, as in that of Francklin, political pressure produced a political trial, before judges who shared the feelings of the ruling powers. In England, as the Glorious Revolution sank into the Hanoverian mire, trials for seditious libel became muddily entangled with royal tyranny and parliamentary corruption. Public protest brought either vindictive prosecution in court or summary punishment at the bar of Commons or Lords; frequently both. By emotional involvement more than by logical connection, the issue of freedom of political expression was brought within the orbit of the approaching American Revolution. It is in England's rough-and-tumble political and social conflict in the four decades after 1750 that we must seek the final outside influence upon the framing of the American Bill of Rights.

CHAPTER 16
Franklin, Francklin, Cato and Wilkes

When Benjamin Franklin, at the age of sixteen, edited and printed the *New England Courant* during the imprisonment of his brother,[1] he dared not make a direct attack on the Massachusetts Assembly for its violation of the freedom of the press and general usurpation of power. Nevertheless, he gave that body a well-deserved rebuke by publishing the following extract "from a London Journal":

"Without freedom of thought, there can be no such thing as wisdom; and no such thing as public liberty without freedom of speech; which is the right of every man, as far as by it he does not hurt or controul the right of another; and this is the only check it ought to suffer and the only bounds it ought to know.

"This sacred privilege is so essential to free government, that the security of property, and the freedom of speech always go together; and in those wretched countries where a man cannot call his tongue his own, he can scarce call any thing else his own. Whoever would overthrow the liberty of a nation must begin by subduing the freeness of speech; a thing terrible to public traitors."

Franklin was quoting the opening paragraphs of No. 15 of "Cato's Letters," which began to appear in the London press in 1720.[2] This one was entitled "Of Freedom of Speech: That the same is inseparable from Publick Liberty." It may have been more than coincidence that "Cato" was echoing William Penn's words to the jury half a century earlier, that if the ancient liberties of Englishmen were not "indispensably maintained, who can say he hath right to the coat upon his back?" By 1720 the British press, freed of the punitive restraint of the Licensing Act, was discussing politics with a new-found vigor that led "Cato" to write in a later letter:

"It it commonly said that no nation in the world would allow such papers to come abroad as England suffers; which is only saying, that no nation in the world enjoys the liberty which England enjoys."

But this was partly defensive exhortation. The country was already moving into the era described by Thomas E. May: "Every one was a libeler who outraged the sentiments of the dominant party." John Trenchard and Thomas Gordon (these two were "Cato") willingly accepted monarchy but denounced the monstrous frauds of the South Sea Bubble. Their castigations of unnamed ministers were protectively offset by fulsome praise of George the First. Whoever vilified and traduced a good prince was an enemy to society and to mankind, and should be punished as such.

"And yet [wrote "Cato"] it is scarce possible, in a free country, to punish by a general law any libel so much as it deserves; since such a law, consisting of so many branches, and being of such vast latitude, would make all writing whatsoever, how innocent soever, and even all speaking, unsafe."

The same words could be written today, not merely by way of warning, but as a historical verdict upon the futility, the folly, and the damage to human liberty, of pursuing for two and a half centuries the course against which Trenchard and Gordon cautiously directed their pens. Caution was imperative, at a time when every ministerial lawyer was searching for an unguarded phrase or even an injudicious silence that could be construed into a besmirching of the king. But the two men had no need to tailor their abstract ideas about personal freedom into a denial of it, and on that score they became the libertarian voice of early Hanoverian England.

"Cato's Letters" abruptly vanished from the London newspapers in 1723, when the driving partner, Trenchard, died. For decades thereafter, collected reprints flooded the bookstalls of England and the American colonies. For a hundred years the pseudonym "Cato" ranked with "Algernon Sidney" as evidence of a public writer's devotion to liberty at the purest level. Time and again,

American newspapers quoted or gave full space to letters from the Trenchard-Gordon collection. "Cato" expressed the fundamental feeling that was gathering force on the western side of the Atlantic:

"That men ought to speak well of their governors, is true; while their governors deserve to be well spoken of; but to do public mischief, without hearing of it, is only the prerogative and felicity of tyranny. A free people will be showing that they are so, by their freedom of speech. . . . Only the wicked governors of men dread what is said of them."

Young Benjamin Franklin, like "Cato" himself, was free of any delusion that speech or press was really free. But in England a kinsman in spirit and almost in name, Richard Francklin (the same who soon afterwards felt the wiry knout of prosecution), gave in 1726 what amounted to Blackstone's 1769 definition of freedom of the press as freedom from *prior restraint*.[3] Wrote Francklin in the second issue of *The Craftsman*:

"By the liberty of the press I mean, as I suppose every body else does, an unreserved, discretionary power for every man to publish his thoughts on any subject, and in any manner, which is not forbidden by the laws of the land, without being obliged to apply for a license or privilege for so doing. In short, where this liberty prevails, every author has a right to print what he pleases, without asking any body leave, and without fearing molestation from authority, so long as he keeps within his proper bounds; which it is his business to take care not to transgress. He knows the laws of his country; and if he rashly offends against them, he must submit to the penalty."

This definition, as Francklin understood it, allowed writers to debate freely on Government and Religion: "For, as the public welfare of every nation depends entirely on these two great articles, so they are the only points on which any tyrant or arbitrary prince would desire to restrain our thoughts." Possessing this freedom, the people "have hereby an opportunity of writing upon subjects of the utmost importance; such as nearly affect our consciences, our liberties, and estates." But it was a freedom restricted by law:

He did not mean "liberty to undermine the fundamentals of government and religion, or to calumniate persons in high power," neither of which ought to be tolerated. The people should have a liberty of giving political and religious opinions freely, of debating the great affairs of peace and war; of freely discussing proposed laws "and of modestly offering our reasons for the repeal of those which are found to be oppressive." Finally, they ought to have "a liberty of setting forth mal-administration, and pleading for the redress of grievances; of exposing mismanagement and corruption in high places, and discovering [i.e. disclosing] the secret designs of wicked and ambitious men."

The trouble with this too-plausible combination of freedom and restraint was that lawful and necessary defenses of good government against mismanagement and corruption were sure to be construed by wicked and ambitious ministers as undermining the fundamentals of government, and calumniating men in high position. The power to abridge freedom is the power to destroy it. Francklin was well aware of this, as shown by the way he damned English conditions, present and past, in *The Craftsman* No. 3, published with No. 2 on December 9, 1726. Discreetly avoiding direct mention of England under Walpole, he said that in some countries, without a licenser, "where the greatest *Liberty* of the Press is supposed to be allowed, very little in reality will be found." In such countries, publishers discovered that their superiors "pretend to leave them at their full *Liberty*, and yet have always some artifice in reserve, to punish them for using this *Liberty*." Libeling was such a pernicious practice that it ought to be punished, but it was undefined in the laws and left to the judgment of the courts, with the result that in bad reigns, patriots lost their ears or their lives for what in good reigns deserved commemoration in bronze statues:

"We have seen, in some reigns, remote allegories, ironical expressions, and the most distant innuendos explained [by tortured constructions], to a man's destruction; we have seen printers and booksellers menaced and intimidated with arbitrary seizures, illegal confinements, and groundless, vexatious prosecutions."

Where such methods are practiced, said Francklin, there can be no real liberty of the press, "since a privilege which is invaded and superceded, in this manner, is no privilege at all; . . . it is a melancholy proof that wicked men in authority will stick at nothing to invalidate the just rights and privileges of their fellow-citizens, when they stand in competition with their corrupt designs."

So besides furnishing Blackstone with his definition of freedom of the press as freedom from prior restraint, Francklin exposed the fallacy of it forty years before it was promulgated under the authority of that name. The printer of *The Craftsman* was a prophet of his own future. Three years after he published this analysis of Walpole's tactics he was tried for seditious libel in publishing "The Alcayde of Seville's Speech." The jury voted him Not Guilty, but the closest approach to a lawbook report of the case is found in a famous ballad written by William Pulteney, whose rhymed attacks on Robert Walpole caused another poetaster to call him, "Of all Bob's foes, The wittiest in verse and prose." This stanza by Pulteney (one of the sponsors of *The Craftsman*) was directed against Attorney General Yorke and hits the case at its heart:

> Sir Philip well knows,
>   That his innuendos
> Will serve him no longer
>   In verse or in prose;
> For twelve honest men have determined the cause,
> Who are judges alike of the facts and the laws.

[Too late for inclusion except in the Bibliographical Notes, the author has found a 1729 account of this case. Turn to page 534.]

For Richard Francklin the acquittal was a mere respite until his trial and conviction in 1731 for publishing Bolingbroke's unsigned "Letter from Ghent" criticizing British foreign policy. The concentrated attention paid to the results of the 1731 trial, through which Chief Justice Raymond stamped Star Chamber libel practices into the common law, has obscured the contemporary reaction to it. The trial was originally set for July 12 but more than half of the jury panel stayed away, delaying the case till the next session. The July courtroom scene was described in Abel Boyer's monthly, *The Political State of Great Britain,* quoted in the *State Trials.* Naming noblemen of both parties who attended, Boyer added:

"It was remarkable that Mr. Pulteney, who is presumed to be one of the patrons of that weekly paper, was loudly huzza'd by the populace, as he went out of Westminster-hall. Which shews the fondness of the people of England for the liberty of the press."

The fondness was for a liberty that the government character-ized as lawless license. There can be no doubt that if Bolingbroke had been in power, and Walpole leading the opposition, roles would have been reversed and freedom no less in the pillory. The historian Ralph pointed out (writing after Walpole's final ouster from the Prime Ministry) that this man who used "all the artillery of ministerial power" to silence his critics "was at a certain period one of the most zealous advocates for the liberty of the press." In particular, Walpole led the debate in 1715 in defense of Richard Steele, a member of Parliament who was cited for seditious libel and expelled from the House for newspaper articles critical of Queen Anne's government. "This violent prosecution [as Ralph quoted Walpole] struck at the liberty of the subject in general." He hoped the House "would not sacrifice one of their members to the resentment and rage of the ministry, for *no other than his crime, exposing their notorious mismanagements.*"

It was in the wake of such conduct that "Cato" wrote: "Only the wicked governors of men dread what is said of them." But the Walpole who championed "Richard Steele and liberty" rose to power himself and his motto changed to "Richard Francklin and tyranny." Still to be learned, but suggested by Francklin himself and taught by the whole record of the eighteenth century, was the fact that freedom existing at the discretion of men in power—be they congressmen, kings, presidents, ministers or judges—is noth-ing but freedom's shadow.

In 1752, a score of years after Francklin's conviction, the trial of William Owen, bookseller, produced a confrontation whose im-portance was little guessed at the time. Owen, in the course of trade, sold a pamphlet criticizing the House of Commons for ousting a member who presented a petition protesting the stealing of a West-minster parliamentary election. Prosecuting the case was Solicitor General William Murray, afterwards the Earl of Mansfield, who as Lord Chief Justice became the most efficient enforcer of the Star Chamber concept of seditious libel disguised as common law. One of Owen's lawyers was Charles Pratt, afterwards Lord Camden, who stepped forward as Mansfield's chief antagonist when the latter's handling of the libel law became an acute political issue in the House of Lords.

In an unwitting preview of the next forty years, the future Lord Mansfield told the jury that the only question before it was whether Owen published the pamphlet. If that fact was proved "the libel proves itself, sedition, disturbance, etc." But that was a question of law with which the jurors had nothing to do, "you being judges of the fact; the judge determines the law."

Defense lawyers Pratt and Ford defended the right of the people to call their governors to account. The doctrine giving the Houses of Parliament immunity from criticism could be full of the most fatal consequences—shutting people's mouths when they would petition for redress of grievances. But in any case, the printing and sale of a book for profit did not prove the charge against their client: malicious publication of a false libel with seditious and scandalous intent.

Chief Justice Lee completely supported the future Lord Mansfield in charging the jury. But the judge permitted character witnesses to testify, and they exalted Owen into such a model of devotion to king and church that the jury found him Not Guilty. Crown and Court twice asked the jury whether it was not proved that Owen did sell the book, but the only response to this hint of attainder was a chorus of "Not Guilty, Not Guilty. That is our verdict, my lord, and we abide by it." Upon which "the Court broke up; and there was a prodigious shout in the hall."

Whatever else that trial did, it placed Lord Mansfield so completely in the line of Clarke (Udall's judge), Hyde, Scroggs and Raymond that by the time he became Chief Justice the new common law born of the Star Chamber had become both law and burning gospel to him.

In 1758 Mansfield and the future Lord Camden resumed their disagreement. Pratt as attorney general prosecuted the pamphleteer Dr. John Shebbeare for seditious libel in his "Sixth Letter" to the people of England, which blamed the country's calamities upon German state influence on England's Hanoverian king. Pratt, who obtained a conviction, not only invited the jury to decide both law and fact, but deliberately kept his back turned to Lord Mansfield throughout his address.

A dual change was taking place in England regarding the restraints on freedom of the press. The courts were moving backward

—back toward the Star Chamber—thus forcing the advocates of liberty to concentrate their attacks on specific restraints rather than advance the freedom proclaimed in principle by Milton and actually sought by "Cato." However, the zone of defense was broadening, as alarm spread among the people. In the House of Commons, on the contrary, a rapidly worsening "rotten borough" system gave the Crown almost limitless opportunity to control elections and protect ministerial corruption. To save itself, the ruling party in both houses became the efficient partner of the courts in the suppression of political freedom.

This conflict, spilling over into many related rights and privileges, came to a sudden climax in April 1763 when John Wilkes, a member of Pitt's opposition party in the House of Commons, published a violent assault on the new ministry of George Grenville. Wilkes was no shining light of personal and political morality, but a notorious reveler in Rabelaisian orgies who had bought a parliamentary seat at Aylsbury with his wife's money. In No. 45 of his anonymous publication, *The North Briton,* discussing the treaty that transferred Silesia to Prussia at the close of the Seven Years' War, he called King George's speech from the throne on that subject "the most abandoned instance of ministerial effrontery ever attempted to be imposed on mankind." He came close to saying that the king knew he was being induced to countenance a lie. As *The North Briton* bore no names, Secretary of State Halifax issued a general warrant requiring "strict and diligent search for the authors, printers and publishers of a seditious and treasonable paper" of that title, and the seizure of them and their papers.

If any magistrate had authority to issue such a blanket warrant, Halifax certainly did not, and it was doubly unlawful when used against a member of Parliament. Wilkes, implicated by his printer, was seized on his way to his house and taken there while the officers ransacked the premises, broke locks, and jammed his political and personal papers into sacks. John Almon, an opposition pamphleteer and bookseller, chanced to come in during the performance and at once notified Pitt's brother-in-law, Lord Temple, of the arrest and seizures.

Temple got Wilkes out of the Tower of London on a writ of habeas corpus issued by Mansfield's adversary, Charles Pratt, who had become Chief Justice of the Court of Common Pleas. The ground was violation of the privilege of a member of the House of Commons. By this time Wilkes faced charges of seditious libel brought by information *ex officio* in Mansfield's Court of the King's Bench. Parliament then stepped in with a resolve that *North Briton* No. 45 was "a false, scandalous, and malicious libel," and ordered it burned by the common hangman. In their fury the lawmakers reversed a rule of hundreds of years' standing by resolving "that privilege of Parliament does not extend to the case of writing and publishing seditious libels, nor ought to be allowed to obstruct the ordinary course of law." Not only did this resolution subject members to a censorship, but (as T. E. May pointed out) Parliament itself obstructed the course of law by declaring an action to be unlawful before the courts found it to be so, and violated the common-law rule against *ex post facto* legislation by withdrawing parliamentary privilege from a completed action.

The civil courts proved independent of crown pressure. Wilkes brought suit and obtained a judgment of £1,000 against Under-Secretary of State Wood, for his connection with the arrest and seizure. At that time he had a suit pending against Lord Halifax from whom he later collected £4,000. With less pleasure, he carried in his pocket a summons to appear for trial at the bar of the House, for contempt of that body, and in his belly two bullets received in an unrelated duel. The situation called urgently for foreign travel, and a surprised House soon received from him, forwarded from Paris, his English physician's certificate that he was too ill to appear. The Commons responded by expelling him.

During his five-year sojourn on the continent, Wilkes was tried *in absentia* by Mansfield's Court of King's Bench. He was found guilty of a wicked and seditious libel (with the word "false" conspicuously omitted) in the *North Briton* article, and in another trial was convicted of blasphemy. The latter charge was based on an anonymous "Essay on Woman," an obscene parody of Pope's "Essay on Man," written by a poetaster of the period. The work was not offered for sale, but twelve copies were printed by Wilkes and put under lock and key for the future edification of a coterie of his intimate friends—nobles and gentlemen whose high social position forbade them the closely related pleasure of writing four-letter words on outhouse walls. A thirteenth copy, secretly made by a printer, was obtained by the government (reputedly purchased at a high price) for the purpose of the prosecution—a collusive transaction that further tainted the trial. The failure of Wilkes to appear for judgment on either conviction enabled Mansfield to enter a decree of outlawry against him.

In 1768 when the Whigs took over the ministry, Wilkes ventured to return to England. The Middlesex voters quickly elected him to Parliament by a large majority. Had the king and his parliamentary partisans possessed a modicum of political sense, they would have left Wilkes free to orate and write and slide into oblivion. Instead, he was once more expelled by the Commons. Before this action was taken, Lord Mansfield committed him to prison on his outlawry. On the way there, a friendly mob halted his carriage; men took the place of horses and drew him for hours around the city, shouting, "Wilkes and Liberty." Finally, he slipped away from his admirers and went to jail alone.

Mansfield, who loved to make such gestures, reversed the outlawry on a trivial technicality unnoticed by the defense lawyers, then smote Wilkes with twenty-two months' imprisonment for libel and blasphemy. He was re-elected to Parliament while in prison, expelled a third time and again re-elected. The House then, in February 1769, declared him permanently incapable of being elected to serve in that Parliament. Twice more his stubborn constituents re-elected him, whereupon the House both halted and heightened the travesty by throwing out all votes cast for Wilkes and seating an opponent who had been defeated four to one. Six times this rakish champion of popular rights was expelled or excluded from the seat to which he was lawfully entitled.

Britons by this time were in a pro-Wilkes frenzy that extended in full force to the American colonies. His affairs were managed by a new "Society of Supporters of the Bill of Rights." Gifts from all over England and from America restored his depleted fortune. The pen of the mighty and mysterious "Junius" came to his support. In the colonies, "45" and "22" became magic symbols—one toast for each month in prison putting many an American banqueter under the table. Wilkes-Barre, Pennsylvania, received its name in 1769 from Wilkes and his pro-American defender, Colonel

Barré. After his release from prison Wilkes was elected alderman of London, sheriff of London and Middlesex counties, and finally Lord Mayor of London. Coincident with this last action, the dissolution of the old Parliament removed the ban against his election, and Middlesex sent him back to the House of Commons by an overwhelming vote. There, working with vigor, persistence and unaccustomed discretion, he not only kept his case before the public but won a seven-year fight to have the resolution disqualifying him from election expunged from the journals as an unlawful act.

The persecution of Wilkes violated more civil rights and liberties than one could readily name, but at the bottom of it all, with special impact in America, was the right of subjects and citizens to call their government to account. This had been challenged, in the Wilkes case, first by a positive denial of the right to criticize public officials; next by violation of the immunities given elected representatives in order to free them from coercive pressures; then by misuse of general warrants of arrest, search and seizure, and finally by arbitrary cancellation of the right of citizens to be represented by persons of their own choosing.

It was this last feature that aroused the greatest tumult among the British people and the minority in Parliament. Lord Camden (promoted now to Lord Chancellor) declared in parliamentary debate that the oversetting of the Middlesex election inflicted a more dangerous wound on the constitution than King Charles did when he forced the country to go twelve years without a Parliament. Out of a union of thought and feeling between tumultuous mobs and responsible statesmen came something new in British history. Thomas Erskine May described the movement:

"The violation of the rights of the electors of Middlesex by the Commons, united, in support of Wilkes, the parliamentary opposition, the wronged electors, the magistrates and citizens of London, a large body of the middle class, the press, and the populace. . . . The throne was approached by addresses and remonstrances. 'Junius' thundered forth his fearful invectives. Political agitation was rife in various forms; but its most memorable feature was that of public meetings, which at this period began to take their place among the institutions of the country. No less than seventeen counties held meetings to support the electors of Middlesex. Never had so general a demonstration of public sentiment been made, in such a form. It was a new phase in the development of public opinion. . . . Association for political purposes, and large assemblies of men, henceforth became the most powerful and impressive form of agitation."

Although British emotions were most deeply stirred by the assault on the electoral system, the fundamental issue was the right of the people to criticize their rulers; to chastise them with tongue and pen if they felt the need to do so. Had that right been protected in England's constitutional law and observed in practice, not one of the other grievances would have arisen. It was this aspect of the conflict that drew the American colonies into the thick of it. They had daily evidence that the full weight of governmental repression in England was being directed against British champions of American rights. Had speech and press been free in England, had elections been fair and representative, the resulting shift of political power would have produced such a change of policy that there would have been no American Revolution based on festering grievances.

As it was, Americans identified *re*pression with *op*pression, and recognized the British government as the instrument of both. Being relatively free of tyranny in the colonial courts, after the chastisement given the prosecutors of John Peter Zenger, they had no such need as the English libertarians felt, to concentrate on the perversions of justice in the libel laws. Unconstitutional taxation, writs of assistance, general warrants, trial in distant courts, quartering of troops in private homes, disallowance of colonial legislation, punitive control of American ports and commerce—these were the grievances that stirred the American colonists to action. But the spectacle of freedom of opinion suppressed in England was always in sight, and the sight of it not only stirred sympathy, but carried a warning that linked freedom of speech, press and assembly with the rights whose infringement was carrying the people of the colonies toward independence. The actual evils in England were potential American evils that merged with the revolutionary grievances of America and built unwritten bills of rights in the minds of the people.

This feeling was dramatically enhanced by what has been called

"The American Wilkes case." This was the prosecution of Alexander MacDougall at the instigation of Royal Governor Colden and the New York Colonial Assembly, which in 1770 voted him guilty of "a false, seditious and infamous libel." MacDougall was the author of a handbill signed "Son of Liberty," addressed "To the betrayed Inhabitants of New-York." In it he denounced a collusive agreement by which the Assembly voted to furnish supplies for the British troops in New York in exchange for Colden's signature to a paper-money bill. Defiantly or astutely choosing to stay eleven weeks in jail rather than put up exorbitant bail, MacDougall passed out articles denouncing the law of seditious libel as one of the "tyrannical tenets . . . invariably associated with the infamous Star Chamber."

Among the people, the excitement stirred by the Zenger trial thirty-five years earlier was more than repeated. MacDougall's arrest represented far more than the personal pique of a governor. The issue that provoked it—colonial support of British soldiery—touched the raw flesh of the approaching Revolution. This added violence and volume to the universal shout for "freedom of the press" with which the Sons of Liberty rallied to MacDougall's support. Governor Colden and the Assembly by their aggressive conduct, and MacDougall by the nature of his provocation and resistance, made the case a genuine replica of the Wilkes affair, and the populace was not slow to recognize it. The symbolic Wilkes number "45," already in use throughout the colonies, became almost as thick in New York as mulberries on a tree.

A grand jury picked for wealth and subserviency indicted MacDougall, but the only witness to his connection with the broadside died and the case collapsed. The Assembly then stepped in with a new arrest for libel, intending to convict him (it had already declared him guilty) at the bar of the Assembly. But his grand-jury indictment had not yet been dismissed and the House got into a Laocoön tangle over double jeopardy, self-incrimination and the extent of its jurisdiction. In a moderate concession, MacDougall was ordered to present written objections to the proceedings against him. He did so with such libertarian vigor that the angered Assembly voted him guilty of fresh libels, sentenced him to prison for an undefined period and ordered the sheriff not to honor any writ of habeas corpus. A judge issued one, but caved in when the sheriff defied it. MacDougall was released when the Assembly adjourned. He found his prison record no obstacle in rising to the rank of major general in the Continental Army.

To those who believe that the American Bill of Rights does not mean what it says, the arrest, trial and imprisonment of Alexander MacDougall furnish evidence that Blackstone correctly defined freedom of the press, that Mansfield was right on seditious libel, and that each house of Congress and of state legislatures has constitutional authority to commit its critics to prison without court action—as some of them actually have done in fits of temper. Yet what was this case, from beginning to end, except an object lesson in the tenets of tyranny which the Constitution of 1787 and the amendments of 1789 were designed to overthrow? The royal prosecutors, royalist grand jurors and corrupt assemblymen were not among the Sons of Liberty who stood by MacDougall and typified the mass force of public sentiment that some years later put the safeguards of liberty into the basic law of the new nation.

CHAPTER 17
Junius, Juries and Judges

In England the primary issue that underlay the Wilkes affair—political freedom in speech, press, assembly, petition and association—boiled up with fresh intensity in 1769. The new case broke at the very moment the outraged electors of Middlesex County were regaining their rights, and in the same year that the MacDougall prosecution aroused similar emotions in America. It was not this coincidence, however, that focused American attention upon the new blow struck against freedom of the press. The challenge in Mansfield's court was against the right of Englishmen to champion the American colonial cause.

The central figure, unseen in person, was the mighty "Junius," whose pen was a jabbing rapier in the ribs of the ministers of George the Third. In this instance, he fleshed the king himself more deeply than Wilkes had done, and did so deliberately. The vehicle was a published "Letter to the * * * * [king]," about which he made this private notation in advance: "I am now meditating a capital, and, I hope, a final piece." Giving a conventional nod to the libel laws by such abbreviations as "k——," "s———n," and "p———t," "Junius" told his *sovereign* that through lack of knowledge he had linked himself with a venal *Parliament* in pursuit of policies that conflicted with the sentiments of the English people and were driving the American colonists to rebellion. Addressing the king:

"They [the colonists] left their native land in search of freedom, and found it in a desert. Divided as they are, into a thousand forms of policy and religion, there is one point in which they all agree:

they equally detest the pageantry of a k——, and the supercilious hypocrisy of a bishop. It is not then from the alienated affections of Ireland or America that you can reasonably look for assistance; still less from the people of England, who are actually contending for their rights, and, in this great question, are parties against you. . . . The affection of your subjects may still be recovered. . . . Come forward to your people. . . . Tell them you have been fatally deceived."

Had King George acted on this advice there would have been no American Revolution, but king, ministers and judges were blind to destiny. Since nobody knew who "Junius" was, Attorney General de Grey moved against the publishers and sellers of the letter. No grand jury could be counted on to indict, so informations *ex officio* were issued against Henry Woodfall, who first published the letter in the *Public Advertiser* of December 19, 1769; against John Miller, who reprinted it that same month in his magazine, the *London Museum;* and against John Almon, the Middlesex bookseller, in whose shop an agent of the Crown purchased a copy of Miller's widely distributed magazine. Perversely, the man least implicated was the first to be put on trial before Lord Mansfield, either to obtain a Middlesex jury (usually more tractable than Londoners) or because of the hatred the Crown felt for Almon, the brainiest publisher linked with the political opposition.

The information charged that Almon, intending "to asperse, scandalize and vilify" the king and his ministers and lawmakers, and with the intent to stir up rebellion, "did publish, and did cause and procure to be published, a most wicked, scandalous, seditious, and malicious libel," etc. Conspicuously omitted from these accusatory adjectives was the basic charge that the libel was "false." Why was it omitted? asked Almon's chief counsel, the libertarian Serjeant-at-Law John Glynn. The answer came from Lord Mansfield to the jury. Such epithets were merely a matter of form, and it was true that "false" used to be among them, but "it was left out many years ago; and the meaning of leaving it out is, that it is totally immaterial in point of proof, true or false."

Omitted *"how many years ago?"* asked a footnote in the pamphletized report of the trial. As a prosecutor, it was pointed out, Mansfield himself had charged William Owen (1752) and Richard

Nutt (1754) with "wicked, *false*" libels, and he presided when Dr. Shebbeare was similarly accused in 1758. The earliest omission, said the notewriter, was only seven years back, in Mansfield's own court:

"It [false] was left out in the information against Mr. Wilkes, because all the crown lawyers know very well, that every word of that North-Briton was true. . . . But it seems to be omitted now, in conformity with, and perhaps the better to enforce that new and absurd doctrine, that any writing, true or false, against a minister, is a libel. It may be so, according to the imperial slavish civil law; but it is contradicted by natural reason, upon which is founded the mild and liberal law of England."

Almon was convicted, but sentence was delayed until November because of a juror's affidavit that he was misled by Mansfield's instruction (held back until it was too late to combat it by available testimony) that exposure of libelous material for sale was *prima facie* proof of a bookseller's guilt even though it was done by a servant without his knowledge or concurrence. By November such a storm had been raised about all the cases that Almon escaped with a trivial fine and security requirement.

In the meantime, the case of Henry Woodfall (the original publisher) went to a jury in London. Serjeant Glynn said he would approve a conviction if the jury found that Woodfall had in fact designed to abuse the king and stir up rebellion and commotion. If on the contrary the letter was published to give the people information made necessary by the temper of the times, both author and publisher should be considered as having acted the parts of good subjects and good citizens. Moreover, "the liberty of the press was immediately concerned," for if Woodfall was convicted, "the hands of every publisher would be tied" while ministerial scribblers would be left free to vilify the opposition.

Lord Mansfield instructed the jury that it had only to decide whether Woodfall published the "Junius" letter and whether "k——" meant "king," etc. They were not to decide whether the letter was malicious or seditious: "the Court were the only judges of that." He then picked up and adopted Blackstone's one-year-old definition of freedom of the press:

"As for the liberty of the press, I will tell you what that is; the liberty of the press is, that a man may print what he pleases without a licenser: so long as it remains so, the liberty of the press is not restrained. It is the same thing as in all other actions: a man may use his arm; but he must not strike his neighbor: a man may use his tongue, but he must not speak blasphemy."

The physiological analogy would have been truer if the Chief Justice had said: "A man may use his feet, but he must not put them on the ground." The jury returned a verdict: "Guilty of printing and publishing only." That produced a three-way wrangle (guilty, not guilty, or new trial), and as in the Almon case, judgment was postponed until November. At that time, after argument, all the judges decided that although the word "only" was not a finding of "no libel," the use of it put the jury's intentions in doubt. So there should be a new trial. There was none, because the Crown could not produce the copy of *The North Briton* on which the case was based. According to report, the foreman of the first jury pocketed and destroyed it.

The trial of John Miller followed a simpler course. The evidence was similar; the defense was the same; and Mansfield's instructions took everything away from the jury except the admitted fact of publication. But the defiant London jury returned a clear, undebatable verdict of "Not Guilty."

With these three cases out of the way, Serjeant Glynn moved in the House of Commons that a committee inquire into the administration of justice, "particularly in cases relating to the Liberty of the Press." It had been confidently affirmed, he said, that the judges laid down false law in order to mislead jurors in their verdicts, denying them the right to pass on the malice or innocence of the published article. This, he said, subverted the doctrine established in the *Case of the Seven Bishops*, wherein the defendants admitted everything except malicious intention and were acquitted with the approval of the judges.

Mansfield's chief defender, Sir Gilbert Elliot, looked back for precedents. He did "not choose to quote Scroggs or Jeffreys, though they cannot, in all cases, be accused of illegal decisions." Instead he would produce the best authority from the best of times—that of Chief Justice Raymond—who in the case of Richard Francklin held "the very opinion and the very language which are now represented to be illegal, and charged upon Lord Mansfield as crimes."

He quoted at length from Raymond's charge in the *Francklin Case*, derived from the Star Chamber by way of Scroggs, that it was immaterial whether the facts involved in a libel were true or false. In reply, Serjeant Glynn quoted from Defense Counsel Bootle's argument for Francklin, describing Raymond's doctrine as tending to "the utter suppression of the liberty of the press"; also Bootle's assertion to the jury that proof should be offered "that it is false, scandalous, and seditious, before you can find it by your verdict to be so."

Commented Glynn: "I think it is very plain from hence, that Lord Chief Justice Raymond's doctrine, about truth and falsehood, was not the known, received and acknowledged law of the land; that the counsel did not acquiesce to it; but on the contrary, did revolt at it. . . . Nor did the Chief Justice establish his doctrine by any instance or authority, though called upon by Mr. Bootle to do so. And shall this unfounded, unsupported, unreceived opinion, established neither on the principles of law or reason—shall it be supposed to have gained in the space of thirty or forty years, solidity and settlement enough to become itself a foundation?"

Glynn's position was bulwarked by John Dunning (later Baron Ashburton), a lawyer of the highest standing. He traced each element in the Mansfield libel doctrine to its source, showing what was derived from the case of John Udall, who "was condemned through the artifice of Baron Clarke"; how this was "greatly exceeded in cruelty and brutality" by Chief Justice Hyde in the case of Keach and his primers of prayer; how much was taken from Scroggs and Jeffreys in the case of Henry Carr, in which it was held that the printing of any news was illegal; how much from Justice Allibone's minority declaration in the case of the *Seven Bishops* "that no private man could take upon him to write concerning the government at all"; and what was derived from Richard Nutt's case, in which Chief Justice Lee declared "that if a servant carries a libel for his master, he certainly is answerable for what he does, though he cannot so much as read or write." Having shown Mansfield's indebtedness to bad judges, Dunning credited him with two instances of originality. He had lately dropped the word "false" from libel charges, making it easier to punish truthful criticism.

And nobody could deny him the "merit" of making *prima facie* evidence conclusive in a criminal case.[1]

The day after this onslaught upon him in the Commons, Lord Mansfield secured a special meeting of the House of Lords. At it the excited and expectant peers were merely told that he had left a paper with the clerk which they might read and copy. It was his November judgment in the Woodfall case. Lord Camden suggested that it be entered in the journals, to make it a topic of discussion and action, but Mansfield cried "No, no!" Thus, as a journalist remarked, his action had no more effect than if he had left the paper at the Calf's-head Club. However, Lord Camden read it and rose next day to tell the peers:

"I consider the paper delivered in by the noble lord on the wool-sack, as a challenge directed personally to me, and I accept of it; he has thrown down the glove, and I take it up. In direct contradiction to him, I maintain that his doctrine is not the law of England. I am ready to enter into the debate whenever the noble lord will fix a day for it. I desire, and insist, that it may be an early one."

Camden submitted six questions to the Chief Justice, who refused to answer them, saying that this was "taking him by surprise." Camden offered to meet him upon his own ground of law and pressed him to fix a day. Lord Mansfield "shuffled a good deal" but finally promised "that the matter should be discussed." The Duke of Richmond tried to nail that down by congratulating the House on the judge's pledge to debate. Lord Mansfield replied that he had only said he would give his own opinion. "And as to fixing a day, he said, No, I will not fix a day."

The mere asking of Camden's questions threatened to strip Lord Mansfield bare of wig and robe. They started with the query (to which the answer must have been yes) whether he meant to declare that the jury had no right by law to determine the innocence or criminality of the paper alleged to be a libel. (Its *power* to do so was not challenged.) The next question followed with devastating naturalness. If the jury should say they found the fact of publishing only, but that the paper was no libel, was that to be entered as a general finding of guilty? Camden had his opponent boxed. To answer Yes would destroy the jury system. To say No would lead only to a stalemate. Mansfield said nothing.

In the crown-controlled Commons, Serjeant Glynn's motion was defeated, 184 to 76, after the government closed the debate with a castigation of Glynn and other "Bill-of-Rights-men . . . that wretched junto, with their miserable faction." A few months later the fight against Mansfield's position was renewed in a bill to declare the rights and powers of juries in libel cases. Edmund Burke, then at the peak of his less-than-lifelong liberalism, stressed the Star Chamber's connection with the original restrictions on printing. "The press and its enemy," he said, "are nearly coeval." The alleged tendency of libels to produce riots and disorders was a mere technical device to give the Star Chamber jurisdiction through its allotted power to punish misdemeanors:

"After the Star Chamber was abolished in the 10th of Charles I, its authority indeed ceased, but its maxims subsisted and survived it. The spirit of the Star Chamber has transmigrated and lives again; and Westminster-hall was obliged to borrow from the Star Chamber for the same reasons as the Star Chamber had borrowed from the Roman Forum, because they had no law, statute, or tradition, of their own."

Burke was no believer in unabridged freedom of the press. His concern was with a fair trial, and even on that issue, his stentorian voice for liberty became at last a falsetto on the other side. During the twenty-one years it took to write jury reform into law, the glaring unfairness of libel procedures made them the principal objects of attack in courts and Parliament. Yet during this development there was a gradual spread of libertarian thought upon the basic rights of free human beings. One of the most efficient agents in this work was Dr. Joseph Towers, author of the multi-volume *British Biography*. In this forerunner of the *Dictionary of National Biography*, Towers threw the weight of his opinions into his work and exposed the fallacies of Mansfield's law and history of seditious libel. At the same time, under the leadership of the great lawyer Thomas Erskine, English liberals organized the Constitutional Society for systematic attack on the Mansfield doctrines. The two efforts coalesced in a pamphlet of the society made up of "right *versus* wrong" extracts from Towers' *Life of John Lilburne* and his *Life of Lord Chief Justice Jefferies*. These conflicting constructions of the rights of juries were followed (in the words of the Erskine pamphlet) by Towers' refutation of the position of "this infamous justice."

Since the sanctified Mansfield was following the same system as the disreputable Jeffreys, nobody could fail to recognize the target of the pamphlet. However, no libel was involved and judicial notice of it was incidental to another and more controversial publication. In September 1783 the Dean of St. Asaph, William Davies Shipley, was brought to trial at Wrexham, England, for seditious libel, with Erskine as defense counsel. The prosecution was a spite affair, pushed by a Tory sheriff who filed charges against the dean for reprinting *The Principles of Government, in a Dialogue between a Gentleman and a Farmer.* Anonymous, this was known to be written by the highly reputable Sir William Jones, supreme judge for Britain's Asiatic empire and brother-in-law of Dean Shipley.

The *Dialogue* was obviously seditious, by the standards of that day, being an argument for apportionment of the House of Commons according to population. A touch of good sense kept the Crown from acting but the sheriff forced a trial on his own initiative. Not liking the jury panel, he falsely charged the dean with trying to influence it by local circulation of the Erskine-Towers pamphlet. By this means the sheriff secured a change of venue to Shrewsbury and brought the case before Justice Buller, a young, strong-minded, ultrareactionary Mansfield disciple.

The charge of libel laid against the Dean of St. Asaph still stands as a classic in bald suppression of freedom of political discussion. The *Dialogue* opens with a request by the Gentleman that the Farmer sign a petition to reapportion Parliament, abolish rotten boroughs and extend suffrage. The Farmer replies:

"Why should humble men, like me, sign or set marks to petitions of this nature? It is better for us farmers to mind our husbandry and leave what we cannot comprehend to the king and parliament."

The Gentleman wins him over by comparing Parliament to a Farmers' Club and the king to a club president. The Farmer, thus brought to realize that he has the right and interest to take part in government, is stirred to indignation by what he hears: that six men out of seven in the kingdom have no votes; and the petition "has nothing for its object, but the restoration of you all to the right of chusing those lawmakers by whom your money or your lives may be taken from you." Says the Farmer:

"Give me your pen—I never wrote my name, ill as it may be written, with greater eagerness."

To publish a paper for such a purpose was highly criminal— indeed, twelve years later it was made high treason, punishable by death, to advocate reapportionment of Parliament. Here the libel was compounded by a dialogue reaffirming in rustic and therefore dangerous language the principle by which the "Glorious Revolution" drove James the Second from his throne:

"Gentleman. . . . Recollect your opinion about your club in the village, and tell me what ought to be the consequence, if the king alone were to insist on making laws, or on altering them at his will and pleasure.

"Farmer. He too must be expelled."

If any one sentence in that pamphlet was seditious or libelous, said Counsel Erskine to the jury, the Bill of Rights "was a seditious libel;—the Revolution was a wicked rebellion; the existing [Hanoverian] government is a traitorous conspiracy against the hereditary monarchy of England." Erskine laid heavy emphasis upon the acquittal of the Seven Bishops (whose trial for libel in 1688 triggered that year's Revolution) by a jury to whom the judges submitted both law and fact. This brought a reply from the crown counsel that the *Case of the Seven Bishops* was "a special miracle wrought for the safety of the nation"—a miracle wrought by jurymen "inspired by God to perjure themselves in the administration of justice."

Justice Buller needed no miracle to persuade him that times had changed. Adhering to Mansfield, he instructed the jury that it had nothing to decide except whether the Dean of St. Asaph published the pamphlet and whether the words "king" and "parliament" applied to those of England. The reluctant jury found him "Guilty of publishing only"—a verdict later modified to read: "Guilty of publishing, but whether a libel or not the jury do not find." Erskine's appeal to the full Court for a new trial was described by Charles James Fox as "the finest argument in the English language," but Mansfield and his colleagues gave complete support to Justice Buller. Erskine then cited a fatal defect in the indictment and the pseudo conviction was set aside.

Although the debate between Erskine and Mansfield centered on the function of the jury, they clashed no less sharply on the nature of freedom of the press. Erskine, as the interest of his client required, tacitly accepted the legality of restraints on the press and linked its freedom with the unrestricted right of the jury to determine innocence or guilt. If judges took away that right, and put the weight and majesty of the crown into the scale against an obscure individual, the freedom of the press was at an end:

"For how can it be said that the press is free because every thing may be published without a previous license, if the publisher of the most meritorious work . . . may be prosecuted by information of the king's Attorney General, without the consent of the grand jury —may be convicted by the petty jury, on the mere fact of publishing . . . and must then depend [for stay of judgment] upon judges, who may be the supporters of the very administration whose measures are questioned by the defendant, and who must therefore either give judgment against him or against themselves?"

To this Lord Mansfield replied in Blackstonian terms:

"The *liberty of the press* consists in printing without any previous license, subject to the consequences of law. The *licentiousness* of the press is *Pandora's* box, the source of every evil. Miserable is the condition of individuals, dangerous is the condition of the state, if there is no certain law, or, which is the same thing, no certain administration of law to protect individuals, or to guard the state."

The Chief Justice reinforced his position by recalling an unpublished case involving *The Craftsman* (Richard Francklin's first trial) in which Chief Justice Raymond left the facts to the jury, the law to the judge, and the jury thus instructed acquitted the defendant. Said Lord Mansfield:

"I recollect it from a famous, witty and ingenious ballad that was made at the time by Mr. Pulteney. . . . It will show you . . . [that] the leaders of the popular party in those days . . . had not an idea of assuming that the jury had a right to determine upon a question of law. . . . The stanza I allude to is this:

"Sir Philip well knows,
That his innuendos
Will serve him no longer

In verse or in prose;
For twelve honest men have decided the cause,
Who are judges of fact, though not judges of laws."

Thomas Erskine was too young to know from personal memory that Mansfield misquoted the ballad, but he was given an ancient printed copy of it in time to use it with devastating effect when the case of the Dean of St. Asaph shifted from the courtroom to the halls of Parliament. Speaking in the House of Commons on May 20, 1791, in support of Fox's Libel Bill, Erskine recited the same stanza with its correct concluding couplet:

"For twelve honest men have determin'd the cause,
Who are judges alike of the facts, and the laws."[2]

Next to the case of the *Seven Bishops*, which put an end to England's Stuart dynasty, the trial of the Dean of St. Asaph produced the most dramatic results of any libel trial in English history. Taken up by press and public, it led in eight years to passage of Fox's Libel Act of 1792, a declaratory law in which Parliament asserted that juries had always possessed the powers that Raymond and Mansfield denied them. That was the limit of the legislative influence of the case, for in that same year the Wars of the French Revolution began and the French National Assembly deposed its dull-witted Bourbon monarch, Louis the Sixteenth. A part of the British populace applauded that action and doubled its outcries against crown control of the House of Commons by "rotten boroughs," purchase of seats and bribery. The British upper classes took fright and England spiraled downward into an antilibertarian panic that gripped the country for more than a quarter of a century. Freedom of speech, press and assembly lost all that they had gained except a jury power that was reduced to a nullity by hysterical fear of French communism.

CHAPTER 18
The Current of Freedom

While the atrocious prosecution of the Dean of St. Asaph focused British reform activities on the perversion of the jury system, it also stirred public indignation against a political practice that made Parliament the object of criticism. The influence of this was deeply felt in the United States, although, as national independence put an end to the deprivations of liberty produced by colonial status, and no home-grown tyranny developed, it was a matter of apprehension for the future rather than revolt against current practices. This gave different directions to public discussion on the two sides of the Atlantic.

Englishmen found themselves in the shadow of prison for repeating, with application to current times, the political sentiments that were part of the nation's glorious history. They turned for relief to emancipation of the jury system from crown control, thus in effect relying on themselves for mutual protection against their own government. American citizens beheld this as an appalling but distant phenomenon, which for them required measures of prevention, not of relief. And as the imbecility of the Confederation forced them to reluctant creation of a new and far stronger national government, their thoughts were on the definition of rights and the restraint of governmental power to interfere with them, not on laws and judicial rules to regulate an authorized restraint of political liberty.

To an American at the time of Dean Shipley's trial, it was unthinkable that publication of a dialogue against the rotten borough system should be construable into a crime, warranting a prison sentence. Such a principle would have put almost every adult American citizen in jeopardy. The framers of the Constitution of 1787 sought to guard against that road to oligarchy and avenue of corruption by requiring that members of the House of Representatives be apportioned according to population. Two years later, the republican form of government was further strengthened by the First Amendment, with its mandate that "Congress shall make no law . . . abridging the freedom of speech, or of the press." Is it conceivable that this prohibition was designed to ratify the Mansfield Doctrine of seditious libel, thus leaving all Americans open to such an ordeal as that of the Dean of St. Asaph?

It cannot be said that imprisonment for criticizing malapportionment was made impossible in the United States by the constitutional requirement of equal representation. Congress and state legislatures afterwards made that a dead letter by failure to enforce it. The legislative department of government, state and federal, first tolerated and then protected a rotten borough system that was steadily growing worse until the Supreme Court stepped in and upset it in 1964. Had the evil been allowed to progress, while freedom of speech and press were subject to abridgment by the "balancing test," public endeavors to equalize representation could have become a crime, as they were in England.

For the distinctive feature of the "rotten borough" system is that the longer it goes without correction, the worse it becomes, and the worse it becomes, the harder it is to correct it through the ordinary channels of legislation. That is because the beneficiaries of unfair apportionment are both the officeholders favored by it and the favored constituents who elect them. As the system worsens, the beneficiaries have increasing power to retain it and a greater interest in doing so. Reform came to England forty-nine years after the trial of the Dean of St. Asaph, when Parliament yielded to the imminent threat of armed revolution. Reform came to the United States through the untrammeled action of an independent judiciary, upholding a Constitution enacted by the people. The ensuing attempt in Congress to override that action and shackle the Court furnished a measure of the danger.

The broad turn given to libertarian thought in England during the 1770s—with immediate repercussions in America—was the combined product of the Wilkes and "Junius" affairs, and the rising protest of Protestant Dissenters against the inadequacy of "religious toleration." The Act of Toleration that was passed after the Revolution of 1688 did not repeal the statutes making dissent from the Church of England a crime, but it freed Protestant Dissenters from the penalties that continued to be imposed on Roman Catholics. They were compelled, however, to subscribe to the Anglican Articles of Faith whose rejection was the core of their dissent. Their sole weapon was the right of petition, which they employed with a vigor that threatened to stir the established church from its lethargic willingness to let the existing law die of inanition while keeping it on the books.

In America shortly before and after the Revolution, freedom of religion was acutely controversial in some regions, especially Virginia, where dissenting preachers were treated as harshly as they had been in England half a century earlier. But, except in its relationship to religion, the issue of freedom of speech and press tended everywhere to be in abstract terms. This was not unnatural. Except during the upsetting strain of the Revolutionary War, there were no considerable abridgments of those freedoms, consequently no feeling of crisis that would lead to sharp definition of the issue. That very fact left an open field for the quiet influence of British writers who went beyond the furious battle over the jury system and resumed the discussion of fundamental rights begun sixty years earlier in the "Cato" letters of Trenchard and Gordon. Indeed, the actual *Letters of Cato* never ceased to extend their transatlantic influence. Clinton Rossiter, after combing the agencies of public expression prior to the American Revolution, put his conclusion in these words:

"No one can spend any time in the newspapers, library inventories, and pamphlets of colonial America without realizing that *Cato's Letters* rather than Locke's *Civil Government* was the most popular, quotable, esteemed source of political ideas in the colonial period."

And nobody can read "Cato" without concluding that Trenchard and Gordon regarded complete freedom of speech and press as inseparable from public liberty. If they were living in the United States, where anybody can verbally challenge the doctrine of seditious libel without running afoul of it, they would be the most absolute sort of absolutists in support of freedom of opinion. What reason is there to think that eighteenth-century Americans who idolized "Cato" were less devoted to liberty than their idol?

The state of mind thus reflected in the press ran counter to the opinion of many prominent colonial lawyers (a perennial phenomenon) yet was recognized even in their challenges of it. In 1753 the New York *Independent Reflector*, organ of Lawyer William Livingston and his associates, said that freedom of the press was abridged when a rival newspaper refused to print a reply to one of its articles. But Livingston made this general comment on a publisher's rights and duties:

"When on the other hand, he prostitutes his art by the publication of any thing injurious to his country, it is criminal . . . high treason against the state. The usual alarm rung in such cases, the common cry of an attack upon the LIBERTY OF THE PRESS, is groundless and trifling. The Press neither has, nor can have such a liberty, and whenever it is assumed, the printer should be punished."

Criminal it was, and subject to punishment, under the prevailing law of England. But Livingston wrote as a lawyer bound by and sympathetic toward those judicial decrees. His own words show that he was not expressing the thought of the American public. He was *combatting the common cry*. And what was the common cry except the voice of the people, claiming a freedom that had been choked off by judges and lawyers following Star Chamber precepts engrafted onto the common law?

Americans had another illuminating choice two decades later, when a 1773 pamphlet collection brought the conflicting views of "Candor" and "Father of Candor" across the water. The former has never been identified, but Horace Walpole named "Father of Candor," by repute, as "one Dunning, a lawyer lately started up, who makes a great noise." If that is correct, the libertarian reply came from John Dunning (the later Lord Ashburton), who had just begun a meteoric rise to the top level of the English bar by his defense of the English East India Company against Dutch competitors.[1] "Candor," writing in the London *Public Advertiser* in 1764, gave the tone of ministerial approval to the rigorous rules of libel laid down by Chief Justices Raymond, Lee and Mansfield. He then exclaimed:

"In God's name, what business have private men to write or to speak about public matters? Such kind of liberty leads to all sorts of license and obloquy. . . . [The prevailing law of libel] seems to me to be really an excellent device for keeping the scribbling race from meddling with political questions, at least from ever drawing their pens a second time upon such subjects."

To which "Father of Candor" replied in what became popularly known as "the celebrated 'Letter to Mr. Almon' '':

"I will venture to prophecy that if the reigning notions concerning libels be pushed a little farther, no man will dare to open his mouth, much less to use his pen, against the worst administration that can take place, however much it may behoove the people to be apprised of the condition they are likely to be in. In short, I do not see what can be the issue of such law, but an universal acquiescence to any man or measures, that is, a downright passive obedience."

Which of these two positions is more consonant with government by and for the people? Which drew the sympathy of most Americans when the two letters were brought to America in 1773? Which came nearer to representing the thoughts of the men who drafted the First Amendment? There was, to be sure, a broad vacant area between the two positions, but "Candor" truly reflected the repressive spirit and purpose of the English libel law: a determination to put down by court action all effective peaceful efforts to alter government or change administrations. "Father of Candor" did not go the whole distance in affirming that freedom should be unabridged. He believed that a "wilfully false" publication deserved punishment, but wanted the question of intent left entirely to the jury. *Willful* falsehood being virtually unprovable on a factual basis, that was close to a complete exemption except when jurors shared the passion or prejudice of prosecutors and judges. This they seldom did except in cases involving religion. Yet even in journalism the middle position had its avowed advocates in colonial America. It was stated with pontifical assurance in the Boston *Gazette* of March 9, 1767:

"Man, in a state of nature, has undoubtedly a right to speak and act without control. In a state of civil society, that right is limited by the law. Political liberty consists in freedom of speech and action, so far as the laws of a community will permit, and no farther; all beyond is criminal, and tends to the destruction of liberty itself."

Among those who apply the "balancing test" to the First Amendment, such an assertion made in 1767 is taken as an indication of what the framers of that amendment had in mind when they wrote that "Congress shall make no law" abridging the freedom of speech or of the press. If that is correct, the meaning of the First Amendment will not be changed if it is reworded in accordance with the opinion thus expressed. It will then read as follows: "Freedom of speech and of the press shall extend as far as the acts of Congress shall permit; all beyond is criminal." The absurdity is manifest. Yet that statement by the Boston *Gazette* accurately describes the law of England as it stood in 1767. It is only by assuming American adoption of the law of England that the First Amendment is reduced from a constitutional mandate to an optionally observed or disregarded counsel of moderation.

Religious opinions, even more harshly restricted than political discussion, were defended in England during the Wilkes and "Junius" upheavals with a latitude that came to embrace speech and press. Here too the libertarian views of laymen, conflicting with the turgid thinking of Mansfield and Blackstone, made an immediate impress in America. In 1775 twenty-four-year-old James Madison, shifting his book-buying from London to Philadelphia, made repeated purchases through the agency of his friend William Bradford, son of the Philadelphia publisher and bookseller. Among the publications asked for were Joseph Priestley's 1768 treatise on government and Philip Furneaux's 1772 *Essay on Toleration,* written to support a petition of dissenting ministers to Parliament. The request for these works leaves little doubt that he possessed the far better known writings of Priestley and Furneaux assailing Blackstone for his benighted treatment of religious dissent in his newly published *Commentaries.* The Furneaux and Priestley pamphlets (including Blackstone's reply to Priestley), published separately in England, were combined in three different editions printed in Philadelphia in 1772 and 1773.[2]

The feeling inspired by the Furneaux-Priestley writings is evident in the sub-title given by one of the Philadelphia publishers, placing genuine religious liberty *"above the reach of all petty Tyrants, who attempt to lord it over the Human Mind."* The suggestion in that title of universal resistance to mental overlords[3] was carried out in Furneaux's pamphlet, written in the form of letters to Blackstone. The magistrate, he remarked, may encourage general principles of religion and morality, but he goes beyond his province if he undertakes to restrain and punish those who embrace and profess what he dislikes *on account of the supposed ill tendency of their principles*. The province of the magistrate, asserted Furneaux, is confined to *those actions* which affect the peace and good order of society. In every step taken beyond that limit, he is in danger of trampling on the rights of conscience:

"For, if the magistrate be possessed of a power to restrain and punish any principles relating to religion because of their tendency, and he be the judge of that tendency . . . religious liberty is entirely at an end; or, which is the same thing, is under the control, and at the mercy of the magistrate."

But, Furneaux went on, if the line of magisterial power be drawn between the *mere tendency* of religious principles, "and those overt acts which affect the public peace and order . . . the boundaries between civil power and liberty, in religious matters, are clearly marked and determined." Even though the tendency of religious principles be *unfavorable* to society, it is not *prejudicial,* Furneaux contended, "till it issues in some overt acts against the public peace and order." The magistrate "may punish the *overt acts,* but not the *tendency,* which is not actually hurtful." Although Furneaux did not specifically apply his reasoning to freedom of speech and press, he carried the distinction between tendencies and overt acts broadly into "cases of a civil nature":

"It would not be difficult to mention customs and manners, as well as principles, which have a tendency unfavourable to society; and which, nevertheless, cannot be restrained by penal laws, except with the total destruction of civil liberty. And here, the magistrate must be contented with pointing his penal laws against the overt acts resulting from them. . . . Punishing a man for the *tendency* of his principles is punishing him *before* he is guilty for fear he *should* be guilty."

Returning later to the interrelation of personal freedoms, Furneaux pointed to the truth that "religious and *civil* liberty have a reciprocal influence in producing and supporting one another." This became one of Madison's deepest convictions, but he made his approach from the opposite angle. Furneaux saw freedom of speech and press as a support to religious liberty. Madison, observing the passions engendered by religious strife, made freedom of religion the *sine qua non* in whose absence all other freedoms would be subverted.

The importance of Furneaux's arguments, powerful in themselves, was vastly increased by being directed squarely against Blackstone. There was no easier task than to rip that commentator to shreds for his treatment of religious dissent as a genuine crime (even Mansfield was against him on that), and toleration as an ill-advised concession. Exposure of his Dark-Ages stand on that subject made him more vulnerable where his fallacious position was more damaging—on freedom of the press—but the basic attack on that score was yet to come.

While the Furneaux pamphlets were making their impress on American thought, other dissenting ministers in England carried forward his arguments in equally broad terms. The dangers that might result from full freedom, wrote the Reverend Ebenezer Ratcliffe in 1773, were "no great price to pay for truth and the privilege of expressing our sentiments without controul." Government had no right to interfere with the public expression "of sentiments and opinions, till they have produced criminal overt acts, evidently injurious to society." In the same year the Reverend Andrew Kippis voiced the same conviction: that only overt acts "criminally injurious to the public," not the mere tendency to produce them, ought to bring the force of the laws into play. "Speculations and fancies about the tendencies of opinions may be carried on to the entire destruction of liberty."

Blackstone was challenged more fundamentally by the greatest of English law reformers, Jeremy Bentham, whose *Fragment on*

Government appeared in 1776. Bentham's great fame was slow in coming, but his tremendous assault on Blackstone could not escape the attention of American students of law and government. "In regard to a government that is *free,* and one that is *despotic,*" he asked rhetorically, "wherein is it then that the difference consists?" The distinction turned, was his answer, not on the bounds of power in each, but on factors in the possession and exercise of power. Those he specified bore a surprising relevance to the basic features of the American Constitution drafted eleven years later, and to the First Amendment. Government was free or despotic depending on:

1. The manner in which the supreme power is *distributed* among the sharers of it. (Separation and balance of powers.)

2. The source from which their titles to power are successively derived. (Sovereignty in the people or in a monarch.)

3. "Frequent and easy *changes* of condition between govern*ors* and govern*ed.*" (Popular elections and short terms.)

4. The right of the subject to know and canvass the reasons of "every act of power that is exerted over him."

5. "The *liberty of the press:* or the security with which every man, be he of the one class or the other, may make known his complaints and remonstrances to the whole community."

6. "The *liberty of public association;* or the security with which malcontents may communicate their sentiments, concert their plans, and practice every mode of opposition short of actual revolt, before the executive power can be legally justified in disturbing them."

Bentham's fifth item was a full resurrection of Trenchard and Gordon, without their protective nod to the libel laws, while public association was a phenomenon just then coming into being.

Bentham conceded that freedom of the press and association, protected up to the point of actual revolt, would make "the road to revolution, if a revolution be necessary . . . more free and easy . . . and upon less provocation," under a free government than under an absolute one. Granting this, until the point of revolt is reached, "resistance is as much too soon under one of them as under the other." This concession was hardly necessary, for in any country with a heritage of freedom, such as England or the United States, the rare danger of revolt is made greater by restricting personal freedom than through its agency. England's two successful revolutions, each of which ended the reign of a Stuart king, were both generated by despotic suppressions of liberty. The American Declaration of Independence is a chronicle of liberties denied by king, courts and Parliament. The American Civil War resulted from the weakness and indecision of the national government in coping with overt acts of openly planned rebellion. It was not brought on by public gatherings or expressions of opinion. Any attempt at suppression of that would have precipitated the evil it was designed to prevent.

The refutation of Blackstone was carried on by Joseph Towers, this time directly on the issue of freedom of the press. Americans were introduced to his 1784 *Observations on the Rights and Duties of Jurors, in Trials for Libel,* in a laudatory review of it in the *Monthly Review* of London. Even those in America who saw only this widely read magazine, learned that Towers was challenging the historical accuracy, the reasoning and the impartiality of Blackstone.

The *Monthly Review* devoted much space to Towers' proof that judges had perverted constitutional law, precedent and justice in the rules under which they conducted trials for criminal libel. But when his pamphlet reached America it was found that he had challenged the whole concept of seditious libel. Referring to a *Letter concerning Libels, Warrants, the Seizure of Papers,* etc., (Baron Ashburton's letter to Almon) published in 1765 during the Wilkes excitement and well known to Americans, Towers wrote:

"It is observed by an acute writer, who has been repeatedly quoted, that 'the whole doctrine of libels, and the criminal mode of prosecuting them by information, grew with that accursed court the Star-Chamber. All the learning intruded upon us *de libellis famosis,* was borrowed at once, or rather translated, from that slavish imperial law, usually denominated the civil law. You will find nothing of it in our books before the time of queen Elizabeth and sir Edward Coke.' "

No less pertinent to the First Amendment was a related and equally notable publication of the Wilkes epoch, *Another Letter to Mr. Almon, in matter of Libel.* From this Towers quoted:

"The notion of pursuing a libeller in a criminal way at all, is alien from the nature of a free constitution. Our ancient law knew of none but a civil remedy, by special action on the case for damages incurred, to be assessed by a jury of his fellows. There was no such thing as a public libel known to the law. It was in order to gratify some of the great men, in the weak reign of Richard the Second, that some acts of parliament were passed to give actions for false tales, news, and slander of peers, or certain great officers of state, which are now termed *de scandalis magnatum.*"[4]

Turning to the doctrine, "so little consonant to common sense," that it is immaterial whether a libel is true or false, Towers ran it back to its origin in *Want's Case.* "Thus it appears, that this maxim originated in the infamous court of Star-chamber, and being retailed from one law reporter or compiler to another, we are at length gravely and confidently informed, that this is a part of the law of England." He noted that in the twenty-three folio volumes of Viner's *General Abridgment of Law and Equity,* only seven pages were devoted to libel cases and these in great part from the Star Chamber:

"In short, almost the whole of what is now called the law of libels, is the mere fabrication of the professors and officers of the law, and was never ratified by the parliament, or the people of England, nor any part of the ancient common law of the land."

Towers' choice of the words "almost the whole," coupled with his failure to mention Sir Edward Coke as one of the fabricators, indicates that he had no answer to the two cases cited by Coke to prove common-law descent of the libel law—the fourteenth-century cases of Adam of Ravensworth and John of Northampton. But as has been shown in Chapter 9, *ante,* those two cases were the grossest fabrications in the entire fictitious history of seditious libel.

It is indeed remarkable that against the mighty but fallacious authority of Coke on libel, laymen and a few lawyers should have come so close to sensing the truth—that seditious libel had no common-law ancestry whatever. Two other writers, a layman and a barrister, came as close as Towers did to this fact. Capel Lofft, whose slight figure and powerful pen caused Boswell to call him "the little David of the popular spirit," placed no limit on the severity with which private individuals might censure the conduct and measures of public men. Not even "the most artful and daring libeller," he averred in his 1785 essay, "can shake a Government worthy of public confidence." "It would be no surprise," he continued, "if the very title of Libel were not to be found" in the code of a free people who shared political rights and had full freedom to investigate the operations of their government. That was no description of England, past or of his time, though it could have been a hopeful forward glance at the new United States of America. Yet it truly applied to the freedom of the ancient common law from the pernicious doctrine encrusted upon it by a Tudor-Stuart invention.

Manasseh Dawes, a member of the London bar, struck even more directly at the concept of criminal libel. Sedition, he declared, could never be committed by words, but only by "violent act." Towers, Lofft and Dawes were writing of what should be in England, not of what was. As practical reformers, they worked to relieve the worst excesses of the law rather than make a vain attempt to get rid of it entirely. To some commentators, the efforts of these men to improve existing conditions furnished circumstantial evidence that American libertarians intended to sanction the law of seditious libel when they produced the mandate that Congress shall make *no law* "abridging the freedom of speech, or of the press."

Let us assume that not only Towers, Lofft and Dawes, but Trenchard and Gordon, Serjeant Glynn, Lord Ashburton, Thomas Erskine and Jeremy Bentham all had the desire to establish absolute freedom of speech and press, for both their own time and the future. It would not be sufficient to revoke the existing laws of libel. England would first have to do what John Lilburne and the Levellers wanted: establish a supreme written constitution based on the sovereignty of the people. In this constitution there would have to be a mandate, appropriately worded: "Parliament shall make no law abridging the freedom of speech, or of the press, *nor shall these freedoms be abridged by the common law or by royal prerogative.*"

In other words, to achieve complete and lasting freedom from the doctrine of seditious libel, England would have to do exactly what was done in the United States through the instrumentality of the written Constitution and its First Amendment, but with a

supplement to prevent circumvention through the common law
or the Crown. Such a supplement would have been out of place
in the First Amendment, since it would have implied that Congress
had a common-law jurisdiction in other respects. Yet, as will be
shown hereafter, the absence of it opened the First Amendment to
damaging assaults whose effects were still being felt after a hundred
and fifty years.

Surveying the turbulent period from 1720 to 1789, from the
publication of the *Letters of Cato* to the drafting of the first ten
amendments to the new American Constitution, it is clearly evident
that two great currents were in motion in the Anglo-Saxon world.
One was a powerful forward motion, setting mind and body free
from the political, religious and monarchic invasions of the basic
rights of humankind. The other was a backward motion—the eddy-
ing currents of resistance to the advance of society. Eddies can have
tremendous undercutting power, and so it was with those in
England. The champions of freedom were sucked down into the
whirlpools of seditious libel and parliamentary privilege. In
America the stream was smoother, the eddies weaker. The current
of freedom ran easily around obstructive islands. The Constitution
of 1787 quickened the flow, in which the amendments of 1789 were
gleaming libertarian cascades. But the river, as often happens below
a waterfall, ran into dark canyons, devious channels and stagnant
lagoons; and many Americans have mistaken the backwater for
the flowing stream.

PART II
The Bill of Rights and Its Foreground

CHAPTER 19
Congress Shall Make No Law

The first ten amendments were added to the Constitution of the United States in a period of uneasy calm. The Americans who were most apprehensive over that untried document, because its guarantees of liberty did not go far enough, included a great many who wanted to cut down its grants of legislative and executive power. But the amendments were drafted and submitted to the nation by men who supported both the substantive powers of the new government and the protection of civil rights and liberties. If some of them had little zest for the amendments they voted for, they at least recognized the force of the popular demand and joined in satisfying it. The major task of Madison and his congressional associates was to place the amending of the Constitution high on the House of Representatives agenda, ahead of important bills that were to fill out the structure of government. With that achieved, the amendments submitted by Madison were taken up, debated and perfected with scarce a single move to weaken them. No such move was successful except the Senate's defeat of the article that would have made the guarantees of the First Amendment and trial by jury binding on the individual states.

One result of this was a harmony in debate that left the meaning of the amendments almost untouched by controversial discussion. That had no significance where basic meanings did not invite dispute, as in jury-trial provisions, self-incrimination, excessive bail, cruel and unusual punishment, general warrants, unreasonable search and seizure, compensation for property taken for public use. There were ambiguities in wording which debate might have cleared up. Does the *right to counsel* cover only the rich man's right to hire a lawyer, or does it require that the ignorant and poor shall have the same protection, even at public expense? Does the guarantee against being put twice in jeopardy for the same offense give protection against duplicate prosecutions in federal and state courts? How comprehensive is the "establishment of religion" that is forbidden? The amendments contain one inescapable ambiguity. "Due process of law" defies definition to cover all conceivable denials of it, present and future. But the framers assuredly would have been surprised if told that the separate specification of various procedural rights served to exclude them from due process as a general requirement. Yet so our highest court began holding after the Civil War, in making comparisons of "due process" in the Fifth and Fourteenth Amendments, and so a majority was holding no less tenaciously throughout the first half of the twentieth century.

Strangely enough, the greatest uncertainty about the meaning of the amendments has developed where the wording seems most clear and definite: in the command that "Congress shall make no law . . . abridging the freedom of speech, or of the press." These were the protections most vociferously demanded by the people. Nobody in Congress challenged them and they were approved without discussion.

This absence of clarifying debate has been interpreted in two ways. To one set of judges and like-minded commentators, it has meant that freedom of speech and press cannot be abridged, *except* —and what a mammoth exception this is—except by punishing such speech and writings as were punishable under the common law of England. For, say they, the framers had read the assertion of Blackstone that freedom of the press meant only freedom from *prior restraint,* and that if any man offended the law by what he said or wrote, he was to be punished for his temerity. To offend the "law," in this respect, was to offend the Crown or the judges. For hundreds of years, Englishmen had been fined, whipped, pilloried, imprisoned and had their ears cut off for speech and writings offensive to government or society. Surely, say those who believe that "NO abridgment" means "abridgment only when, on balance, it is thought necessary," the framers of the First Amendment could not have intended to wipe out abridgments of speech and press so thoroughly and respectably established. If they had such an intention they would have not used so ambiguous a term as "Congress shall MAKE NO LAW." They would have said "no law WHATSOEVER."

To be sure, those who construe the Constitution in this fashion do not use such plain words to uphold the power of Congress to abridge the freedoms it is forbidden to abridge. But that is exactly what it comes to. What the framers should have done, perhaps, was add a second section to the First Amendment, saying: "The preceding section means what it says." But that might require a third section with the same wording, and perhaps a fourth and a fifth, to prove that "no" means "no."

To those who believe that the First Amendment *does* mean what it says, the sponsors of it were men who were well aware of the way their British cousins had been fined, whipped, pilloried, jailed and mutilated for daring to say what they thought about their government. They saw signs of the same system developing in America, both in the attitude of some judges and in the tyrannical conduct of some colonial assemblies. They wrote an amendment designed to stop it and plainly worded to achieve that result.

One of the arguments against a literal reading of the free-press guarantee is that the silence of Madison on the meaning of the clause, when he submitted it to the House, is evidence that he did not intend to prohibit prosecutions for writings that the courts or Congress would regard as exceeding proper bounds. If he did intend to prohibit them, it is argued, surely he would have said so in presenting the amendment. But surely he would not! The amendment required a two-thirds majority in each house. If there were members (as assuredly there were) who agreed with the Blackstone-Mansfield concept, the sponsor of the amendment would not risk stirring them to intransigence by needlessly raising that issue. The Blackstonians, however few or numerous they might be, were being brought into line by the pressure of public opinion—a nationwide upsurge stirred by fear of a repetition, under the new federal government, of the atrocious spectacle of repression in England. If anybody was to put forward the Blackstone definition, in the face of words conflicting with it, the Blackstonians were the ones to do it. If the Blackstone definition was intended, the natural course would have been to write it into the amendment. But in this instance, the clause on freedom of the press was actually stiffened in committee. As Madison presented the amendments, religion and press were in separate articles, the one on religion concluding with the words: "nor shall the full and equal rights of conscience be in any manner, or on any pretext, abridged." This article followed:

"The people shall not be deprived of their right to speak, to write, or to publish their sentiments, and the freedom of the press, as one of the great bulwarks of liberty, shall be inviolable."

This article offered double-barreled protection to freedom of the press. "Shall not be *deprived*" was at least a ban on prior restraint. That gave a broader meaning to the ensuing words, "and the freedom of the press, as one of the great bulwarks of liberty, shall be inviolable." Distinct, as this clause was, from the guarantee of freedom to write and publish, it was meaningless unless it protected what was written and published.

Madison's two articles were blended into one by a committee of which he was the leading member. In the clause forbidding abridgment of freedom of religion, the redundant words of emphasis, "in any manner, or on any pretext," were dropped without altering the mandate. In the clause on the press, "inviolable" had its meaning made more definite by the substitute words that went into the Constitution, "Congress shall make no law." Thus an original wording that repudiated the Blackstone concept of freedom of the press was made still stronger, if words mean what they say.

In all the two months' proceedings, not one voice was lifted to assert that the amendment embodied the British law of seditious libel. If that had been the intention, silently understood by all, would not at least one person have stood up, to point out that the amendment as worded was a mandate to the contrary? No corresponding burden lay on the advocates of a strong guarantee. No ambiguity in the English language made it necessary for them to say to the House: "The words 'Congress shall make no law' mean that Congress shall make no law." But those who contend that "no law" means "no unreasonable law" cite the following from Madison to Jefferson (October 17, 1788) concerning the proper articles of a bill of rights:

"I am inclined to think that *absolute* restrictions in cases that are doubtful, or where emergencies may overrule them, ought to be avoided. The restrictions however strongly marked on paper will never be regarded when opposed to the decided sense of the public, and after repeated violations in extraordinary cases they will lose even their ordinary efficacy."

Does that mean that Madison regarded the guarantees of the First Amendment as doubtful cases or of a sort to be legitimately overruled by emergencies? His words can be given that meaning only when taken out of context. His own explanation of them in the next two sentences showed that he had something very different in mind:

"Should a rebellion or insurrection alarm the people as well as the government, and a suspension of the Habeas Corpus be dictated by the alarm, no written prohibitions on earth would prevent the measure. Should an army in time of peace be gradually established in our neighborhood by Britain or Spain, declarations on paper would have as little effect in preventing a standing force for the public safety."

That he was not placing the great personal liberties among the cases requiring less than absolute protection is further indicated by an earlier passage in that letter, written before the amendments were drafted. Explaining why, although always in favor of a bill of rights, he was not anxious for amendments except to satisfy the anxiety of others, Madison gave this as one of his reasons:

"Because there is great reason to fear that a positive declaration of some of the most essential rights could not be obtained in the requisite latitude. I am sure that the rights of conscience in partic-ular, if submitted to public definition would be narrowed much more than they are likely ever to be by an assumed power."

That fear was made groundless a few months later, by his own drafting of the public definition. Had he specified another of the "most essential rights" whose narrowing he feared, undoubtedly it would have been freedom of the press. These were the rights concerning which he said in his speech proposing the ten amend-ments: "The freedom of the press and rights of conscience, those choicest privileges of the people, are unguarded in the British Constitution." It is inconceivable that a person who called the

British constitution completely void of any protection to freedom of the press could have looked to that constitution for the meaning of his own prohibition of its abridgment.

But, what about congressmen who did not share Madison's desire for absolute protection of freedom of the press? Would they have accepted a federal amendment knowing that the protection it gave was unqualified? They might indeed. Their first wish was to still the clamor against the Constitution and terminate the agitation for another convention to revise it. Nothing would do more to achieve this than a total ban on federal interference with the press. Easing the way to such action, for those who had no wish to establish total freedom, was the fact that the First Amendment placed no limitation on state action.

In 1789 five of the thirteen states had no constitutional guarantee of freedom of the press. Six had maxims of the "ought" or "ought not" variety, sound in principle but weak in effect. Two declared this freedom to be inviolate.

In all thirteen states the common law of England had been incorporated into state law. In the absence of a constitutional provision or statute to the contrary, adoption of the common law carried with it the power of prosecution for libel. Consider then the situation of a man like Fisher Ames, who scoffed at the Bill of Rights yet helped Madison secure powerful guarantees. His state of Massachusetts had this "ought not" admonition in its 1780 constitution:

"The liberty of the press is essential to the security of freedom in a state; it ought not, therefore, to be restricted in this commonwealth."

The same constitution decreed that all laws theretofore adopted, used and approved in the colony or state should remain in force, "such parts only excepted as are repugnant to the rights and liberties contained in this constitution." One need not be a 110 per cent libertarian to conclude that the common law of libel was repugnant to the declaration that freedom of the press "ought not" to be restricted. But to expect such a ruling from the hardshelled Federalists who governed Massachusetts would have been about as fanciful as to expect Chief Justice Taney to rule that a slave who entered free territory became free. So Fisher Ames, who regarded Berkshire farmers as horned cattle, could cheerfully help Madison forbid *Congress* to make *any law* abridging the freedom of the press, knowing full well that his own state retained its power to proclaim freedom in principle and deny it in practice.

The effect of state adoption of the common law had been brought out, though not specifically explained, in the debates over ratification of the Constitution. In the Maryland convention a committee drafted a set of amendments to be recommended to Congress, but they were not acted on. One of them provided "That the freedom of the press be inviolably preserved." To this the committee added the explanatory comment: "In prosecutions in the federal courts for libels, the constitutional preservation of this great and fundamental right may prove invaluable." Maryland's constitution, adopted in 1776, contained those same words on freedom of the press and also declared the common law to be effective in the state. The effect was the same as saying that freedom of the press should be inviolate except as abridged by adoption of the common law. The Maryland committee apparently assumed that the common law would be enforceable in the federal courts and would have the same effect there, regarding libel, as in the states.

The same reliance on the common law for state action underlay the remarks of James Wilson in the Pennsylvania ratifying convention, but he denied the existence of any corresponding federal power. Replying to a query about danger to freedom of the press, he said there was no need of a constitutional guarantee on the subject because "there is given to the general government no power whatsoever concerning it; and no law, in pursuance of the Constitution, can possibly be enacted to destroy that liberty." Wilson defined liberty of the press in Blackstonian terms—no antecedent restraint upon it but every author was liable to prosecution for libel. The United States had no jurisdiction in this field, but suppose it did have: "Is the person prosecuted in a worse situation under the general government, even if it had the power to make laws on this subject, than he is at present under the state government?"

Wilson's position was logical as far as it reflected current practices. Pennsylvania, on gaining independence, tacitly continued the common law, by a constitutional reference to "the penal laws as heretofore used." So libel laws remained in force in spite of a declaration that "the freedom of the press ought not to be restrained." Wilson's assertion that the federal government had "no power whatsoever" in this field was explained by him *to bar federal trials for libel,* although state trials were not barred.

In the North Carolina convention, Samuel Iredell took a still narrower view of federal power. A member expressed fear that Congress might make it misprision of treason to write against the most arbitrary proceedings. "Where," asked Iredell, "is the power given to them to do this? They have power to define and punish piracies and felonies committed on the high seas, and offences against the law of nations. They have no power to define any other crimes whatever." Iredell overstated his case. He took no account of the large area of federal criminal law relating to commerce, taxation, mails, public lands and other enumerated objects of federal power. But that did not invalidate his argument that the jurisdiction was limited to their enumerated powers.

Here were positive declarations by two men, both of whom became justices of the United States Supreme Court, that Congress had no power whatever to restrict freedom of the press by prosecutions for seditious libel. Considering their very different later opinions, one might suspect that they had mental reservations concerning federal jurisdiction under the common law. However, their earlier attitude can be explained without presupposing deception.

North Carolina's 1776 constitution declared "That the freedom of the press is one of the great bulwarks of liberty, and therefore ought never to be restrained." But the article on freedom of religion ended with this proviso, "That nothing herein contained shall be construed to exempt preachers of treasonable or seditious discourses, from legal trial and punishment." Clearly, then, the British law of seditious libel was not regarded as overridden by the "ought not" axiom about restraint of the press. In contrast, both Iredell and Wilson categorically denied that any corresponding power would be possessed by Congress under the new federal Constitution, even in the absence of a Bill of Rights. Silence on the subject, Iredell told the convention, excluded such a power as effectively as "the strongest negative clause that could be framed."

No person with that honest belief could object to a strong negative. In 1789, under the spur of public demand, Congress proceeded to place in the Constitution a prohibition that the conservatives had said was already in it, though not expressed in words. Conservatives and liberals joined in drafting and proposing for adoption "the strongest negative clause that could be framed," forbidding Congress to make any laws abridging the freedom of the press. In the discussions leading to that action, the most conservative supporters of the Constitution and the most apprehensive of its opponents made an approach to common ground. One group held that there *was not,* the other that there *must not be,* any power in the new national government to abridge the freedom of the press. To summarize, here are the reasons why there was no revolt, protest, denial or debate, when the amendment to effect that end was given a wording which denied the power to prosecute for seditious libel:

1. Because those who feared a free press expected the individual states to continue to abridge its freedom under the common law or statutes, unchecked by the weaker axioms in state constitutions.

2. Because of widespread fear among both "Whigs" and "Tories," of a power to punish political opinion, by a government just coming into existence, alien to American experience and of unknown powers and disposition.

3. Because no political conditions were present or visibly prospective, in 1789, to make any class of men feel the need of a congressional weapon against the free expression of political opinion.

Here was a combination of circumstances that might not recur in a century, making it possible to place guarantees of freedom in the federal Constitution that went far beyond the views that would have prevailed in a period of political storm and strife. That happy condition did not last. Although the skies were calm in 1789, storm clouds were not far below the horizon, some blowing from the French Revolution, others brought up by domestic faction. By 1792, the differences between Democratic Republicans and Federalists, between Jeffersonians and Hamiltonians, had become broad in public policy and sharp in acrimony. The rival parties had their vitriolic publicists, whose zestful scurrilities stirred and reflected new political passions but did not produce a resort to legal action. Madison, writing anonymously for Philip Freneau's *National Gazette*, touched close to the subject of seditious libel and gave a clear indication of his own position. Under the title "Who are the best Keepers of the People's Liberties?" he wrote a dialogue between "Republican" and "anti-Republican" (Federalist). The former found the best keeper in the people themselves. The latter scorned the people as stupid, suspicious and licentious. They broke off their heated discussion with this final exchange:

"Anti-Republican. . . . I denounce you to the government as an accomplice of atheism and anarchy.

"Republican. And I forbear to denounce you to the people, though a blasphemer of their rights and an idolator of tyranny.— Liberty disdains to persecute."

Had it been "Republican" who said "I denounce you to the government," that would have been equivalent to saying that the First Amendment permitted trials for seditious libel. For obviously, "Republican" spoke for Madison and his party. Had he even said, in that role, "Liberty disdains to *prosecute*," instead of *persecute*, it would have implied the *power* to prosecute, although rejecting the exercise of it. But in putting the threat of prosecution into the mouth of "an idolator of tyranny," Madison rejected the idea of such a power. He rejected it again in the contrast between denunciation to the government and to the people—the former an appeal to power, the latter to public opinion—and doubled the rejection by contrasting the tyrannous threat to *prose*cute with the libertarian refusal to *perse*cute. The article is a revelation of what the author of the First Amendment believed it to mean, not an afterthought drawn from him by the threat or reality of repressive legislation. It is a revealing primer of the opposing views of the idolator of tyranny and the champion of liberty.

During the six months before this dialogue was published, the three-year-old French Revolution precipitated France and England into twenty years of warfare. The Revolution itself began its swift conversion from an uprising for political liberty into a savage and bloody conflict of social classes. Thousands of royalists were slain in the streets of Paris, the Tuileries was sacked, the National Assembly abolished the monarchy. Americans, who had unitedly hailed the original uprising, now divided almost along the lines of Federalists and Republicans. Those who had expressed their enthusiasm by forming Jacobin Societies generally stood by the French Revolution, though lamenting its excesses. Federalists, already fearful of what the "filthy democrats" would do if they ousted "the wise, the good, the rich" (of Fisher Ames) from control of the federal government, found their fears rising to terror at the continued sympathy of the American "Jacobins" for the decidedly dissimilar bearers of that name in France. But for two more years there was not a hint of abridging the right of the people to hold and express what opinions they pleased.

Then came a change. In the summer of 1794, some hundreds of farmers in western Pennsylvania came together in armed resistance to the collection of a federal excise on whisky and burned a collector's house. In that mountainous region, where corn could not be transported across lofty ridges, whisky was the farmer's only money. The excise therefore was a straight income tax, doubled by the fees paid to the distiller for turning corn into whisky. It resulted in close to a 50 cent tax on what was commonly a $600 income. An equal burden, heaped on everybody in the United States, would have defeated or hanged every congressman who voted for it. The Whisky Rebellion, however, had virtually no support outside of its participants and few sympathizers except their neighbors. Men of all political factions were among the 15,000 militiamen who, with President Washington at their head, marched to save the country some time after Albert Gallatin, Henry Hugh Brackenridge and Congressmen Smilie and Findley had persuaded the farmers to go home. Two farmers were tried for treason under a strained construction of "two witnesses to the same overt act," sentenced to death and pardoned.

In relation to civil liberties, the most serious features of the Whisky Rebellion were the fictitious treatment of frontier lawlessness as a treasonable uprising against the government, and the political maneuvers resulting from this attitude. Secretary of the Treasury Alexander Hamilton, who induced the President to send the overwhelming military force and who managed the operations of it, wrote from his Pennsylvania camp that the constitutional guarantees of civil liberty should give way to "a peace process of outlawry." He offered this argument to Rufus King for canceling constitutional rights:

"The best objects of punishment will fly, and they ought to be compelled by outlawry to abandon their property, homes, and the United States."

Hamilton was not talking about scuttling the Constitution merely to cope with rifle-toting farmers. "The political putrefaction of Pennsylvania," he told King, "is greater than I had any idea of." A week later, writing to Washington, he said the military arm was to make summary seizure "of all who are worth the trouble," on the common-law principle "that every man may of right apprehend a Traitor." Brackenridge had been "the worst of all scoundrels"— a remark that pointed to Gallatin, Smilie and Findley as co-targets of wrath.

The next Federalist maneuver was directed against the Democratic Societies"—the newly sown grass roots of Jeffersonian Democracy—then sprouting over the United States. "The game was," as Madison accurately described the maneuver, "to connect the Democratic Societies with the odium of the insurrection—to connect the Republicans [Democrats] in Congress with those societies—to put the President ostensibly at the head of the other party, in opposition to both [the insurrection and the societies]," and thus hold the North to its political illusions while trying to spread them to the South.

Madison was referring to Washington's annual message to Congress in November 1794, written by Hamilton, in which he blamed the Pennsylvania uprising on "the arts of delusion" practiced by "certain self-created societies." "Self-created" was a dirty word in 1794. It denoted a coming together of common people without the sanction of either the government or their social superiors. Alert to his cue, Representative Fitzsimons of Philadelphia moved to insert the following in a pending resolution condemning the insurrection:

"As part of this subject, we cannot withhold our reprobation of the self-created societies, which have risen up in some parts of the Union, misrepresenting the conduct of the government, and disturbing the operation of the laws, and which, by deceiving and inflaming the ignorant and the weak, may naturally be supposed to have stimulated and urged the insurrection."

Madison took the lead against the motion. It was an attempt to have Congress interpose in the reserved rights of the people. "He conceived it to be a sound principle that an action innocent in the eye of the law could not be the object of censure to a legislative body. . . . Opinions are not the objects of legislation." Congress, he asserted, could properly investigate the conduct of persons in the public service, but start criticizing people for abuse of their reserved rights and how far would it go? "It may extend to the liberty of speech and of the press."

Here was an assertion, not merely that Congress had no power to pass laws abridging freedom of speech or press, but that the Constitution outlawed any congressional criticism of private persons that might have the effect of limiting their freedom to speak and write. He also saw in the wording of this resolution a violation of a closely related constitutional protection:

"It is in vain to say that this indiscriminate censure is no punishment. If it falls on classes, or individuals, it will be a severe punishment. He wished it to be considered how extremely guarded the Constitution was in respect to cases not within its limits. . . . Is not this proposition, if voted, a vote of attainder?"

As Madison construed the constitutional mandate that "No bill of attainder . . . shall be passed," the clause is more than a denial to Congress of the power to enact formal laws subjecting particular persons *to punishment without a judicial trial.* It is a denial of power *to use any legislative process* to subject individuals to punishment, either singly or as identifiable groups, *by the infliction of infamy* through criticism of conduct that does not violate the law. The House of Representatives could and did unanimously denounce those, whoever they might be, who resisted the federal excise law. But for the House to say that the Democratic Societies (unnamed but identifiable) "may naturally be supposed to have stimulated and urged the insurrection"—that would be an infliction of infamy by legislative action: a violation of the ban on bills of attainder. Madison made it perfectly clear that what Congress cannot do, no part of Congress can do. "If it be admitted," he told the House, "that the law cannot animadvert on a particular case, neither can we do it." And they did not. The Fitzsimons resolution, ruinously amended by the tie-breaking vote of the Speaker, went down to overwhelming defeat and its author went down also in the next election.

This was not the full extent to which the fundamentals of political freedom were clarified in the debate over the Democratic Societies. Madison capped his speech by laying down a maxim that set the United States apart from the monarchic England of that day and from all the royal governments of continental Europe:

"If we advert to the nature of Republican Government we shall find that the censorial power is in the people over the Government, and not in the Government over the people."

That truth goes to the very heart of free government and personal freedom. By its nature, hereditary monarchy needs to control, direct and restrain political opinion in order to ensure its continuance. (This does not apply, of course, where royalty has shrunk to a social showpiece in a political democracy.) By its nature a self-governing republic cannot be truly self-governing where the government is vested with power to punish its critics, and thus may silence them by the threat of punishment. Such a republic may preserve the forms of representative democracy, but the reality—either chronically or at recurring periods—will be enforced conformity, passive acquiescence, or revolt.

No truth was better known than this to the framers of the Constitution of 1787 and its first ten amendments. Yet no truth has been more severely challenged in the country governed by that Constitution, first and most acutely in the decade of its adoption; again and more dangerously (because recurring illness tends to become incurable) in the century of turbulence that was ushered in by the First World War.

CHAPTER 20
A Time Lag in Madness

"If we advert to the nature of republican government, we shall find that the censorial power is in the people over the government, and not in the government over the people."

Madison's protesting words to Congress cannot be too often repeated. Had that thought been voiced five years earlier, it would have been hailed as an immortal truth by at least some of the men whose deeds and words rejected it in 1794. Seldom in the world's history, within so short a time, have events so deeply shaken the mental bearings of men of good will, or so quickly and decisively turned the half-believers in freedom into total disbelievers. Under the combined impact of the French Revolution and the broadening base of American politics, men's faculties gave way and destructive emotions took over. The most powerful of these was fear—fear of the distant, the strange and the unknown; fear also of one's neighbors when their ways showed a pattern of change.

What happened in the United States in the 1790s was no unique phenomenon. It was imitative of England, representing a time lag of a few years in the development of public policies to match the quicker alteration of thoughts and emotions. In each country there was a divided reaction to events at home and across the water: across the English Channel for one people, across the Atlantic Ocean for the other. The British people and the American people divided in similar fashion, each country producing a faction friendly to the French Revolution; each country a faction and a government hostile to it. The domestic division followed the same lines as the international one, with similar objectives and reactions. In England the party out of power sought the right to vote and to be represented in Parliament through fair elections. In the United States the party out of power sought office through the exercise of existing political rights. In both countries the sympathy felt for France, by the party out of power, was for the French people striving to throw off the chains of absolute monarchy. And in both countries the party in power either mistook that sympathy, or pretended to mistake it, for disloyalty and sedition. In both countries—but here the American time lag was greater—the domestic political cleavage produced savage repression of the freedoms of speech and of the press.

Standing as a virtual symbol of the decline of liberty, first in England and later in the United States, was the sedition trial, in 1792, of Thomas Paine, the British subject and Philadelphia resident whose pamphlet *Common Sense* touched a spark to the American Revolution. Returning to Europe in 1787 for business reasons, Paine projected himself into the early polemics of the French Revolution as a devotee of freedom, American style. When English Whigs, most notably Edmund Burke, turned violently against the French Revolution and against the English liberties they once had defended, Paine fired upon them with a verbal broadside. The first part of his *Rights of Man*, published in 1791 and dedicated to George Washington, escaped libel action because its appeal was intellectual. A year later came Part Two, saying much the same thing in phrases that everybody could understand, and the sales ran into the hundreds of thousands. The British government launched a nationwide campaign of slanderous vituperation against Paine, and struck through the courts with all its power.

Indicted for publishing the second part of *The Rights of Man*, and warned of a plot to murder him, Paine escaped to France. He was tried *in absentia* on December 18, 1792, in a country whose state of mind was described in these words by T. E. May:

"None of the causes that precipitated the revolution in France were in existence here. . . . We had a free constitution, of which Englishmen were proud. . . . Yet their very loyalty [to the king] was now adverse to the public liberties. It showed itself in dread and hatred of democracy. Repression and severity were popular, and sure of cordial support. The influential classes, more alarmed than

the government, eagerly fomented the prevailing spirit of reaction. . . . The democratic spirit of the people was betraying itself;
and must be crushed out, in the cause of order."

Two weeks before Paine's trial, the government deliberately
built up anti-French hysteria by calling out the militia to cope with
a spirit of tumult and disorder (totally nonexistent) inspired by
"evil-disposed persons" acting in concert with persons in foreign
parts. Five days before the trial the king informed Parliament—
called in special session—that they were faced with a domestic and
foreign conspiracy to destroy the constitution. The ensuing panic
was not allayed by the assertion of minority leader Charles James
Fox that these allegations were "an intolerable calumny upon the
people of Great Britain."

In such an atmosphere the trial of Thomas Paine for publishing
The Rights of Man opened. Written to defend the French Revolution in its early libertarian phase, the force of the book lay in its
contrast of British monarchism and American republicanism. First
and highest place in the 11,000-word information *ex officio* was
given to the following passage:

"All hereditary government is in its nature tyranny. An
heritable crown, or an heritable throne, or by what other fanciful
name such things may be called, have no other significant explanation than that mankind are heritable property. To inherit a government, is to inherit the people, as if they were flocks and herds!"

Different principles, Paine said, ruled the independent American people, whose 1787 constitutional convention he described.
His account of the framing and ratification of the basic charter by
delegates of the people concluded with this comparison, so seditious
that it froze the blood of bishops and judges, between the American
action and England's post-Stuart changes of dynasty:

"For this purpose they did not, like a cabal of courtiers, send
for a Dutch Stadtholder [William III] or a German Elector [George
I]; but they referred the whole matter to the sense and interest of
the country."

To link Paine with the fictitious Anglo-French insurrectionary
plot and offset his praise of American self-government, Attorney
General Archibald MacDonald brought American politics into the
trial. He quoted at length from "a very able writer" in America,

who, he had reason to believe, held second place in the executive branch of government; "that is, he is second in the exercise of the regal part of the government of the country." The author of the quoted articles, "Publicola," was actually 23-year-old John Quincy Adams, writing in defense of his father, but nearly all Americans shared the British belief that the tract was the work of Vice President John Adams himself. The Attorney General emphasized this passage:

"His [Paine's] intention appears evidently to be, to convince the people of Great Britain, that they have neither liberty nor a constitution; that their only possible means to produce those blessings to themselves is to topple down headlong their present government, and follow implicitly the example of the French."

The Adams onslaught upon Paine was actually a hardly veiled attack on Secretary of State Thomas Jefferson, whose letter to a Philadelphia publisher praising *The Rights of Man* was used without permission as the foreword to the American edition of Part One. The stinger in it was Jefferson's expression of pleasure "that something is to be publicly said against the political heresies which have sprung up among us." Americans easily recognized this as a reference to John Adams' *Discourses of Davila,* wrongly regarded as monarchic by a large part of the public. As intended, the Adams denunciation of Paine as a French-type revolutionary agitator pinned the same tag on Jefferson, and thus brought the ensuing sedition trial of Paine into the stream of American politics. Metaphorically it was a trial of Jefferson before an English jury.

What Paine had in mind, in his appeal to the British public, was hardly of jacobinical origin. The central theme of *The Rights of Man,* placed before the jury, was a blend of John Locke, Algernon Sidney, the American Declaration of Independence, and the final clause of the Fifth Amendment. Wrote Paine:

"The end of all political associations is, the preservation of the rights of man, which rights are liberty, property, and security; that the nation is the source of all sovereignty derived from it; the right of property being secured and inviolable, no one ought to be deprived of it, except in cases of evident public necessity, legally ascertained, and on condition of a previous just indemnity."

These, said Defense Counsel Thomas Erskine, were undoubtedly the rights of man—"the rights for which all governments are established—and the only rights Mr. Paine contends for; but which he thinks, no matter whether right or wrong, are better to be secured by a republican constitution than by the forms of the English government."

Erskine with Paine's absentee approval conceded (as he had to, English law being what it was) that his client should be convicted if his intent was to stir revolution. But the charge of sedition, he said, was "notoriously paper and packthread," because it had been built up by enlarging the sense or ordinary construction of words. On that account the case involved a question of the deepest importance to all, "the nature and extent of the liberty of the English press."

Erskine argued for hours. He showed that Paine had said no more than was said by Locke, and by Edmund Burke in his liberal days. If Englishmen had not possessed an inalienable right to criticize their government, to awaken the people to errors and abuses in it (he asked in a blend of fact, fancy and satire), how could that government "have passed on from stage to stage, through reformation and revolution, so as to have arrived from barbarism to such a pitch of happiness and perfection, that the Attorney-General considers it as profanation to touch it farther, or to look for any future amendment?" In every age, said Erskine, the government had considered itself perfect and untouchable, "but a free press has examined and detected its errors, and the people have from time to time reformed them."

This was pure fancy, for the press had not a vestige of freedom—not even from licensing—when the seditious libel trial of the Seven Bishops touched off the Glorious Revolution. Erskine struck much closer to the truth, but he was in effect contrasting American freedom with British repression when he told the jury:

"Other liberties are held *under* governments, but the liberty of opinion keeps GOVERNMENTS THEMSELVES in due subjection to their duties. This has produced the martyrdom of truth in every age; and the world has been only purged from ignorance with the innocent blood of those who have enlightened it."

The words of Erskine furnished a foretaste of those of Madison two years later—that *by the nature of republican government* the people have the power to censure it. In England the censorial power was in the government over the people, not only in the power of prosecution but in the use of propaganda to aid the prosecuting arm. Erskine had felt the force of this. Under the banners of freedom of the press, he said early in his argument, "I stand up to defend Thomas Paine. But how, alas! shall this task be accomplished? . . . Has not this cause been prejudged through a thousand channels? . . . Has not the public mind been excited, by crying down the very phrase and idea of the Rights of Man?" The lawyer's final words to the jury were a prophecy of the verdict:

"I can reason with the people of England but I cannot fight against the thunder of authority."

In this instance the people of England (the Paine jurors) did not wait for the thunder to roll. When the Attorney General rose to reply to Erskine, the jury foreman forestalled him with these unprecedented words to Lord Chief Justice Kenyon:

"My lord, I am authorized by the jury to inform the Attorney General, that a reply is not necessary for them, unless the Attorney General wishes to make it, or your lordship. Mr. Attorney General sat down, and the jury gave in their verdict, GUILTY."

In England, following Paine's conviction, there was a quick but limited upsurge of libertarian public opinion, not in a hopeless effort to modify the law of libel, but to rescue England from government by vigilante committees operating through the courts or as a substitute for them. A month and a day after Paine's conviction, nineteen hundred "Friends of the Liberty of the Press" met at the Crown and Anchor Tavern in London and adopted resolutions drafted by Thomas Erskine. "A sudden alarm," they said, "has been spread through the kingdom by the Ministers of the Crown, of imminent danger to the Constitution, and to all order and government. The nation has been represented to be fermenting into sedition and insurrection," and though no insurrectionists had been discovered, it was not surprising that large classes gave credence to the charges and that some used lawless methods of appealing to the law.

"We assemble [said the resolution] . . . to enter our solemn protest against the propriety or justice of those Associations, which by the contagion of example are spreading fast over England, supported by the subscriptions of opulent men for the avowed purpose of *suppressing and prosecuting writings*: more especially when accompanied with rewards to Informers."

Such rewards, it was charged, had been extended even to procure the punishment of opinions delivered in the privacy of family life, but the worst of it was the intrusion of these vigilantes into the work of the courts. What was become of trial by jury when the panels "come reeking from vestry-rooms, where they have been listening to harangues" against those whom they are to condemn by their verdicts? If justice was thus tainted in the superior courts, what must it be in the lesser but co-ordinate ones "where the judges are the very gentlemen who lead those Associations in every county and city in the kingdom, and where the jurors are either their tenants and dependents, or their neighbors," looking up to them as friends and protectors? "It would be infinitely more manly, and less injurious to the accused, to condemn him at once without a hearing, than to mock him with the empty forms of the British Constitution, when the substance and effect of it are destroyed."

A few hardy individuals raised their voices against the whole idea behind the law of libel. Saying that under the pretense of sedition "the most alarming attempts are made to wrest the liberty of the press out of our hands," Baptist Minister Robert Hall asserted that the world's experience furnished no cause of violent alarm at the greatest liberty of discussion. "This dread of certain opinions on account of their tendency," he wrote, "has been the copious offspring of all those religious wars and persecutions, which are the disgrace and calamity of modern times." The government might properly proceed "against *overt acts* of sedition and disorder, [but] to suppress *mere opinions* by any other method than reasoning and argument is the height of tyranny."

Dr. Joseph Towers, the biographer-historian, took the same stand as Hall. In "a country professedly free," opinions were to be combatted by reason and argument, not by force and violence. To the claim of vigilantes that books were being published to subvert the government, Towers replied that "the law, or what is called the law, respecting libels," would take care of that. In that wording, Towers rejected the legitimacy of the law of libel, even when citing it as an argument against lawless vigilantism.

Had the British libertarians confined themselves to abstract invocations of freedom, they might have escaped with light libel penalties or none at all. But when they added such monumental heresies as equal representation in Parliament, universal suffrage and annual elections, the government and upper classes were thrown into a frenzy of fear. Trials multiplied in numbers and severity.

A young Scotch lawyer, Thomas Muir, tried at Edinburgh for advocating parliamentary reform, heard his highest judge, Lord Braxfield, tell the twelve jurors (every one of them an enrolled vigilante) that "the landed interest . . . alone has a right to be represented; as for the rabble, who have nothing but personal property, what hold has the nation of them?" (Fox denounced that language in Parliament.) He heard a second judge say, after the verdict of "Guilty," that the applause of the courtroom crowd at Muir's speech defending himself was a proper measure of the crime and of the punishment they were giving him—fourteen years transportation to the penal colony in Australia. Muir heard a third judge lament that "punishment adequate to the crime of sedition . . . could not be found in our law, *now that torture is happily abolished.*"

The defect in severity was soon remedied. The British government in 1795 suspended the writ of habeas corpus, seized the papers and arrested the leaders of societies devoted to parliamentary reform. They made pretended discoveries of insurrectionary plots (the most ludicrous was the Pop-Gun Plot based on a cache of children's toys) and put twelve outstanding libertarians on trial for high treason. In this instance the government's misconduct was so atrocious that jurors rebelled, and Thomas Erskine secured acquittals in the memorable cases of Thomas Hardy and John Horne Tooke.

But the national shift of sentiment increased the official madness, especially after 150,000 persons, many of them jobless and hungry because of industrial depression, assembled to petition the king for parliamentary reform, the removal of his ministers, and an end to the war with France. Parliament replied with laws that stayed on the books for a score of years, making it high treason to attempt, by writing, to compel a change of government measures or councils. Under that law men could be hanged for publicly advocating an end to the "rotten borough" system. No public meeting of more than fifty persons could be held, to petition the king, except in the presence of a magistrate with authority to arrest everybody present. Death was the penalty for resisting him. That was England in the middle 1790s—a veritable madhouse of terrorization by men who were themselves beset with irrational fears.

The impact of all this upon America was tremendous, but it ran in two directions, that of protest and that of emulation, and the latter was the more portentous. Accounts of Thomas Muir's trial reached the United States in pamphlets, newspapers and parliamentary debates. The intensity of the reaction may be judged by the fitting out of a private expedition to rescue Muir and a fellow martyr, the Reverend Thomas Fyshe Palmer, from the Australian penal colony at Botany Bay. It failed, but eight years later—two years after Palmer died of dysentery—an American sea captain exhumed his remains and brought them to this country for burial in a Boston cemetery. It was a symbol as distinct as "The Martyr's Monument" erected on Calton Hill, Edinburgh, just fifty years after these men laid down their lives (for it amounted to that) to obtain in Great Britain the rights of free speech and equal representation that were written into the Constitution of the United States.

But while one party in America reacted in this fashion, a more powerful one shared the general panic of the British public and aped its actions. In the earliest stage of emulation the Federalist attack upon the Democratic Societies met defeat, but the general attitude of Congress threw a shadow into the future as dark and prophetic as the one cast in Great Britain by the trials of the three Thomases—Paine, Muir and Palmer. Six years after the verdict against Thomas Paine by an English jury, three years after the British Parliament deepened seditious libel into treason, American Tories followed that same pattern and wrote into law the infamous Sedition Act of 1798. Here was the contest whose somber outline was visible in Madison's 1792 dialogue between Republican and anti-Republican: between the "champions of liberty" and the "idolators of tyranny." It was a contest in which the champions of liberty lost every battle except the one that decided the conflict.

CHAPTER 21
Idolators of Tyranny

The earliest judicial blow against the First Amendment was struck by Justice Thomas Iredell of the United States Supreme Court in his lesser capacity as circuit judge. Addressing the federal grand jury in Richmond, Virginia, in the spring of 1797, he delivered a philippic against members of Congress who wrote circular letters to their constituents assailing the Adams Administration for its belligerent attitude toward France. Nine years earlier, when asked whether the new Constitution might not allow Congress to punish its critics, this same Thomas Iredell had assured the North Carolina ratifying convention that such a thing was impossible. Congress was barred from such action by the silence of the Constitution as completely "as they could be by the strongest negative clause that could be framed." Now times had changed and he changed with them.

In 1797, six years after ratification of the First Amendment broke the silence of the Constitution by forbidding Congress to pass any law abridging freedom of the press, Iredell assured the grand jurors that no law was needed. The federal courts could send these members of Congress to prison for seditious libel under the unwritten common law brought from England. The Federalist grand jurors, thus incited, returned a presentment against Representative Samuel J. Cabell of the Albemarle-Orange district, whose constituents included Jefferson and Madison. The congressman was accused of "endeavoring at a time of real national danger to disseminate unfounded calumnies against the happy government of the United States . . . and to increase or produce a foreign influence, ruinous to the peace, happiness and independence of these United States."

Vice President Jefferson, at his Virginia home, drafted a petition of protest to the General Assembly. Approved by Madison with a few verbal changes, it was signed throughout the district and adopted by the House of Delegates. The presentment was denounced as "a violation of the fundamental principles of representation . . . an usurpation of power . . . and a subjection of a natural right of speaking and writing freely."

This legislative blast caused Attorney General Charles Lee to drop the intended trial, for which he was eager, but did not check the flooding current of repression. Emotions had been mounting in America ever since 1793, when "Citizen" Genet, the minister of the French revolutionary republic, misgauged the meaning of pro-French sentiment and tried to rally public opinion to a repudiation of President Washington's policy of neutrality toward the European war. On paper, the United States was still bound to France by the 1778 treaty of mutual assistance, made with Louis XVI; under the altered circumstances not even the upholders of the treaty construed it to require military aid to Robespierre and company. However, the adopted policy of neutrality and trade left the United States subject to assaults on maritime commerce by both belligerents. John Jay's treaty with England, ratified in 1795, pledged the United States not to go to the help of France and came close to making the country a wartime commercial satellite of England. France, governed now by the conservative, almost antirevolutionary. Directory, broke diplomatic relations with the United States. Continental triumphs of French armies created deep alarm. President Adams (easily overheated) indulged in superpatriotic jingoism, while more purposeful Federalist leaders began to drum up a war spirit to overcome the political drift toward democracy. The Federalist press was filled with vituperation of Jefferson during and after the election of 1796, by which, under the constitutional rule then in force, his defeat for the Presidency made him Vice President.

It was in this atmosphere that Justice Iredell made his abortive attempt to prosecute Congressman Cabell. President Adams, not at heart a war man, sent commissioners to negotiate a settlement with France. Their report of demands for bribe money by French agents (the XYZ affair) revealed by the President on April 3, 1798, started Adams on a new round of jingoism and gave immense stimulus to the real war party, headed by Hamilton and Secretary of State Timothy Pickering. Genuine patriotism swept the country and soon mounted to hysteria. Congress lost its senses. It was a perfect reproduction, partly imitative and partly the result of similar provocations and motivations, of the still-dominant British pattern of panic, repression, and resistance to rule by the people.

First notable product in Congress was the Alien Act of 1798, designed to drive Frenchmen and English radicals (like Dr. Priestley) out of the country. As an aid to expulsion, the House bill made it a crime for any person to harbor a suspected alien. Not only, protested Representative Albert Gallatin, was such legislation "contrary to every principle of justice and reason," but it violated the constitutional provision that no person should be deprived of life, liberty, or property, without due process of law. Since no offense was defined, said Gallatin, the whole of it might as well be made to read: "The President of the United States shall have the power to remove, restrict, or confine the alien enemies and citizens whom he may consider as suspected persons."

Some senators may have been listening to the House debate, for a couple of weeks later the Senate passed a bill that almost embodied Gallatin's words and enlarged the net to take in alien friends. Without a solitary safeguard, the President was empowered to expel "all such aliens as he shall judge dangerous to the peace and safety of the United States." Again Gallatin protested that this denied due process, to which Representative William Gordon retorted that "due process" was to be given men accused of crime, but here no crime was charged. Aliens were to be removed on suspicion, not as criminals, so they were not entitled to due process. On that monstrous perversion of the Constitution the bill was enacted into law, passing the House by a six-vote margin. Suspected aliens, without waiting for the President to expel them, said good-by to the country to which they had fled to escape a kindred tyranny.

Even before the debate on aliens there were indications that a sedition act was to follow. The Federalist press likened Jefferson, Madison and Gallatin to a traitorous American Directory in the

service of France. President Adams exhorted the nation in a flood
of responses to addresses of support. His replies were a potpourri
of patriotic appeal, denunciation of France and aliens, and castigation of citizens who failed to fall in with administration policies.
Vice President Jefferson observed the movement as it developed
around him in Philadelphia and wrote prophetically to Madison
on April 26, 1798:

"One of the war party, in a fit of unguarded passion, declared
sometime ago they would pass a citizen [naturalization] bill, an
alien bill, and a sedition bill. . . . There is now only wanting, to
accomplish the whole declaration before mentioned, a sedition
bill, which we shall certainly soon see proposed. The object of that,
is the suppression of the Whig presses. Bache's [Philadelphia
Aurora] has been particularly named."

A week later Jefferson found evidence that President Adams
was putting himself behind the movement, and sensed also that
part of the purpose was to break the line of communication between
Republican congressmen and the public—to do by statute what
Judge Iredell had been blocked from doing under the common law
of England. On May 3 Jefferson wrote to Madison about the President's response, published in Fenno's *Gazette of the United States*,
to a New Jersey message of support. Said the Vice President:

"Nor is it France alone, but his own fellow-citizens, against
whom his threats are uttered. In Fenno, of yesterday, you will see
one, wherein he says to the address from Newark, 'the delusions
and misrepresentations which have misled so many citizens, must
be discountenanced by authority as well as by the citizens at large.' "

It was evident to Jefferson that they were referring to letters
from Republican members of Congress which their constituents
"have been in the habit of seeking after and publishing; while those
sent by the Tory part of the House to their constituents, are ten
times more numerous and replete with the most atrocious falsehoods and calumnies." But what new law they would pass on the
subject, to curb the writing of letters by congressmen, "has not
yet leaked out."

On July 4, banqueters at Orange Courthouse, Virginia, drank
to this toast defiantly offered by James Madison: "The Freedom
of the Press—The Scourge of the Guilty and the support of virtuous

Government." That was no conventional felicitation, but a hail and farewell to freedom, in a country where the press, unless it chose the virtue of silence, was to be scourged by a guilty government. The United States Senate chose that same day, dedicated to "life, liberty, and the pursuit of happiness," to pass a sedition bill with no recorded debate (sessions were secret then) and a final roll call of sixteen to six. The six opponents consisted of the two Virginia senators and one each from Tennessee, Kentucky, New Hampshire and Maryland. It was a dismaying revelation of the inroads made on the ideals of freedom and justice which the Fourth of July stood for in the young republic. The sedition bill imposed maximum penalties of five years in prison and a fine of $5,000 on the following classes:

Persons who should conspire to oppose any measures of the government or impede the operation of any law, or to intimidate or prevent an officer from exercising his trust. (The Jefferson-Madison petition against prosecution of Cabell would violate that provision.)

Any person who, by writing, speaking or printing, should threaten such officer with damage to his character, person, or estate. (Any effective public criticism of a federal officer would be criminal.)

Any person who should advise or attempt any riot or insurrection, whether it had the desired effect or not. (Idle words at a dinner party could send the speaker to prison.)

Penalties up to two years in prison and a fine of $2,000 were provided for any person who by printing or publishing should traduce or defame Congress, with intent to create a belief that it was moved by hostility to the Constitution or the liberties and happiness of the people. (Two years in prison for telling why this law was enacted, or for citing loss of liberty under it as a reason for defeating its supporters.)

The same penalties were provided for any person who should similarly traduce the President of the United States, or any court or judge, by declarations tending to criminate their motives. (That too could send Jefferson and Madison to prison for such criticism as they had directed against the courts in the prosecution of Cabell.)

Then began one of the most crucial debates in American history

—the first discussion, in the generation of their adoption, of the guarantees of liberty implanted in the Constitution. In effect it transferred to the halls of Congress, with human liberty actually at stake, the hypothetical dialogue Madison had chronicled half a dozen years before, between "Republican" and "anti-Republican" —between the "champion of liberty" and the "idolator of tyranny."

Edward Livingston of New York, who became President Jackson's Secretary of State, moved to reject the bill, and John Allen of Connecticut took the lead in its support. Allen's first words confirmed the belief of Thomas Jefferson that the immediate purpose of the bill was to silence the Philadelphia *Aurora,* which stood first among the handful of newspapers (outnumbered five or ten to one) that would be supporting Jefferson for President in the next election. Said Allen:

"If ever there was a nation which required a law of this kind, it is this. Let gentlemen look at certain papers printed in this city [Philadelphia] and elsewhere, and ask themselves whether an unwarrantable and dangerous combination does not exist to overturn and ruin the Government by publishing the most shameless falsehoods against the Representatives of the people of all denominations, that they are hostile to free Governments and genuine liberty; that they ought, therefore, to be displaced, and that the people ought to raise an *insurrection* against the Government."

Allen proceeded to quote the paragraph in which the *Aurora* raised the standard of revolt:

"It is a curious fact, America is making war with France for NOT treating, at the very moment the Minister for Foreign Affairs fixes upon the very day for opening a negotiation with Mr. Gerry. What think you of this, Americans?"

This item reflected the fact that Talleyrand had refused to treat with all three American commissioners, regarding two of them as partisans of England, but was willing to negotiate with Republican Elbridge Gerry—an objectionable arrangement. The *Aurora's* purpose, said Allen, "is to persuade the people that peace with France is in our power . . . on proper terms, but that we reject her offers, and proceed to plunge our country into a destructive war."

The *Aurora's* malicious paragraph, said Allen, was in the very spirit of a speech delivered some days earlier by Representative

Livingston, who had made a motion that President Adams direct Mr. Gerry to treat with France. This, in Livingston's opinion, Gerry had authority to do, the powers given the commissioners being joint and several. Allen described the teamwork between Livingston and Editor Bache, in terms that would subject both of them (unless congressional immunity saved the legislator) to prison sentences under the proposed Sedition Act:

"Here are circumstances of what I call *a combination against the government,* in attempts to persuade the people of certain facts, which a majority of this House, at least, and of the people at large, I believe, know to be unfounded."

As further proof "that a revolution is intended," Allen quoted another *Aurora* statement, referring to the sedition bill, that it would soon be "difficult to determine, whether there is more safety and liberty to be enjoyed at Constantinople or Philadelphia." Once again, identifying Livingston as the fountainhead of insurrection, Allen went on:

"Who can doubt the existence of a combination against the real liberty, the real safety of the United States? I say, sir, a combination, a conspiracy, against the Constitution, the Government, the peace and safety of this country, is formed, and is in full operation."

To take Allen's words at their ordinary meaning would be to stamp him as a near lunatic. But they make sense when one realizes that by a "dangerous combination to overturn and ruin the Government," he meant the uniting of enough voters to transfer political power from Adams and the Federalists to Jefferson and the Republicans. The "insurrection against the Government" was to be an insurrection at the ballot box, not by force of arms. Its success would end "the real liberty, the real safety of the United States," which depended on keeping conservatives in office. In the eyes of New England Federalists, such a transfer of authority would be a genuine insurrection, since it would take political power away from those who were born to rule, and give it to those who were born to be ruled. To anybody holding such views (and nearly all Federalist leaders held them), there was genuine sedition in the *Aurora*'s "What think you of this, Americans?" designed to persuade voters that the Adams Administration was moving of its own volition toward an avoidable war. To avert a political calamity the press had to be muzzled.

This alleged conspiracy against the government was rather narrow, with only Congressman Livingston and the *Aurora*'s Editor Bache (Benjamin Franklin's grandson) as identifiable participants. However, Allen widened the field by bringing in the New York *Time-Piece*, a new triweekly owned by Matthew L. Davis, Aaron Burr's zealous henchman. Quoting a long paragraph, he repeated its high points in denouncing it:

"Gentlemen contend for the liberty of opinions and of the press. Let me ask them whether they seriously think the liberty of the press authorizes such publications? The President of the United States is here called 'a person without patriotism, without philosophy, and a mock monarch,' and the free election of the people is pronounced 'a jostling him into the Chief Magistracy by the ominous combination of old Tories with old opinions, and old Whigs with new.' "

Monarchies, the *Time-Piece* observed, had drawn the tears and execrations of mankind, to which the editors promised to add "derision and contempt" of the Adams mock-monarchy. To Allen this was treason twice compounded:

"If this be not a conspiracy against Government and people, I know not what to understand from the 'threat of tears, execrations, derision and contempt.' Because the Constitution guaranties the right of expressing our opinions, and the freedom of the press, am I at liberty to falsely call you a thief, a murderer, an atheist? Because I have the liberty of locomotion, of going where I please, have I a right to ride over the footman in the path? The freedom of the press was never understood to give the right of publishing falsehoods and slanders, nor of exciting sedition, insurrection, and slaughter, with impunity. A man was always answerable for the malicious publication of falsehood; and what more does this bill require?"

Allen then reverted to his favorite target, the *Aurora*, citing an editorial which asked whether, when an unconstitutional law should be passed "making it criminal to expose the crimes, the official vices or abuses, or the attempts of men in power to usurp a despotic authority, is there any alternative between an abandonment of the Constitution and resistance?" This, Allen explained, was a virtual repetition of what Livingston had said about the sedition bill on the floor of the House.[1] It was proof of a subversive conspiracy:

"The gentleman [Mr. Livingston] makes his proclamation of war on the Government in the House on Monday, and this infamous printer [Bache] follows it up with the tocsin of insurrection on Tuesday. . . . This is an awful, horrible example of 'the liberty of opinion and freedom of the press.' Can gentlemen hear these things and lie quietly on their pillows? . . . God deliver us from such liberty, the liberty of vomiting on the public floods of falsehood and hatred to everything sacred, human and divine."

Twitted by a member who suggested that Allen supported the *Aurora* by subscribing to it, the Federalist replied that he read it at public expense and only to see how far the Jacobinic press could go in iniquity. Unlike some men in public life, he was "not daily and nightly closeted with its editor." He would mention no names, but the paper was "perfectly well understood, by all parties and persons, to contain the opinions of certain great men, and certain gentlemen in this House." Since Allen had already labeled those opinions treasonable, and Fenno's *Gazette* had been picturing Jefferson as a midnight conferee with Bache, he was in effect calling the Vice President a traitorous conspirator, along with Livingston, Gallatin, and anybody else who might be thrown into the kettleful of insinuations.

Allen's final outburst was about the published letter of an unnamed Virginia congressman to his constituents, saying that Congress in the past nine years had produced "a dangerous preponderance of Executive power" by studiously augmenting and funding the national debt and creating a bank connected with the government. "Such representations," said Allen, "are outrages on the national authority, which ought not to be suffered; and I have no doubt that Congress have power to remedy the evil."

John Allen was no crackpot. He was a conservative lawyer of high standing, whose leadership of the Federalist drive for the Sedition Act was followed by his appointment to the Connecticut Supreme Court of Errors. Although he did not specifically limit freedom of the press to Blackstone's "freedom from prior restraint," his exclusions from it had that effect. Except as a ban on licensing, he reduced the First Amendment to a cipher. Under his concept of the mandate that Congress should make no law abridging the freedom of the press, laws could be passed to punish every attack on administration that had been punishable under the Star Chamber, or later in the common-law courts of Hyde, Scroggs, Jeffreys, Raymond and Mansfield. His metaphors were *non sequiturs* that equated overt criminal actions with opinions that he considered dangerous. It was equally criminal, in his eyes, to deliberately ride down and trample a pedestrian in the street and to ask the rhetorical question whether the Sedition Act would leave more freedom in America than existed in Turkey. Criminality was heightened, not lessened, if the published criticism of the government had previously been made in debate by a subversive (i.e. a Jeffersonian) congressman.

Robert Goodloe Harper of South Carolina, the most influential of the Federalists, took up the theme. He had often heard "harangues on the liberty of the press, as if it were to swallow up all other liberties; as if all law and reason, and every right, human and divine, was to fall prostrate before the liberty of the Press; whereas, the true meaning of it is no more than that a man shall be at liberty to print what he pleases, provided he does not offend against the laws." There was nothing in the Constitution, Harper asserted, to say that "no law shall be passed to *regulate* this liberty of the press. . . . Nor would the rational liberty of the press be restricted by a well defined law, provided persons have a fair trial by jury." But the liberty of the press desired by those who wished to overturn society "ought not to be allowed, either in speaking or writing, in any country."

Harper had not worried much about this matter of freedom as long as the abuse was confined to the press, but now that a member of Congress (Livingston) was pronouncing invectives against the government, his speech "may have a very different effect from the filthy streams of certain newspapers; it may gain a credit with the community, and produce consequences which all former abuse has failed to do. . . . It was for this reason that he wished a law to pass to punish treasonable and seditious writings."

In a later speech Harper declared that the presence of a pro-

French party when war was imminent made restriction of the press imperative. As John Allen had done, he asserted that liberty of the press stood on the same ground in law as lawless action. A legal right to violently abuse the President and Congress was the same as a legal right to rob or assassinate. But to lift this bill above the level of the common law, he offered amendments, which were adopted, making truth a defense against libel charges, and empowering juries to pass on both law and fact.

Harrison G. Otis of Massachusetts, third speaker of the Federalist triumvirate, carried the emasculation of the First Amendment to its logical conclusion. Every independent government, he said, had a right "to preserve and defend itself against injuries and outrages which endanger its existence." The sedition bill was directed against specified activities that tended to the destruction of the Constitution. "And if gentlemen would agree that these were acts of a criminal nature, it follows that all means calculated to produce these effects, whether by speaking, writing, or printing, were also criminal." American adoption of the common law of England, he said, produced those results in the several states and was intended to be embodied in the national Constitution.

That left only one question, Otis argued: whether the amendments to the Constitution divested the federal government of this power. The terms "freedom of speech and of the press" were borrowed from the only country in which these freedoms had been tolerated. Citing Blackstone's *Commentaries,* he declared that "the Liberty of the press is merely an exemption from all previous restraints." Any person who exercised this liberty was answerable "for false, malicious, and seditious expressions, whether spoken or written." The New Hampshire Constitution, he pointed out, declared that liberty of the press ought "to be inviolably preserved." Yet thereafter a law was passed to punish any person "publishing a lie or libel, tending to the defamation of any person." Massachusetts had a constitutional article saying that freedom of the press "ought not to be restricted," yet the courts there were given cognizance of offenses "tending to . . . raising of faction, controversy or debate." In Pennsylvania, the Chief Justice had given a similar interpretation of the state's constitutional provision for freedom of the press. Virginia's Declaration of Rights asserted "that the freedom of the press cannot be restrained, except in despotic governments," yet that state's legislature imposed any penalty short of death or mutilation (in 1785 and 1792) for any spoken or published words to instigate the setting up of a separate government in Kentucky.

How, then, asked Otis, was a line to be drawn between the liberty and licentiousness of the press? "An honest jury was competent to such a discrimination, they could decide upon the falsehood and malice of the intention. . . . But if twelve honest men cannot be found to acquit a libelist, he ought to be convicted." The present bill, he asserted, allows free animadversion upon the proceedings of Congress and the conduct of its members: "it merely prohibits calumny and deception."

The arguments of Otis were more plausible than those of Allen and Harper, who did not hide their vindictive purposes. But Otis's soothing plausibility was merely a gloss on fallacy. His case was based on the supposition that, by some mysterious magic, the common law of England became embedded in the federal Constitution, placed there nobody knew how, by nobody knew whom. Being there, it silently transcended the enumerated powers of Congress, wiped out the Tenth Amendment, and automatically broadened the jurisdiction of the federal courts to the limitless latitude of those in England.

All this was pure conjecture on the part of Otis. To support it he offered not one atom of evidence, and there was no improvement in logic when he sought to buttress the argument with citations of state bills of rights. Here his method was to treat dissimilar things as identical. Not one of the states mentioned by the Massachusetts Federalist had a free-press guarantee similar to the First Amendment, mandatory and unqualified, denying Congress the power to do what it was now about to do. New Hampshire and Massachusetts had the "ought to" brand of defense of freedom, sound in principle but undermined by constitutional recognition of the common law. Virginia's article was a mere protest against despotism, which a despotic legislature could and did brush aside.[2] The Pennsylvania provision, as revised by a reactionary convention in 1790, had resounding phrases about liberty, but the substance of it was a rewording of Blackstone: "every citizen may freely write, print or speak on any subject, being responsible for the abuse of that liberty."

To realize the worthlessness of analogy with state bills of rights, as a measure of the force of the First Amendment, one need merely go back to the words of Madison when he submitted the constitutional amendments in 1789:

"Besides, some states have no bills of rights, there are others provided with very defective ones, and there are others whose bills of rights are not only defective, but absolutely improper; instead of securing some in the full extent which republican principles would require, they limit them too much to agree with the common ideas of liberty."

That statement invites analysis. By making "republican principles" the test of adequacy, Madison showed that he was talking about civil rights and liberties essential to political self-government, not about due process of law and other rights that belong to man as man, regardless of the form of government. In other words, he was talking about freedom of political opinion—about the clauses on freedom of speech and press—when he disparaged state articles as nonexistent, very defective or "absolutely improper." And whose ideas were to be followed, in protecting political rights to "the full extent which republican principles would require"? Did he have in mind the ideas of Blackstonian judges hostile to those freedoms? Evidently not. The new federal guarantees were to measure up to "the *common ideas* of liberty." But it was precisely those "common ideas" of liberty against which the Scroggses and Mansfields and Blackstones in England, the Iredells and Otises and Harpers and Allens in America, had been railing.

In the several states, as Madison's comment indicated, the "common ideas of liberty" went beyond the defective or improper ideas that conservative lawyers and lawmakers made constitutional either by commission, omission or interpretation. But these common ideas continued to gain effectiveness in quiet years, through the force of a public opinion that bore against either state or federal interference with the press. An English traveler testified to this in a pamphlet, *Emigration to America Candidly Considered*, published in London only a few months before passage of the Sedition Act turned his eulogy into an ironic falsehood:

"The grand bulwark of liberty in America is the freedom of the press—its latitude is infinite—it cannot be restrained—whether for or against the government, there is no power that can prevent the voice of truth from being heard. Conscious of that greatest of blessings, the American dares to bring every deliberation of his mind before the eye of his fellow citizens, without fear or dread. He can only be censured by the public opinion."

No doubt that English traveler had the First Amendment primarily in mind, and was expressing the "common ideas" of its force. But he would hardly have expressed himself so sweepingly if he had encountered a different condition of the press, or different ideas about its freedom resulting from abridgments of that freedom by the states. This throws additional light on the speeches of Allen, Harper and Otis, which encompassed the entire argument for validity of the Sedition Act. They were not genuine interpretations of the First Amendment at all. They were *arguments against its being in the Constitution.* That can best be realized by rewriting the free-press clause of the amendment to make its wording express the legal meaning (minus torrid oratory) given it by these Federalist congressmen:

To fit the views of Allen: "Congress shall make no law abridging the freedom of the press, except to protect Congress and the President from such criticism as tends to undermine or weaken public confidence in them."

To fit the views of Harper: "Congress shall not abridge but may regulate the freedom of the press. No well-defined law to regulate it shall be considered an abridgment, provided the right of trial by jury be preserved."

To fit the views of Otis: "Congress shall not abridge the freedom of the press by licensing or other form of prior restraint, but may impose any restriction that is sanctioned by the common law of England."

These three statements amount to three ways of stating a single proposition. If any Federalist in Congress disagreed with them, it did not show up in debate or in the votes. If a single Republican member accepted these interpretations of the clause, it was undiscoverable. Such unanimity within each of two opposing parties is a rare phenomenon, even when factional antagonism runs so high. It naturally raises the question whether, in taking their conflicting positions, the members of Congress and other spokesmen were governed by the situation immediately confronting them, or were consistently maintaining positions previously taken.

With regard to two men of prime importance the record is clear. James Madison, chief architect of the ten amendments, never deviated from the purpose to make freedom of opinion absolute, or from the conviction that the constitutional mandate engineered by him achieved that purpose. Judge Iredell, whose 1797 charge to a federal grand jury set the campaign for a sedition act in motion, completely reversed his 1788 contention that the federal government would have no constitutional power to restrain the press. The contrasting conduct of two outstanding spokesmen does not establish a pattern, although it suggests one. But let us assume that Iredell, instead of being impelled by altered circumstances to reverse his earlier position, believed in 1788 what he proclaimed in 1797, and was merely trying to fool the people when he denied the existence of federal power to abridge freedom. That would be eloquent evidence of the need to fool them—evidence that the "common idea of liberty" was total liberty, which lawyers and judges would first proclaim and then proceed to take away. It seems fairer to Iredell to postulate a genuine reversal of opinion, under the conviction that freedom of the press must be abridged by the federal government to save the country from Napoleon Bonaparte or Thomas Jefferson, if not from both of them.[3]

Since Allen, Harper and Otis present no record of a change of front, it may be assumed that their arguments for the sedition bill expressed long-held convictions. If so, they must at all times have approved the basic feature of the British common law of seditious libel—that men were to be sent to prison for political comments offensive to the government. But if that is the meaning of the First Amendment, and was intended to be its meaning, it necessarily follows that Madison and his zealous associates had a like understanding, a like intent, and that their attitude likewise resulted from approval of the way "freedom of the press" had worked in England under the concept of it described by Blackstone. More specifically, any such unified acceptance of the British system required united approval of the system of "freedom" under which Thomas Paine was condemned to prison in London for praising the political institutions of the United States. In his case truth was pleaded as a defense and the jury judged both law and fact—two deviations from the common law that were imitated in the Sedition Act. The failure of those defenses in Paine's case made a general travesty of them and stripped the issue of freedom to its essential: that any *power* of abridgment puts the *extent* of abridgment into the hands of those who hold the power.

It is with that in mind that we must proceed to the arguments of those who spoke against the Sedition Act of 1798. It is relatively unimportant whether the supporters of that iniquitous bill were consistent adherents of a system of repression, or late converts to tyranny. Not so with respect to its opponents. The force of the First Amendment, it is true, depends only in part on the known or conjectured purpose of its framers and supporters. Its ultimate strength will be determined less by its uncompromising wording than by the growth or decay of the concept of freedom. But to the extent that knowledge of history aids or hinders growth, the crucial element is the integrity of its supporters in the generation that gave it birth. That is to be judged in the great testing places of public opinion— the debates in Congress when freedom was assailed in 1798 and the reaction of the American people and libertarian leaders to its denial. The defenders of freedom in Congress were not silenced by the menaces they faced.

CHAPTER 22
Champions of Liberty

Representative John Nicholas of Virginia, the youngest of three brothers who rose to fame in the building of Jeffersonian Democracy, opened the arguments against the sedition bill on July 5, 1798. Preliminary to his main speech, Nicholas rose to remark that Messrs. Allen and Harper seemed "most afraid of the speeches and letters of gentlemen in this House." Since they could not silence the members, what was their aim? He could not tell, unless it was "to prevent the publication of their sentiments to their constituents and to the world." He would give liberal support to the war with France, which seemed unavoidable, "but he was not ready to create a *domestic tyranny*. . . . It was striking at the root of free republican government, to restrict the use of speaking and writing."

Resuming the subject later, Nicholas assailed the sedition bill as unconstitutional. He looked in vain in the Constitution for authority to enact such a law, "but he found what he considered as an express prohibition against passing it." Gentlemen were saying that "this bill is not to restrict the liberty of the press, but its licentiousness." Where did they draw the line between this liberty and licentiousness?

"Will they say the one is truth, and the other falsehood! Gentlemen cannot believe for a moment that such a definition will satisfy the inquiry. . . . It has been the object of all regulations with respect to the press, to destroy the only means by which the people can examine and become acquainted with the conduct of persons employed in their Government."

The American people, said Nicholas, had no intention to place such a power in the General Government, where persons accused of speaking falsely about it would be tried by judges appointed by the President and by juries selected by the presidentially appointed marshal. Under such circumstances, "printers of papers would be deterred from printing anything which should be in the least offensive to a power which might so greatly harass them. . . . This bill would, therefore, go to the suppression of every printing press in the country, which is not obsequious to the will of Government."

It was said, Nicholas continued, that Congress had power to pass this bill because of "the common law being part of the law of the United States." Where did gentlemen find an account of its adoption? What common law? Was it the common law of England? If so, adoption of it in the Constitution made it unchangeable and Congress had no power to pass this bill, which would modify the common law. Akin to the common-law argument was the argument by analogy, that all the states took cognizance of offenses by the press. Did it follow, asked Nicholas, that this gave a similar power to the General Government? Such reasoning would give Congress a concurrent power with the states over all offenses—a novel idea indeed! In fact, he was utterly at a loss to find any ground whatever upon which to base a federal law of this sort, and he was confident there was none.

His own state, the Virginia congressman said, had taken the same position in 1788, in ratifying the Constitution. He quoted the declaration of the Virginia convention, that every power not granted by the Constitution remained with them, "and that, among other essential rights, the liberty of conscience and of the press cannot be cancelled, abridged, restrained, or modified, by any authority of the United States." In pursuance of the same idea, the Congress of the United States, and the State Governments, proceeded to declare the meaning of the Constitution in the most express terms. "And yet, in direct opposition to the clause of the Constitution which says, 'Congress shall pass no law to abridge the freedom of the press,' Congress is now about to pass such a law."

Nathaniel Macon of North Carolina pointed out that religious establishments were prohibited in the same section of the Constitution and by the same wording that forbids interference with speech and press. He looked upon the sedition bill as the commencement of a system that could extend to establishment of a national religion as readily as to restraint of speaking and writing. When the words of the Constitution were so express in defense of these freedoms, it seemed impossible that they could be understood as the supporters of the bill contended. He quoted Iredell and other leading members of the ratifying conventions of 1787 and 1788, to show that friends of the Constitution never understood that the federal government could prosecute for libel. "Not a single member in any of the conventions gave an opinion to the contrary." What the federal government lacked of power in this field would be found in the states, which would exercise it when necessity called for it.

Edward Livingston took the floor, to endeavor to show that this bill was not only contrary to the spirit, but to the letter of the Constitution. He quoted the clause forbidding Congress to make any law abridging the liberty of speech and of the press, and asked whether citizens would have the same liberty after this bill was passed that they enjoyed when the amendment was adopted. If not, and if they still enjoy that same freedom, must it not be allowed "that the Constitution [by forbidding abridgment] is positive in prohibiting any change in this respect? Gentlemen may call this liberty an evil, if they please; if it be an evil (which he was far from believing) it is an evil perpetrated by the Constitution."

The Constitution, Livingston said, seemed to look forward to a day (not yet arrived, he added astutely) when a corrupt congressional majority "might wish to pass laws to suppress the only means by which its corrupt views might be made known to the people, and therefore says, *no* law shall be passed to abridge the liberty of speech and of the press." Like Macon, he linked this guarantee with another "dear and valuable privilege—the liberty of conscience." Under the opinion of the present majority, "gentlemen may tomorrow establish a national religion . . . on the ground of an uniformity of worship being more consistent with public happiness than a diversity of worship. The doing of this is not less forbidden than the act which the House is about to do." How would they deal with a man who should charge that in "passing an unconstitutional act [we are] violating our oaths? . . . We are not to disprove the fact, and let the public judge between us, but we are immediately to prosecute the man who makes the charge."

To make the Federalists squirm still more, Livingston read a long extract from John Adams' *Defence of the Constitutions of the United States*, ostensibly written in reply to a French criticism of the state constitutions. In this extract, Adams described the transition from freedom to despotism in a republic swayed by demagogy, with all power concentrated in one House. A few persons, gaining control through opulence, superior birth and connections, would remain in power by bestowal of offices and contracts. Control of the courts, bar and church would follow. Then would come the final stroke of tyranny:

"The press, that great barrier and bulwark of the rights of mankind, when it is protected in its freedom by law, can now no longer be free." Authors, writers and printers must either accept the line that is offered or submit to ruin. "The presses will be made the vehicles of calumny against the minority, and of panegyric and empirical applause of the leaders of the majority, and no remedy can possibly be obtained . . . but *in arms.*"

There was a widespread belief, in 1787, that Adams was predicting developments in the United States should a democratic constitution be adopted. He actually presented a perfect description of what the Adams Sedition Act promised to produce, in governmental mastery of public opinion, and of what the First Amendment was designed to prevent. Livingston supplemented it with a forecast of his own:

"The effect of this bill may be to lift a few men into consequence who were never of any before, and to ruin two or three others; but it will be in vain to attempt to hide the misconduct of Government from the people. The thing will defeat its own end. They will, besides, be struck with the flagrant breach which it makes in the Constitution, compared with which, he looked upon war, pestilence, and every other calamity, as of trifling consequence."

Albert Gallatin continued the argument, attacking the contention that the Constitution originally gave Congress power to punish libels and other offenses at common law, and that this original power was not taken away by the First Amendment. The first assertion was unfounded, he said, for the Constitution confined the jurisdiction of the courts to specified fields and to cases arising under the Constitution, treaties, and laws *made* under the authority of that Constitution. That excluded cases not arising under any of these, excluding therefore cases arising under the common law. It was preposterous to suppose, as Mr. Otis did, that technical expressions in the Constitution, such as *habeas corpus,* derived from the common law, implied a recognition of common-law jurisdiction. "He had there confounded two very distinct ideas—the principles of the common law, and the jurisdiction over cases arising under it."

But, said Gallatin, had the gentleman succeeded in proving that federal courts had jurisdiction over offenses at common law, it would be the strongest argument against the passing of this bill. For if the jurisdiction already existed, where was the necessity of conferring it on the courts? He denied that power to pass any such law existed in a government of limited and enumerated powers, and then turned to the First Amendment.

This bill, he said, justified the suspicions felt when the Constitution was submitted to the states, that the authority to pass laws "necessary and proper" to carry the granted powers into effect might be distorted into a power to abridge the freedoms of speech and of the press. To remove those suspicions, the amendment was proposed and adopted, declaring that Congress shall pass no law abridging them. As Gallatin and his friends understood this amendment, "Congress could not pass any law to punish any real or supposed abuse of the press." As construed by supporters of the pending bill, the amendment did not prevent them from punishing what they called the licentiousness of the press, but merely forbade previous restraints. Said Gallatin:

"It appeared to him preposterous to say, that to punish a certain act was not an abridgement of the liberty of doing that act. It appeared to him that it was an insulting evasion of the Constitution for gentlemen to say, 'We claim no power to abridge the liberty of the press; *that,* you shall enjoy unrestrained. You may write and publish what you please, but if you publish anything against us, we will punish you for it.' "

To prove that the intention was merely to forbid previous restraint, Gallatin argued, it would be necessary to show that a power to impose previous restraint existed before the amendment was adopted—"a suggestion which never was hinted, even by the most violent opponents of the Constitution, at the time of its adoption."

Finally, that construction was inconsistent with the First Amendment itself. It provided against the passing of laws abridging either the liberty of the press or of speech, and a sound construction must be such as to be applicable to both. But the forbidding of prior restraint would have been absurd, so far as it related to speech, "unless gentlemen chose to assert that the Constitution had given Congress a power to seal the mouths or to cut the tongues of the citizens of the Union." Since previous restraint could not be laid upon freedom of speech, was it not evident that a clause forbidding its abridgment meant that "no punishment should by law be inflicted upon it"?

Although Nicholas, Macon, Livingston and Gallatin almost monopolized the vocal fight against the sedition bill, it is obvious that they voiced the views of all who voted against the narrowly adopted bill. In the entire debate, and in the entire known record of the participants, there is not the slightest suggestion of a departure from long-held convictions.

To break down the presumption that Madison, Jefferson and the congressional and other libertarians held the same views in 1789 that they expressed in 1798, only one argument is commonly offered. It is contended that Blackstone's definition of freedom of the press as freedom from "prior restraint" was generally accepted in 1789, when the First Amendment was drafted, and a repudiation of it in 1798 came too late to be a valid indication of earlier opinion on the subject. We may readily grant that few of the Federalists of 1798-1800 believed in freedom of the press in 1789. Iredell and Wilson, it is true, did complete and well-recorded flip-flops, but one can hardly suspect Allen, Harper and Otis of being the opposite in 1789 of what they were in 1798. They and other leaders of their party, like Fisher Ames, simply did not realize in 1789 that they would ever need the *federal* power which they were willing to exclude because *the states* retained a similar power.

To draw erroneous deductions based on lapse of time is one of the commonest failings of historians. It has been soberly argued that after the Revolutionary War came to an end, the American people must have been pretty well satisfied with the Articles of Confederation as a peacetime institution because so many years elapsed before revisionary machinery was set in motion. How long was that period of supposed satisfaction? Six months longer than John F. Kennedy was President of the United States.[1] To say that lapse of time invalidates the 1798 judgments on the meaning of the First Amendment is like saying that by the time President Eisenhower left the White House, nothing said by Democrats about the Truman Administration could be relied on because it was so far back in history.

However, one can find plenty of evidence that both libertarian leaders and a large part of the American people rejected the idea of abridging the freedom of the press before the Federalists undertook to abridge it. The evidence is in Jefferson's Statute of Religious Freedom, written in 1779, adopted in 1785, with wording that applied as naturally to speech and press as to religion. It is in Madison's 1789 rejection of the Blackstone definition, when he told Congress that freedom of the press was unguarded in the British Constitution. It is in his protest, during that same debate, that state bills of rights did not measure up to "the common ideas of liberty." It is in the observation of the English traveler, visiting the United States in 1797, who said of freedom of the press: "its latitude is infinite—it cannot be restrained" except by public opinion. It is in the 1798 speech of Congressman Harper, lamenting that he had so often heard "harangues on the liberty of the press" that put it beyond restraint. How could there be such harangues if the belief expressed in them was not widespread?

Harper himself made one last effort to find support for the Blackstone definition outside the coterie of Federalist politicians and judges who were using it to convert the guarantee of the press's freedom into a weapon for its destruction. Speaking in final rebuttal for the sedition bill, he quoted (with careful selectivity and effectual distortion) from a facetious article published by Benjamin Franklin in 1789. Satirizing the venom-filled newspapers of Philadelphia as "the Supremest Court of Judicature in Pennsylvania," Franklin suggested what the state legislature might do about it. Owing to "the length of the essay, and the lateness of the hour," said Harper, he would omit Franklin's opening observations. The portion thus deleted made it evident that Franklin was concerned entirely with personal defamation, not seditious libel, and that he carried freedom of the press far beyond Blackstone. Harper omitted the following:

"If, by the liberty of the press, were understood merely the liberty of discussing the propriety of public measures and political opinions, let us have as much of it as you please; but if it means the liberty of affronting, calumniating, and defaming one another, I, for my part, own myself willing to part with my share of it, whenever our legislators shall please so to alter the law."

Harper quoted Franklin's remark that he had given much thought to the problem of checking this abuse, but had "been at a loss to imagine any that may not be construed an infringement of the sacred *liberty of the press*." At last he had thought of a way: restore to the people "a species of liberty of which they have been deprived by our laws; I mean the *liberty of the cudgel*." Said old Ben:

"My proposal then, is to leave the liberty of the press untouched, to be exercised in its full extent, force, and vigor, but to permit the liberty of the cudgel to go with it *pari passu*. Thus, my fellow-citizens, if an impudent writer attacks your reputation, dearer to you perhaps than your life, and puts his name to the charge, you may go to him, as openly, and break his head."

All this was no more than a facetious argument for more effective resort to civil defamation suits. An ensuing statement, *as quoted by Harper*, appeared to be a repudiation by Franklin of his lifelong opposition to prosecutions for seditious libel of government (italics are here added to the key word):

"But if the *Government* should ever happen to be affronted, as it ought to be, with the conduct of such writers, I would not advise proceeding immediately to these extremities, but that we should, in moderation, content ourselves with tarring and feathering and tossing them in a blanket."

The word "Government" tied this to seditious libel and gave an inescapable suggestion of prison penalties if lesser measures failed. And such was Harper's interpretation of the passage:

"Thus we see that this great man, the champion of liberty, who spent his life in promoting her cause, did not think that liberty of the press would be abridged by an explicit law for curbing its licentiousness. Supported by this great authority, I can never believe that a law to punish the publication of false, scandalous, and malicious libels, on conviction by a judge, is a law 'to abridge the liberty of the press,' as intended by the Constitution."

Harper's whole case was built on misquotation. Franklin said nothing about writings that affronted the government. His words were "if the *public* should ever happen to be affronted"—a mere reference to the widespread dislike of obnoxious journalism. Instead of employing his sense of humor to support seditious libel prosecutions, he was approving suits for defamation of character. Although Harper's position collapses utterly when the distortion is exposed, his illogic is best revealed by accepting, for the sake of argument, his contention that Franklin intended to sanction federal laws to punish libelous political comment in the press. On that supposition, *what Franklin actually said* about freedom of the press, and Harper's interpretation of what Franklin said, form a valid composite. It will read as follows:

"My proposal then, is to leave the liberty of the press untouched, to be exercised in its full extent, force, and vigor, . . . but to punish the publication of false, scandalous, and malicious libels."

That is a flat contradiction in terms, since *liability to trial* for seditious libel abridges all three characteristics of liberty listed by Franklin as untouchable—extent, force, and vigor. However, let us suppose not only that Franklin desired such an abridgment (abandoning long-held principles), but that James Madison had a similar desire when he proposed an amendment whose wording indicated the opposite. Suppose further that while Madison was on his way from Virginia to New York City, to attend the opening session of the First Congress, he stopped in Philadelphia to discuss freedom of the press with his friend, the eighty-four-year-old Franklin. This colloquy ensues:

Franklin: My proposal is to leave the liberty of the press untouched, to be exercised in its full extent, force, and vigor, but to punish the publication of false, scandalous, and malicious libels.

Madison: That is exactly my idea too. My state has already declared that under the Federal Constitution as it stands, the general government has no power whatever to abridge the liberty of the press. What puzzles me is how to implant that mandate in the Constitution, to protect the most precious of our liberties, and at the same time make it clear that Congress shall have power to enact laws to punish false, scandalous, and malicious libels.

Franklin: Perfectly simple. Just adopt an amendment with this wording: "Congress shall make no law to abridge the freedom of the press."

The absurdity of such an exchange requires no comment. Yet on precisely that distorted reasoning the House of Representatives passed the sedition bill of 1798, 47 to 37. And on precisely such reasoning, buried under a deeper and deeper gloss of words, the Supreme Court and Congress and most legal commentators were construing the First Amendment in the middle of the twentieth century.

In legal effectiveness, the perversion began on July 14, 1798, when President John Adams signed the famous and infamous Sedition Act—an act so destructive to freedom that under its terms (to use a slightly anachronistic illustration) a newspaper publisher could be sent to prison for charging the President of the United States with cruelty to animals in lifting a beagle by the ears.

CHAPTER 23
Freedom Enchained

In adopting Harper's amendments to the sedition bill, the Federalists kissed the skirt of the Goddess of Justice but avoided her lips. Submitting both law and fact to the jury, they made the law conform to Fox's British Libel Act of 1792. Allowing truth to be offered as a defense, they added a reform of the common law long clamored for in England but only occasionally granted by judges. The amendments were a shrewdly offered sop to public opinion and gave the Federalists nothing to fear. *They* had the federal judges, and *their* marshals picked the jury panels. Under such circumstances, *truth* would be whatever Federalist editors wrote about that Frenchified traitor, Vice President Thomas Jefferson. *Falsehood* would be whatever Republican editors wrote about that noble patriot, President John Adams. And so it turned out. During the next two years, Federalist editors shot poisoned arrows that flashed in the sunshine of government approval. Republican editors looked at the sunshine through prison windows.

For Secretary of State Timothy Pickering—generalissimo of the enforcement campaign—there was only one cause of regret. God took care of *Aurora*'s editor Bache before the law could do so. The law tried; indeed it jumped the gun. Bache was arrested for seditious libel under the common law of England eighteen days before the Sedition Act was signed. Ten days earlier he had obtained and printed a still-secret dispatch from Talleyrand, offensive in wording but pointing toward a peaceful settlement with the United States. Bache's real "crime" was in disclosing the possibility of peace. To discredit him, Adams' cabinet members spread a story that he was in secret communication with Talleyrand, evidence of which was a packet from the French Foreign Office, addressed to him but deflected to the State Department and still unopened. Bache secured a public opening of the packet, and it was found to contain a couple of pamphlets on English affairs sent by Louis Pichon, former secretary of the French legation in Philadelphia. Libel was charged in Bache's criticism of the conduct of the men who defamed him, but he died of yellow fever before he came to trial. His death, many Federalists seemed to believe, was the most striking intervention of the Lord on the side of good government since the acquittal of the Seven Bishops in 1688.

The first victim of the Sedition Act was Congressman Matthew Lyon of Vermont, a hot-tempered Irishman. He was indicted for writing to a newspaper that he would zealously support the Executive in measures to promote the happiness of the people, but would not be its humble advocate "whenever I shall, on the part of the Executive, see every consideration of the public welfare swallowed up in a continual grasp for power, in an unbounded thirst for ridiculous pomp, foolish adulation, and selfish avarice." As a second count in his indictment, he was accused of libeling the President and Senate in his electoral campaign. During it he had repeatedly quoted a letter from Joel Barlow to his brother-in-law, Congressman Abraham Baldwin of Georgia, expressing surprise that the Senate had not responded to one of the President's messages with "an order to send him to a madhouse."

Those were the formal charges against Lyon. But everybody in the country knew, and a good many rejoiced, that in reality he was being sent to prison because he spat in the face of Congressman Roger Griswold of Connecticut when Griswold called him a coward. The results of the conviction were not precisely what the government hoped for. Lyon, while serving his prison sentence, was re-elected to Congress by two to one over his highest opponent. His fine of $1,000, which kept him in prison after his four-month sentence expired, was raised twice over by public subscriptions in Vermont and Virginia. Jefferson, Madison, Monroe, John Taylor and Senator S. T. Mason took the lead in raising and subscribing to the latter fund. The constantly changing triumphal procession that escorted Lyon from Vermont to the national capital, after his release, took hours to pass given points along the way.

By its own terms, the Sedition Act of 1798 was to expire on March 3, 1801—the last day of President Adams' term of office. That in itself was a proclamation of the purpose of the legislation: to shut down or intimidate the Jeffersonian press during the presidential campaign, yet make sure that, if the misguided voters did bring in a Democratic-Republican administration, there would be no sedition law on the statute books to be turned against the party that put it there. If any further evidence of the partisan purpose was needed, it was furnished by the triviality of the charges against Congressman Lyon. But there was nothing in the conduct of Justice William Paterson of the United States Supreme Court, who presided over the trial in Vermont, to suggest that the jurors faced anything but a momentous issue affecting the safety of the American government.

Paterson sidestepped the issue of constitutionality, yet in effect upheld the statute, by saying that the Sedition Act must be considered valid until declared otherwise by a competent tribunal—that is, by the Supreme Court *en banc.* There was no reason, however, to suspect him of having constitutional doubts. He told the jurymen that their only duty (the fact of publication being admitted by Lyon) was to consider whether "language such as that here complained of could have been uttered with any other intent than that of making odious or contemptible the President and government, and bringing them both into disrepute. If you find such is the case, the offense is made out, and you must render a verdict of guilty." This left no room for acquittal based on Lyon's real intent, which was to build up political opposition to a President and Congress who had brought themselves into disrepute. It did not allow an acquittal on the ground that, even with a bad intent, the publications were insufficient to make the President and government odious and contemptible. It threw completely out of sight the defense basic to all political liberty, that Congress was commanded by the Constitution to "make no law abridging the freedom of the press."

Had Justice Paterson been so minded, he could have gone far

back in English history and found support for his position all the way. He could have found it in judges who served tyrannical kings, and in the ministers, lawyers and churchmen who read evil intent into words intended for the public good. He could have found it in the acts and utterances of better-intentioned judges who nevertheless subscribed to the fundamental rule of monarchic society that any criticism of men in power is a peril to government, and that the act of publication denotes seditious intent.

Justice Paterson accepted the basic tenet of the English common law (born in the Star Chamber) that any criticism that reflects on rulers is seditious. His rulings were in complete accord with the intent of Congress as revealed in the speeches of Allen, Harper and Otis. The entire purpose and principle of the Sedition Act, and of all similar abridgments of political expression, can be summed up by reversing Madison's 1794 axiom about the libertarian nature of republican government:

"If we advert to the nature of *authoritarian government*, we shall find that the censorial power is in the government over the people, and not in the people over the government."

The trial of Matthew Lyon gave full notice that political freedom was at an end in the United States, unless the people reversed the course of the government. Two men who were intent on reversing it were Thomas Jefferson and James Madison. When first informed by the Vice President that the sedition bill was pending in Congress, Madison replied that it left only one recourse against desperate measures. Enough virtue might remain in the public mind to make arbitrary attacks on the freedom of the press "recoil on the wicked authors." All other hope was gone:

"The sanguinary faction ought not however to adopt the spirit of Robespierre, without recollecting the shortness of his triumphs and the perpetuity of his infamy."

Jefferson saw a glint of hope for the future, though none for the present, as he considered the verdict against Matthew Lyon. "I know not which mortifies me most," he wrote to John Taylor, "that I should fear to write what I think, or my country bear such a state of things." Yet Lyon's judges had produced national fear, and that might start a restoration of sanity. Jefferson's apprehension for himself was not of prosecution, but that "the infidelities of the postoffice" might open his letters to interception and publication, giving Federalist editors some months of unremitting slander. At the time he wrote, in November 1798, Jefferson and Madison had just completed a divided task that made both of them fair targets for Fenno, Cobbett and other masters of vituperation.

Impelled by the indictment and arraignment of Lyon, which left no doubt that the federal judiciary was in league with the administration, the two men launched an appeal to public opinion against the Alien and Sedition Acts. The impetus came from Jefferson, but the method was Madison's, previously outlined by him in his 1789 speech proposing the Ten Amendments. He had predicted then that if "independent tribunals of justice" failed to protect the rights guaranteed in the Constitution, the state legislatures would jealously watch the operations of the general government and would "be able to resist with more effect every assumption of power than any other power on earth can do."

To call that force into play, Jefferson wrote "The Kentucky Resolutions," Madison "The Virginia Resolutions," of 1798, adopted in November and December by the two state legislatures. Identical in purpose and closely akin in basic argument, their difference in tone and content reflected the wide divergence of their authors in emotional and mental traits. The Kentucky Resolutions were powerful in exhortation against the hated statutes, but the constitutional arguments probably would have drawn revisionary criticism from Madison if he had seen the paper before it was sent to Kentucky. The Federalists were able to distract attention from the heavy blast Jefferson delivered against the Sedition Act, as a liberty-destroying usurpation of power, by pointing to minor flaws in his position and emphasizing one of major importance. This was his contention that, the states being parties to the compact setting up a general government of limited powers, each state had an equal right to judge for itself when those powers were exceeded, and the mode and measure of redress. For relief in this instance, it was resolved "that the co-States, recurring to their natural right in cases not made federal, will concur in declaring these acts void and of no force, and will unite with this Commonwealth in requesting their repeal at the next session of Congress." The final softening clause about repeal was added by Kentucky legislators.

Jefferson was heavily assailed as an alleged nullifier and insurrectionist, after his authorship became known, but in the long look of history his overemphasis on the Alien Act and lack of system in the remainder has caused the Kentucky Resolutions to drop into obscurity. The Virginia Resolutions, on the contrary, have remained a living influence through the centuries, though less for their virtues than for intentional ambiguities in wording that led to unintended misconceptions of their meaning.

Madison's resolves opened by declaring firm support of the Union, and of the Constitution as the only basis of the Union's existence. The Assembly then did "explicitly and peremptorily declare" that the powers of the general government were limited to those authorized by the constitutional compact, "and that in case of a deliberate, palpable and dangerous exercise of other powers, not granted by the said compact, the States who are parties thereto, have the right, and are in duty bound, to interpose for arresting the progress of the evil, and for maintaining within their respective limits, the authorities, rights and liberties appertaining to them."

The Assembly protested in particular against "the palpable and alarming infractions of the Constitution" by passage of the Alien and Sedition Acts, one of which subverted the general principles of free government by transferring legislative and judicial powers to the Executive, while the other exercised a power expressly and positively forbidden by one of the amendments to the Constitution. The power thus exercised in the Sedition Act ought more than any other "to produce universal alarm, because it is leveled against that right of freely examining public characters and measures, and of free communication among the people thereon, which has ever been justly deemed, the only effectual guardian of every other right."

Harking back to the resolution by which Virginia ratified the Constitution in 1788, Madison quoted its declaration that, among other essential rights, "the liberty of Conscience and of the Press cannot be cancelled, abridged, restrained, or modified by any authority of the United States." In their extreme anxiety to guard these rights from every possible attack of sophistry and ambition, Virginia and other states had recommended an amendment for that purpose which in due time was annexed to the Constitution. After such a record it would be "criminal degeneracy" to be indifferent now "to the most palpable violation of one of the Rights, thus declared and secured; and to the establishment of a precedent which may be fatal to the other."

So, with sincere affection for their brethren of other states and the truest anxiety to preserve the Union, the General Assembly appealed to other legislatures to "concur with this Commonwealth in declaring, as it does hereby declare, that the acts aforesaid, are unconstitutional; and that the necessary and proper measures will be taken by each, for cooperating with this State, in maintaining the Authorities, Rights, and Liberties, reserved to the States respectively, or to the People."

There were two essential differences between the Virginia and Kentucky Resolutions. Madison affirmed the *constitutional* right of the states to "interpose" *collectively* to maintain their *respective* authorities, rights and liberties. Jefferson affirmed the *natural* right of *each state* to redress federal violations of the constitutional compact. Madison's resolutions called the Alien and Sedition Acts *unconstitutional.* Jefferson's declared them *void and of no force.* Thus Madison restricted himself to undefined constitutional measures, while Jefferson relied on the unquestioned natural right of the people—that is, their revolutionary right—to do whatever they might choose to do in the realm of government.

The Virginia and Kentucky Resolutions were duly dispatched to all state legislatures and reached the public via newspapers and pamphlets. They came to governments and people wrought to frenzy by the war drive against France, at a moment when the political party led by Jefferson seemed to be disintegrating. Virginia was accused of plotting a revolutionary uprising to support a foreign foe. The suggestions of nullification, implicit in the Kentucky Resolutions, were transferred by Federalist propaganda to the resolutions of Virginia, and the transfer was made easier by Madison's studied failure to spell out the means of "interposition." Seven states—New York, Delaware, and all of New England —replied during 1799 to Virginia's call for collective action. All of them rejected it and nearly all upheld and praised the Alien and Sedition Acts.

At the same time, enforcement of the sedition law mounted in extent and savagery. David Brown, a wandering cracker-box orator, was fined $480 and given eighteen months in prison for inspiring Massachusetts Democrats to erect a Liberty Pole whose incitement to "insurrection and civil war" reached its fearful climax in the words: "downfall to the Tyrants of America, peace and retirement to the President, Long Live the Vice-President and the Minority; May moral virtue be the basis of civil government." Benjamin Fairbanks, a wealthy citizen charged with abetting Brown, crawled on his belly to beg forgiveness of Supreme Court Justice Samuel Chase and was let off with a five-shilling fine and six hours in jail.

It was not until 1800, at the outset of the presidential campaign, that the Federalist judges made their maximum effort to hamstring the Jeffersonian press. Virulence of accusation and partisan zeal in prosecution marked the conduct of Justice Chase in the seditious libel trial of Dr. Thomas Cooper of Sunbury, Pennsylvania, and James T. Callender of Virginia. Dr. Cooper, lawyer, editor, scientist, physician and teacher, was brought to trial by information *ex officio* for writing that President Adams had saddled the country with the expense of a permanent navy, imperiled it with a standing army, borrowed money at 8 per cent in peacetime, and delivered up an American seaman, Jonathan Robbins, "to the mock trial of a British court martial." Cooper's defense, based on the truth of these assertions, brought the countercharge from Prosecutor Rawle that the defendant was compounding his crime by pleading the truth. He was addressing the country rather than the jurors, "evincing in the clearest manner a settled design to persuade the public that the President of the United States is not fit for the high office he bears."

Justice Chase added his judicial voice to the excoriation. "Take this publication in all its parts," he said to the jury, "and it is the boldest statement I have known to poison the minds of the people." The delivery of Robbins was defended as a simple case of extradition, required by treaty, of a man accused of murder. The judge then turned to political motivation. Noting that Cooper, in his published article, had declared his intention of making the Robbins case better known to the voters, Chase said to the jury:

"Here, then, the evident design of the traverser was, to arouse the people against the President so as to influence their minds against him on the next election. I think it right to explain this to you, because it proves, that the traverser was actuated by improper motives, to make this charge against the President."

Chase's position can be expressed perfectly in a syllogism. Criticism of a President's actions, with an improper motive, is criminal. The design to influence people against his re-election is an improper motive. Therefore it is criminal to try to influence people against his re-election by criticism of his actions. A minute or two later, Chase virtually ordered a conviction by describing each alleged libel as false and malicious. To this he added a general denunciation in which he blurted out even more plainly the political purpose of the Sedition Act:

"This publication is evidently intended to mislead the ignorant, and inflame their minds against the President, and to influence their votes on the next election."

The trial of Cooper added little to that of Lyon in constitutional controversy, but it did clarify the opposing positions on freedom of the press. To United States District Attorney Rawle the situation was simple. The defendant stood charged "with attempts which the practice and policy of all civilized nations have thought it right at all times to punish with severity." He had falsely and maliciously attacked the President "with an intent to excite the hatred and contempt of the people of this country against the man of their choice." It was atrocious conduct to abuse the men entrusted with national affairs, "to withdraw from them the confidence of the people, so necessary for conducting the public business." The peace of the country would be endangered if such mischief were tolerated, for "Error leads to discontent, discontent to a fancied idea of oppression, and that to insurrection," of which examples had been given in the Whisky Rebellion and a recent smaller Pennsylvania uprising against taxes.

What Rawle's stand amounted to, taken in April of a presidential election year, was that it was a crime for supporters of Jefferson to give specific reasons why President Adams did not merit re-election. Lawyer-Editor Cooper had contrary ideas. Conducting his own defense, he freely acknowledged the need of a certain degree of confidence in the executive government, then added:

"But this confidence ought . . . [to] be earned before it be reposed. . . . It cannot be exacted by the guarded provisions of sedition laws, by attacks on the freedom of the press, by prosecutions, pains and penalties on those which boldly express the truth, or who may honestly and innocently err in their political sentiments."

In the present state of things, said Cooper, the press was free to those who would praise the conduct of the men in power, while the threat of the law hung over those who blamed them. Praise was welcomed with avidity, "while those who venture to express a sentiment of opposition must do it in fear and trembling, and run the hazard of being dragged like myself before the frowning tribunal, erected by the Sedition Law. . . . Nor do I see how the people can exercise on rational grounds their elective franchise, if perfect freedom of discussion of public characters be not allowed."

Justice Chase, like Rawle, ignored the First Amendment. Said he to the jury:

"All governments which I have ever read or heard of punish libels against themselves. If a man attempts to destroy the confidence of the people in their officers, their supreme magistrate, and their legislature, he effectually saps the foundation of the government. A republican government can only be destroyed in two ways; the introduction of luxury, or the licentiousness of the press. This latter is the more slow, but most sure and certain, means of bringing about the destruction of the government. The legislature of this country, knowing this maxim, has thought proper to pass a law to check this licentiousness of the press. . . ."

The lines of conflict were closely drawn between Cooper and Chase, but no more closely than between Chase and the Constitution. To protect the foundation of republican government, the Constitution decreed that Congress should pass no law to abridge the freedom of the press. Congress, in order to make republican government secure (as Chase viewed it), abridged the freedom of the press to prevent its licentiousness. For authority Chase looked away from the Constitution to all governments he had "ever read or heard of." Implicit in his stand was the common attempt to restrict the meaning of "freedom" to exclude whatever freedom was regarded as obnoxious. But in relation to a free republic he damned his own position by the application of it—finding licentiousness of the press, warranting punishment by fine and imprisonment, in the always vitriolic arguments of a presidential campaign.

The trial of Publisher Callender was no less blatantly designed to silence the newspaper support of Jefferson for President, this time in his own state. Callender was a drunken roué of vicious character. His extravagant denunciations of the Adams Administration would have been self-defeating had they been ignored by the government. But the political motive for his indictment and conviction was clearly revealed in this sentence, cited as libelous, in his offending editorial: "Take your choice, then, between Adams, war and beggary, and Jefferson, peace and competency." Callender's trial won its conspicuous place in history by a savagery of prosecution that led (together with the Cooper case) to the impeachment of Justice Chase, and his narrow escape from actual removal from office, after political power shifted to the opposing party.

All of these trials, reeking with political rancor, furnished overwhelming proof of the folly and menace of the Sedition Act. They verified all that was said in the Kentucky and Virginia Resolutions about the destruction of liberty. They added the reinforcing effect of fulfilled prediction to what had been said in the congressional debates of 1798 on the fundamental conflict with the First Amendment. On that subject the author of the amendment was unremittingly at work, expounding and clarifying the issues placed before the country by his Virginia Resolutions.

CHAPTER 24
Madison vs. Marshall vs. Iredell

In drafting the Virginia Resolutions of 1798, Madison presented no detailed argument to support his summary declaration that the Sedition Act violated the Constitution. That omission was taken care of in January 1799, in an *Address of the General Assembly to the People*, also written by Madison. Coincident with it came an "Address of the Minority" from the pen of John Marshall, late envoy to France, who was both a Federalist member of the Virginia House of Delegates and member-elect of Congress. The two papers expounded the conflicting positions taken by the Republican majority and Federalist minority in the fight over adoption of the Virginia Resolutions. They were not summaries of debates, but constitutional expositions by the opposing protagonists. Madison's address was distributed by the state, Marshall's less extensively by the signers of it.

The Sedition Act, Madison wrote, "presents a scene which was never expected by the early friends of the Constitution." At the time of its adoption, the principle was admitted that federal power was limited to enumerated powers and to implied powers necessary to carry these specified powers into effect. Now, far broader federal authority was being deduced by implication. "From the existence of state law, it is inferred that Congress possess a similar power of legislation." Such a pretension, if admitted, would endow Congress with legislative power in all cases whatsoever. This would strip the states of every reserved right, because federal power is paramount when powers are concurrent. As understood in 1789, said Madison:

283

"Every libellous writing or expression might receive its punishment in the State courts, from juries summoned by an officer, who does not receive his appointment from the President, and is under no influence to court the pleasure of Government, whether it injured public officers or private citizens. . . . In answer to this, it is [now] urged that every Government possesses an inherent power of self-preservation, entitling it to do whatever it shall judge necessary for that purpose."

Powers drawn from such a source, Madison declared, could only be the creatures of uncontrollable ambition; for if the claim were correct, the defining of powers would have been superfluous. From this foundation he turned to freedom of the press:

"So insatiable is a love of power that it has resorted to a distinction between the freedom and licentiousness of the press for the purpose of converting the [First] amendment of the Constitution, which was dictated by the most lively anxiety to preserve that freedom, into an instrument for abridging it. Thus usurpation even justifies itself by a precaution against usurpation; and thus an amendment universally designed to quiet every fear is adduced as the source of an act which has produced general terror and alarm."

The distinction between liberty and licentiousness, Madison elaborated, was merely a new shape of the doctrine of implication. By its help, the judge of what was licentious could find a way through any constitutional restriction. Congress might find a religion to be heretical and licentious and proceed to suppress it. "The sophistry of a distinction between the liberty and the licentiousness of the press," he said, had been so forcibly exposed by the American envoys to France (John Marshall, C. C. Pinckney and Elbridge Gerry) that he would present it in their own words. Replying to Talleyrand's complaints about American newspaper criticism the envoys said in a 1797 memorial (recognized as the product of Marshall's pen):

"The genius of the Constitution, and the opinion of the people of the United States, cannot be overruled by those who administer the Government. Among those principles deemed sacred in America, among those sacred rights considered as forming the bulwark of their liberty, which the Government contemplates with awful reverence and would approach only with the most cautious circumspection, there is no one of which the importance is more deeply impressed on the public mind than the liberty of the press. That this *liberty* is often carried to excess; that it has sometimes degenerated into *licentiousness,* is seen and lamented, *but the remedy has not yet been discovered.*"

Perhaps, the quotation from the envoys went on, this licentiousness "is an evil inseparable from the good with which it is allied; perhaps it is a shoot which cannot be stripped from the stalk without wounding vitally the plant from which it is torn." However desirable remedial measures might be, to "correct without enslaving the press, they have never yet been devised in America." No regulations existed to suppress calumnies, nor to punish them "otherwise than by a legal prosecution in [state] courts which are alike open to all who consider themselves as injured."

Marshall's 1797 defense of a free press had previously attracted wide attention. In the 1798 debate on the sedition bill, Nathaniel Macon cited these same words, saying that "this subject had been so well handled by our Envoys in their reply to Mr. Talleyrand" that he wondered at the attempt to pass a bill of this kind. But there was a special significance to Madison's citation, for Marshall had just won election to Congress by declaring himself opposed to the Alien and Sedition Acts and promising to work and vote for their repeal.

"Had I been in Congress when they passed," Marshall wrote for publication in September 1798, ". . . I should have opposed them because I think them useless; and because they are calculated to create unnecessary discontents and jealousies at a time when our very existence, as a nation, may depend on our union."

This did not prevent Marshall from taking the lead in the Virginia legislature, three months later, in upholding the constitutionality of the acts. So when Madison eulogized the envoys for exposing "the sophistry of a distinction between the liberty of the press and its licentiousness," he was saying in effect that Marshall, in 1797, had exposed the sophistry of the position he took a year later in the Virginia legislature, where he made the distinction between liberty and licentiousness an essential element in the constitutionality of the Sedition Act.

Continuing his address to the people, Madison declared that the clause in the Sedition Act permitting a defendant to plead the truth would "not for a moment disguise the unconstitutionality of the act." Opinions as well as facts were made punishable and "the truth of an opinion is not susceptible of proof." Under this precedent "the truth of religion itself may be ascertained, and its pretended licentiousness punished by a jury of a different creed from that held by the person accused."

This brought Madison to what he regarded as not only the greatest danger but the greatest fallacy in the notion that allowing truth as a defense in libel permitted Congress to override the mandate that it should make no law abridging freedom of speech or press. The danger and the fallacy lay in the source from which the alleged power to legislate was derived—the common law of England. Madison stated the anomaly and portrayed its disastrous consequences:

"But where does the Constitution allow Congress to create crimes and inflict punishment, provided they allow the accused to exhibit evidence in his defense? This doctrine, united with the assertion, that sedition is a common law offence, and therefore within the correcting power of Congress, opens at once the hideous volumes of penal law, and turns loose upon us the utmost invention of insatiable malice and ambition, which, in all ages, have debauched morals, depressed liberty, shackled religion, supported despotism, and deluged the scaffold with blood."

These words came from an American to whom the history of the world was an open scroll. They linked our constitutional guarantees of freedom with the struggles against tyranny and cruelty in all the ages and in all countries—in England, France, Spain, Rome, Greece and the Oriental despotisms. But the link was especially with England, through the pretended incorporation in our Constitution of a common law that provided no protection for the great rights that formed the foundation stones of republican government.

Yet what is the fundamental assumption that has to be made, and is made, by those who contend that the mandates of the American Bill of Rights, unqualified in wording, carry within themselves the weakening provisions of the English common law? They are bound to assume that Madison, and those who stood with him in the shaping of these guarantees, wrote them with deliberate intent (for knowledge of effect is the same as design) to allow "the utmost invention of insatiable malice and ambition" to be turned loose upon the American people whenever that might be the will and pleasure of Congress. That must have been the intention of those having such a view of the common law, if they intended that the First Amendment should be subordinate to it.

As Madison answered Marshall, so Marshall answered Madison in the "Address of the Minority." In his 1797 memorial to Talleyrand, Marshall had denied a legal distinction between liberty and licentiousness and defended freedom of the press in terms that lacked little of being absolute. But he left a loophole within his denial of the power of Congress to override "the genius of the Constitution." Freedom of the press was so sacred that the lawmakers would approach the subject only with "awful reverence" and "the most cautious circumspection." Marshall now told how and why, being free to approach the subject, they had power to subject the press to the Sedition Act:

"To contend that there does not exist a power to punish writings coming within the description of this law, would be to assert the inability of our nation to preserve its own peace, and to protect themselves from the attempts of wicked citizens, who, incapable of quiet themselves, are incessantly employed in devising means to disturb the public repose. . . . This the people have a right to prevent: and therefore, in all the nations of the earth, where presses are known, some corrective of their licentiousness has been deemed indispensable."

Marshall found constitutional authority in the combined effect of the "necessary and proper" clause and the English common law *as the law of the individual states.* Congress had power to pass penal laws "necessary and proper" to prevent resistance to the execution of laws. Did not that clause, then, "also authorize the punishment of those acts which are criminal in themselves, and which obviously lead to and prepare resistance?" Such was the effect of continued calumnies against the government.

The federal courts, Marshall said, had power to try cases arising *under the Constitution* OR *the laws* of the United States. Those arising under the Constitution, but not under federal laws, "must be cases triable by a rule which exists independent of any act of the legislature of the union. That rule is the common or unwritten law which pervades all America, and which declaring libels against government to be a punishable offence, applies itself to, and protects any government which the will of the people may establish."

Marshall avoided saying that there was any such thing as a federal common law, and he carefully limited the scope of his reasoning to the subject of libel. But having set up a common-law jurisdiction for *federal* judges because the common law "pervades all America"—that is, *pervades the states*—he employed it to transfer the power from the courts to Congress:

"The judicial power of the United States, then, being extended to the punishment of libels against the government, as a common law offense, arising under the Constitution which creates the government, the general [necessary and proper] clause gives to the legislature of the union the right to make such laws as shall give that power effect."

That argument, less cleverly worded, had been answered again and again in the congressional debates on the sedition bill: If the judges had the power under common law, no statute was needed to give it effect, so the need of the law disproved the existence of the power. Marshall's whole case was predicated on the supposition that "cases arising under the Constitution" *must be* cases arising under the common law instead of statutes. Common sense and history both disprove this. By judicial interpretation and application, the words refer to constitutional provisions that are self-enforcing—provisions so elemental, clear and positive that no law is needed to put them into effect. Consider, for instance, the clause forbidding Congress to pass bills of attainder. Would anybody suggest that the courts could not enforce it unless Congress first passed a law forbidding itself to pass such bills? Would anybody suggest that a court's power of enforcement was derived from the common law, which presents no obstacles whatever to bills of attainder?

No less fallacious was Marshall's contention that, because libels against the government were punishable under common law in all the states, the common law reached up and protected "any government which the will of the people may establish." Actions might indeed be brought *in state courts* for libel of *federal* officials as individuals. But Marshall was saying that because the will of the people established the federal government by constitutional compact, and because libels against government were punishable at common law in all the states, the existence of this power *in the states* established a similar jurisdiction in the *federal* courts. Such an argument might be called upside-down "interposition" run wild.

This brought Marshall to his highest hurdle—the First Amendment. Here he had no alternative but to turn to Blackstone and in effect repudiate his memorial to Talleyrand. The amendment, he pointed out, employed different language concerning religion and the press. "Congress is prohibited from making any law *respecting* a religious establishment, but not from making any law *respecting* the press"—only from *abridging* its freedom. For two reasons the Sedition Act did not abridge the freedom of the press:

"1. A punishment of the licentiousness is not considered as a restriction of the freedom of the press.

"2. The act complained of does not punish any writing not before punishable, nor does it inflict a more severe penalty than that to which the same writing was before liable."

The liberty of the press, Marshall explained without mentioning Blackstone, "signifies a liberty to publish, free from previous restraint, any thing and every thing at the discretion of the printer only, but not the liberty of spreading with impunity false and scandalous slanders, which may destroy the peace and mangle the reputation, of an individual or a community." On the second point, freedom of the press was unabridged as long as writers were not punished more severely than they had been previous to the Revolution, when "the common law was the law of the land throughout the United States."

That reasoning made degree of punishment a constitutional test of the law's validity. A sedition law would be beyond the power of Congress if it provided the death penalty for writers who called President Adams a tyrant. It would be constitutional, as far as the common law was concerned, if the maximum punishment did not exceed life imprisonment, slicing off the ears and slitting the nose.

In adopting Blackstone's definition of freedom of the press,

Marshall threw his memorial to Talleyrand into the discard and struck down "the genius of the Constitution." If freedom meant no more than the absence of a government licenser, the whole subject had been moot for a hundred years. The best answer to Marshall had already been made by Marshall himself, when he wrote to the French Foreign Minister that the "calumnies and invectives" of the American press, directed as much against the American government as against France, were "*a calamity incident to the nature of liberty.*"

But the "Address of the Minority" was a partisan tract, not a judicial opinion. Never, as Chief Justice, would John Marshall have indulged in the manifold sophistries of his legislative address. Yet his partisanship was hardly more than political rote, for Marshall had cut all ties with the New England advocates of the Sedition Act when he promised, as a candidate for Congress, to work for its repeal. To Fisher Ames he had proved himself by his apostasy one of "the meanest of cowards, the falsest of hypocrites." Ames's temper had in it the distemper of the times.

The ambivalence in Marshall's position—defending as legally "necessary and proper" a law that he had politically condemned as unnecessary and improper—made both parties reject him and helped to consign his minority address to virtual oblivion. The real challenge to Madison, Jefferson, Gallatin, Livingston and other defenders of the First Amendment came from Supreme Court judges, and especially from Justice Iredell.

For two years Iredell had been in a state of silent rage because of his inability to send Congressman Cabell to prison. No early case under the Sedition Act came to his circuit, but he found an opportunity to discuss that law in April 1799, while asking a federal grand jury in Philadelphia to indict a tax-resisting German farmer, Jacob Fries, for high treason.[1] The Alien and Sedition Acts were not involved, he told the grand jurors, but the Virginia and Kentucky legislatures having pronounced those laws unconstitutional, he deemed it his duty to discuss that subject.

Taking up the Sedition Act, Iredell reversed the position he had taken in 1788, when he denied that Congress had power to restrict the freedom of the press. He was now "convinced it was an erroneous opinion." And so it was, in the sense that he had stated the penal powers of the federal government much too narrowly. Now, however, he went still farther on the opposite tangent, saying that under the "necessary and proper" clause, Congress could enact laws in a period of confusion and disorder that "would not, perhaps, be necessary and proper in a time of tranquillity and order." Why did Fries resist taxes? Because "the government had been vilely misrepresented" in the press. "The liberty of the press is, indeed, valuable—long may it preserve its lustre!" But the nearly $2,000,000 spent to put down the Whisky Rebellion "might be deemed the price of libels" that went unpunished.

Thus Iredell, like Marshall, found the power to punish libels arising out of the power to pass laws "necessary and proper." But while Marshall tried to restrict his reasoning to libel alone (apparently to avoid the limitless expanse of a federal common law), Iredell took the position that necessity created power. But necessity of that sort had no limit except the imagination. If confusion and disorder in the country created new and unspecified powers in Congress, every safeguard of liberty could be wiped out by confused and disorderly lawmakers.

Both Marshall and Iredell, in relying on the "necessary and proper" clause, for restraint of the press, were giving as a source of power the very section of the Constitution against which the First Amendment was meant to be a protection. Iredell, contending that the Sedition Act was "necessary and proper" to ensure the collection of federal taxes, revealed the pin-point accuracy of Madison's warning to Congress that this general power must be restrained by a Bill of Rights. Said Madison in 1789:

"The General Government has a right to pass all laws which shall be necessary to collect its revenue; the means of enforcing the collection are within the direction of the Legislature: may not general warrants be considered necessary for this purpose?"

If instead of "general warrants," Madison had warned of a possible attempt to collect revenue by abridging freedom of the press, the whole House might have roared with laughter at such a chimera. Yet here, ten years later, was that precise argument, advanced by a justice of the Supreme Court to justify the abridgment of that freedom by another Congress.

Iredell also repeated Marshall in contending that the change from "respecting" to "abridging" in two clauses of the First Amendment, gave Congress a power to make laws "respecting" the press without abridging its freedom. But not content, as Marshall had been, with merely adopting the Blackstone definition as his own, Iredell pillared his position on the English commentator's writings. Nowhere, said he, had the meaning of freedom of the press been more happily, more justly, or more definitely expressed than in the great *Commentaries* of Blackstone, which for nearly thirty years "has been the manual of almost every student of law in the United States," and often was the favorite reading of private gentlemen. Blackstone's definition of it as freedom from *previous* restraint, with punishment for "improper, mischievous, or illegal" publications, "could scarcely be unknown to those who framed the Amendments to the Constitution." Even if it was unknown, said the judge, his explanation must have been satisfactory to them. For if not, "I presume the amendment would have been more particularly worded, to guard against any possible mistake."

Iredell's argument came down to two points: (1) that since Blackstone's definition was known to the framers of the First Amendment, they must have accepted it; (2) that words similar to the First Amendment in state bills of rights did not prevent punishment of seditious libel under "the common law principles concerning libels."

Iredell's first conclusion was unsupported guesswork; the second was built on a false premise. Not one of the state bills of rights contained the mandatory language of the First Amendment. Since the common law was established by state constitutions, it was easy for courts and legislatures to override the weakly worded maxim that freedom of the press *ought to* be inviolable. From the standpoint of the people in general, such ineffectual clauses were in themselves an argument for a stronger federal guarantee. Madison made that very point in 1789, when he spoke in Congress of state bills of rights being "absolutely improper" because they did not "agree with *the common ideas of liberty.*"

On the factual side, Iredell's whole edifice of logic had a single underpinning—that because the men who wrote the First Amendment were no doubt familiar with Blackstone's definition, they must have agreed with it. The easiest way to disprove that assumption is to accept it. Doing so puts Framer Madison in full harmony with Interpreter Iredell, both of them recognizing England's common law of seditious libel as an unwritten part of the United States Constitution. Agreeing thus, they should have agreed no less on the results of this recognition. Did they?

Iredell, using the words of Blackstone, said that making sedition a common-law offense was necessary "for the preservation of peace and good order, of government and religion, the only solid foundations of civil liberty."

Madison said that making sedition a common-law offense "opens at once the hideous volumes of penal law, and turns loose upon us the utmost invention of insatiable malice and ambition, which, in all ages, have debauched morals, depressed liberty, shackled religion, supported despotism, and deluged the scaffold with blood."

Does one need a microscope to detect a difference between those two statements? But it has been said that nothing Madison or anybody else wrote after the passage of the Sedition Act can be accepted as a measure of earlier opinions, because their attitudes may have been warped by that law. Supposing, momentarily, that such was the case, let us consider what the ardent advocates of freedom of the press must have been ready to accept, in 1789, if at that time they agreed with Blackstone's definition of freedom of the press and approved the common law of seditious libel.

Such a premise would force us to conclude that the people who forbade Congress to abridge freedom of the press placidly accepted, for the United States, the conditions that developed in England after licensing was abolished in 1694. As T. E. May described them: "To speak ill of the government was a crime. . . . Every one was a libeler who outraged the sentiments of the dominant party." That was the universally known condition in England and the potential condition anywhere, under such a system. It was also the exact situation brought about in the United States by the Sedition Act. To speak ill of the government was a crime. That perfectly represented the political thinking of the congressmen who passed the Sedition Act and the judges who upheld and enforced it. But to say that it fell within the design of those who framed the First Amendment, or the countless thousands of Americans who unitedly demanded it, is so preposterous a contention that one can only marvel at the state of mind that has given credence to it.

The question of original purpose can be resolved without difficulty if all persons concerned are credited, as they should be, with honest presentation of the views they held during the brief period of framing and testing the guarantees. But that does not decide the underlying constitutional issue on which the validity of the Sedition Act—and all federal libel prosecutions—was deemed to turn. Were the individual members of the Supreme Court correct, in 1798-1800, in holding that the common law of England was imbedded in the Constitution and determined the meaning of the First Amendment? If they were wrong, if there was no federal common law, the original basis for rejecting the literal meaning of the First Amendment vanishes completely. The final answer to that question was to come from the United States Supreme Court, as a body, a dozen years after Marshall became Chief Justice. But the immediate answer came from the State of Virginia. The instrument of it was Madison's famous 1800 Report to the General Assembly on the Virginia Resolutions of 1798.

CHAPTER 25
A Textbook on Liberty

Madison's *Report on the Virginia Resolutions of 1798*, presented by a legislative committee and adopted by the Virginia General Assembly on January 7, 1800, had two distinct but related purposes. The first was to remove the impression prevailing in several states that Virginia's call for "interposition" by the states against the Alien and Sedition Acts meant nullification of them by state action. The other purpose was to demonstrate that these two laws violated the Constitution, and in that connection to rebut the Federalist contention that seditious libel was punishable at common law in the federal courts of the United States.

In defining "interposition" *by the states*, Madison observed that the word "states" was variously used. It might mean territories occupied by the political societies within them, or the governments established by those societies, or those societies as organized into governments. "Lastly, it means the people composing those political societies, in their highest sovereign capacity." It was in this highest sense that the Constitution was submitted to "the States" and ratified by them. It was in this sense that the Resolutions of 1798 asked "the States," as makers of the federal compact, to "interpose" to uphold it against the "deliberate, palpable and dangerous" exercise of powers not granted by the Constitution. Reverting to this theme after dealing with the Alien and Sedition Acts, Madison asserted that the means of "interposition" were to be constitutional, consisting in the main of expressions of opinions, exertion of influence for repeal of laws, or exercise of the power of the states to revise the national Constitution. There was a sharp distinction, he said, between declarations of the meaning of the Constitution by judges, or by peoples and legislatures. The latter, in calling a law unconstitutional, did not assume the office of the judge:

"The declarations in such cases, are expressions of opinion, unaccompanied with any other effect, than what they may produce on opinion, by exciting reflection. The expositions of the judiciary, on the other hand, are carried into immediate effect by force."

State "interposition" against a law as unconstitutional, said Madison, "may lead to a change in the legislative expression of the general will; possibly to a change in the opinion of the judiciary." But until the law goes off the statute books, or the courts alter their decisions, it must be considered that their upholding of the law "enforces the general will." In taking this position Madison was supporting the judicial power even in cases where he believed it was being grossly misused. Of far greater ultimate importance, his 1800 repudiation of nullification helped to hold the nation together in the 1830s, when that doctrine was pressed by South Carolina. But the immediate effect, in 1800, was to give greater force to the main body of the *Report*, which was directed against the constitutionality of the Alien and Sedition Acts.

Conceding that Congress through its war power had ample authority over enemy aliens, Madison pointed out that two laws on aliens had been passed, one specifically limited to enemy nationals, the other applying alike to enemies and to aliens who were members of friendly nations. Only with respect to the latter did Virginia protest the law. Defenders of the statute contended that not even friendly aliens could demand due process of law because this was not a *penal*, but a *preventive* measure. Even admitting such a distinction, said Madison, the law violated the principles of preventive justice. Due process required that some probable ground of suspicion be exhibited before some judicial authority; that it be supported by oath or affirmation; that the party be allowed to avoid confinement by producing pledges for legal conduct; that a person must be able to obtain release by habeas corpus if wrongly confined; and that he could be restored to his former rights and liberties by judicial order, if found to be entitled to them.

All these principles of American law were violated by a statute that threw total power into the hands of the President with no judicial safeguards whatever. "His will is the law. . . . His suspicion is the only evidence which is to convict: his order the only judgment which is to be executed." This union of powers subverted both "the general principles of free government" and the positive provisions of the Federal Constitution separating the legislative, executive and judicial branches.

Turning to the Sedition Act, Madison's *Report* struck instantly at the main support of it. This was "the doctrine lately advanced . . . 'that the common or unwritten law,' a law of vast extent and complexity, and embracing almost every possible subject of legislation, both civil and criminal 'makes a part of the law of these States; in their united and national capacity.' " This pretension was so novel and extravagant that it might have been passed over in silence, except for the auspices under which it was presented.

Although Madison did not identify "the auspices," the nature and sequence of his argument identified his principal target (though not the only one) as the report of a select committee of the national House of Representatives, adopted on February 25, 1799, by a vote of 52 to 48. The House at that time was being flooded with petitions for repeal of the Alien and Sedition Acts, with more than 18,000 signers in a dozen counties of Pennsylvania, New York, New Jersey, Virginia and Vermont. Instead of being disposed of without comment in Committee of the Whole, declared Representative Gallatin the moment the motion to refer was made, they were being used to produce a partisan report that would be circulated throughout the United States to halt the flow of petitions. An incidental effect, if not an intended one, was to guide Federalist state legislatures in their replies to the Virginia and Kentucky Resolutions. The committee report, presented by Chauncey Goodrich of Connecticut, was in general distilled out of the 1798 speeches of Otis, Harper and Allen. The nature of it is indicated in Madison's rebuttal.

Prior to the American Revolution, wrote Madison in his 1800 *Report*, the common law under various limitations made a part of the colonial codes. But it was the separate law of each colony within its limits, and totally unknown as a law pervading all of them as one society. It could not be otherwise, for it was not the same in any two colonies, nor was there any common legislature or magistracy by which a common will could be expressed or carried into practice. England could not impose it on the colonies, for the Revolution was a denial of Parliament's power to legislate for them.

The Articles of Confederation, Madison averred, did not contain a sentence or a syllable that could be tortured into a construction that the states formed one community with respect to the common law. Such an inference was "absolutely precluded" by the Second Article, reserving to each state every power, jurisdiction and right that was not expressly delegated to the United States in Congress Assembled. That left only one question: "Is this exclusion revoked, and the common law introduced as a national law, by the present Constitution of the United States?"

Madison's answer was No. He would readily admit that particular parts of the common law might have received a sanction from the Constitution, so far as they were necessarily comprehended in the technical wording of the enumerated powers, or were necessary and proper for carrying those powers into execution. But the question at issue "relates to the common law, beyond these limitations." The *Report* analyzed various provisions of the Constitution to show that the wording of the document did not embrace the common law. Nearly a dozen hypothetical questions produced as many reasons why so diverse a mass of unwritten laws, variously modified by British statutes and those of the American states, could not be shaped by implication into an American national code. If it could be so shaped, he said, it would either be unchangeable by Congress, being in the Constitution, or, through the power to change it, Congress would be vested with a power of legislation coextensive with the common law. That would give it power to legislate in all cases whatsoever. The system argued for would give the President enforcement powers coextensive with the common law, if not with British crown prerogatives growing out of that law. It would give the courts a legislative power hardly short of that of Congress, except as overruled by statutes that would require ages to enact.

The *Report* concluded "that the common law never was, nor by any fair construction ever can be, deemed a law for the American people as one community." To hold it to be so "would sap the foundation of the Constitution as a system of limited and specified powers." There could be no severer reproach on the Constitution, or on those who framed or those who established it, than such a supposition would throw on them.

This argument alone should have been enough for anybody who wished to maintain the federal system, but it was only a prelude to Madison's attack on the Sedition Act as a specific violation of the Constitution. Nobody pretended that Congress had express power to pass such an act. Was there any express power for whose execution a law of this kind was necessary and proper? Claim was made that the power of "suppressing insurrections" implied a power of *preventing* them by punishing whatever might *lead* or *tend* to them. This brought the comment from Madison:

"But it surely cannot, with the least plausibility, be said, that a regulation of the press, and a punishment of libels, are exercises of a power to suppress insurrections. The most that could be said, would be, that the punishment of libels, if it had the tendency ascribed to it, might prevent the occasion, of passing or executing laws, necessary and proper for the suppression of insurrections."

The federal government, Madison said, had ample power to pass laws in advance to punish insurrections, and to enforce them when the occasion arose. But "if the power to *suppress insurrections,* includes a power to *punish libels;* or if the power to *punish,* includes a power to *prevent,* by all the means that may have that tendency," then the interrelationship of the subjects of legislation was such that "a power over a very few, would carry with it a power over all." Moreover, if Congress was not limited in its *choice of means* to those having an appropriate relation to the powers specified in the Constitution, judicial review was reduced to a nullity. The actions of Congress would be governed by "mere policy and expediency; on which legislative discretion alone can decide, and from which the judicial interposition and controul are completely excluded."

Madison's argument up to this point had taken no account of the First Amendment, or of the particularly vicious details of the Sedition Act. He was denying the power of Congress, even under the unamended Constitution, to pass *any sort of criminal libel law.* He now turned to the mandate that "Congress shall make no law . . . abridging the freedom of speech or of the press." The common law, he had shown, was not American national law, but the question remained whether its definitions were implied in the Constitution:

"In the attempts to vindicate the 'Sedition Act,' it has been contended, 1. That the 'freedom of the press' is to be determined by the meaning of these terms in the common law. 2. That the article supposes the power over the press to be in Congress, and prohibits them only from *abridging* the freedom allowed to it by the common law."

Actually, said Madison, some of the crimes defined in the Sedition Act abridged even the freedom of publication recognized by the common law in England. But, passing over that, the contention of the law's defenders was that freedom of the press under the common law consisted of exemption from all *previous* restraint on publication. Said Madison's committee *Report:*

"It appears to the committee, that this idea of the freedom of the press, can never be admitted to be the American idea of it: since a law inflicting penalties on printed publications, would have a familiar effect with a law authorizing a previous restraint on them. It would seem a mockery to say, that no law should be passed, preventing publications from being made, but that laws might be passed for punishing them in case they should be made."

To clarify the subject Madison pointed to "the essential difference between the British government, and the American Constitution." In England the danger of encroachment on rights was understood to be confined to the Executive. Magna Carta and the British bills of rights were reared against royal usurpations of power. It was to guard against the danger from the Executive that the powers of Parliament became unlimited. Under such a government as Britain's, "an exemption of the press from previous restraint by licensers appointed by the king, is all the freedom that can be secured to it." Not so in the American system:

"In the United States, the case is altogether different. The people, not the government, possess the absolute sovereignty. The legislature, no less than the executive, is under limitations of power. Hence in the United States, the great and essential rights of the people are secured . . . not by laws paramount to prerogative, but by constitutions paramount to laws. This security of the freedom of the press, requires that it should be exempt, not only from previous restraint by the executive, as in Great Britain; but from legislative restraint also; and this exemption, to be effective, must be an exemption, not only from the previous inspection of licensers, but from the subsequent penalty of laws."

It was natural, Madison thought, that liberty of the press should be less extensive in England, where the greater part of the government was hereditary and not responsible, than in the United States, where executive magistrates were not held to be infallible nor legislatures to be omnipotent. Yet in England, in reference to the responsible part of the government—the House of Commons and ministers subject to impeachment[1]—the press acted with a freedom that went far beyond the limits prescribed by the ordinary rules of law. So too in probably every state of the Union, a press legally restricted by the common law was in the habit of unrestrained animadversions on state governments and officials. "On this footing, the freedom of the press has stood; on this footing it yet stands."

Having demolished the lofty edifice of argument built on these dormant state restrictions, Madison went on: "Some degree of abuse is inseparable from the proper use of every thing; and in no instance is this more true, than in that of the press." Paraphrasing John Marshall's words to Talleyrand on American refusal to restrain the licentiousness of the press, Madison said that the states found it better "to leave a few of its noxious branches, to their luxuriant growth, than by pruning them away, to injure the vigor of those yielding the proper fruits.

"And can the wisdom of this policy be doubted by any who reflect, that to the press alone, checquered as it is with abuses, the world is indebted for all the triumphs which have been gained by reason and humanity, over error and oppression; who reflect that to the same beneficent source, the United States owe much of the lights which conducted them to the rank of a free and independent nation; and which have improved their political system, into a shape so auspicious to their happiness."

Had sedition acts been uniformly enforced against the press, for bringing the constituted agents of government into contempt, "might not the United States have been languishing at this day, under the infirmities of a sickly confederation? Might they not possibly be miserable colonies, groaning under a foreign yoke?" The Madison *Report,* however, did not rest its case on a demonstration that the common law of England was a false guide to the freedom whose abridgment was forbidden:

"They [the committee] contend that the article of amendment, instead of supposing in Congress, a power that might be exercised over the press, provided its freedom be not abridged, was meant as a positive denial to Congress, of any power whatever on the subject."

To demonstrate "that this was the true object of the article," Madison recalled the great apprehension expressed in 1787 and 1788, lest the omission of some positive guarantee of the freedom of the press might expose it to the danger of being drawn by construction within the powers of Congress. Especially was there fear of this through the power to make all laws necessary and proper for carrying the other powers into execution. In reply, it was invariably urged that all powers not given by the Constitution were reserved; that power over the press was neither enumerated nor implied, and any exercise of such power would be a manifest usurpation. "It is painful to remark, how much the arguments now employed in behalf of the Sedition Act are at variance with the reasoning which then justified the Constitution, and invited its ratification."

It was to remove doubts and dangers on this point that the First Amendment was adopted. Congress itself declared, in submitting the amendments, that it did so because a number of state conventions, in ratifying the Constitution, had "expressed a desire, in order to prevent misconstructions or abuse of its powers, that further declaratory and restrictive clauses should be added." Here, said Madison, "is the most satisfactory and authentic proof, that the several amendments proposed, were to be considered as either declaratory or restrictive," and as corresponding with the desires of the states. Only by a construction holding the press "to be wholly exempt from the power of Congress" could the amendment correspond with those desires:

"Nay more; the construction employed to justify the Sedition Act, would exhibit a phenomenon without a parallel in the political world. It would exhibit a number of respectable states, as denying first that any power over the press was delegated by the Constitution, as proposing next, that an amendment to it, should explicitly declare that no such power was delegated; and finally, as concurring in an amendment actually recognizing or delegating such a power."

"Is then the Federal government [Madison asked in conclusion] destitute of every authority for restraining the licentiousness of the press, and for shielding itself against the libellous attacks which may be made on those who administer it?" The Constitution alone could answer this question. And if no such power was expressly delegated, if it was not both necessary and proper to carry out an express power; "above all, if it be expressly forbidden by a declaratory amendment to the Constitution, the answer must be, that the federal government is destitute of all such authority."

For this prohibition, the *Report* said, there were many reasons, including the magnitude of some of the federal powers and the almost sole reliance on the press for information on affairs at a distant seat of government. Would not these account for "binding the hand of the federal government . . . and of leaving those who administer it, to a remedy for injured reputations, under the same laws, and in the same tribunals, which protect their lives, their liberties, and their properties?" But beyond all this, should any elective officers violate their duties, it was natural and proper that "they should be brought into contempt or disrepute, and incur the hatred of the people." The great remedial rights of the people were to be found in pure elections. A free press was their instrument of information and communication, and only a press that was wholly free could serve the electoral process, which was the essence of a free and responsible government.

Madison's *Report* had flaws in it due to its nature—an attempt to preserve the *force* of state "interposition" while confining its *substance* to the influence of public opinion. But as an argument against the Sedition Act it was overwhelming both in constitutional law and as an exposition of public policy in a free society. Widely distributed, and accepted at once as a Republican textbook, it gradually broke through party lines and helped to establish a national consensus against the existence of a federal common law. But the *Report* went further. *It assailed every basis so far advanced for asserting the power of Congress to punish seditious libel by statute.*

With the common law eliminated, that power was stripped down to the contention that Congress, in order to carry out its specified powers, could pass a law punishing any speech or writings that *tended* to hamper the making or enforcement of laws. It could do this even though the Constitution—to prevent that very construction—was specifically amended to forbid it. Madison shattered that contention by irrefutable reasoning and illustration. He did the same to the one point left—that freedom of the press consisted of nothing but the absence of a government licenser. But Federalists in Congress and on the bench gave no sign of accepting his arguments or the similar ones advanced in Congress.

CHAPTER 26
Revival of Freedom

Two weeks after the Virginia legislature adopted Madison's *Report*, Congressman Macon of North Carolina offered a resolution to repeal Section 2 of the Sedition Act. His motion did not touch Section 1—dealing with insurrections—but was directed against the portion that was producing the trials and convictions: making it seditious libel to defame the government or the President.

As he had done in 1798, the North Carolinian denied that the Sedition Act was constitutional, and in this year of a presidential election he emphasized the need of free political discussion. Purity in government depended on free elections, and elections could not be free unless the people had "the liberty of freely investigating the character, conduct, and ability of each candidate."

Replying to Macon, Federalist James A. Bayard of Delaware cried out: "Can the freedom of the press require the liberty to publish malicious lies? Can any one hesitate in saying that such a liberty would be licentiousness? The law had said no more." Nothing could induce Mr. Bayard to vote for repeal, but not knowing how the vote would go in that closely divided House, he would offer an amendment to render the resolution as harmless as possible. He moved the following addition:

"And the offences therein specified shall remain punishable as at common law; provided, that upon any prosecution it shall be lawful for the defendant to give in his defence the truth of the matters charged as a libel."[1]

Gallatin saw a trick in this and jumped onto the word RE-MAIN. By phrasing it thus, Bayard was seeking an implied declaration that a certain class of persons were already punishable at common law in the courts of the United States. Nicholas of Virginia suspected that Bayard had a larger hidden design, "to bring into force in this country all the common law of England, and with it all the punishments and penalties there inflicted."

Bayard resumed the floor. He did not know why he was accused of hiding his purpose behind a veil. Far from being hidden, his intention was open. The word "remain" was not intended to *introduce* the common law into the Constitution but to testify to its *existence*. He had always been of that opinion, and he was informed that the same view was held by all but one of the Supreme Court judges. (Justice Chase had rejected it some years earlier.)

This roused Gallatin to ask: "Where did the judges get that power of making the common law the law of our land?" Such a doctrine "was clearly the same as setting aside at one stroke all the restrictions and limitations of power as expressed in the Constitution." Indeed it would go farther. Congress could legislate only on subjects specially granted to them by the Constitution, but if the judiciary had common-law powers, it could make decisions on subjects upon which Congress could not legislate.

Harper of South Carolina, taking his cue from Marshall's minority pamphlet, said there was no need to decide whether the common law was generally in force in the United States. The question was whether libel of the government was punishable without a statute. "Of this he never had a doubt." The Sedition Act was merely an affirmation of the "common or universal law" that such libel is punishable. If the subject matter existed, the law operated upon it. "When the Constitution created the Government, it brought into existence the subject matter; the offence therefore arises under the Constitution, and in that view the judiciary can punish libels against the Government of the United States."

It was not quite clear, in Harper's paraphrase of Marshall, whether "the subject matter" was "the Government," or "libel," but it made no difference. Either one was adequate to the argument, which could as well have been based on the slant of the Leaning Tower of Pisa. Harper did, however, arouse curiosity. Nicholas had never yet seen a man who could explain the common law, and now Harper had found something new: the Bayard Amendment was "part of the universal law." Where was he to look for this universal law? Was it the practice of all nations, and was no government to deviate from it?

Otis of Massachusetts rescued Harper by rising from universal to heavenly law. It was not the common law of England "in its full extent" that had been absorbed into the United States Constitution, but so much as had been found applicable to America. The right to punish misdemeanors that had a tendency to destroy the Government was inherent in the people of every State. "It was a principle of common law essential to the preservation of social order and of every Government under Heaven."

The author of the original resolution stood up for a closing comment on Bayard's addition to it: "Mr. Macon thought it the most extraordinary amendment that ever was tacked to a resolution." It meant, when coupled with the resolution, "that the law ought to be repealed, and yet continued in force!" But if the common law was in force, and could punish crime, there could be no reason for declaring so by statute. If it was not in force, he feared this amendment would establish it.

Instead of voting first on the amendment, the House by some quirk, or slip, or subtle design, reversed the order. The original resolution was approved 50 to 48. The amendment then carried, 51 to 47. Speaker Jonathan Dayton attempted to treat this as a final action, since both parts had been approved. But amid the protests of the Republicans against this finesse, "Mr. Otis relieved the House from the embarrassment by moving the question on the whole resolution," and it was defeated, 87 to 11.

So ended this bizarre attempt to have Congress declare that the common law of England, or so much of it as would enable federal judges to punish seditious libel, was part of the law of the United States. Late in the contest John Nicholas voiced a conclusion drawn from the words and actions of those who attempted this maneuver:

"Mr. Nicholas conceived the common law was at its last push, and that if gentlemen, who were friends to it, could not get this, or some such provision, to support it, it was beginning to appear so monstrous that it never could be executed in this country. There might be found court after court who could give opinions in favor of its existence and force, but he should venture to say that public opinion must finally make them abandon the doctrine."

That was an accurate forecast, and also foreshadowed the political upheaval against the Sedition Act, about to be registered in the presidential and congressional elections, but it brought an immediate protest from one of the leading Federalists, Samuel W. Dana of Connecticut. He found evidence throughout the Constitution (in such things as reference to "excessive bail" and other terms) that common law was established in the American code. Gallatin replied, as he had done two years earlier, that the adoption of certain common-law procedures in the courts was vastly different from the principle that offenses were brought within the jurisdiction of the federal courts by the mere fact that they were offenses at common law. Concede that, and the country would have two constitutions. One would be the Constitution established by the people, the other would be the common law, and the latter would erase all the limitations placed by the people on the former.

No member, probably, listened to the debate with more acute interest than silent Congressman John Marshall. He heard his own arguments used by the Federalists, along with their own more sweeping contentions, to support the Sedition Act. He fulfilled his campaign promise by voting with the Republicans against the extension of it, but his opinion on common-law jurisdiction remained locked within his breast.

The country early in 1800 was rumbling with portents of political change, but there was no hint of this in the conduct of Supreme Court justices on circuit. They went from one mad prosecution to another in their drive to silence the Jeffersonian press during the presidential campaign. The Alien and Sedition Acts had depended from the beginning, for passage and support, on hysterical fear of France. The whole tipsy edifice crashed to the ground when President Adams, the statesman triumphing over the passionate egotist, ousted his cabinet warmongers, made John Marshall Secretary of State, and sent new commissioners to France in an effort to end the naval half-war. The mere sending of them went far to dissolve the international crisis.

For his political future, the President's mixing of patriotism, common sense and righteous anger proved a witches' brew. It racked and divided his own party, and ended the delusion of danger that had won him Republican support. It also gave new sway to two deep-seated American characteristics: hatred of government curbs on tongue and press, and violent dislike of taxes. The infliction of war taxes without a war may have done more than was done by voice and press to persuade the people of the iniquity of the Sedition Act and its sponsors.

Among the private words of protest, however, were some that provided a fundamental message to America on the meaning of free speech in a self-governing society. Tunis Wortman, a prominent New York lawyer, took time enough from his practice in 1800 to write a book-length *Treatise Concerning Political Enquiry and the Liberty of the Press.* Calm in tone, persuasive in content, it marshaled the accumulated and developing libertarian thought of several centuries.

"Public liberty," wrote Wortman, "is the greatest blessing of the social state," and freedom of speech and opinion is "indispensably requisite to the perpetuation of civil liberty." The age-long suppression of liberty resulted from a belief that people could be governed only by stratagem and imposture; that they would lose their reverence for public institutions the moment they were asked to support them by the conviction of their understanding. On the contrary, investigation was dangerous only "to the systems which are founded in despotism and corruption, but it confers additional energy on those that are established upon the genuine foundation of truth."

"There is no species of tyranny [wrote Wortman] more pernicious in its consequences than that which is exerted to impede the progress of intellect. Slavery will inevitably produce mental debility and degradation. . . . Wherever freedom of enquiry is established, improvement is inevitable; the smallest spark of knowledge will be cherished and kindled into flame."

In contrast with this, the attempt of government to coerce thought and expression was a grafting of slavery upon the trunk of liberty, altering its natural properties. To prevent an inferior and almost imaginary evil should we resort to a system accompanied by formidable calamities? "In the exuberance of our zeal against malignant calumny and misrepresentation, shall we consent to paralyze and cripple the most beneficial powers of society?"

Prosecutions for personal slander, Wortman observed, were

founded in real damage, but private action at the suit of the injured party furnished a sufficient remedy. So too, civil suits by injured officers of government were a sufficient restraint upon the licentiousness of the press. Far different in purpose and effect was the instrument of seditious libel:

"The interference of Government, to punish men for their assertions respecting itself, ever has been, and ever will be, subject to the most odious oppression. Public prosecutions for libel are, therefore, more dangerous to society than the misrepresentation which they are intended to punish. . . . The infliction of penalty, instead of being a wholesome corrective of falsehood . . . will infallibly destroy that censorial jurisdiction of society which is the only salutary preservative of Public Liberty and Justice."

Wortman disposed of Blackstone's definition of freedom of the press with the usual reply of thinking men who believed deeply enough in that freedom: "Of what use is the liberty of doing that for which I am punishable afterwards?" He concluded with a warning drawn from colonial and European history:

"It should ever be remembered that the present system of libel, is the offspring of a monarchy. However it may correspond with hereditary establishments, and the existence of privileged orders, the dangerous exotic can never be reconciled to the genius and constitution of a Representative Commonwealth."

Wortman's powerful treatise was not of a sort to shift votes in the presidential election of 1800. Its appeal was to those who were already roused by the iniquities of the Sedition Act. However the credit be apportioned, the political upheaval of 1800 swept the Federalists out of the Executive branch, shattered their control of Congress, and left them only the Judiciary (solidly of their party) as a possible entrenchment for the future.

The Sedition Act by its own terms was to expire on March 3, 1801, the day on which Federalist control of the government would come to an end. Still having time in which to legislate, the alarmed leaders of that party undertook to extend the repudiated law in the short final session of the old Congress. Their reasoning, taking it to be sincere, was ludicrously logical. They had proved (they said), and judges had similarly decided, that seditious libel could be punished in federal court under the unwritten common law. The Sedition Act meliorated the common law by making truth a defense. Without that restraint, the incoming Jeffersonians would prosecute seditious libel under the common law with all the fanatic zeal that could be expected from such extremists.

"I wish to revive this law, sir," said Robert Goodloe Harper, "as a shield for the liberty of the press and the freedom of opinion." Shielded by the benign provisions of the Sedition Act, the Federalists might hope to conduct "a manly, dignified, candid and patriotic opposition" to the government, without being subjected to "the overbearing sway of that tyrannical spirit, by which a certain political party in this country is actuated; that spirit which . . . knows neither moderation, mercy nor justice; regards neither feeling, principle nor right; and sweeps down with relentless fury, all that dares to detect its follies, oppose its progress, or resist its domination." In other words, the Federalists could skin the hides off their victorious adversaries, and Federalist judges would keep them out of prison as long as the Sedition Act continued to modify the common law by making truth a defense.

The fear of such prosecutions was logical, if the Jeffersonians actually intended to pursue the less-than-Golden Rule of "do as you are done by." But Republican speakers assured Harper, Otis, Bayard, Dana and the others that the period of repression was over, and they denied that prosecutions were possible under common law. Even Congressman Matthew Lyon, after telling how he was kept four months in a cold, fireless, stinking cell when warmed rooms were empty, heaped coals of fire on the men who sent him there by saying: "Had I, therefore, a wish for revenge, I would vote for the bill." Speaker Dayton's vote broke a 48-to-48 tie, carrying the resolution, but it was heard of no more.

Thomas Jefferson became President and issued pardons that opened the prison doors to all remaining victims of the Sedition Act. Dismissed also was an indictment against William Duane, Bache's successor as publisher of the Philadelphia *Aurora*, accused of libeling the United States Senate. In ordering the dismissal, Jefferson directed that a new action be brought against Duane "on whatever other law might be in evidence against the offence." That meant the common law, but it was no maneuver to establish it. The directive went to the new District Attorney, Alexander J. Dallas, the foremost libertarian lawyer of Philadelphia. He had made the argument against federal common-law jurisdiction in *Worrall's Case,* and was attorney for Duane (until he took office) in the pending charge under the Sedition Act. As expected, the indictment was not renewed, but Dallas's public record on that point was enough to account for the inaction.

Vituperative assaults in the Federalist press soon put President Jefferson to a test in which he rated far above his predecessor but somewhat under A Plus. He had been in office two years when Governor Thomas McKean of Pennsylvania, who as Chief Justice had been a rigorous enforcer of state libel laws, wrote to him that "The infamous and seditious libels published almost daily in our newspapers are become intolerable." He thought it could be "greatly checked by a few prosecutions," but as the President and Congress would figure in the charges he did not want to do it without presidential advice and consent. Jefferson replied that the Federalists, "having failed in destroying the freedom of the press by their gag-law," seemed intent on doing so "by pushing its licentiousness and its lying to such a degree of prostitution as to deprive it of all credit." He had long thought that a few prosecutions under state law would have a wholesome effect in restoring the integrity of the presses, but "not a general prosecution, for that would look like persecution."

The mutual advice bore fruit in an idiotic prosecution by Attorney General Joseph McKean (the governor's son) of Joseph Dennie, editor of the fanatical Federalist weekly *Port-folio.* Dennie published an editorial denouncing democracy in Athens, Sparta, Rome, Revolutionary France and Cromwellian England. "It is on trial here," he wrote, "and its issue will be civil war, desolation and anarchy . . . no brave man but draws his sword against its force." Dennie was tried under Pennsylvania law for libeling the American form of government. Judge Yeates told the jury that if they believed the publication was intended to "infect insidiously the public mind with a subtile poison," producing a dangerous tendency to anarchy, sedition and civil war, they should convict the defendant. If they thought the purpose was to inform the public mind, no matter how erroneous the expressed opinions might be, they should acquit Mr. Dennie. This the jury promptly did. The instructions plainly contemplated an acquittal, but partook of the underlying fallacy of the prosecution—that evil intent or bad tendency can make speech or writing criminal.

Appealing the conviction of Publisher Harry Crosswell, convicted under New York law of libeling President Jefferson, defense lawyers headed by Alexander Hamilton assailed "the despotic tribunal of the Star Chamber" as the "polluted source" of the doctrine that truth is no defense in libel. But since the entire system of seditious libel, misbranded as common law, originated in that same polluted despotic source, the argument goes to cast it all out even though Hamilton had no such thought.

In 1806 a United States attorney in Connecticut on his own initiative secured common-law indictments in federal court against five persons, for seditious libel of President Jefferson and Congress. One indictment was against two publishers of the *Connecticut Courant* for printing a political canard, that $2,000,000 secretly appropriated for part payment of a projected purchase of Florida was a bribe to Napoleon. President Jefferson knew nothing of the indictments until Gideon Granger of Connecticut warned him that the defendants were being made martyrs, but he did not order the actions dismissed until Madison and John Nicholas added their protests. Madison's argument that federal power did not embrace the common law of libel furnished legal ground of dismissal. These abortive indictments were the sole deviation from complete freedom from federal prosecution for seditious libel in the entire nineteenth century.

Ordinarily, the dropping of an indictment ends further proceedings. But in the case of the Hartford editors, two federal judges had divided on constitutionality and certified that question to the Supreme Court. Five years after the case became moot, the Court picked that appeal out of a pigeonhole and set the case of *United States* v. *Hudson* and *Goodwin* for argument. The sole apparent reason was to determine whether or not there was a federal common law. The record of its disposition opens with this astonishing entry:

"*Pinkney*, Attorney General, in behalf of the United States, and *Dana*, for the defendants, declined arguing the case."

Standing unexplained, that is as mystifying as it is unparalleled.

But there were compelling reasons for it. If William Pinkney and Samuel Dana had argued the case, each would have argued against his own convictions and the Attorney General would have had to assail the firmly held views of President Madison. Dana, by this time a United States Senator, would have had to repudiate the strong stand he took in 1800 for libel prosecutions at common law. And the outcome meant nothing to his clients, since the whole case was five years dead.

So the judges dealt with the question in conference, and it was in the main a contention between Justices William Johnson and Joseph Story. Of the seven justices who enforced the Sedition Act so ruthlessly on circuit, only Bushrod Washington (the mildest of them) was still on the bench. Chief Justice John Marshall took office in 1801, followed by five appointees of Presidents Jefferson and Madison. Story, thirty-two years old, only three months on the bench, was an ardent nationalist, highly wrought up by New England's resistance to the impending declaration of war against England for assaults on American commerce and navigation.

Justice Johnson delivered "the opinion of the majority of this court" on the last day of the term. The only question, he stated, was whether the circuit courts of the United States could exercise a common-law jurisdiction in criminal cases. Although the question was brought up now for the first time, "we consider it as having been long since settled in public opinion." The long absence of other such cases and the general acquiescence of legal men showed that the prevalent opinion favored the negative. The Court regarded that opinion as correct. It was not necessary, Justice Johnson said, to inquire whether Congress had power to confer jurisdiction of this sort on the circuit courts. It was enough that they had not done so. In this quiet fashion the Supreme Court took one of the most decisive steps in American history for the safeguarding of civil liberties.

Four months later the United States was at war with Great Britain and New England was seething with sedition. Justice Story, from his home in Salem, Massachusetts, wrote to Attorney General Pinkney urging that Congress pass a law making any prejudicial or injurious act, which would be an offense at common law, an offense against the United States. That would arm the courts with plenary power. Pinkney forwarded the letter to President Madison, who silently disregarded it but expressed his opinion to another pleader for counteraction, that the "wicked project of destroying the Union" would be defeated by the loyalty of the great body of the people of New England. In May 1813, with sedition still rampant and slander of the President a hundred times worse than anything John Adams had suffered, Justice Story tried a new approach. He furnished the Attorney General with an outline of amendments to the "barbarously deficient" criminal statutes, to cope with traitorous activities. Again the President chose to let the seditionists hang themselves on their own rope.

The persistent Justice tried a new tack. Before him in Circuit Court, in the term of October 1813, came the case of Cornelius Coolidge and others, indicted at common law for rescuing a prize captured by two privateers. Both Story and District Judge Davis of Massachusetts regarded the indictment as valid, but to get a new test that might upset the 1812 decision, they decided to disagree on constitutionality and certify the case to the Supreme Court "as upon a division of the judges."

Story felt justified in raising the question again, he wrote in his Circuit Court opinion, because the 1812 decision had been made without argument and by a divided court. But he was quickly challenged when the Supreme Court took up the appeal in 1816. Attorney General Richard Rush told the justices that he had given the case anxious attention, and examined the opinion delivered in 1812. "Considering the point as decided in that case, . . . he desired respectfully to state, without saying more, that it was not his [in]tention to argue it now." The defense counsel did not show up and this exchange ensued:

"Mr. Justice Story. I do not take the question to be settled by that case.

"Mr. Justice Johnson. I consider it to be settled by the authority of that case."

Once more Justice Johnson wrote for the Court. The former difference of opinion, he said, still existed; the Attorney General had declined to argue; and no counsel had appeared for the defendant. "Under these circumstances the Court would not choose to review their former decision . . . or draw it into doubt." Thus for a second time, and for all time, the Supreme Court held that the Constitution does not give federal judges the power to subject Americans to fines and imprisonment under the common law, without an act of Congress defining the crime and fixing the punishment.

During the discussions in both cases, the one voice not heard was that of Chief Justice Marshall. It has sometimes been conjectured that because he wrote the address of the Virginia minority, which utilized the common law of seditious libel to support the constitutionality of the federal Sedition Act, he may have been one of the Story minority in the *Hudson-Goodwin* and *Coolidge* cases. It seems far more likely that Story was joined only by Bushrod Washington, whose record in circuit court put him on that side.

If Marshall in 1798 believed along with Iredell, Wilson and others that the Constitution gave federal judges a general power to punish common-law crimes, there was no reason on earth why he should have taken a narrower position in his Virginia minority address. In 1798-1800, federal common law was an avowed weapon of the Federalist party against the Republicans. In 1812-1816, it was a potential weapon of the Republicans against the antiwar Federalists, of whom Marshall was one. Why should he vote to put that weapon into the hands of his party's enemies, when he had never given it either legal sanction or moral approval in the hands of his friends?

The Chief Justice had in fact given a clear indication of his position in 1807, when Erich Bollman, charged with complicity in the Burr Conspiracy, was released by the Supreme Court through habeas corpus. In determining the source of the Court's authority to do so, Marshall rejected the argument of Bollman's lawyer that the power was vested in it by analogy with the common law. "For the meaning of the term *habeas corpus*," said Marshall, "resort may unquestionably be had to the common law, but the power to award the writ by any of the courts of the United States, must be given by written law." That was the exact position taken by Madison, Gallatin and others in denying the existence of a federal common law as the basis of the Sedition Act.

If the common-law decisions of 1812 and 1816 had gone the other way, there would have been a monstrous and indefinite enlargement of federal criminal jurisdiction, with undefined penalties variable at the whim of judges. This great amorphous jurisdiction would have been uncontrollable by government, except as it might be hacked away, bit by bit, through statutory restriction. Such a system undoubtedly would have been fixed on the country by judicial decree, had the question been decided *collectively* by the judges who upheld that system *individually* before 1801. Such a decree could not have survived the storm of its own creating, unless the American people were ready to relinquish their liberties.

But the Marshall Court did more than save the country from the rigors of a federal common law and the legal confusion and political turmoil that would have resulted from it. The Court ratified the basic position taken by Madison in his *Report,* previously supported in Congress by Gallatin, Livingston, Nicholas and Macon, against the constitutionality of the Sedition Act. In doing so, it struck fundamentally at the power of Congress to enact any law of criminal libel. It did not do so in words, for the opinion of the Court was limited to a denial that the Constitution gave federal judges power to enforce the common law in matters criminal. But the consensus of public opinion, which Justice Johnson cited in support of the decision, was a total verdict against the validity of the Sedition Act on any basis whatsoever. Taken together, public opinion and the Supreme Court dealt such a blow that federal seditious libel was not heard of again for a hundred years.

CHAPTER 27
The Fourteenth Amendment: Its First Form

There was more genuinely seditious speech and printing to the square foot in the United States during the War of 1812 than to the square mile during the period of the Sedition Act. But the author of the First Amendment was now the President. In prior years he had taken the position that unabridged freedom of speech and press, guaranteed by the Constitution, meant freedom to speak and write seditiously. As President he lived up to his principles. Among the thousands of Federalists whose utterances had in them the full spirit of treason, not one felt the restraining hand of government. And what was the result?

When President Madison left office, resolutions adopted by the citizens of the District of Columbia eulogized him for conducting the war to a successful conclusion "without infringing a political, civil or religious right." The Federalist party melted out of existence, destroyed by its own disloyalty. Thanks to the absence of punitive measures during the war, a nationwide consensus was achieved that made the next eight years the Era of Good Feeling. Gradually, as the nineteenth century moved toward its middle years, the dreadful institution of human slavery became the country's plague and scourge. Still there was no official interference with freedom of opinion. A Northern mob, feeling that the advocates of liberty were moving too far too fast, might express its displeasure by burning the printshop of an abolitionist editor, or even murder him, as happened to Elijah Lovejoy in 1837. But the federal government placed no restraints on the working out of national policy, for good or ill, by public discussion.

The South, however, had become the slave of slavery. Bound

to an inferior labor system and having no substitute, it became more and more dependent on the instrument that victimized both master and slave. Partly in reaction against Northern criticism, partly in self-defense against self-accusation, slaveowners turned to deification of the system which their ancestors condemned but had not the will power to abolish. Slavery became a divine as well as a human order, and the will of God was ratified by Chief Justice Taney in the *Dred Scott* case, when he ruled that a Negro had no rights that a white man was bound to respect.

That 1857 ruling, plus the imbecility of a do-nothing President, plunged the country into civil war, and when the four-year holocaust came to an end the Southern slaves were free. Lincoln's Emancipation Proclamation did not free those in the nonseceding border states, and one of the first actions in national reconstruction was the submission and adoption of the Thirteenth Amendment prohibiting slavery or involuntary servitude, except as a punishment of crime, within the United States or any place subject to its jurisdiction. It was the first significant postwar action of the new Republican Party.

On the convening of the Thirty-Ninth Congress, December 4, 1865, the Joint Committee on Reconstruction was set up, with nine House members and six from the Senate. It was headed by the moderate Senator William Pitt Fessenden of Maine, but the dominant figure was the House subchairman, Representative Thaddeus Stevens of Pennsylvania, whose lifelong hostility to slavery became mixed with a vengeful attitude toward the defeated South. His aggressive personality helped to give the Joint Committee almost dictatorial power over the Radical Republican majority in both houses of a Congress that included no representatives from the eleven states of the Confederacy. Less influential than Stevens but much fairer, and ardently devoted to civil rights and liberties, was Representative John A. Bingham of Ohio. His title to fame rests upon authorship (except for the first sentence) of Section 1 of the Fourteenth Amendment, which reads:

"All persons born or naturalized in the United States, and subject to the jurisdiction thereof, are citizens of the United States and of the State wherein they reside. No State shall make or enforce any law which shall abridge the privileges or immunities of citizens of the United States; nor shall any State deprive any person of life, liberty, or property, without due process of law; nor deny to any person within its jurisdiction the equal protection of the laws."

Other sections, designed to limit the political rights of persons and the power of states lately in rebellion, attracted far greater controversial attention during the drafting and ratification, but they soon dropped from sight. Today, as a vital part of the Constitution—and a throbbingly vital part of it—the Fourteenth Amendment consists of Section 1, supplemented by Section 5, which gives Congress power to enforce it by appropriate legislation. Combine this with two other articles of the Bill of Rights—the First and Fifth Amendments—and the three of them form today the most dynamic and controversial portion of the entire Constitution. The Fourteenth Amendment, after being almost destroyed by vitiating court decisions, has grown tremendously in authority and importance in recent decades, through increasing recurrence by courts and Congress to its original purposes. Long strides in that direction—especially those taken in 1954 and 1964—left the process still incomplete and resisted by strenuous denials that such purposes ever existed.

During the greater part of the century after adoption of the amendment, the conflicting interpretations were based largely on what judges, lawyers, teachers, politicians and lay writers wished to believe about its purpose, meaning and force. Even after Dr. Howard Edgar Flack of Johns Hopkins University published in 1908 a careful study of *The Adoption of the Fourteenth Amendment,* demonstrating that the framers intended much more than the Supreme Court allowed, reluctant judges and like-minded commentators clung to the decisions and opinions that had emasculated it.

Early narrowing decisions on the scope of the amendment were by a closely divided court, but as the memory and spirit of original protective purposes faded, so did judicial support of them. In the last twenty years of the nineteenth century one famous member of the Supreme Court, Justice John Marshall Harlan, repeatedly raised his voice in behalf of reason and justice, the twin victims of the restrictive decisions. All that his many dissents achieved for him in his lifetime was a reputation for legal oddity. By a common quirk of the human mind, this impression became so deeply fixed that it did not vanish even as the feeling spread that he was not only morally right (which often is injurious to a judge's standing) but legally correct.

The legislative history of the Fourteenth Amendment received its first judicial exposition in the dissenting opinion of Justice Hugo Black in *Adamson* v. *California,* a 1947 decison which repeated earlier denials that the "due process" requirement of the Fourteenth Amendment makes the privilege against compulsory self-incrimination binding on state courts. Justice Black contended that one of the chief objects of that amendment "was to make the Bill of Rights applicable to the states," thereby throwing all the protections of the first eight amendments around persons who were put to hazard by state action. Justice Douglas joined in this opinion, which was approved also by Justices Murphy and Rutledge with the enlarging reservation that "due process" *includes* but is not *limited to* the guarantees of the eight amendments.

To support his position, Justice Black appended a 33-page summary of the congressional debates during the framing of the amendment in 1866, quoting chiefly the speeches of its author, Representative Bingham. Outside the Court, both among those who agreed and those who disagreed with Justice Black, his dissent lighted a stronger fire than the affirming opinions of Justices Reed and Frankfurter. Reed, writing for the Court, merely stood on former decisions. Frankfurter disagreed strongly with Black on philosophical grounds, but took no account of the supporting evidence gathered by Black and dismissed Harlan as "an eccentric exception."

The task of refuting the team of Black and Flack was taken up by writers in law journals, who went still more extensively into the framing and adoption of the amendment and presented the sponsors of it as floundering in a sea of confusion about what they were trying to do and what they did. This tended to destroy the force of what the congressmen said in 1866 when they spoke with clarity, as in the passages quoted by Flack and Black. The main opposing contention has been that Congressman Bingham talked in a general way about "this immortal Bill of Rights" and the "privileges and immunities of citizens" being made binding on the states by his amendment, without specifically saying that by these terms he meant the guarantees of the first eight amendments. Senator Howard of Michigan, in laying the House-passed amendment before the Senate, did say specifically that the purpose was to compel the states to respect the first eight amendments, but his statement is dismissed because no other senator repeated (or contradicted) it.

This manner of refuting Black and Flack has been highly effective, because the course pursued by Congressman Bingham, *when presented without explanation*, does make him appear to be a confused flounderer. But his purposes, and the purposes of the amendment, become perfectly clear when one takes account of the cause of his initial confusion. When Bingham offered his amendment, he had the erroneous impression that the first eight amendments were intended to restrict both the federal and state governments. That belief was widely held among legislators, laity and lawyers during the first half century after the amendments were adopted, and it persisted even after Marshall's Supreme Court decided in *Barron* v. *Baltimore* (1833) that they did not apply to the states. In fact the erroneous belief gained new force as the Abolitionist movement spread through the North and West in the next quarter century.

The author of the Fourteenth Amendment was a leading figure among the Abolitionists. Sharing their error about *Barron* v. *Baltimore*, he drafted an amendment designed to overcome that decision by giving Congress the enforcement power which the Supreme Court said Congress did not possess. Learning, during the debate, that he had misread Marshall's opinion, and accepting that opinion as valid, he recast the amendment to reach the same end in a different way. That change of position, and the reason for it, have to be understood to make Bingham's course intelligible and the purpose of Congress clear.

The basis of Bingham's approach was the spreading conviction, voiced by him in an Ohio speech in September 1865, that "every free Negro born and residing in the United States . . . is a natural-born citizen of the United States." If that was true it necessarily followed that "Free black citizens are as fully entitled to every guarantee of the Constitution as any white citizen. And among others, to that guarantee [Article IV, Section 2] which declares the citizens of each State shall be entitled to all the privileges and immunities of citizens in the several States."

Here was the Abolitionist credo and the genesis of the Fourteenth Amendment. The same doctrine was voiced by Senator Lyman Trumbull of Illinois in opening the debate on his Civil Rights bill of 1866. Said he on January 29, a month before Bingham presented his amendment:

"In my judgment, persons of African descent, born in the United States, are as much citizens as white persons who are born in the country. . . . They being now free and citizens of the United States, as citizens they are entitled, as I have undertaken to show, to the great fundamental rights belonging to free citizens, and we have a right to protect them in the enjoyment of them."

This could be done, in Trumbull's opinion, under the Thirteenth Amendment, since slavery was not actually abolished until its vestiges were wiped out. Or it could be achieved under the original "privileges and immunities" clause, Article IV, Section 2, whose intention, as described in Story's *Commentaries on the Constitution*, was to confer on citizens "a general citizenship, and to communicate all the privileges and immunities which the citizens of the same State would be entitled to under the like circumstances." There were many state laws, said Trumbull, that did not make a man an absolute slave yet denied him the rights of a freeman:

"It is perhaps difficult to draw the precise line where freedom ceases and slavery begins, but a law that does not allow a colored man to go from one county to another is certainly a law in derogation of the rights of a freeman. A law that does not allow a colored man to hold property, does not allow him to teach, does not allow him to preach, is certainly a law in violation of the rights of a freeman, and being so may properly be declared void."

Here Trumbull interpreted the "privileges and immunities" clause of the original Constitution to cover two freedoms specifically protected by the First Amendment—speech and religion—as well as the implied right of travel, and he also brought in the Fifth Amendment's protection of life, liberty and property. His position was virtually a duplicate of Bingham's. Both took their stand on the equality of men whose fundamental rights were set forth in the Declaration of Independence, the preamble to the Constitution, and the amendments setting forth specific guarantees of rights and liberties.

So Bingham offered his amendment on the supposition that although the eight amendments were binding on the states, the Supreme Court had ruled that the Constitution gave Congress no power to enforce them. His purpose was to give Congress that power. Apparently the Joint Committee shared his error and approved his purpose, for it authorized him to place this amendment before the House:

"The Congress shall have power to make all laws which shall be necessary and proper to secure to the citizens of each State all privileges and immunities of citizens in the several States (Art. 4, sec. 2); and to all persons in the several States equal protection in the rights of life, liberty, and property (5th amendment)."

Owing to the absence of that power of enforcement, said Bingham, "this immortal bill of rights embodied in the Constitution, rested for its execution and enforcement hitherto upon the fidelity of the states." And how faithful had they been? The whole civilized world knew that the officers of eleven states, in utter disregard of their oath to uphold the Constitution, "have violated in every sense of the word these provisions" whose enforcement was absolutely essential to American nationality.

Read in the light of a true understanding of *Barron* v. *Baltimore,* neither Bingham's speech nor his amendment was logical. He was denouncing state officers for violating a Bill of Rights that was solely a restriction on the federal government. He was seeking an amendment to give Congress an enforcement power it already possessed (in the power to pass "necessary and proper" laws) for any purpose comprehended by the Bill of Rights. Yet the misunderstanding was not surprising. Article IV, section 2 provides that "the Citizens of each State shall be entitled to all Privileges and Immunities of Citizens in the several States." That vague wording, squeezed to its narrowest possible meaning, guarantees that a citizen traveling from one state to another shall enjoy all the privileges and immunities possessed by citizens of the state he enters. Bingham, however, construed it to mean that all citizens, wherever they were, shall enjoy all the privileges and immunities that appertain to citizenship in a free republic. Believing that such privileges and immunities had been systematized in the first eight amendments, he construed Article IV, section 2 as a constitutional source of power to enforce those amendments "in the several States." Consequently, the *Barron* v. *Baltimore* decision was to him a denial to Congress of power to enforce the Bill of Rights against the states under the "privileges and immunities" clause of Article IV. His remedy was to grant that power by constitutional amendment.

But if Bingham thought that his clause on "privileges and immunities" made the first eight amendments binding on the states, why did he add a specific guarantee already found in the Fifth Amendment's command that no person shall "be deprived of life, liberty, or property without due process of law"? Unexplained, that would seem unnecessary if he intended the amendment to incorporate the first eight amendments. But a sound reason for it is found in the wording of the Bingham draft: "to secure . . . to all persons in the several states *equal protection* in the rights of life, liberty, and property."

Those two words, "equal protection," furnished the final mandate needed (once the eight amendments were made enforceable against the states) to give the freed slaves complete and assured protection against deprivation of "life, liberty, or property, without due process of law." Thus Bingham picked out two provisions of the existing Constitution that seemed to comprehend the whole sweep of protected rights and liberties, and added all that was needed to raise the emancipated slaves and their posterity to a legal parity with other free Americans. He was truly giving universality to "this immortal bill of rights."

There was no misunderstanding in Congress of this purpose, even though the precise nature of the obstacle to be overcome was misunderstood by Bingham and others. When debate opened on the Bingham amendment the day after it was introduced, Congressman Rogers of New Jersey, an aggressive opponent of the amendment, quoted a Massachusetts case in which Chief Justice Parker said that the constitutional provision on privileges and immunities was "necessarily limited and qualified." For some purposes the states remained foreign to each other, as in the residence requirements for voting, regulation of property, marriage and divorce.

Would they still be foreign to each other in these respects, asked Rogers, if this amendment was adopted? No, it proposed to em- power the Federal Government "to exercise an absolute, despotic, uncontrollable power" to compel the states to repeal their laws "wherever they do not give to the colored population of the country the same rights and privileges to which [their] white citizens are entitled."

Rogers said the whole amendment was part of a plan to reduce the Southern states to mere dependencies, with Congress exercising unlimited control, "embracing in its jurisdiction all the most valu- able rights of life, liberty, and property, which our Constitution designed to be under the guardianship of the individual States." How extensive were the rights thus affected? "Sir, I defy any man upon the other side of the House to name to me any right of the citizen which is not included in the words 'life, liberty, property, privileges, and immunities,' unless it should be the right of suff- rage"; and that too (he added) had been included by the United States Circuit Court in *Corfield* v. *Coryell.*

Rogers undertook to correct Bingham on the scope of the first eight amendments, saying that repeated decisions of the Supreme Court had held the clause on "due process of law, as well as the other guarantees of the Constitution" to apply only to cases affect- ing the Federal Government. Bingham saw no distinction between this and his own contention that the Court had denied the power of Congress to enforce guarantees that were intended to include the states. Taking the floor next day, he said he had been challenged to cite a decision showing such a denial. He now quoted Chief Justice Marshall's statement in *Barron* v. *Baltimore,* that in a Con- stitution setting up a government of limited powers, any "limita- tions of power, if expressed in general terms," must apply to the government created by that instrument. So, wrote Marshall, the Fifth Amendment—the one directly involved—"must be under- stood as restraining the power of the General Government, not as applicable to the States." Bingham quoted further from a later case involving the Seventh Amendment, in which the Court used similar language. Those rulings prevented federal enforcement of the guarantees.

As a gauge of what Bingham was trying to do, it is utterly irrele- vant whether he thought his amendment was needed to overcome *wrongful* or *rightful* decisions of the Supreme Court. The point that counts is that the Fourteenth Amendment *was intended to overcome those decisions.* Believing that the Court erroneously allowed state officials to flout the Bill of Rights, Bingham said after quoting the two cases:

"The question is, simply, whether you will give by this amendment to the people of the United States the power, by legislative enactment, to punish officials of States for violation of the oaths enjoined upon them by their Constitution? . . . Is the bill of rights to stand in our Constitution hereafter, as in the past five years within eleven states, a mere dead letter? It is absolutely essential to the safety of the people that it should be enforced."

One may argue, with good reason, that state officials had not violated their oaths by disregarding the Bill of Rights. But does it follow that the Fourteenth Amendment was not intended to make them subject to these provisions of the Constitution? Bingham put the intention beyond doubt by his ensuing remarks:

"What more could have been added to that instrument to secure the enforcement of these provisions of the bill of rights in every State, other than the additional grant of power which we ask this day? . . . Gentlemen who oppose this amendment oppose the grant of power to enforce the bill of rights. Gentlemen who oppose this amendment simply declare to these rebel States, go on with your confiscation statutes, your statutes of banishment, your statutes of unjust imprisonment, your statutes of murder and death against men because of their loyalty to the Constitution and Government of the United States."

The breadth of purpose was brought out in the questioning of Bingham. Hale of New York had asked the day before whether he was correct in believing that the amendment, in practical effect, would serve only to protect "American citizens of African descent" in the eleven states lately in rebellion. Bingham replied to him that it would also protect "the thousands and tens of thousands . . . of loyal white citizens" who had suffered banishment and confiscation of property. And it would apply to other states whose constitutions and laws "were in direct violation of every principle of our Constitution." Asked to specify he said: "It applies unquestionably to the State of Oregon."

There was no need for him to recite the clause in Oregon's

Constitution of 1857 forbidding free Negroes or mulattoes, not already residing there, to enter the state, reside there, hold real estate, make contracts, or sue in state courts. With Bingham's purpose broadened next day by the declared intention to overset *Barron* v. *Baltimore*, there was ample warrant for the question by Hale that followed. Would the amendment, if adopted, confer upon Congress "general powers of legislation in regard to the protection of life, liberty, and personal property"? Replied the author of the amendment:

"It certainly does this: it confers upon Congress power to see to it that the protection given by the laws of the States shall be equal in respect to life and liberty and property to all persons."

This stirred Representative Hotchkiss of New York to protest that Section 1 went too far in one direction and not far enough to secure what was intended. As worded, it authorized Congress "to establish uniform laws throughout the United States upon the subject named, the protection of life, liberty, and property." He was unwilling to transfer primary legislation of that sort from the states to the nation.

Bingham replied that there was no such intention. The amendment was exactly in the language of the Constitution and the intent was "to secure to the citizen of each State all the privileges and immunities of citizens of the United States in the several States. If the State laws do not interfere, those immunities follow under the Constitution."

Hotchkiss said he was not talking about the clause on privileges and immunities, but the one that followed, on life, liberty and property. He supposed the object was to provide against exclusion of any class from the privileges other classes enjoyed. If so, the amendment was not strong enough to achieve its object:

"It should be a constitutional right that cannot be wrested from any class of citizens, or from the citizens of any state by mere legislation. But this amendment proposes to leave it to the caprice of Congress; and your legislation upon the subject would depend upon the political majority of Congress, and not upon two thirds of Congress and three fourths of the States.

"Now, I desire that the very privileges for which the gentleman is contending shall be secured to the citizens; but I want them secured by a constitutional provision that legislation cannot override. Then if the gentleman wishes to go further, and provide by laws of Congress for the enforcement of these rights, I will go with him. . . . I want him to go to the root of this matter. . . . Why not provide by an amendment to the Constitution that no State shall discriminate against any class of its citizens; and let that amendment stand as a part of the organic law of the land, subject only to be defeated by another constitutional amendment."

By taking a little more time and comparing views, Hotchkiss advised the House, they could "agree upon an amendment that shall secure beyond question what the gentleman desires to secure." The House majority, *including Bingham,* saw the force of this, and by a vote of 110 to 37 the subject was postponed (from February 28) until the second Monday in April. This was a great turning point. Hotchkiss was proposing at one stroke to reduce the power of Congress below the level Bingham sought, but to increase greatly the force of the amendment. Worded as a prohibition upon the states, said Hotchkiss, it would be effective even though Congress failed to enforce it. (That is, the courts could enforce it without statutory aid, in cases properly before them.) The change presented another opportunity to which he did not refer. With primary responsibility for protection of civil rights still resting upon the states, and the federal government constitutionally empowered to prevent violations of them, the prohibitions could be made more extensive without upsetting the federal system.

CHAPTER 28
The Fourteenth Amendment: Its Final Form

After laying aside the draft of a fourteenth amendment, the House took up the Senate-passed Civil Rights bill, whose purpose, as described by Chairman Trumbull of the Senate Judiciary Committee, was to destroy the discriminations against Negroes and mulattoes "running through all the statutes of the late slaveholding states." The Thirteenth Amendment, abolishing slavery, was cited as the source of constitutional power, but the debate kept jumping to the proposed fourteenth.

Congressman Bingham, to the surprise of his colleagues, opposed the bill as a violation of the Constitution, unwarranted by the Thirteenth Amendment. His speeches revealed that he now understood and accepted *Barron* v. *Baltimore.* By the text of the Constitution, its past interpretations and "the manifest and declared intent of the men who framed it," the enforcement of the Bill of Rights fell within the reserved powers of the states, to be enforced by state tribunals. Having said time and again in earlier debate that this meant no enforcement, Bingham assured the House manager of the Civil Rights bill, Wilson of Iowa, that he stood with him "in an earnest desire to have the bill of rights in your Constitution enforced everywhere. But I ask that it be enforced in accordance with the Constitution of my country."

As to the extent of those rights: "I submit that the term civil rights includes every right that pertains to the citizen under the Constitution, laws, and Government of this country." Blackstone, who was so exact in definitions, everywhere used "civil liberty" and "political liberty" as synonymous. If civil rights had this extent, the proposed Civil Rights Act would strike down *by congressional enactment* every state constitution that contained "a discrimination on account of race or color in any of the civil rights of the citizens," and this meant nearly all the states, including his own. He would say, with all his heart, that the proposed law should be the law of every state, by its voluntary act. Since that could not be expected: "I should remedy that not by an arbitrary assumption of power, but by amending the Constitution of the United States, expressly prohibiting the States from any such abuse of power in the future."

Bingham asserted that his amendment, if it should be reworded as a prohibition of the violation of the civil rights of the citizen, would still leave to the states the primary "care of the property, the liberty, and the life of the citizen." That duty always had rested upon the states and he sought no change in that respect. What he advocated was an amendment that would arm Congress with power to punish all violations of the Bill of Rights by state officers, but would leave them to discharge the duties imposed upon them by the Constitution and their oath to uphold it.

Wilson replied that these were the very rights his bill was to protect against violation by the states. If he ever had heard of *Barron* v. *Baltimore,* he must have thought an act of Congress would override it. The House evidently thought so too, for it disregarded Bingham's constitutional objections and sent the Civil Rights bill to the White House. President Johnson vetoed it on the grounds stated by Bingham, and Congress repassed it over his veto. In these proceedings the author of the Fourteenth Amendment, the House manager of the Civil Rights bill, and more than two thirds of the House, all came together on one agreed fact—that their common purpose by one means or the other was to throw federal protection over the whole range of civil rights belonging to American citizens, against violation by the states.

Still broader purposes were embodied in Bingham's proposed amendment after the Joint Committee resumed its sessions in mid-April. Recasting Section 1 in the negative form Representative Hotchkiss had suggested, Bingham after preliminary jockeying obtained 10-to-3 approval of a three-part provision that went word for word into the Constitution:

"No State shall make or enforce any law which shall abridge the privileges or immunities of citizens of the United States; nor shall any State deprive any person of life, liberty, or property without due process of law; nor deny to any person within its jurisdiction the equal protection of the laws."

This produced five essential changes from the original Bingham resolution:

1. Instead of granting Congress primary power to protect privileges and immunities and furnish equal protection to life, liberty and property, it prohibited violation of those rights by the states. That avoided a vast extension of federal power, and left the primary duty of protection with the states.

2. The shift to a prohibition upon the states permitted enforcement by either Congress or the federal courts, or by both.

3. The rewording of the "privileges and immunities" clause (if truly interpreted) carried it beyond Article IV, Section 2 of the original Constitution, which merely placed a citizen moving from one state to another on an equality with citizens of the latter state. By forbidding any state to abridge "the privileges or immunities *of citizens of the United States*" the clause was to protect all such rights possessed by native-born or naturalized citizens wherever they might be.

4. Bingham's original proposal to give Congress power to secure "to all persons equal protection in the rights of life, liberty, and property," was converted into a far more comprehensive clause forbidding any state to "deprive any person of life, liberty or property without due process of law." It no longer was confined to equality in such rights as a state might grant by its laws, but protected all rights to which all persons were entitled by the Constitution or by the law and customs of free nations.

5. The throwing of "equal protection" into a separate clause maintained the original scope of it and gave it additional force through emphasis.

In their new form, these provisions of Section 1 went forward to adoption by both houses, together with an important prefix inserted by the Senate, declaring who are citizens. But to understand the controversy over the meaning of Section 1 it is necessary to take further account of the reason for the change of wording. In 1871, five years after Congress approved the amendment, Bingham was asked in debate by Representative John F. Farnsworth of Illinois why he altered the form from a grant of power to a prohibition. His answer omitted the great credit due to Hotchkiss, but was in perfect harmony with the course of his own thinking. He did so because "in re-examining that case of Barron . . . I noted and apprehended as I never did before, certain words in that opinion of Marshall." The Chief Justice said in *Barron* v. *Baltimore,* referring to the first eight amendments, "Had the framers of these amendments intended them to be limitations on the powers of the State governments they would have imitated the framers of the original Constitution, and have expressed that intention." So, continued Bingham:

"Acting upon this suggestion I did imitate the framers of the original Constitution. As they had said 'no State shall emit bills of credit, pass any bill of attainder, *ex post facto* law, or law impairing the obligations of contracts,' imitating their example and imitating it to the letter, I prepared the provision of the first section of the fourteenth amendment as it stands in the Constitution."

Bingham then proceeded to state the purpose of the amendment as revised and adopted:

"Mr. Speaker, that the scope and meaning of the limitations imposed by the first section, fourteenth amendment of the Constitution may be more fully understood, permit me to say that the privileges and immunities of citizens of the United States, as contradistinguished from citizens of a State, are chiefly defined in the first eight amendments to the Constitution of the United States. . . . These eight articles I have shown never were limitations upon the power of the States, until made so by the Fourteenth Amendment."

That 1871 statement, of course, is not part of the 1866 legislative record, but it so perfectly supports everything Bingham said and did in 1866 that few impartial persons with the full record before them could fail to give it credence. That record is clear and lucid only if one knows, at every stage of the congressional proceedings, that Bingham presented his original draft under a mistaken belief that the Bill of Rights was already binding on the states, and revised the wording when he learned that *it must be made binding on them.*

As Bingham viewed the Constitution, its libertarian guarantees formed an equilateral triangle, each side of which was an equation: Bill of Rights equals privileges and immunities; privileges and immunities equal the first eight amendments; the eight amendments equal the Bill of Rights. These were the natural rights of all men, the guaranteed rights of American citizens, and they could be summed up as privileges and immunities, or as the rights of life, liberty and property, protected by due process of law.

This interlinking may be observed in his closing speech of May 10, 1866, when he said his amendment was needed to supply the one thing that was wanting in the Constitution, power "to protect by national law the privileges and immunities of all the citizens of the Republic and the inborn rights of every person within its jurisdiction whenever the same shall be abridged or denied by the unconstitutional acts of any State." The privileges and immunities to which all citizens were entitled (by Article IV, section 2) "include, among other privileges, the right to bear true allegiance to the Constitution and laws of the United States, and to be protected in life, liberty and property." The right of national allegiance, he asserted, had been expressly denied by South Carolina's nullification ordinance of 1833, and "many instances of State injustice and oppression have already occurred in the State legislation of this Union, of flagrant violations of the guarantied privileges of citizens of the United States," for which the national government could provide no remedy. Said Bingham:

"Contrary to the express letter of your Constitution, 'cruel and unusual punishments' have been inflicted under State laws within this Union upon citizens, not only for crimes committed, but for sacred duty done. . . . It was an opprobrium to the Republic that for fidelity to the United States they could not by national law be protected against the degrading punishment inflicted on slaves and felons by State law. That great want . . . is supplied by the first section of this amendment."

Cruel and unusual punishment, prohibited by the Eighth Amendment, was cited by the author of the Fourteenth Amendment *during the drafting* to illustrate the privileges and immunities which the states would be forbidden to abridge. After Congress approved the amendment, urging ratification by his own state,

Bingham asserted in an Ohio speech that there could be no peace and safety for the Republic "if, as in the past, States are permitted to take away freedom of speech, and to condemn men, as felons, to the penitentiary for teaching their fellow men that there is a hereafter, and a reward for those who learn to do well." With the First and Eighth Amendments thus directly specified as binding upon the States, what ones of those between could he have intended to exclude?

Even these illustrations were not needed. The broad sweep of Bingham's call for federal protection in the states of "the Bill of Rights," "privileges and immunities," the rights of "life, liberty and property," "every right that pertains to the citizen under the Constitution, laws and government"—these all-inclusive phrases of the 1866 debate, combined with the declared purpose to overcome the restriction which *Barron* v. *Baltimore* placed upon the eight amendments, leave nothing to the rejection of Bingham's construction of his own amendment except the wish to escape it.

In the Senate the application of the amendment to the first eight amendments was set forth in the opening speech of its manager, Senator Jacob M. Howard of Michigan, who took charge because Chairman Fessenden's ill-health kept him out of sustained debate. Howard went through the amendment section by section and clause by clause. He regarded the protection of "privileges and immunities . . . as very important." It would be "a curious question" to determine what were the privileges and immunities covered by Article IV, Section 2 of the Constitution, which belonged to "citizens of each of the States in the several States." They had never been defined by the Supreme Court, said Howard, but in 1823 Justice Bushrod Washington in circuit court had confined them to those "which are, in their nature fundamental; which belong of right to the citizens of all free Governments" and have been enjoyed by citizens of the several states of the Union. They included, said Washington, "protection by the government; the enjoyment of life and liberty, with the right to acquire and possess property"; the right of travel, the benefit of habeas corpus, the right to sue in the courts, exemption from discriminatory taxes. These were "some of the privileges and immunities . . . deemed to be fundamental," to which could be added the elective franchise and many other privileges that would promote friendship and intercourse among the people of different states.

Such, said Senator Howard at the conclusion of the long quotation from Washington, "is the character of the privileges and immunities spoken of in the second section of the fourth article of the Constitution." He enlarged the list in turning to the Fourteenth Amendment:

"To these privileges and immunities, whatever they may be— for they are not and cannot be fully defined in their entire extent and precise nature—to these should be added the personal rights guarantied and secured by the first eight amendments of the Constitution; such as the freedom of speech and of the press; the right of the people peaceably to assemble and petition the Government for a redress of grievances, a right appertaining to each and all the people; the right to keep and bear arms; the right to be exempted from the quartering of soldiers in a house without the consent of the owner; the right to be exempt from unreasonable searches and seizures . . ."

His list ended with the Eighth Amendment's guarantee against cruel and unusual punishments. Then Senator Howard summed up:

"Now sir, here is a mass of privileges, immunities and rights, some of them secured by the second section of the fourth article of the Constitution, which I have recited, some by the first eight amendments of the Constitution . . . secured to the citizens solely as a citizen of the United States and as a party in their courts. They do not operate in the slightest degree as a restraint or prohibition upon State legislation. . . . The great object of the first section of this amendment is, therefore, to restrain the power of the States and compel them at all times to respect these great fundamental guarantees."

Proceeding to the remaining clauses of Section 1, on "due process of law" and "equal protection of the laws," Senator Howard said: "This abolishes all class legislation in the States and does away with the injustice of subjecting one caste of persons to a code not applicable to another." The whole section, combined with Section 5 giving Congress power of enforcement, would have a most important effect:

"It will, if adopted by the states, forever disable every one of them from passing laws trenching upon those fundamental rights and privileges which pertain to citizens of the United States, and to all persons who happen to be within their jurisdiction. It establishes equality before the law, and it gives to the humblest, the poorest, the most despised of the race the same rights and the same protection before the law as it gives to the most powerful, the most wealthy, or the most haughty."

In the entire Senate debate on the Fourteenth Amendment, running from May 23 to June 8, *not a single senator challenged Senator Howard's declaration that Section 1 made the first eight amendments enforceable against the states.* He was spokesman for the Joint Committee of both houses. Combing the debates from beginning to end, one cannot find a single sentence that conflicts with Howard's speech. The nearest suggestion of inconsistency is this remark by Senator Luke Poland of Vermont on June 5:

"The clause of the first proposed amendment, that 'no State shall make or enforce any law which shall abridge the privileges or immunities of citizens of the United States,' secures nothing beyond what was intended by the original provision in the Constitution, that 'the citizens of each State shall be entitled to all privileges and immunities of citizens in the several States.' "

To determine whether that agreed with or diverged from Howard's statement, one would need to know how broadly or narrowly Poland interpreted the clause in the original Constitution. There was no hint of disagreement in Poland's opening remark that all questions involved in the proposed amendment "have been so elaborately and ably discussed on former occasions during the present session that I do not feel at liberty to argue them at length and in detail." That comment took in a good deal of ground, but in relation to the clause on privileges and immunities the eulogy applied to Senator Howard and to nobody else, for Howard was the only member who had discussed it before the Vermont senator took the floor. Poland was debating a prefix to Section 1 offered by Howard on May 30 and approved the same day. Designed to overturn the ruling in the *Dred Scott* case that Negroes were ineligible to national or state citizenship, it read as follows:

"All persons born or naturalized in the United States, and

subject to the jurisdiction thereof, are citizens of the United States and of the State where they reside."

Senator Hendricks of Indiana, an unreconstructed Democrat who even opposed the amendment abolishing slavery, made a slashing attack on that clause after its approval. Put it in the Constitution, he said, and it would force the descendants of "the great races of people who inhabit the countries of Europe" to share the proud rank and title of citizens, "with the negroes, the coolies, and the Indians." Senator Poland, an outstanding champion of Negro rights, answered Hendricks next day by urging an immediate extension of suffrage, to whatever extent was practicable, without regard to race or previous condition of servitude. (A preview of the Fifteenth Amendment.) His position on that subject hardly marked him as a narrow construer of privileges and immunities.

The two subjects coalesced on June 8 in a discussion of Section 2 of the amendment, cutting down the representation of states that "denied or in any way abridged" the right to vote. Howard did not know, and could not find anybody who did know, what it meant to "abridge" a person's right to vote. Being indivisible, suffrage could be denied but not abridged.

If the meaning of "abridged" was so uncertain, rejoined Senator Hendricks, was it proper to use it in the more important Section 1, forbidding the states to "abridge the privileges or immunities of citizens of the United States"?

"I think so, undoubtedly," replied Senator Howard, "because it is easy to apply the term 'abridged' to the privileges and immunities of citizens, which necessarily include within themselves a great number of particulars. They are not a unit, an indivisible unit, like the right to vote."

Hendricks went on with his speech, in the course of which he twisted Howard's answer into this perverted form: "What is meant by 'abridging' the rights and immunities of citizens? We do not know, the Senator from Michigan says." Taken out of context, and without the corrective quotation of Howard's actual remark, that can be and has been used to disparage the Michigan senator's clear-cut inclusion of the first eight amendments in the privileges and immunities of citizens.

Bingham and Howard were not speaking for themselves alone

in describing the purposes of the Fourteenth Amendment. Back of them was the Joint Committee, guiding the course of both Houses, which had given advance approval to every clause they were advocating and supporting. Their speeches were not merely expressions of approval. They were formal expositions of purpose by the men in charge of the amendment. Had Section 1 been presented by itself, without such backing, it no doubt would have been subjected to debate on every possible nuance of meaning. But besides having the powerful sponsorship of the Joint Committee, it was overshadowed polemically by the punitive sections of the amendment directed against participants in the Rebellion—a subject on which the Radical Republicans themselves were radically split.

In spite of this concentration on the "rebel clauses," the handful of Democrats opposing the amendment took time enough to denounce Section 1 as an instrument of "absolute, despotic, uncontrollable power." Could anyone have gone much further than Representative Rogers did, in describing breadth of coverage, when he defied any man on the other side "to name me any right of the citizen, which is not included in the words 'life, liberty, property, privileges, and immunities' "?

Members who agreed with Bingham and Howard had no need to spell out their agreement. The absence of dissenting interpretations is what counts. Is it conceivable that in a Congress where a majority disagreed with these men, *not one man* would have stood up to tell them they were wrong and wherein and why they were wrong? Bring the matter a hundred years closer. Imagine that the Fourteenth Amendment did not exist, and that racial discrimination and other denials of civil rights and liberties produced the conditions that led Congress to pass the Civil Rights Act of 1964. The first need, in such a case, would be to obtain the constitutional power to legislate. So an amendment is introduced in 1964, containing the same wording as Sections 1 and 5 of the Fourteenth Amendment.

What follows, in this imaginary scene in American history? Senator Hubert Humphrey of Minnesota, the man who steered the Civil Rights bill of 1964 to passage, takes charge of the proposed amendment. He tells the Senate, as spokesman for a special Joint Committee appointed to deal with the emergency, that the purpose is to give the federal government *power to enforce the first eight amendments of the Constitution against violation by the states.* The debate begins on May 23, 1964, and the Senate votes on June 8. (No filibuster.) In all that time, not a single senator disputes what has been said by the manager of the amendment about the meaning of it, and the Senate approves it by more than two to one. Could that happen, could anything like that conceivably happen within the compass of human nature, in 1964 or 1866 or 200 B.C., if the Senate did not substantially agree with what the sponsor of the amendment said about its meaning?

In the process of ratification, the Fourteenth Amendment was dealt with by state legislators chiefly in relation to the hotly controversial Sections 2, 3, and 4, punishing the South for its rebellion. Those were the acute public issues. Most of the states ratified the amendment with little attention to the meaning of Section 1 outside the immediate field of race relations. Yet in Ohio, where Negro rights were the focal point, Governor J. D. Cox in placing the amendment before the legislature said Section 1 was needed because it was notorious "long before the war . . . that any attempt to exercise freedom of discussion [in regard to slavery] was not tolerated in the Southern States; and the State laws gave no real protection to immunities of this kind, which are of the very essence of free government." In Bingham's state, evidently, it was thought that the Fourteenth Amendment made the First Amendment effective against violation by the states.

More striking declarations were made in states where the debate went into extremes, for or against federal power to curb state violations of civil rights. In such states the emphasis was upon the great extent of the power that was either desired or disliked. In Florida, Governor David S. Walker declared that Sections 1 and 5 left "no further use for the State governments," so vast was the power given Congress "to legislate in all cases touching the citizenship, life, liberty or property of every individual in the Union, of whatever race or color."

In Massachusetts, the Bingham-Howard scope-of-power concept was upheld by both sides in a split of the huge Republican majority in the General Court (legislature). The Radical Abolitionists, numbering little more than a tenth of the House of Representatives, but having four votes on the seven-man joint Committee on Federal Relations, defined Section 1 in terms of the federal Bill of Rights, but opposed the whole amendment on the ground that it abridged, instead of protecting, the voting rights of Negroes. With them in opposition, for exactly the opposite reason, were the handful of Democrats. The moderate Republicans, numbering five sixths of the House, agreed with the Abolitionists on the scope of Section 1, but stood firmly for ratification. It was the Republican extremists, through their control of the joint committee, who presented the issue to the legislature.

The four-man majority opposed ratification on two grounds: (1) the strong provisions of Section 1 were already in the Constitution and binding on the states; (2) Section 2 allowed the Southern states, by accepting a cut in congressional representation, "to exclude from voting every colored citizen." The greater part of the committee report dealt with this potential restriction of Negro suffrage, but the significant part was the view taken of Section 1.

Many of the ablest jurists of that state, the majority report declared, "agree with the opinion of the late Attorney-General Bates, that all native-born inhabitants and naturalized aliens, without distinction of color or sex, are citizens of the United States." This settled the definition of citizenship "quite as authoritatively as an amendment could do." Proceeding to the remainder of Section 1, the committee set forth various provisions of the original Constitution that it considered to be within the compass of the Fourteenth Amendment. These consisted of the Preamble, which declared the purpose to "secure the blessings of liberty to ourselves and our posterity"; the federal guarantee to every state of a republican form of government; and the article declaring that citizens of each state shall be entitled to all privileges and immunities of citizens in the several states.

The committee then listed numerous guarantees of the first eight amendments that would be enforceable against state violation, under Section 1 of the Fourteenth. Those mentioned were freedom of religion, speech and press; assembly and petition; the right to bear arms; no deprivation of life, liberty or property without due process of law; right of accused persons to a speedy and impartial trial, confrontation of witnesses, etc.; right to have the assistance of counsel; trial by jury in civil suits; no excessive bail or excessive fines; no cruel and unusual punishments.

As shown by what followed, these were meant as illustrations, not as an exclusive list. The report went on to say that "Nearly every one of the amendments to the Constitution grew out of a jealousy for the rights of the people, and is in the direction, more or less direct, of a guarantee of human rights." After discussing the citizenship clause of Section 1, the committee said that the remainder of the Fourteenth Amendment, with the possible exception of the clause on equal protection of the laws, "is covered in terms by the provisions of the Constitution as it stands, *illustrated, as these express provisions are, by the whole tenor and spirit of the amendments.*"

Here is proof beyond question that the Massachusetts committee considered the first eight amendments to be covered by the Fourteenth Amendment, even though it mistakenly believed the Fourteenth to be already in the original Constitution. The clause on equal protection, the committee went on, "though not found in these precise words in the Constitution, is inevitably inferable from its whole scope and true interpretation." In consequence of all this, the Radical Abolitionists concluded that the first section was "mere surplusage," and the amendment should be rejected to avoid a backward step in Negro suffrage through the operations of Section 2. The three dissenters, in a minority report, called ratification extremely important. "As a declaration of the true intent and meaning of American citizenship, it appeals to freemen everywhere," and it marked an advance in popular rights which, when completed, would "make our Constitution and laws accordant with the highest principles of free civil organization."

The Boston *Advertiser,* the leading Republican newspaper of Massachusetts, gave the amendment its powerful support. The majority, it noted, regarded Section 1 as "mere surplusage" and its provisions already inferable in the Constitution and effective against the states. Perhaps they were *inferable* but they had not been and were not being *inferred.* To put those guarantees in the Constitution was simply a prudent precaution, and Section 1, "so far from being surplusage, will establish forever that which as mere matter of construction would probably have been judicially denied ten years ago" (at the time of the *Dred Scott* decision).

To bring the resolution for ratification before the House, the minority report was substituted for that of the majority, 120 to 22, and the amendment was approved. From beginning to end of these Massachusetts proceedings, there is not the slightest suggestion of disagreement as to the broad scope of the powers contained in Section 1. In the majority report, the minority report, the speeches of the advocates of power and the opponents of power, and in the guiding editorial of the leading newspaper supporter of the amendment, there is complete unity as to the purpose of the libertarian guarantees. Nowhere is there either a denial or a questioning of the committee report insofar as it equated Section 1 with the earlier amendments of the Constitution. And in denying, as well they might, that these amendments were already binding on the states, the advocates of ratification emphasized alike the force and the necessity of the new constitutional provisions. One group praised the provisions, but said they were already in the Constitution, the other group was determined to put them there, but to everybody they were the first eight amendments.

Considering the fact that Massachusetts furnished the only clear-cut discussion of Section 1 that took place in any state, considering also the intellectual, political and moral leadership of Massachusetts in the long struggle to strike down the chains of slavery, there could hardly be more striking support of the fundamental facts about the Fourteenth Amendment. It was advocated, framed and adopted during a great national upsurge of feeling for liberty and equality. But it received its effective interpretation in the branch of government least touched by such feelings at the time, and at the beginning of a regressive decline that lasted well into the twentieth century.

CHAPTER 29
The Privilege of No Privilege

The first legal test of the Fourteenth Amendment came in a field far removed from the purposes for which it was written. In 1869 the Louisiana legislature prohibited the landing, keeping or slaughtering of cattle in three parishes (counties) centering in New Orleans except on the property of one specified company. The monopoly thus created absorbed the butchering business of a thousand persons in an area of 1,154 square miles, subject to the requirement that the favored company provide facilities at rates fixed by law, for the butchering of all livestock that passed inspection.

The excluded merchants, after losing five cases in the state courts, asked the United States Supreme Court to strike down the legislation on the multiple grounds that it imposed involuntary servitude on them, abridged the privileges and immunities of citizens of the United States, denied them the equal protection of the laws, and deprived them of property without due process of law. When the cases came before the Supreme Court in 1873, argument was presented almost entirely on the issue of privileges and immunities. The other grounds were cursorily dismissed by Justice Miller in the Court opinion. Dividing five to four, the majority upheld the statute as a valid police regulation for the health and comfort of the people—a decision that would have been forgotten in a week except for one fact. Instead of merely holding that butchering cattle in a city was not a constitutional privilege or property right, five members of the Court indulged in a refinement of reasoning that virtually knocked the "privileges and immunities" clause out of the Constitution.

The Fourteenth Amendment, said Justice Miller, "opens with

344

a definition of citizenship—not only citizenship of the United States, but citizenship of the States." By its wording "the distinction between citizenship of the United States and citizenship of a State is clearly recognized and established . . . a man . . . must reside within a State to make him a citizen of it, but it is only necessary that he should be born or naturalized in the United States to be a citizen of the Union." This distinction was of great weight because the next paragraph of Section 1, chiefly relied on by appellants, "speaks only of privileges and immunities of citizens of the United States, and does not speak of those of citizens of the several States. . . . It is too clear for argument that the change in phraseology was adopted understandingly and with a purpose." Only the former —"the privileges and immunities *belonging to a citizen of the United States* AS SUCH"—were placed under the protection of the Federal Constitution. For the protection of privileges and immunities derived from state citizenship, a citizen of the state must look to the state for protection.

And what was the relative extent of these two classes of privileges and immunities? Those belonging to a person *as citizen of a state,* said Justice Miller, embrace "nearly every civil right for the establishment and protection of which organized government is instituted." Listing the great array of privileges and immunities set down by Justice Washington in *Corfield* v. *Coryell* he asked: could it be the purpose of the Fourteenth Amendment, by mere prohibition of the violation of the privileges and immunities of *citizens of the United States,* "to transfer the security and protection of all the civil rights which we have mentioned, from the States to the Federal Government"?

"We admit," said Miller, that an argument against the existence of a power, drawn from the consequences urged against adoption of a particular construction, "is not always the most conclusive." But "when the effect is to fetter and degrade the State governments by subjecting them to the control of Congress, in the exercise of powers heretofore universally conceded to them of the most ordinary and fundamental character . . . the argument has a force that is irresistible, in the absence of language which expresses such a purpose too clearly to admit of doubt."

If the privileges and immunities left exclusively to the states were so vast in extent, what were the ones that were placed by this article "under the special care of the Federal government"? Lest it be said none such could be found, "we venture to suggest some which owe their existence to the Federal government, its National character, its Constitution, or its laws." His list included:

The right to come to the seat of national government, to seek its protection, to hold federal office.

The right of free access to national seaports, to subtreasuries, land offices, and federal courts.

The right to care and protection on the high seas or in foreign countries.

The right to assemble to petition Congress; the privilege of the writ of habeas corpus.

The right to use the navigable waters of the United States.

The right to become a citizen of a state.

That ended Miller's list. So the Constitution was amended to endow emancipated slaves with these rights, every one of which (except the last) *they already possessed without an amendment* and with no threat of molestation by the states. Such were the rights for which Bingham, Howard, Trumbull, Hotchkiss, Garfield and others waged and won their mighty battle. If Justice Miller was correct in holding that the Fourteenth Amendment was intended to mean what he said it meant, these senators and representatives were the most colossal hypocrites that ever sat in the Congress of the United States. If the Court majority was right, these congressional leaders demanded full and equal rights for three million emancipated slaves with the secret design to hold them as close as they could to the slavery from which Abraham Lincoln and the Thirteenth Amendment set them free.

Said Senator Trumbull on January 29, 1866: "A law that does not allow a colored man to go from one county to another is certainly a law in derogation of the rights of a freeman." Under the Supreme Court's ruling, the Constitution protected the right of a colored man to go from any state to Washington, D.C., but he could still be sent to jail if he crossed a county line. A freed slave could make a tour of Europe, he could operate his yacht on navigable waters, he could enter any subtreasury building to cash his government bonds; indeed, he could be appointed Secretary of the

Treasury, and no state dare say him nay. Beyond that, what were his constitutional rights?

By virtue of the Fourteenth Amendment, according to the Miller thesis, any citizen of the United States had the right to become a citizen of any state. As such, the privileges and immunities of a colored citizen of the state equalled those of a white citizen and embraced "nearly every civil right for the establishment and protection of which organized government is instituted." But if a state systematically violated the privileges and immunities of one class of its citizens, or of all of its citizens, what remedy did the victims have under this clause of the Constitution? They could walk into a federal courthouse and walk out again, enjoying the full protection of the Fourteenth Amendment until they reached the sidewalk.

Such was the practical effect of the well-named *Slaughter-House Cases*—for this was truly a slaughter of the Constitution as far as privileges and immunities were concerned. But the destructive effect of the decision was matched by the illogic of the opinion declaring it. Justice Miller steadily confused the meanings of "citizen" and "citizenship." He opened his argument and even his wording by treating the broadest possible definition of "citizen of the United States" as if it were the narrowest possible definition of "national citizenship"—a term not used in the amendment and, as a limitation, foreign to his history. The whole fabric of his argument collapses if one rewords the clause by replacing "citizens of the United States" with the constitutional definition of those words:

"No State shall make or enforce any law which shall abridge the privileges or immunities of persons born or naturalized in the United States."

Only by doing violence to the language and known purpose of the amendment can the Court's interpretation be maintained, and Justice Miller came close to admitting that he was doing just that. Speaking of all three Civil War amendments, he said (too narrowly but with basic accuracy) that on the most casual examination of their language, "no one can fail to be impressed with the one pervading purpose found in them all . . . we mean the freedom of the slave race, the security and firm establishment of that freedom, and the protection of the newly-made freeman and citizen from the oppressions of those who had formerly exercised unlimited dominion over him." Recognizing this, Miller must also have recognized that there was not a trace of such a purpose in his interpretation of the "privileges and immunities" clause. That is why he said "the argument we admit is not always the most conclusive" when a power is argued against because of the consequences of recognizing it. In this case, the Court knowingly set itself up against the purposes of a constitutional provision whose validity it acknowledged[1] in the very act of emasculating it. That intention was jubilantly admitted by Charles Wallace Collins of the Alabama bar, an extreme opponent of the Fourteenth Amendment, who wrote in 1912 about the *Slaughter-House Cases* of 1873 and the *Cruikshank Case* of 1875:

"Several years after the adoption of the Amendment, when the various clauses thereof came up to the Supreme Court of the United States for interpretation, the majority of the Court followed, in effect, the reasoning of the Democratic opposition, and refused to give effect to the ideals of the Radical Republicans. . . . These two cases . . . marked the practical overthrow of the Congressional ideal for the Fourteenth Amendment within seven years after its victorious adoption . . . and reduced the bill of rights of section one to distant potentialities."

The ideal thus rejected was liberty and equality. But Justice Miller misstated the nature of the amendment in reaching the conclusion that it must be emasculated because of its probable consequences. His basic premise was that under the broader interpretation the amendment would "transfer the security and protection of all the civil rights which we have mentioned from the States to the Federal Government." That same complaint was made with some reason against Bingham's first draft, which gave Congress the primary power and responsibility of maintaining those rights. But the amendment as revised and adopted left the primary duty of protection to the states. Neither Congress nor the courts could lift a finger against any state that obeyed this constitutional mandate, any more than they could against a state that refrained from passing bills of attainder or *ex post facto* laws, forbidden by the original Constitution. The plain and virtually admitted truth was that five members of the Court were not willing to extend freedom from slavery into equality with white freemen, because it would upset the established political and social order of racial inequality, and produce very serious transitional problems.

Four members of the Court had no such qualms. Justices Field, Bradley, and Swayne and Chief Justice Chase all stood together in Field's dissent, and Bradley and Swayne added dissents of their own. Justice Field squarely challenged the majority position on state and national citizenship in relation to privileges and immunities:

"A citizen of a State is now only a citizen of the United States residing in that State. The fundamental rights, privileges, and immunities which belong to him as a free man and a free citizen, now belong to him as a citizen of the United States, and are not dependent upon his citizenship of any State. . . . The amendment . . . ordains that they shall not be abridged by State legislation. If this inhibition has no reference to privileges and immunities of this character, but only refers [to those described] by the majority of the court in their opinion . . . it was a vain and idle enactment, which accomplished nothing. . . . But if the amendment refers to the natural and inalienable rights which belong to all citizens, the inhibition has a profound significance and consequence."

Justice Bradley, joined by Swayne, said it was "now settled by the Fourteenth amendment itself, that citizenship of the United States is the primary citizenship in this country; and that State citizenship is secondary and derivative," depending on the citizen's place of residence. What, then, "in general, are the privileges of a citizen of the United States?" He found them in Magna Carta, in the 1774 Declaration of Rights by the Continental Congress,[2] in the Declaration of Independence, and in the Constitution itself, where "some of the most important" were set forth. They were found in the clauses forbidding the states to pass bills of attainder, *ex post facto* laws, or laws impairing the value of contracts:

"But others of the greatest consequence were enumerated, although they were only secured, in express terms, from invasion by the Federal government, such as the right of habeas corpus, the right of trial by jury, of free exercise of religious worship, the right of free speech and a free press, the right peaceably to assemble for the discussion of public measures, the right to be secure against unreasonable searches and seizures, and above all, and including almost all the rest, the right of *not being deprived of life, liberty, or property, without due process of law*. These, and still others are specified in the original Constitution, or in the early amendments of it, as among the privileges and immunities of citizens of the United States, or, what is still stronger for the force of the argument, the rights of all persons, whether citizens or not."

Even if the Constitution were silent, Bradley contended, "the fundamental privileges and immunities of citizens, as such, would be no less real and no less inviolable than they now are." But admitting that formerly the states were not prohibited from infringing these fundamental rights, except in a few specified cases, "that cannot be said now, since the adoption of the fourteenth amendment. In my judgment, it was the intention of the people of this country in adopting that amendment to provide National security against violation by the States of the fundamental rights of the citizen." The mischief to be remedied was not merely slavery and its incidents and consequences. The amendment was designed to cover the spirit of insubordination and disloyalty that had troubled the country for so many years in some states, "and that intolerance of free speech and free discussion which often rendered life and property insecure, and led to much unequal legislation."

Great fears were expressed, Bradley noted, that this construction of the amendment would lead to interference by Congress with the internal affairs of the states, establishing civil and criminal codes and thus abolishing the state governments in everything but name. In his judgment nothing of the sort would happen. Very little if any legislation would be needed. The amendment would execute itself, as in the case of impairment of contracts, through suits at law. As the privileges and immunities protected "are only those fundamental ones which belong to every citizen," they would soon become well defined in the federal courts, and "the recognized existence of the law would prevent its frequent violation."

The principles laid down by the majority on the pretense of regulating slaughterhouses were speedily transferred to the arena of human rights. In the Enforcement Act of 1870, Congress had supplemented earlier legislation in order to put the validating force of the Fourteenth Amendment behind the protections of civil rights. In 1876 the Supreme Court dismissed indictments, based on the 1870 law, against leaders of a mob that prevented Negroes from attending a meeting called for discussion of public affairs. The decision in *United States* v. *Cruikshank* was unanimous, presumably because the indictments were defective, but Chief Justice Waite (a new appointee) took occasion to reaffirm the *Slaughter-House* position on privileges and immunities.

The Fourteenth Amendment, he wrote, protected the right of assembly only for purposes connected with the powers or duties of the national government. Had it been averred in the indictments that such was the purpose of this meeting, the case would have been within the scope of national sovereignty. Lacking grounds of federal jurisdiction, the complainants must look to the states for protection of their right to assemble. By implication, this was saying that if the meeting was called to protest house-burnings by the Ku Klux Klan, either the Klan or the police could break up the meeting without violating any right covered by the Fourteenth Amendment.

Since the intended scope of that amendment reached far beyond racial matters, the effect of the *Slaughter-House* decision was correspondingly broad. John O'Neil of Whitehall, New York, was a wholesale and retail liquor dealer who in the early 1890s took mail orders from thirsty Vermonters and shipped gallon jugs C.O.D. by express across the state line to nearby Rutland. This was a moral and economic issue on which Vermont prohibitionists, cider makers, bootleggers, prosecutors and judges could see eye to eye. New Yorker O'Neil was tried by a Vermont justice of the peace on the charge of unlawfully selling liquor *in Vermont* "at divers times." Found guilty of making 457 distinct sales and given the maximum penalty for each sale, he was fined $9140 and sentenced to 79 years in jail at hard labor. On appeal, a county court jury scrutinized the evidence more closely and cut the "divers times" to 307. This reduced the punishment to a $6140 fine and a mere 54 years in prison.

The Vermont Supreme Court concluded that these sales took place in Vermont and did not involve interstate commerce. It spurned the plea that 54 years imprisonment for "selling intoxicating liquor without authority" was "cruel and unusual punishment," which the state constitution forbade. The $20.00 fine and jail sentence for each offense were not excessive and if the total was severe, it was "simply because he has committed *a great many* such offenses." The United States Supreme Court held that the question of interstate commerce had not been raised clearly enough to give jurisdiction. As for cruel and unusual punishment, the Court declined even to discuss it. The provision concerning it in the state constitution "is not within our province," while as a federal question it was not assigned as an error. Moreover, "it has always been ruled that the 8th Amendment . . . does not apply to the States." (That is, so ruled prior to the Fourteenth Amendment.)

No more biting dissent ever came from Justice Field than the one he delivered in this case, with the support of Justices Harlan and Brewer in a separate dissent. The sentence, said Field, was six times as great as any Vermont court could have imposed for manslaughter, forgery or perjury; greater than the maximum for burglary or highway robbery. The term "cruel and unusual" punishment was usually applied to the infliction of torture, such as the rack, the thumbscrew, the stretching of limbs, and the like, but the inhibition embodied in the English Bill of Rights and our own Eighth Amendment was directed also against all punishments greatly disproportioned to the offense charged.

Fifty-four years in prison for the acts here committed was a punishment at which, he believed, no "man of right feeling and heart can refrain from shuddering." It was true that the Eighth and Fourteenth Amendments were not set forth in the assignment of errors, but when the Court took jurisdiction of a case affecting life or liberty it should look into the entire record. Immunity from cruel and unusual punishment was claimed in the court below. The Eighth Amendment, forbidding such punishment, was formerly applicable only to the federal government. But this and the other early amendments were given a new status by the provision of the Fourteenth Amendment that "no State shall make or enforce any law which shall abridge the privileges or immunities of citizens of the United States." The rights of persons so protected "are rights belonging to them as citizens of the United States under the Constitution," and the Fourteenth Amendment forbade abridgment of them by the states:

"If I am right in this view, then every citizen of the United States is protected from punishments which are cruel and unusual. It is an immunity which belongs to him, against both state and Federal action. The State cannot apply to him, any more than the United States, the torture, the rack or thumbscrew, or any cruel and unusual punishment, any more than it can deny him security in his house, papers and effects against unreasonable searches and seizures, or compel him to be a witness against himself in a criminal prosecution."

Justice Harlan, with whom Justice Brewer concurred "in the main," contended (as did Field) that the transactions were interstate, but took his stand for reversal solely on the issue of "cruel and unusual" punishment. In doing so he stood for general application of the Bill of Rights to the states. "I fully concur with Mr. Justice Field [wrote Harlan] that since the adoption of the Fourteenth Amendment, no one of the fundamental rights of life, liberty or property, recognized and guaranteed by the Constitution of the United States, can be denied or abridged by a State in respect to any person within its jurisdiction. These rights are, principally, enumerated in the earlier Amendments of the Constitution," and among them was immunity from cruel and unusual punishments.

In this almost incredible case of *O'Neil* v. *Vermont*, Field, Harlan and apparently Brewer were reasserting the position taken nineteen years earlier by the four dissenters in the *Slaughter-House Cases*. Field, one of the 1873 quartet, was the only member of that Court still on the bench, and *stare decisis* was uniting with callousness to reduce the minority. Yet if one more member of the Court had stood with the original dissenters, it would have tipped the balance the other way and the amendment would have meant in law what its framers intended it to mean. It would have escaped the further erosion that took place when its other clauses—"due process" and "equal protection of the laws"—came before the Court. And the nation, though suffering an initial shock to convenience and complacency, would have escaped the dreadful accumulation of wrongs and grievances that did not reach their shattering climax until the middle of the twentieth century.

The same can be said about the total neglect during that period of the Fifteenth Amendment, with its mandate that "The right of citizens of the United States to vote shall not be denied or abridged by the United States or by any State on account of race, color, or previous condition of servitude." This arsenal of power was left untouched because of its potency, not out of any doubt of its meaning. Had it been enforced from the outset, under the restraint of a fair and honest literacy test applied to both races, the ex-slaves and their descendants would have risen gradually toward universal suffrage, winning the means of a broader advance through the power of the ballot, with no menace to an orderly society.

CHAPTER 30
The Due Process of No Process

The Fourteenth Amendment offered a second sweeping libertarian protection in the command that no state should deprive *any person* of "life, liberty or property without due process of law." That wording, it was made clear in the debates of 1866, was designed to cover the rights of aliens as well as citizens, and to extend the protection of civil rights and liberties beyond those strictly pertaining to citizens and citizenship. Broadly construed and treated as a genuine protection of personal rights and liberties, "due process" would accomplish all that was expected from the "privileges and immunities" clause. The Court gave it an interpretation that stretched and narrowed it. Accepting a mythical conjecture of purpose that blossomed in the fertile brain of Roscoe Conkling, corporation lawyer and incidentally a member of Congress, the Court held in a Southern Pacific Railroad case that a corporation was a "person" within the meaning of the Fourteenth Amendment.

It had long been recognized that the corporation, an artificial entity, had some human or at least anthropoid characteristics, in addition to paying taxes unwillingly. In 1827 an English lawyer, Howel Walsh, conceded this entity a body and head, "a throat to swallow the rights of the community, and a stomach to digest them!" But, he asked at the Tralee Assize, "whoever yet discovered in the anatomy of any corporation, either bowels, or a heart?" Today, in America, we might credit corporations with either of these organs, alternatively, depending on whether they do or do not pollute the rivers of the country. But for Conkling's contention there was not one word of support in the debates on the Fourteenth Amendment. Indeed, the author of the concept barely refrained from overt admission that treating a corporation as a person in this particular connection was a flight of fancy. He said to the judges in oral argument:

"Those who devised the Fourteenth Amendment wrought in grave sincerity. They may have builded better than they knew. . . . To some of them, the sunset of life may have given mystical lore."

It soon became the established rule that due process was violated by any state or federal law or administrative action that reduced or threatened to reduce the profits of a corporate "person" below the level that the judges thought fitting; or by any legal restraints that impressed them as arbitrary. An avalanche of "due process" cases overflowed the courts. For more than sixty years, it became the principal political business of the financial community to seek the election of presidents who would appoint judges who would make the kind of decisions that would suit the digestive processes of these all-too-natural "persons." There were few indications during those halcyon years that the word also took in the human race. That situation lasted until 1940, when the teamwork of Justices Stone, Black and Douglas culminated in the *Olsen Case*. The corporation remained a "person," but "substantive due process" no longer guaranteed profits or exempted that "person" from the regulatory power of government.

In his *Adamson* dissent, Justice Black listed the privileges and immunities of citizens, and personal rights of life, liberty and property, that the states had been given leave to violate with impunity. It amounted to a Bill of Rights in reverse. The states could:

Inflict cruel and unusual punishments;

Compel persons accused of crime to incriminate themselves;

Subject accused persons to double jeopardy;

Dispense with grand-jury indictments even when the death penalty was involved;

Deny jury trials in civil cases;

Deny the right to keep and bear arms;

Abridge freedom of assembly;

Abridge freedom of speech.

This erosion of genuine "due process," made easier by the earlier washing out of "privileges and immunities," started with the gaping hole produced by *Hurtado* v. *California*, decided in

1884, with Justice John Marshall Harlan as the lone dissenter. The California constitution of 1879 allowed prosecution by information in all cases where grand-jury action had previously been compulsory. Joseph Hurtado, sentenced to death for murder, appealed on the ground that trial without an indictment by a grand jury conflicted with the Fifth and Fourteenth Amendments and would deprive him of life without due process of law.

Hurtado's counsel did not argue that the Fourteenth Amendment made the first eight amendments binding on the states. To have done so would have been a sure way to lose the case, after the Court had held repeatedly to the contrary. Instead, Counsel A. L. Hart contended that the phrase "due process of law" was equivalent to "the law of the land" in Magna Carta, that by immemorial usage it included certain ancient legal institutions found necessary for the preservation of those principles. Among these institutions was the grand jury, whose presentment or indictment was intended to be a safeguard, in cases of felony, against prosecutions founded on private malice or popular fury.

Justice Stanley Matthews, speaking for the Court, accepted the historical criterion but denied the conclusion. It was true that Chief Justice Shaw of Massachusetts, a jurist of high repute, had written that grand-jury action, "in case of high offences, is justly regarded as one of the securities to the innocent against hasty, malicious, and oppressive public prosecutions, and as one of the ancient immunities and privileges of English liberty." It was true that Lord Coke had said to illustrate Magna Carta's "law of the land" that no man could be restrained of liberty "unless it be by indictment or presentment of good and lawfull men, where such deeds be done."

Coke's statement, said Matthews, had been too broadly interpreted, for it tended to outlaw prosecution by information even in cases of misdemeanors. True enough, but Coke merely made a slip which he corrected elsewhere, as Matthews himself noted. The Justice then proceeded to make errors of his own. To prove that the finding of a grand jury was not mandatory *in a capital case*, he cited the argument of Sir Bartholomew Shower in *The King* v. *Berchet*, "in which, with great thoroughness, he arrays all the learning of the time on the subject." But nothing that Shower wrote affected the *Hurtado* case except a statement, *which Matthews omitted,* that directly contradicted his position: "In matters *merely criminal, but not capital*, the finding of a [grand jury] is not requisite."

Justice Matthews went on, building up his case from the English courts, and mishandling everything he touched. Citing *Rex* v. *Joliffe*, a slander action against a man who had charged the plaintiff with felony, Matthews offered this paraphrase of Justice Buller: that if the slander jury found the charge of felony to be justified, "that of itself amounts to an indictment, as if it had been found by the grand jury, and is sufficient to put the party thus accused on his trial." What Buller actually said was that the petit jury had not taken the oath (required of a grand jury) "to inquire for the King; but inasmuch as it is found by a jury of 12 men, it is sufficient to put the party thus accused on his trial." Thus the petit jury became a grand jury, and the fundamental principle of the grand jury was maintained, that no person should be put to hazard of life or limb without preliminary and final denunciation by two juries.

No more legitimate was Justice Matthews' citation of an 1864 English court decision, in which, he said, it was held that upon a finding of murder or manslaughter returned by a coroner's jury, "the offender may be prosecuted and tried without the intervention of a grand jury." What the court held, in this case of *Regina* v. *Ingham*, 5 B. and S. 257, was that an 1861 act of Parliament on grand-jury requirements applied also to an 1843 law authorizing coroners' juries to make presentments. This too preserved the principle of the dual jury, the coroner's jury doubling as a grand jury. But even aside from that, Matthews was arguing that a nineteenth-century statute *modifying* the common law proved the nonexistence of the common law that it altered.

Going still farther afield to demonstrate that the grand jury was not part of due process, Matthews wrote that the medieval practice of "trial by appeal" in murder cases (that is, trial without grand-jury action, by virtue of a writ demanded by a relative of the murdered person) was never thought of as contrary to Magna Carta. "On the contrary, the appeal of death was by Lord Holt 'esteemed a noble remedy and a badge of the rights and liberties of an Englishman.' *Rex* v. *Toler*." In Maryland, in 1765, Justice Matthews went on, "a Negro was convicted and executed upon such an appeal," and in England an appeal of murder was brought "as lately as 1817, but defeated by the appellant's declining to accept the wager of battel."

If the citation of the Negro's execution as an argument *against* the grand jury seems incredible today, it at least reveals the state of mind that governed the opinion-writer in *Hurtado* v. *California.* As for the 1817 "appeal," any newspaper researcher could have knocked to shreds Matthews' use of it against the jury system by writing a journalistic resumé of the affair. Such as this imaginary one:

"The people of England were shocked in 1817 by a resort to the unrepealed 'law of appeal'—unused for more than a century— by which William Ashford, a Stafford County laborer, sought to force a retrial of Abraham Thornton, who had been acquitted of murdering Ashford's sister Mary by drowning her in a pond after raping her. Thornton's lawyers on their part resurrected the likewise unrepealed 'trial by battel,' which allowed the defendant in an 'appeal' to choose between a jury trial and a fight to the death with his accuser. Ashford refused the duel, and such was the public clamor that both 'appeal' and 'battel' were abolished at the next session of Parliament."

So much for the legal lynching of the Maryland Negro and the judicial farce in England. But what about Lord Holt and the "noble remedy" of "trial by appeal," eulogized by him in *Rex* v. *Toler?* Lord Holt *took no part in deciding that case.* Here is what happened. An influential justice of the peace, Spencer Cooper, another lawyer and their two legmen had been acquitted of the diabolical murder of Mrs. S. Stout, "a Quaker woman." Mrs. Stout's mother obtained a writ of appeal to retry the case. The writ was issued to the murdered woman's heir, a twelve-year-old boy (not her son), but it was invalid because of his age, which was concealed. Lord Holt, indignant at the acquittal of the lawyers, undertook to validate the writ by appointing Mrs. Stout's mother temporary guardian of the boy. Cooper and the other lawyer then won the support of *the boy's mother* and suborned a deputy sheriff to give her the writ, which she destroyed.

The suit of *Rex* v. *Toler* was brought to reinstate the writ of appeal. To exclude Lord Holt from the trial without embarrassment, the Lord Keeper gave the case to a special three-judge court headed by Lord Chief Justice Treby of the Court of Common Pleas. Lord Treby, in denying the writ, said that trial by appeal, which put an acquitted person again in jeopardy, was "a revengeful, odious prosecution" that ought to receive no encouragement. Lord Holt, stung by those words, described the case in his reports without Treby's remark but with his own rebutting comment. So that is how Justice Matthews was able to present this "revengeful, odious" system as "a badge of the rights and liberties of an Englishman," making it, by the implications of his remark, *a noble substitute for the grand jury.*

It is really remarkable that in an opinion depending for its force on the history of the grand jury in English common law, Justice Matthews should have gone astray at every point. He was sound enough in saying that there was nothing in Magna Carta, rightly construed, that ought to exclude the best ideas of all systems and of every age. But when he assailed the grand-jury requirement on the ground that "the primitive grand jury heard no witnesses in support of the truth of the charges to be preferred, but . . . indicted upon common fame and general suspicion," he made early imperfections (often useful in a primitive society) the excuse for abandoning the developed and well-proved system.

It is easy enough to justify trial by "information" in police court cases, which always have been below the grand-jury level, and in more serious misdemeanors that do not touch the field of politics. Trials brought about by the "information" of a district attorney do passably well in felonies such as forgery and grand larceny, which come within the definition of "infamous" crimes but do not reach the higher levels of punishment. But the "information *ex officio*" has two lines of descent. It is the short-cut to speedy justice (or at least to speedy disposal of cases) in minor crimes. But it has been the instrument of terror used by kings, royal cabinets and tyrannous republics to take the lives of political adversaries and to repress freedom through the instrument of seditious libel. Against these evils, the grand jury has been the first line of defense, most effective when there is antagonism between the government and the people. Witness the agitation in the British Parliament after the trials of Almon, Miller and Woodfall without prior indictment by a grand jury. Said Captain Constantine Phipps (no Wilkesite, but a member of the king's own party) in the House of Commons on November 27, 1770:

"Sir, no one can deny that a general cry has gone abroad against the exercise of the power lodged in the Attorney General to file informations *ex officio*. The country, from one extremity to the other, rings with outcries for its extirpation. And no wonder, Sir, for it is but a cousin-german of the Star-chamber. Its very nature and constitution is arbitrary, and incompatible with the spirit of a free government."

Solicitor General Edward Thurlow replied that prosecution by "information" was indispensable in cases of seditious libel:

"If no other process is left, but the common one of bringing the affair before a grand jury . . . the press will teem with scurrility, abuse and falsehood. The minds of the people will be poisoned with vile aspersions, and misled by scandalous misrepresentations. The many-headed beast [the people] will swallow the poison, and the land will consequently be one scene of anarchy and confusion."

It was in that swirling miasma of political intolerance that the grand jury, long before put aside by the Star Chamber and High Commission as an obstacle to Tudor and Stuart "justice," was weakened in the common law by Georgian ministers and judges. And it was with eyes open to what was going on in England that the First Congress and the people of the United States placed these words in the Constitution (with a reservation excluding the armed forces): "No person shall be held to answer for a capital, or otherwise infamous crime, unless on presentment or indictment of a Grand Jury."

The specific reference to capital punishment said volumes for the state of mind that produced the safeguard. And because Joseph Hurtado was under sentence of death, Justice John M. Harlan directed his dissent to that specific aspect of the case. He took up the contention of Justice Matthews that when a general and a specific guarantee are included in the same article (in this instance "due process of law" and the grand jury requirement) the specific guarantee cannot be part of the general clause because that would make the mention of it superfluous. So, Matthews argued, a grand jury indictment not being part of "due process" in the Fifth Amendment, it could not be part of it in the Fourteenth Amendment—due process necessarily having the same meaning in both.

Before proceeding to Harlan's answer let us clarify Matthews' argument. By natural extension it excluded all of the specific guarantees of the first eight amendments from "due process" unless the Court found some independent reason for including them. The irresistible logic of that reasoning can be better appreciated by duplicating it in a more familiar setting. Suppose that the Constitution contained an article reading: "The people of each state shall have exclusive fishing rights in all streams, rivers, creeks and brooks within the state, but no state shall obstruct the flow of any stream without the consent of Congress." It is obvious, we can imagine Justice Matthews writing, that rivers, creeks and brooks are not streams, and may be obstructed at will by the states, because if they were streams there would have been no need to mention them in the fishing clause.

Justice Harlan, without the aid of analogy, proceeded to challenge the Court's precisely similar conclusion. He agreed that the phrase "due process" had the same meaning in both amendments. The Court itself had said (in 1856) that its meaning in the Constitution was to be looked for in *"those settled usages and modes of proceeding existing in the common and statute law of England before the emigration of our ancestors, and which are shown not to have been unsuited to their civil and political condition by having been acted on by them after the settlement of this country."* He quoted Erskine, Blackstone, Hawkins, Bacon and Hale to show that no person in England could be put on trial for his life without arraignment by a grand jury. If it was true, as the Court now held, that the specific provision in our Constitution for grand juries meant that due process did not require a grand jury in capital cases, inexorable logic would likewise require a holding that due process did not prohibit compulsory self-incrimination, or double jeopardy, or the right of persons to just compensation for private property taken for public use.

The same reasoning, wrote Justice Harlan, would naturally apply to all the procedural safeguards specified in all the amendments. It would mean that rights to a fair trial universally recognized as secured by "that due process of law which for centuries had been the foundation of Anglo-Saxon liberty—were not deemed by our fathers as essential in the due process of law prescribed by our Constitution." These rights, Harlan asserted, were set forth specifically because they were "of a character so essential to the safety of the people that it was deemed wise to avoid the possibility that Congress, in regulating the processes of law, would impair or destroy them." To them was added a general requirement of due process "broad enough to cover every right of life, liberty or property secured by the settled usages and modes of proceeding existing under the common and statute law of England at the time our government was founded."

Thus Harlan showed that the reasoning employed by the Founding Fathers to make protection doubly sure was being used to make it nonexistent. That was the great evil of the *Hurtado* decision. Grand-jury action required by due process would come to a point where the application was uncertain, in relation to non-capital crimes. The dreaded "information *ex officio*," against which the grand jury was the prime defense in monarchic England, was less subject to systematic abuse in republican America. But the value of the grand jury in capital cases and the smallness of the inconvenience of it in prosecution of other "infamous crimes" make its maintenance a low price to pay as a bulwark of the more vital elements of due process.

Justice Harlan either had second sight or was a better prophet than he knew. For as year followed year, the Supreme Court proceeded to strip out of due process, and out of the Fourteenth Amendment, one after another of the protections that Harlan pointed to as equally subject to attack under the *Hurtado* ruling. Thirty years passed before the Court began the slow, intermittent, difficult and painful restoration of the constitutional rights thus taken away.

CHAPTER 31
Equal Rights and Segregation

In the first court test of "equal protection of the laws," this final libertarian clause of the Fourteenth Amendment was given the meaning intended for it. By the laws of West Virginia no colored man was eligible to sit on the grand or petit jury. Taylor Strauder, an ex-slave convicted of murder in 1874, appealed to the United States Supreme Court on the ground that this racial discrimination deprived him of full and equal benefit of the laws. The question, said Justice Strong in the Court's 1879 decision, was not whether Strauder had a right to trial by a jury with Negroes on it, but whether all persons of his color could be excluded by law from sitting on his jury. The Constitution forbade the states to deny any person the equal protection of the laws:

"What is this but declaring that the law in the States shall be the same for the black as for the white; that all persons, whether colored or white, shall stand equal before the laws of the States, and, in regard to the colored race, for whose protection the amendment was primarily designed, that no discrimination shall be made against them by law because of their color?"

It could not be doubted, said the Court, that this jury statute was such a discrimination. Singling men out because of their color, "though they are citizens, and may be in other respects fully qualified, is practically a brand upon them, affixed by the law, an assertion of their inferiority, and a stimulant to that race prejudice which is an impediment to securing to individuals of the race that equal justice which the law aims to secure to all others."

Had the Supreme Court held firmly to the definition and the standard thus set forth, American history would have followed a different course. But this was not to be. The decision came at a period of transition. The end of "reconstruction," marked by withdrawal of Union military forces from the South and restoration of self-government, also ended the brief period during which freed slaves had varying degrees of protection in their civil rights. The garrisons of occupation almost literally marched north flanked by the white robes and hoods of the Ku Klux Klan, waiting to solve the South's new problem by force and terror.

In the Civil Rights Act of 1875, popularly known as the Ku Klux Klan Act, Congress declared that all persons were entitled to full and equal enjoyment of all accommodations of inns, public conveyances, theaters and other places of public amusement. Any denial of such accommodations, except for reasons applicable to citizens of every race and color, should subject the violator either to a civil suit for damages or prosecution for a misdemeanor. The Supreme Court in 1883, through Justice Bradley, held these provisions unconstitutional.

Individual invasion of individual rights, said Bradley in the *Civil Rights Cases*, was not the subject matter of the Fourteenth Amendment. "It nullifies and makes void all State legislation, and State action of every kind," that conflicts with the rights protected by the amendment. Also, Congress was given power *to enforce the prohibition*. It could nullify state laws and state acts, and that was the whole of its power. "Such legislation cannot properly cover the whole domain of rights appertaining to life, liberty, and property, defining them and providing for their vindication." That would be to make Congress supersede the state legislatures. This portion of the Civil Rights Act did not profess to correct any constitutional wrong committed by the states. It laid down rules for the conduct of individuals in society toward each other, without referring in any manner to any supposed action of the state or its authorities.

The wrongful act of an individual, "unsupported by State authority in the shape of laws, customs, or judicial or executive proceedings," was simply a private wrong or crime, to be vindicated, the Court said, by a resort to state law. A right to equal accommodations and privileges of inns, public conveyances and places of amusement "is one of the essential rights of the citizens which no State can abridge or interfere with." But this Act of Congress did not correct abridgment by the state. It took immediate and primary possession of the subject, with no constitutional authority for doing so. Bradley added a significant exception:

"Of course, these remarks do not apply to those cases in which Congress is clothed with direct and plenary powers of legislation over the whole subject, accompanied with an express or implied denial of such power to the States, as in the regulation of commerce. . . . And whether Congress . . . might or might not pass a law regulating rights in public conveyances passing from one State to another, is also a question which is not now before us. . . ."

Turning to the Thirteenth Amendment, Justice Bradley dismissed the argument that denial of equal accommodations imposed an unconstitutional badge of servitude on the colored race. It was true that decrees of the National Assembly of France wiped out "a long list of burdens and disabilities of a servile character . . . imposed by the old law, or by long custom, which had the force of law . . . But is there any similarity between such servitudes and a denial by the owner of an inn, a public conveyance, or a theatre, of its accommodations and privileges to an individual, even though the denial be founded on the race or color of that individual?"

The answer to that question in Justice Harlan's dissent was an emphatic Yes. He could not "resist the conclusion that the substance and spirit of the recent amendments of the Constitution have been sacrificed by a subtle and ingenious verbal criticism." The Court, he said, admitted in this case that the Thirteenth Amendment "established and decreed universal *civil freedom* throughout the United States," and that Congress had *direct and primary power* to enforce that freedom. "Was nothing more intended than to forbid one man from owning another as property? . . . Were the States against whose protest the institution was destroyed, to be left free, so far as national interference was concerned, to make or allow discriminations against that race, as such, in the enjoyment of those fundamental rights which by universal concession, inhere in a state of freedom?" Harlan thought not:

"I do not contend that the Thirteenth Amendment invests Congress with authority, by legislation, to define and regulate the entire body of the civil rights which citizens enjoy, or may enjoy, in the several States. But I hold that since slavery, as the court has repeatedly declared, . . . was the moving or principal cause of the adoption of that amendment, and since that institution rested wholly upon the inferiority, as a race, of those held in bondage, their freedom necessarily involved immunity from, and protection against, all discrimination against them, because of their race, in respect of such civil rights as belong to freemen of other races."

Harlan then turned to equal rights in public accommodations. Running through railroad decisions from 1848 onward, he found that "The sum of the adjudged cases is that a railroad corporation is a governmental agency, created primarily for public purposes, and subject to be controlled for the public benefit." Such being the case, it would seem that the right of a colored man to use an improved public highway, upon the terms accorded to freemen of other races, was as fundamental as other rights conceded to be of that quality. Harlan quoted Blackstone's statement that "Personal liberty consists in the power of locomotion, of changing situation," without restraint unless by due course of law. But the burdens laid on locomotion, and other burdens which Congress by the Act of 1875 intended to remove, "are burdens which lay at the very foundation of the institution of slavery as it once existed." He let Justice Story (*On Bailments* 475-6) state the common-law requirements laid on both public carriers and innkeepers:

"They (carriers of passengers) are no more at liberty to refuse a passenger, if they have sufficient room and accommodations, than an innkeeper is to refuse suitable room and accommodations to a guest."

As to places of amusement: The managers of these, it was contended, had no public duties to perform, so the exclusion of a black man on account of race violated no legal right for whose protection he could invoke the aid of the courts. "My answer is," said Harlan, "that places of public amusement, within the meaning of the Act of 1875, are such as are established and maintained under direct license of the law. The authority to establish and maintain them comes from the public. The colored race is a part of that public. . . . A license from the public to establish a place of public amusement, imports, in law, equality of right, at such places, among all the members of that public."

Taking up the Fourteenth Amendment, Harlan challenged

the assumption that it consisted wholly of prohibitions upon state laws and proceedings. No one, he supposed, would for a moment question that by that amendment, colored citizens were covered by the guaranty of Article IV, section 2, and thus were entitled "to all privileges and immunities of citizens in the several States." To hold that Congress, after the creation of that new constitutional right, could not uphold it until it was assailed by state laws or proceedings, "reverses the policy which the general government has pursued from its very organization." Such an interpretation would lead, declared Harlan, to this anomalous result: that whereas Congress during the period of slavery had passed the most stringent laws in order to enforce the requirement that fugitive slaves be given up, they could "not now, by legislation of a like primary and direct character, guard, protect, and secure the freedom established, and the most essential right of the citizenship granted, by the constitutional amendments.

"With all respect for the opinion of others [wrote Harlan], I insist that the national legislature may, without transcending the limits of the Constitution, do for human liberty and the fundamental rights of American citizenship, what it did, with the sanction of this court, for the protection of slavery and the rights of the masters of fugitive slaves."

Thus did Justice Harlan hold to the purpose of the Civil War Amendments at a time when the nation was forgetting them. It was a portent of what lay ahead. During the next thirty years, first by organized vigilantes and then by Southern legislatures, the Negro was subjected to a constantly deepening pattern of racial discrimination. In the former slave states he was excluded from all the facilities that Congress had attempted to assure for him. He was refused the right to vote, pushed into Jim Crow railroad cars, given the most primitive separate schooling or none at all, crowded into black ghettoes in city and village, and held to manual labor or agricultural semipeonage. On a recognized basis of master and man, this ill-treatment was relieved by the goodwill of individual plantation owners and by benevolent friendliness toward servants and workmen. White families looked out for "our niggers," or, when that expression became too crude, for "our Nigras." As long as white supremacy remained unchallenged, there was more and freer association of the races in the South than in the North or West.

In Northern states the segregation pattern was repeated, in housing, hotels, restaurants, theaters, with a spotting of it in the schools. Crowded ghettoes were walled in with racial covenants. Negroes were rigidly excluded from labor unions and virtually all employment was closed to them except personal service and rough labor. In all sections of the country the belief prevailed (or was deliberately fostered, as it had been in defense of slavery) that the Negro race was inherently inferior to the white. This belief was utilized in both South and North to justify the separation of the races and to excuse the enforced semiliteracy and economic degradation of the former slaves and their descendants.

By 1896 the Fourteenth Amendment was virtually nonexistent except as a bulwark of the rights of corporations. Of the Court that struck down the Civil Rights Act of 1875, only Harlan and Field were still on the bench and Field was sinking rapidly into senility. To this new Court, then, a colored citizen of Louisiana brought that state's law, passed in 1890, requiring all railway companies carrying passengers in the state to "provide equal but separate accommodations for the white, and colored races," and commanding that no persons be admitted to coaches other than those "assigned to them on account of the race they belong to." In the plaintiff's motivation, this was hardly a civil rights case at all, since Homer Plessy, seven-eighths white and looking like a white man, was complaining that his forced occupation of a Jim Crow car deprived him of the property rights accruing to him from his light complexion.

The way the Court handled the case was what made it stand out in history. The contention about property rights in being *almost* white was tossed out. If Plessy was a white man he could sue the railroad; if not, he had lost nothing to which he was entitled. Justice Henry B. Brown then surveyed the Court's past record, which showed a tendency to outlaw state laws impairing the political equality of the Negro, but so far had discovered no power in Congress or the courts to interfere with laws requiring separation of the races. Coming to the point at issue, the Court went far beyond the subject of Jim Crow cars. The question, said Justice Brown, was whether the Louisiana legislature had made a reasonable regulation:

"In determining the question of reasonableness it is at liberty to act with reference to the established usages, customs and traditions of the people, and with a view to the promotion of their comfort, and the preservation of the public peace and good order. Gauged by this standard, we cannot say that a law which authorizes or even requires the separation of the two races in public conveyances is unreasonable, *or more obnoxious to the Fourteenth Amendment than the Acts of Congress requiring separate schools for colored children in the District of Columbia, the constitutionality of which does·not seem to have been questioned, or the corresponding acts of state legislatures.*" (Italics added.)

In the course of years, the reference to segregated schools submerged all other aspects of the decision. The next two sentences furnish the most illuminating revelation of judicial cynicism (unless in charity one can call it naïveté) to come from the Supreme Court since Chief Justice Taney said that a Negro had no rights that a white man was bound to respect:

"We consider the underlying fallacy of the plaintiff's argument to consist in the assumption that the enforced separation of the two races stamps the colored race with a badge of inferiority. If this be so, it is not by reason of anything found in the act, but solely because the colored race chooses to put that construction on it."

What followed smacks not of cynicism, but of shallow reasoning. The argument, said Justice Brown, necessarily assumes that if the colored race should dominate a legislature and establish segregation in reverse, "it would thereby relegate the white race to an inferior position. We imagine that the white race, at least, would not acquiesce in this assumption." Certainly not, considering the comparative status of the two races in the recent past. But suppose the white man had been the slave of the colored man for two hundred years. What then would he think about compulsory separation of the races in every facility devoted to public service and accommodation, especially when enforced with systematic disregard of everything fair and decent in human relationships?

The argument against segregation, said Justice Brown in conclusion, also assumed that social prejudices could be overcome by legislation, and that equal rights could not be secured except by an enforced commingling of the two races. The Court could not accept that proposition:

"If the two races are to meet upon terms of social equality, it must be the result of natural affinities, a mutual appreciation of each other's merits and a voluntary consent of individuals. . . . Legislation is powerless to eradicate racial instincts or to abolish distinctions based upon physical differences, and the attempt to do so can only result in accentuating the difficulties of the present situation. If the civil and political rights of both races be equal one cannot be inferior to the other civilly or politically. If one race be inferior to the other socially, the Constitution of the United States cannot put them upon the same plane."

But how can individuals of two races meet on the basis of mutual appreciation of each other's merits, when both law and custom forbid them to meet? And how can there be civil and political equality in the face of compulsory ostracism of one race by the other? The concept "separate but equal," used in the Louisiana "Jim Crow" law, originated in Massachusetts in 1848. There the state supreme court, rejecting the argument that separate schools for colored children tend "to deepen and perpetuate the odious distinction of caste," held that it was not unreasonable to require five-year-old Sarah Roberts to walk seventy rods beyond a school for whites. So it was not Southern judges who affixed the term "separate but equal" to this insidious justification of racial inequality.

The Court opinion in *Plessy* was followed by the familiar line, "Mr. Justice Harlan dissenting." It was his greatest dissent. As Justice Brown had done, Harlan surveyed past cases dealing with the Civil War Amendments, but he did so to emphasize the reiteration, time after time, of the intention to endow the colored man with all the rights and privileges of his white fellow citizen, and to secure them for him by the force of law. "These notable additions to the fundamental law," he said, "were welcomed by the friends of liberty throughout the world. They removed the race line from our governmental systems." It was said in argument that the statute of Louisiana did not discriminate, but prescribed a rule applicable alike to white and colored citizens. Everybody knew that the actual purpose was something else:

"The thing to accomplish was, under the guise of giving equal accommodations for whites and blacks, to compel the latter to keep to themselves while traveling in railroad passenger coaches. No one would be so wanting in candor as to assert the contrary. The fundamental objection, therefore, to the statute is that it interferes with the personal freedom of citizens. . . . If a white man and a black man choose to occupy the same public conveyance on a public highway, it is their right to do so, and no government, proceeding alone on grounds of race, can prevent it without infringing the personal liberty of each."

Harlan cut then to the heart of the matter, the attempt to write racial supremacy into law:

"The white race deems itself to be the dominant race in this country. And so it is, in prestige, in achievements, in education, in wealth and in power. So, I doubt not, it will continue to be for all time, if it remains true to its great heritage and holds fast to the principles of constitutional liberty. But in view of the Constitution, in the eye of the law, there is in this country no superior, dominant, ruling class of citizens. There is no caste here. Our Constitution is color-blind, and neither knows nor tolerates classes among citizens."

In respect of civil rights, Harlan went on, the law regards man as man, and the humblest is the peer of the most powerful. It was to be regretted, therefore, that this high tribunal, the final expositor of fundamental law, had found it competent for a state to set up a racial basis for the enjoyment of civil rights:

"In my opinion, the judgment this day rendered will, in time, prove to be as pernicious as the decision made in the *Dred Scott* case. . . . The present decision, it may well be apprehended, will not only stimulate aggressions, more or less brutal and irritating, upon the admitted rights of colored citizens, but will encourage the belief that it is possible, by means of state enactments, to defeat the beneficent purposes which the people of the United States had in view when they adopted the recent amendments of the Constitution. . . . The destinies of the two races, in this country, are indissolubly linked together, and the interests of both require that the common government of all shall not permit the seeds of race hatred to be planted under the sanction of law."

Harlan in conclusion laid down his own rejected pattern for the future, in contrast with the accepted evil alternative:

"The sure guarantee of the peace and security of each race is the clear, distinct, unconditional recognition by our governments, National and State, of every right that inheres in civil freedom, and of the equality before the law of all citizens of the United States without regard to race. State enactments, regulating the enjoyment of civil rights, upon the basis of race, and cunningly devised to defeat legitimate results of the war, under the pretence of recognizing equality of rights, can have no other result than to render permanent peace impossible, and to keep alive a conflict of races, the continuance of which must do harm to all concerned."

If ever a prophecy was fulfilled with overflowing measure, it was this one. Yet as Jim Crowism spread and deepened, and as "separate but equal" became and remained a farcical synonym for gross inequality, the Supreme Court continued to protect it against renewed attacks. In 1914 the matter was settled for all time, or so the Court seemed to believe, when it upheld a railroad segregation law of the lately admitted State of Oklahoma. There was no reason, wrote Justice Charles Evans Hughes, to doubt the correctness of the "separate but equal" rule laid down in *Plessy* v. *Ferguson.* "The question could no longer be considered an open one." It remained closed until 1938, by which time a vast amount of turbulent water had flowed over the racial dam. These are the significant decisions affecting Negro rights during the fifty-eight-year life span of *Plessy* v. *Ferguson:*

In 1899, the Supreme Court upheld educational qualifications for voting that discriminated in fact though not in form.

In 1903, it refused to order the registration of a qualified Negro under an Alabama law described by the complainant as fraudulent, on the fantastic ground that to give him his rights under a fraudulent law would be upholding the validity of the fraud. (Three justices dissented from the Holmes opinion.)

In 1914, the Court upheld Jim Crow railroad cars.

In 1917, ordinances requiring racial separation in housing were declared to be invalid, violating due process of law.

In 1926, real estate covenants excluding Negroes from ownership or tenancy were upheld.

In 1927, the "separate but equal" doctrine of *Plessy* was reaffirmed in the case of a Chinese girl who for racial reasons was assigned to a school for colored children.

In 1927, state laws excluding Negroes from participation in party primaries were held to violate the Fourteenth Amendment.

In 1935, exclusion of Negroes from primaries, by decision of a party convention without the aid of a statute, was held to be lawful.

In 1938, it was ruled that a state maintaining a law school for whites must either admit qualified Negroes to it or immediately establish a law school of equal quality for them.

In 1939, the Court upheld an action for damages brought by a Negro who was excluded from the ballot for life because he had failed to register during a twelve-day period in 1916 that was set aside for registration of persons previously disqualified by the "grandfather clause."

In 1944, qualified Negroes were ordered admitted to all party primaries, which were now held to be part of the system of public elections.

In 1946, state laws requiring racial segregation in interstate buses were held to be unconstitutional under the Commerce Clause.

In 1948, the Court forbade discriminatory delay in furnishing a legal education to a qualified Negro.

In 1948, it was held that real estate covenants based on race, though not unlawful as private actions between individuals, could not be enforced in state courts.

In 1949, discriminatory purpose and use of a requirement that voters be able to explain and understand the Constitution were held to invalidate the statute requiring it.

In 1950, a state was required to drop racial barriers to its all-white law school because its law school for Negroes was inferior in fact. On the same day, the segregation of a Negro *after* admission to college was held to deprive him of equal facilities for study.

In 1954, a unanimous Supreme Court abandoned *Plessy* v. *Ferguson,* holding that racially segregated schools were inherently unequal, depriving the segregated race of the equal protection of the laws. But certain questions were to be reargued in the next term, as an aid to the formulation of a system of enforcement.

In 1955, after reargument, the Court ordered the affected states to proceed "with all deliberate speed" to admit pupils to public schools "on a racially nondiscriminatory basis."

Of several desegregation cases argued and decided together in 1954—cases from Kansas, Delaware, Virginia, South Carolina and the District of Columbia—that of *Brown* v. *Board of Education* was the most basic. It was conceded that the schools for colored children in Topeka, Kansas, were equal to those for whites in all the tangible factors of education—buildings, equipment, faculties and curricula. The case turned therefore on compulsory "separate" education in relation to equal protection of the laws. Four years earlier, in requiring the University of Texas to open its law school to Negroes, the Court had held that even though standards of teaching might be equal, a minor and segregated law school could not provide its students with the qualities that "make for greatness in a law school." Advantages available for all must be open to all, regardless of race. Such considerations, wrote Chief Justice Warren in the case from Topeka, "apply with added force to children in grade and high schools. To separate them from others of similar age and qualifications solely because of their race generates a feeling of inferiority as to their status in the community that may affect their hearts and minds in a way unlikely ever to be undone."

"We conclude," wrote Warren for all nine justices, "that in the field of public education the doctrine of 'separate but equal' has no place. Separate educational facilities are inherently unequal. Therefore we hold that plaintiffs and others similarly situated for whom the actions have been brought are, by reason of the segregation complained of, deprived of the equal protection of the laws guaranteed by the Fourteenth Amendment."

Thus, eighty-six years after "equal protection" was written into the charter of American government, that clause woke from its drugged sleep and became in reality a part of the law of the land. It was not yet, however, a full part of the national consciousness. In the District of Columbia and border states, the requirement of "deliberate speed" was met or exceeded. In the deep South, scores of state laws were passed in an attempt to evade the constitutional requirement and were as rapidly struck down by the Supreme Court. Partly through additional federal court decisions, partly through uneven white acceptance of the new order, but chiefly because American Negroes firmly and forcefully demanded the rights admitted to be theirs in law, Jim Crowism began to crumble. Parks, theaters, restaurants, hotels, depots, buses, ocean beaches were progressively desegregated. Counterpressures built up, marked in the South by a revival of Ku Klux Klan outrages against Negroes, by social ostracism of white sympathizers, and by economic reprisals against both.

In the North, Negroes met resistance no less intense in their efforts to break out of city ghettoes and to gain an entry into the industrial life of the community—especially into labor unions— on a parity with the white population. Offsetting all this was the tremendous increase in the political strength of the Negro, first in the Northern industrial states to which millions had migrated, then in the South as barriers to voting were broken down. Underlying the entire "revolution" was the advance achieved by the Negro race in spite of obstacles old and new—an advance that lifted individuals to high standing in literature, the arts, science, government, the professions, sports and entertainment, and that produced educational and cultural parity with the whites wherever equality of opportunity existed.

This last factor had as much to do with the decisions in the *Desegregation Cases* as did the reasoning set forth in the judicial opinions. By destroying the ancient illusion of inherent racial inferiority, the cultural and economic rise of the colored population turned their compulsory subordination into an unconcealable stain upon those who enforced it. There was no real need for the Supreme Court to base its *Brown* decision on the psychological trauma inflicted by segregation on Negro children. The traumatic effect had been universal, on whites and colored alike, and it grew worse upon the whites as the injustice became more manifest. All that was needed was for the Court to say: "There can be no equality in a caste system; we have been wrong from the start, and it is time to correct the error."

If the "deliberate speed" called for by the Supreme Court in 1955 turned out to be foot-dragging in many sections, part of the responsibility rested at a high level. Seven years of inertia and moral indifference in the White House came to an end in 1961. President John F. Kennedy on entering office undertook to arouse a national consensus and put the executive and legislative branches of government behind the principle of human equality. The leadership he offered coincided with and stimulated a natural stirring of conscience which in varying degrees was almost nationwide. President Lyndon B. Johnson took up and carried forward the banner that fell from a lifeless hand in Dallas. The Civil Rights Act of 1964, enacted under his skilled and determined leadership, brought to legal fruition all that a once-aroused nation had attempted in 1866. The acceptance of that law by the most responsible political leaders of the South—national, state and local—had far greater significance than the outbursts of violence against it in the dregs of Southern society or the "housing backlash" in Northern slums and suburbs.

Quickly and unanimously, in December 1964, the Supreme Court upheld the desegregation of public accommodations. Justice Tom C. Clark, writing for the full Court, justified the Civil Rights Act of that year as a regulation of commerce among the states. In three separate concurrences, Justices Black, Douglas and Goldberg indicated their belief that the accommodations section was likewise a valid enforcement by Congress of the "equal protection" clause of the Fourteenth Amendment. Justice Clark was careful to say that the Court's silence on that point meant only that the Commerce Clause was sufficient. The inference seemed clear that racial discrimination based on state custom having the force of law, with no bearing on interstate commerce, would likewise be condemned if brought before the Court on that issue.

With like unanimity, the Court in March 1965 outlawed the Louisiana "civics test" for voting, Justice Black calling it "not a test but a trap." Through it, election registrars had rejected Negro doctors of philosophy and registered (in one typical instance) a white citizen who wrote this constitutional interpretation of freedom of speech: "Frdum foof spetgh."

Mississippi mobs and Alabama state police might resist the future under the banner of Murder Rampant, but their actions testified only to the degeneration and defeat of the social order they sought to preserve. The colored race had come of age. The Negro had earned the right to exercise his rights, and the nation recognized that this was true. With years of difficult work yet to be done, and extremists still to be handled, the way at last was opened to a true equality and union of the races in seeking to enjoy the blessings of liberty that belong to all.

CHAPTER 32
Thou Shalt (Not) Accuse Thyself

During the half century after *Plessy* v. *Ferguson* wrote *"un"* before the constitutional command for *"equal* protection of the laws," the Supreme Court held firmly to its restrictive interpretations of other parts of the Fourteenth Amendment. With vigor and consistency it continued to rule that the privileges and immunities of citizens of the United States were not abridged when the states abridged the privileges and immunities set forth in the first eight amendments to the Constitution. Again and again, though with occasional escape by another route, it repeated its arguments in *Hurtado* v. *California* that due process of law, which the states were forbidden to violate, did not include the rights enumerated in these eight amendments, because the Fifth Amendment contained a "due process" clause that would have made the other guarantees of the Bill of Rights superfluous if they were included in due process.

This is so difficult for laymen to understand, or, if understood, to acquiesce in, that it may be worth while to clarify it by another fishing analogy. In place of "due process" read "game fish." Suppose that there is common administration of game laws in a national park and a state park adjacent to it. A sign in the national park warns that "no game fish, trout, bass, pike or crappie" shall be taken before May 1. A sign in the state park reads: "No game fish shall be taken before May 1." One might think that it would be unwise, in April, to display a string of trout or bass in either park. But no; it is quite safe to do so in the state park. Under the *Hurtado* reasoning, trout, bass, pike and crappie are not game fish, because if they were, it would be superfluous to name them in the national park sign.

In his vain protest in 1884 against such reasoning, Harlan had pointed out that the Court's argument for excluding the grand-jury requirement from due process would apply just as logically to the petit jury, to immunity from compulsory self-incrimination, to double jeopardy and to the various elements of a fair trial. When fifteen years later the Supreme Court began to turn his warning into a fulfilled prophecy, it held in *Maxwell* v. *Dow*, on the same reasoning as before, that a Utah law reducing a trial jury to eight persons in noncapital cases did not infringe any privilege of a citizen of the United States or deprive any person of due process of law. The make-up of a jury was within the state's discretion. For the first time, in this case, counsel quoted the speech of Senator Howard in 1866, laying the Fourteenth Amendment before the Senate and saying that the purpose was to make the first eight amendments binding on the states. The meaning of the article, replied Justice Peckham for the Court, is "to be determined by the language actually therein used and not by the speeches made regarding it."

But in this case as in *Plessy* and *Hurtado* and the *Slaughter-House Cases*, the Court was misconstruing the plain language of the amendment as well as disregarding the evidence of congressional intent. Justice Harlan made that clear enough in his dissent, saying also that the power to cut a jury to eight persons implied a power to cut it to three or even to a single judge, all without violation of the established privileges of a citizen of the United States or the historic right of trial by jury. Maxwell was in prison, he asserted, as the result of a mode of trial that would have caused the rejection of the Constitution by every state of the Union had that method been sanctioned in it.

Harlan was still on the bench in 1908, when the Court brought its restrictive course to a climax in *Twining* v. *New Jersey* by holding that the Fourteenth Amendment did not protect a person against compulsory self-incrimination. With bad taste but undeniable logic, Justice Moody grounded the current action upon Harlan's repeated warnings of possible future extensions. His past dissents, said Moody, pointed out "that the inexorable logic of the reasoning of the court was to allow the States, so far as the Federal Constitution was concerned, to compel any person to be a witness against himself." That was what the Court now proceeded to do.

The *Twining Case* involved adverse comment made by a trial judge upon the failure of two bank officers to take the stand to rebut the charge of exhibiting a false paper to a state bank examiner. New Jersey, alone among the states of the Union, furnished no constitutional protection against compulsory self-incrimination, but recognized it as a common-law immunity. The New Jersey Supreme Court denied that this was infringed by the comments of the trial judge, and the case came to the national tribunal as a violation of the Fourteenth Amendment.

The Supreme Court confined itself to the constitutional issue, holding first that protection against compulsory self-incrimination was not a privilege or immunity of *national* citizenship. Neither, asserted Moody, was it a part of due process of law either in England, the colonies or the United States. He conceded (quoting from *Hurtado*) that a process of law not otherwise forbidden "must be taken to be due process of law, if it can show the sanction of settled usage both in England and this country." But that did not mean that all settled procedures were essential elements of due process. That would be to let the past bind the future, and forbid improvement. As the Court had once said,[1] it was a sufficient definition of due process "to say that there are certain immutable principles of justice which inhere in the very idea of free government which no member of the Union may disregard."

Justice Moody denied that the privilege against self-incrimination was fundamental or immutable. Englishmen had been forced to testify against themselves for 400 years after Magna Carta and the practice did not entirely cease until the eighteenth century. In Massachusetts, in 1637, Anne Hutchinson had been compelled by Governor Winthrop to incriminate herself. At the time of the drafting of the Constitution, only six of the thirteen states had constitutional provisions against self-incrimination. In the ratifying conventions only four states petitioned Congress for an amendment against self-incrimination.[2] In later years, all but two of the states (New Jersey and Iowa) protected the privilege in their constitutions, although virtually all had a separate "due process" clause. So, concluded Justice Moody:

"The inference is irresistible that it has been the opinion of constitution makers that the privilege, if fundamental in any sense, is not fundamental in due process of law, nor an essential part of it. . . . Many doubt [the wisdom of] it today, and it is best defended not as an unchangeable principle of universal justice but as a law proved by experience to be expedient."

Other inferences seem more rational than the one drawn by Justice Moody:

First. That since every one of the thirteen original states treated the privilege against self-incrimination as a right enforceable at common law, the fortifying of the guarantee in six state constitutions was much more significant than the failure to do so in seven others.

Second. That the subsequent spread of the constitutional guarantee to all states except New Jersey (Iowa having it as a recognized part of due process) furnishes prime evidence of the fundamental nature of the immunity.

By a strange inversion of reasoning, Justice Moody established a case for the growth of due process through the gradual improvement of legal procedures, yet treated the growth of it, in the case of self-incrimination, as evidence that it was not due process. It could not be, in his opinion, because it did not date back to Magna Carta nor reach complete acceptance in England until the eighteenth century. Let us look back at the actual manner of development. Compulsory self-incrimination came into the ecclesiastical courts of England in the Middle Ages, from Roman law through Canon Law, as a method of extorting evidence in heresy and other clerical offenses. The methods employed were torture and the oath *ex officio* (introduced in 1236) which bound the person under examination to make a true answer to all questions that might be asked. The purpose was to force him to destroy himself by his own testimony.

The system reached a climax in the High Commission and the Court of the Star Chamber during the reigns of the Tudors and Stuarts. The abolition of those two tribunals in 1641 left only vanishing vestiges of compulsory self-incrimination. The disappearance became substantially complete in 1662 when an act of Parliament put an end to the oath *ex officio*. Compulsory extraction of evidence against one's self continued for a few years in preliminary examinations, but this died out shortly after the Revolution of 1688.

What then is the basis for asserting that immunity from self-incrimination was not recognized at common law until four hundred years after Magna Carta? Nobody, certainly, would cite the ecclesiastical devices for forcing confessions by heretics as proof of it. In reality it is an illusion growing out of Star Chamber and High Commission practices, and the attempts of Tudor judges to transfer torture and the oath *ex officio* to the common-law courts. Resistance to it by all classes culminated in the destruction of those two inquisitorial courts.

Look once more at the case of John Udall in 1590. He asserted that "by law I need not answer" the question whether he wrote a schismatical book. Chief Justice Anderson replied: "That is true, if it concerned the loss of your life." What made it true? Nothing except ancient law and settled practice, during a time when death was the penalty for every major crime. When a member of the Crown Council demanded that Udall take the oath *ex officio*, he replied that they had no law to make him "swear to accuse myself or others." At this, the Solicitor General could do nothing but protest that Udall—an Anglican parson—was behaving the way Catholic priests did, "for they say, 'there is no law to compel them to take an oath to accuse themselves.' "

That was in 1590. In 1629 "all the judges of England" met and were asked by the Attorney General whether any subject having knowledge of a treason or treasonable intent ought not to disclose to the king, when it was demanded of him, all that he knew concerning the matter. "And if he refuses, whether it be not a high contempt in him, punishable in the Star-Chamber, as an offence against the general justice and government of the kingdom?"

The judges delivered their answer:

"That it is an offence punishable as aforesaid, so that this do not concern himself, but another, nor draw him to danger of treason or contempt by his answer."[3]

Eight years later, in 1637, the Star Chamber ordered John Lilburne to take the oath *ex officio*, swearing to answer to he knew not what. He made the famous reply: "I know it is warrantable by the law of God, and I think by the law of the land, that I may stand upon my just defence, and not answer to your interrogatories; and that my accusers ought to be brought face to face, to justify what they accuse me of." For this refusal he was fined, whipped, pilloried and imprisoned in irons until the Long Parliament in 1640 ordered him set free. Five years after that, the House of Lords remitted his fine of £500 and ordered an inquiry into the legality of his trial. The Commons' action might perhaps be ascribed to Puritan ascendancy: that of the Lords could not be.

Lilburne's lawyer, John Bradshaw, proved by Star Chamber record that the sentence was imposed on him solely for his refusal to take the oath *ex officio*, whereas, said Bradshaw, it was "contrary to the laws of God, nature and the kingdom, for any man to be his own accuser." The Lords vacated the sentence "as illegal, and most unjust, against the liberty of the subject, and law of the land, and Magna Charta, and unfit to continue upon record."

Lilburne's defiant protest and the parliamentary support of it have sometimes been referred to as marking the origin of the principle that no man shall be compelled to accuse himself, with Magna Carta and the law of the land drawn in to give the appearance of antiquity. True it is that an article proclaiming such immunity *as a universal rule* would have been out of place in Magna Carta. Compulsory self-accusation was a prized feature of ecclesiastical law, even though confession under torture was not yet an essential preliminary to the burning of heretics. But in declaring that immunity from self-accusation was part of "the law of the land," the House of Lords (England's highest court) carried the privilege indefinitely back *toward* Magna Carta as due process *at common law*—or as phrased by the counsel whose petition was accepted, process required by the laws of God, of nature and the kingdom.

The House of Lords in 1645 used almost the same words—but with opposite import—that were employed by our Supreme Court in 1908 concerning the privilege against self-incrimination. England's highest court specified the qualities that *made this privilege due process of law.* The highest American court listed the same qualities *for lack of which it was not due process.* The House of Lords upheld the immunity in tones of moral indignation (imagine Congress doing so in behalf of invokers of the Fifth Amendment!), but back of that was the calm judicial exposition of "all the judges of England," who informed the king in 1629 that the privilege against self-accusation was the settled law and practice of the land. And those twelve judges were restating, as an established principle of the common law, the same defensive rights that John Udall had wrung out of hostile jurists and prosecutors in the darker days of Tudor England.

Against this record what did our Supreme Court have to offer in the *Twining Case?* It presented an action by the first governor of Massachusetts that is remembered in history only because it was so revolting to the American conscience—the action of Governor Winthrop who in 1637 brought Anne Hutchinson before a court headed by himself, forced her to confess heretical religious beliefs and banished her from the colony. Governor Winthrop, Justice Moody observed, had been an active English lawyer with membership in London's Inner Temple, but "an examination of the report of this trial will show that he was not aware of any privilege against self-incrimination or conscious of any duty to respect it." Quite true, and of what import?

It was in that same year, 1637, that John Lilburne defied the Star Chamber's attempt to force him to accuse himself. Winthrop, being in America, could not know of this. With less reason, he seemed unaware of the 1629 declaration of the twelve highest judges of England that no person questioned about treason could be required to "draw him[self] to danger of treason or contempt by his answer."[4] His ignorance did not make his action lawful. The question as applied to *Twining* v. *New Jersey* was whether the unjust and arbitrary edict of a colonial governor, contradicted by the twelve highest judges of England and by the House of Lords, should be allowed to nullify the plain words of the United States Constitution.

Justice Harlan was the sole dissenter in *Twining.* He quoted from seven state constitutions adopted between 1776 and 1784 to support his assertion that "the wise men who laid the foundations of our constitutional government would have stood aghast at the suggestion that immunity from self-incrimination was not among the essential, fundamental principles of English law." But Harlan scarcely needed to do more, in order to expose the fallacy of the Court's position, than to quote (as he did) from an introductory paragraph of Justice Moody's majority opinion:

"The exemption from testimonial compulsion, that is, from disclosure as a witness of evidence against oneself, forced by any form of legal process, is universal in American law, though there may be differences as to its exact scope and limits. At the time of the formation of the Union the principle that no person could be compelled to be a witness against himself had become embodied in the common law and distinguished it from all other systems of jurisprudence. It was generally regarded then, as now, as a privilege of great value, a protection to the innocent though a shelter to the guilty, and a safeguard against heedless, unfounded or tyrannical prosecutions."

If that is not the very tissue and essence of due process of law, either as an ancient right brought down intact or as a protection built up through the centuries, what meaning does due process have?

Twenty-nine years elapsed before the next downward step was taken. Then in *Palko* v. *Connecticut,* in 1937, the Supreme Court held that the Fourteenth Amendment did not protect a person against being put twice in jeopardy for the same offense. Justice Cardozo rejected offhand, on the basis of precedent, "the argument for appellant . . . that whatever is forbidden by the Fifth Amendment is forbidden by the Fourteenth Amendment." Palko had been convicted of murder in the second degree and given a life sentence. The state obtained a new trial on the ground that a confession had been improperly excluded by the judge. He was retried and sentenced to death.

Justice Cardozo observed that in past cases the Court had found no deep-rooted principle of justice in grand-jury indictments, jury trials or immunity from self-incrimination. He saw nothing more fundamental in this case. If a court procedure was "of the very essence of a scheme of ordered liberty," it must be followed; otherwise the question of due process depended on the circumstances of the case. This, he said, had been the ruling consideration in the 1932 case of *Powell* v. *Alabama,* in which seven "ignorant defendants in a capital case" (the "Scottsboro Boys") had been unlawfully condemned to death through refusal, in fact though not in form, of the aid of counsel.

The convictions of those boys were reversed, Justice Cardozo said, not because the requirement of counsel in federal cases, under the Sixth Amendment, established a similar requirement in state cases, but because the aid of counsel was essential to a fair trial in that particular case. Was the kind of double jeopardy in Palko's retrial "a hardship so acute and shocking that our polity will not endure it?" The Court thought not, so there was no denial of due process, while as for privileges and immunities, "*Maxwell* v. *Dow* . . . gives all the answer that is necessary."

This five-year step from *Powell* to *Palko* was actually a reversal of the growth of due process of law. In the former case—the original test of "right to counsel" as due process under the Fourteenth Amendment—Justice Sutherland had said that no such right was recognized by the common law of England at the time our Constitution was written. However, in twelve out of the thirteen states the English rule had been definitely rejected "and the right to counsel fully recognized in all criminal prosecutions, save that in one or two instances the right was limited to capital offenses or to the most serious crimes." By 1932 every state in the Union had such a requirement either by statute or by court decrees.

On the other hand, Sutherland continued, the opinion of Justice Matthews in *Hurtado* if followed in *Powell* would exclude the right to counsel from due process because there is a specific guarantee of that right in the Sixth Amendment, apart from the "due process" clause of the Fifth Amendment. But the *Hurtado* rule had been departed from in cases involving freedom of speech and press and the taking of private property without just compensation. "The rule is an aid to construction, and in some instances may be conclusive; but it must yield to more compelling considerations whenever such considerations exist." They existed in the case of these seven boys, where the poverty, ignorance, illiteracy or feeble-mindedness of a defendant made it "the duty of the court, whether requested or not, to assign counsel for him as a necessary requisite of due process of law."

Had the decision in *Powell* v. *Alabama* been based on a simple and logical holding that the Fourteenth Amendment makes the Sixth Amendment binding on the states, it would have fulfilled the purpose of the Constitution and put the right to counsel beyond cavil or assault. It would have given lasting verity to the superiority of American over English law that Judge Cooley claimed in his *Constitutional Limitations:* "With us it is a universal principle of constitutional law, that the prisoner shall be allowed a defense by counsel." But recognition of the *"Hurtado* rule" in this and other cases made it necessary to find escape routes in resounding phrases, "fundamental principles of liberty and justice which lie at the base of all our civil and political institutions," "immutable principles which inhere in the very idea of free government," "the very essence of a scheme of ordered liberty." The trouble with such expressions is their flexibility of application. They can be used as readily to deny rights and liberties as to affirm them. They have in fact been employed chiefly as a gloss on such denials, spreading from one field to another in their application.

That is precisely what happened *in the same field* just ten years after the Scottsboro episode. Smith Betts, a penniless unemployed farm hand of little education, was indicted in Maryland for robbery. His petition to have counsel appointed was rejected on the ground that provision of counsel was not the practice except in prosecutions for murder and rape. Adverse state action on a writ of habeas corpus brought his eight-year sentence to the Supreme Court, which affirmed the Maryland judgment. The Sixth Amendment, Justice Roberts conceded, had been construed to make counsel mandatory in federal trials of this sort, but the question was whether that "expresses a rule so fundamental and essential to a fair trial, and so, to due process, that it is made obligatory upon the States by the Fourteenth Amendment." He judged from the common law of England, which barred defense counsel in felony trials, that the purpose in American constitutions was to *permit* a defense by counsel, not to compel the state to provide it. All states but one had some constitutional provision on the subject, but only twenty-two states made it mandatory by constitution or statute to provide counsel *in all cases* where defendants were unable to do so for themselves. This demonstrated that in the considered judgment of the great majority, appointment of counsel "is not a fundamental right, essential to a fair trial." That which may, "in one setting, constitute a denial of fundamental fairness, shocking to the universal sense of justice, may, in other circumstances, and in the light of other considerations, fall short of such denial."

These words, as well as the Court's mathematics, shocked the sense of justice felt by Justices Black, Douglas and Murphy. Justice Black itemized the constitutions, statutes, judicial decisions and judicially approved practices by which thirty-five states required that indigent defendants in noncapital as well as capital criminal cases be provided with counsel on request. Eleven states were indefinite and only in Maryland and Texas was the requirement affirmatively rejected. The protest voiced in Justice Black's dissent was in full harmony with the words he quoted from the Supreme Court of Indiana, uttered in 1854:

"It is not to be thought of, in a civilized community, for a moment, that any citizen put in jeopardy of life or liberty, should be debarred of counsel because he was too poor to employ such aid. No court could be respected, or respect itself, to sit and hear such a trial."

To return to the subject of compulsory self-incrimination: one might have thought that due process struck the bottom of the well in the 1908 case of *Twining* v. *New Jersey*. But with the *Palko* and *Betts* decisions as new toeholds, the Supreme Court really got down to bedrock in the 1947 case of *Adamson* v. *California*. This produced the memorable confrontation between Justices Black and Frankfurter on the basic issue of the Bill of Rights and the Fourteenth Amendment. In this engagement Justice Black stood forth as the spiritual descendant of the great dissenter Harlan. Justice Frankfurter took his stand behind the many-ply shield of *stare decisis*, backed by the ghostly phalanx of Miller, Waite, Matthews, Moody and lesser luminaries of the law.

The case involved damaging comments by a California prosecuting attorney to the jury upon the failure of a murder

defendant to take the stand as a witness. The decision would have
been a routine repetition of *Twining* v. *New Jersey* had not Justice
Black in his dissent advocated the overruling of the *Twining* decision and supported his argument by a comprehensive study of
the legislative purpose of the framers and backers of the Fourteenth
Amendment.[5] Justice Black took note that the Court's opinion
was careful to point out that coerced confessions violate the
Federal Constitution if secured "by fear of hurt, torture or exhaustion." Nor could a defendant be compelled to testify against
himself by "any other type of coercion that falls within the scope of
due process." That admission, said Justice Black, "repudiates the
foundation" of the *Twining* opinion, which was that compelling
a man to incriminate himself does not violate a fundamental right
or privilege. If the Fifth Amendment's prohibition of compulsory
self-incrimination was so fundamental that the Fourteenth Amendment "absorbed" *part* of it, what reason was there for not
absorbing it in full? In the years since the *Twining* decision, the
Court had found the First Amendment to be part of "due process"
and enforceable under the Fourteenth against state violation.
Thus it accepted or rejected constitutional mandates according to
its own view of them. Justice Black did not trust this piecemeal
application:

"I cannot consider the Bill of Rights to be an outworn 18th
century 'strait jacket' as the *Twining* opinion did. Its provisions
may be thought outdated abstractions by some. And it is true
that they were designed to meet ancient evils. But they are the
same kind of human evils that have emerged from century to
century wherever excessive power is sought by the few at the expense of the many. . . . I fear to see the consequences of the Court's
practice of substituting its own concepts of decency and fundamental justice for the language of the Bill of Rights as its point of
departure in interpreting and enforcing that Bill of Rights. . . . I
would follow what I believe was the original purpose of the
Fourteenth Amendment—to extend to all the people of the
nation the complete protection of the Bill of Rights. To hold that
this Court can determine what, if any, provisions of the Bill of
Rights will be enforced, and if so to what degree, is to frustrate
the great design of a written Constitution."

Justice Douglas joined in Black's opinion, and Justices Murphy and Rutledge agreed "that the specific guarantees of the Bill of Rights should be carried over intact into the First Section of the Fourteenth Amendment." But the latter two would not say that due process was necessarily limited to those guarantees.

Thus, sixty years after the *Hurtado* decision, the position initiated by Justice Harlan—that the Fourteenth Amendment applied the whole Bill of Rights to the states—lacked but one vote of becoming the law of the land. It was this evidence of rising strength that brought Justice Frankfurter so vigorously into the *Adamson* case as a defender of early interpretations. In an opinion concurring with Justice Reed's official disposition of the case, Frankfurter launched into eulogies of the men, decisions and opinions that led to the holding in *Adamson*. Less than ten years had elapsed, he said, since Justice Cardozo (in *Palko*, referring back to *Twining*) "announced as settled law" that the Fourteenth Amendment did not require immunity from self-crimination. Now Justice Frankfurter could not say too much for *Twining*:

"Decisions of this Court do not have equal intrinsic authority. The *Twining* case shows the judicial process at its best—comprehensive briefs and powerful arguments on both sides, followed by long deliberation, resulting in an opinion by Mr. Justice Moody which at once gained and has ever since retained recognition as one of the outstanding opinions in the history of the Court. After enjoying unquestioned prestige for forty years, the *Twining* case should not now be diluted, even unwittingly, either in its judicial philosophy or in its particulars. As the surest way of keeping the *Twining* case intact, I would affirm this case on its authority."

This was not all aimed at Justice Black. The "unwitting dilution" was Justice Reed's remark in the official opinion that although the Fourteenth Amendment does not embody the privilege against self-incrimination "to its full scope under the Fifth Amendment," it does forbid "compulsion to testify by fear or hurt, torture or exhaustion . . . [and] forbids any other type of coercion that falls within the scope of due process." Justice Frankfurter's protest against this language did not mark him as a supporter of torture or other extremities of coercion. In fact, Reed supported his concession by citing Justice Frankfurter's concurring opinion in the 1945 case of *Malinski* v. *New York*, reversed on account of a coerced confession.

Justice Reed's offense was in failure to observe that in the *Malinski* case Justice Frankfurter said that the self-incrimination clause of the Fifth Amendment had nothing to do with his position. His own ground of reversal was that the mishandling of Malinski by the New York police "offend[ed] those canons of decency and fairness which express the notions of justice of English-speaking peoples even toward those charged with the most heinous offenses." The difference was subtle in nature but vast in consequence. Call the action of the police a violation of the Fifth and Fourteenth Amendments and it points logically toward a ban on *any violation* of the Bill of Rights by the states. Call it a violation of English-speaking peoples' "canons of decency and fairness" and it leaves the states free to violate all the guarantees of the Bill of Rights, except as the Supreme Court may find one or another of their actions to be so indecent and unfair as to violate those canons.

To buttress this position Justice Frankfurter argued (as Matthews had done in *Hurtado* in 1884) that because the Fifth Amendment requires indictment or presentment by a grand jury, forbids double jeopardy, and bars compulsory self-accusation, these cannot be included in the clause of the same amendment precluding deprivation "of life, liberty, or property without due process of law." Said Frankfurter in *Adamson*:

"Art Madison and his contemporaries in the framing of the Bill of Rights to be charged with writing into it a meaningless clause? To consider 'due process of law' as merely a shorthand statement of other specific clauses in the same amendment is to attribute to the authors and proponents of this Amendment ignorance of, or indifference to, a historic conception which was one of the great instruments in the arsenal of constitutional freedom which the Bill of Rights was to protect and strengthen."

This seems to say that Justice Black unduly restricted the scope of due process in saying that it was intended "to extend to all the people of the nation the complete protection of the Bill of Rights."

If so, Justices Murphy and Rutledge showed the way out by saying that due process of law *included* but was not *limited to* the provisions of the Bill of Rights.

In practice the Matthews-Frankfurter concept, advocated as a way of enlarging procedural rights, has operated steadily to contract them—a result that certainly was not contemplated by "Madison and his contemporaries." The fallacy of the position was evident in Justice Frankfurter's own illustration of it. Listing the clauses that could not be included in due process because they were specified separately in the Fifth Amendment, he omitted the one reading "nor shall private property be taken for public use, without just compensation." Why was this omitted? Because it was so manifestly a part of due process, both in essence and by court decisions, that the mention of it would destroy the argument. If one right can be specified separately from due process, and still be part of it, so can the others. This points to what "Madison and his contemporaries" actually did—itemize certain procedural guarantees and blanket them and other rights with a "due process" clause.

The untimely deaths of Justices Rutledge and Murphy gave the Supreme Court a setback from which it did not recover for considerably more than a decade. The landmark case of *Bill of Rights* v. *Canons of Decency* was pushed into the future, awaiting reargument under some new writ of certiorari. More was involved, however, than mere changes in the personnel of the Court. There was to be a new look at the history of the Fourteenth Amendment, under the spur of the Black dissent in *Adamson*. There was to be a far-reaching reappraisal of the clause on "equal protection of the law," starting nearly half a century after its almost fatal wound in *Plessy* v. *Ferguson*. Paralleling these developments, throughout the first half of the twentieth century, the age-old issues of political freedom and religious liberty came up to throw old shadows and new lights on the American scene.

CHAPTER 33
Due Process in Speech and Press

The First Amendment had been part of the Constitution for 116 years before the Supreme Court had occasion to decide what was meant by "freedom of the press." The question came obliquely but fully before it in 1907, in the appeal of United States Senator Thomas M. Patterson, publisher of the Denver *Times* and the *Rocky Mountain News*, from a $1,000 fine for contempt of court. Colorado at that time was the private political domain of the Colorado Fuel and Iron Company and assorted public utilities and railways, exercising control through William G. Evans, president of the Denver City Tramway Company and Republican "boss" of the state.

In a political upheaval against this control the state constitution had lately been amended to give Denver a charter form of government and require a vote of the people for the granting or extension of public utility franchises. The boss-controlled (two to one) supreme court was to be enlarged to five in 1905 and a newly elected reform governor was to make the appointments. But the outgoing governor appointed two judges to positions not yet in existence. As a further safeguard the new governor was ousted by the legislature after his inauguration, on a fictional recount of ballots ordered by and supervised by the supreme court. The enlarged court (four to one) proceeded to declare the new constitutional amendment unconstitutional, holding that city government by charter (common in the United States) conflicted with the republican form of government. Keeping well inside the facts, Senator Patterson wrote next day in the *Times*:

"For the first time in the country's judicial history it is announced that the people may amend their state constitutions only just so far as a supreme court is willing that they should. . . . What next? If somebody will let us know what next the utility corporations of Denver and the political machine they control will demand the question will be answered."

The Attorney General was directed to hale Patterson before the bar of the supreme court for "constructive contempt"— contempt not committed in the presence of the judges. The publisher took his stand on the declaration in the Colorado constitution that "every person shall be free to speak, write or publish whatever he will on any subject, being responsible for all abuse of that liberty, and that in all suits and prosecutions for libel, the truth thereof may be given in evidence . . ." But the court held that since the offense was contempt, not libel, "the truth of published charges of corrupt motives . . . is no defense." Furthermore, *by pleading the truth of the charges in his answer,* Patterson had converted his offense from constructive contempt to direct contempt and was subject to summary punishment without a trial by jury required by the state law on contempt procedures.

Senator Patterson was asked if he had any comment to make before judgment was passed. His 1,500-word reply was made part of the dissenting opinion of Justice Steele, who introduced it by saying that the court had set aside both the state constitution on freedom of the press and the statutory provisions governing contempt of court. Quoted with approval by Steele was Patterson's remark that the court's conduct was "the most stupendous indictment that can be framed against this whole doctrine of constructive contempt; or, has it come to this in the United States, that the publisher of a newspaper, because men are judges, may not speak the truth of them as to their official actions, except at the peril of confinement in the common jail, the payment of heavy monetary penalties, or both?"

This judgment, descending to the level of Scroggs or Jeffreys in depravity, came before the United States Supreme Court in 1907. Justice Holmes, in a seven-to-two decision, held that no ground of appeal could be considered federally except the claim that the Fourteenth Amendment was violated by the refusal to allow Patterson to prove the truth of his charges. However, "even if we were to assume that freedom of speech and freedom of the press were protected from abridgment by the states," that would be far from proving its involvement here:

"In the first place, the main purpose of such constitutional provisions is 'to prevent all such previous restraints upon publications as had been practiced by other governments,' *Commonwealth* v. *Blanding*, 3 Pickering 304 [1825], . . . and they do not prevent the subsequent punishment of such as may be deemed contrary to the public welfare. The preliminary freedom extends as well to the false as to the true; the subsequent punishment may extend as well to the true as to the false. This was the rule of criminal libel apart from statute in most cases, if not in all."

His words "apart from statute" were significant, for the *Blanding* decision created such a furore in Massachusetts that the legislature in 1826 passed a law making truth a defense in libel cases. Thus Justice Holmes disregarded even the amelioration of the common law in his own state and gave a definition of freedom of the press that carried the full measure of Star Chamber tyranny minus the licensing system. On that basis, he found that no federal question at all was involved in the *Patterson* case.

From that holding Justices Harlan and Brewer dissented, the latter merely stating that the Court should have considered the constitutional question on its merits. That is what Harlan proceeded to do. It seemed clear to him that as the First Amendment guaranteed the rights of free speech and a free press against hostile action by the United States, the Fourteenth Amendment had a like effect upon the states. The Court, he noted, left that question undecided yet proceeded to hold that the main purpose of the First Amendment was to prevent *previous restraint* upon the press, but that it did not prevent subsequent punishment of publications *deemed contrary to the public welfare.* Harlan could not assent to that view:

"The public welfare cannot override constitutional privileges, and if the rights of free speech and of a free press are, in their essence, attributes of national citizenship, as I think they are, then neither Congress nor any State since the adoption of the Fourteenth Amendment can by legislative enactments or by judicial action, impair or abridge them. . . . I go further and hold that the privileges of free speech and of a free press, belonging to every citizen of the United States, constitute essential parts of every man's liberty, and are protected against violation by that clause of the Fourteenth Amendment forbidding a State to deprive any person of his liberty without due process of law."

Here indeed was Janus-headed Justice facing fore and aft: Holmes, the future apostle of liberty, looking back to a British constitution that made freedom of speech and press empty words in a judicial void, Harlan offering a new formula for bringing the Fourteenth Amendment to life through enlarged application of the "due process" clause. One year later these two justices stood together in protest against that misuse of due process to block humanitarian legislation, both of them dissenting in *Lochner* v. *New York,* when the Court nullified a New York law limiting the hours of employment in bakeries. Years were to elapse, however, before the Court again would face the question whether a person was deprived of liberty without due process of law when a state abridged the "liberties" guaranteed to him by the First Amendment.

In the meantime, those liberties had the misfortune to be caught in the hysteria that swept the United States upon our entry into the First World War. The First Amendment lost its meaning even as a federal protection. It was a period in which midnight patriots smeared yellow paint on the doors of German-American neighbors. Fritz Kreisler, Johanna Gadski and Frieda Hempel were driven off the concert and opera stage. The German language was banned by law from high school curricula. And Congress passed the Espionage acts of 1917 and 1918, the latter of which, modeled on the Sedition Act of 1798, fell just short of making it a penal offense to say *Gesundheit* at a sneeze. Many states followed the pattern. Among the results:

A Minnesota man was sent to prison for saying to patriotic knitters: "No soldier ever sees those socks."

Rose Pastor Stokes was given a ten-year sentence for writing a letter in which she said: "I am for the people and the government is for the profiteers."

Louis C. Fraina went to prison for saying that he was a conscientious objector, not because of his father's Quaker religion (which would have absolved him) but because by experience, thinking and action he had "felt it flow into my conscience and my life."

Sentencing a New Hampshire man to three years in prison for saying "This was a Morgan war and not a war of the people," U.S. Judge Aldrich remarked: "This is no time for fooling. . . . Out west, they are hanging men for saying such things as this man is accused of saying."

Eugene V. Debs and Congressman Victor Berger went to prison for saying *during the war*, in sharper language, substantially what President Woodrow Wilson said at St. Louis on September 5, 1919: "Why, my fellow citizens, is there any man or woman here who does not know the seed of war in the modern world is industrial and commercial rivalry? This war was a commercial and industrial war. It was not a political war."

In that period of madness the only fault of the judges was that nearly all of them were like most other Americans. Federal Judge Amidon, who tried to maintain the ordinary rules of law in North Dakota, wrote afterwards that his instructions were disregarded by juries made up of "candid, sober, intelligent business men," as he had previously known them, "but during that period they looked back into my eyes with the savagery of wild animals, saying by their manner, 'Away with this twiddling, let us get at him.' Men believed during that period that the only verdict in a war case, which could show loyalty, was a verdict of guilty."

In such a climate there could be little hope of bringing the First Amendment to life, yet there were stirrings of vitality. When the Postmaster General excluded the pacifist and socialistic magazine *Masses* from the mails, for "willfully" publishing "false statements" with intent to impede prosecution of the war, District Judge Learned Hand ruled that the law was not violated by *erroneous opinions* which the utterer obviously believed to be true. Judge Hand was slapped down hard by the United States Circuit Court of Appeals, in which Judge Rogers, quoting Blackstone and the Holmes opinion in *Patterson* v. *Colorado*, construed freedom of the press to be freedom from prior restraint.

But Justice Holmes by this time was beginning to advance from his 1907 position. The first step forward came in 1919 when he wrote the opinion upholding the conviction of Charles T.

Schenck for distributing Socialist circulars contending that military conscription was involuntary servitude. Schenck relied on the mandate that Congress shall make no law abridging the freedom of the press, and it was emphasized and admitted that the words chiefly complained of were utterances of responsible public men. In rejecting this defense Justice Holmes wrote that "it well may be that the prohibition of laws abridging the freedom of speech is not confined to previous restraints, although to prevent them may have been the main purpose, as intimated in *Patterson* v. *Colorado*." In many places and in ordinary times the defendants would have been within their constitutional rights in saying all that was said in the circular. "But the character of every act depends upon the circumstances in which it was done." His ensuing words became dominant in free-speech polemics—though far from ruling the decisions—of the next four decades:

"The most stringent protection of free speech would not protect a man in falsely shouting fire in a theatre and causing a panic. It does not even protect a man from an injunction against uttering words that may have all the effect of force. . . . The question in every case is whether the words used are used in such circumstances and are of such a nature as to create a clear and present danger that they will bring about the substantive evils that Congress has a right to prevent. It is a question of proximity and degree."

Although this was said to support the conviction of Schenck, in the belief that his circular did present "a clear and present danger," the underlying intent was to find a halting place in the abridgment of the freedoms that Congress was forbidden to abridge. *Schenck* was decided in March 1919. In the following November Justice Holmes took a second step away from Blackstone and *Patterson*. Following the Allied military invasion of Russia designed to put down the new Bolshevik regime, a quintet of Russian-born Socialists had printed two circulars filled with the flamboyant jargon of their class and period. Declaring that President Wilson's "shameful silence about the intervention in Russia reveals the hypocrisy of the plutocratic gang in Washington and vicinity," they issued this earth-shaking call to the American proletariat:

"The Russian Revolution cries: Workers of the World! Awake!

Arise! Put down your enemy and mine! Yes! friends, there is only one enemy of the workers of the world and that is CAPITALISM."

German militarism also was denounced, and workers were warned that the bullets they were making were to murder "your dearest, best, who are in Russia," as well as Germans. A handful of these pamphlets, pitched out of a high New York window, fluttered to the pavement without starting a revolution. The biggest flutter was in the Department of Justice. Jacob Abrams, a tailor, and four others were tried and convicted under the 1918 Espionage Act of conspiring to write and publish "disloyal, scurrilous and abusive language about the form of Government of the United States," with the design to bring its government into contempt, to incite resistance to the war against Germany, and to incite and advocate curtailment of arms and ammunition essential to fight that war.

The Supreme Court's postwar decision upholding those convictions is notable only for the Court's state of mind and for the way it aroused the scornful indignation of Justice Holmes. Joined by Justice Brandeis, he dissented as he would have done in *Patterson* v. *Colorado* had the realities of freedom and its suppression come home to him with equal clarity in his younger days. Holmes opened with a measured analysis of the "silly" leaflets to show that, repellent as they were, they did not show an intent to do any of the things charged in the indictment. They were written to oppose American intervention in Russia, not to impede the war with Germany, and even if they had the *effect* of impeding it, conviction would require proof of a specific *intent* to do so, and such proof was totally lacking. From this Justice Holmes turned to the underlying issue of freedom to speak and write:

"In this case sentences of twenty years imprisonment have been imposed for the publishing of two leaflets that I believe the defendants had as much right to publish as the Government has to publish the Constitution of the United States now vainly invoked by them."

Even if he were technically wrong "and enough can be squeezed from these poor and puny anonymities to turn the color of legal litmus paper," the most nominal punishment would be enough unless the men were to suffer not for what they did "but for the creed that they avow—a creed that I believe to be the creed of ignorance and immaturity . . . but which . . . no one has a right even to consider in dealing with the charges before the Court."

Persecution for the expression of opinions, said Justice Holmes, seemed perfectly logical when practiced by those who had no doubt of their power or their premises. "But when men have realized that time has upset many fighting faiths, they may come to believe . . . that the ultimate good desired is better reached by free trade in ideas—that the best test of truth is the power of the thought to get itself accepted in the competition of the market, and that truth is the only ground upon which their wishes safely can be carried out. That at any rate is the theory of our Constitution."

Limitless freedom for the expression of thought was an experiment, "as all life is an experiment," and every day it was necessary to wager salvation on some prophecy based upon imperfect knowledge:

"While that experiment is part of our system I think that we should be extremely vigilant against attempts to check the expression of opinions that we loath and believe to be fraught with death, unless they so imminently threaten immediate interference with the lawful and pressing purposes of the law that an immediate check is required to save the country. I WHOLLY DISAGREE WITH THE ARGUMENT OF THE GOVERNMENT THAT THE FIRST AMENDMENT LEFT THE COMMON LAW AS TO SEDITIOUS LIBEL IN FORCE. History seems to me against the notion. I had conceived that the United States through many years had shown its repentance for the Sedition Act of 1798 by repaying fines that it imposed." (Emphasis added.)

This was like a reply to himself in the *Patterson* case. Justice Holmes did not go the whole distance toward freedom of opinion, but his dissent cut through the murky atmosphere of 1919 like a shaft of lightning and led quite naturally to a further advance in his position in 1925. Here, in the memorable *Gitlow* case, seven members of the Court held that "The Left-Wing Manifesto" of a communistic element in the Socialist Party created an *"immediate danger"* of *"ultimate* revolution," and warranted punishment under the New York statute against criminal anarchy. Illogical as that was, the case had a more rational aspect. Accepting jurisdiction in order to uphold the New York action, the Court said through Justice Sanford:

"For present purposes we may and do assume that freedom of speech and of the press—which are protected by the First Amendment from abridgment by Congress—are among the fundamental personal rights and 'liberties' protected by the due process clause of the Fourteenth Amendment from impairment by the States."

Justice Holmes in his dissent (again supported by Brandeis) did not merely assume this but asserted it:

"The general principle of free speech, it seems to me, must be taken to be included in the Fourteenth Amendment, in view of the scope that has been given to the word 'liberty' as there used, although perhaps it may be accepted with a somewhat larger latitude of interpretation than is allowed to Congress by the sweeping language that governs or ought to govern the laws of the United States."

Applying his own test of "clear and present danger," Holmes saw nothing whatever in the left-wing manifesto that would create a present danger of an attempt to overthrow the government. It was called more than a theory, an incitement. "Every idea is an incitement," which is acted on only if it is believed and is not outweighed by some other belief. "If in the long run the beliefs expressed in proletarian dictatorship are destined to be accepted by the dominant forces of the community, the only meaning of free speech is that they should be given their chance and have their way."

Here was an expression of faith in the force of reason strong enough to make freedom both reasonable and safe. Holmes and Brandeis held to that faith but weakened the expression of it by their vote, when the Court in 1926 upheld the conviction of Anita Whitney under the California law against criminal syndicalism. She had helped in 1919 to organize the Communist Labor Party of California, whose Marxist-Trotzkyite platform proclaimed that "the revolutionary industrial proletariat of America," when organized, was going to put capitalism out of business by strikes "proceeding without the authority of the old reactionary Trade Union officials." The language was inflammatory, but the only political action advised was to vote for C.P.L. candidates, who were legally on the ballot. The Supreme Court upheld her conviction, as a participant in a party convention, on the ground that the guarantee of free speech does not provide "unrestricted and unbridled license giving immunity for every possible use of language." Justice Sanford wrote for seven members:

"[A State] in the exercise of its police power may punish those who abuse this freedom by utterances inimical to the public welfare, tending to incite to crime, disturb public peace, or endanger the foundations of organized government and threaten its overthrow by unlawful means."

Justices Brandeis and Holmes concurred in the result, finding some evidence of a criminal conspiracy between the C.P.L. and the I.W.W. (though it took a long kitestring to draw Anita Whitney into that), but they dissented sharply from Sanford's opinion. The two justices could not agree that the Fourteenth Amendment offered no protection to the assembling of a political party formed to advocate the desirability of a proletarian revolution by mass action, at some date necessarily far in the future. Fear of serious injury, wrote Brandeis, "cannot alone justify suppression of free speech and assembly. Men feared witches and burnt women." Many lawful acts and utterances increased the danger that laws would be violated:

"But even advocacy of violation, however reprehensible morally, is not a justification for denying free speech where the advocacy falls short of incitement and there is nothing to indicate that the advocacy would be immediately acted on. The wide difference between advocacy and incitement, between preparation and attempt, between assembling and conspiracy, must be borne in mind."

In spite of these well-spoken words, one can hardly imagine Holmes and Brandeis voting to uphold the conviction of Miss Whitney, had their vote been based on proof that two *nonrevolutionary* labor groups intended to break some law in attaining their objectives. In retrospect, it is evident that the most important effect of the revolutionary hoopla of that California convention was to arouse trade-union members against the left-wing extremists who were trying to gain control of unions. Revolutionary utterances, which so easily produce judicial condemnation, have achieved nothing in the United States at any stage except to expose and weaken those who do the uttering.

Hesitant though it was, the Supreme Court was moving forward on the basic matter of constitutional coverage. By 1931 a majority of the justices found it "no longer open to doubt that the liberty of the press, and of speech, is within the liberty safeguarded by the due process clause of the Fourteenth Amendment from invasion by state action." This was a case in which the Court protected a Minneapolis scandal sheet against immediate suppression and future censorship, but Chief Justice Hughes kept the road open for subsequent punishment by saying that the First Amendment still left the law of criminal libel upon the "secure foundation" of common-law rules for public prosecution and private damage suits.

Louisiana produced a landmark case on freedom of the press in 1936, when the Supreme Court in *Grosjean* v. *American Press Company* unanimously struck down a tax on the advertising revenue of the larger newspapers of the state. The manner in which the decision was reached (related to the author of this book by Justice Harlan F. Stone) illustrates as in a microcosm the growth of constitutional law by judicial review. In conference, a majority voted to bypass the issue of freedom of the press and annul the statute as a commercial discrimination that denied the equal protection of the laws. Justice Sutherland wrote for the Court along that line. Justice Cardozo, who contended that freedom of the press was violated, put his own rejected oral argument on paper and circulated it as a concurring opinion. It proved so persuasive that the Court approved it, Justice Sutherland embodied it in his opinion and cut his original holding down to the remark that "we deem it unnecessary to consider the further ground assigned that it also constitutes a denial of the equal protection of the laws."

Thus Justice Sutherland won plaudits that belonged to his colleague, but demonstrated his own capacity for growth and submergence of pride of opinion. Exactly those same qualities, spread over twenty years and grounded in a deep understanding of human nature and a humanitarian philosophy, lifted Justice Oliver Wendell Holmes from constrictive legalism to the heights of judicial protest and deserved renown.

The Sutherland-Cardozo opinion surveyed English history to show that taxation of newspapers had been persistently employed in Great Britain to prevent or abridge adverse criticism of the government, and had been as persistently resisted. The framers of the First Amendment, familiar with that history, could not have intended to adopt merely the narrow view that freedom of the press "consisted only in immunity from previous censorship; for this abuse had then permanently disappeared from previous practice." The intention evidently was to forbid all forms of previous restraint.

This was far from proclaiming total freedom, but since the *Grosjean* case was factually limited to previous restraint, there was no need to go beyond that odious evil. The significant fact was that the English common law was formally rejected as a measure of the freedoms guaranteed by the First and Fourteenth Amendments. Blackstone's definition of freedom of the press was reduced to his personal affirmation of what he thought it included: he was no longer a sacrosanct authority on what it did not include. But this was not an instance of the present overruling the past. It was a return, though not a complete return, to the principles that governed the framers of the First Amendment, as demonstrated in the congressional debates of 1789 and 1798 and in Madison's *Report* of 1800.

The Court's enlarging view of political freedom was made evident a year after *Grosjean* when it upheld the right of left-wing unionists in Oregon to meet for the purpose of supporting striking seamen and stevedores and to solicit membership in the Communist Party. An Oregon criminal syndicalism law making it a crime for an *unlawful* body to meet for a *lawful* purpose was held to violate the guarantees of freedom of speech, press and assembly. Those rights, wrote Chief Justice Hughes, "may be abused by using speech or press or assembly in order to incite to violence and crime," but the rights themselves must not be curtailed. Free political discussion must be maintained "to the end that government may be responsive to the will of the people, and that changes, if desired, may be obtained by peaceful means. . . . The holding of meetings for peaceable political action cannot be proscribed." This notable decision of *De Jonge* v. *Oregon* went far to protect the right of assembly, but furnished no license to speak freely when assembled, since almost anything repugnant to authority could be held an incitement to unlawful action.

The Constitution, in its First Amendment, measures up completely to the thought of Euripedes: "This is true liberty, when free-born men / Having to advise the public, may speak free." But Congress, the courts and the public had yet to concede the right of freeborn men to give bad advice in an obnoxious manner.

CHAPTER 34
Freedom of Religion

With freedom of speech, press and assembly inside the compass of the Fourteenth Amendment there could be no logical reason to exclude the remaining command of the First Amendment: "Congress shall make no law respecting an establishment of religion, or prohibiting the free exercise thereof." What is an establishment of religion? The earliest official though nonjudicial interpretation came from the author of the amendment. In 1811 a Baptist meetinghouse stood on public lands in Mississippi Territory. Congress, in confirming certain land grants, provided in the bill that five acres "be reserved for the use of the Baptist Church, at said meeting-house." Nobody objected to the gift, worth about $10.00. But President Madison vetoed the measure, informing the House that he did so "because the bill, in reserving a certain parcel of land of the United States for the use of said Baptist Church, comprises a principle and precedent, for the appropriation of funds of the United States, for the use and support of religious societies; contrary to the article of the Constitution which declares that Congress shall make no law respecting a religious establishment."

What room does that interpretation leave for tax support of religious schools? The House of Representatives had passed the bill without evidence of opposition, but only thirty-three members voted to override the veto. This short veto message has received little attention, although, coming from the man most looked to for the meaning of the establishment clause, it is one of the most significant utterances ever made upon the subject.

The second clause concerning religion, "nor prohibit the free exercise thereof," was given its first judicial construction in 1879, when the Supreme Court had to decide whether the plural marriage system of the Mormons in Utah Territory was bigamy or a lawful feature of their religious practices. Chief Justice Waite wrote that religious freedom gave no sanction to "an act made criminal by the law of the land," and this applied as much to polygamy as it would to the immolation of widows on a funeral pyre. Such a conclusion, the Chief Justice emphasized, was consistent with the great breadth of the guarantee of religious freedom. He cited Madison's Memorial and Remonstrance of 1785, in which, said Waite, "he demonstrated 'that religion, or the duty we owe the Creator,' was not within the cognizance of civil government." This was followed, said Waite, by passage of the Virginia statute "for establishing religious freedom," written by Jefferson, which proclaimed complete liberty of opinion and allowed no interference by government until ill tendencies "break out into overt acts against peace and good order." Finally, the Chief Justice cited Jefferson's letter of 1802 to the Danbury Baptist Association, describing the First Amendment as "building a wall of separation between church and state." Coming as this does, said Waite, "from an acknowledged leader of the advocates of the measure, it may be accepted almost as an authoritative declaration of the scope and effect of the amendment thus secured."

Chief Justice Waite endorsed that "wall of separation" in 1879. Not until 1925 did the bearing of the Fourteenth Amendment upon the subject come before the Supreme Court. The high tribunal upset an Oregon law requiring all children between the ages of eight and sixteen to be sent to public schools. Counsel for the state argued that separation of church and state called for an educational system totally free of church influence. A special brief for Governor Pierce (presumably not intended to sabotage his own case) suggested that the people may have voted to eliminate parochial schools in order to check the current juvenile crime wave and to guard against possible future control of education "by bolshevists, syndicalists and communists." The Supreme Court evaded a strictly religious decision by holding that the law "unreasonably interferes with the liberty of parents and guardians to direct the upbringing and education of children under their control."

Five years later the Court held that a Louisiana law furnishing free textbooks to all school children did not violate the Fourteenth Amendment. The obvious purpose of the law was to bring Catholic parochial schools into the state's free textbook system, but the legal argument against it was that public purchase of books for private schools "constituted a taking of public property for a private purpose." Chief Justice Hughes upheld the law as a broad and comprehensive measure to promote education.

Ten more years elapsed before the Supreme Court directly and completely included freedom of religion within the protection of the Fourteenth Amendment. Jesse Cantwell and his two sons, members of Jehovah's Witnesses, were convicted in Connecticut of selling religious tracts without a license and in an offensive manner. Justice Roberts said for a unanimous Court that these men were deprived of their liberty "without due process of law in contravention of the Fourteenth Amendment." The Court then made this sweeping declaration:

"The fundamental concept of liberty embodied in that Amendment embraces the liberties guaranteed by the First Amendment. The First Amendment declares that Congress shall make no law respecting an establishment of religion or prohibiting the free exercise thereof. The Fourteenth Amendment has rendered the legislatures of the states as incompetent as Congress to enact such laws."

Jehovah's Witnesses furnished occasion for several other decisions, the Court usually upholding their aggressive methods of seeking converts, though it condemned the use of loud and raucous noises in the street. The *cause célèbre*, however, was the Pennsylvania *Flag Salute Case*, decided June 3, 1940. Speaking through Justice Frankfurter, eight justices upheld a state regulation under which Lillian and William Gobitis, aged twelve and ten, were expelled from school for refusing to join in a compulsory salute to the national flag. Their family religion taught them that such a salute violated the injunction in Chapter 20 of Exodus that "Thou shalt not bow down thyself to" any graven image or any likeness of anything in heaven or earth that would place "other gods before me."

The Court held that "the mere possession of religious convictions which contradict the relevant concerns of a political society does not relieve the citizen from the discharge of political responsibilities." We live by symbols, said Justice Frankfurter, and "The flag is the symbol of our national unity, transcending all internal differences, however large, within the framework of the Constitution." It is not for the courts to interfere with a school board's right "to awaken in the child's mind considerations as to the significance of the flag contrary to those implanted by the parent."

The law thus sustained, said Justice Stone in dissent, did more than suppress freedom of speech and more than prohibit the free exercise of religion. "For by this law the state seeks to coerce these children to express a sentiment which, as they interpret it, they do not entertain, and which violates their deepest religious convictions." There are other ways to teach loyalty and patriotism than by compelling the pupil to affirm what he does not believe and by commanding a form of affirmance that is repugnant to his religion. The very essence of the liberty guaranteed by the Constitution "is the freedom of the individual from compulsion as to what he shall think and what he shall say, at least where the compulsion is to bear false witness to his religion." The Constitution, said Justice Stone in conclusion, "expresses more than the conviction of the people that democratic processes must be preserved at all costs. It is also an expression of faith and a command that freedom of mind and spirit must be preserved, which government must obey, if it is to adhere to that justice and moderation without which no free government can exist."

Following the *Gobitis* decision, the West Virginia Board of Education embodied the Court's language in a resolution making the flag salute compulsory in all public, private and parochial schools. Jehovah's Witnesses carried a new challenge to the Supreme Court. This time, after a lapse of three years and with two changes in membership, the Court held the compulsory salute unconstitutional by a vote of six to three. Justice Jackson wrote this *Barnette* opinion. There was much talk among lawyers about "the mutability of the Court," but in the nation at large, the dissenting *Gobitis* opinion of Justice Stone had made such an impression that the result was widely applauded.[1]

Supreme Court justices are like everybody else. When novel subjects come up they study them. But unlike most people, they sometimes have to take a public stand before the study is completed.

That happened not only in the *Flag Salute* cases, but in the more controversial area of the First Amendment "respecting an establishment of religion." The Louisiana textbook case was decided without any real inquiry into its bearing on the relations of church and state. It served, however, as a precedent for the five-to-four decison in 1947 that payment of bus fares of New Jersey children attending Catholic schools is part of a general public service to all school children and is not financial assistance to the parochial school system.

In this case of *Everson* v. *Board of Education* there was a thorough exploration of principles and purposes underlying the establishment clause. Justice Black wrote for the majority. Justice Rutledge wrote a lengthy dissent in which he was joined by Justices Frankfurter, Jackson and Burton, while Jackson emphasized his position in a dissent of his own. But all three members who wrote opinions—Black, Rutledge and Jackson—stood together so completely on basic principles that the actual decision as to bus fares almost dropped out of sight. Their common conclusion was that the First Amendment erected a "wall of separation" between church and state, and that any form whatsoever of financial support of a religious institution made a breach in the wall. The main support for this conclusion was found in Madison's 1785 "Memorial and Remonstrance against Religious Assessments," which defeated "A Bill establishing a provision for Teachers of the Christian Religion." Justice Rutledge printed both documents in full as an appendix to his dissent. The complaint of the minority was that the Court opinion established a conclusive case *against* the constitutionality of bus-fare payments, which were nevertheless held to be valid.

In reverse fashion, the same reaction came from those in the Roman Catholic Church who were striving to obtain general tax support of parochial schools. They welcomed the decision regarding bus fares, but objected as strongly to the opinion supporting it as they did to the dissents. For while opening a chink in the wall large enough for a bus token, the Court appeared to be cementing it against the passage of a dollar. Justice Black wrote that the "establishment of religion" clause *means at least this:*

"Neither a state nor the Federal Government can set up a church.

"Neither can pass laws which aid one religion, aid all religions, or prefer one religion over another.

"Neither can force nor influence a person to go to or remain away from church against his will or force him to profess a belief or disbelief in any religion.

"No person can be punished for entertaining or professing religious beliefs or disbeliefs, for church attendance or non-attendance.

"No tax in any amount, large or small, can be levied to support any religious activities or institutions, whatever they may be called, or whatever form they may adopt to teach or practice religion. . . .

"In the words of Jefferson, the clause against establishment of religion by law was intended to erect 'a wall of separation between church and state.' "

Justice Rutledge's dissent from the decision reinforced these definitions. He went extensively into the religious controversy in Virginia, which produced Madison's epochal remonstrance. In no phase of this struggle, commented Rutledge, was Madison "more unrelentingly absolute than in opposing state support or aid by taxation." New Jersey's payment of school transportation costs "exactly fits the type of exaction and the kind of evil at which Madison and Jefferson struck." It is precisely because the instruction is religious, he said, that children are sent to religious schools, and the cost of transportation is a substantial part of the cost of education and religious instruction. The two elements, religious and secular, are inseparable, "Yet this very admixture is what was disestablished when the First Amendment forbade 'an establishment of religion.' "

Only one year went by before the subject of "establishment" came before the Court in a new form—that of "released time"—a system by which clergymen of various denominations give religious instruction in public schools during regular class hours. Instruction was given in the schools of Champaign, Illinois, to pupils whose participation was authorized by their parents. Other pupils were required to leave the room and pursue secular studies in another part of the building. The Court held in this McCollum case (Justice Reed alone dissenting) that tax-supported property was being used for religious instruction and that the school authorities and a religious council were jointly promoting a program of religious teaching carried on by separate sects. "This," wrote Justice Black for the Court, "is beyond all question a utilization of the tax-established and tax-supported public school system to aid religious groups to spread their faith." As such, it fell squarely under the ban of the First and Fourteenth Amendments.

Justice Frankfurter's concurring opinion, approved by Justices Jackson, Rutledge and Burton, carried forward the historical study begun by Justice Rutledge in *Everson*. Starting with Madison's Remonstrance, "an event basic in the history of religious liberty," Justice Frankfurter showed how the Virginia conflict had been duplicated in state after state, as the newly developing system of public schools competed with older church schools for support by taxation. It was not out of hostility to religion, but to avoid fierce sectarian strife, that public schools were dissociated from religious teaching and tax funds were denied to schools in which sectarian doctrine was taught. By 1875 the separation of public education from church entanglements "was firmly established in the consciousness of the nation," without federal compulsion.

The issue of "released time" came back to the Supreme Court in 1952, in a challenge of the New York system of religious instruction for public school children. The only significant divergence from the Illinois arrangement was that pupils were released to attend services in religious centers set up outside the school grounds. The Court upheld this, in *Zorach* v. *Clauson*, six to three, over the dissents of Justices Black, Frankfurter and Jackson. Justice Douglas moved to the other side and wrote the Court's opinion, but the deaths of Justices Murphy and Rutledge were the decisive factor in the change of position. Justice Douglas held that in New York there was no use of state property for religious purposes and no use of force to promote instruction. Here, "the public schools do no more than accommodate their schedules to a program of outside religious instruction. . . . We are a religious people whose institutions presuppose a Supreme Being," said the Justice, and "when the state encourages religious instruction or cooperates with religious authorities by adjusting the schedule of public events to sectarian needs, it follows the best of our traditions."

The three dissenters, writing separately, all found the machinery of the state running through the New York system from end to end, with compulsion at every point except in the decision of who should be authorized to attend the religious classes. "In considering whether a state has entered this forbidden field," wrote Justice Black, "the question is not whether it has entered too far but whether it has entered at all. New York is manipulating its compulsory education laws to help religious sects get pupils. This is not separation but combination of Church and State."

Justice Frankfurter protested against the Court's reliance upon the "absence from the record of evidence of coercion in the operation of the system," when its absence was due to the refusal of the New York court to allow proof of coercion to be presented. Justice Jackson challenged "the Court's suggestion that opposition to this plan can only be antireligious, atheistic, or agnostic," then added:

"The day that this country ceases to be free for irreligion it will cease to be free for religion—except for the sect that can win political power."

That remark went to the heart of the matter, both as it was understood by the highly religious men of the eighteenth century who decreed the separation of Church and State, and as it will have to be understood by the American people if they are not to revert to the sectarian vendettas that have disfigured nearly all the religions in the world's history. "Under our system of religious freedom," wrote Justice Black in his *Zorach* dissent, "people have gone to their religious sanctuaries not because they feared the law but because they loved their God. . . . State help to religion injects political and party prejudices into a holy field. It too often substitutes force for prayer, hate for love, and persecution for persuasion."

That observation furnished a preview of the next great religious issue, placed before the Court after a ten-year interval—that of employing the force of the state to establish prayers in the public schools. Only three of the justices who had taken part in the *Zorach* decision were part of the seven-man court that heard the 1962 arguments in *Engel* v. *Vitale*. With Justice Potter Stewart as the only dissenter, and with Justice Black as spokesman, the Court held that the New York State "Regents' Prayer" conflicted with the constitutional prohibition of any law respecting an establishment of religion. The nature of the prayer, the manner of its invocation, and the bearing of these on the Court's decison, are all set forth in the official syllabus of the opinion:

"State officials may not compose an official state prayer and require that it be recited in the public schools of the State at the beginning of each school day—even if the prayer is denominationally neutral and pupils who wish to do so may remain silent or be excused from the room while the prayer is being recited."

The simple prayer involved in the case could readily be joined in by nearly all Christian sects: "Almighty God, we acknowledge our dependence upon Thee, and we beg Thy blessings upon us, our parents, our teachers and our Country." The Court's objection, in addition to actual violation of the constitutional prohibition, was that in its innocent wording it brought the camel's head into the tent: admit that, and almost anything could follow, depending on the will of the dominant religious group in the community.

"There can be no doubt," wrote Justice Black, "that New York's state prayer program officially establishes the religious beliefs embodied in the Regents' prayer." It had been argued that the prayer was nondenominational and that observance was voluntary. At most, said Black, that could only free the official prayer from the limitations of the clause on "free exercise" of religion, not from the Establishment Clause, whose purposes go much further. The ban on establishment "is violated by the enactment of laws which establish an official religion whether those laws operate directly to coerce nonobserving individuals or not." The Founders of this country were aware that in England an Act of Uniformity compelled all persons to attend services based on the Book of Common Prayer and made it a criminal offense to conduct or attend religious gatherings of any other kind. That was what produced the resistance and sufferings of such men as John Bunyan:

"It was in large part to get completely away from this sort of systematic religious persecution that the Founders brought into being our Nation, our Constitution, and our Bill of Rights with its prohibition of any governmental establishment of religion. The New York laws officially prescribing the Regents' prayer are inconsistent both with the purposes of the Establishment Clause and with the Establishment Clause itself."

It had been said, Justice Black noted, that such an interpretation of the Constitution indicated a hostility toward religion or toward prayer. "Nothing, of course, could be more wrong. The history of man is inseparable from the history of religion." The First Amendment was written to quiet well-justified fears "arising out of an awareness that governments of the past had shackled men's tongues to make them speak only the religious thoughts that government wanted them to speak and to pray only to the God that government wanted them to pray to. It is neither sacrilegious nor antireligious to say that each separate government in this country should stay out of the business of writing or sanctioning official prayers and leave that purely religious function to the people themselves and to those the people choose to look to for religious guidance." To those who thought the Regents' official prayer so brief and general that the establishment of it created no hazard to religious freedom, Justice Black submitted the words of James Madison in his Memorial and Remonstrance:

"It is proper to take alarm at the first experiment on our liberties. . . . Who does not see that the same authority which can establish Christianity, in exclusion of all other Religions, may establish with the same ease any particular sect of Christians, in exclusion of all other Sects? That the same authority which can force a citizen to contribute three pence only of his property[2] for the support of any one establishment, may force him to conform to any other establishment in all cases whatsoever?"

Significant in this prayer decision was the fact that Justice Douglas, who had written the opinion upholding religious exercises in the *Zorach* case, stood with the majority in this instance. He emphasized his concurrence by taking a stand that would have reversed the position of the Court in the New Jersey parochial school bus-fare case had it been taken in 1947. "The *Everson* case," he wrote, "seems in retrospect to be out of line with the First Amendment. . . . Mr. Justice Rutledge stated in dissent what I think is durable First Amendment philosophy." The lengthy quotation that followed, from the Rutledge dissent, was a condensation of various passages from Madison's Remonstrance of 1785. It all came down to the conclusion that any form of state support of religion produces a struggle of sect against sect, the end of which (wrote Rutledge) "cannot be other than to destroy the cherished liberty."

Justice Stewart's dissent in this case embodied the thought of millions of Americans who looked at the innocuous wording of the Regents' Prayer and did not take adequate account of its official character. "I cannot see how an 'official religion' is established," he wrote, "by letting those who want to say a prayer say it." What was important was not the history of religious persecutions in England but "the religious traditions of our people, reflected in countless practices of the institutions and officials of our government." He listed many of them: the Supreme Court's own historic invocation, "God save the United States and this Honorable Court"; the opening of each day's House and Senate sessions with prayer; the asking of God's help by all Presidents from Washington onward; the words "In God We Trust" impressed on coins; the words "under God" in the pledge of Allegiance to the Flag; the passage by Congress, in 1952, of an act requiring the President each year to proclaim a National Day of Prayer.

A flaw in this reasoning was the assumption that the decision of the Court made it unconstitutional for a government official to express his religious sentiments, as examples of which the Justice cited invocations of divine aid by Presidents Washington, Adams, Jefferson, Madison, Lincoln, Cleveland, Wilson, Eisenhower and Kennedy. Quoted from Washington were his inaugural words on April 30, 1789, "It would be peculiarly improper to omit in this first official act my fervent supplications to that Almighty Being who rules over the universe, who presides in the councils of nations, and whose providential aids can supply every human defect . . ."

The relevance of this, if it were relevant, could be doubled by mentioning that Washington on May 5 sent a note of thanks to Madison for writing that address. But it was a personal expression of piety, just as personal as Washington's request to Tench Tilghman on March 24, 1784, to send him an indentured house joiner and a bricklayer, who, "if they are good workmen . . . may be Mohametans, Jews or Christian of an[y] Sect, or they may be Athiests [sic]." Between the piety of Washington's inaugural address and the levity of his letter to Tilghman there is room for a six months' investigation by the House Committee on Un-American Activities. But both of them were personal expressions, neither one a governmental act.

A truer analogy would be the adoption by law of a Congressional Prayer to be recited in unison each day by the members of the House and Senate—voluntarily, of course, so as to exempt the hardy handful who would match the courage of ostracized school children. The same principle is reached in the Supreme Court's daily request that "God save the United States and this Honorable Court." If Congress has constitutional power to compel the utterance of those words, it has unlimited power to establish religion. Coming voluntarily from the Court it is a personal expression, reflecting anything from historic piety to urgent present need for the help invoked.

For an official statement of the relationship of the American government to Christianity, as understood when the country was founded, one can go to the treaty of 1796-1797 between the United States and Tripoli. Negotiated by the Washington Administration, ratified by the Senate and proclaimed by President Adams on June 10, 1797, it contained the following language:

"Article eleven. As the government of the United States of America is not in any sense founded on the Christian religion— and as it has in itself no character of enmity against the laws, religion or tranquility of Musselmen . . . it is declared by the parties that no pretext arising from religious opinions shall ever produce an interruption of the harmony between the two countries."[3]

It is hard to visualize a President accepting or the Senate ratifying such an article today, nor would it have been done in 1797 in the absence of a clear understanding of what was meant by the separation of church and state. In the present day, religious phraseology is less an expression of feeling than a cloak to hide the absence of it. Congress in 1952 gave legal status to the Thanksgiving holiday, but not all turkey-stuffed, motor-smashing Americans would recognize its identity in the wording of the law: "The President shall set aside and proclaim a suitable day each year, other than a Sunday, as a National Day of prayer, on which the people of the United States may turn to God in prayer and meditation at churches, in groups, and as individuals." The Constitution would certainly prohibit the giving of such a command to the President, if the act were not carefully worded to exclude any element of compulsion or admonition addressed to the public. The reference to what the people MAY do on that day could well be patterned on President Madison's proclamation of June 19, 1812, unwillingly issued in response to a joint resolution of Congress after the declaration of war on Great Britain. He cited the request of Congress "that a day may be recommended to be observed by the people . . . as a day of public humiliation and prayer," but he limited his own action to setting "a convenient day" that would "enable the several religious denominations and societies *so disposed*" to offer their common vows and adorations. The wording, he wrote many years later, was chosen to make it a mere intimation of a timely day for a "voluntary concurrence of those who approved a general union on such an occasion." In July 1813, when the war with England was going marvelously well at sea and very badly on land, Madison again complied to a minimum extent with a joint resolution of Congress. He recommended "to all who shall be piously disposed," that they unite their hearts and voices in thanking the Great Parent and Sovereign of the Universe for our naval victories, bountiful harvests, the expansion of munition factories, and the possession of a Constitution "guaranteeing to each individual security, not only of his person and his property, but of those sacred rights of conscience so essential to his present happiness and so dear to his future hopes." With that as a prelude, Madison expanded his proclamation into an exposition of the meaning of freedom of religion in the Constitution:

"If the public homage of a people can ever be worthy the favorable regard of the Holy and Omniscient Being to whom it is addressed, it must be that in which those who join in it are guided only by their free choice, by the impulse of their hearts and the dictates of their consciences; and such a spectacle must be interesting to all Christian nations as proving that religion, that gift of Heaven for the good of man, freed from all coercive edicts, from that unhallowed connection with the powers of this world which corrupts religion into an instrument or an usurper of the policy of the state, and making no appeal but to reason, to the heart, and to the conscience, can spread its benign influence everywhere and can attract to the divine altar those freewill offerings of humble supplication, thanksgiving, and praise which alone can be acceptable to Him whom no hypocrisy can deceive and no forced sacrifices propitiate."

If it is meaningful that the author of the First Amendment, as President, willingly or unwillingly proclaimed days of prayer and thanksgiving, it is tenfold more signficant that the wording of them destroys the claims that are based upon the fact that he proclaimed them. Where, in the words quoted from his proclamation, is there even microscopic room for the official prayer that the State of New York required to be recited every day in every schoolroom? Judicial sanction of that prayer would either open the way to establishment of any prayer, no matter how sectarian, or would make the Supreme Court a permanent censor of official prayers, in manifest violation of the Constitution.

It is easily conceivable that twelve representatives of twelve religious sects could draft and deliver twelve prayers that would be gratefully received and promptly granted by the Holy and Omniscient Being to whom they were addressed, but that eleven of these prayers would be heatedly rejected by each of the twelve supplicants. Something like that, but in a more wholesome sense, became manifest in the ultimate reaction to the decision in *Engel* v. *Vitale*. It was greeted at first with nearly universal condemnation. The Supreme Court was driving prayer out of American life, depriving children of contact with their Maker, yielding to atheism. The halls of Congress resounded with denunciation, some of it from members who had not prayed in fifty years. Constitutional amendments were offered by the bushel to put prayer back into the charter of government. The House Committee on the Judiciary held hearings that ran on week after week.

Under the wise chairmanship of Representative Emanuel Celler, the House Committee let everybody have his say. During the process light began to dawn. Those who wanted to modify the First Amendment could not agree on how to change it without opening the way to all the evils that the Amendment was designed to prevent. Important church organizations began to speak, not only in defense of the Constitution as it stands, but in support of the prayer decision. The change of view extended to the press and to

Congress itself. In the last stages of the dying agitation, it was merely a whip in the hands of those who were attacking the Supreme Court for other reasons. One year after the prayer decision there was hardly a ripple of protest when the Court unanimously banned compulsory Bible reading in the schools. In 1964, the justices declined to review a New York State decision that the Constitution was not violated by the presence of the words "under God" in the pledge of allegiance to the flag, when recited without compulsion in public schools. That produced a double sigh of relief, as it clearly indicated by analogy that "in God we trust" could continue to sustain the national veneration of the dollar.

To realize what these turbulent politico-religious reactions could do to the separation of church and state, if yielded to, we may go back to hearings held by the House Judiciary Committee on March 11, 1896. Representatives of various religious organizations appeared to support or oppose a resolution to amend the Preamble of the Constitution by giving it the following opening:

"We the people of the United States, acknowledging Almighty God as the source of all power and authority in civil government, the Lord Jesus Christ as the ruler of nations, and His revealed word as of supreme authority in civil affairs, in order to form a more perfect Union," etc.

Dr. Stockton, moderator of the Presbyterian Synod of Pennsylvania, stated the purpose: "I wish to call your attention simply to one point—that this is a Christian nation, and ask you to bring the Constitution of the nation in line with what we believe is the unwritten constitution of the nation." In the course of the hearing the Reverend Mr. Cole was asked whether this amendment would permit a Jew to accept an election to Congress.

"Mr. Cole. Logically I think he could not."

As the hearing progressed, Dr. David McAllister of Allegheny, Pennsylvania, editor of the *Christian Statesman*, began to suspect that the members of the Judiciary Committee did not understand their country. Said he:

"I wish you to understand that . . . this country was settled by Christian people, as has already been said—not by Jews, not by Mohammedans, not by Confucians, but by Christian forebears, from whom you and I, Mr. Chairman, and you, gentlemen, are proud to be descended, whether they be Quakers . . . Episcopalians

. . . Presbyterians, or any other denomination. . . . We have as a nation called upon God; we have acknowledged Jesus Christ as the appointed way through whom to seek God's blessing."

The acting chairman, Representative Ray of New York, asked Dr. McAllister to be more specific. What did the amendment mean by "His revealed will"?

"Dr. McAllister. The Bible.

"The Chairman. Then you wish the Constitution to recognize the Bible as supreme authority in civil affairs, do you?

"Dr. McAllister. Yes, sir."

Asked for an example of a biblical injunction to be enforced by Congress, Dr. McAllister responded: "Remember the Sabbath Day to keep it holy." At this point a voice came from the audience: "That is the seventh day."

"It is not the seventh day," firmly replied the witness. In the ensuing colloquy it was brought out that Jews and Seventh-Day Adventists would have the right, under this amendment, to observe Saturday as their Sabbath and to work in their own houses on Sunday. They could not plow corn "to the disturbance of those who pass to church," and it would be criminal to play Sunday baseball. Suppose, he was asked, that the Supreme Court should decide that the Bible did not fix the Sabbath to be on Sunday. Replied the witness: "If the Court should say that, and the nation think it is not right, we must change it."

Dr. McAllister told the committee that Congress itself had made this amendment essential by holding "sessions on the Lord's day" when there was no real necessity of it. Representative Connolly of Illinois doubted that amending the Constitution would lift the level of congressional piety. He asked:

"If the devil should make a constitution for hell and acknowledge the supremacy of God in that constitution, would it make hell any better?"

The hearing was brought back to earth by Representative Broderick of Kansas. "Is it not true," he asked, "that Christianity has grown in this country because it has been free" of arbitrary legislation?

"Dr. McAllister. Is it arbitrary legislation to have Congress opened by prayer?

"Mr. Broderick. No.

"Dr. McAllister. Do you think it is arbitrary legislation that we should have prayers in our public schools?

"Mr. Broderick. I am not certain about it.

"Dr. McAllister. Should not the children in the schools be taught that there is a God? Should they not be taught that there is a judgment seat?

"Several Gentlemen. No, no.

"Dr. McAllister. These gentlemen say no. That shows where the conflict is. The conflict is between the denial of the judgment seat, the denial of our responsibility to the God in whose name we swear, and those who hold Christian principles sacred. . . . What is the unwritten constitution of this country? It embodies Christianity. It is Christian in all the facts of our life, as shown by the appointment of chaplains, in the administration of oaths, in the appointment of days of thanksgiving and fasting. . . ."

There is a clearly discernible resemblance between the language and thought of Dr. McAllister and the dissenting opinion in *Engel* v. *Vitale*. The difference between them—an enormous one—lies in the fact that Dr. McAllister carried small beginnings to their ultimate consequences when used to breach the constitutional "wall of separation between State and Church." That 1896 hearing leaves no doubt of what would happen in this country if the First Amendment should be broken down. We should then witness the calamitous results of that "unhallowed connection," as Madison called it in his 1813 proclamation, "with the powers of this world which corrupts religion into an instrument or an usurper of the policy of the state." Apply it to tax support of all schools and there would soon be a strangulation of parochial schools in some sections, a strangulation of public schools in other localities, a multiplying of sectarian school systems, a shift to federal control of education to escape local strife, and then a ferocious struggle between religious sects for the control of Congress. All these are possible—even the bombing of churches and schools—in a civilized country which forgets that harmony grows and religion thrives only as long as it and its institutions remain outside the purview of government.

Since 1896 there has been a vast enlightenment in the councils of American churches, spreading through all major denominations and most minor ones. Yet no consensus has been reached on the meaning of constitutional guarantees of freedom or even on the desirability of them. In every instance, those who would weaken or breach the barrier point to the paid services of congressional and military chaplains as conflicting with the decisions of the Supreme Court and inferentially invalidating them. Why, it is asked, did not James Madison, the author of the First Amendment, protest against such appointments when he was in Congress?

Chaplainships of both Congress and the armed services were established sixteen years before the First Amendment was adopted. It would have been fatuous folly for anybody to stir a major controversy over a minor matter before the meaning of the amendment had been threshed out in weightier matters. But Madison did foresee the danger that minor deviations from the constitutional path would deepen into dangerous precedents. He took care of one of them by his veto of the appropriation for a Baptist church. Others he dealt with in his "Essay on Monopolies," unpublished until 1946. Here he wrote:

"Is the appointment of Chaplains to the two Houses of Congress consistent with the Constitution, and with the pure principle of religious freedom? In strictness the answer on both points must be in the negative. The Constitution of the U.S. forbids everything like an establishment of a national religion. The law appointing Chaplains establishes a religious worship for the national representatives, to be performed by Ministers of religion, elected by a majority of them, and these are to be paid out of the national taxes. Does not this involve the principle of a national establishment . . . ?"

The appointments, he said, were also a palpable violation of equal rights. Could a Catholic clergyman ever hope to be appointed a Chaplain? "To say that his religious principles are obnoxious or that his sect is small, is to lift the veil at once and exhibit in its naked deformity the doctrine that religious truth is to be tested by numbers, or that the major sects have a right to govern the minor." The problem, said the author of the First Amendment, was how to prevent "this step beyond the landmarks of power [from having] the effect of a legitimate precedent." Rather than let that happen, it would "be better to apply to it the legal aphorism *de minimis non curat lex* [the law takes no account of trifles]." Or, he said (likewise in Latin) , class it with "faults that result from carelessness or that human nature could scarcely avoid."

"Better also," he went on, "to disarm in the same way, the

precedent of Chaplainships for the army and navy, than erect them into a political authority in matters of religion." The motive for them was laudable, but it would be safer to adhere to a right principle. If the spirit of an army was devout, there would seldom be a failure of volunteer means for expression of it, "and if such be not the spirit of armies, the official services of their Teachers are not likely to produce it." The case of navies with insulated crews was different, yet even here "the chance of a devout officer, might be of as much worth to religion, as the service of an ordinary chaplain." The deviations from constitutional principles went further:

"Religious proclamations by the Executive recommending thanksgivings and fasts are shoots from the same root with the legislative acts reviewed. Altho' recommendations only, they imply a religious agency, making no part of the trust delegated to political rulers."

On a full survey of the Supreme Court's decisions on religion and the criticisms of those decisions, a clear pattern emerges. The Court is working to protect the country against a breakdown of constitutional guarantees that would hurl the American people into a vortex of sectarian bitterness and strife. To do so it is obliged to call a halt to practices that range in effect from trivial harm to minor good. Popular dislike of these decisions is played upon by those who desire to break the barriers between state and church. Others join in, seizing any weapon within reach to discredit the Court because of the stand it takes in other areas of national policy.

It is this last element that poses real danger for the country, particularly as it finds expression in the legislative branch of government. Free and fair discussion can be counted on to dispose of the contention over religion, and to maintain the centuries-long trend toward complete freedom of conscience and total separation between civil and religious establishments. But American democracy faces a far more dangerous menace in the growing belief of Congress that it possesses inherent censorial power over the people.

CHAPTER 35
Lex et Consuetudo Congressi

In December 1795 two land speculators named Robert Randall and Charles Whitney arrived in Philadelphia to present Congress with a memorial in behalf of themselves, two or three other New Englanders, and several Canadian merchants, asking for a grant of twenty million acres in Michigan Territory. For this vast area, covering most of the lower peninsula of Michigan, they were willing to pay $500,000, or two and one-half cents per acre. But the United States would reap a great benefit, for the Canadian associates had sufficient influence over the Wyandot Indians, lately on the warpath, to acquire title to their land and induce them to resettle north of the lakes. That would establish peace on the frontier. To encourage congressional action, twelve million acres had been reserved for members of Congress who felt like coming into the project on the same terms as the original associates.

Randall outlined the scheme to Representative William Smith of South Carolina, chairman of the Land Office committee. Smith, alarmed, consulted William Vans Murray of Maryland, whose advice was to draw Randall out and inform President Washington. By the time that was done, the speculator was spreading the word that thirty or forty members of the House had approved the project and a majority of senators were "snug." At this point he was lodged in the city jail by order of the President, on a common-law charge of attempted bribery.

Chairman Smith had more reason than anybody else to wear the robes of Caesar's wife, owing to the publicity given his late speculation in depreciated public securities, bought up for a few

425

cents on the dollar before their owners learned that Congress had voted to pay them in full. The South Carolinian took the floor to denounce the two men and argued strongly that they be brought to the bar of the House and punished for violation of congressional privilege. Murray warned that such a course would merely spread the false story about members accepting the offer and might thus "afford to malice an opportunity of affixing a stigma to any thirty or forty names at which personal enmity might point." By order of the House, Randall was brought up from jail. His request to be allowed counsel was granted, "as a matter of right," said most speakers; "as a matter of favor," said Chairman Smith. Randall secured the services of Edward Tilghman, the "Mr. Big" of the Philadelphia bar, and the hardly less eminent William Lewis.

Under Tilghman's questioning, three of the four complaining witnesses confirmed what their depositions came near to saying, that they did not construe the offer as a bribe but as an invitation to share in the speculation, including the expenses of purchasing the land and acquiring the Indian title. The fourth witness (Murray) drew a contrary inference from a debatable set of facts. Thus, by the time the House reached a vote, the bribery charge had faded and the decision turned on Randall's statement, regarded as a slander upon the House, that thirty members had told him they would support his scheme.

The real import of the case was that a conviction for contempt would set a precedent establishing the inherent power of either House of Congress to punish conduct outside the Capitol—conduct that did not interfere with the work of the House—without the sanction of any law, without trial in the courts, and in disregard of the limited privileges granted the two Houses by the Constitution. That document contains two sections on congressional privilege. Article II, section 5 deals with the relations between each House and its own members, conferring the power to punish them "for disorderly behavior" and to expel them for misconduct. Section 6 covers relations with the public:

"The Senators and Representatives . . . shall in all cases, except treason, felony and breach of the peace, be privileged from arrest during their attendance at the session of their respective Houses, and in going to and returning from the same; and for any speech or debate in either House, they shall not be questioned in any other place."

Certainly, to protect its activities and its members, each House has ordinary police power to halt disorder created by nonmembers. Also the "necessary and proper" clause furnishes ample authority to *enact laws* punishing disorder, bribery, and other obstructions to its work. But in a Constitution establishing a government of limited and enumerated powers, the specifying of allowable privileges could have no purpose or effect except to deny the indefinite and unlimited privileges exercised by an omnipotent legislature. The power to punish members is an exception from the separation of legislative and judicial powers—a totally needless exception if unlimited privilege existed. That, however, was not the way it looked to Chairman Smith when he moved that Randall be brought before the House for trial and punishment:

"As every jurisdiction had certain powers necessary for its preservation, so the Legislature possessed certain privileges incident to its nature, and essential for its very existence. This is called in England the parliamentary law; and as from that law are derived the usages and proceedings of the several State Legislatures, so will the proceedings of this House be generally guided by the long-established usages of the State Legislatures."

As Smith understood the British precedents, Randall and Whitney could be tried at the bar and if found guilty, imprisoned, though not beyond the end of the term. But if there was weight to what he had heard some members saying (about honoring the rights the men would have if tried in a court of law), "then the House would have to tread back all the unconstitutional steps they had been taking," and discharge both prisoners without delay. For the arrests were not based on any law and were justifiable only on the ground of "the inherent and indispensable power of self-preservation."

This opinion was sharply challenged. Protested John S. Sherburne of New Hampshire:

"When we speak of privileges of the House, it seems a word of cabalistic meaning. Will any gentleman define or point out those privileges? In what book of the laws are they written? If they are indefinite, we may come to be hereafter as irregular as a Convention, and our sentences as dreadful as those of a revolutionary tribunal. . . . The term of *leges non scriptae* had been used by the gentleman last up as to the privileges of the House. The phrase Mr. S. thought to be derived from the First Constitutional Assembly of France. They had applied it, along with the word inviolability, to Louis XVI, and soon after cut off his head."

Defense Counsel Tilghman, arguing for his client, asserted that "The Constitution says nothing of privilege that reaches to the case of the prisoner." The House, in his opinion, had the privilege essential to its existence to defend itself from any insult from within or from without, but not further. In this case there was no threat to the safety of Congress. The analogy with Great Britain was not a valid one. "The privileges of an English Parliament rested on immemorial usage; those of this House, on a written Constitution, which had considerably narrowed them, in comparison with those of British Parliaments." Counsel Lewis took a similar stand. "It was hazardous to quote precedents from an English Parliament," an omnipotent body whose privileges had no limit.

Just before the decisive vote on Randall, John Nicholas of Virginia arose to say that he had felt doubts about the affair from the first. "His scruples had gradually augmented," and he was now of opinion that Randall should not have been meddled with "in the present way. The right of privilege had been given up, unless in cases of absolute necessity."

John Page of Virginia (the man who brought William Penn's hat into the 1789 debate on freedom of assembly) spoke still more positively. He "did not think parliamentary precedents respecting cases of breach of privilege, by any means applicable to the situation or powers of Congress. The Constitution had defined those powers, and he hoped never to exceed them." Page would go as far as any member to protect House members from insults offered by the gallery, or by persons in the street, but the protection should be afforded by passage of laws establishing uniform rules for proceeding against offenders. It was improper for members "in their own cause, to be prosecutors, witnesses, judges, and jurors."

Randall was found guilty of contempt, reprimanded, held in custody another week and discharged. The division, 78 to 17, appeared on the surface to uphold the contempt power by the same margin. But the "aye" votes undoubtedly were swollen by those who feared that a suspicious public would include them among the nonexistent thirty of Randall's "come-on" story. It took a hardy man to vote "no" in that roll call.

With Randall disposed of and the House heartily sick of the case, all it wished to do with Whitney was get rid of him. A motion was made that the overt act charged against him—soliciting a member of Congress in Vermont—did not amount to a breach of privilege. Why then, it was asked, was he in jail? After an all-day debate, the House passed a plain motion that he be discharged from custody. Whitney walked out of jail into the arms of his frightened creditors who straightway clapped him back into prison for debt. Congress inflicted punishment by inflicting infamy.

In dealing with these two men the House spread suspicions against itself that never would have arisen if the legislators had done what Lawyer Lewis suggested and simply "kicked my client out of the room." There would not have been a breath of scandal if some member had presented the Randall-Whitney memorial "by request" and moved its immediate rejection. The Senate, by ignoring the matter, escaped unscathed, although Randall had been saying that he had a majority of its members in the bag.

James Madison kept out of the Randall controversy, which developed just as he was trying to form a bipartisan majority against implementation of Jay's Treaty with England. But he voted "No" on the contempt resolution and stated his position when the case of Whitney was taken up. As recorded in the *Annals*, "it appeared to him that the House could have no privileges, unless what arises from the necessity of the case. He differed from the opinion of the House," but thought that the principle adopted in the case of Randall ought to be applied in dealing with Whitney. What Madison would have said, had he given expression to his feelings, was made clear enough in a letter to Jefferson. There was no truth, he wrote, in what Randall said about thirty members of Congress approving his plan, but consider the consequences if Congress has power to punish slander as a matter of privilege:

"What an engine may such a privilege become, in the hands of a body once corrupted, for protecting its corruptions against public animadversion, under the pretext of maintaining its dignity and preserving the necessary confidence of the public! . . . Apply the principle to other transactions and the strictures which the press has made on them, and the extent of its mischief will be seen at once."

Madison's concern over future corruption was well warranted, but the greater abuses of privilege have come when pride, passion, lust of power or misdirected patriotism has stimulated House or Senate to enforce its assumed prerogative. What the House actually did in 1795-96 was disregard the closely limited privileges of Congress set forth in the Constitution, and take to itself the unlimited and undefined *Lex et Consuetudo Parliamenti,* through which the legislative branch of the British government developed and maintained its supremacy. There was excuse for placing the Law and Custom of Parliament above challenge in England during the centuries when the struggle to attain popular government depended on pulling down the power of kings. But in a self-governing republic, where government is the servant of a sovereign people and all rights and powers are expressed in a written Constitution, the assertion of a *Lex et Consuetudo Congressi* is a cancerous growth in the organs of the body politic.

The second invocation of privilege verified what Madison said about use of such an arbitrary power to curb "the strictures of the press." The Senate in February 1800 had before it a bill to establish a "Grand Committee of Thirteen"—six members from each House chaired by the Chief Justice—which was to make a secret inquiry into the legality of electoral votes in the coming presidential election, discard illegal votes, and determine who should be President. The Philadelphia *Aurora* published the text of the nefarious bill. Publisher William Duane was cited for contempt, both in publishing the bill without authority, and for describing it as an offspring of the "spirit of faction secretly working" to control an election "that may involve the fate of the country and posterity."

Senator Charles Pinckney of South Carolina led the handful of Jeffersonian Democrats in opposition to the preliminary motion for an inquiry into the publication. The Constitution, said Pinckney, was drafted by men (he was one of them) who had before them the example of the unlimited privileges of the British Parliament and those assumed by colonial assemblies. Knowing the consequences of indefinite powers, they carefully defined those of Congress in the manner fixed in the Constitution—limiting them to the protection of members against disturbance while engaged on public affairs. Pinckney read the pertinent sections of the Constitution and commented:

"That is all that is said on the subject of privilege; and surely no words can be more explicit, nor any subject more clearly defined. . . . Nor is there a word or a sentence in the whole that can by any possible construction be made to mean that for any libels or printed attack on the public conduct or opinions of either House of Congress, or of any of its members, that their privilege shall extend to ordering the persons charged with the offence before them, and imprisoning them at their will."

Pinckney would allow that the Senate was following the doctrine and practice of the British Parliament, "but it was because the doctrines there held are utterly inadmissible in a free government; and to prevent any influence from them, and their precedents, and the improper practice of the Colonial and State Legislatures, that this limitation of the privileges of Congress was here purposely introduced." The Carolina senator denounced the action as a violation of the freedom of the press, which he defined in terms of the Pennsylvania constitution of 1790 providing that "every citizen may freely speak, write, and print, on any subject, being responsible for the abuse of that liberty." That foundation was true and safe, he thought, if coupled with trial by jury, but his defense of freedom went further. Among the ancients, he noted, "we find Tiberius, and Trajan, and Titus, allowing absolute liberty of speech and writing, suppressing the laws against seditious words and writings, and punishing informers."

It was difficult, Pinckney conceded, in preserving the privileges of the press "to guard against its licentiousness; but it is infinitely better that some instances of this sort should arise, than that a particle of its freedom should be lost." Few men had been "attacked in the papers with more acrimony than myself; but as I know it is impossible to touch the freedom of the press without destroying it, and as I believe it to be the only true means of preserving rational liberty in the world, I trust that our country, which has received such important benefits from its operations, will never cease to cherish and protect it."

Senator William Cocke of Tennessee had opened the debate by

declaring that the Constitution gave the Senate no authority for the action it was taking: "the privilege of the House and the members did not extend beyond the walls of the Chamber in which they were sitting, in cases of comment upon their official proceedings." Now he reinforced Pinckney on freedom of the press. The motion concerning Duane, of the *Aurora,* he noted, was partly designed to find out who (i.e. what senator) gave him the text of the bill. If he said he was pledged not to tell, would they subject him to torture?

"While you are straining his muscles and dislocating his joints, what becomes of the grand palladium of American freedom? . . . The Constitution declares that you shall not infringe upon the liberty of the press; and a power expressly denied to the whole Government, a single branch may not assume."

Senator Uriah Tracy of Connecticut, sponsor of the move against Duane, rose to answer Pinckney and Cocke. The *Aurora,* he said, had asserted that the electoral bill had passed the Senate, when every member knew it was still on the table.[1] "Surely gentlemen will not advocate such liberty as this—the liberty of publishing nothing but lies and falsehoods." He would not sacrifice the security of the government to the licentiousness of the press. "If it is admitted that we have the right of protecting ourselves within these walls, from attacks made on us in our presence, it follows of course that we are not to be slandered and questioned elsewhere . . . The defamation and calumny of yesterday, circulated in the newspapers, out-travel the slow and tardy steps of truth; they have spread over the face of the country and entered every cottage, where the contradiction may never penetrate."

Senator S. T. Mason of Virginia punctured these sophistries with a question. Since calumny was charged in falsely reporting that the bill had passed the Senate, was not the Connecticut senator saying in effect that a Senate committee had reported a bill which it would be scandalous to pass? Nevertheless the Senate ordered Duane brought before the bar to answer for publishing false, scandalous, defamatory assertions. He appeared and was granted the right to counsel who could be heard in denial of facts or extenuation of guilt, but would not be allowed to challenge the authority of the Senate or attempt to justify the article. The lawyers, Alexander J. Dallas and Thomas Cooper, thus hamstrung, refused to serve, and Duane consequently refused to appear. The Sergeant-at-Arms searched vainly for him for seven weeks—looking everywhere, some cynics thought, except in the *Aurora* office. Just before adjournment the unmollified Senate passed a resolution calling for Duane's prosecution under the Sedition Act. He was indicted but not tried.

It was from such a background of tyranny and futility that the contempt power of Congress came before the Supreme Court in 1821. Colonel John Anderson of Michigan Territory, a volunteer officer in the War of 1812 whose naïveté far exceeded his iniquity, tried to expedite various damage claims by asking the chairman of the House Claims Committee *in writing,* to accept "the small sum of five hundred dollars, as part pay, for the extra trouble I give you" in passing on them. Anderson's sacrificial war record and general integrity, testified to by his wartime commander, Congressman Richard M. Johnson of Kentucky, reduced his punishment to imprisonment during the thirteen days the House debated its power to imprison him.

The debate, more extensive than all previous ones put together, was nevertheless a repetition of them. One group of congressmen, including Philemon Beecher of Ohio, John C. Spencer of New York and Philip P. Barbour of Virginia, denied that the Constitution permitted Congress to absorb the limitless privileges of the British Parliament. The other group, headed by John Forsyth of Georgia, affirmed inherent power to extend congressional privileges beyond those defined in the Constitution. Great stress was laid by the supporters of privilege on the Randall-Whitney precedent. A motion to discharge Anderson because "this House does not possess the Constitutional power to try, or right to punish" him was defeated 47 to 119. He was brought to the bar, testified that his only motive was to speed up relief for the still-suffering survivors of the Raisin River Massacre, and was discharged with an admonition to "endeavor to obliterate, as far as it may be possible, the stain . . . on the high and honorable character you appear to have previously sustained."

Niles' Weekly Register (January 24, 1818) said that Colonel Anderson's "silly, or infamous," proposal was in the "true spirit of what *common fame* has said was the best way to get an account *settled* at Washington," but that the general practice was to pay a subordinate official to expedite a claim.

A damage suit for false imprisonment put the contempt power of Congress before the Supreme Court in *Anderson* v. *Dunn*. To escape the Court's previous holding that the English common law was not in the Constitution, Attorney General Wirt argued that the power exerted by the House was not derived from that source but was "rather a principle of universal law growing out of the natural right of self-defence belonging to all persons." The power of punishing contempts was incidental to all courts of justice, and each branch of Congress had "certain powers of judicature under the Constitution," as in impeachments and the punishing of members for disorderly conduct. This sufficed to show that the warrant for Anderson's arrest "was issued by a Court of competent jurisdiction," and, if the House possessed this jurisdiction, "its exercise cannot be questioned or re-examined elsewhere."

Justice Johnson, writing the Court's opinion, did not completely accept this view of the House of Representatives as a court. But he did accept the analogy with the power of a court to commit for contempt, and upon it built an edifice of congressional power as high as that of the House of Commons. "That a deliberate assembly, clothed with the majesty of the people . . . composed of the most distinguished citizens . . . whose decisions must be clothed with all that sanctity which unlimited confidence in their wisdom and purity can inspire; that such an assembly should not possess the power to suppress rudeness, or repel insult, is a supposition too wild to be suggested."

Justice Johnson conceded that no power was "given by the Constitution to either House to punish for contempts, except when committed by their own members." But if, as seemed to be admitted in the arguments, the Houses had absolute control within their own walls, that gave up the objection based on the absence of an express grant of power. Consequently it wiped out any distinction based on the locale of insults. "For why should the House be at liberty to exercise an ungranted, an unlimited, and undefined power within their walls, any more than without them?"

Nor, said Johnson, was legislation needed to deal with remote contempts, "which, from their very nature, admit of no precise definition." But if the *offense* of contempt was undefinable, its *punishment* need not be indefinite. What then was the permissible extent of the punishing power on the principle of self-preservation? *"The least possible power adequate to the end proposed."* That was "the power of imprisonment," which must terminate with adjournment, for at that time the legislative body ceased to exist. Though recognizing that what he said placed no actual limit on congressional punishing power, Justice Johnson saw no danger that the House would employ it to inflict "corporal punishment, or even death, and exercise it in cases affecting the liberty of speech and of the press." The restraint was moral:

"The Constitution was formed in and for an advanced state of society, and rests at every point on received opinions and fixed ideas. . . . It is not, therefore, reasoning upon things as they are, to suppose that any deliberative assembly, constituted under it, would ever assert any other rights and powers than those which had been established by long practice, and conceded by public opinion. Melancholy, also, would be that state of distrust which rests not a hope upon a moral influence."

If the Bill of Rights had been written on that basis, four words would suffice for it: "Lawmakers should be good"—which is indeed the basis of the "admonition" concept of that document. The opinion in *Anderson* v. *Dunn* avoided overt analogy with British parliamentary privilege as a source of congressional authority. Justice Johnson thus protected the 1812 and 1816 decisions of the Supreme Court, written by himself, denying that common-law powers exist by implication in our Constitution. But in this very act of avoidance he set up an inherent power that was untouched either by the limitations on privilege that are found in our Constitution or by the moderate but definite restrictions that British courts were placing on the Law and Custom of Parliament.

The *Anderson* v. *Dunn* opinion came down to this: for protection against an unlimited, undefined privilege that produced periodic tyranny in England—a power that Madison warned against as a likely shield of corruption and a threat to freedom of the press— American citizens were informed that Congress would always be "composed of the most distinguished citizens" whose "wisdom and purity" made it safe to "hope upon a moral influence." That was presented not only as constitutional law, but as a justification for ignoring the limitations of the Constitution.

The wisdom and purity of Congress, as a substitute for constitutional limitations, was not apparent to James W. Simonton, Washington correspondent of the *New York Times,* when he wrote in the issue of January 6, 1857, that the Committee on Public Lands was about to report a bill turning a great part of Minnesota Territory over to a group of private speculators as a pretended aid to the building of a useless strip of railway. The proportion of honest men having anything to do with the bill, he wrote, "would have been scarcely sufficient to save Sodom and Gomorrah from destruction, while there is hardly an individual hanging about the Capitol living upon ill-gotten gains, and whose hands reek with the slime of congressional corruption, who does not look to this Minnesota land bill as the present Mecca of his hopes."

Congress might have taken this in stride had not Henry J. Raymond, founder and editor of the *Times,* denounced this "new and magnificent land-stealing scheme" as the work of "a thorough combination" of corruptionists in and out of Congress. Said the *Times* editorial: "Unless rumor, confirmed by a hundred acts which speak louder than words, is false, the Minnesota Land Bill numbers among its supporters who are to profit by its success, at least thirty and probably forty members of the House of Representatives." Their reported price was $1,000 per vote.

Simonton, the obvious source of the charge, was called before a quickly set up committee "to investigate the existence of corrupt combinations among members of Congress." He had accused nobody, he told the committee, but had a moral conviction that the reports reaching him were true. Asked whether he had direct knowledge of corruption, he said that two members of the House had come to him, obtained his promise not to disclose what they were going to say, and asked him to arrange with the lobbyists for the Minnesota land bill to pay them for their votes. He could not name these members without violating his pledge of confidence, and would suffer anything rather than do so. The committee gave him a day to think it over and advised him to read the opinion in *Anderson* v. *Dunn.* He did so and wrote that night for the *Times:*

"I suppose . . . that the House will usurp the power [to take me in custody], and violate the constitutional provision against depriving a citizen of liberty without due process of law."

Anderson v. *Dunn,* he told the committee next day, confirmed him in his refusal to answer. (Presumably by what it said about unlimited power being safe because of the purity of Congress.) Adhering to this position at the bar of the House, he was declared to be in contempt and was ordered held in custody until the end of the session or until he purged himself by testifying. The investigation of "corrupt combinations" caused two House members to resign to escape expulsion for *isolated acts* of corruption. The actual subject under investigation—*concerted* solicitation of bribes—came before the committee when the president of the Des Moines Railroad Company produced and identified a letter to him signed O. B. M. soliciting a huge gift of land "in addition to what Stryker arranged," to put through Congress a grant of 275,000 acres to the railway. His further testimony was that Representative Orasmus B. Matteson of New York demanded and obtained $100,000 to satisfy "a large number of the members" of the House who (to quote the resolution to expel Matteson) "had associated themselves together, and pledged themselves each to the other not to vote for any law or resolution granting money or lands, unless they were paid for it."

Congressman Matteson had resigned earlier in the day and his friends argued that no longer being a member he could not be expelled. But the House would not let such criminality escape unrebuked. The miscreant was expelled for having *"falsely and willfully assailed and defamed the character of this House"* in asserting that others were associated with him in the bribery.

As a further demonstration of its wisdom and purity, the House took up with zeal the committee motion to expel a Connecticut congressman who allegedly demanded $50.00 from a widow for passage of an invalid pension act. The evidence was dubious, the amount too small to make the charge credible, and the man accused had not been allowed to confront his accusers. A freshman congressman from Ohio, Benjamin Stanton, told his colleagues that even in the semi-barbarous days of the Tudors and Stuarts, the procedures by which men were tried, condemned and executed by Parliament seemed somewhat more enlightened than those the House was pursuing. Instead of giving the man a fair trial, by due process of law, they were being governed by a committee's report on what was and what was not evidence.

Then Stanton exploded a bomb which others tried vainly to throw out of a window before it went off. To show what was *not evidence,* he would read a passage *deleted by the committee.* ("Dishonoring" the committee by a paper "surreptitiously obtained," shouted Orr of South Carolina. Oh no, replied Stanton, copied from a manuscript that is a public record.) Sustained by the Speaker, Stanton read what a witness, presumably Simonton, told the committee about a statement by "Mr. Chubb, the banker," that he was forced to deliver $15,000 to a congressman to be divided among thirty members who otherwise would vote against the California war bond bill of 1856. Congressman Stanton had made his point. The House voted that the charge of extracting $50.00 from the widow was not proved.

That was on February 27, 1857, four days before the dissolution of the Thirty-Fourth Congress. James W. Simonton was still in custody and would have to be released on adjournment—too slight a punishment for the man who had stirred up all these reflections on the purity of Congress. So the House passed a resolution expelling Simonton from the privileges of the floor on the fictitious charge of violating the pledge required of every newspaper correspondent that he would not "be employed as an agent to prosecute any claims pending in Congress."[2]

This contemptible falsehood typified the entire course of the House in this pretended protection of the privileges of Congress. Simonton in reality was not cited and held in custody for contempt because he refused to identify bribetakers. He was cited, held under arrest and attainted for having compelled the House to investigate the notorious criminality of a portion of its members, or go through the motions of doing so. The failure to subpoena Banker Chubb is a sufficient commentary on the deletion of the testimony about him and the nature of the investigation.

Yet from this Congress, through a paradoxical combination of circumstances, came a legislative act that both stiffened the penalties for contempt of Congress and led to ultimate abandonment of the arbitrary power to punish for contempt by direct action. The investigating committee presented a bill, which passed both Houses in two days, under which any person summoned to appear or produce papers before a congressional committee, who should wilfully make default or who should "refuse to answer any question pertinent to the matter of inquiry," should be liable to prosecution for a misdemeanor in any federal court. Maximum penalties were a fine of $1,000 and imprisonment for one year—these to be "in addition to the pains and penalties now existing" through direct action by either House.

The driving force behind this bill in the House appeared to combine passion against Simonton and a desire of members to demonstrate their innocence by their zeal for inquiry. In the Senate there was a brief, intelligent debate. Hale of New Hampshire opposed the bill because it would "strike down a principle which has been held sacred for centuries wherever the common law is practiced—the principle which protects a witness from answering to matters which shall criminate or disgrace himself." He looked upon this bill as "one of the greatest invasions of popular right ever attempted by this Government."

Tombs of Georgia, an eminent lawyer, thought the guarantee against self-incrimination sufficiently preserved by a section that forbade use of forced testimony against a witness in any federal court, even though federal immunity did not extend to state prosecutions. He took occasion to say, however, that "I totally disbelieve that doctrine," supported by many members of the House and Senate, that "they have the power, sometimes very vaguely called an inherent power, to punish for contempt. . . . We brought no common law here, either parliamentary or any other. We have no other law but what we put here."

Senator Bayard of Delaware emphasized the importance of the word "pertinent." A witness was not subject to penalties if he refused to answer an irrelevant question. "The question must be pertinent to the subject-matter, and that will have to be decided by the courts of justice on the indictment. That power is not given to Congress; it is given appropriately to the judiciary." One of the greatest recommendations of this bill, said Bayard, was that it transferred the power of punishment for contempt from Congress to a court of justice after judicial inquiry. "I am aware," said he, "that legislative bodies have transcended their powers—that under the influence of passion and political excitement they have very often invaded the rights of individuals, and may have invaded the rights of co-ordinate branches of the Government." If our institutions were to last, there could be no greater safeguard than to transfer that indefinite power of punishment to the courts of justice:

"When a case of this kind comes before a court, will not the first inquiry be, have Congress jurisdiction of the subject-matter—has the House which undertakes to inquire, jurisdiction of the subject? If they have not, the whole proceedings are *coram non judice* and void, and the party cannot be held under indictment. The court would quash the indictment if this fact appeared on its face; and if it appeared on the trial they would direct the jury to acquit."

Andrew P. Butler of South Carolina, protégé of Calhoun and chairman of the Senate Committee on the Judiciary, didn't care for all this twiddle-twaddle about the constitutional rights of witnesses. Congress had been mocked long enough by contumacious newspapermen. He recalled what happened in 1848 when they brought up Correspondent Nugent of the New York *Herald* for publishing the treaty of peace with Mexico. He was held in custody for a week "and we paid the Sergeant-at-Arms five hundred dollars for entertaining him at his house very handsomely." Butler's opinion always had been that each House had power to defend itself against any assault or insult. It had that power under the law of self-preservation, of self-defense, "the organic law of vitality—yes, sir, the vitality of resentment, if you choose to call it so." He would vote for this bill, though he thought it reduced instead of strengthened the power of Congress to deal with such men as Simonton:

"I say, on the contrary, that Congress should proceed at once to make exhibitions of people of this kind. . . . I should wish to see the time come when—like the hardy English law, the common law—we could punish a man so that he should feel the force of your law. . . . This man—I do not know who he is—says that he will not answer because it will implicate him. [Simonton said no such thing.] Men are not likely to be approached unless they are approachable. How came he to be approached in preference to other people?"

If Butler had to be told the answer to that question, he must have been the only man in Congress who was unaware that the Minnesota Land Bill lobby was headed by the New York City Chief of Police, whom Simonton exposed. The chairman of the Senate Judiciary Committee lived a hundred years ahead of his time. It was not in his spirit that the Senate in 1857 voted to turn contempt proceedings over to the courts. But his call to punish witnesses under "the organic law of vitality . . . the vitality of resentment" met with a full response when the House a few weeks later expelled Simonton on an accusation it knew to be false and infamous. A much milder attempt to use such a power, against the Democratic Societies in 1794, had been denounced and beaten by Madison as a violation of the constitutional prohibition of bills of attainder. But in 1857, in the very process of eliminating the worst misuses of congressional privilege, the chairman of the Senate Judiciary Committee and the House of Representatives gave a perfect preview of the system by which congressional committees, a century later, would pervert the power of investigation into a wholesale system of trial and punishment for political heresy.

CHAPTER 36
Forging the Sword of Inquisition

John Brown's raid on the Harper's Ferry arsenal, October 16, 1859, led to the appointment of a senatorial investigating committee whose membership, powers and policies, by deliberate intent of all factions, were determined by proslavery senators headed by James M. Mason of Virginia. This produced in effect a supergrand-jury, empowered not only to inquire into the physical aspects of the armed invasion of Virginia, but to ascertain whether any citizens of the United States *not present* were implicated in it by contributions of money, supplies, etc., or by organized efforts to subvert any state government. To give the proceedings an assured constitutional cast, the committee was to determine what legislation, if any, was needed to preserve peace and public property.

When Thaddeus Hyatt of New York City and three others resisted the committee, the Senate ignored the 1857 act authorizing prosecution in the courts. Hyatt, as Senator Jefferson Davis described his conduct, discussed the subpoena for some weeks with committee members and his own friends in Congress, then left for Boston without testifying and was forcibly brought back to the bar of the Senate.[1] His friends came sufficiently to his support to force the reading of his Boston lawyers' 9,000-word brief challenging the Senate's power. The main function of the committee, wrote Counsels S. E. Sewall and John A. Andrew, was to find out who committed certain crimes and who were accessory to them. That was a judicial inquiry, constitutionally assigned to the courts and subsidiary agencies.

"We know it will be urged [said they] that the proceeding authorized by the resolution is not a trial or judicial proceeding, because the Senate does not propose to punish any one. . . . Under the resolution, the committee have power to report that such and such persons have been guilty of treason or other offenses. Here, then, we find a trial and conviction. And though it is not pretended that the Senate has any power to punish crime, yet such a conviction, by blasting a man's character, may, in this as in other cases, become the most tremendous punishment."

That agrees precisely with what Madison said in Congress in 1794, with far less provocation, when it was proposed to charge several unnamed but identifiable societies with responsibility for the Whisky Rebellion: "It is in vain to say that this indiscriminate censure is no punishment. . . . Is not this proposition, if voted, a vote of attainder?"

In the Sewall-Andrew brief, Congress was informed that the British Privy Council (which included such legal lights as Chief Justice Denman and Lord Brougham) had lately held that the Law and Custom of Parliament was not a general parliamentary law, enforceable in all the legislatures of the British Empire. It had no existence apart from the Houses of Lords and Commons through whose customs it developed. So, in *Kielley* v. *Carson*, the Privy Council held that the House of Assembly in Newfoundland had no power to arrest a person for a contempt committed outside the House, such an arrest not being essential to its functioning. Consequently, no such power could be deduced for American state legislatures or Congress from British precedent.

Hyatt's lawyers would assume (though disbelieving it) that the House and Senate formerly had power to arrest a citizen for a contempt not committed in their presence. They would grant that Congress intended to retain that power by writing the words "in addition to existing pains and penalties" into the 1857 law making contempt of Congress a misdemeanor. But, said they, that power was given up by making contempt an indictable crime. That brought the offense within the purview of the requirement that *all crimes* be tried by jury, with the safeguards of due process of law.

There was no immediate discussion of the brief, but Committee Chairman Mason's motion that Hyatt be kept in close custody till he purged himself of contempt brought a query from Hale of New Hampshire, who had already branded the whole procedure unconstitutional. Did the chairman agree that such a commitment, with no time limit specified, must terminate at the end of the session? "The Senate is a continuous body," replied Mason, always in existence though not always in session. He presumed that unless the Senate, before adjournment, ordered "something to be done with him, he will remain in custody."

Mason was saying in effect that because the Senate elected one third of its members every two years, it had power to keep Hyatt in prison for life. Not even the hereditary House of Lords asserted the power to imprison for contempt beyond the day of adjournment, except during a period of usurpation. Those assertions of privilege were protested in the Commons, rejected by Chief Justice Holt, argued against by Lord Chancellor Nottingham (when he was solicitor general), and condemned in the writings of Sir Matthew Hale. Wrote the eminent Francis Hargrave, after summarizing these denials: "Not the least trace can I find of any opinion from our judges in favor of such an arbitrary power in the lords over the king's subjects without trial by jury."

Hyatt's brief, after senators had studied it, produced a debate between Senators Charles Sumner of Massachusetts, a fervent Abolitionist, and William P. Fessenden of Maine, a less outspoken foe of slavery. Sumner rejected the idea of senatorial power based on that of Parliament, which was "without the constraint of a written constitution." He would recognize "that just and universal right of self-defense inherent in every parliamentary body, as in every court, and also in every individual; but which is limited closely by the simple necessities of the case." Now it was proposed to take a step without any support either in the words or intendments of the Constitution, and with no support in the inherent right of self-defense. If the Senate could rush to the assistance of grand juries in the District of Columbia or Virginia on any occasion of alleged crime, be it treason, or murder, or riot, it will be "so transcendent in its powers, that by its side the local inquest will be dwarfed into insignificance." Establish this power, declared Sumner, and "You take into your hands a sword, whose handle will be in this Chamber, to be clutched by a mere party majority, and whose point will

be in every corner of the Republic." With a little more foreknowl-
edge, Sumner could have said that the handle would be grasped by
Senator Joe McCarthy, Representative Martin Dies, or any of their
less illustrious successors in the field of attainder by investigation.

Senator Fessenden agreed with Sumner that the resolution
under which Hyatt was arrested contained unconstitutional provisions. He and his friends "did not examine that question, from the
desire we had to afford the largest liberty of inquiry on the subject."
But part of the authority conveyed was within the powers of the
Senate—the power to legislate—and the valid portion sustained the
subpoena. A witness was not supposed to know what questions
would be asked of him. Hyatt's proper course, therefore, was to appear, refuse to answer any question he regarded as improper, and
let the Senate decide the point thus raised. Of the Senate's general
power to punish contempt Fessenden had no doubt. It was true that
Congress differed from the English Parliament, but parliamentary
law was part of the common law of England and "all of it that was
applicable to us, that was fitted to our position and Constitution,
was adopted by us." It was true "that the Constitution confers only
specific powers upon us. . . . It told what subjects were within our
control; but it did not undertake to tell us the form and manner of
proceeding by which we should accomplish the purposes of that
legislation." It was conceded, said the senator from Maine, that the
Senate had power to clear its galleries, eject disturbers and arrest
attackers from the outside. Where do you go, then, to draw the line?

"You go outside the Constitution. . . . You go to the parliamentary law, which is recognized as part of the common law. Where will
you stop? Stop, I say, just at the point where we have gone far
enough to accomplish the purposes for which we were created . . . I
speak of legislation as the principal purpose. . . . Who is to judge of
the necessity? We. Senators may say there is danger in it; they may
object that we are judges in our own case. Sir, we are judges for the
good of the nation, for the good of the people."

In this speech, Fessenden put his finger on the weak spot in Hyatt's position, his refusal to appear for questioning, rather than refusal, after appearing, to answer improper questions. The senator
validly defended the broad scope of congressional inquiry for purposes of legislation. There was a suggestion, however, of rejection

of all restraints when he added that "we should rid ourselves of all these ideas that we are simply a body under a written Constitution," obliged to find some one power absolutely essential to accomplish the purposes for which the legislature was created. The conflict of views came out clearly when Hale asked the senator from Maine to restate his position.

"I said," replied Fessenden, "we had all the powers necessary to accomplish the purposes for which we are created, and within that limit we had the power to take the means to accomplish that end. Of what was necessary to accomplish that, we were judges."

"He says," commented his New Hampshire neighbor, "that within what is granted to us, we have the power to do everything that is necessary, and we are the judges of that necessity. . . . I put it to my honorable friend from Maine, that a more perfect despotism never was inaugurated since government was talked of."

Neither senator stated the true position, which was that within the limits of its constitutional powers, Congress has the right to judge *what laws are necessary* to accomplish a legitimate end, but *both the laws and the aids to enacting them* must conform to the Constitution. On both of these points the actions of Congress are subject to constitutional restraints and consequently to judicial review.

Hyatt was held in the common jail from March until near the June adjournment, when Chairman Mason sprang a little surprise. Senator Fitch of Indiana, a Northern despiser of free Negroes, had been denouncing Sumner for the "insult" of presenting a petition from Massachusetts Negroes, *as citizens,* for the release of Hyatt, when everybody knew (since the *Dred Scott* decision) that no Negro could be a citizen. Senator Mason made a report two days later rejecting this and other petitions for Hyatt and then moved that the prisoner be discharged from custody.

Senator Sumner, welcoming the motion with pleasure, "was unwilling that this act of justice should be done a much-injured citizen, without for one moment exposing the injustice which he has received at your hands." He repeated the argument he had made before, that the Senate had no power to *compel* testimony in aid of legislation. "*Convenient,* at times it may be; but *necessary, never.*" From such a power, if it existed, Cabinet or President could claim no immunity that did not belong equally to the humblest citizen. Turning to the precedents of the British Parliament, "all more or less inapplicable . . . under a written Constitution," Sumner mentioned the severe criticism of them by Lord Chief Justice Denman in *Stockdale* v. *Hansard.* He quoted the comment of the Earl of Stanhope after he had served a score of years in both Houses. Wrote Stanhope in his *History of England:*

"I may observe, in passing, that, throughout the reign of George II, the privileges of the House of Commons flourished in the rankest luxuriance. . . . So long as men in authority are enabled to go beyond the law on the plea of their own dignity and power, *the* ONLY *limit to their encroachments will be that of the public endurance."*

Nothing could be more true, observed Sumner. Even more applicable, if possible, to the case before the Senate were the words spoken by Lord Brougham in debate: "All rights are now utterly disregarded by the advocates of privilege, excepting that of exposing their own short-sighted impolicy and thoughtless inconsistency."[2] With these remarks, said Sumner, "I quit this question, anxious only that the recent usurpation of the Senate may not be drawn into a precedent hereafter."

For a brief period that seemed a valid hope. In the general revision of federal statutes in 1873, the 1857 law punishing contumacious witnesses was modified by striking out the words "in addition to existing pains and penalties." The evident purpose was to transfer all contempt cases involving nonmembers to the courts, or at a minimum to strike out double jeopardy. Nevertheless, three years later an employe of the Jay Cooke & Co. banking house was held forty-five days in jail by direct order of the House of Representatives for refusing to answer questions or produce books called for by a House committee. Released on a writ of habeas corpus, Hallet Kilbourn sued the Sergeant-at-Arms for false imprisonment and the case came to the Supreme Court in 1880.

By modern standards the Jay Cooke investigation was completely within the legislative function of Congress and its power to investigate corruption in government. But as seen by the Supreme Court in *Kilbourn* v. *Thompson* an inquiry into "improvident" deposits of naval funds in a bankrupt bank was an invasion of private property rights beyond the powers of Congress as well as an interference with judicial proceedings in bankruptcy. The Court held, however, that damages could not be recovered from an employee of Congress who had merely obeyed his orders.

Had Justice Miller not used his talents to restrict the legitimate functions of Congress, the sound features of his opinion would have placed it among the great Supreme Court decisions, protecting civil liberties, restraining arbitrary power, and putting the contempt power in its true perspective in English and American history. The Constitution, Miller wrote, conferred on Congress no general power of inflicting punishment. The strongest implication against such a power was found in the provision that no "person shall be deprived of life, liberty or property, without due process of law." The Court had repeatedly decided that due process "means a trial in which the rights of the party shall be decided by a tribunal appointed by law, which tribunal is to be governed by rules of law previously established."

Since the Constitution gave Congress no express power to punish contempts, except those committed by its own members, advocates of that power had tried to find it by implication in two sources: the practice of the English House of Commons, and the necessity of it to enable Congress to perform its work. In England, said Miller, the contempt power of Lords and Commons was uniformly held to be judicial in nature, derived from the ancient period when the two Houses were united in a single High Court of Parliament. At a time when parliamentary privilege ran high, notably in 1771 and again in 1811, English judges ruled that the House of Commons had power to determine its own privileges and contempts. But "in the celebrated case of *Stockdale* v. *Hansard*, decided in 1839, this doctrine of the omnipotence of the House of Commons in the assertion of its privileges received its first serious check in a court of law."

In that case, wrote Miller, Lord Chief Justice Denman "in a masterly opinion, concurred in by the other judges of the King's Bench, ridicules the idea of the existence of a body of laws and customs of Parliament unknown and unknowable to anybody else but the members of the two Houses, and holds with an incontrovertible logic that when the rights of the citizen are at stake in a court of justice, it must, if these privileges are set up to his prejudice, examine for itself into the nature and character of those laws, and decide upon their extent and effect upon the rights of the parties before the court."

In the ensuing conflict between King's Bench and Commons, the judges did not risk their own decapitation. After the House imprisoned the Sheriff of Middlesex County for obeying the Court's order to enforce a judgment for Stockdale,[3] the judges disclaimed power to release the sheriff by habeas corpus. They could not reach within the walls of Parliament on suspicion that the House in a commitment for contempt "would suppress facts which, if discussed, might entitle the person committed to his liberty." But Denman reaffirmed the Court's fundamental holding "that there was no power in this country above being questioned by law," and added that the attempt of the House to place its privilege beyond review "tended to a despotic power which could not be recognized or exist in this country."

Justice Miller did not go into these details, but proceeded to take up British Empire cases, *Kielley* v. *Carson* (1841) and later ones, showing that the highest English courts were striking down the contempt power that colonial assemblies had been trying to exercise in imitation of Parliament. The Privy Council in *Kielley* decided also, "according to the principles of the common law," that these colonial assemblies possessed no privileges beyond those "reasonably necessary for the exercise of their functions and duties." These did not include the exclusive privileges which the House of Commons had acquired through ancient usage and prescription, "that of punishment for contempt being one."

From these cases it was evident, said Justice Miller, that the powers and privileges of the House of Commons had no application to the House of Representatives of the United States, which was "in no sense a court," and whose functions, so far as they were in any sense judicial, were limited to punishing their own members and determining their election. Consequently the right of the House to punish a citizen for contempt "can derive no support from the precedents and practices of the two Houses of the English Parliament." Neither did English judges give much aid to the doctrine that such power existed of necessity to enable either House to exercise its legislative function, but Miller saw no need to go into that because the Court did not consider the Jay Cooke inquiry to be an aid to legislation.

Anderson v. *Dunn*, Justice Miller noted, undoubtedly was decided "under the pressure of strong rulings of the English courts"— rulings that had since been upset by *Stockdale* v. *Hansard, Kielley* v. *Carson,* etc. Miller went into the English cases at length, but did not bring out the striking features of their interrelationship with what he called the "first impression" of the American court in *Anderson* v. *Dunn.* That invites attention.

In 1811, in *Burdett* v. *Abbott*, the court of King's Bench sweepingly upheld the privileges of the House of Commons, with Lord Ellenborough putting in a lengthy dictum that was construed to recognize analogous contempt powers in all legislative assemblies. The *Burdett* decision was closely adhered to in 1821 by the United States Supreme Court in *Anderson* v. *Dunn*, the Attorney General's argument overtly resting the contempt power of Congress upon it, Justice Johnson doing likewise without naming it. *Burdett* was similarly followed by the Queen's Bench in 1836, in *Beaumont* v. *Barrett*, a case of privilege appealed from Jamaica. That opinion was written by Mr. Baron Parke.

When *Kielley* v. *Carson* was appealed to the Privy Council in 1841, the Newfoundland Assembly pinned its case on *Burdett* and the Jamaica case, with a comment also that the United States Supreme Court had upheld the power of Congress to punish a stranger for contempt. This was done, said the colony lawyers, in spite of the fact that the Constitution gave Congress only specially delegated powers, among which was the power to commit its members for contempt, but "no such power was given over strangers."

Kielley v. *Carson* was argued twice, the second time before the Lord Chancellor and ten others of the highest judges of England, including Baron Parke, who had written the only opinion that ever upheld the inherent contempt power of a British colonial assembly. Parke now wrote the *Kielley* opinion for a unanimous Court, and *overruled himself.* The decision in *Beaumont* v. *Barrett*, he said, had been based entirely on Lord Ellenborough's *dictum* in *Burdett*, and that *dictum* had been misunderstood: it referred only to the powers of the Lords and Commons. The colonial assemblies possessed no such powers, either by analogy with Parliament or by derivation from the common law.

Except for the absence of jurisdiction, the decision in *Kielley* v. *Carson* overruled the Supreme Court in *Anderson* v. *Dunn* as much as it did *Beaumont* v. *Barrett*. It struck down completely the 1811 *dictum* of Lord Ellenborough on which both were built. Indeed, it undermined the congressional power to punish nonmembers for contempt even more completely than it did the colonial power to do so. For there was no source of the congressional power by analogy with Parliament, no source of it in the common law, no source in colonial or in state precedents, no grant of it in the Constitution; instead a clear presumption of the lack of it because the contempt powers *specifically granted* did not include it.

How then, it may be asked, can Congress protect itself against obstruction of its work if it cannot do so by arrest and punishment of the obstructors? By the same means that the British courts of appeal recognized in the colonial assemblies, the means that our Constitution conferred upon Congress—the power to pass laws necessary and proper to carry out its granted powers.

That process, authorized by the Act of 1857, received no judicial test until 1897 when it was upheld by the Supreme Court. Elverton R. Chapman, a stockbroker, was indicted and convicted in district court of contempt of the Senate, in refusing to disclose purchases by senators of stock in a sugar refining company while Congress was revising the tariff on sugar. The Supreme Court held that the inquiry was a proper one, within the Senate's power to expel a member, and overruled Chapman's contention that the Act of 1857 was an unconstitutional delegation of the contempt power of Congress to the courts. "We grant," wrote Justice Fuller, "that Congress could not divest itself or either of its Houses, of the essential and inherent power to punish for contempt in cases to which the power of either House properly extended; but because Congress, by the Act of 1857, sought to aid each of the Houses in discharge of its constitutional functions, it does not follow that any delegation of the power in each to punish for contempt was involved."

It is certainly true that Congress could not, by law, take away the privilege given to each House by the Constitution, to punish or expel its own members. But if Justice Fuller meant (as his words have been taken to mean) that each House has an inherent contempt power derived from outside the Constitution, and superior to the legislative power conferred by the Constitution, what he offered was a formula for setting up two independent dictatorships in the United States, incapable of being terminated even by the joint will of the dictators themselves.

Twenty more years passed before the action of an angry House of Representatives again brought a direct contempt commitment before the Supreme Court. In 1916 H. Snowden Marshall, a United States district attorney, heatedly accused a House subcommittee of trying to block the indictment of a congressman by a New York grand jury. The House declared that Marshall's published letter was "defamatory and insulting and tends to bring the House into public contempt and ridicule." Arrested by the Sergeant-at-Arms, he was denied release by habeas corpus and appealed the denial to the Supreme Court.

Chief Justice White, after a long review of American and English cases, upheld in a general way the power of the House "to deal with contempt in so far as that authority was necessary to preserve and carry out the legislative authority given." But, said he, "we think from the very nature of that power it is clear that it does not embrace punishment for contempt as punishment, since it rests only upon the right of self-preservation, that is, the right to prevent acts which in and of themselves inherently obstruct or prevent the discharge of legislative duty . . ." The contempt deemed to result from the Marshall letter was not due to any obstruction of the legislative process, but to the effect "which the irritating and ill-tempered statements made in the letter would produce upon the public mind or because of the sense of indignation" engendered by the letter upon members of the House. The Court rejected any such authority in the House, saying that it transferred the limited contempt power, meant for self-preservation, into the comprehensive legislative power to punish wrongful acts; and also transformed the legislative into judicial power.

Thus it was held, in 1916, that the power of Congress to punish for contempt does not include the power to punish libels of Congress or its members—a belated confirmation of what Madison wrote in 1796 about the Randall-Whitney proceedings. During the 1920s, the scandals of the Harding Administration brought back the question dealt with in the Jay Cooke inquiry—the power of Congress to investigate corruption in the executive department and to compel witnesses to answer questions in aid of legislation. That power was sweepingly upheld in contempt cases against Banker Mally S. Daugherty, brother of President Harding's Attorney General, and Harry F. Sinclair, lessee of the Teapot Dome naval oil reserves. Against Daugherty the Senate acted directly, against Sinclair through the courts. Both methods were held to be valid, subject to the requirement that questions must be pertinent to the subject matter.

The issue came still more broadly before the Supreme Court in 1935, when William P. MacCracken sought release by habeas corpus from imprisonment by the Senate for contempt. The case of *Jurney* v. *MacCracken* was one to stir indignation against the culprit. Ordered to produce papers required in an investigation of Ocean and Air Mail Contracts, he refused on the ground that they involved the confidential relations of lawyer and client. An airline agent went to MacCracken's law office, took away some of the subpoenaed papers and tore up others (which the government retrieved from sacks of waste). Jailed by the Senate, MacCracken was released by the Circuit Court of Appeals on a habeas corpus writ that was appealed to the Supreme Court.

At this stage of the case, the sole contention for MacCracken was that the Senate had no power to inflict punishment on him, *simply as punishment*, especially for a completed past action whose effect had been undone as far as was possible and where coercion could have no influence on future proceedings. The Court, speaking through Justice Brandeis, rejected this argument. The power to punish "for a past and completed act" had been asserted before the Revolution "by the colonial assemblies, in imitation of the British House of Commons," and later by state legislatures. Congress exerted it in 1795 in the cases of Randall and Whitney. In *Anderson* v. *Dunn*, the Supreme Court in 1821 upheld the power of the House to punish an attempt at bribery—a completed past action. Protests in Congress from time to time, against particular contempt proceedings, "concerned not the power to punish, as such, but the broad, undefined privileges which it was believed might find sanction in that power."

The ground for such fears, said Justice Brandeis, had been effectively removed by the Court's decision in *Kilbourn* v. *Thompson* that assertions of congressional privilege were subject to judicial review, and by the later holding in *Marshall* v. *Gordon* that the power to punish did not extend to slanderous attacks which presented no immediate obstruction to legislative processes. The power to punish for a past contempt, the Court now declared, was an appropriate means of vindicating "the established and essential privilege of requiring the production of evidence."

This decision very naturally won the applause of every American who looked at it from the standpoint of giving a bad guy what he deserved, or of expediting the legislative process by the quickest possible route. But it verified once more the saying that hard cases make bad law. Frank J. Hogan, one of the great lawyers of his day, presented an argument for MacCracken that was not answered in the opinion. He granted that Congress had the right to force a witness to attend, testify, and produce material documents, and to coerce him by imprisonment until he should do what was commanded. But the power was remedial and coercive, not punitive. In this case the witness attended, testified, and produced what papers it was still in his power to produce. For what had been done there was no remedy, and coercion would produce no effect on the Senate's future work.

Tested by any standard, said Hogan, the offense with which MacCracken was charged constituted a criminal contempt, and "in vain do we search the Constitution for any provision authorizing either House of Congress to try and imprison a private citizen for any offense." Not only is punishment for crime a judicial function, sharply separated from the executive and legislative powers, "but it is contrary to the spirit of our institutions to treat anything as a crime unless it be defined and its punishment fixed beforehand." That spirit was equally violated by permitting imprisonment to be imposed, *as punishment,* by any branch of government other than the judiciary. Hogan ran through past American and English cases to show that a decision upholding the imprisonment of Mac-Cracken *for a past and completed action* would run counter both to earlier decisions of the Supreme Court and to the restrictive decisions of the British courts in *Kielley* v. *Carson,* etc. This brought the conclusion:

"In the present case it is patent that the Senate now asserts on the ground of necessity the existence of practically the full power belonging to the House of Lords, though this Court has distinctly held [in the *Kilbourn* and *Marshall* cases] that it has no such power by express grant or by analogy to that body."

To this view Justice Brandeis presented three offsets: (1) Congressional privilege is subject to judicial review. (2) American colonial assemblies, state legislatures and Congress had consistently punished past offenses by imprisonment. (3) A completed act is not punishable "unless it is of a nature to obstruct the performance of the legislature." If it is of such a nature, the removal of the obstruction or inability to remove it "is without legal significance."

These precedents break down on examination. State actions for contempt were generally regulated by state constitutions or laws, often reflecting distrust of the power. What were the outstanding colonial cases of imprisonment for the purpose of punishing contempt? The most notable were the jailing of Publisher James Franklin by the Massachusetts Assembly and of Alexander Mc-Dougall by the New York Assembly, in each instance for libeling the lawmaking body. Both assemblies violated British constitutional law as defined later in *Kielley* v. *Carson*. Both actions were in direct conflict with the Constitution of the United States as interpreted in *Marshall* v. *Gordon*.

These colonial cases, involving libel, collapse also under Justice Brandeis's third criterion—that to be punishable, the contemptuous act must be of a nature to obstruct the performance of legislative duties. Here likewise the first and foremost congressional precedent falls down. Speculator Randall, in 1795, was originally cited for making corrupt proposals to congressmen, but that accusation was abandoned at the bar of the House. He was committed to jail for telling some members, falsely, that thirty others had said they would support his memorial for a land grant. Since the memorial never was presented to Congress, there was not the slightest obstruction to the legislative process. There was nothing to obstruct. Randall was punished for damaging the reputation of the House—the exact charge and punishment held to be unconstitutional in *Marshall* v. *Gordon*.

In *Jurney* v. *MacCracken*, the Court's final justification for congressional punishment of a completed action was that it would deter a repetition. But punishment as a deterrent is the very essence of criminal law and is not only assigned solely to the judiciary, by our Constitution, but is wrapped with all the constitutional safe-guards of due process of law.

The *MacCracken* opinion dismissed "the apprehensions ex-pressed from time to time in congressional debates," concerning exercises of the contempt power, saying that they "concerned not the power to punish, as such, but the broad, undefined privileges which it was believed might find sanction in that power." But the power to *punish* for contempt was in itself the broadest of those undefined privileges. With that gate opened, the whole field could be overrun. In every congressional debate from 1795 onward, the argument against undefined privilege centered in the slogan: hold to the constitutional limitation *or there is no limit.* The power to punish exterior acts was denied *in toto.*

Nowhere was this denial expressed more strongly than in the 1832 contempt case against General Samuel Houston, cited in *Mac-Cracken* as outstanding proof of the power of the House to impose punishment. In an encounter in the street, the one-armed general caned a congressman carrying two pistols.[4] Libertarian lawyer Francis Scott Key, counsel for Houston, sought "to impress upon the minds of others the strong feelings and convictions of my own; . . . [of the] danger to our free institutions from maintaining the power here assumed." The House, argued the man who wrote "The Star-Spangled Banner," derived its existence and all its powers from the Constitution, which gave no such power as this. It could not be derived from English precedent without bringing with it all the abuses that had disgraced British practice. Necessity did not create the power, since an assault of this sort did not interfere with the work of Congress and "our courts are competent to try all such offences." Neither was the asserted power a proper one. "It can never be proper that a party prosecuting for offences against itself shall be the judges to try and punish." The action, Key asserted, was inconsistent with the powers expressly given to the judiciary and conflicted with the prohibition of punishment for criminal of-fenses except through trial by an impartial jury in a court of law.

No less basic were the final contentions of Representative James

K. Polk in Houston's behalf. After three weeks of debate this future President was confirmed in his original opinion "that this House is invested with no authority under the constitution or laws of the land to punish as for a contempt, or violation of its privileges, any offence committed not in the presence of the House during its session, or in such manner as to disturb its proceedings." What was the House really doing?

"To the neglect of our appropriate functions . . . we are in reality trying an assault and battery, under the parliamentary name of privilege. We hear of contempt, of breach of privilege. These constitute the offence, the crime committed, and yet in vain do we look to our powers in the constitution for a sanction for this proceeding. In vain do we search the laws to learn what these privileges are, and wherein a contempt consists. The whole doctrine is borrowed from the practice of the British Parliament, between which and the American Congress there exist, as to this matter, no points of analogy. . . . The Parliament of England is omnipotent. The Congress is limited in its powers by a written constitution."

The House, by a vote of 106 to 89, declared General Houston to be in contempt of the House, and the Speaker was directed to deliver a reprimand. He did so, with the result that crowded galleries and nearly half of the House gave the one-armed general a cheering, clapping, standing ovation. The demonstration for Houston proved nothing except the futility of the whole proceeding. Taking them one after another, the votes in Congress, colonial assemblies and state legislatures, to punish contempt, have been mere explosions of anger and injured pride. The tendency of them is to make heroes or martyrs of the victims.

Analysis of the contempt actions cited in *Jurney* v. *MacCracken* brings the judicial conclusions down to this formula: *unconstitutional precedents create constitutionality*. Why, in the case of MacCracken, was there this too-ready sacrifice of constitutional principles by senators and justices who most cherished them? Emotionally, because they shared the reaction of nearly all Americans, "Don't let this scamp escape." Basically, however, the harm was done more than a hundred years earlier, when a thoughtless court gave its blessing in *Anderson* v. *Dunn* to congressional powers drawn by imitation from the parliamentary law of England in its worst period of exaggeration and misuse. All this could have been avoided had the Court adhered in 1821 to the limited powers of privilege set forth in the Constitution and to the constitutional separation of the judicial from the legislative power. That would have left Congress with all the protection it needs, in its granted power to punish its own members and to *provide by necessary and proper laws* for the punishment of private citizens who obstruct the legislative processes.

Nor is the refusal of witnesses to answer questions an actual obstacle to the framing and passage of laws. It is more likely to be an aid. The destruction of the papers demanded of MacCracken sent the Holding Company Bill sailing through Congress with the support of members who otherwise would have labored to stall or defeat it. As a matter of policy, if not of constitutional power, the record through two centuries fully supports the assertion of Senator Sumner in 1860, that to *compel* testimony in aid of legislation may at times be convenient, "but *necessary, never.*"

Barely half a dozen years were needed, after the sweeping affirmation of the contempt power in 1935, to swing it completely from the field of legislation to that of punishment in which it got its start 140 years earlier. Ruthlessly employed by congressional committees for systematic punishment of American citizens, it has made the mid-twentieth century an age of attainder in a country where not one person in a hundred knows the meaning of the word. "What an engine may such a privilege become," exclaimed Madison, after the precedent was set in 1795, to protect the corruptions of a body once corrupted. He did not visualize the engine that would be created to serve unrecognized corruptions of the mind and heart.

CHAPTER 37
Attainder by Congressional Committees

It has frequently been said, and most truly, that since an early date in the nineteenth century the South has been ruled by the Negro. That is, the presence first of a slave population, then of its free descendants, has dominated the thoughts, feelings, politics, public policies, economic system and social structure of the entire community. In much the same way, but minus the personal social aspect, the American people have let themselves be ruled since 1917 by dread of the Soviet Union and the shadow of international communism thrown by it around the world. This first broke out in the abortive allied military intervention in Russia in 1918, based on the fantastic notion that Lenin, Trotzky and the rest of the Bolsheviki were hirelings of the German Kaiser.

During fifteen uneasy years, successive Presidents of the United States refused to admit the existence of a Russian government, apparently hoping that the Soviet mirage would fade away. Diplomatic recognition of Soviet Russia by President Roosevelt in 1933 lessened the old tensions. World War II forced the United States and Russia into a military partnership that drove the differences of political and social systems temporarily out of mind. Victory was followed by the Cold War between East and West. Regardless of its causes, the natural and inevitable effect of peacetime military confrontation was a deepening of fear in every country affected.

During these developments, all conventional systems of defense were rendered obsolete in major warfare, by the atom bomb, the hydrogen bomb, the intercontinental missile. The heartland of every country in the world became the prospective front, center and rear in a war of mutual annihilation that might be over in twenty minutes or twenty hours, with the slow tortures of radioactive poisons to carry off those who survived the blast. The effect of this was to produce a still greater state of tension, admirably sustained by persons of good emotional balance, but causing a rapid sprouting in the United States of reactionary political and propaganda groups, some of the crackpot variety, others utilizing popular apprehensions and misapprehensions to advance political programs that could not otherwise gain a foothold.

In actual dealings with the Soviet Union, under the high provocations of mutual suspicion, the American government has in common parlance "kept its shirt on." Furthermore, the antagonisms at governmental level have never turned the people of the two countries against each other. How can these facts be reconciled with the way the United States was thrown into terror, during the quarter century beginning about 1938, by that minuscule offshoot of sovietism, the American Communist Party? It is explainable at bottom through the numbing effects of a century and a half of isolation from international peril, and the intense hostility of many people to inescapable social change in the new age of technology. To these influences must be added the shrewd employment of modern instruments of propaganda by men seeking to attain their own objectives under the guise of combatting a nonexistent domestic "Communist peril."

This was made easier by the fact, so obvious as to need no evidence but sight and sound, that the American Communist Party came into being as the sycophantic servant of the Soviet Union, wheeling to right or left at every swing of Soviet policy. But that was the germ of the party's dissolution. Built up during the Great Depression by the twin recruiting agents—unemployment and hunger—the party by 1945 had reached the anthill summit of 80,000 members in a population of 140,000,000. Prosperity and disillusionment with the Soviet Union crumbled it to 7,000 by 1962, not counting 1,500 FBI informants holding Communist Party cards.

There was a time, prior to 1945, when an unknown proportion of American Communists could have been thought of as a potential "fifth column" in the event of war with Russia. Little was left of that hazard after organized labor wiped out a medium-sized Communist foothold in the trade unions. The very concept of a "fifth column" went into limbo with the development of nuclear weapons. This put all humanity into the same basket—soldiers, civilians, Communists, anti-Communists, Russians, Americans and bystanders—all swinging through space into a future in which nothing was certain except being smashed into a glutinous mess if the basket dropped.

With the world perforce divided, at the atomic level, into an international peace party on one side and morons led by a possible lunatic on the other, there remained plenty to worry about in the contention between international communism and capitalism. But the planting of American Communists at the target end of the Soviet missile trajectory was the final element in their demoralization and virtual obliteration as a party.

By the most elementary rule of logic, the temperature of the domestic Communist issue, which never had reason to rise above the freezing point, ought to have been reduced by these developments to fifty below zero. Instead it boiled along as usual in all the propaganda agencies that had been keeping it alive for a score of years. The phenomenon becomes understandable when one realizes what is actually meant by domestic communism in the current political vocabulary. In Phoenix, Arizona, communism is the graduated income tax. In Alabama and Mississippi it is the effort to enforce equal rights for Negroes. In some minds it is the TVA, Social Security, the New Deal, the Fair Deal, the New Frontier, the Great Society, the post office, or even Dwight Eisenhower.

In other words, by 1960 the words "Communist" and "communism," applied to Americans, had become political epithets to be hurled against any person, party or objective regarded by the hurler as obnoxious. That leads to the inquiry, how did this come about in a supposedly rational society? The tangible physical answer is furnished by the record of the congressional investigating committees that took their start in 1938 with the creation of the House Un-American Activities Committee (HUAC) and soon spread to the Senate.

The story of the House Committee and its cruel inanities has been too well told in the books of Father August R. Ogden, Robert

K. Carr, Walter Gellhorn, Alan Barth and others to need even a brief recapitulation here. With hardly a glance at the native fascism that presents a real peril to the country, and with no rational consideration of the actual status of the American Communist Party, the committee plunged into a campaign directed against political liberals from the Roosevelt cabinet down. The glitter of political gold in the Communist hills was not lost on Senator Joseph Mc-Carthy of Wisconsin, with a Senate subcommittee as his pick and shovel. Taking the State Department as his special target, his technique of the "big lie" followed by the bigger one grew in power like a stream from a hydraulic hose, washing out everything in its path in the search for Communists who have not yet been found. For many years, by sheer force of piling accusation on accusation, McCarthy dominated Congress, terrorized the executive branch of government and swayed a gullible public as completely as Titus Oates and his crew ruled England through the perjuries of the "Popish Plot."

In the Senate committee, below the level of McCarthy himself, there was an effort during his ascendancy to give some value to committee investigations of Communist methods and objectives. No such trivial inquiries held back the House Committee or stunted its methods. Using co-operative ex-Communists as instruments, it "exposed" enough genuine Communists to give a cast of authenticity to its operations, and employed an infallible system of incriminating others. Accusation proved guilt, denial doubled it, and guilt by association brought in new victims with the speed and thoroughness of measles in a schoolroom. The glaring light of publicity in an overwrought nation produced the inescapable punishment—social infamy, loss of livelihood, blasted families, physical breakdown, and at times the suicide's bullet.

Under the irrational pressures engendered by these proceedings, combined with apprehensions growing out of the Cold War with Russia, Congress passed the "Smith Act" of 1940, slightly modified in 1948, making it unlawful for any person to "knowingly or willfully advocate, abet, advise or teach" the desirability of overthrowing the government of the United States or any state government by force or violence. It was similarly made unlawful, with such an intent, to publish, sell, circulate or publicly display any written or printed matter advising the propriety of overthrowing any such government. Finally, it was made a criminal offense to help or attempt to organize any society or assembly teaching or encouraging such overthrow, or to become a member or affiliate of it knowing its purposes. Penalties extended to a $10,000 fine and ten years in prison.

The Smith Act clearly abridged freedom of speech and press. This act of Congress made it unlawful to express the most distant approval of violence as a means of overthrowing a government in the United States—even of a Communist government, if one should be elected and hold on by force. Such a statute, plus the penalties of the Stuart period, would have sent Algernon Sidney to his death without perverting the law of treason to that end. It would have ended the careers of Patrick Henry and other patriots years before British intransigence drove them into a course they wished to avoid. It could have sent Thomas Jefferson to prison for saying that he continued to believe what he wrote in the Declaration of Independence. All this not being enough, the McCarran Act of 1950 was passed, violating the privilege against self-incrimination by requiring Communists to register as such, thus subjecting themselves to imprisonment under the Smith Act. The one redeeming feature of the latter law was that (as the Supreme Court held in 1956) federal occupation of the field made state sedition laws inoperative. That eliminated a brood of illegitimate offspring even uglier than their sire.

Passage of these federal laws gave Communists an "out" as far as investigation by committees of Congress was concerned. To avoid self-incrimination, they could refuse to answer any question that would link them with the practices of political groups condemned by the Smith Act. But the method of defense thus forced on them intensified the punishment—infamy—meted out by the committees. This the committees employed to the full, asking repetitious questions—a dozen or a hundred it might be—each question forcing the witness to invoke a protection that was popularly taken to be a confession of criminality. The televised public spectacle intensified the punishment.

No well-disposed person could object to an orderly procedure in Congress to ensure the exclusion of Communists from sensitive governmental positions affecting the national security. But this piti-less system of exposure under the Klieg lights was not designed for that. The purpose and effect were akin to the pillory and the slitting of noses. Men were branded as criminals in the face of society be-cause of political beliefs that are anathema to the general public. The effect was to drive such persons out of all employment, public or private, unless somebody with a sense of mercy gave them a spot in which to hide.

Non-Communist victims of the committees suffered the same fate if, after listening to testimony they knew to be false, they in-voked the Fifth Amendment to escape being charged with perjury on the word of perjurors. A final effect was the discrediting of one of the great safeguards of liberty in the mind of the public. Few people realize that the privilege against compulsory self-incrimina-tion is a shield of the innocent as well as the guilty. Few recognize it as a protection, built up in Anglo-American society, against the once universal employment of torture to extract confessions. All that is seen in committee questioning of Communists is the spec-tacle of witnesses claiming for themselves the freedoms of speech and press, the protection against self-incrimination, that no Com-munist regime in power would grant to its opponents. So, cries the loud voice of unreason, take away the rights that are thus abused. Few hear the smaller voice of reason adding, "and thus take away those rights from all of us."

As the years passed, an amazing dichotomy developed in Con-gress. The lawmakers in their legislative capacity moved more and more to the support of equal rights for all Americans. But the con-gressional investigators of "Un-Americanism," partly as a result of the seniority system, partly through a natural affinity in their dis-likes, began more and more to direct their activities against white residents of the South who had the vision and courage to speak out in support of the civil and political rights of Negroes. Hearings were called in various Southern cities, timed apparently with reference to regional conferences on civil rights. The ostensible purpose was to investigate the spread of communism, in states where the entire membership of the Communist Party could dance the Virginia reel in a telephone booth.

Typically subpoenaed were white men and women who dared

to speak out against racial segregation. They had Hobson's choice. They could take the stand and deny Communist affiliation, as some did when called before Senator Eastland's Subcommittee on Internal Security in New Orleans in 1954. As a result they were blazoned in their home towns and over the country as Communists or fellow travelers, on the sworn testimony of an ex-Communist informer whose past perjuries had ended his usefulness in judicial prosecutions. Or the persons subpoenaed might refuse to answer any questions about their political beliefs and associations, on the ground that these were none of the business of Congress and were protected by the constitutional guarantees of freedom of speech and assembly. Carl Braden and Frank Wilkinson, noted civil rights leaders who took this course before the HUAC in Atlanta, in 1958, served a year in prison over the dissenting protests of four members of the Supreme Court.

That brings us to the congressional dichotomy. How could the same House of Representatives that passed the Civil Rights Act of 1964 appropriate close to $400,000 to the House Committee on Un-American Activities, knowing that it would be used largely to frustrate the purposes of the Civil Rights Act? There is a simple answer. It did so for the same reason that caused the House of Lords to send Viscount Stafford to the scaffold in 1680, though believing him to be innocent of the Popish Plot. The death of Stafford, Lord Halifax told Lord Temple, "was necessary to the people's satisfaction." The Popish Plot "must be handled as if it were true, whether it were so or not."

So it has been with the House Committee on Un-American Activities. Vote to abolish the odious institution, or cut its appropriations, in the face of a fanatic right-wing minority, and every congressman patriotic enough to do so could expect an adversary in the next election crying out that he was "soft on communism" if not an outright subversive. It was much easier to give the committee its usual appropriation, worse than wasted from a public standpoint, but amounting to a $1,500 insurance premium for each member of the House against challenge at the polls by the political forces built up by the committee itself.

The Supreme Court has at times attempted to curb the excesses of the Un-American Activities Committee by holding it to definite limits of action, determined by the resolution creating it or by the announced purposes of its own inquiries. At other times the Court has appeared to give the committee virtually free license to override the First Amendment, though steadily upholding the less flexible privilege against self-incrimination. Seldom has the Court done worse than when it refused to hear an appeal of the 1948 decision in *Barsky* v. *United States,* in which the support of the HUAC by the District of Columbia Court of Appeals (Judge Edgerton dissenting) rivaled the most savage heresy inquisitions of the Tudor period.

In *Watkins* v. *United States,* decided in 1957, the Court overturned the conviction of a labor union leader who, though not a party member, had co-operated with Communists. Watkins testified freely to the House Committee about himself and persons he knew to be Communists, but refused to name other past associates and thus subject them to obloquy. The questions, he contended, infringed his rights under the First Amendment and were not pertinent to the inquiry.

The Supreme Court reversed his conviction on the combined grounds of vagueness in the House resolution creating the committee, vagueness in the purpose of the inquiry, and irrelevancy of the questions to the stated purpose. But the opinion of Chief Justice Warren set up general standards that appeared to go much farther. Congressional investigations were subject to the command that Congress shall make no law abridging the freedom of speech or press. "There is no congressional power to expose for the sake of exposure." The power to obtain information for the benefit of the public "cannot be inflated into a general power to expose where the predominant result can only be an invasion of the private rights of individuals."

These declarations seemed to condemn a great part of the conduct of the HUAC during the previous two decades as violations of the constitutional freedoms of speech, press and association. But when Lloyd Barenblatt, psychology teacher at Vassar College, relied on the First Amendment in refusing to answer questions about alleged Communist connections when he was a student at the University of Michigan, his conviction of contempt of Congress was upheld five to four. The majority held that the questions were pertinent to an authorized inquiry and that the "balancing test" over-rode the First Amendment. That is, the need to abridge freedom of speech, in the public interest, made it lawful for Congress to do what the Constitution unqualifiedly forbids it to do. "We conclude," said the Court, speaking through the grandson and namesake of the first Justice Harlan, "that the balance between the individual and the government interests here at stake must be struck in favor of the latter." Justice Black's dissent, approved by Chief Justice Warren and Justices Douglas and Brennan, made a three-way attack on the Court's decision:

"(1) Rule XI creating the Committee authorizes such a sweeping, unlimited, all-inclusive and undiscriminating compulsory examination of witnesses in the field of speech, press, petition and assembly that it violates the procedural requirements of the Due Process Clause of the Fifth Amendment.

"(2) Compelling an answer to the questions asked Barenblatt abridges freedom of speech and association in contravention of the First Amendment.

"(3) The Committee proceedings were part of a legislative program to stigmatize and punish by public identification and exposure all witnesses considered by the Committee to be guilty of Communist affiliations, as well as all witnesses who refused to answer Committee questions on constitutional grounds."

By this last tactic, said Justice Black, the committee was "improperly seeking to try, convict, and punish suspects, a task which the Constitution expressly denies to Congress and grants exclusively to the courts, to be exercised by them only after indictment and in full compliance with all the safeguards provided by the Bill of Rights." The Justice piled up evidence from the committee's own reports that it was pursuing a course of "pitiless publicity and exposure" (HUAC's own words) in order to drive suspected Communists and "subversives" out of virtually all fields of employment, public and private. Its purpose was clearly stated in a 1951 report, when, after telling how it had driven Communists, ex-Communists and suspected Communists out of employment, the Committee said: "The time has come now when even the fellow traveler must get out." The HUAC, said Justice Black, had told Congress of its success in what it called "the real purpose of the House Committee . . .

468 The Bill of Rights

the task of protecting our constitutional democracy by turning the light of pitiless publicity on [these] organizations." The method, however, was to turn that pitiless light on individuals, in all sorts of organizations.

"I do not question the Committee's patriotism and sincerity in doing all this," wrote Justice Black. "I merely feel that it cannot be done by Congress under our Constitution." In 1943, he recalled, the House Committee reported that the "views and philosophies" of three government workers "as expressed in various statements and writings constitute subversive activities within the definition adopted by your committee," and they were unfit for government employment. By a House "rider" stubbornly affixed to a vital war bill, the Treasury was ordered not to pay their salaries. Justice Black recorded the ensuing action:

"We held that statute void as a bill of attainder in *United States* v. *Lovett* . . . stating that its 'effect was to inflict punishment without the safeguards of a judicial trial' and that this 'cannot be done either by a State or by the United States.' "[1]

The House Committee, in spite of this rebuff, held to its self-described conduct as "the only agency of government that has the power of exposure." "I cannot agree," wrote Justice Black in his *Barenblatt* dissent, "that this is a legislative function. Such publicity is clearly punishment, and the Constitution allows only one way in which people can be convicted and punished . . . by court and jury after a trial with all judicial safeguards." It was no answer to suggest that legislative committees should be allowed to inflict punishment if they grant the accused some rules of courtesy or the right of counsel. "For the Constitution proscribes *all* bills of attainder by State or Nation, not merely those which lack counsel or courtesy."

The Founders, said Black, "believed that punishment was too serious a matter to be entrusted to any group other than an independent judiciary and a jury of twelve men acting on previously passed, unambiguous laws, with all the procedural safeguards they put in the Constitution as essential to a fair trial." John Lilburne's "attack on trials by such committees and his warning that 'what is done unto any one, may be done unto every one' was part of the history of the times which moved those who wrote our Constitution to determine that no such arbitrary punishments should ever occur here." Justice Black's concluding words put the issue up to the American people as well as to fellow jurists:

"Ultimately all the questions in this case really boil down to one —whether we as a people will try fearfully and futilely to preserve Democracy by adopting totalitarian methods, or whether in accordance with our traditions and our Constitution we will have the confidence and courage to be free."

Those words supported the conclusion of four justices that congressional committees violated the constitutional prohibition of bills of attainder when they punished American citizens by the infliction of infamy without a judicial trial. This did not make it absolutely certain that five or more members of the Supreme Court, holding that same conviction, would have "the confidence and courage" to enforce it as the law of the land. That might perhaps have been done, had the full evil been manifest when Madison halted congressional criticism of the Democratic Societies by denouncing it as "a vote of attainder." But in 1794 people knew at least the formal shape of attainder. Not even the frightened and desperate men who resorted to the Sedition Act of 1798 would have risked their own future liberty by erecting themselves into such an agency of terror as Cromwell's Parliament or its Stuart successor.

The need today is to recapture a lost sense of the preciousness of individual liberty, and a lost knowledge of the historic methods of its destruction. The day has long since vanished when every American educated in law and history, on hearing the name "Earl of Strafford," would think instantly of the way good men disposed of a bad minister in 1640 by piling his blunders and misdemeanors into a package labeled "treason by accumulation"; then sent him to death through a bill of attainder to which Parliament turned because evidence was lacking to prove a crime.

Our Supreme Court in 1868 gave an authentic definition of this instrument of injustice: "A bill of attainder is a legislative act which inflicts punishment without a judicial trial. If the punishment be less than death, the act is termed a bill of pains and penalties. Within the meaning of the Constitution, bills of attainder include bills of pains and penalties." That was said in the 1868 case of *Cummings* v. *Missouri,* in which a Catholic priest resisted, on principle, a Missouri law requiring clergymen to swear that they had never given aid or comfort to enemies of the United States. On the same day the Court struck down an act of Congress imposing a similar loyalty oath on members of the federal bar. Any statute like these, the Court held, "operates as a legislative decree of perpetual exclusion" from a chosen profession.

Those two laws, like the action that doomed the Earl of Strafford, presented bills of attainder in the full form of a statutory enactment. Application to congressional committees like the HUAC and the Senate Subcommittee on Internal Security requires affirmative answers to two questions: Is the deliberate infliction of infamy, for the purpose of punishment, an act which inflicts punishment without a judicial trial? Does the constitutional mandate, "No bill of attainder or *ex post facto* law shall be passed," forbid the separate Houses or committees of Congress to do what would be unlawful if done by the whole Congress? Both of these questions were answered by Madison in 1794, in supporting his assertion that denunciation of the Democratic Societies by a vote of the House would be "a vote of attainder":

"If it be admitted that the law cannot animadvert on a particular case, neither can we.

"It is vain to say that this indiscriminate censure is no punishment. If it falls on classes, or individuals, it will be a severe punishment."

Both of these positions have been repeatedly affirmed in congressional proceedings on the contempt power. Said Senator Cocke of Tennessee in 1800: "A power expressly denied to the whole government, a single branch may not assume." Defending General Sam Houston in 1832, Francis Scott Key pointed to the constitutional guarantees of trial by jury and due process of law. If Congress, in disregard of these provisions, should *pass a law* authorizing each House to punish contempts by its own action, "could there be a doubt of the courts of the United States deciding it to be unconstitutional and void? And yet the assumption now is, that this House can do without a law that which the whole Congress, with the sanction of the Executive, could not accomplish."

The noted lawyers who defended Thaddeus Hyatt in 1859 had two thousand years of law behind them when they declared that the Senate had tried, convicted and *punished* him by issuing a subpoena with the intended purpose of linking him with John Brown's raid. "Such a conviction," declared Sewall and Andrew, "by blasting a man's character, may . . . become the most tremendous punishment."

The very words, "to *brand* with infamy," are derived from the ancient Roman practice of burning the letter "K" (for Kalumnia) in the forehead of a false informer. This reaches the United States Congress with startling directness in the statement of Carl Ludwig von Bar that "the peculiarly arbitrary character of the Roman criminal law" is due in part to the transition from monarchy to republic. Immediately after that the entire criminal jurisdiction "devolved upon the popular assembly which also possessed the legislative power; it passed upon the person—the character of the accused—more frequently than upon the facts, which constituted the basis of the complaint." Could attainder by Congressional committees have a more perfect antecedent?

Montesquieu said in *Lettres persanes:* "The hopelessness of infamy causes torment to a Frenchman condemned to a punishment that would not deprive a Turk of a quarter hour of sleep."

Beccaria, whose *Essay on Crimes and Punishment* helped shape our Fifth and Eighth Amendments, wrote in it "Of infamy, considered as a Punishment." Said this defender of human rights in an inhuman world: "Infamy is a mark of the public disapprobation, which deprives the object of all consideration in the eyes of his fellow citizens, of the confidence of his country, and of that fraternity which exists among members of the same society."

Wrote Brissot de Warville, friend of Jefferson and Madison, whose American travels in the 1780s spread the influence of his books: "It is more in the power of moral custom rather than in the hands of legislators that there resides this terrible weapon of infamy, this kind of civil excommunication, which deprives the victim of all consideration, which ruptures all the ties that attach his fellow citizens to him, which isolates him in the midst of society."

In English common law, "infamy" is the condition, resulting from conviction of a crime, that renders a person incompetent as a witness in court. That is obsolete both in England and the United States. The term "infamous crime," as used in the grand-jury requirement of the Fifth Amendment, was interpreted by our

Supreme Court in 1885 to depend on the severity of punishment defined by law. Such uses of the word do not cover the infliction of infamy *as a punishment* in itself, by exposure *for that purpose* in the stocks or pillory, by cutting off ears, slitting the nose, branding the forehead, or by public flogging at the cart's tail. No different in kind are the exposure, branding and flogging inflicted upon individuals by congressional committees. Brissot de Warville gave a true account of that "terrible weapon" of public execration, and Jeremy Bentham testified to its duration. "Any kind of infamy, howsoever inflicted or contracted," wrote Bentham, "may chance to prove perpetual; since the idea of the offense, or, what comes to the same thing, of the punishment, may very well chance to remain more or less fresh in men's minds to the end of the delinquent's life."

By no possible twist of argument can the infliction of such punishment be anything but attainder of the victim—a civil excommunication that exposes him to lasting and ruinous chastisement by society. Congress, by the express words of the Constitution, is forbidden to pass any law having such an effect. By no system of reasoning can either house of Congress authorize a committee to do what is forbidden to the whole Congress.

To put an end to these unconstitutional practices, the Supreme Court need but add three letters, *"ion,"* to its 1868 definition of a bill of attainder. It will then read: "A bill of attainder is a legislative act*ion* which inflicts punishment without a judicial trial." There is universal agreement that where the Constitution forbids Congress to legislate, the prohibition extends to the executive and judicial branches of government. By inescapable logic, committees of Congress come within a similar restriction. If they can escape by lifting congressional privilege above the prohibition of bills of attainder, there is no limit to what may be done by that same means. Could not the House or Senate, after committing a citizen to prison for contempt, proceed likewise against any judge who should release him on a writ of habeas corpus? That would carry us back to the darkest days of England, or, possibly, forward to a hazard that cannot be dismissed in any country where arbitrary controls of any sort are tolerated: the danger that a military force corrupted by congressional example would act on the pattern placed before it.

This hazard was considered so great, in the early days of the Republic, that strenuous efforts were made to prohibit the maintenance of standing armies in time of peace. The absence of any threat from that source, even in periods of national stress and distress, is a testimonial to the fidelity and patriotism of those who have borne arms for their country, from the highest generals to the lowest ranks. The principle of civilian control of the military, steadily adhered to, has helped to ensure the supremacy of law. What deviations there have been from sound policy in this respect have been minor and temporary, yet of a sort to reveal the crucial position of due process of law, and especially of habeas corpus, in the maintenance of freedom.

During the War of 1812, military commanders encroached at times on civilian rights and were speedily checked by the courts or the Executive. In the fall of 1812 Attorney General Pinkney and President Madison considered the case of Elijah Clark, an American citizen living in Canada, serving in the British army, and captured spying in New York. The commanding general was notified that "the said Clark being considered a citizen of the United States and not liable to be tried by a court martial as a spy, the President is pleased to direct that unless he should be arraigned by the Civil Courts for treason or a minor crime under the laws of the State of New York, he must be discharged."[2]

A year later Congressman Robert Wright of Maryland, famed in the Revolution for hanging Tories on the Eastern Shore, offered a motion to extend the army rules on spies to citizens of the United States. The resolution vanished under a flood of speeches denouncing it as going "to subvert every principle of civil liberty, to place the citizens under the ban of martial law, to prostrate courts of justice and the trial by jury," and take away the sacred right of habeas corpus—the right of a man in prison to be taken in person before a judge to determine whether he should be released or held.

In 1815, Major General Andrew Jackson continued martial law in New Orleans after a British admiral brought news of the treaty of peace and the defeated British army had put to sea. He imprisoned a Louisiana legislator who published a criticism of his actions, defied a writ of habeas corpus ordering the man's release, and banished the federal judge who issued the writ. The noted constitutional lawyer A. J. Dallas was then Secretary of War. With the approval of President Madison, he wrote to Jackson that he had full authority to protect his garrison, but possessed no powers incompatible with the rights of citizens and the independence of the judiciary. If he undertook to suspend the writ of habeas corpus and restrain the liberty of the press, he might be justified by the law of necessity but he could not resort for vindication to the established law of the land. After the proclamation of peace, General Jackson was summoned before Judge Hall and fined $1,000 for contempt of court. The people of New Orleans paid it, but the law was vindicated.

The tendency to deal with military usurpation after the crisis is past was manifest in the Civil War. Lambdin P. Milligan, an Indiana civilian, was arrested in October 1864 and condemned to death by a military commission for having joined the reputedly insurrectionary Order of American Knights or Sons of Liberty. The Supreme Court in 1866 ordered him released on a writ of habeas corpus, holding that no military commission could try a civilian resident of an uninvaded, nonrebelling state *in which the federal courts were open*. Such had been the rule of law, said Justice David Davis, from the time the British Parliament reversed the attainder of the Earl of Lancaster in the year 1326. The principle then established was that in time of peace no man was to be adjudged to death without arraignment and trial and that "when the king's courts are open it is a time of peace in judgment of law." That rule was reinforced by the absence of enemy forces or military operations. Said the Court in *Milligan*:

"Martial law can never exist where the courts are open, and in the proper and unobstructed exercise of their jurisdiction. It is also confined to the locality of actual war."

Another guarantee of freedom was broken, the Court held, when Milligan was denied a trial by jury. "This privilege is a vital principle, underlying the whole administration of criminal justice." Military discipline requires other and swifter modes of trial for offenders in the army or navy, but if a military commander has power "to suspend all civil rights and their remedies, and subject citizens as well as soldiers to the rule of *his will* . . . republican government is a failure, and there is an end of liberty regulated by law."

The worst violations are in the states, on the pretense that labor disorders constitute insurrection. During the State of Colorado's subjection to the rule of the Colorado Fuel and Iron Company, President Moyer of the Western Federation of Miners was carried by force into a county where martial law had been proclaimed by the governor. In this strike-breaking tactic he was imprisoned three months by the state militia, with no charges against him. Habeas corpus was denied although the courts were open. The United States Supreme Court, through the yet-unawakened Justice Holmes, held that the governor's proclamation of a state of insurrection was conclusive, and prevented redress under the act of Congress dealing with deprivation of constitutional rights under color of state law or usage.

A score of years earlier (1886-1893), in the misnamed trials of the "Haymarket Anarchists," resort to the open courts of Illinois produced prejudiced prosecutors, judges and juries, unlawful seizures and compulsory self-incrimination (though not proof of guilt)—all stemming from panic over socialistic labor groups. A courageous new governor, John P. Altgeld, halted the tragic travesty by pardoning the convicted men not already hanged, and suffered thereby the blighting of his political career and reputation.

The principle that war does not suspend the Constitution has been praised more consistently than it has been maintained. The military orders issued and enforced in World War II, forcibly removing American citizens of Japanese ancestry from the Pacific Coast, are recognized today as the product of a monstrous misjudgment of character and loyalty by the officer who ordered it and by the government and nation. The Supreme Court entered gingerly into these cases by unanimously upholding a curfew for Japanese-Americans, on the ground that espionage and sabotage might occur before there was time to distinguish between loyal and disloyal citizens of that ancestry. Chief Justice Stone's reasoning led to a similar decision, with Justice Black writing for the Court, when the whole Japanese-American population was uprooted and transported to concentration camps a thousand miles inland. This time Justices

Roberts, Murphy and Jackson dissented, Jackson saying that a decision upholding the order was worse than the order itself, for by holding it to be constitutional "the Court for all time has validated the principle of racial discrimination in criminal procedure and of transplanting American citizens."

The subject of trial by military commissions came thumping back in 1946, after a commission set up by General Douglas MacArthur condemned Japanese General Tomoyuki Yamashita to death for failing to prevent atrocities by his troops during the American invasion of Luzon, in the Philippines. Failure of a commanding general to control his troops, wrote Chief Justice Stone, was a violation of the laws of war, punishable under martial law even after hostilities ended. Admission of hearsay evidence and opinion did not violate any Act of Congress. The military commission's rulings on evidence were not reviewable in the courts but only by higher military authorities. Consequently it was not necessary to decide whether, under other situations, the course followed would have violated the Fifth Amendment by depriving the defendant of his life without due process of law.

Yamashita is dead but *Yamashita* lives in history both for its demonstration of what the war psychology will do to judicial judgment and for the dissents of Justices Rutledge and Murphy. The grave issue raised in this case, said Justice Murphy, was whether, under the power of Congress "to define and punish . . . offenses against the Law of Nations," a military commission may disregard procedural rights guaranteed by the Constitution. The answer, said he, is plain:

"The Fifth Amendment guarantee of due process of law applies to 'any person' who is accused of a crime by the Federal Government or any of its agencies. No exception is made as to those who are accused of war crimes or as to those who possess the status of an enemy belligerent. Indeed, such an exception would be contrary to the whole philosophy of human rights which makes the Constitution the great living document that it is."

The military commission, Justice Murphy declared, rushed the defendant to trial under an improper charge, without sufficient time to prepare a defense, in violation of some of the elemental rules of evidence, and summarily sentenced him to be hanged. It was not charged that he ordered or condoned the atrocities. "Not even knowledge of these crimes was attributed to him." It was simply alleged that he failed to discharge his duties as commander to control his troops. "The recorded annals of warfare and the established principles of international law afford not the slightest precedent for such a charge."

Justice Rutledge endorsed all that Murphy had said and turned to the subject he thought most at stake, that even taking Yamashita to be guilty of the atrocities for which his death was sought, "there can be and should be justice administered according to law." His concern at bottom was "that our system of military justice shall not alone among all our forms of judging be above or beyond the fundamental law or the control of Congress within its orbit of authority; and that this Court shall not fail in its part under the Constitution to see that these things do not happen."

This trial, said Rutledge, was unprecedented in American history. Never before had an enemy general been tried and convicted for action taken during hostilities. Much less had we condemned one for failing to take action. It was not in our tradition for anyone to be charged with a crime which is defined after his conduct, alleged to be criminal, had taken place. (An *ex post facto* law.) In this case mass guilt was imputed to an individual, without making the charge definite enough to enable him to make a defense. Part of the evidence was "hearsay, once, twice or thrice removed." He was convicted on affidavits that did not permit cross-examination of the accuser, on *ex parte* documents prepared by the prosecution, including not only opinion but conclusions of guilt. Whether taken singly as departures from specific guarantees or as a total denial of due process, "a trial so vitiated cannot withstand constitutional scrutiny.

"The fountainhead of the commission's authority," wrote Rutledge, was a directive by General MacArthur, so broad and loose that "a more complete abrogation of customary safeguards . . . hardly could have been made. So far as the admissibility and probative value of evidence was concerned, the directive made the commission a law unto itself." In one respect only, said the dissenting Justice, did Yamashita have a fair trial. He was furnished with lawyers, officers of the United States Army, who performed their difficult assignment "with extraordinary fidelity, not only to the accused, but to their high conception of military justice," always to be in subordination to the Constitution, laws and treaties.

But the commission consistently ruled against the defense, reprimanded counsel for raising constitutional questions, declined to receive further objections, and even reversed its rulings to admit evidence it had previously declined to receive. Unverified rumor was accepted as evidence and "perhaps the greatest prejudice arose from the admission of untrustworthy, unverified, unauthenticated evidence which could not be probed by cross-examination or other means of testing credibility, probative value or authenticity." In a case where *knowledge of the crime* was an essential element of criminality, the sole attempted proof of knowledge was in the form of *ex parte* affidavits and depositions which "Congress has expressly commanded shall not be received in such cases tried by military commissions and other military tribunals."

Not only did the trial of Yamashita violate the statutory Articles of War, said Justice Rutledge, but in denying him the protection of those Articles the United States violated the Geneva Convention of 1929. And never before this decision had it ever been held that any human being was beyond the protecting spread of the Fifth Amendment's guarantee of a fair trial in the most fundamental sense:

"That door is dangerous to open. I will have no part in opening it. For once it is ajar, even for enemy belligerents, it can be pushed back wider for others, perhaps ultimately for all."

Reverting in conclusion to this all-inclusive coverage of due process of law, Rutledge wrote: "I cannot consent to even implied departure from that great absolute. It was a great patriot [Thomas Paine] who said:

" 'He that would make his own liberty secure must guard even his enemy from oppression; for if he violates this duty he establishes a precedent that will reach to himself.' "

That closing statement forges a link between the unintentional hazarding of our own rights in emotional reaction to the misconduct of our enemies in war, and the actual destruction of those rights in panicky revulsion against a hated philosophy of government or social system. There is no essential difference, either legally or in the resulting danger to democracy and individual liberty, between the overriding of constitutional restraints by a military commission and similar action by congressional committees, when both are done with the approval of the courts. In the military field the larger danger is remote and contingent. In the congressional field the door of attainder has already been pushed wide open for all. In dealing with both of these menaces the Supreme Court has followed the same course. It has affirmed—as it ought to—the basic power of judicial review, but has failed to exercise it effectively when the evil is lodged in a citadel of power that makes the dislodging of it more difficult and more urgent. Yet it is in this same field of due process, under both the Fifth and Fourteenth Amendments, that the latest and greatest forward steps have been taken by the Court.

CHAPTER 38
Resurgent Rights

For a score of years the Supreme Court decisions in *Betts* v. *Brady* and *Adamson* v. *California* formed a dark cloud over American justice, casting a helpless minority into prison gloom and leaving nothing certain except the guilt of society. In each case the question was whether the due process clause of the Fourteenth Amendment made a federal guarantee of liberty binding on the states. In *Betts* (1942) it was held that the right of an accused person to assistance of counsel, mandatory in federal cases under the Fifth Amendment, "is not a fundamental right, essential to a fair trial." The Fourteenth Amendment establishes that right only when the circumstances are "shocking to the universal sense of justice." In *Adamson* (1947) the decision was that the privilege against self-incrimination is not enforceable against the states, as due process of law, unless torture or similar coercion is involved.

From both of these decisions Justices Black, Douglas and Murphy dissented, joined in *Adamson* by a later appointee, Justice Rutledge. Year after year the dissents persisted in similar cases. Then in 1962, after every member of the *Betts* majority had departed, a near duplicate of that case came into view. The Court received the petition of Clarence Earl Gideon, handwritten on prison stationery, asking for a review of his eight-year sentence for larcenous entry of a Florida pool hall. At his trial his request for counsel as an indigent had been denied under state law. The Supreme Court's appointment of Abe Fortas to present Gideon's case gave ample notice that *Betts* v. *Brady* was to receive a decisive test, and twenty-four state attorneys-general intervened as *amici curiae*. Twenty-two took the side of Gideon, an amazing demonstration of the influence of Justice Black's dissent in *Betts*. The Court unanimously overruled that decision and reversed Gideon's conviction. On Gideon's retrial in Florida, his lawyer demolished the state's evidence and he was acquitted.

The overruling of *Betts* v. *Brady* was relatively easy because—to quote the brief of the twenty-two intervening states—that decision was "an anachronism when handed down"; a backtracking from the enlightened stand taken in the case of the "Scottsboro Boys." The Court held in *Gideon* that the assistance of counsel was a fundamental right that could not be abridged. The noble ideal that every defendant stands equal before the law, wrote Justice Black, "cannot be realized if the poor man charged with crime has to face his accusers without a lawyer to assist him." Although the decision was unanimous, Justice Harlan in concurring rejected "the concept that the Fourteenth Amendment 'incorporates' the Sixth Amendment as such." On the same day, the Court upset a California rule allowing a judge to decide whether appointment of counsel would be useful to an indigent appellant. Such a rule, wrote Justice Douglas for the Court, does not distinguish between good and bad cases, but between rich and poor appellants. Justices Clark, Harlan and Stewart dissented.

These divisions made it obvious that unanimity was achieved in *Gideon* because the Court did not rest its decision on the contention that the Fourteenth Amendment makes all of the provisions of the first eight amendments binding on the states. In a concurring opinion, however, Justice Douglas named ten members of the Court who had taken that position since 1868—Justices Field, Bradley, Swayne, probably Clifford, the first Harlan, probably Brewer, Black, Douglas, Murphy and Rutledge. That view, remarked Douglas, had "never commanded a Court," but constitutional questions were always open and "what we do today does not foreclose the matter."

The *Gideon* case marked in fact a sharp acceleration in that direction. The first isolated move was made in 1897, when it was held that due process under the Fourteenth Amendment forbade the states to take private property without just compensation. Apart from that, the stream of denials continued until 1925, when the

Court began in a long series of cases to recognize the Fourteenth Amendment as protector of the freedoms of speech, press, religion, assembly and petition. In 1961, in *Mapp* v. *Ohio,* the Court in an opinion by Justice Clark expanded a previous partial ban on unreasonable searches and seizures by holding that evidence unlawfully obtained could not be used by the states to secure conviction. A year later, with Justice Stewart speaking for the Court, the Eighth Amendment's prohibition of cruel and unusual punishment was extended to the states. The second Justice Harlan concurred solely on the ground that the case involved an arbitrary statute. Thus he did not take part in making his grandfather's 1892 dissent in *O'Neil* v. *Vermont* the law of the land.

By such an approach the Supreme Court came in 1964 to the privilege against self-incrimination—the most crucial, because most keenly controverted, of all the questions about due process under the Fourteenth Amendment. The case, *Malloy* v. *Hogan,* produced a minor division on the question whether the privilege had been properly invoked, but the basic issue was set forth in the opening words of Justice Brennan's opinion:

"In this case we are asked to reconsider prior decisions holding that the privilege against self-incrimination is not safeguarded against state action by the Fourteenth Amendment. *Twining* v. *New Jersey,* 211 U.S. 78; *Adamson* v. *California, 332 U.S. 46.*"

That question was decided with staccato clearness: "We reverse. We hold that the Fourteenth Amendment guaranteed the petitioner the protection of the Fifth Amendment's privilege against self-incrimination." The opinion reviewed the Court's evolution of thinking on this and related matters arising under the Fourteenth Amendment, and took care to tell exactly what it was doing in this case.

"Although," wrote Justice Brennan, "many Justices have deemed the Amendment to incorporate all eight of the Amendments, the view which has thus far prevailed" was that of determining, clause by clause, whether the various guarantees were covered by the due process requirement of the Fourteenth. Following that course, "The Court has not hesitated to re-examine past decisions according the Fourteenth Amendment a less central role in the preservation of basic liberties than that which was contemplated by its Framers when they added the Amendment to our constitutional scheme."

This was equivalent to saying that in the past the Court had disregarded the intended purpose of the amendment and was proceeding now to correct its errors. Since the intended purpose, as indicated in the 1866 debates, was to make the first eight amendments binding on the states, the *Malloy* opinion revealed a clear intention to proceed, clause by clause, until all the "basic liberties" were incorporated in the Fourteenth Amendment. This purpose brought a strong dissent from Justice Harlan, writing also for his Brother Clark:

"I can only read the Court's opinion as accepting in fact what it rejects in theory: the application to the States, via the Fourteenth Amendment, of the forms of federal criminal procedure embodied in the first eight Amendments to the Constitution."

It was just as improper, said Justice Harlan, to do that step by step as all at once. He would agree that the Fourteenth Amendment forbids a state to imprison a person "*solely* because he refuses to give evidence which may incriminate him" under state law. But he thought that blanket application of federal guarantees to the states took no account of relevant differences between federal and state criminal law. What he desired was to continue the test of "fundamental fairness" in deciding what was due process under the Amendment.

There are two objections to that plausible course. One is that it took ninety-six years for five members of the Supreme Court to discover fundamental fairness in the privilege against self-incrimination. The second is that it is a *substitute* for the Fourteenth Amendment, not an *observance* of it. Furthermore, the essential differences between state and federal criminal law, though immense in subject matter, have little bearing on "fundamental fairness" or "basic liberties." These are involved when overlapping jurisdictions produce double jeopardy, but the fundamentals of fairness are not different in state and federal courts. Every one of the vital amendments involving *procedural* due process—the Fourth, Fifth, Sixth and Eighth—was modeled on state procedures. The First Amendment, involving *substantive* due process, also has the same meaning in states and nation. The great divergencies in due process, wherever they are found, represent variations in fidelity to tested and time-honored principles of liberty.

The one major due-process problem really caused by federalism —double jeopardy arising under two jurisdictions—was dealt with by the Supreme Court on the same day that it set the new standard for the Fourteenth Amendment. Twenty years earlier, in 1944, the Court in a four-to-three decision upheld the *federal* conviction of a man on testimony he had been compelled to give in a *state* court under a law granting immunity from prosecution by the state. The majority saw no violation of the Fifth Amendment because the self-incriminating evidence thus given in federal court was not extorted by federal officers. In 1958, this principle was extended so that it became possible for either the United States or a state to convict a person on testimony given by compulsion in the other jurisdiction, even though neither government could use the testimony it had itself extracted. The result, said Justice Black in dissent, was that "a person can be whipsawed into incriminating himself under both state and federal law," in the face of guarantees against self-incrimination in each jurisdiction.

On June 15, 1964, the Supreme Court used a scalpel on this form of self-accusation. It held that neither state nor nation can compel the giving of incriminating testimony, under a grant of immunity, unless similar immunity is extended in the other jurisdiction. The opinion by Justice Arthur Goldberg in *Murphy* v. *Waterfront Commission* approved the earlier "whipsaw" objection of Justice Black, and demonstrated that previous contrary decisions had been based on a misreading of controlling cases in England, with a like misunderstanding of an opinion delivered by Chief Justice Marshall in 1828. In England, Justice Goldberg pointed out, the Court of Chancery Appeal upheld, in 1867, the refusal of an American Confederate agent, McRae, to answer questions in a "fraud discovery" inquiry, on the ground that to do so would incriminate him in the United States.

Justice Harlan concurred narrowly in the judgment but dissented from the Goldberg opinion. He contended that the *McRae* decision did not follow the English rule, but was "distinguished" from it because the Chancery action was based on the fact that the United States Government propounded the questions in the English court. One must conclude that Justice Harlan did not notice the reason given by Lord Chancellor Chelmsford (on another page of his opinion) why the participation of the United States Government was decisive. It was because *that put it beyond question that the answers would be incriminating,* in contrast with an earlier case where "it was not shown that the Defendants had rendered themselves liable to criminal prosecution."

The decisions in these 1964 self-incrimination cases did not reach the core of state-and-federal double jeopardy, which was found in the "Lanza Rule" of 1922. Chief Justice Taft then wrote concerning a violation of federal and Washington State liquor laws: "An act denounced as a crime by both national and state sovereignties is an offense against the peace and dignity of both, and may be punished by each." That is equivalent to saying that justice is established for sovereignties, not for men. The "Lanza Rule" was based on earlier American decisions supposedly in line with English precedents but actually in conflict with them. In 1662, the acquittal of a man tried in Wales for murder was held to bar an indictment of him in England for the same crime. Sixteen years later the same rule was applied to an Englishman who was brought to trial in England for a killing of which he had been acquitted in Portugal. "For the rule is," wrote Hawkins in his *Pleas of the Crown,* "that a man's life shall not be brought into danger for the same offence more than once."

The rule laid down in *United States* v. *Lanza* was rigidly adhered to and powerfully attacked in 1959. Alfonse Bartkus, accused of robbing a bank in Cicero, Illinois, was tried and acquitted in federal court; then tried and convicted of the same robbery by the state. Justice Frankfurter, for a Court divided five to four, said that to bar this on the ground of double jeopardy "would be disregard of a long, unbroken, unquestioned course of impressive adjudication." His word "unquestioned" was open to question, since Justices Johnson and Story dissented from the first decision of that sort, in 1820, and dissents continued. Most "pre-Lanza" cases touched the issue slantwise, and an increasing number of state decisions and statutes have come to prohibit this form of double jeopardy.

Justice Black's *Bartkus* dissent, joined in by Chief Justice War-

ren and Justice Douglas, called it a misuse and desecration of the
concept of "federalism" to hold that the notion of two "Sovereigns"
opened the way to double prosecutions, held in "almost universal
abhorrence." Justice Brennan dissented separately on a showing
that federal officials obtained the state indictment, furnished the
evidence, and took part to such an extent that the state trial was
"actually a second federal prosecution of Bartkus." There seems no
reason to doubt that if the 1964 cases had presented the basic issue
of state and federal trials for the same offense, the "Lanza Rule"
would have been stricken down.

The course charted by the Supreme Court in 1964, broadening
the coverage of due process under the Fourteenth Amendment,
raised anew an old question concerning application to the states of
the first eight amendments as a body. That, it has long been argued,
would force minor, vexatious, outdated rules onto the states and
interfere with workable modern experiments. That is like saying
that a law requiring all horses to be shod would force the digging
up of dead ones.

The Third Amendment, on quartering soldiers in private
houses, faced backward toward colonial days when adopted and
has meant nothing since. The Second Amendment, popularly misread, comes to life chiefly on the parade floats of rifle associations
and in the propaganda of mail-order houses selling pistols to teen-
age gangsters: "A well regulated Militia, being necessary to the
security of a free State, the right of the people to keep and bear
Arms, shall not be infringed." As the wording reveals, this article
relates entirely to the militia—a fact that was made even clearer
by a clause dropped from Madison's original wording: "but no
person religiously scrupulous of bearing arms should be compelled
to render military service in person." It was made clearest of all
in the congressional debate on the amendment. Why was a militia
necessary to "the security of a free state"? Elbridge Gerry asked
and answered that question: "What, sir, is the use of a militia? It is
to prevent the establishment of a standing army, the bane of
liberty." Thus, the purpose of the Second Amendment was to
forbid Congress to prohibit the maintenance of a state militia. By
its nature, that amendment cannot be transformed into a personal

right to bear arms, enforceable by federal compulsion upon the states.

The next bogie is the Seventh Amendment, providing that "in suits at common law, where the value in controversy shall exceed twenty dollars, the right of trial by jury shall be preserved." That amendment was destroyed ages ago by the devaluation of money. Adopted to allay idle fears, long outmoded in federal practice, it is subject also to discard, as far as the Fourteenth Amendment is concerned, under the rule *de minimis*—the law takes no account of trifles.

With these trivialities eliminated, there is just one spot at which application of the first eight amendments to the states runs into a serious problem. That is in the command of the Fifth Amendment that no civilian "shall be held to a capital, or otherwise infamous crime, unless on presentment or indictment of a Grand Jury." In 1868, when the Fourteenth Amendment was ratified, the grand-jury requirement was close to universal in the several states, either by constitutional provision or by statute. In eleven out of twelve states admitted to the Union since then, it is optional, and has been made optional in some of the older states. This unquestionably shows a drifting away from the grand jury, but it is far from rendering so many independent verdicts on the meaning of the Fourteenth Amendment. In that respect, it is merely a by-product of the near destruction of that amendment in the *Slaughter-House* and *Hurtado* cases.

The principle of the grand jury is as sound today as it ever was, in relation to treason, the major forms of felony, and all crimes in which there is a strong emotional basis for unjust prosecution. The grand-jury clause of the Bill of Rights, if applied to the states, would not interfere with prosecutions "by information" in the great mass of minor actions. At a higher level, some latitude of application can be found in the phrase "otherwise infamous crime." Or, if the Court continues to proceed clause by clause in applying the Fourteenth Amendment, there is nothing to compel it to put aside *stare decisis* when change is difficult. And in a period when past values are being recaptured, there is the possibility of aid through a new national consensus.

Nothing could do more to help restore the grand jury than universal familiarity with *In re Oliver,* in which the Supreme Court in 1948 upset the work of a Michigan circuit judge who was acting under a 1917 statute as a "one-man grand jury." Investigating crime in secret session, the judge concluded from a conflict with other secret testimony that the witness Oliver was not telling the truth. So the "judge-grand jury" charged him with contempt of court, immediately pronounced him guilty and sentenced him to sixty days in jail. The Michigan Supreme Court upheld these proceedings.

The United States Supreme Court, speaking through Justice Black, concluded that the shift from investigation to contempt proceedings made this a criminal trial. In the conduct of it the defendant was deprived of his constitutional right to "a speedy and public trial," his right to counsel, to be advised of the charges against him, to call witnesses in his behalf and to confront the witness whose testimony he was said to have contradicted. Justice Rutledge, in a concurring opinion, said that this was "the immediate offspring of *Hurtado* v. *California"* (1884) and later like cases, in which the Court had permitted selective departure by the states from the scheme of personal liberty established by the Bill of Rights.

If the grand jury is to be restored, the impetus will hardly come from the organized legal fraternity. This one-man Michigan substitute was the brain child of the State Bar Association, which also put in a brief to defend Oliver's secret and arbitrary trial, likened by the Supreme Court to the "practice of the Spanish Inquisition, to the excesses of the English Court of Star Chamber, and to the French monarchy's abuse of the *lettre de cachet."* But the uncertainty concerning the grand jury does not affect the general course of events. In the broad field of procedural due process, the Bill of Rights is at last on its way to becoming an All-American Bill, protecting all persons in all states and under all jurisdictions.

The great questions yet unanswered lie in another area—the extent and meaning of the freedoms of the First Amendment. Here some of the unmade decisions are crucial but not difficult, others difficult but not crucial, and there is one that could be both crucial and hard to make. This concerns the constitutionality of government grants to church-related colleges and universities under the National Defense Education Act for scientific research and many other matters connected either with national defense or the general welfare. There is a potential hazard, here, both of weaving religious schools into the fabric of government and of making all higher education an adjunct of the military system. The constitutional difficulty lies both in the immense force of the pull of national defense in a period of world crisis, and in the absence of action by complainants who would have standing in court. Judicial decisions can be made only in litigated cases.

In the category of difficult but not crucial problems, yet unresolved under the First Amendment, two stand out: (1) Does the prohibition of government aid to religious establishments make it unlawful to exempt church property from taxation? (2) Is "obscenity" to be treated in the same way as speech and press in general?

The First Amendment is construed to prohibit any form of financial aid to religious institutions, but to permit their inclusion in public services such as police and fire protection, zoning, etc. Exemption from taxation unquestionably is a financial benefit, but the constitutional question is more complex. Property devoted to religion is exempted along with that of many other nonprofit institutions serving community purposes—libraries, museums, art galleries, hospitals, schools, colleges, charitable establishments, cemeteries, churches. So the question can be worded in several ways:

Is tax exemption unconstitutional because it is a financial benefit conferred by the government?

Must churches be singled out because they are devoted to religion, and forced to pay a tax from which all other nonprofit institutions with community values are exempted?

Is there a constitutional difference between prohibiting the use of public funds to aid a church, and omitting the church from a requirement selectively made to use private funds to aid the public? It would be rash to look to past judicial decisions for answers to questions such as these.

From religion to obscenity is a short jump over the high hurdle of morality. All of the forces arrayed for the one are deployed against the other. But what is obscenity? There lies the trouble. What is it? The fireside banter of Chaucer's Canterbury Pilgrims was disgusting obscenity to Victorian-type moralists whose co-ed granddaughters shock the Victorian-type moralists of today. Words that are obscene in England have not a hint of impropriety in the United States, and *vice versa*. The English language is full of innocent words and phrases with obscene ancestry.

The courts have tried from the start to establish workable tests of what is obscene and who is to decide it. It seemed in 1884 that the New York Court of Appeals settled the matter when it upheld the conviction of August Muller, a New York City bookstore clerk, on the charge of "selling indecent and obscene photographs, representing nude females in lewd, obscene, indecent, scandalous and lascivious attitudes and postures." The words of the statute, said Judge Charles Andrews, "are words in common use, and everybody of ordinary intelligence understands their meaning." The issue was not whether the photographs were obscene or indecent *in the opinion* of witnesses, or of a class of people, but whether they were so *in fact*. That question was "one of the plainest that can be presented to a jury, and under the guidance of a discreet judge there is little danger of their reaching a wrong conclusion." So the discreet New York judges upheld the conviction of Book Clerk Muller for selling replicas of world-famous paintings that had been exhibited at the Salon of Paris, the Philadelphia Centennial Exposition, and elsewhere, and would be considered obscene today only if somebody put fig leaves on them.

The Muller decision was based on an English case, *Regina* v. *Hicklin* (1868), which stated that the test of an obscene book was whether the tendency of the matter objected to was to deprave or corrupt those whose minds were open to such immoral influences, and who might come in contact with the offensive article. The *Hicklin* test was followed for a good many years in American courts but gradually gave way to a test described by the United States Supreme Court in 1957 as: "whether to the average person, applying contemporary community standards, the dominant theme of the material taken as a whole appeals to prurient interest." To have a "prurient interest," the Court said, is to have "a tendency to stir lustful thoughts." Applied to persons rather than books, and tested by the reaction of the average male, might that not lead to a five-to-four decision either way on the comparative stimulus to lustful thoughts of female nudity and the sarong and veil?

In obscenity cases juries often agree, witnesses never do and judges almost never. The reasons are not far to seek. First, obscenity is a matter of taste and social custom, not of fact. Secondly, the restraint of obscenity inevitably impinges upon freedom of speech and of the press, now including motion pictures and television. This impingement was acknowledged and approved in the 1957 case referred to above, *Roth* v. *United States.* Here Justice Brennan wrote for the majority: "We hold that obscenity is not within the area of constitutionally protected speech and press." That was firing a ten-inch shell to hit a polecat in a henhouse. It was tempered by contrasting the protection given "all ideas having even the slightest redeeming social importance" with "the rejection of obscenity as utterly without" that quality. That seemed to imply that nothing is obscene, in law, if it has the slightest social importance. But Justices Douglas and Black asserted in dissent that "any test that turns on what is offensive to the community's standards is too loose, too capricious, too destructive of freedom of expression to be squared with the First Amendment. . . . Government should be concerned with antisocial conduct, not with utterances."

The *Roth* decision actually seemed to multiply standards instead of creating one. Several *per curiam* decisions (without opinions) were followed in 1964, in *Jacobellis* v. *Ohio,* by a six-to-three decision absolving the French film *Les Amants* of obscenity, but with a five-way disagreement on the reasons for absolution and two different reasons for dissent. In this case Justices Brennan and Goldberg sought a national standard, in line with the *Roth* decision, to determine what is obscene. Chief Justice Warren was ready to turn that problem back to the states. Justice Stewart considered everything except "hardcore pornography" to be protected by the First Amendment. What that was he could not define but, said he, "I know it when I see it." Justices Black and Douglas, adhering to the "absolutes" of liberty, declared that the conviction of anybody for "exhibiting a motion picture abridges freedom of the press as safeguarded by the First Amendment."

What is the reason for this multiple sclerosis of the judicial faculty? It is due to the fact stated above, that obscenity is a matter of taste and social custom, not of fact. The ban on obscenity is a tabu, as deeply imbedded in civilized society as in that of the most primitive savage tribe; subject to constant alteration by society itself, but completely dominant in its period of power. The resulting conflict cannot be resolved by constitutional law, but there may be an approach to a solution in practice. That is to treat violation of the universal tabu in words and pictures as disorderly action, akin to nakedness in a public street. That furnishes no guide whatever in the actual drawing of a line between speech and action. It merely sets up the tabu as a supreme court of human fallibility, and leaves the way open for absolute protection of the human freedoms whose protection is the overriding imperative in a free society.

CHAPTER 39
Fear of Freedom

"Congress shall make no law . . . abridging the freedom of speech or of the press."

Judging these words by what they say, they form a mandate, clear in meaning, absolute in force. Yet for the greater part of two centuries they have been treated by Congress, the Supreme Court and the nation as a flexible admonition, applied with varying degrees of strictness and laxity. In general, the protection of freedom has been lax when there was most need to be strict, with gains in strictness when there was little to risk by being lax.

For such an anomaly there is but one explanation—fear of the freedom that the words proclaim. Blessed with a form of government that requires universal liberty of thought and expression, blessed with a social and economic system built on that same foundation, the American people have created the danger they fear by denying to themselves the liberties they cherish. The abridgments of freedom are not thrust upon the nation by a hereditary monarch, hereditary peers, proprietors of entailed estates and crown-appointed judges, as they were in England from the Middle Ages up to the middle of the nineteenth century. In the United States the denials of liberty are a by-product of the power of the people to establish or destroy that liberty. Guarantees planted in a written Constitution as a safeguard against impulsive legislatures, arbitrary executives and thoughtless popular majorities have been reduced to feeble maxims unheeded by those who give them that misnomer.

Fear, translated into a supposed necessity for self-preservation, produced the first great denial of freedom in passage of the Sedition Act of 1798. Fifty years later its unconstitutionality was acknowledged and asserted by Congress, in the wording of the act reimbursing the descendants of those who had paid illegal fines. But another three quarters of a century went by before the first member of the Supreme Court spoke up—and this in dissent—to reject the legal concept on which that violation of the Constitution was based. Had such a freedom-destroying precept of freedom been written into the Constitution in 1798 it could have received a composite wording from the speeches in support of the sedition bill. Freedom of the press would then have been safeguarded in approximately these terms:

"Congress shall make no law abridging the freedom of the press, but may impose any restriction upon it that is sanctioned by the common law of England, or that is necessary to protect Congress and the President from such criticism as tends to undermine or weaken public confidence in them; and no well-defined law to regulate that freedom shall be considered an abridgment of it, provided the right of trial by jury be preserved and truth be admitted as a defense in any trial."

Except for the eleven words actually taken from the Constitution, this imaginary amendment is an almost literal transcript of outstanding phrases in the speeches of Harrison G. Otis, Robert Goodloe Harper and John Allen, the three Federalist lawyers who almost monopolized the argument for constitutionality of the sedition bill in 1798. Atrocious as such a draft is seen to be, in the lurid light cast on it by the history of that iniquitous law, there is not a glint of power in it that does not glare also through the chinks and loopholes of the "balancing test"—the twentieth-century method of reducing the First Amendment from a mandate to an admonition.

The transition from one test to the other—from misused common law to discretionary abridgment—shows plainly the paramount effect of fear. In 1798 there was at least a pretense of upholding the literal command of the Constitution. Congressional supporters and judicial interpreters of the Sedition Act affirmed that this law did not "abridge" freedom of the press because that freedom was merely what Blackstone called it—the absence of prior restraint. A publisher could not be prohibited by law from printing the statement that President John Adams delivered up Jonathan Robbins "to the mock trial of a British court martial." But if he did print it he could be sent to prison for doing so, as Editor Thomas Cooper did and was.

The modern "balancing test" follows a different formula to the same end. It is admitted that punishment of a publisher for what he prints *does "abridge"* the freedom of the press. It is admitted that the Constitution says it shall not be abridged. But, say the balancers, it is no violation of the Constitution to do what it says shall not be done, if there are reasonable grounds for doing it. Balance these two tests against each other. The one employing Blackstone's common-law definition does no violence to the English language and no more damage to the victim. The balance is perfect in the grievous wounds the two systems of evasion inflict on the Constitution.

As an actual source of federal power, the English common law of seditious libel vanished in 1812, when Marshall's Supreme Court held that the common law is not in the Constitution. But it could still be asserted, by those who wished to believe it, that the framers of the First Amendment intended to authorize the British system of abridgment when they wrote the command that there should be NO abridgment. Those who feared freedom did so assert. St. George Tucker, in his 1803 annotated edition of Blackstone's *Commentaries,* so completely discredited the Blackstone definition of freedom of the press that it might have passed out of the American lawyer's lexicon—except that the need of later annotations caused Tucker's work to be supplanted and his words to be forgotten. Not completely so, for in the famous *Abrams* case of 1919, Defense Counsel Harry Weinberger quoted Tucker's statement of what the framers intended and the people understood to be the political freedom protected by the First Amendment. Said Tucker in his Note G:

"Every individual, certainly, has a right to speak or publish, his sentiments on the measures of government; to do this without restraint, control, or fear of punishment for so doing, is that which constitutes genuine freedom of the press."

The government's attempt to refute this early statement of libertarian purposes is what brought the protesting words of Justice Holmes: "I wholly disagree with the argument of the Government that the First Amendment left the common law as to seditious libel in force." Other issues in the *Abrams* prosecution caused that feature of the case to be undeveloped in the Court opinions, but the attempt of the government to refute Tucker lays bare the basic struggle between freedom of the mind and tyrannical repression in English and American history.

The almost inconceivable fact is that the Solicitor General's attempted reply to Tucker was overtly and admittedly grounded on the "Goodrich Report" presented to the House of Representatives on February 21, 1799, defending the obnoxious Sedition Act against the rising demand of the public for its repeal. Quoting the First Amendment, Solicitor General Alexander C. King emphasized (as the 1798-1800 supporters of the Sedition Act did) that Congress was to make no law *respecting* an establishment of religion or *prohibiting* the free exercise thereof, whereas "in regard to the freedom of the press it is merely provided that the right thereto shall not be *abridged*." The purpose, said he, was "to fix the liberty of the press" by the law on the subject prior to the adoption of the Constitution. What that liberty was then "it shall continue to be, no more, no less." King then revealed and sanctified the source of the meaning he intended to give it:

"This meaning is attributed to the Constitution by the committee of the House of Representatives reporting on the alien and sedition laws in 1799 (citation). It is inconceivable that a committee of the House would have dared at that time to give an incorrect interpretation of the meaning of the Constitution on such an important point."

As a tribute to the cherubic innocence and political piety of Congress, that remark by a hard-boiled South Carolina railroad lawyer deserves a place beside Justice Johnson's 1821 opinion in *Anderson* v. *Dunn*. The Solicitor General proceeded to define freedom of the press as understood in English law at the time the First Amendment was written. It was not necessary, he thought, to adopt the view of Blackstone that the liberty of the press "consisted merely in freedom from censorship or licensing, although this view has great authority in its favor." The better way to look at the matter was that of Sir James Stephen in his *History of the Criminal*

Law of England, vol. 2, pp. 348, 349. There, after citing Lord Mansfield and Lord Kenyon in support of Blackstone's definition as the law of England, Stephen "states that such, however, was not public opinion, and hence 'the law and common practice had come into direct contradiction to each other.' " This prospective modification of English law, in the Solicitor General's opinion, embodied the original purpose of the First Amendment:

"In other words, it was a transition period, and it would be unfair to the makers of the Constitution to suppose that they meant to adopt a view which the English people were about to discard."

The First Amendment was written in 1789. Stephen published his *History* in 1883. So what the Solicitor General of the United States was telling the Supreme Court in 1919 was that freedom of the press was and "shall continue to be" what it was in 1789 under the common law then current. But since by 1883 British public opinion had overthrown that law, it must be considered that the American framers intended freedom of the press to mean in 1789 what it came to mean in England in 1883.

That argument was something more than a display of reasoning for men to marvel at. It was a reluctant admission that public opinion can override the common law, that freedom was not frozen by Blackstone, Mansfield, or the 1799 House committee on which Mr. King so touchingly relied. What then were the permissible abridgments of the freedom that Congress was forbidden to abridge? For this too the Solicitor General relied on Sir James Stephen, whose definition of seditious libel was accepted by "all the judges" in 1886. This in its major aspect was any utterance intended to bring the queen or government "into hatred or contempt." That applied perfectly to the indictment of Jacob Abrams (based on the wording of the Espionage Act of May 16, 1918) charging him with "language intended to bring the form of government of the United States into contempt, scorn, contumely and disrepute." Here then, we are told, was the original meaning of freedom of the press as understood by everybody except St. George Tucker. Having made this much of a concession to progress the Solicitor General set up a stop sign:

"It is, however, proper to claim that no liberty of the press was conceived of which included the unlimited right to publish a seditious libel. No claim of that sort was ever made by any respectable person."

Apparently James Madison was no more respectable than Tucker. For Madison was *refuting the same House committee report relied on in the Abrams brief* when he said that the First Amendment "declared the press to be wholly exempt from the power of Congress." He was addressing himself to those same congressional upholders of the Sedition Act when he asked rhetorically, "Is then the Federal government . . . destitute of every authority for restraining the licentiousness of the press, and for shielding itself against the libelous attacks which may be made on those who administer it?" Answering his own question he rejected suggested sources of power, and said that "above all, if it be expressly forbidden by a declaratory amendment to the Constitution, the answer must be, that the Federal government is destitute of all such authority."

Seemingly familiar with that devastating contradiction of the government's position in *Abrams,* the Solicitor General sought to escape it by this limitation of the common-law offense of seditious libel as carried into American law:

"It is an offense, like treason and seditious conspiracy, of a nature directly affecting the existence of the Government itself. The act of May 16, 1918, however, does not adopt the common law offense in its full stature, but limits it to publications concerning the very form of government itself, as distinguished from criticism, no matter how violent and abusive, of public officials."

Justice Holmes replied in his dissenting opinion that the Abrams circulars "in no way attack the form of government of the United States." True, but he said too little. False conviction on such a charge is trivial (except to the man spending twenty years in prison) compared with the violence done to our form of government by making it a crime to attack it by even the most abusive spoken or published words. Such a statutory offense is not merely "like treason." It is an exact adaptation to our form of government of that part of the 1351 treason statute of Edward III that the framers omitted from the American Constitution: "compassing or imagining the death of the king." Here in the Espionage Act of

1918 was the crime of "compassing or imagining the death of republican government"[1]—a virtual resurrection of constructive treason, which Chief Justice Marshall was supposed to have destroyed forever with his opinion in *Ex parte Bollman* and his rulings in the treason trial of Aaron Burr.

Like all laws that undertake to punish words instead of actions, the 1918 espionage act was conceived in fear and enforced in terror. Justice Holmes was a man who felt no fear, but he wrote in an age of fear for men who feared. His rejection of the common law as a source of power to punish seditious libel did not by any means eliminate that power, even in his own mind. It hastened the shift to the "balancing test," which earlier in 1919 he had sought to restrict by the doctrine of "clear and present danger." Words could be punished only if they created imminent danger of producing the evils that Congress had a right to prevent. Libertarians hailed that doctrine with joy. They continued to applaud it until thirty years' trial proved that every danger—dim, distant or totally nonexistent —was clear and present to judges who thought it to be so.

The shortcomings of that test were manifest at all times, but were at their minimum during the all-too-brief period—from 1943 to 1946—when seven appointees of President Franklin D. Roosevelt were simultaneously on the Court. Four of these—Justices Black, Douglas, Murphy and Rutledge—almost invariably stood together in upholding the Bill of Rights, and they gained a fifth recruit often enough to give the Court a libertarian cast. By the beginning of the term in October 1949, the deaths of Chief Justice Stone and Justices Murphy and Rutledge had more than reversed the balance. Three more years passed, with alarming erosion of civil liberties, before the appointment of Earl Warren as Chief Justice to succeed Fred Vinson began the creation of what came to be known as the "Warren Court." By a combination of what some called "happy accidents" in the Eisenhower selections and deliberate design in that of John F. Kennedy, the Court by October 1962 ranged from a consistent majority to unanimity in support of the rights and liberties of all Americans—and was assailed with cries for impeachment by the enemies of those rights.

The low point for the Bill of Rights was reached in 1951, in what appeared on its face to be a striking victory for a mistreated minority. In *Beauharnais* v. *Illinois* the Supreme Court upheld the criminal-libel conviction of an anti-Negro agitator under a state law punishing slanderous attacks on racial or religious groups. The defamatory circular—a petition for a city ordinance to keep Negroes in their ghetto—had no sympathizers among the four justices who defended it as an exercise of the constitutional right to petition. There was ample warrant, however, for Justice Black's warning that minority groups should consider the ancient remark, "Another such victory and I am undone." Justice Frankfurter, writing for the Court, upheld the Illinois antidefamation law, on the ground that "libel of an individual was a common-law crime," punished as such in the colonies and all the states. Libel of a well-defined group being no less a threat to the peace and welfare of the state, it was equally subject to restriction.

Such reasoning undermined the Fourteenth Amendment and threatened to vitiate the First as a federal restraint. But the Frankfurter opinion did not so much as mention the First Amendment, thus heightening the impression, made by reliance on the common law, that the Court was silently repudiating the absorption of the First into the Fourteenth Amendment. Justices Black and Douglas, in the former's dissenting opinion, hammered on this point and the weakening of the liberties themselves. A devastating blow had been struck against the "unequivocal First Amendment command that its defined freedoms shall not be abridged." Justices Reed and Jackson dissented more narrowly, but the latter took occasion to agree with Holmes and Brandeis (in their *Abrams* dissent) that the Sedition Act of 1798 violated the Constitution.

Eleven years passed before the damaging potential of the *Beauharnais* decision became fully manifest, but by that time the personnel of the Court was greatly altered. The issue was faced, surprisingly, in the field of civil law, in the damage suit of an Alabama police commissioner against the *New York Times,* decided March 9, 1964. The alleged offense was publication of an advertisement charging unnamed Birmingham police authorities with contributing to a wave of terror against Negroes. An Alabama jury awarded the full amount sued for, $500,000, and the state supreme court affirmed the verdict, relying principally on a statement in *Beauharnais* v. *Illinois* that the Constitution does not protect libelous publications. The suit, judgment and affirmation all smacked of action *in terrorem* against a free press.

The United States Supreme Court, in reversing this judgment, presented some *dicta* on seditious libel that came close to wiping the slate clean. "In the court of history," wrote Justice Brennan, the judicially untested Sedition Act of 1798 had been held invalid. Quoting Madison's statement that in a republic "the censorial power is in the people over the government," he declared that neither factual error nor defamatory content removes the constitutional shield from criticism of official conduct. And what a state could not do by means of a criminal statute was likewise beyond the reach of its civil law of libel. Here was the limitation:

"The constitutional guarantees require, we think, a federal rule that prohibits a public official from recovering damages for a defamatory falsehood relating to his official conduct unless he proves that the statement was made with 'actual malice'—that is, with knowledge that it was false or with reckless disregard of whether it was false or not. . . . As to the *Times*, we . . . conclude that the facts do not support a finding of actual malice."

Justices Black and Douglas, concurring through the former, regarded the concept of "actual malice" as too abstract and elusive to be an effective protector of free speech. "I base my vote to reverse," wrote Justice Black, "on the belief that the First and Fourteenth Amendments do not merely 'delimit' a State's power to award damages to 'a public official against critics of his official conduct,' but completely prohibit a State from exercising such a power." The power of the federal government to award civil damages was in his opinion "perfectly nil," and the state's power to do so was taken away when the First Amendment became binding on the states. "An unconditional right to say what one pleases about public affairs is what I consider to be the minimum guarantee of the First Amendment."

Justice Goldberg, likewise joined by Justice Douglas, took a position between the Court and Black opinions. From "the impressive array of history and precedent marshaled by the Court," he was confirmed in his belief that the constitutional protection of the right of public criticism was not met by the standard of "actual malice." This was not to say that the Constitution protects defamatory statements directed against the *private conduct* of a public official or private citizen. But in his view the First and Fourteenth Amendments "afford to the citizen and to the press an absolute, unconditional privilege to criticize official conduct despite the harm which may flow from excesses and abuses."

All three opinions in the *New York Times* case put the stamp of unconstitutionality on the Sedition Act of 1798, either by flat averment (Black and Goldberg plus Douglas) or by the tenor and documentation of the Court's statement that it had been so held "in the court of history." (A formal ruling against a *criminal* statute would have been out of place in a *civil* case.) That seemed to point to the rejection of any federal law making it a crime (in the words of the Sedition Act of 1798) to engage in "false, scandalous *and malicious*" criticism of public officials. Yet criticism with actual malice was left punishable by civil damages under state law. Thus the decision and opinions left areas of uncertainty capable of dangerous expansion by judges and juries. The uncertainties lay in the meaning of "actual malice," in the distinction drawn but not defined between defamation of public and private persons, in the distinction between the public and private conduct of public officials, and in the question whether criminal prosecution and civil suits were on a complete or partial constitutional parity.

The last question cannot be answered by a simple conclusion that the First Amendment forbids both or permits both. Civil actions for slander and libel developed in early ages as a substitute for the duel and a deterrent to murder. They lie within the genuine orbit of the common law, and in the distribution of American sovereignty they fall exclusively within the jurisdiction of the states. The First Amendment further assures their exclusion from the federal domain. The Fourteenth Amendment, by absorbing the First, unquestionably gives the Supreme Court authority to block state use of civil suits as a substitute for laws of seditious libel. But considering the differences in derivation, in purpose, in value to society, and in the natural location of power, there seems to be no compelling constitutional reason to bar private suits. The most absolute construction of the First Amendment, as applied to the states by the Fourteenth, would permit a line to be drawn between the spurious common law of seditious libel and the genuine common law of civil liability for defamation of private character. It is the misuse of civil liability that offends the Constitution.

If this reasoning has validity, there is but one point at which the literal application of the First Amendment to the states may be at odds with "instant justice." That is in the banning of criminal action against the publishers of blackmail sheets—publishers who are immune to civil damage suits because they have no property. But levying blackmail is a crime in itself and criminal prosecution for publication of slanderous articles is an easy substitute for enforcing or strengthening the blackmail laws. A cry went up, all over the country, when the Supreme Court in repeated decisions cracked down on police who chose the easy method of obtaining convictions of criminals through the use of confessions unlawfully obtained. That, replied defenders of the Court, called for better police work and was no excuse for violating the Constitution. No more should the Court sanction a violation of the Constitution in order to cope with those who violate the laws against blackmail. There is no difference in principle between disregarding the Constitution in order to achieve a good objective and doing so to let in the nefarious criminal law of libel.

Further light but less than full illumination was thrown on the issues raised in the *New York Times* case when *Garrison* v. *Louisiana* came up for re-argument in November 1964. It was a tough case, in which the Court had been unable to muster a majority either way in the previous spring. District Attorney Jim Garrison of New Orleans was convicted under a Louisiana defamation statute for the published observation (mild by Louisiana standards) that eight judges of the Criminal District Court had let a backlog of cases build up because of inefficiency, laziness, excessive vacations, and restrictive actions that hampered investigations of vice in New Orleans. The conviction was reversed unanimously, but with a rather sharp division between the Court opinion and three concurring opinions by Justices Black, Douglas and Goldberg.

All nine justices accepted the Court's view, expressed by Justice Brennan for six members, that the Louisiana statute was unconstitutional. The three other members did not disagree with but went beyond the Court's statement of its fatal defects, which were (1) that it punished *true* statements made with "actual malice," defined by the Louisiana courts to mean "hatred, ill will or enmity," and (2) that it punished *false* statements if made with ill will, regardless of whether they were *known* to be false. The whole Court moved away from the idea of "criminal prosecution for private defamation." Finally, all the judges agreed that where criticism of public officials is concerned, civil libel laws and criminal libel statutes are governed by the same constitutional standards. The cleavage came on what those standards should be.

The Court applied to criminal libel the *New York Times* civil-suit rule of "actual malice," which was stated in both cases to be "knowing or reckless falsehood." In the case of public officials, wrote Justice Brennan, "the interest in private reputation is overborne by the larger public interest, secured by the Constitution, in the dissemination of truth." The rule held "even where the utterance is false," unless the falsehood was knowing or reckless:

"The use of calculated falsehood, however, would put a different cast on the constitutional question. Although honest utterance, even if inaccurate, may further the fruitful exercise of the right of free speech, it does not follow that the lie, knowingly and deliberately published about a public official, should enjoy a like immunity. . . . For the use of the known lie as a tool is at once at odds with the premises of democratic government and with the orderly manner in which economic, social, or political change is to be effected."

This brought the demurrer from Justice Douglas, joined by Justice Black, that if malice, evidenced by a knowingly false statement, is all that is needed to sustain a conviction for seditious libel, "inferences from facts as found by the jury will easily oblige." (That is, go back to the old common-law system of accusation by "innuendoes" concerning the meaning and intent of words.) It was a commonplace of life, he said, "that heat and passion subtly turn to malice in actual fact." When that is allowed to become a gloss on the First Amendment, freedom of political discussion is robbed of vitality and turns into something "pale and tame."

Justice Black, with Douglas concurring, expressed his belief that the First Amendment protects every person from either state or federal penalties, criminal or civil, for criticism of public officials. Requiring proof of malice in criticisms would not prevent public officials from punishing their critics, and such prosecutions would stifle the public discussion our Constitution guarantees. Justice Goldberg, writing briefly, reached much the same conclusion.

In the closing sentence of his concurring opinion Justice Black referred to the Court's unqualified affirmation in *Gideon* of the right to counsel after years of partial recognition, and said (emphasis added):

"I would hold now *and not wait to hold later* . . . that there is absolutely no place in this country for the old, discredited English Star Chamber law of seditious criminal libel." The Court did not accept that emphatic advice, but taking the *New York Times* and *Garrison* cases together, there was a distinct move in that direction. Justice Brennan's opinion in *Garrison* did not actually put him on the other side. His was a "Court opinion," not written to express his own view but to secure a unanimous decision (as it astonishingly did) among nine judges who according to report had split four ways at the first argument of the case.

The basis for a further advance was established by putting criminal libel and civil damage suits on a parity. Thus the limitations on libel laid down in the *New York Times* case were extended to the criminal field. This narrowed seditious libel to whatever the courts might find to represent "actual malice," evidenced by "knowing falsehood," "calculated falsehood," "reckless disregard of truth or falsity." All the implications were that this test would be applied with the strictness implicit in the famous exclamation "not while this Court sits." Such an application would frustrate terroristic civil suits for damages (though possibly piling heavy work on the Supreme Court) and come close to wiping out criminal libel *under state laws.* But what if future judges should sit on a different woolsack? What if Congress, goaded by some new excitement, should enact a law to punish *knowing or reckless falsehoods* uttered against public officials?

Here is the real question. How free, *constitutionally*, is freedom of speech that leaves "calculated falsehood" indictable under a seditious libel law? To realize the true nature of such a test, imagine that after reading *Garrison* v. *Louisiana* a few dozen "John Birchite" grand juries should return indictments against all the persons within their jurisdiction who had said publicly during the campaign, "Barry Goldwater is trigger-happy." The Supreme Court would unanimously strike down every conviction. But submit that question to a jury of 65,000,000 voters—submit it with instructions that "knowing falsehood" is punishable as "actual malice" under state law—and would not that jury vote 25,000,000 for conviction, 40,000,000 for acquittal? If those figures chanced to be reversed, with political power shifted accordingly, and with Supreme Court justices emotionally divided in the same ratio and direction, what would their decision be? Fantastic as this illustration is, it points to the truth of Justice Douglas's remark that "heat and passion subtly turn to malice in actual fact." In every such instance, under such a constitutional rule, conviction or acquittal would depend on the direction taken by heat and passion in the jury, if not also in the judges.

There is no greater fallacy than the belief that government can or ought to separate truth from error. Error, protected by freedom of speech, may outlive truth. But freedom dies when error is repressed by law, and error multiplies when freedom dies.

CHAPTER 40
Freedom from Fear

The great need of the present day is to cast off fear of freedom, and recapture the courage and vision of those who first erected the standard of American liberty. Basic to all liberties is freedom to think, to speak, to write, to publish one's thoughts, not merely without restraint, but without even thinking about the possibility of restraint. Men are truly free only when they do not have to ask themselves whether they are free.

Often and truly it has been said that the intent of the Constitution is to protect not only the ideas we cherish, but those we loathe. Yet so far has the opposite idea been carried, at various times and in various places, that people are frequently looked upon as enemies of the Constitution for praising and upholding its guarantees of liberty. All of this springs from a distrust of human society, which means at bottom a distrust of one's self. Those who feel the need to be told what to do, and to be made to do it, are most certain to endeavor to inflict their collective will on others, either through the medium of government or with disregard of it. These are the extremists—the Communists, the Fascists, the Minutemen, the superpatriots who think they honor the flag by compelling their neighbors to salute it. But the fear extends further. It reaches those who dread the uncertainties of the world they live in, the society whose present problems they cannot fathom, the future whose nature nobody can foretell.

What these fears have led to is directly visible in the fields of government and law. It is to be seen in the excesses of congressional investigating committees and the exaggerated emphasis on "secur-

507

ity checks" in government employment, extending far beyond the legitimate needs connected with national defense. It is seen in the almost hysterical fear that foreign spies or domestic traitors are penetrating the secrets of the State Department, in whose lower echelons, it is not too much of an exaggeration to say, the "top secret" label has been most useful in concealing from our own people the blunders already known to our adversaries. Indeed, one is moved to wonder whether the chief effect of turning the entire files of the State Department over to a potential enemy might not be to reassure him that our policies are what he refuses to believe they are.

These considerations do not in any way palliate the criminality of betraying such documents. Yet looking at the famous "Pumpkin Papers" of Alger Hiss, bizarrely hidden by Whittaker Chambers to dramatize his disclosure of them, one can only wonder, at a minimum, whether their political significance marked the incompetence of Hiss as a Soviet agent or the absence of anything worth delivering. Stalin robbed the Soviet treasury if he paid Chambers twenty rubles for them.

It is in the general field of political expression, however, that unthinking fears produce a blight upon the human mind. Such was not the attitude of those who wrote our guarantees of freedom. All that they feared was an open road or twisted bypath through which tyranny could strike in America as they had seen it strike in England and on the European Continent. They set up instruments of protection and barriers against attack: an independent judiciary, habeas corpus, trial by jury, strict limitation of treason, no bills of attainder, the manifold safeguards of due process of law, and above all else, the absolute command that no laws should be made to prohibit or curtail the freedoms of religion, speech, press and assembly.

Experience during nearly two centuries of American national life has shown that the defects lie in ourselves, not in those who proclaimed the freedoms. The bars those men set up were high enough, but a Congress smitten by panic pulled them down. The ignominy of the Sedition Act of 1798 produced a hiatus in repression that lasted more than a hundred years. When the pattern was resumed in 1917, the stigma still attaching to the word "sedition" was avoided by branding the new restrictions on speech and press a defense against "espionage." But the asserted source of power was the same as in 1798. The unqualified commands of the United States Constitution were made subordinate to the English common law of seditious libel.

And whence came this English common law of libel, so magisterially traced back to the fourteenth century through Mansfield, Blackstone, Raymond and the long arm of Coke? As has been shown in these pages it is not common law at all. It is a Star Chamber invention embossed with the antique heraldry of Lord Coke's imagination. The 1336 letter of Adam de Ravensworth, discovered by Coke in 1628 in the ancient King's Bench rolls, quoted by him in direct contradiction of its wording and meaning, furnishes the sole testimony in English history to the common-law heredity of seditious libel. This illegitimate offspring of the Goddess of Justice was conceived and delivered under the roof of the Star Chamber, and none knew this better than Coke himself, who was the consummating agent in both phases of the operation.

In resorting to common-law libel as a source of authority in 1798, the authors of the Sedition Act sought to hide its iniquity by permitting truth to be presented as a defense. That, their argument implied, was a greater freedom than was intended by the words of the First Amendment. Read once more Madison's reply to those who said they were *punishing only malicious falsehood:*

"This doctrine, united with the assertion, that sedition is a common law offense, and therefore within the correcting power of Congress, opens at once the hideous volume of penal law, and turns loose upon us the utmost invention of insatiable malice and ambition, which, in all ages, have debauched morals, depressed liberty, shackled religion, supported despotism, and deluged the scaffold with blood."

In all ages. It was Tudor and Stuart judges who deluged the scaffold with blood, but every other attribute of tyranny belonged to their sanctified successors in England, who reached back to the Star Chamber for the fictitious "common law of libel" that depressed liberty and debauched morals throughout the eighteenth century. In the United States that same common-law abridgment of freedom, metamorphosed into a "balancing test" between the positive commands of the Constitution and the negative inclinations of Congress, continues to vitiate the constitutional command that there shall be no abridgment.

With the common law of libel revealed to be what its early English critics believed but could not prove it to be—a sham and a fiction—what remaining excuse is there for not deciding that "make no law" means "make no law"? Some answer, *stare decisis*. But long-established precedent, as Justice Black observed in *Garrison*, did not prevent the injustice of *Betts* from being overruled in *Gideon*. The true answer is fear: fear of letting other people set forth ideas that fill us with horror. Justice Holmes voiced that thought, though not for himself, when he put forward his doctrine that freedom of speech and press may not be abridged except when the exercise of it creates a "clear and present danger." The illustration he gave, to support that limitation, has been repeated a hundred thousand times:

"The most stringent protection of free speech would not protect a man in falsely shouting fire in a theatre and causing a panic."

No, it would not. But free speech would not be involved. Such a false shout in such a place would be part of an inseparable combination of speech, action and criminal intent, with the action dominating and the intent proved by the falsity. Give the shout of "Fire" another setting. Let it be the command of a Gestapo officer, bringing death to a dozen victims lined up before his soldiers. Could he, tried at Nuremberg before Supreme Court Justice Jackson, plead our constitutional command that no law shall be made to abridge freedom of speech? As well claim that freedom of association would protect him, if he said nothing and brought his fist down in a gesture of command.

The rule of "clear and present danger" has failed, as it was bound to. Its defect was congenital. The rule was first applied to confirm a conviction, not to reverse it. Charles Schenck's circular, exhorting readers to petition Congress to repeal the 1917 Draft Act, was replete with the jargon of a socialistic pacifist who believed that Wall Street plutocrats had dragged the United States into World War I to serve the interests of England. The typical reaction of a nonpacifist reader was indignation and anger, quickly transmuted into alarm. But what actual or potential effect did these wild phrases have? Newspaper reproduction extended their circulation from a few thousand into tens of millions, and they did nothing except stimulate the sale of Liberty Bonds.

Extend the inquiry into all suppressions of speech and press designed to save the country from "clear and present danger" both in war and peace. What is the result? The punishments testify without exception to the unwarranted fears of those who inflicted them, or to the impelling force of righteous or unrighteous anger. There is a point, not always easy to ascertain, at which inciting speech shades into disorderly action, clearly unlawful. Spoken or published words may be overt acts of treason, as when troop movements in wartime are disclosed to an enemy through coded broadcasts or cryptic want ads. In a zone of battle, the laws of war surmount all others or may themselves be forgotten. But these are matters to be handled initially by the executive agencies of government and ultimately by judges, all aiming at security and justice in an aura of liberty. Necessity without law may sometimes have to breach the wall of freedom, but the breach cannot be made by constitutional law without opening the way to limitless invasion of human rights.

The First Amendment stands where it does, numerically, because two trivial articles ahead of it were not ratified. But the substance of it is what makes it truly First. It will hold that place only if the American people support the freedoms it endows them with. "The people," in the sense here meant, are not merely the millions of individuals living within a national area. They are also the state and the institutions of state that reflect the collective will: Congress, the Executive, the Courts, state governments, the newspapers, the wireless media, the schools and churches. From them is needed a consensus on the theme of liberty that will either make the First Amendment a symbol of the freedom of fearless men and women, or take it out of the Constitution as a broken monument to the vision of the country's Founders. If the decision is to make that vision a reality, the political freedoms of the First Amendment cannot mean less than this:

Congress has no power to restrain, license or censor speech or publications;

No power to define or punish any form of slander or libel;

No power to prohibit or abolish any political party or association or to punish membership or activity therein;

No power to restrain peaceable assembly for political purposes;

No power to compel testimony concerning political beliefs or associations.

By the force of the Fourteenth Amendment, all of these limitations on congressional action are equally binding on the individual states. Liberty cannot properly be less in state than in federal law, merely because state governments have lagged behind the popular ideas of liberty that found expression in the federal Constitution. Still less can this be so when the states have been misled by the fiction of a common law of libel that was invented by despots to serve the ends of tyranny.

Most of the animus built up against the Supreme Court during its libertarian periods has been grounded on opposition to specific decisions sustaining liberty, establishing equality, or upholding due process of law. In milder mood, some have objected that the Court was moving too far or too fast, with scant regard for long-established precedents. The impression of haste and disrespect is an illusion. The course taken by the Court has been forced on it by a hundred years of accumulated error. Where property rights are concerned, there may be reason to say that *knowing* what the law is, is more important than *what* it is. But human rights cannot be reduced to any such level. Where they are concerned it is the business of the Court to get rid of inherited error, not necessarily by going the whole distance in one step, but with due regard to justice when the steps are short. Human rights are not to be denied because some judge went wrong a hundred years ago. Judicial disagreements produce dissenting opinions, and dissenting opinions publicize the disagreements. They also educate the public, which then helps to turn the remedial dissents into the law of the land.

The most ancient errors are hardest to correct, partly because they become indurated by their antiquity. How greatly simplified the restoration of the Bill of Rights would be if the Supreme Court should put back into the Constitution the clause that it took out in the 1873 *Slaughter-House Cases.* Instead of struggling to make Canons of Decency cover "due process of law," or vice versa, and getting a bewildering sequence of conflicting answers, the judges would soon set up a logical, consistent, easily identifiable list of privileges and immunities that the states are forbidden to abridge. That would not solve a greater problem. The difficulty is vastly increased—indeed it is hard to maintain well-established liberties —when the wrong people ask for the right remedies. Lawyers who have the courage and sense of professional duty to act as counsel for Communists, though hating their doctrine and despising their conduct, are assailed as sympathizers with the system they condemn. Judges who insist on fair procedures for persons accused of crime are described as "bleeding hearts." Courts that protect the rights of citizens, lawlessly attainted by congressional committees, invite not only the scurrility of extremists but concerted attacks in Congress that put the very foundations of government in peril.

In 1958, half a dozen bills to override libertarian Court decisions or restrict the appellate power of the Supreme Court were defeated in the Senate by the skill and determination of Democratic Majority Leader Lyndon B. Johnson. In 1964, to undo the decision that outlawed "rotten boroughs" as a denial of equal protection of the laws, the House passed a bill to strip the Court of any jurisdiction in that field. The deadly aspect of all this lies in the fact that such a movement should ever reach the danger point in Congress.

Supreme Court decisions on the meaning and application of the Constitution may be right or wrong, good or bad, wise or rash. But when the power to make them is taken away by a vote in Congress, the Constitution ceases to be anything more than the gaunt skeleton of a frame of government, open to all the conflicting blasts of the winds of passion. Under the mounting effect of such a limitation there would soon be sixty constitutions of the United States, a different one in each of the ten federal circuit jurisdictions, and fifty different ones in the fifty states. But it never was intended that Congress should have such a destructive power. As construed in that body, Article III gives the Court appellate jurisdiction "with such exceptions, and under such regulations, as the Congress shall make." But with full support in the history of the clause, with complete logic, and with equal reliance on wording, the meaning is that Congress may make exceptions to the appellate power *to decide both law and fact.* The sole purpose of the "exceptions," as explained by Alexander Hamilton in *The Federalist* No. 81, was to guard against the possible extension of *equity* rules to cases in law, in which facts found by a jury are not reviewable on appeal.

The Supreme Court can and should reject any law curtailing its appellate jurisdiction, beyond the true meaning of the "exceptions" clause. But only the alert, intelligent, responsible part of the American people—from hod carrier to President—can furnish protection in advance against these rash and destructive attacks. Such a national understanding would work wonders in building a sense of responsibility in Congress, where few indeed are intentional destroyers.

As happens in virtually every area of public policy, this matter of popular support depends on the fundamental fitness of the people for self-government. That in turn is totally dependent on freedom of the mind. So we come back to the First Amendment as the foundation stone of the edifice of freedom, and to unrestricted freedom of thought and expression as the only sure guard against its crumbling. But there can be no freedom of thought without freedom from fear; no freedom from fear when there is fear of freedom.

The form of government so cherished by the American people would not be worth preserving if it could be blown over by the spoken or written words of any political minority. Still less would it be worth saving if nothing but forcible repression could maintain it. Time and again in history, proof has been given of American strength and stability founded on freedom and democracy. But again and again, irrational fears have swept the people and the government into destructive assaults on the very liberties to which we pin our existence as a self-governing republic and our happiness and dignity as individuals.

To be worthy of the American heritage, the people must live up to it. To retain it, they must shape their institutions and their thoughts for its retention. That calls for full recognition by the courts, the Congress, and most of all by the great body of the people, of the true nature of the complete Bill of Rights. They must accept, support and defend it as the bastion of the social order, the bulwark of the state, the guardian of the family and the individual. That will not put an end to political acrimony, or eliminate the extremists of the Left or Right. But it will establish a climate in which no political storm can become an irresistible whirlwind.

"If we advert to the nature of republican government," said Madison, "we shall find that the censorial power is in the people over the government, and not in the government over the people." When the American people recognize that profound truth, it will prevail and when it truly prevails it will vanish from the mind. For then there will be little need of a censorial power over the government, and no possibility of a censorial power over the people. Government and people will be one, in a nation free of fear and dedicated to freedom.

NOTES

Chapter 1

[1] Section 2 further provides that any abridgment of suffrage in a state shall proportionately reduce its representation. Sections 3 and 4 imposed penalties relating to participation in the war.

[2] The Twenty-Fourth Amendment was resorted to because the Senate filibuster was weaker against it than against the antipoll-tax bill that repeatedly passed the House of Representatives. The Supreme Court, with Justice Stone speaking for the majority in *United States* v. *Classic* (313 U. S. 299), virtually notified Congress that such a law would be upheld. Justice Stone said to the author of this book, "I showed them the way, didn't I?"

Chapter 2

[1] Gouverneur and Robert Morris both were delegates.

[2] To Americanize the British statute, "against the United States within their territories" was substituted for "against our Lord the King within his realm." The highest of high treasons at the time of Edward III was "compassing or imagining the death of the King." To that the framers paid no heed.

Chapter 3

[1] The library of John Mercer, Virginia lawyer, catalogued in 1770, contained approximately 315 general works, mostly of his-

tory, and 200 law books. Catalogue in Brock Collection, Huntington Library, San Marino, California.

Chapter 5

[1] In the *Annals of Congress,* the third person is used to some extent in reporting speeches.

Chapter 6

[1] Vermont's admission to the Union on March 4, 1791, made it necessary to have eleven states ratify, but the new state at once produced the extra ratification, before Virginia became No. 11.

Chapter 7

[1] "We fought not to free ourselves from a Constitution, but to preserve it. Ours was not a true revolution. It was a territorial secession and a resort to arms to preserve our existing Constitution. When we wrote our Constitution we naturally brought forward in the main our former unwritten Constitution."—Representative Hatton W. Sumners, chairman of the House Committee on the Judiciary, arguing orally for the House of Representatives as *amicus curiae* in *Jurney* v. *MacCracken,* 294 U.S. 125, at 132 (1935).

[2] Statute of Westminster the First, 3 Edw. 1, c. 34 (1275), printed in *British Statutes:* Revised Edition (1870), I, 24.

Chapter 8

[1] Penry was the real Martin Marprelate, or head of the group that wrote under that name.

[2] "All the judges of England" meant the twelve highest, drawn equally from the three courts of King's Bench, Common Pleas and Exchequer. They were brought together occasionally to give advisory opinions to the Crown, decide questions referred to them by trial courts before passing judgment, or, infrequently, to act as a court of appeals of lesser rank than the House of Lords.

[3] *State Trials,* IV, 1362.

[4] Rushworth, Thurloe and Clarendon, important sources for

the Lilburne story, all were among Madison's 1783 recommendations for reading by the Continental Congress.

Chapter 9

[1] Most of this chapter, and parts of Chapters 7 and 10, were
published in the *New York University Law Review*, January 1964,
Vol. 39, p. 1, under the title, "Seditious Libel: Myth and Reality."

[2] Quoted in 6 *Oxford English Dictionary* 237 (Murray ed. 1908).
Lord Clarendon in 1702-04 referred to John Lilburne collecting
and reading "all those libels and books, which had anciently, as well
as lately, been written against the church." *State Trials*, III, 1416.

Chapter 10

[1] Milton was referring to the Council of Trent, 1545-1563.

[2] The weight given to Twyn's Case is revealed by the citation
of it in William Hawkins' *Pleas of the Crown,* with this description: "It has also been adjudged, that . . . printing treasonable
positions, as that the king is accountable to the people, and that
they ought to take the government into their own hands, or publishing a book to prove that the king's government is antichristian
and heretical, etc., may be alleged as overt acts to prove the compassing the king's death."

Chapter 11

[1] Actually named Edmund Berry Godfrey but universally
known as Sir Edmundbury.

[2] Nathaniel Reading had acted as Bedloe's attorney, without fee,
in obtaining a pardon needed to qualify this convicted arsonist as
a witness against the men he was accusing of treason. Later, with
approval in royal circles, he became procedural counsel to the "Five
Popish lords" in the Tower. The lawyer transmitted messages between Bedloe and the lords concerning a softening of his intended
testimony against them. Bedloe betrayed Reading, who was convicted of a misdemeanor on his own statement that he delivered
Bedloe's application for a bribe.

Chapter 12

[1] Dr. Wakeman did furnish Father Ashby with a prescription, which the pharmacist who filled it produced in court. It was for a harmless remedy for gout and was written by the doctor's assistant.

[2] Miles Prance confessed in open court that every story he had told was false. Dangerfield was whipped and pilloried for the falsehoods in his published *Narrative*, and on his way back to prison was jabbed in the eye with a cane, dying of the blow.

Chapter 13

[1] Sidney's death obscured a minor monstrosity of the Rye-House trials—the decision to get troublesome Henry Cornish out of the London Council by convicting him of treason. This was not easy, for the only direct witness against him, Rumsey, had to contradict his own testimony given in an earlier trial. This exchange resulted:

"Cornish. But, Colonel, what is the reason that you have not accused me all this while?

"Rumsey. . . . I think I suffer for it and not you. It was compassion."

Three centuries later, compassion moved Whittaker Chambers, before denouncing Alger Hiss as his accomplice, to swear again and again that he knew of no espionage by him. Anybody, either with the piercing sarcasm of Sir John Hawles or as inescapable fact, can repeat about Chambers what Hawles said of Rumsey: "he perjured himself to save the prisoner, and then swore truth to hang him." *State Trials*, XI, 381, 455. Fred J. Cook, *The Unfinished Story of Alger Hiss* (1958).

Chapter 14

[1] John Tutchin is probably the only man in history who ever petitioned the King of England that he be put to death to escape the punishment inflicted on him. Tried by Chief Justice Jeffreys as a Monmouth rebel and acquitted when no witnesses appeared

against him, he was given a sentence for using a false name that worked out to seven years in prison with a flogging every two weeks. After he petitioned to be hanged, friends bribed Jeffreys into including him in a pardon. He was expected after that treatment to love the government.

[2] By cutting off the reading with an *"et cetera,"* the Attorney General avoided reading the part that showed the statute to be for the *discovery* of the *originator* of the falsehood, rather than to punish the repeater of it. See page 91 *ante.*

[3] Francklin was fined £100, imprisoned for a year, and required to furnish a large security for seven years' good behavior.

Chapter 16

[1] See Chapter 3 *ante.*

[2] Franklin's quotations agree completely with the 1724 edition of *Cato's Letters.* In later editions of *Cato,* "freeness" is changed to "freedom," with other minor alterations.

[3] It seems likely that Blackstone took his definition from Francklin, since it was not in the lawbooks, and Francklin's words were reprinted in James Ralph's widely read *Critical History of the Administration of Sir Robert Walpole.*

Chapter 17

[1] Lord Mansfield's deserved and lasting fame as a creator of merchant law has helped to obscure his bias and injustice in the field of criminal libel.

[2] See page 186 *ante.*

Chapter 18

[1] There was a less definite report that "Father of Candor" was Lord Chief Justice Pratt (Lord Camden) of the Court of Common

Pleas, but that probably reflected the hunt for somebody high enough to bestow the credit on.

[2] One of the Priestley-Blackstone-Furneaux pamphlets printed in Philadelphia, now owned by the University of Virginia, has an inventory of farm property penciled on the flyleaf.

[3] Compare Jefferson's immortal slogan: "I have sworn upon the altar of God eternal hostility against every form of tyranny over the human mind."

[4] The act of 2 Richard II (1378) broadened Edward I's statute of 1275 by which a repeater of "false news or tales" that threatened discord between *king and nobles* was to be imprisoned till he should bring in "the first author of the tale." Richard extended the law to cover "horrible and false lies" told about great men, "whereby debates and discords might arise betwixt the said Lords, or betwixt the Lords and Commons." Serjeant Maynard, defense counsel in the slander suit of *Lord Townsend* v. *Dr. Hughes* (2 Modern 150), told the Court in 1677 that "Upon this Statute of 2 Rich. 2, c. 5, there was no action brought till 13 Henry 7, which was above an hundred years after the making of that law." Later christened *"De Scandalis Magnatum"* (of the slander of great men), it became highly popular after Charles the Second's judges ruled (1 Ventris 60) that debatable words, always construed with minimum offensiveness in slander suits at common law, must be "understood in the worst sense" under this statute, "that the honour of such great persons be preserved." Never was it a libel law or part of the common law. Sir John Comyn's *Digest of the Laws of England* placed it under Action upon the Case. (5th edition, I, 360.) See *Statutes at Large* (1870), I, 24, 222, 238.

Chapter 21

[1] Livingston, as previously reported in the *Aurora:* "The people of America . . . will resist this tyrannic system! The people will oppose, the States will not submit to its operation. They ought not to acquiesce, and I pray to God they never may."

[2] In punishing speech or writing designed to promote a separate government for Kentucky, the Virginia legislature had the excuse that another provision of the State Constitution made such an attempt criminal.

[3] Iredell's 1788 position is clarified in Chapter 23 *post.*

Chapter 22

¹ Peace was proclaimed on April 11, 1783. The Annapolis Convention on September 14, 1786, asked the Continental Congress to summon a constitutional convention to meet in Philadelphia on the second Monday in May next.

Chapter 24

¹ Fries, one of the "Northampton Insurgents" who organized to resist collection of the "French war" taxes, was sentenced to death for (among equally monstrous acts of treason) threatening to lock a tax assessor in a stable and feed him on rotten corn. President Adams pardoned Fries.

Chapter 25

¹ That is, the House of Commons was responsible to the people and the ministers were responsible to Parliament.

Chapter 26

¹ The *Annals of Congress* (X, 404) by error include Bayard's amendment in Macon's original resolution.

Chapter 29

¹ The amendment has been assailed, though never in the courts, because ratification of it was one of the preconditions set up by law for the full restoration of the seceding states to participation in the government of the Union.

² The 1774 Declaration of Rights, asserting that the American colonists possessed the natural and inalienable rights, liberties and immunities of natural-born British subjects, placed heavy emphasis

on the right of petition, and of being tried by a jury of the vicinage. *Journals of the Continental Congress,* October 14, 1774.

Chapter 32

[1] In *Holden* v. *Hardy,* 169 U. S. 366, holding that due process of law required just compensation for private property taken for public use.

[2] The four included two that were not among the six, raising to eight the number that had or desired constitutional protection. Vermont had such a provision before statehood, raising the total to nine out of the fourteen states that ratified the first ten amendments.

[3] Rushworth, *Collections,* I, 663, the Monday after April 25, 1629.

[4] The year 1629 was the busiest one in John Winthrop's life. He obtained the charter of the Massachusetts Bay Colony in March, dropped his law practice and was absorbed for the next year in organization of the colonial expedition, which sailed in March 1630.

[5] See Chapter 27.

Chapter 34

[1] The shift of opinion inside the Court was more apparent than real. Owing to the rush of work at the close of the term, in June 1940, Justice Stone's dissenting opinion was not read by other justices until after the decision was announced. Justices Black, Douglas and Murphy at once told Justice Stone that they agreed with him and would stand with him at the first opportunity. This information was given to the author by Justice Stone more than a year before the change of position took place, which was in *Jones* v. *Opelika,* 316 U.S. 584 (1942).

[2] The three-penny tax on tea that led to the American Revolution.

[3] The treaty with Tripoli reached the United States after John Adams became President. It had been accepted and signed on

February 10, 1797, by Commissioner Plenipotentiary David Humphreys, President Washington's personal representative in Europe and his trusted friend.

Chapter 35

[1] The *Aurora* had corrected this error. The bill ultimately passed the Senate but was defeated in the House.

[2] In 1873, when Simonton as general manager of the Associated Press was exposing the stupendous corruptions of the Grant Administration, this 1857 vote of expulsion was made the core of scurrilous anonymous assaults on his character.

Chapter 36

[1] A second subpoenaed witness was protected from a United States marshal by his armed neighbors in Ohio. A third was arrested in Massachusetts but freed on a writ of habeas corpus by the state supreme court. The fourth could not be found.

[2] Impolitic indeed was the Hyatt imprisonment. The way his attorney, John Andrew, faced up to the committee led to his election as governor of Massachusetts that same year. Through prodigious foresighted efforts he raised state troops that safeguarded the national capital before President Lincoln had time to organize its defense.

[3] Hansard, the official printer, was ordered to pay damages to Stockdale for publishing a defamatory document by order of the House.

[4] The congressman, to strike at the Jackson Administration, had made unwarranted charges of criminal misconduct in Indian trade affairs against Houston.

Chapter 37

[1] Chairman Martin Dies started the movement for the "rider" through a speech in the House, February 1, 1943, denouncing Lovett, Dodd, Watson and thirty-six others as "irresponsible, unrep-

resentative, crackpot, radical bureaucrats" (i.e., New Dealers) and affiliates of "Communist front associations." The *Lovett* decision was unanimous, but Justice Frankfurter in a concurring opinion rejected the conclusion that the "rider" was a bill of attainder. There was no infliction of punishment, he argued, because the "rider" did not say why the payment of salaries was forbidden; the Senate, by rejecting the "rider" five times, showed that it had no animus against the men and so did the President when he said that he signed the bill with reluctance and wished to keep the three officials in office. 328 U.S. 303. So the protests of the Senate and the President validated what they protested against!

[2] Secretary of War Eustis to Attorney General Pinkney, October 2, 1812; Pinkney to Major General Hall, October 20, 1812, National Archives, Military Book 6: 179, 202.

Chapter 39

[1] The author was not familiar with the *Abrams* brief when he wrote conjecturally in Chapter 2 about the omission from the Constitution of treason by "compassing or imagining the death of the republic," and the probable fanatic defense of it in modern times if it had been put in.

BIBLIOGRAPHICAL NOTES

These bibliographical notes are not intended as a reading guide to the immense amount of primary and secondary material bearing on the Bill of Rights. They are designed to aid the reader who wishes to consult the principal documentary material drawn on by the author, and to indicate books and articles that have brought his attention to various facets of the subject. The author especially regrets that, except at the cost of long delay in the writing of this book, he could not explore the rich resources of law journals on the subject. The result may well be that thoughts here presented have been earlier and better expressed elsewhere, and that such a study would have averted various errors of omission or commission. For whatever there may be of these nobody else bears responsibility.

Citations of *State Trials* in these notes are to the volumes and pages of Howell's *State Trials,* the complete collection published in 1816. In nearly every instance, however, state trials held early enough to have been familiar to Americans at the time of the constitutional convention of 1787 were described in Emlyn's 1730 edition of the *State Trials,* or in the supplementary volumes that were published from time to time during the next half century. Except occasionally for flavor, the spelling and capitalization of quoted material have been modernized. Adherence to ancient script would subordinate its meaning to antiquarian curiosity.

Chapter 1 of this book requires no notes.

Chapter 2
James Madison, *Notes of Debates in the Federal Convention of 1787,* various editions. Proceedings of August 20.

Trial of Thomas Becket, A.D. 1163, *State Trials*, I, 1.

Sir Matthew Hale, *Pleas of the Crown* (1736), chapters 10, 11 and 12.

J. W. Willis-Bund, *A Selection of Cases from the State Trials . . . Trials for Treason, 1327-1681* (1879-82). Treason statute of Edward III, vol. I, 7; repeal of treason statute of Edward III, 21-22; cases of Jack Cade, Thomas Burdett and the Duke of Clarence, 33-35. See also pages 46, 49, 59, 64 (on burning heretics), 111, 219 (Northern Rebellion), 282 (traitor O'Rourke). *State Trials*, I, 275 (1478) on Burdett and Duke of Clarence.

Trial of Nicholas Throckmorton, 1554, *State Trials*, I, 869.

Trial of Peter Messenger and 14 others, 1668, *State Trials*, VI, 879.

Trial of Sir Richard Grahme, 1691, *State Trials*, XII, at 678.

Colyer v. Skeffington, 285 Fed. 17 (1920) habeas corpus action through which U.S. Circuit Judge George W. Anderson released victims of the Palmer Red Raids.

Zechariah Chafee, *Freedom of Speech* (1920), for description of these raids.

Willard Hurst, "Treason in the United States," *Harvard Law Review*, vol. 58, (1944-1945).

Hurst, "Historic Background of the Treason Clause," *Federal Bar Association Journal*, VI, 305 (January 1945).

Chapter 3

Papers of James Madison, edited by William T. Hutchinson and William M. E. Rachal, I, 103, 105 (1962).

Catalogue of Library Company of Philadelphia, 1770 and supplement of 1838.

Benjamin Franklin, *Autobiography*, and continuation by Dr. George Stueber.

Madison, Notes of Debates, *op. cit.*, August 28, 30, September 12, 14, 1787.

Journals of the Continental Congress, January 24, 1783.

Paul de Rapin-Thoyras, *History of England*, I, Book X, 469.

Chapter 4

Jonathan Elliot, *Debates in the Several State Conventions . . .* (1836).

Annals of Congress, House of Representatives, June 8, 1789.

R. E. Rutland, *The Birth of the Bill of Rights* (1955).

Brant, *James Madison: Father of the Constitution* (1950), chapter 21.

Chapter 5

Annals of Congress, (House) July 21, August 13, 15, 17-22, September 10, 21; (Senate) August 25, September 2, 7, 9, 10, 1789.

Senate Journal, First Congress, first session, page 77.

Trial of William Penn and William Mead at the Old Bailey, 1670, written by themselves, *State Trials,* VI, 951.

Case of imprisonment of Edward Bushell for alleged misconduct as a juryman, 1670, *State Trials,* VI, 999.

Edward Dumbauld, "State Precedents for the Bill of Rights," *Journal of Public Law,* VII, No. 2 (1958).

Chapter 6

Brant, *James Madison: Father of the Constitution,* 286-87, 491.

Virginia General Assembly, *Journal of the Senate,* December 8, 11, 12, 1789.

Learned Hand, *Address before the New York State Board of Regents,* October, 1952.

Learned Hand, *The Bill of Rights* (lectures at Harvard University) (1958).

Roscoe Pound, *The Development of Constitutional Guarantees of Liberty* (1957), preface.

Edmond Cahn, "The Doubter and the Bill of Rights," *New York University Law Review,* November, 1958.

Hurtado v. California, 110 U. S. 516 (1884).

Chapter 7

Sir Edward Coke, *Second Institute of the Laws of England* (1628); *Third Institute* (1628), 174.

W. S. McKechnie, *Magna Carta: A Commentary on the Great Charter of King John* (1914).

Magna Carta as re-affirmed in 25 Edward I (1297), *The (British) Statutes:* Revised Edition (1870), I, 89.

Julius Goebel, *Cases and Materials on the Development of Legal Institutions* (1930).

Impeachment and attainder of Thomas, Earl of Lancaster, A.D. 1322, *State Trials,* I, 39; attainder reversed, 1327.

Case of Edmond Peacham, *State Trials,* II, 869 (1615).

Case of Hugh Pine, *State Trials,* III, 359 (1628).

I. S. Leadam, *Select Cases before the . . . Court of Star Chamber, 1477-1544* (1903-1911, Selden Society Publications).

Vale v. *Broke, ibid,* page 38.

Thomas Starkie, *Treatise on the Law of Slander and Libel* (1812).

Sir Edward Coke, *Reports,* 5 Coke 124, 125; 9 Coke 59.

Sir William Blackstone, *Commentaries on the Laws of England* (1765-69) , Book IV, chapter 11.

Thomas Erskine May, *Constitutional History of England* (1861-63), 1875 edition, II, 239-44.

Patterson v. *Colorado,* 205 U.S. 454 (1907); *Schenck* v. *United States,* 249 U.S. 47, 51-52 (1919); *Abrams* v. *United States,* 250 U.S. 616, 630 (1919).

Chapter 8

Proceedings against John Wickliffe, for Heresy, 1377, *State Trials,* I, 67.

Trial of Sir Thomas More, 1535, *State Trials,* I, 385.

John Strype, biography of John Whitgift, Archbishop of Canterbury (1718 edition in Huntington Library, republished by Clarendon Press in Strype's *Complete Works,* 1822-1840).

Trial of John Udall for felony, 1590, *State Trials,* I, 1271.

Trial of William Prynne for libel, in Star Chamber, 1633, Rushworth *Collections,* II, 220; *State Trials,* III, 561.

Trials of John Lilburne, *State Trials,* III, 1315 (1637); IV, 1269-1470 (1649). Proceedings in Parliament against Lilburne, Rushworth *Collections,* VII, 769. *Ibid,* VII, 844. Cf. *Dictionary of National Biography.*

A Collection of the State Papers of John Thurloe, I, 320, 367 (1742).

Trial of Charles I before the House of Commons Commission, 1649, *State Trials,* IV, 990, especially 1085-92.

A. V. Dicey, *Law of the Constitution,* tenth edition (1959), page 267.

The Leveller Tracts, 1647-1653, William Haller, editor (1944).

Alan Barth, "The Levellers and Civil Liberties," *Civil Liberties* (American Civil Liberties Union), March 1964.

Chapter 9

"The Case de Libellis Famosis, or of Scandalous Libels," 5 Coke 124, 125. John Lamb's Case, 9 Coke 59. *Third Institute,* 174.

Case of Adam of Ravensworth, A.D. 1336, in *Select Cases in the Court of King's Bench, Edward III,* edited by G. O. Sayles, Selden Society Publications vol. 76.

Case of the Archdeacon of Norfolk and his official, A.D. 1315, in Sayles' *Select Cases . . . Edward II,* Selden Society Publications vol. 74.

Chapter 10

Proceedings of the House of Commons against James Nayler for blasphemy, December 5-16, 1656, *State Trials,* V, 801.

Treason trial of John Twyn, 1663, 1 Kelyng 22; *State Trials,* VI, 513.

Trial of Benjamin Keach for libel, 1665, *State Trials,* VI, 701.

Trial of Benjamin Harris for libel, 1680, *State Trials,* VII, 925.

John Milton, Areopagitica, in *Works,* II, 427, 435, 436, 440 (1698).

Chapter 11

Memoirs of Sir John Reresby, 1634-1689, edited by Andrew Brown, 1936, page 365.

"Introduction to the Trials for the Popish Plot," including Bishop Burnet's account and Oates's narrative to the House of Lords, *State Trials,* VI, 1401. Oates's narrative is also in the *Journal of the House of Lords,* vol. 13, following October 31, 1678, pages 313-330.

Testimony of Sir Philip Lloyd, *State Trials,* VII, 651.

Hansard, *Parliamentary History of England,* October 21, 1678, IV, 1015-16, 1075-79.

Trial of Edward Coleman, November 27, 1678, *State Trials,* VII, 1.

Trial of Robert Green, Henry Barry and Lawrence Hill, February 5, 1679, *State Trials,* VII, 159.

Trial of Fathers Fenwick, Harcourt, Whitebread, Gavan and Turner, June 13, 1679, *State Trials,* VII, 311.

Trial of Richard Langhorn, June 14, 1679, *State Trials,* 417, especially pages 424, 431, 446-47, 490, 527.

Jane Lane (Elaine Dakers), *Titus Oates* (1949).

Articles in *Dictionary of National Biography* on Titus Oates, William Bedloe, Edward Coleman, Thomas Dangerfield, Sir Edmund Berry Godfrey, William Ireland, Sir Roger L'Estrange, Miles Prance and Israel Tonge.

Chapter 12

Trial of Sir George Wakeman *et al*, July 18, 1679, *State Trials*, VII, 591, especially 592, 619, 652-53, 685, 703.

Speech of L. C. J. Scroggs on libelous pamphlets, *State Trials*, VII, 701.

Trial of Lionel Anderson *et al*, January 17, 1680, *State Trials*, VII, 811.

Trial of Elizabeth Cellier, June 1680, *State Trials*, VII, 1043.

Account of the "Meal-tub Plot," *State Trials*, VII, 1055.

Trial of the Earl of Castlemaine, June 23, 1680, *State Trials*, 1067.

Memoirs of Sir John Reresby, op. cit., December 26, 1680. (Reinserted in part by error on same date 1681.)

Sir William Temple, *Works*, I, 339 (1740).

Proceedings in Parliament against the Five Popish Lords, Powis, Stafford, Petre, Arundell, Belasyse, October 25, 1678, to June 4, 1685, *State Trials*, VII, 1217-1576.

Trial of William Viscount Stafford before the Lords on impeachment for high treason, November 30-December 7, 1680, *State Trials*, VII, 1293-1568.

Slander action of Duke of York against Titus Oates, 1684, *State Trials*, X, 125; judgment reversed, 1327.

Trial of Titus Oates for perjury, May 8, 1685, *State Trials*, X, 1079, especially 1097-99, 1175.

Trial of Oates for another perjury, May 9, 1685, and later proceedings, *State Trials*, X, 1227-1330.

Sentencing of Miles Prance for perjury, on his confession, June 15, 1686, *State Trials*, VII, 228n.

Chapter 13

Seymour Schofield, *Jeffreys of the Bloody Assizes* (1937).

Sir John Hawles, Remarks on Colonel Algernon Sidney's Trial, *State Trials*, IX, 999.

Algernon Sidney, *Thoughts on Government*.

Gilbert Burnet, *History of His Own Time* (1753).

Trial of Algernon Sidney for high treason, 1683, *State Trials*, IX, 817.

Trial of the Seven Bishops for libel, 1688, *State Trials*, XII, 183-524.

Thomas B. Macaulay, *History of England* (1849), in *Works* (1875), II, 173.

Chapter 14
Trial of Thomas Paine for libel, 1792, *State Trials*, XXII, 357.
Trial of William Fuller for a cheat in publishing a false, scandalous and defamatory libel, 1702, *State Trials*, XIV, 517.
Trial of John Tutchin for libel, 1704, *State Trials*, XIV, 1095.
The Queen v. *Dr. Brown*, Holt 425 (1706).
Trial of Richard Francklin for a libel, 1731, *State Trials*, XVII, 625.

Chapter 15
Trial of John Peter Zenger for libel, 1735, *State Trials*, XVII, 675, especially pages 675, 694, 696, 699, 703-04, 706-07, 718, 722-24.
Joseph Towers, *Observations on the Rights and Duties of Juries* (1784), 112.

Chapter 16
Benjamin Franklin, *Autobiography*.
New England Courant, July 9, 1722, quoted in *The Papers of Benjamin Franklin*, Leonard W. Labaree, editor, I, 27 (1959).
Cato's Letters (by Trenchard and Gordon), 1720-1723. Letters No. 15 and 32, edition of 1724.
T. E. May, *Constitutional History of England* (1875 ed.), II, 2-26; 248-61; 267-70.
James Ralph, *Critical History of the Administration of Sir Robert Walpole* (1743), pages 306-11 and Section 8.
The Craftsman, Richard Francklin, editor, Nos. 2 and 3 combined, December 9, 1726.
State Trials, XVII, 626, quoting Abel Boyer.
Trial of William Owen, 1752, *State Trials*, XVIII, 1203.
Case of John Wilkes, *State Trials*, XIX, 981, 1075. Hansard, XVI, 423, 589-93, 786, 810-30, 874-966.
Richard J. Hooker, "The American Revolution Seen Through a Wine Glass," *William & Mary Quarterly*, 3d series, XI, 52-57 (toasts to Wilkes).
Leonard W. Levy, *Legacy of Suppression* (1960), 79-85 (*re* case of Alexander MacDougall).
Hansard, May 16, 1792, XXIX, 1408 (Lord Camden on the case of Dr. Shebbeare).

Abel Boyer, in his *Political State of Great Britain* for December 1729, recorded that Richard Francklin was tried for seditious libel on December 3, for publishing *The Craftsman* of March 8, 1729, and was acquitted after a six-hour trial. Neither in the March 8 issue (which contains only a harmless pasquinade) nor any other *Craftsman* can the pretended Alcayde speech be found. The reason for that can be deduced from circumstances. After his 1729 acquittal, Francklin published a pretended letter to himself advising him never again to print the "vain and insolent braggadocios" of the Spaniards, lest they "be construed in a *criminal* light." The collected *Craftsman* was republished in book form *while Francklin was awaiting his famous 1731 trial.* He took his own advice and omitted the Alcayde composition, whose republication might have brought an additional charge and doubled the likelihood of conviction.

In the 1729 trial, Boyer reported, Francklin's counsel argued at length that the published Spanish boasts were not necessarily directed against King George II and England, since other "most potent princes" and "most formidable maritime" powers might have been intended. Lord Chief Justice Raymond submitted that question to the jury, and also "the nature of the publication"—that is, whether the speech was genuine or written for *The Craftsman*—as it no doubt was, by Bolingbroke or Pulteney. "It was also argued," said Boyer, "whether the jury were not judges of law, as well as fact." The answer to that major question is found in the Pulteney ballad and in the complaint of a Walpole organ, which Francklin gleefully reprinted, that the jury decided the case contrary to the truth and to "the CHARGE of the Court." Thus Raymond's first attempt to overrule Lord Holt and resurrect the Scroggs-Hyde doctrine ended in failure, thanks to the jury's rebellion. See *The Craftsman*, March 8, December 20, 27, 1729, vol. V, pp. 225, 239, and Boyer, vol. 38, p. 591, both in the Huntington Library. *State Trials*, XVII, 625, 627, for reference to The Alcayde of Seville's Speech, and to Boyer's comment on the 1731 trial scene.

Chapter 17
Letters of Junius, G. Woodfall edition, II, 62 (*re* destruction of evidence).

Trials of John Almon, Henry Woodfall and John Miller for selling or publishing Junius' Letter to the King, 1770, *State Trials*, XX, 803, 869, 895. The Junius letter occupies pages 805-19.

Hansard, December 10, 11, 1770, XVI, 1211, 1312, 1321, debate on motion for inquiry into the administration of justice. See Hansard, May 20, 1791, for Erskine's correction of Mansfield's misquotation of the Pulteney ballad.

Trial of the Dean of St. Asaph, for seditious libel, 1783-84, *State Trials*, XXI, 847.

Chapter 18

Clinton Rossiter, *Seedtime of the Republic* (1953).

The quotations from the New York *Independent Reflector*, Boston *Gazette*, Ebenezer Ratcliffe, Andrew Kippis, Capel Lofft and Manasseh Dawes will be found in Leonard W. Levy, *Legacy of Suppression*. Although the present writer cannot agree with Dean Levy that the framers of the First Amendment accepted Blackstone's definition of freedom of the press, he has found this book of great value for its extensive and accurate presentation of colonial cases and the views of little-known English libertarians of the eighteenth century.

Jeremy Bentham, *A Fragment on Government* (1776), in *Works*, I, 287-88.

Philip Furneaux's letters to Blackstone, Philadelphia reprint of 1772, pages 33-34.

Joseph Towers, *Observations*, etc., *op. cit.* (London, 1784), 67, 69-71.

Monthly Review (London, January-June, 1785), review of Towers's *Observations*, etc.

Chapter 19

Annals of Congress, (House) June 8, July 21, August 13-22, September 21, 24; (Senate) August 25, September 2, 7-9, 21, 25, 1789.

James Madison, essay, "Who are the Best Keepers of the People's Liberties?" in *Writings*, Gaillard Hunt, editor, VI, 120-23.

Brant, *James Madison: Father of the Constitution*, 415-20 (on Whisky Rebellion).

Alexander Hamilton to Rufus King, October 30, to George Washington, November 8, 1794, in Hamilton *Works* and Princeton University Library.

Chapter 20

Thomas Paine, *The Rights of Man* (1791, 1792) in *Complete Writings* (1945).

Proceedings against Thomas Paine for libel, December 18, 1792, *State Trials*, XXII, 357, especially pages 360, 394, 414, 416-17, 437, 472.

T. E. May, *History, op cit.* II, 284-92; 292-310 (*re* Muir, Palmer, Hardy, Horne Tooke); 317-23, 344.

Robert Hall, *An Apology for the Freedom of the Press and for General Liberty* (London 1793).

Joseph Towers, *A Dialogue between an Associator and a Well-Informed Englishman* (London 1793), bound with trial of Horne Tooke for libeling Charles James Fox, Huntington Library.

Thomas Erskine, *Declaration of the Friends of the Liberty of the Press*, January 19, 1793, also bound with Horne Tooke.

Trials of Thomas Muir and T. Fysche Palmer for sedition, August 30 and September 12, 1793, *State Trials*, XXIII, 117, 237.

Hansard, (Lords) January 29, April 25, (Commons) March 10, 1794, regarding the trial of Thomas Muir.

Chapter 21

Adrienne Koch and Harry Ammon, "The Virginia and Kentucky Resolutions . . ." *William and Mary Quarterly*, April 1948 (*re* Iredell and Cabell).

Jefferson-Madison petition to Virginia General Assembly against grand-jury presentment of Congressman Cabell, in Jefferson's *Writings*.

Annals of Congress, (House) July 5, 1798, especially pages 2093-94, 2096-97, 2101-02, 2146, 2148-50.

John C. Miller, *Crisis in Freedom: The Alien and Sedition Acts* (1951), quoting English traveler in America, page 83.

Chapter 22

Annals of Congress, (House) July 5, 1798, especially pages 2103-04, 2139-42, 2152-57, 2159-61, 2169.

James M. Smith, *Freedom's Fetters; the Alien and Sedition Laws and American Civil Liberties* (1956).

Chapter 23

Trial of Matthew Lyon, in Francis Wharton, *State Trials of the United States during the Administrations of Washington and Adams* (1849), especially pages 333-34.

Virginia Resolutions of 1798, in Madison, *Writings*, edited by Hunt. Kentucky Resolutions in *Writings* of Jefferson.

Trial of Thomas Cooper, in Wharton, *op. cit.*, especially pages
662-63, 665, 669-71, 674-76.

Chapter 24
Madison, "Address of the General Assembly to the People of
the Commonwealth of Virginia," January 1799, in Madison,
Writings (Hunt, editor), VI, 332.

John Marshall, "Address of the Minority," *Journal*, Virginia
House of Delegates, 1799.

Albert J. Beveridge, *The Life of John Marshall*, II, 328-31,
387-91, 574-77.

Thomas Iredell, charge to the federal grand jury, District of
Pennsylvania, April 11, 1799, in Wharton, *op. cit.*, 473.

Chapter 25
Madison, *Report on the Virginia Resolutions of 1798*, adopted
by the General Assembly in January 1800, *Writings* (Hunt, ed.),
VI, 341-406.

Chapter 26
Annals of Congress, (House) January 23, 1800; January 21, 22,
23, 1801, on repeal or extension of the Sedition Act of 1798, especially pages 406, 408-11, 413-15, 418, 420-21, 424, 939-40, 974.

Tunis Wortman, *A Treatise Concerning Political Enquiry
and the Liberty of the Press* (1800), pages iv, 30, 128, 168, 170, 262.

Thomas McKean to Jefferson, February 7, Jefferson to McKean,
February 19, 1803, on libel prosecutions under state law, Jefferson
Papers, Library of Congress.

Respublica against *Joseph Dennie*, 4 Yeates 267; *American Decisions*, II, 402. Dennie was indicted for libel in the Mayor's Court,
Philadelphia, but the case was transferred to the Pennsylvania Supreme Court in December 1803 and tried at *nisi prius* before a jury
in the November term, 1805, by Justices Yeates, Smith and Brackenridge.

Case of Harry Crosswell, 3 Johnson Cases (N.Y.) 344 (1804).

Brant, *James Madison: Secretary of State*, 354-55 (on Granger);
James Madison: Commander in Chief, 32, 200 (on Cary).

United States v. *Hudson and Goodwin*, 7 Cranch 32 (1812).

United States v. *Coolidge*, 1 Wheaton 415 (1816). The Circuit
Court opinion is in 1 Gallison 488.

Chapter 27

Howard Edgar Flack, *The Adoption of the Fourteenth Amendment* (1908).

John B. Smith, *The Framing of the Fourteenth Amendment* (1956).

Benjamin B. Kendrick, *The Journal of the Joint Committee of Fifteen on Reconstruction* (1914).

Adamson v. *California*, 332 U.S. 46 (1947).

Charles Fairman, "Does the Fourteenth Amendment Incorporate the Bill of Rights? The Original Understanding," *Stanford Law Review*, II, No. 1, December 1949. (The outstanding denial that it does.)

Alfred H. Kelly, "The Fourteenth Amendment Reconsidered," *Michigan Law Review*, June 1956. (Dealing with the Abolitionist credo.)

Congressional Globe, 39th Congress, 1st session, pages (Trumbull) 474-75; (Bingham) 1033-34, 1064-66, 1088-95; (Hale) 1065-66, 1094; (Hotchkiss) 1095; (Rogers) Appendix 133, 135.

Barron v. *Baltimore*, 7 Peters 243 (1833).

Lessee of Livingston v. *Moore* and others, 7 Peters 551.

Corfield v. *Coryell*, 6 Federal Cases 546 (Circuit Court of Eastern District of Pennsylvania, 1823).

Abbott v. *Bayley*, 6 Pickering 89 (Massachusetts 1827).

Chapter 28

Congressional Globe, 39th Congress, first session, pages (Bingham) 1291, 2542-43; (Wilson) 1294; (Senator Howard) 2765-66, 2890, 3039; (Hendricks) 2939, 3039; (Poland) 2961.

Ibid, 42d Congress, first session, Appendix, p. 83, Bingham's speech of March 31, 1871.

Massachusetts Legislative Documents, House 112-474, 1867; House Document 149, Report of the Committee on Federal Relations, February 28, 1867, especially pages 1-4, 23, 25.

Boston *Advertiser,* March 4 (editorial on 14th amendment), 13-14 (legislative debates), 1867.

Cincinnati *Commercial* (speeches of Bingham in Ohio), September 19, 1865; August 27, 1866.

Chapter 29

Slaughter-House Cases, 16 Wallace 36 (1873), especially 72-79, 95-96, 118-19, 123-24.

Charles W. Collins, *The Fourteenth Amendment and the States* (1912).

United States v. *Cruikshank*, 92 U.S. 542 (1875).

O'Neil v. *Vermont*, 144 U.S. 323 (1892), especially 331-32, 340, 370.

Chapter 30

Adamson v. *California*, 332 U.S. 46 (1947). Justice Black's dissent at 78-79.

Hurtado v. *California*, 110 U.S. 516 (1884).

Roscoe Conkling, brief in *County of San Mateo* v. *Southern Pacific RR. Co.*, filed January 16, 1883, File Copies of Briefs, vol. 6, No. 106, 1885, United States Supreme Court Library.

William Hone, *The Table Book* (London 1827), I, 524, quoting Howel Walsh at the Tralee Assize.

The King v. *Berchet*, 1 Shower 106 (1690) .

Rex v. *Joliffe*, 4 Term Reports 285-93 (1791).

Ashford v. *Thornton*, 1 Barnewall & Alderson 405 (1818).

Rex v. *Toler*, 1 Lord Raymond 555; 12 Modern 375; Holt 483 (1700).

Hansard, November 27, 1770 (speech of C. Phipps).

Olsen v. *Nebraska*, 313 U.S. 236 (1941).

Chapter 31

Strauder v. *West Virginia*, 100 U.S. 303 (1880).

Civil Rights Cases, 109 U.S. 3 (1883).

Plessy v. *Ferguson*, 163 U.S. 537 (1896).

Roberts v. *City of Boston*, 5 Cushing 198 (Massachusetts 1849).

McCabe v. *A. T. & S. F. Railway Co.*, 218 U.S. 71 (1914).

Gong Lum v. *Rice*, 275 U.S. 78 (1927).

Missouri ex rel. Gaines v. *Canada*, 305 U.S. 337 (1938).

Sweatt v. *Painter*, 339 U.S. 629 (1950).

Nixon v. *Herndon*, 273 U.S. 536 (1927).

Terry v. *Adams*, 345 U.S. 461 (1953).

Brown v. *Board of Education*, 347 U.S. 483 (1954); supplemental decision, 349 U.S. 294 (1955).

Heart of Atlanta Motel, Inc., v. *United States*, 379 U.S. 241 (1964).

Louisiana v. *United States*, decided March 8, 1965.

Robert J. Harris, *The Quest for Equality* (1960).

Race Relations Law Reporter, February 1956 (Vanderbilt University School of Law).

Chapter 32

Maxwell v. *Dow*, 176 U.S. 581 (1900).

Trial of John Lilburne and John Wharton for printing and publishing seditious books, 1637, *State Trials*, III, at 1318, 1349, 1358.

Twining v. *New Jersey*, 211 U.S. 78, especially 101-02, 110, 113, 91 (1908).

Powell v. *Alabama*, 287 U.S. 45 (1932).

Palko v. *Connecticut*, 302 U.S. 319 (1937).

Betts v. *Brady*, 316 U.S. 455 (1942).

Adamson v. *California*, 332 U.S. 46, especially 87-89, 124, 59, 54.

Malinski v. *New York*, 324 U.S. 401, especially 416-17 (1945).

John Raeburn Green, "The Bill of Rights, the Fourteenth Amendment and the Supreme Court," *Michigan Law Review*, May, 1948.

Chapter 33

Patterson v. *Colorado*, 205 U.S. 454 (1907).

Colorado v. *News-Times Publishing Co.*, 84 Pacific 912 (1906).

Commonwealth v. *Blanding*, 3 Pickering 304 (Massachusetts 1825).

Fraina v. *United States*, 255 Federal 28 (1918).

Schenck v. *United States*, 249 U.S. 47 (1919).

Abrams v. *United States*, 250 U.S. 616 (1919).

Gitlow v. *People of New York*, 268 U.S. 652 (1925).

Masses Publishing Co. v. *Patten*, 244 Federal 535 (District Judge Hand, July 1917); 246 Federal 24 (Circuit Judge Rogers, December 1917).

Whitney v. *California*, 274 U.S. 357 (1927).

Near v. *Minnesota*, 283 U.S. 697 (1931).

Grosjean v. *American Press Co.*, 297 U.S. 233 (1936).

De Jonge v. *Oregon*, 299 U.S. 353 (1937).

Zechariah Chafee, *Freedom of Speech* (1920), for conditions during and after World War I.

Edward G. Hudon, *Freedom of Speech and Press in America* (1963).

William O. Douglas, *The Right of the People* (1958).

Chapter 34

Reynolds v. *United States,* 98 U.S. 148 (1878), on polygamy.

Pierce v. *Society of Sisters,* 268 U.S. 510 (1925).

Cochran v. *Louisiana State Board of Education,* 281 U.S. 370 (1930).

Cantwell v. *Connecticut,* 310 U.S. 296 (1940).

Minersville School District v. *Gobitis,* 310 U.S. 586 (1940).

West Virginia Board of Education v. *Barnette,* 319 U.S. 624 (1943).

Jones v. *Opelika,* 316 U.S. 584 (1942).

Everson v. *Board of Education,* 330 U.S. 1 (1947).

McCollum v. *Illinois,* 333 U.S. 203 (1948).

Zorach v. *Clauson,* 343 U.S. 306 (1952).

Engel v. *Vitale,* 370 U.S. 421 (1962).

Hunter Miller, *Treaties and International Acts of the United States,* II, 365 (treaty of 1796-97 with Tripoli).

James D. Richardson, *Messages and Papers of the Presidents,* II, 498, 517.

Hearings on House Joint Resolution 28, House Committee on the Judiciary, Fifty-Fourth Congress, first session, March 11, 1896.

Elizabeth Fleet, "Madison's Detached Memoranda," 3 *William & Mary Quarterly,* third series (1946), 554-62.

Chapter 35

Contempt cases of Robert Randall and Charles Whitney, *Annals of Congress,* (House) December 28-31, 1795; January 1, 4-8, 12, 13, 1796.

Contempt case of William Duane, *Annals of Congress,* (Senate) February 26, March 5, 8, 19, 20, 22, 24, 26-28, May 14, 1800.

Contempt case of John Anderson, *Annals of Congress,* (House) January 7-18, 1818.

Contempt proceedings against James W. Simonton, *Congressional Globe,* (House) January 9, 12, 21-23, February 19, 21, 27, 28, (Senate) January 23, 1857. See especially pages 403, 411, 434-45, 764-68, 925-27, 929-35, 952.

Anderson v. *Dunn,* 6 Wheaton 204 (1821).

James M. Smith, *Freedom's Fetters* (1956), chapter 13.

Chapter 36

Contempt case of Stanley Hyatt, *Congressional Globe,* 36th Congress, (Senate) January 24, March 6, 9, 12, May 28, June 13, 15,

1860. See especially pages 999-1000, 1076-86 (Hyatt's brief), 1100-09 (speeches of Sumner, Fessenden, Hale, Jefferson Davis), 2908 (petitions for Hyatt's release), 3006 (final committee report on Hyatt and absentee witnesses), 3007 (Sumner).

Kilbourn v. *Thompson,* 103 U.S. 168 (1880).

In re Chapman, 166 U.S. 661 (1897).

Marshall v. *Gordon, Sergeant-at-Arms,* 243 U.S. 521 (1927).

McGrain v. *Daugherty,* 273 U.S. 135 (1927).

Sinclair v. *United States,* 279 U.S. 263 (1929).

Jurney v. *MacCracken,* 294 U.S. 125 (1935).

Francis Hargrave, *Juridical Arguments and Collections,* II, 183-220 (1797-99).

Contempt case of General Houston, *Register of Debates,* 22nd Congress, (House) April 14 to May 14, 1832, especially pages 2512, 2540, 2597-2620 (Key), 2822 (Polk), 3017, 3018.

Chapter 37

Walter Gellhorn, *Security, Loyalty & Science* (1950); *American Rights* (1960).

Alan Barth, *The Loyalty of Free Men* (1951); *Government by Investigation* (1955).

Robert K. Carr, *Federal Protection of Civil Rights* (1947); *The House Committee on Un-American Activities, 1945-1950* (1952).

Gellhorn, "Report on a Report of the House Committee on Un-American Activities," 60 *Harvard Law Review* 1193 (1946-1947).

Beccaria, *Essay on Crimes and Punishment,* 1770 edition, chapter 23.

Mitchell Franklin, "The *Encyclopediste* Origin and Meaning of the Fifth Amendment," *Lawyers Guild Review,* XV, 41 (1955), quoting Montesquieu, Brissot, Bentham.

Erwin N. Griswold, *The Fifth Amendment Today* (1955).

Pennsylvania v. *Nelson,* 350 U.S. 497 (1956).

Watkins v. *United States,* 354 U.S. 178 (1957).

Barenblatt v. *United States,* 360 U.S. 109 (1959).

Braden v. *United States,* 365 U.S. 431 (1961).

Barsky v. *United States,* 167 Fed. 2d 241 (1948 United States Court of Appeals, D.C.), dissenting opinion of Judge Henry W. Edgerton.

Ex Parte Milligan, 4 Wallace 2, especially 123-24, 127-28 (1866).

Moyer v. *Peabody,* 212 U.S. 78 (1909). *In re Moyer,* 85 Pacific 190 (1904).

For the Haymarket Riots and Governor Altgeld, see *Spies* v. *Illinois*, 123 U.S. 131 (1887), and Harry Barnard, *Eagle Forgotten* (1938).

Hirabayashi v. *United States*, 320 U.S. 81 (1943).

Korematsu v. *United States*, 323 U.S. 214 (1944).

In re Yamashita, 327 U.S. 1 (1946).

Annals of Congress, January 10, 1814, pages 879-88, *re* civilian spies.

Brant, *James Madison: Commander in Chief* (1961), 383-85, *re* General Jackson at New Orleans.

Chapter 38

Betts v. *Brady*, 316 U.S. 455 (1942).

Adamson v. *California*, 332 U.S. 46 (1947).

Gideon v. *Wainwright*, 372 U.S. 335 (1963).

Anthony Lewis, *Gideon's Trumpet*, 1964.

Douglas v. *California*, 372 U.S. 353 (1963).

Robinson v. *California*, 370 U.S. 660 (1962), on cruel and unusual punishment.

Mapp v. *Ohio*, 367 U.S. 643 (1961).

Malloy v. *Hogan*, 378 U.S. 1 (1964).

Murphy v. *Waterfront Commission*, 378 U.S. 52 (1964).

Feldman v. *United States*, 322 U.S. 487 (1944).

United States of America v. *McRae*, L.R. 3 Chancery 79 (1867).

Knapp v. *Schweitzer*, 357 U.S. 371 (1958).

United States v. *Saline Bank of Virginia*, 1 Peters 100 (1828).

Anson Phelps Stokes and Leo Pfeffer, *Church and State in the United States* (1950, revised 1964), chapter 18.

United States v. *Lanza*, 260 U.S. 377 (1922).

J. A. C. Grant, "The Lanza Rule of Successive Prosecutions," *Columbia Law Review*, XXXII, 1309-31 (1932).

Bartkus v. *Illinois*, 359 U.S. 121 (1959).

In re Oliver, 333 U.S. 257 (1948).

People of New York v. *August Muller*, 96 N.Y. 408 (1884).

Regina v. *Hicklin*, Law Reports 3 Queens Bench 360 (1868).

Roth v. *United States*, 354 U.S. 476 (1957).

Jacobellis v. *Ohio*, 378 U.S. 184 (1964).

Milton R. Konvitz, *First Amendment Freedoms* (1963).

The First Freedom, Robert B. Downs, editor (1960).

Chapter 39

Schenck v. *United States*, 249 U.S. 41 (1919), and File Copies of Briefs, 1918 term, vol. 87, No. 437, Supreme Court Library.

Abrams v. *United States*, 250 U.S. 216, and File Copies of Briefs, 1919 term, vol. 84, No. 316, Supreme Court Library.

Beauharnais v. *Illinois*, 343 U.S. 250 (1951).

New York Times Co. v. *Sullivan*, 376 U.S. 254 (1964).

Garrison v. *Louisiana*, No. 4, October term, 1964.

Alexander Meiklejohn, *Free Speech and Its Relation to Self-Government* (1948).

Chapter 40

Karl N. Llewellyn, *The Common Law Tradition: Deciding Appeals* (1960).

Irving Dilliard, "Dissent from Llewellyn on Dissent," *Washington University Law Quarterly*, February 1962.

INDEX

As an aid to identification of the persons named in this book, parenthetical abbreviations are used in the Index to indicate the position or status of nearly all of them. This does not seem necessary in the case of presidents of the United States. Also, membership in the British House of Lords is implicit in titles denoting the peerage. The abbreviations do not necessarily represent the highest rank achieved by the persons named. Thus, Sir Francis Bacon is identified only as a British prosecutor, Blackstone as a writer, with no reference to their ultimate rank as jurists. The occasional multiple listings point to corresponding activities dealt with in the narrative. The abbreviations follow:

(apr) American prosecutor

(bj) British judge or other officer with judicial functions

(bpr) British prosecutor

(cab) cabinet member or other minister of state

(cc) delegate to constitutional convention, federal or ratifying

(cjcp) Lord Chief Justice of the Court of Common Pleas

(cjkb) Lord Chief Justice of the Court of King's Bench

(cjsc) Chief Justice of the United States Supreme Court

(csl) counsel for defendant or civil litigant

(def) defendant in court or legislative proceeding

(fj) American federal judge

(gv) governor of a state or colony

(inf) informer

(jsc) associate justice of the United States Supreme Court

(mp) member of Parliament (House of Commons)

(pl) plantiff or complainant

(rep) member of the United States House of Representatives

(sen) member of the United States Senate

(sj) state or colonial judge

(wit) witness

(wr) writer, editor, printer or publisher

INDEX

A

Abolitionists, 318, 322, 340, 342, 444

Abrams v. *United States,* 398–400, 495–98, 526

Adam of Ravensworth (def), 115–19, 217, 509

Adams, John, 240, 246, 247, 249, 252, 253, 265, 271, 272, 274, 279, 280, 282, 289, 308, 315, 416, 417, 495, 523, 524

Adams, John Quincy, 240

Adams v. *California,* 321, 356, 388–92, 480, 482

Alabama, 348, 373, 377, 461, 500

Aldrich, Edgar (fj), 397

Alexander, James (csl), 176

Aliens and Alien Act of 1798, 25, 248, 277, 296f, 355

Allen, John (rep), 251–54, 256–60 *passim,* 262, 267, 275, 297, 494

Allibone, Sir Richard (bj), 161, 162, 200

Almon, John (def), 189, 197f, 216, 360

Altgeld, John P. (gv), 475

Ames, Fisher (rep), 53, 66, 80, 228, 233, 267, 290

Amidon, Charles F. (fj), 397

Anabaptists, 27

Anarchism and criminal syndicalism, 400, 401, 404

Ancient rights and privileges, 17–20 *passim,* 58, 82, 84, 111, 151, 166, 182, 362f, 385

Anderson, Father Lionel (def), 146

Anderson, Sir Edmund (cjcp) 102f, 382

Anderson v. *Dunn,* 434–37, 450–51, 453, 457, 496

Andrew, John A. (csl), 442f, 471, 525

Andrews, Charles (sj), 490

Anglicans (Episcopalians), 22, 30, 99, 100, 101f, 131, 158–59, 209, 382, 414, 420

Annals of Congress, 518, 523

Anne, Queen, 165, 187

Apportionment, legislative, 14, 208, 338, 517. *See* Rotten boroughs

Arbitrary power, 31, 88, 109, 111, 248, 297, 446, 447, 448, 449

Arizona, 461

Armies, standing, 227, 486

Arms, right to bear, 13, 336, 356, 486f

Articles of Confederation, 63, 207, 267f, 298, 301

Arundel, Archbishop Thomas, 123

Arundell, Henry, Baron (def), 135

Ashburton, Baron (*see* John Dunning)

Ashby, Richard (def), 144, 520

Ashford, William (pl), 359

Assembly, freedom of, 13, 54–62, 244–45, 336, 346, 349f, 356, 402, 404f, 512

Associated Press, 515

Association, freedom of, 215, 233, 234, 240, 466, 467, 510, 512; guilt by, 105, 234–36, 462